Electronic and Experimental Music

Electronic and Experimental Music: Technology, Music, and Culture provides a comprehensive history of electronic music, covering key composers, genres, and techniques used in both analog and digital synthesis. This textbook has been greatly expanded and revised with the needs of both students and instructors in mind. The fourth edition's reader-friendly style, logical organization, and pedagogical features provide easy access to key ideas, milestones, and concepts.

New to this edition

* Audio CD Companion, a first for this book, including more than a dozen historically significant works selected by the author for this edition.
* Listening Guides providing a moment-by-moment annotated exploration of key works of electronic music, including those found on the accompanying audio CD.
* New discussions of classic electronic music in the United Kingdom, Italy, Latin America, and Asia, expanding the global representation of the history of electronic music.
* New discussion of early experiments with jazz and electronic music.
* Expanded discussion of the roots of electronic rock music.
* Additional accounts of the vastly under-reported contributions of women composers in the field, including new discussions of Daphne Oram, Delia Derbyshire, Lily Greenham, Teresa Rampazzi, and Jacqueline Nova.
* Additional photos, scores, and illustrations throughout.
* Two appendices that trace the evolution of analog and digital synthesis technology.
* A four-part text with fourteen chapters—perfect for a one-semester course.

The Companion Website includes a number of student and instructor resources, such as additional Listening Guides, links to audio and video resources on the Internet, PowerPoint slides, and interactive quizzes.

Thom Holmes is a composer and music historian. He studied composition with Paul Epstein in Philadelphia, was the longtime publisher of the magazine *Recordings of Experimental Music* (1979–85), and worked with John Cage.

Dedicated waveforms

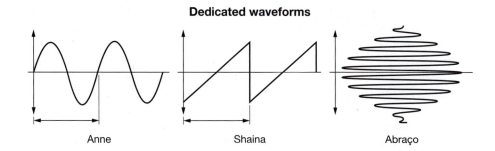

Anne   Shaina   Abraço

Electronic and Experimental Music

Technology, Music, and Culture

FOURTH EDITION

Thom Holmes

with contributions by
Terence M. Pender
Associate Director, Columbia
University Computer Music Center

Routledge
Taylor & Francis Group
NEW YORK AND LONDON

Please visit the companion website at www.routledge.com/cw/holmes

Fourth edition published 2012
by Routledge
711 Third Avenue, New York, NY 10017

Simultaneously published in the UK
by Routledge
2 Park Square, Milton Park, Abingdon, Oxon OX14 4RN

Routledge is an imprint of the Taylor & Francis Group, an informa business

First edition published by Scribner 1985
Third edition published by Routledge 2008

Library of Congress Cataloging in Publication Data
Holmes, Thom.
   Electronic and experimental music: technology, music, and
   culture/Thom Holmes.—4th ed.
   p. cm.
   Includes bibliographical references and index.
   1. Electronic music—History and criticism. 2. Computer music—
   History and criticism. I. Title.
   ML1380.H64 2008
   786.7—dc22
   2007038213

ISBN: 978-0-415-89646-7 (hbk)
ISBN: 978-0-415-89636-8 (pbk)
ISBN: 978-0-203-12842-8 (ebk)

Typeset in Bembo and Helvetica Neue
by Florence Production Ltd, Stoodleigh, Devon
Printed and bound in the United States of America
on acid-free paper by Sheridan Books, Inc.

Contents

Illustrations

FIGURES

TABLES

Preface

One night many years ago, in the heyday of tape music, British electronic music pioneer Delia Derbyshire was crossing the Putney Bridge in West London with her composer friend Brian Hodgson. Both were employed making theme music and sound effects for the BBC Radiophonic Workshop. They paused while crossing and Derbyshire turned to Hodgson. "What we are doing now is not important for itself," she said, "but one day someone might be interested enough to carry things forward and create something wonderful on these foundations."[1]

Derbyshire's pragmatic and visionary words were spoken more than 45 years ago. A *history* of electronic music scarcely existed at that time. The intervening years have seen the invention of analog synthesizers, the rise of MIDI as a bridge between analog and digital synthesis, and the adoption of computers as the key ingredient in the creation, editing, and performance of electronic music. What was once an exclusively experimental kind of musical expression formed a foundation on which nearly every familiar genre of music has since constructed a room of its own.

Electronic and Experimental Music is the story of where electronic music came from and how it has changed over the past decades from early analog technology to the present. It is also the story of musical ideas that evolved in parallel with the technology, sometimes inspired by the machine but just as frequently leading to the invention of technology to fulfill new musical ideas. This new edition remains an account of the history of technology, musical styles, and figures associated with electronic music, paying particular attention to:

- the invention of the key technologies of electronic music;
- the people who first explored new musical ideas using electronics;
- key works of electronic music, their genesis, and influence;
- a reflection on the cultural impact of electronic music over the years.

Many questions about electronic music can only be answered historically. What qualities are uniquely inherent in electronic music? Why do we play sounds in reverse? How did the concept of a sound's envelope become part of the composer's toolkit? Why was the music of early practitioners, such as Schaeffer, Stockhausen, Cage, and Varèse viewed as distinctly different approaches to the medium? What prevented jazz musicians from embracing electronic music as early as musicians in other genres of music, such as classical, pop, and rock? The answers to these questions have been obscured by many years of established practice in the field. Still, understanding the history of such developments remains essential for today's composers and listeners if we are to fully appreciate and comprehend the beauty, complexity, and scope of this thing we call electronic music.

The title of this book invites a little discussion. There has been a debate for many years over the general terminology used for classifying the kind of music described in these pages. Terms such as *electroacoustic*, *electronica*, *acousmatic*, *organized sound*, and *musique concrète* all have their historical connotations and contemporary supporters. While the distinctions between these classifications of electronic music are worth exploring, I have reserved that debate for Chapter 12, the first chapter in Part IV, *The Music*. For the purposes of my book, I have long adopted the term "electronic music" because it is categorically broad and simple to understand. I also use the word "experimental" to underscore that this book is primarily about historical beginnings in the art of electronic music, both technologically and musically. These beginnings span a broad range of years and developments, from the late nineteenth century to the present.

Although the book has roots in European, American, and Japanese electronic music, the story of electronic is truly global. Accordingly, I have broadened the scope throughout, specifically with more history about Latin America (see Chapter 3) and Southeast Asia and China (see Chapter 4). One will also find the discussion of early British and Italian electronic music greatly expanded in Chapter 2.

My opening story about Delia Derbyshire reminds us that women have always played a key role in the development of electronic music. This edition of *Electronic and Experimental Music* uses many opportunities to broaden the discussion of the compelling and under-reported accomplishments of women from many countries, notably the astonishing work of Derbyshire, Daphne Oram, and Lily Greenham in the United Kingdom, Teresa Rampazzi in Italy, and Jacqueline Nova in Colombia. Their stories echo alongside those already included in the book about such innovators as Pauline Oliveros, Wendy Carlos, Maggie Payne, Yoko Ono, Laurie Spiegel, Annea Lockwood, Zeena Parkins, Alice Shields, Marina Rosenfeld, and many others.

The area of digital synthesis continues to evolve rapidly. To help enable the book to remain as timely and relevant as possible in the field of contemporary computer music, I sought the know-how of Terry M. Pender, Associate Director of the Columbia University Computer Music Center. Terry hails from perhaps the most legendary educational program for electronic and computer music in America. He served as a contributing editor on this edition, scouring many of the chapters and especially those regarding digital synthesis. His valued input has resulted in significant updates regarding the computer hardware and software used by today's practitioners.

NEW AUDIO CD AND *LISTENING GUIDES*

Another important addition to this edition is my first-ever collection of musical examples assembled especially for the book. This companion audio CD features more than a dozen historically significant works, each of which is accompanied by an associated *Listening Guide* in the book. With the addition of this audio CD, *Electronic and Experimental Music* now provides three ways to supplement the reading with related listening:

- *Listening Guides*. Found in most chapters, these guides provide a moment-by-moment annotated exploration of key works. *Listening Guides* provide background on a work and the composer, the way in which a work was composed, and a set of production notes explaining how the music was produced, keyed to timings throughout the work. For the purpose of comparing and contrasting similar works, I've also included with each guide a short list of additional tracks, both historic and contemporary. *Listening Guides* are provided in the book for each track on the accompanying audio CD. *Listening Guides* for other, more easily available, tracks are found on the companion website, for example "Tomorrow Never Knows" by The Beatles.
- *Listen* **Playlists**. Each chapter includes one or more *Listen* playlists, a collection of recommended musical tracks that are commercially available through music download sites such as Apple iTunes or Amazon.
- **Pioneering Works of Electronic Music**. In the back of the book is an annotated guide to additional recordings of historically important works of electronic music. This is provided for those who seek to build a library of "greatest hits" in the field.

FEATURES AND ORGANIZATION

The following features are designed to assist the reader throughout:

- **Chapter organization**—*Electronic and Experimental Music* is designed for learning, the first text in the field to incorporate a contemporary pedagogical design based on proven learning techniques for the classroom. Each chapter is structured for easy access to key ideas, people, listening examples, and content that is most useful for self-assessment by the student. Chapters open with a list of chapter contents, a photo, and a quote to set the tone for the discussion. Features found within the body of the chapter include *Listening Guides* and *Listen* playlists to supplement the reading with musical examples. Each chapter concludes with a *Summary* of key points, a list of *Key People*, a list of *Key Terms*, and a *Milestones* table highlighting key technological and artistic achievements.
- **Table of contents**—The organization of the text has been developed for teaching purposes. The book has 14 chapters, an ideal number for a one-semester course. The chapters are divided into four parts, including early history (Part I), analog synthesis (Part II), computer synthesis (Part III), and a survey of the music itself (Part IV).
- **Extensive photos and figures**—The rich history of electronic music is sometimes best told with vivid images, schematics, and sample scores, all of which have been expanded in this edition of the book.

NEW TO THIS EDITION

Responding to the suggestions of instructors and students, the fourth edition includes key changes to several aspects of the text:

- New feature: **Audio CD** (see above).

- New feature: *Listening Guides* found in most chapters (see above).
- New feature: *Glossary*. Key terms are highlighted in bold within the chapters and collected with definitions in a newly added Glossary in the back of the book.
- New feature: Two *Appendices* trace the evolution of electronic music technology. In the previous edition, two chapters were devoted to diagramming the evolution of analog and digital music synthesis. In this edition, I have preserved this feature, but moved it to the back of the book in the form of two new appendices. Appendix I covers the *Evolution of Analog Synthesizers* and Appendix II covers the *Evolution of Computer Music*. Each has been significantly updated.

Chapter by Chapter Changes

Each chapter includes updates to keep pace with changes in our understanding of the history of this field, including new key terms, revised *Listen* playlists, and updates to the book's generous illustration program. Other specific changes worth noting are summarized below.

Chapter 1, Electronic Music Before 1945: New or expanded information and photographs regarding early electronic music technologies, including the musical telegraph, the Telharmonium, photoelectric organs, the Hammond Novachord, and the Phonautograph.

Chapter 2, Early Electronic Music in Europe: Expanded discussion of the early tape music work of Egyptian composer Halim El-Dabh; new discussion about the historial roots of electronic music in Europe; new and expanded discussion of tape music in Italy and the Milan school, including the work of Pietro Grossi, Enore Zaffiri, and Teresa Rampazzi; new comprehensive discussion of the BBC Radiophonic Workshop, its founding, history, composers, and instrumentation; and new discussions of the work of composers Daphne Oram, Delia Derbyshire, David Cain, Brian Hodgson, and Lily Greenham of the UK.

Chapter 3, Early Electronic Music in the United States and Latin America: Revised discussion of John Cage's approach to composing electronic music using chance operations; new discussion of the press response to early electronic music performances; new section discussing the early development of electronic music in Latin America, highlighting composers, studios, and works from Argentina, Brazil, Colombia, Cuba, Mexico, and other countries; Latin composers whose work is newly discussed include Mauricio Kagel, Hilda Dianda, Mario Davidovsky, Guillermo Gregorio (Argentina), Reginaldo Carvalho and Jorge Antunes (Brazil), Jacqueline Nova (Colombia), and Juan Blanco (Cuba). Institutions discussed in this section include the Centro Latinoamericano de Altos Estudios Musicales (CLAEM) and the Laboratorio de Investigación y Producción Musical (LIPM), both in Buenos Aires. In addition, there is a discussion of the Third Inter-American Biennial of Art in Córdoba, Argentina, in October, 1966, which brought together many pioneers of electronic music arts in South America.

Chapter 4, Early Electronic Music in Japan, Southeast Asia, and China: New and expanded discussion of the origins of electronic music in Asia, including the relationship of electronic music of European influence and indigenous music in Japan; additional discussion of Stockhausen's influence on early Japanese electronic music; a new section discussing the early development of electronic and computer music in Southeast Asia and China, including the work of composers Slamet Sjukur and Sapto

Raharjo (Indonesia), José Maceda (the Philippines), Zhang Xiaofu (China), and the Center of Electroacoustic Music of China at the Central Conservatory of Music in Beijing.

Chapter 6, Early Synthesizers and Experimenters: Expanded discussion of the work of Canadian inventor Hugh Le Caine and related musical work by Pauline Oliveros, particularly the techniques used to compose her piece *I of IV* (1966).

Chapter 9, Early Computer Music (1953–85): Updated and expanded discussion of the history and extensions of Bell Laboratory music programming languages, including *Music IV*; the development by Lansky and Vercoe of *Csound* and *Cmix*; new discussions of IRCAM programs, including *PatchWork*; new discussion of spectral analysis and related composition tools; new discussion of Fast Fourier Transform (FFT) and data mapping for spectral analysis; expanded and updated discussion of external computer controllers for music production; new *Listen* playlist for spectral music; and an updated discussion of hardware and software developments for large-scale computers.

Chapter 10, The Microprocessor Revolution (1975–2011): This chapter has been updated to reflect changes to personal computer music technology and software during the past ten years. It includes updates regarding versions and applications for *Max/MSP*; a new figure showing a simple way to use *Max/MSP* audio input to control a video image; new discussions of laptop audio development environments for a variety of musical applications, including the recent history of *Max/MSP/Jitter*; spectral editors, including IRCAM's *AudioSculpt*; percussion synthesis and hardware controllers; musical notation programs; a detailed discussion of physical modeling software; and a new *Listen* playlist for physical modeling and interactive music.

Chapter 11, The Principles of Computer Music: Inclusion of new topics such as spectral editors, the MPEG4 codec, and definition of sequential crossfading.

Chapter 12, Classical and Experimental Music: New and expanded discussions in this first chapter in Part IV on music include a historical view of the current debate over terminology in the field; definition of the term graphic score and several new illustrated examples of different types of electronic music scores; a new discussion examining the method of composition used for Ligeti's *Artikulation* (1958); and a note about Steve Reich's personal manifesto about his process-oriented approach to composing music.

Chapter 13, Jazz, Live Electronic Music, and Ambient Music: This chapter has been extensively updated to explore the subject of early experiments with electronic music and jazz, a long-overlooked subplot in the history of electronic music. This discussion touches on various approaches to combining electronic music and jazz before the advent of synthesizers, and the pioneering work of jazz composers, including André Hodeir, Sun Ra, Terry Riley with the Chet Baker quartet, Walter De Maria's drum experiments, the Bob James Trio, Barney Wilen, Bob Thiele with Jon Appleton, George Russell, İlhan Mimaroğlu and Freddie Hubbard, Eddie Harris, and Gil Mellé. The chapter includes a new *Listen* playlist on electronic jazz.

Chapter 14, Rock, Space Age Pop, and Turntablism: An expanded discussion of electronic rock music includes a new view of Paul McCartney's early experiments with tape music, The Beatles' production of "Revolution 9" and the group's use of the Moog Modular Synthesizer on *Abbey Road*. Other new discussions about electronic rock include the use of such early electronic organs as the Clavioline, a short history of the Mellotron, a magnetic tape-based sound sampler; pioneering artists Pink Floyd, Silver

Apples, and Gary Numan; the use of the Moog Modular Synthesizer by such artists as the Byrds, Monkees, and Keith Emerson; and the rise of contemporary electronic rock with a listing of key artists from around the world.

INTERNET RESOURCES

The author and publisher have created a resource on the Internet at the dedicated website for the fourth edition of *Electronic and Experimental Music*. Go to **www.routledge.com/cw/holmes** to explore self-quiz questions, additional *Listening Guides*, PowerPoint® slides outlining the major points in the chapters, and other features.

Acknowledgments

Many people have contributed to the success of *Electronic and Experimental Music* over the years. I would especially like to thank Constance Ditzel, my editor at Routledge, for working with me to continue making the book a success, especially in the classroom. I would also like to express my gratitude to Denny Tek, assistant editor at Routledge, for working with me on many important details related to the chapters, design, cover, music rights, and companion website for the text. Thanks also go to Rosie Stewart and Sue Leaper of Florence Production Ltd and to Sue Edwards for the superb copy-editing and many fine suggestions.

A special note of thanks goes to my contributing writer for this edition, Terry Pender, who teaches computer music practices at the Columbia University Computer Music Center. His experience as a practicing composer, music instructor, and Assistant Director at this esteemed institution greatly informed the discussions of computer synthesis and new technology for this edition. Terry also guided me through the archives of the Columbia Computer Music Center so that I could tell a more informed history of the original center.

This edition continues to benefit from those with whom I have consulted on past editions. My affection for this topic is largely due to the people I have met along the way who created the technology, culture, and music being discussed in these pages. For allowing me to collect their first-hand accounts of the history of electronic music I wish to thank Robert Ashley, Alvin Lucier, David Behrman, Gordon Mumma, Wendy Carlos, Bob Moog (1934–2005), Matt Rogalsky, Nic Collins, Tetsu Inoue, Alice Shields, Yoko Ono, Halim El-Dabh, Gary Numan, Klaus Schulze, Donald Buchla, Thurston Moore, Marina Rosenfeld, Pauline Oliveros, Annea Lockwood, Laurie Spiegel, David Lee Myers, Charles Cohen, DJ Olive, Bebe Barron (1925–2008), John Bischoff, Harold Budd, Joel Chadabe, Ken Montgomery, Ikue Mori, Pete Namlook, Zeena Parkins, Maggi Payne, Karlheinz Stockhausen (1928–2007), and many others. David Badagnani, composer and adjunct faculty member, ethnomusicology/musicology, Kent State University, was instrumental in making it possible for me to interview Halim El-Dabh. Jeff Winner keeps the flame alive for the Raymond Scott archives and was instrumental in making my version of the Scott story as accurate as possible. My friend Probyn Gregory plays the electro-Theremin in the Brian Wilson band and provided valued insight into the history of this instrument. Thanks to Michael Evans for reigniting my interest in the work of Oskar Sala. My story about Sala and the Trautonium is much richer because of his help.

As for my own personal exploration of music, I must also acknowledge John Cage (1912–92), without whose encouragement as a young composer I would not have developed such a passion for new music. It was always a pleasure to visit John, when our conversations freely drifted from new music to new mushrooms and green tea. I also wish to thank Laura Kuhn, Executive Director of the John Cage Trust, who has provided access for me to materials in the Cage archives. The first person I studied music with was composer Paul Epstein, who taught me how to compose beyond the moment and think about the process. The things I learned from Paul continue to influence the words that I write and the music that I compose. Thanks to Mercedes Santos-Miller, Museum Manager at Caramoor, the estate of Walter and Lucie Rosen, for granting access to Lucie Rosen's Theremin and papers related to her work with the instrument. My history of the Theremin also benefited greatly from the help of David Miller, who has documented the story behind the Paul Tanner electro-Theremin.

The biggest thank you of all goes to Anne, who gives me insight and encouragement and shows unrelenting patience so that I may pursue this endeavor.

FIGURE CREDITS

Unless otherwise credited, all of the originals used for illustrations in this book come from the author's private collection. Every effort has been made to locate all holders of rights to such images. If we have been unable to inform them in some cases, we ask such holders to contact the publisher.

Where references are given for figures, the details are as follows:

Chapter 1 Opener: Edgard Varèse Collection, Paul Sacher Foundation, Basel.
Figure 1.2: R. Wormell, *Electricity in the Service of Man* (London: Cassell & Co., 1886).
Figures 1.25 and *1.26*: Reiner Pfisterer.
Figures 2.2–2.4: Abraham Moles, *Les Musiques expérimentales* (Paris: Éditions du Cercle d'Art Contemporain, 1960).
Figure 2.15: Fondazione Archivio LN.
Figure 2.18–2.20: Ray White.
Figure 2.21: Philips International BV, Eindhoven.
Chapter 4 Opener: Photo, Kiyoji Otsuji. Courtesy of Taka Ishii Gallery.
Figure 4.2: Koichi Fujii, "Chronology of Early Electroacoustic Music in Japan: What Types of Source Materials Are Available?," *Organized Sound* 9(1) (2004).
Figure 4.4: T. Takatsuji, "Mixer kara mita denshi ongaku (Elektronische Musik from a Mixer's Viewpoint)," *Hosogijutsu* 9(3) (1956), 11–17.
Figure 5.9: Benjamin Robert Levy, *The Electronic Works of György Ligeti and Their Influence on His Later Style*. Doctoral dissertation submitted to the Faculty of the Graduate School of the University of Maryland, College Park (2006), 3. Available online: http://drum.umd.edu/dspace/handle/1903/3457?mode=simple (accessed June 14, 2007).
Figures 6.1–6.5: Harry F. Olson, *Music, Physics, and Engineering* (New York: Dover, 1952; 2nd edn, 1967).
Figures 7.1, 7.2, 7.13, and 7.14: Dean Friedman, *Synthesizer Basics* (New York: Amsco Publications, 1986).

Figures 7.3, 7.6, 7.8–7.10, and 7.15–21: Allen Strange, *Electronic Music: Systems, Techniques, and Controls*, 2nd edn (Dubuque, IA: W. C. Brown, 1983).

Figures 7.4, 7.5, 7.7, and 7.12: Joel Naumann and James D. Wagoner, *Analog Electronic Music Techniques* (New York: Schirmer Books, 1985).

Figures 7.22 and 7.23: David Crombie, *The Complete Synthesizer* (London: Omnibus Press, 1982).

Figure 8.18: Tom Scarff. Available online: http://tomscarff.tripod.com/midi_analyser/note_on_off_messages.htm (accessed July 14, 2007).

Figure 9.2: Charles Dodge and Thomas A. Jerse, *Computer Music: Synthesis, Composition, and Performance* (New York: Schirmer Books, 1985).

Figure 11.2: Richard Boulanger, *Sound Design in Csound*. Available online: www.csounds.com/chapter1/index.html (accessed July 18, 2007).

Figures 11.3 and 11.4: Max V. Mathews, *The Technology of Computer Music* (Cambridge, MA: MIT Press, 1969).

Figure 11.5: David Brian Williams, *Experiencing Music Technology*, 2nd edn (New York: McGraw-Hill, 1999), 175.

Figure 11.7: Robert Bristow-Johnson, "Wavetable Synthesis 101, a Fundamental Perspective (2007), figure 1. Available online: www.musicdsp.org/files/Wavetable-101.pdf (accessed February 6, 2008).

Figure 11.8: Jim Aikin, *Software Synthesizers* (San Francisco: Backbeat Books, 2003), 274.

Figure 11.9: J. M. Chowning, "The Synthesis of Complex Audio Spectra by Means of Frequency Modulation," *Journal of the Audio Engineering Society* 21 (1973), 526–34.

Figure 11.10: Curtis Roads, *Foundations of Computer Music* (Cambridge, MA: MIT Press, 1991).

Figure 11.11: Tamara Smythe, "Waveshaping Synthesis," Simon Fraser University, 2007. Available online: www.cs.sfu.ca/~tamaras/waveshapeSynth (accessed June 10, 2011).

Figure 11.12: Curtis Roads, *Foundations of Computer Music* (Cambridge, MA: MIT Press, 1991), 157.

Chapter 12 Opener: Edgard Varèse Collection, Paul Sacher Foundation, Basel.

Figure 12.4: Edgard Varèse Collection, Paul Sacher Foundation, Basel.

Figure 12.8: E. B. Marks Music Corp.

Figure 12.9: C. F. Peters Music Corp.

Figure 12.12: Pierre Schaeffer, *À la recherche d'une musique concrète* (Paris: Éditions du Seuil, 1952).

PART I

Early History

Predecessors and Pioneers
(1874 to 1960)

CHAPTER 1

Electronic Music Before 1945

I dream of instruments obedient to my thought and which with their contribution of a whole new world of unsuspected sounds, will lend themselves to the exigencies of my inner rhythm.
—Edgard Varèse

Edgard Varèse used the sound studios of Philips in Eindhoven to compose *Poème électronique* (1957–58). He is pictured here with Philips engineer, J. W. de Bruyn, recording sounds such as that of a wood block for incorporation into his work of *musique concrète*.
(Edgard Varèse Collection, Paul Sacher Foundation, Basel)

If a turning point in the art of electronic music can be singled out, it began with the somber tolling of a cathedral bell during the opening moments of *Poème électronique* by Edgard Varèse (1883–1965). The work was composed using three synchronized tracks of magnetic tape and premiered on May 5, 1958 in the Philips Pavilion of the World's Fair in Brussels. The score began as shown in Figure 1.1.

Poème électronique was a short work, lasting only 8′ 8″. The music combined the familiar with the unfamiliar in an appealing way and it did so without any formal structure or rhythm. It was a carefully constructed montage of sounds, including bells, machines, human voices, sirens, percussion instruments, and electronic tones, that were processed electronically and edited together moment by moment for dramatic effect. *Poème électronique* was a "shock and awe" assault on musical culture.

Poème électronique was not the first work of electronic music. Nor was it composed using especially unique technology for 1958. The written score was itself an experiment—a visual sketch of sound sequences rather than a prescription for particular instruments. The sound material included concrete sounds from the real world combined with purely electronic signals, although this, too, was not a unique approach to composing electronic music, having already been used by dozens of composers before 1958.

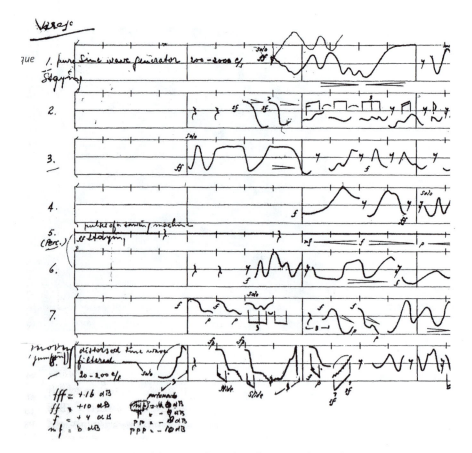

Figure 1.1   Early sketch of the score for *Poème électronique* by Varèse. (Philips International BV, Eindhoven)

What made *Poème électronique* a turning point was that it brought one era of electronic music to a close and opened another. Until this piece by Varèse, electronic music was largely produced and performed within the confines of institutions and academia. By contrast, *Poème électronique* was created expressly for public consumption and was heard by 500 people at a time, many times a day, in a pavilion designed especially for its performance. From April to October 1958, more than two million visitors experienced the work and its accompanying visual projections. *Poème électronique* had an astounding impact on public awareness of electronic music and inspired a new generation of musicians, composers, and inventors to explore the medium. Following the Brussels World's Fair, electronic music studios, both private and institutional, sprung up rapidly around the world.

MUSIC, INVENTION, AND CULTURE

Underlying this book are three themes that inform and amplify the story of electronic music and its history. The first is that *the marriage of technology and music is inescapable* but sometimes imperfect, like any civil union. Rising above dysfunction in this field is a challenge for composers and musicians and also for inventors—the instrument makers of electronic music. *The history of invention* is a second theme of this story, illustrating how the development of new technologies continually benefits and sometimes thwarts the creation of new music. Bringing together the story of electronic music history and invention leads to the third theme, *the diffusion of electronic music into worldwide musical culture.*

The themes of this book are no better illustrated than by Varèse and the creation of *Poème électronique*. It is the work of an artist with deep roots in classical music who, by the age of 74, was finally able to realize a vision for music for which he had long hoped. As early as 1930, Varèse had begun canvassing corporations for financial support to create a sound laboratory for the development of electrical instruments. One of his goals was to create a kind of mechanized means for composing and playing music wherein the composer's ideas would "no longer be desecrated by adaptation or performance as all the past classics were."[1] By the 1950s, with the availability of magnetic tape recorders, microphones, and audio signal generators, Varèse was finally afforded a means for marrying his musical vision with the electronic equipment needed to produce it. The further triumph of *Poème électronique* is that it remains as vital today as it did 50 years ago; so much so that its essential musicality has been largely absorbed into the vocabulary of mainstream musical culture. Hearing the work today, nobody puzzles over just how the piece was constructed but only how it was imagined.

The determination and ingenuity of Varèse is a hallmark of composers and inventors alike in the field of electronic music. Melvin Kranzberg (1917–95), a renowned scholar on the history of technology, once twisted a familiar aphorism by stating that "invention is the mother of necessity."[2] The field of electronic music has often been led by composers and inventors with a need to invent a way to realize their musical visions. This chapter traces the early history of electronic music to its roots in a variety of early **hardwired** analog technologies.

EARLIEST EXPERIMENTS

Rudimentary experiments in the electrical production of sound were taking place before the end of the nineteenth century. In the quest to invent the telephone, several inventors had experimented with the electrical transmission of sound. Among them, German engineer Philip Reis (1834–74) first demonstrated his Reis Telephone in 1861, a simple device for detecting sound and transmitting it from one vibrating membrane to another using a connecting wire charged by a battery (see Figure 1.2). His earliest model was fashioned from a beer barrel and the receiver was carved into the shape of a very large human ear (see Figure 1.3). Although unable to transmit a clearly articulated speaking voice, the Reis Telephone was capable of electrically reproducing an octave's worth of tones if they were sung loudly enough into the transmitting membrane of the beer barrel.

A slightly more practical application of musical tones for the communication of information was the multiple harmonic telegraph, the most musical of which was invented in 1874 by American Elisha Gray (1835–1901). Gray was involved in the field of telegraph communication. He obtained his first telegraph patent in 1867 and was employed by the Western Electric Company as a supervisor. Gray is best known for his contentious patent dispute with Alexander Graham Bell over the design of the original telephone in 1876, a claim that Reis may have also contested had he not died in 1874.

The first of Gray's so-called **Musical Telegraphs**, dating from 1874, had two telegraph keys, each with an electromagnet and a small strip of metal called a reed (see Figures 1.4 and 1.5). When a telegraph key was pressed, an electrical circuit was closed, causing the metal reed to vibrate at a certain **frequency** that was audible when electrically amplified. The resistance of each electromagnet was different, resulting in the creation of two different buzzing tones. Gray fashioned a loudspeaker using a membrane not unlike the one invented by Reis. Each key produced its own distinct tone and the keys could be pressed separately or at the same time. Gray created versions of his Musical Telegraph with piano-like keys that could play one or two octaves. The instrument was **polyphonic**, and capable of playing as many notes simultaneously as the number of keys that one could depress at the same time—a design that predated the introduction of the first practical electric organ by 60 years. Soon after its invention, Gray staged demonstrations in which the Musical Telegraph transmitted musical signals over ordinary telegraph wires to a receiver stationed as far away as 200 miles.[3] But the inventor soon lost interest in the musical applications of the harmonic telegraph, seeing instead its potential for sending several telegraph signals at once—a conceptual predecessor of today's communication multiplexer. Gray was followed by others who saw the musical potential of the telegraph. In 1885, a German inventor named Ernst Lorenz further developed the sound-generating circuits demonstrated by Gray and investigated ways of controlling the **envelope** of the sound. Although his device was patented, it apparently never enjoyed any practical use outside of the laboratory. For more than thirty years, G. P. Hachenburg, a Civil War-era surgeon from Austin, Texas, promoted a means for operating musical instruments remotely through the use of telegraph signals. In 1891, he described a plan to connect ten pianos or pipe organs that could be played remotely by a single person through signals delivered by telegraph. Calling the result "electro-music," Hachenburg's invention was never constructed but his vision was certainly ahead of its time.[4]

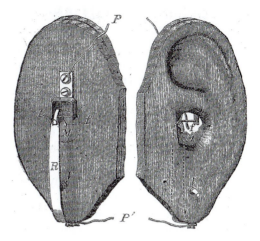

Figure 1.2 Reis Telephone design illustration, 1861. The Reis Telephone was an early device for electrically detecting and amplifying the human voice. (US Patent Office)

Figure 1.3 The microphone of the Reis Telephone was fashioned out of wood in the shape of a human ear. A person spoke into a diaphragm in the "ear" and the signal was amplified by batteries and reproduced by another diaphragm. (US Patent Office)

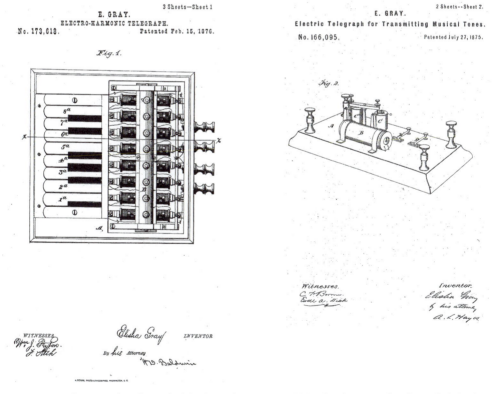

Figure 1.4 Gray's Musical Telegraph (1875) used a small keyboard to trigger buzzing telegraph signals of various pitches. (US Patent Office)

Figure 1.5 Gray's Musical Telegraph (1875) patent. (US Patent Office)

THADDEUS CAHILL AND THE TELHARMONIUM

The study of electromagnetic waves, including sound, gained momentum in scientific circles by the late nineteenth century. The German physicist Hermann von Helmholtz (1821–94), also a prominent physician, was particularly interested in the science of human perception. In 1863, Helmholtz published *On the Sensations of Tone as a Physiological Basis for the Theory of Music*, a classic work on acoustics and tone generation. For his lectures about musical tone, Helmholtz devised a precisely engineered set of chimes, or "resonators," to demonstrate the theory of complex tone quality. By adding and subtracting chimes, he could construct tones ranging from the complex to the elemental—principles adopted by electronic music synthesizers using sound wave generators a century later.

One young American who took an especially keen interest in the work of Helmholtz was Thaddeus Cahill (1867–1934). In 1884, the 17-year-old Cahill was enrolled in the Oberlin Academy Conservatory of Music in Ohio when he first became aware of the elder physicist's work in acoustics. Cahill was inspired by this work to devise an electrical method for fabricating musical sound and putting the power of a synthetic orchestra in the hands of a single performer. He filed his first patent for such a device on August 10, 1895, but finding the original design overly complicated and impractical, he assimilated its pertinent features into a better-conceived 45-page patent opus in 1896. Cahill stated his purpose in the patent to be to construct a machine to produce what he described as "electrical music." In Cahill's own words, the "grand objects" of his invention were:

> [to] generate music electrically with tones of good quality and great power and with perfect musical expression, and to distribute music electrically generated by what we may term "original electrical generation" from a central station to translating instruments located at different points.

Cahill's plan was to build an electronic music **synthesizer** and pipe live music to remote locations.

Cahill was a spirited American inventor who had the technical know-how, creative genius, and marketing foresight to complete what can only be described as the most ambitious electronic music project ever attempted by an individual. Not only was he working against great technological odds—his hardwired instrument preceded the availability of power amplifiers and vacuum tubes by 15 years—but his unique idea to market live electronic music over a telephone network foreshadowed the concepts of radio and cable broadcasting by decades. Cahill was the first person to possess a sense for the commercial potential of electronic music as well as the means and persistence to make it happen.

The patent that he obtained in 1897 described his system in great detail (see Figure 1.6). The instrument itself became known by two different names: the Dynamophone and the *Telharmonium*, Cahill preferring the second. The original patent described a device with electrical tone-generating mechanics, devices for building and shaping individual tones, a **touch-sensitive** polyphonic keyboard for activating the tone-generating circuitry and a speaker system for reproducing the sound. The opening paragraph of the patent even uses the word "synthesizing" to describe the way the Telharmonium

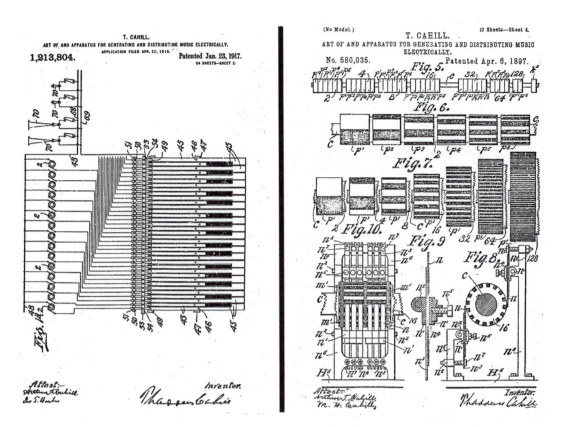

Figure 1.6   Two pages from different patents for Cahill's Telharmonium. The page on the left (1917) illustrates the switch relays for the keyboard. The page on the right (1897) depicts Cahill's ingenious use of rotating cogged wheels to generate tones of the chromatic scale. (US Patent Office)

would combine individual tones to create composite sounds, and we can credit Cahill with coining the term in this field.

The Telharmonium used an ingenious method to produce music. The tone-generating mechanism consisted of "pitch shafts," or axles, upon which were mounted a series of notched metal **tone wheels**. Rotating the pitch shafts brought each tone wheel into contact with a metal brush that was part of an electrical circuit. The width and spacing of the notches on a given tone wheel governed the rate of contact with the metal brush and created an electrical oscillation of a given frequency or tone. The notches of the tone wheels were hand-milled to correspond to specific notes. Borrowing from Helmholtz's concept of resonating chimes, Cahill devised a way for adding and subtracting complementary overtones to fabricate a pleasing full-bodied sound. He did this by using as many as five additional tone wheels for any given note of the scale, each providing a complementary overtone to the base tone.

The first Telharmonium was a prototype capable of playing one octave. It was built in Washington, DC, where Cahill first demonstrated the transmission of "telharmonic music" over telephone wires during 1900 and 1901. After securing financial support, Cahill moved his lab to Holyoke, Massachusetts, where he built his largest model and launched the Cahill Telharmonium Company to market his electronic music service (see Figure 1.7). After a number of well-received local demonstrations in Massachusetts, Cahill found backers to install the Telharmonium in the heart of New York City (see Figure 1.8).

The Telharmonium was nothing short of massive. It consisted of three basic components: a performing console with two keyboards like those of a pipe organ; the bulky tone-generating machinery to which the console was wired; and the listening room where the music was projected using loudspeakers similar in design to early telephone receivers using the principle of a simple vibrating diaphragm. Each of the 12 pitch shafts was 30 feet long. The rotating shafts were bolted to a plate of 18 inch-thick steel girders mounted on brick supports and extending 60 feet. Nearly 2,000 switches were required to connect the keyboard with the tone wheels and various electrical devices needed to synthesize the sounds and maintain their amplification. The entire instrument weighed about 200 tons. The casual observer could have easily mistaken the whirring machinery of the Telharmonium chamber for that of a power plant. The keyboard console was stationed far enough away from the machinery, usually on a different floor, to escape the rumbling dynamo and used a telephone-like receiver to monitor the music being played.

Moving the Telharmonium to New York required more than 30 railroad flatcars. Cahill set up shop in a new building in midtown Manhattan at 39th Street and Broadway, across the street from the original Metropolitan Opera House. The building was later dubbed Telharmonic Hall and consisted of a main floor with a listening room. The Telharmonium keyboard console was located on a small stage in the listening space, tucked into an alcove and framed by giant ferns. Its jungle of wires were discreetly

Figure 1.7 Two musicians playing the Telharmonium in Holyoke in 1906 from a control room equipped with two keyboards. Wiring can be seen leading out from the back of the keyboard console, connecting to the massive Telharmonium tone-generating machinery installed in another part of the building. Two large phonograph-style acoustic horns can be seen above the players; these were wired to the instrument and used to monitor its sound. (*The World's Work*, 1906)

Figure 1.8 Images of Telharmonic Hall in New York City, 1908. The keyboard console (left) resembled that of a pipe organ. The network of wires behind the keyboard console connected the Telharmonium machinery in the basement (right)—a complex hardwired device that required enormous amounts of electrical power. (*Electrical World*, 1908)

channeled through the floor to the bulky sound-generating dynamo located in the basement. Potted plants and ferns, many hiding loudspeakers, were strategically placed around the room.

Concerts in New York began on September 26, 1906. Subscribers for the electronic music service were actively recruited up and down Broadway. A dozen leading hotels and restaurants became subscribers, including the Waldorf-Astoria, the Victoria, and the Café Martin.[5] Several wealthy clients began to have the music piped directly into their homes. There was an active public concert series that increased from two to four performances a day. The public was even enticed by the promise of live telharmonic music being played on trolley cars through the overhead power wires.[6]

Being the first large-scale electronic music instrument of any type certainly lent the Telharmonium an air of novelty that Cahill leveraged with great success. Most newspaper writers were incapable of understanding just how the instrument worked or seeing its technical limitations. This could have led to skepticism on their part, but Cahill was an excellent publicist. He overcame the cynicism of journalists by impressing them with the enormity and complexity of the technical achievement and then focusing on the musicianship required to play the instrument. Cahill's instincts foreshadowed a recurring objection to electronic music that is still with us today—that the ability to produce music using technological means is a shortcut to musicianship. Therefore, contemporary accounts of the Telharmonium were loaded with trivialized evaluations of the technology. Typical were comments such as, "The vibrations stand for notes and tones, and they scurry along to do their work the instant they are released." The same articles were filled with laudatory comments about the Telharmonium's "limitless" potential as a new musical instrument, "for not only can it produce the tones of almost all the known orchestral instruments, but it creates musical sounds never heard before."[7] One writer wrote, "In the new art of telharmony we have the latest gift of electricity to civilization."[8] This suggests the intriguing idea that, had Cahill's instrument been a huge success, we might be using the word "telharmony" today instead of "electronic music" to describe this musical art. But it was not to be.

Despite some early success, technical, regulatory, and business problems soon took their toll on the enterprise. The instrument required an enormous amount of direct current but the power supply could not grow exponentially. Pressing more keys on the keyboard had the effect of reducing the power and volume available to each note. Cahill's ingenious circuits for shaping the texture of the sounds also sapped the power source, causing the volume of the music to diminish as more notes were played.

Cahill leased local phone lines to distribute his music to other locations and this, too, soon became a problem. Because of the massive amount of power needed to drive the music through the telephone network, other telephone wires running alongside those used for the Telharmonium began to experience noise and crosstalk. The music of the Telharmonium was creeping into the conversations of unsuspecting telephone users. Complaints from other customers led the phone company to terminate its agreement with Cahill. These factors combined with a dwindling subscriber base to bring the final curtain down on Telharmonic Hall in February 1908.[9]

While no recordings of the Telharmonium exist, published accounts describe the sound of the instrument as consisting of "singularly clear, sweet, perfect tones"[10] and as being "remarkably pure and beautiful."[11] For all of its purity of tone, the Telharmonium was evidently not the most expressive of instruments for its sound was sometimes characterized as being unemotional and detached. One of the novel features of the instrument was its ability to imitate familiar orchestral instruments. Performances often demonstrated this capability through the replication of oboes, flutes, French horns, bugles, and cellos. The settings for making these sounds were not stored or programmed, but were set manually, just as one would set the stops on a pipe organ. Some of the musical selections known to have been adapted for the Telharmonium included such works as Schumann's *Träumerei*, Beethoven's *Trio in C Major for Two Oboes and Cor Anglais*, selections by Bach and Schubert, and popular songs such as *Arkansas Traveler* and a rousing imitation of a fife-and-drum corps playing *Dixie*.

Cahill's achievement was prototypical of a story to be retold many times since in the development of electronic musical instruments. In creating his synthesizer, Cahill encountered the same basic technical problems still faced by the designers of modern synthesizers: the method of tone generation, tuning, keyboard design, power supply, mixing and amplification, and the control of dynamic features for the shaping of sounds. As a business person, Cahill was also challenged to educate the public, members of the mass media, regulatory functionaries, musicians, and potential financial backers about the potential and benefits of electronically produced music. Unfortunately for Cahill, telharmonic music was unsuccessful as a business concept and the most ambitious achievement in the history of electronic music was soon forgotten. Its legacy lived on, however, in the tone wheel principles used to develop the popular Hammond organ in the late 1920s—a much more compact instrument that took advantage of vacuum tubes to miniaturize its components.

CHILDREN OF THE MACHINE

The Telharmonium was the product of an inventor's mind. Its development was a good example of an often-repeated storyline in the history of electronic music—that of an engineer who nurtures a technological breakthrough for the creation of music. Another familiar story is that of the composer or musician with a radical new musical idea but who must search for a technical means to realize it. The union of these two spirits—the inventor and composer—is a given today in a world diffused with affordable technology for making music. But in the early years of the twentieth century, during the rise of the electronic industrial revolution, the union of technology and music was most often in the purview of artistic radicals and engineering experimenters.

An early advocate of new musical technology was Feruccio Busoni (1866–1924)—an influential Italian musician, composer, and teacher. Living in the long shadow of Italy's immense musical heritage, Busoni was nonetheless dissatisfied with the direction of traditional music. He was interested in freeing music from its "hallowed traditions," daring to put aside the rules, principles, and "laws" that shackled music to the past. As a product of the machine age, Busoni was compelled to use his music as a means for discarding the past in order to link to the future. Busoni documented his activist musical ideas in 1907 with the publication of a short paper, *Sketch of a New Aesthetic of Music.* He was a proponent of alternative tonal scales that divided the octave into more than the customary 12 notes used in Western music. More ideally, Busoni felt that "music was born free; and to win freedom is its destiny," an attitude that inspired a younger generation of composers to open their minds to the use of any and all sounds in music.[12]

Busoni is important to the history of electronic music because he was one of the first composers to realize that technology might be a means to fulfill his musical ideas. Having read an account of Cahill's Telharmonium in a popular magazine, Busoni immediately grasped the relevance of the achievement to his own quest for a means of creating **microtonal** music. He thought so highly of Cahill's synthesizer that he wrote about it in his *Sketch of a New Aesthetic of Music.* Sweeping aside all hyperbole, Busoni lucidly explained the value of an electronic music machine such as the Telharmonium:

> Dr. Thaddeus Cahill . . . has constructed a comprehensive apparatus which makes it possible to transform an electric current into a fixed and mathematically exact number of vibrations. As pitch depends on the number of vibrations, and the apparatus may be "set" on any number desired, the infinite gradation of the octave may be accomplished by merely moving a lever corresponding to the pointer of a quadrant.[13]

In that brief passage, Busoni revealed an understanding of the physics behind sound production and the way that the Telharmonium worked. His innate curiosity about technical matters is a trait seen in many musicians interested in electronic music. Busoni had an immediate grasp of the special relationship between inventors and musicians, stating "I almost think that in the new great music, machines will be necessary and will be assigned a share in it. Perhaps industry, too, will bring forth her share in the artistic ascent."[14] Busoni passed along his enthusiasm for technology to other rising artistic minds of the machine age, not the least of whom would be Edgard Varèse, who became friends with Busoni after reading *Sketch of a New Aesthetic of Music.*

Busoni himself never pursued the development of electronic music in his own work but his advocacy of a new music free from convention registered with many sympathetic ears. Among them was a small coalition of Italian artists, poets, composers, and writers that became known as the Futurists.

The first important document of Futurism was "The Futurist Manifesto" published in 1909. Written by the spiritual leader of the group, the Italian poet Filippo Tommaso

Marinetti (1876–1944), "The Futurist Manifesto" was a paroxysm of condemnation hurled at Italian culture by those who considered themselves to be artistically marginalized. Implicitly militant in style, Marinetti's words eerily anticipated the later rise of Fascism with which some Futurists would later be associated. "Beauty exists only in struggle," wrote the poet. "There is no masterpiece that has not an aggressive character. Poetry must be a violent assault on the forces of the unknown, to force them to bow before man."[15]

Marinetti gathered around him many painters whose works would become the best-known creative output of the Futurists. Futurism gained legitimacy as an art movement by about 1912, when its works were being featured in the same Paris galleries that showcased the art of the Cubists. These paintings were the visual embodiment of the themes first articulated in Marinetti's "Manifesto":

> [the] great crowds agitated by work, pleasure and revolt; . . . the nocturnal vibration of the arsenals and the workshops beneath their violent electric moons; . . . gluttonous railway stations devouring smoking serpents; . . . factories suspended from the clouds by the thread of their smoke; . . . great-breasted locomotives; . . . and the gliding flight of aeroplanes.[16]

The Futurist movement's fascination with machinery, technology, and a general defiance of the cultural status quo led some of its members to explore radical new and unconventional music.

Among the leaders of this Futurist cell was the composer Francesco Balilla Pratella (1880–1955), who published his own manifesto, *Futurista Musica* (*Futurist Music*) in 1911. Like Busoni, Pratella was interested in expanding the range of harmonic music through the use of semitones and agreed with the use of a "chromatic atonal mode," as previously introduced by Schoenberg, although he claimed this development as "a magnificent conquest by Futurism." Pratella's hope to "crush the domination of dance rhythm" in order to create a freer approach to tempo was a startling anticipation of noise music and free jazz alike. But even though Pratella's contributions to the pedagogy of **Futurist music** were vital, it was the painter Luigi Russolo (1885–1947) whose name is most closely associated with the extraordinary musical experiments of this movement. Inspired by Pratella's manifesto, Russolo wrote his own called *L'Arte dei rumori* (*The Art of Noise*, 1913). Russolo's ideas were more extreme than Pratella's. Whereas Pratella was intent on expanding the repertoire of existing musical instruments, Russolo envisioned entirely new ways of making music through the use of noise. So devoted was he to this concept that he abandoned painting for a time to devote every working hour to the design and invention of new mechanical noisemakers to produce his music.

Russolo's manifesto anticipated the use of noise in modern music and naturally appeals to experimental music composers. As was natural for a child of the machine, Russolo equated the diminishing relevance of classical music to its being out of step with modern industrialized society. "Thus we are approaching noise-sound," he wrote in his preamble addressed to Pratella. He continued:

> This revolution of music is paralleled by the increasing proliferation of machinery sharing in human labor. In the pounding atmosphere of great cities as well as in the formerly silent countryside, machines create today such a large number of

varied noises that pure sound, with its littleness and its monotony, now fails to arouse any emotion.[17]

Russolo's solution for freeing music from its tonal prison was to "break at all cost from this restrictive circle of pure sounds and conquer the infinite variety of noise-sounds." He proposed making music from ambient noise and sounds from the environment, an idea that predated by many years any effective way of making remote audio recordings:

> We will have fun imagining our orchestration of department stores' sliding doors, the hubbub of the crowds, the different roars of railroad stations, iron foundries, textile mills, printing houses, power plants and subways. And we must not forget the very new noises of Modern Warfare.[18]

The Futurists' love of public spectacle and demonstration led Russolo to devise a means for orchestrating noise music in a live setting. Both recording and electronic music technologies were still in their infancy in 1913, so the painter focused his energies on the construction of a set of mechanical, hand-cranked noise instruments that did not require electricity. Teaming up with fellow painter Ugo Piatti, he constructed a variety of mechanical noise-producing instruments that the pair called *Intonarumori* ("noise-intoners"). The *Intonarumori* were designed to produce "families" of sounds ranging from roars (thunders, explosions) to whistles (hisses, puffs), whispers (murmurs, grumbles), screeches (creaks, rustles), percussive noises (metal, wood), and imitations of animal and human voices. Outwardly, each instrument consisted of an oblong wooden box with a large metal megaphone to amplify the sound. Inside, there were various mechanical devices used to generate the desired sounds by turning cranks, tapping stretched membranes, and other means. Some had levers and wires to rattle pots or cardboard canisters filled with objects. One used an air bellows to create wind or breath sounds. Another device, used to imitate the starting of an automobile engine, used a skin stretched like a drum head that, when scraped or tapped across its diameter, produced a sequence of pitched tones. Russolo also found that he could adjust the timbre of these stretched membranes by preparing them beforehand using various chemical baths. The noise-intoners were usually played by holding a lever with the left hand to control the pitch range and turning a crank with the right hand to evoke the noise.

By April 1914, an entire orchestra of roarers, whistlers, whisperers, screechers, and howlers had been constructed and Russolo's first Futurist concert was performed in Rome, presided over by Marinetti, Russolo, and their comrades. A number of set pieces were played, each engaging the noise-intoners in unison to create a variety of sound environments reminiscent of the city and nature. An audience disturbance ensued with scores of rotten fruits and vegetables hurled at the performers for the duration of the concert.[19] Marinetti and Russolo were arrested at the conclusion of the concert for having incited a riot. Bruised but triumphant, Russolo and Marinetti next presented a series of 12 performances in London in June 1914. The ensemble was arranged on stage with the megaphones of the noise-intoners aimed squarely at the audience. A musician stood behind each noise-intoner and read from a musical score mounted on a music stand. The formal stage appearance of the troupe was purposefully ironic and contrasted sharply with the noise music played by the musicians. Marinetti remarked that playing

Figure 1.9
Luigi Russolo and his
assistant Ugo Piatti
with *Intonarumori*, 1914.
(Philadelphia Museum of Art)

the noise-intoners for the unsuspecting public was like "showing the first steam engine to a herd of cows."[20]

A critique of the opening London concert in the London *Times* likened the music to the sounds heard "in the rigging of a channel-steamer during a bad crossing." The same critic suggested that it had been "unwise" of the musicians to proceed after their first piece was greeted by "the pathetic cries of 'no more' from all parts of the auditorium." Marinetti himself claimed that the performances were a huge success and attracted as many as 30,000 people.[21]

World War I largely brought the Futurist movement to an end. Some members, including Marinetti, became more politically minded and attached themselves to the rise of Nazism in post-war Germany. Russolo received a serious head injury during World War I, but after a long recovery period returned to Paris to continue his exploration of noise-making machines. One was the *Rumorarmonio*—the "noise harmonium"—which put several of his noise-making devices under the control of a piano-style keyboard.[22]

Sadly, all of Russolo's scores and noise-intoners were lost during World War II, and only a few low-fidelity recordings exist of their performances between 1913 and 1921. Beginning in the 1970s, several efforts have been mounted to reconstruct Russolo's noise-intoners and pay homage to this pioneer of noise music. The greatest legacy of Futurist musicians, however, survives to this day in the acceptance of ambient sounds, noise, verbal, and other non-tonal audio material in the composition of electronic and **electroacoustic** music.

INTO THE AGE OF ELECTRONICS

When Edgard Varèse created *Poème électronique* in 1958, he was nearing the end of a long, fruitful career as a composer. By all reports, he was not fully enamored with the clumsy technology of tape composition—a method for creating music that we shall see was dramatically different from that of writing for the conventional instruments of an orchestra. His perseverance with the new medium was a testament to his long-standing vision for a new kind of music comprised of all possible sounds—a dream that he began to nurture during his friendship with Busoni as early as 1907. Varèse was one of the first composers to anticipate the development of electronic music as a means for realizing entirely new musical experiences.

Edgard Varèse was in his early twenties when he moved from his native France to Berlin in 1907. His reason for leaving Paris was ostensibly dissatisfaction with the French music scene, which his wife later described as static and unimaginative, vices that did not sit well with the rebellious young composer. Varèse had been stirred by reading *Sketch of a New Aesthetic of Music* and chose Berlin in part because its author, Busoni, was living there.[23] The two quickly became friends and for seven years the elder composer tutored Varèse and reviewed his compositions. Before leaving Europe for America during World War I, Varèse continued to travel between Berlin and Paris, becoming friends with many of the poets, writers, and painters associated with Cubism and Futurism.

Varèse moved to New York City in 1915. Although his work with electronic instrumentation lay many years ahead of him, his early work with orchestral sound textures, percussion, and alternative tonal systems brought him early notoriety as an experimenter. He often took his case for new music directly to the popular press. In one of his very first interviews with the American press he told a journalist from the *New York Telegraph*:

> Our musical alphabet must be enriched . . . I refuse to limit myself to sounds that have already been heard . . . What I am looking for is new mechanical mediums which will lend themselves to every expression of thought and keep up with thought.[24]

Writing for the art periodical *391* in 1917, Varèse wrote even more prophetically that, "I dream of instruments obedient to my thought and which with their contribution of a whole new world of unsuspected sounds, will lend themselves to the exigencies of my inner rhythm."[25] Just how to achieve these sounds was unknown to Varèse, but his knowledge of Cahill's Telharmonium and continuing advances in the development of radio technology clearly pointed to an eventual collaboration between inventors and musicians. In an interview in 1922 he continued to speak about the necessity for new instruments and the likely marriage of electronics with music. "Speed and synthesis are characteristics of our own epoch," he said. ". . . The composer and electrician will have to labor together to get it."[26]

Varèse was an interested eyewitness to both Cahill's Telharmonium and the music of the Futurists, acknowledging the relative achievements of each but dismissing them on grounds that they were musically unoriginal. Varèse evidently attended a demonstration of a later model of the Telharmonium, an instrument that Cahill continued to develop long after the closing of Telharmonic Hall in 1908, remarking that he was "disappointed," evidently because so remarkable an engineering achievement was being applied to the production of such mundane, conventional music. Varèse was personally acquainted with Marinetti and Russolo, the "Futurist composers," and although he initially shared many of the tenets of Futurism, he found their music to be an uninteresting attempt to replicate the sounds of everyday life. "Why is it, Italian Futurists," asked

Varèse in 1917, "that you slavishly imitate only what is superficial and most boring in the trepidation of our daily lives!"[27]

Varèse's greatest output as a composer was during the 1920s and 1930s. Unlike most of his contemporaries, he did not prefer to work in either 12-tone or neoclassic music. It wasn't that he disdained tonality; instead, he shaped his music around rhythms and timbres, a move that instantly branded his approach as radical. He used **dissonance** unabated and energized his music with striking rhythms, clashes of timbres, and unusual combinations of instruments. He found support in some of the leading conductors of the time, including most prominently Leopold Stokowski (1882–1977) of the Philadelphia Orchestra, without whose support many of Varèse's works would never have been heard.

The introduction of the vacuum tube made possible a variety of new, electronic performing instruments. Varèse was quick to incorporate new instruments such as the *Ondes Martenot* and *Theremin* into his orchestral arrangements. By the early 1940s, even after having succeeded in establishing a repertoire of singularly iconoclastic works, Varèse still found it necessary to defend his approach to music by saying:

> I prefer to use the expression "organized sound" and avoid the monotonous question: "But is it music?" "Organized sound" seems better to take in the dual aspect of music as an art-science, with all the recent laboratory discoveries which permit us to hope for the unconditional liberation of music, as well as covering, without dispute, my own music in progress and its requirements.[28]

This statement came ten years before the availability of the tape recorder made the modern age of electronic music a reality.

EARLY ELECTRONIC MUSIC PERFORMANCE INSTRUMENTS

If Varèse can be called the father of electronic music, then the American inventor Lee De Forest (1873–1961) might be called the father of the "electronic age" that made electronic music possible. De Forest ushered in the first age of miniaturized electronics with the invention of the audion, or **vacuum tube**, in 1907. The function of a vacuum tube is to take a relatively weak electrical signal and amplify it. With its widespread availability by about 1919, electronic devices no longer required the enormous, power-sapping mechanical dynamos that made the Telharmonium ultimately impractical. The vacuum tube led to radio broadcasting, the amplification of musical instruments and microphones, and later innovations such as television and high-fidelity recording.

Between 1920 and 1945 there arose a vital community of inventors of musically related devices, including record players, loudspeakers, and amplified mechanical musical instruments. The vacuum tube also led directly to the development of a new generation of electronic musical instruments. Without the ability to record and edit sounds— a technology that would not become widely available until after World War II—this era was marked by the rise of the electronic performing instrument that could be played in real time along with other musical instruments.

An electronic phenomenon called **heterodyning** was the underlying principle of many early electronic musical instruments. Using heterodyning, two ultrasonic radio

LUIGI RUSSOLO AND *THE ART OF NOISE*

Luigi Russolo published his manifesto of Futurist music, *L'Arte dei rumori* (*The Art of Noise*), in 1913. Russolo's manifesto was an influential precursor of modern experimental music. His concept of creating music from common noises preceded the widespread adoption of this idea by electronic music composers by some 30 years. Following are some representative statements translated from *The Art of Noise.* Note how these ideas continue to be relevant to much of today's music, from rock to hip-hop to experimental music.

Figure 1.10 The cover of the original *Art of Noise* (1913). The Futurists advocated the complete destruction of musical order by celebrating noise as music.

Ancient life was all silence. In the nineteenth century, with the invention of the machine, Noise was born. Today, Noise triumphs and reigns supreme over the sensibility of men.

At first the art of music sought purity, limpidity, and sweetness of sound. Then different sounds were amalgamated, care being taken, however, to caress the ear with gentle harmonies. Today, music, as it becomes continually more complicated, strives to amalgamate the most dissonant, strange, and harsh sounds. In this way we come ever closer to noise-sound.

The musical evolution is paralleled by the multiplication of machines, which collaborate with man on every front. Not only in the roaring atmosphere of major cities, but in the country, too, which until yesterday was totally silent, the machine today has created such a variety and rivalry of noises that pure sound, in its exiguity and monotony, no longer arouses any feeling.

On the other hand, musical sound is too limited in its qualitative variety of tones . . . this limited circle of pure sounds must be broken, and the infinite variety of noise-sound conquered.

We Futurists have deeply loved and enjoyed the harmonies of the great masters. For many years Beethoven and Wagner shook our nerves and hearts. Now we are satiated and we find far more enjoyment in the combination of the noises of trams, backfiring motors, carriages, and bawling crowds than in listening again, for example, to the Eroica or the Pastorale.

Away! Let us break out since we cannot much longer restrain our desire to create finally a new musical reality, with a generous distribution of resonant slaps in the face, discarding violins, pianos, double basses, and plaintive organs. Let us break out!

We want to attune and regulate this tremendous variety of noises harmonically and rhythmically.[29]

INNOVATION

frequency signals of nearly equal frequency are mixed. The combination of the two results in a third signal that is equal to the difference between the first two frequencies. The remaining, audible tone is the "beat frequency" played by the performer. De Forest himself was one of the first inventors to adapt this principle to the creation of a musical instrument, the Audion Piano, in 1915. The Audion Piano was a simple keyboard device that could play one note at a time. De Forest likened the sounds to those of "a violin, cello, woodwind, muted brass and other sounds resembling nothing ever heard from an orchestra." The pitch of the notes could also be changed by rubbing the finger on part of the circuit, making vibrato and sliding notes possible.[30]

The Theremin and its Offspring

The De Forest Audion Piano was the precursor of the *Theremin*, one of the most familiar electronic musical instruments to gain widespread acceptance. The instrument was invented by the Russian electrical engineer and cellist, Lev Sergeyevich Termen (1896–1993), who was more commonly known by the anglicized version of his name, Leon Theremin. Originally called the Etherophone or Thereminovox, but later simply the Theremin, this device was first built in Russia around 1920. Although Theremin applied for patents in Germany and America during 1924 and 1925, it wasn't until 1927 that Americans first heard public performances of the instrument. Like the Audion Piano, the Theremin used a beat frequency method to produce its haunting sonorities. But instead of having a keyboard to trigger its sounds, the Theremin was played by moving the hands in the vicinity of two antennae. An upright antenna, about 18 inches tall, controlled pitch and was played by moving the right hand within an invisible frequency sphere surrounding the antenna. The loudness, or **amplitude** of the sound was controlled by placing the left hand near a second, circular antenna. The sound was continuous unless the left hand was actually touching the circular antenna. This design made the Theremin the first gesture-controlled electronic musical instrument.

The smooth, wavering tone of the Theremin is unmistakable. It is a familiar sound to those who have seen old science fiction or horror movies, where the Theremin was often used to create unearthly sound effects. The original Theremin had a range of five

Figure 1.11 Leon Theremin and his instrument, 1928. The cabinet is open to reveal the circuitry inside. (Robert Moog)

octaves. Its sound played continuously, somewhat like a violin that never stopped being bowed, unless a hand was moved in and out of the vicinity of the antenna. Special effects such as **vibrato** and **tremolo** were easy to produce with simple movements of the hand. Being monophonic, the Theremin was useful as a melodic instrument and was often given parts that might otherwise have been suited for a violin, flute, or other melodic voice of the orchestra.

The Theremin attracted the attention of American radio maker RCA, which signed the inventor to an agreement to manufacture and market a commercial version of his instrument. The RCA Theremin was introduced in 1929 and had a frequency range of about three and a half octaves. RCA product literature for the Theremin described the instrument as being capable of "exceptional individuality of expression," mainly because it lacked such "limitations" as a keyboard or the stops found on an organ.[31] Though only requiring a pair of hands to play it, the Theremin proved quite difficult to master. Only

Figure 1.12   RCA Theremin advertisement, 1930.

500 were sold by RCA. The instrument remained a quaint novelty at music recitals throughout the 1930s. Composers who wrote for the instrument barely explored its breadth of sound capabilities. The Theremin repertoire was quickly filled with trivial and programmatic solo parts, any of which could have been played as easily on a violin or cello.

The instrument was difficult to play with precision and consistency and required much practice. One had to literally learn to pluck a series of notes out of thin air with great accuracy. There was little room for error. The most revered thereminist of the day, Clara Rockmore (1910–98), knew the inventor and made the rounds of classical music recitals playing conventional music on this unconventional instrument. Her selections frequently included adaptations of string parts from works by Rachmaninoff,

Saint-Saëns, Stravinsky, Ravel, and Tchaikovsky. She once likened playing the Theremin to playing an entire string concerto on only one string. Rockmore is lovingly remembered as the greatest master of the instrument, and fortunately some audio recordings survive of her stunning performances.

Not surprisingly, many felt that the promise of the Theremin was trivialized by using it to perform conventional instrumental music. Composer John Cage (1912–92) echoed the sentiments of many serious composers when in 1937 he said:

Figure 1.13   Clara Rockmore, the foremost interpreter of classical Theremin music, 1932. (Robert Moog)

When Theremin provided an instrument with genuinely new possibilities, Thereminists did their utmost to make the instrument sound like some old instrument, giving it a sickeningly sweet vibrato, and performing upon it, with difficulty, masterpieces from the past. Although the instrument is capable of a wide variety of sound qualities, obtained by the turning of a dial, Thereminists act as censors, giving the public those sounds they think the public will like. We are shielded from new sound experiences.[32]

While Clara Rockmore was responsible for greatly advancing the artistry of Theremin performance, we can thank one of her contemporaries for expanding the original repertoire of the instrument into new musical territory. Lucie Bigelow Rosen (1890–1968), wife of prominent lawyer, banker, and art patron Walter Rosen, befriended Theremin around 1930. Theremin hand-built two instruments for her, and she took lessons from him. Under his tutelage, she joined Clara Rockmore as one of the most skilled thereminists ever to play the original instrument. She performed many concerts, including one at Carnegie Hall with the Philadelphia Orchestra.

Rosen was interested in exploring the new musical possibilities of the Theremin. She commissioned several prominent composers, including Bohuslav Martinů (1890–1959) and Isidor Achron (1892–1948), to write original works for her. These pieces explored the outer ranges of the Theremin's pitches, dynamics, and timbres. Martinů's work, the *Fantasia for Theremin, Oboe, Piano and Strings* (1944)—which Rosen premiered in 1945—used the composer's characteristically long melodic lines and blended and contrasted the tonalities of the Theremin with the strings and oboe. The 15-minute piece is beyond the skills of the average thereminist, which is a tribute to Lucie Rosen's virtuosity on the instrument. She premiered this work at Town Hall in New York in November 1945, along with a shorter work, *Improvisation* (1945) for piano and Theremin, by Achron. Rosen never made any professional recordings of her performances, leaving any documentary evidence of her skills at the Theremin strictly to the imagination, until recently.

In 2002, while visiting the Rosen's Caramoor estate to examine her Theremin, museum facility manager Bill Bullock mentioned to the author that there were several old disc recordings in one of the storage areas. Upon further examination, the recordings consisted of 21 78 rpm discs that Lucie Rosen had recorded privately in New York during the 1940s. Working with Caramoor, the author undertook the digital restoration of the recordings. The discs represent the only known recordings of Lucie Rosen playing the Theremin and appear to consist primarily of practice sessions and rehearsals. With material ranging from her rendition of the popular song *Danny Boy* to adapted short classics by Grieg, Bizet, and Tchaikovsky, the full extent of her skill is apparent. At least two of the discs contain orchestral music only, recorded presumably so that Rosen could practice her Theremin part in preparation for a concert. One most impressive track, the title of which is unknown, displays Rosen's most virtuosic Theremin techniques: a rapid series of notes played up and down the scale; sharp attacks; glissandi; and wide ranges in amplitude.

Figure 1.14 Lucie Bigelow Rosen performing with the Theremin, made for her by Leon Theremin, late 1930s. (Caramoor Center for Music and the Arts)

Lucie Bigelow Rosen did much to advance the art of Theremin playing. She was among the first people to commission works solely for the instrument and through her frequent concertizing continued to keep the art of the Theremin alive into the 1940s.

Among the treasures in Rosen's archive of Theremin scores is a unique transcription of Erik Satie's *Trois Gymnopédies* for three thereminists. She was no slouch when it came to technical aspects of the instrument either and kept meticulous notes about its care and maintenance. Rosen was part musician and part patron, one of the first enthusiastic supporters of the art of electronic music. Summing up her sentiments about the Theremin for some concert notes, Rosen once wrote, "I do not think there is any other instrument so responsive as this to the artist when he has learned to control it, and that must be its eternal fascination."[33]

Lucie Rosen and her husband became Theremin's chief benefactors while he lived in New York. During the 1930s, they provided a town house for him at a low monthly rent next to their own on West 54th Street. Theremin had several productive years at this location as he took on commissions to construct a variety of electronic musical instruments. During this time he invented the Rhythmicon, an early form of drum machine using **photoelectric** principles and a keyboard; the keyboard Theremin, a primitive synthesizer designed to emulate other musical instruments; and the Terpsitone, a small space-controlled dance platform upon which the foot movements of a dancer would trigger the sounds of the Theremin. The Terpsitone also provided evidence for Theremin's interest in the association of colored light with electronic sounds. An often-ignored aspect of the foot-controlled instrument was a bank of colored lights mounted on the wall behind it. Each was wired to correspond to a given pitch.[34]

Interest in Theremin's work quieted as the 1930s unfolded and the Depression took hold. Despite his fortunate association with the Rosens, Theremin was constantly in a state of debt and trying to find additional work to remain solvent. Complicating matters more was a secret of which even the Rosens were unaware. Theremin was a Russian spy and had been passing American technological secrets to the Soviet Union since his arrival in America in 1927.[35] As 1938 arrived, he had been living in the States for ten years on a long-expired visa. Time was running out for him. When he became unable to pay his rent, Lucie Rosen's husband was finally forced to threaten the inventor with eviction. Before that could happen, Theremin suddenly left the country—some say under Soviet arrest—and was not heard from again for almost 30 years.[36] His parting gesture before disappearing was to finish the second of two custom-made Theremins that he had agreed to make for Lucie. One of his assignments back in the mother country was to create a new type of electronic surveillance device: the wireless bug.

Several composers were so fascinated by the Theremin that they approached the inventor with some of their own ideas for electronic musical instruments. Two of Leon Theremin's most notable collaborations were with Henry Cowell (1897–1965) and Edgard Varèse.

In 1931, Cowell asked Theremin to make a special keyboard instrument that came to be known as the Rhythmicon. Depressing one of the keys resulted in a pitched rhythm that could be repeated automatically. It was possible to play multiple notes and rhythms by depressing more than one key at a time. The Rhythmicon worked on the principle of light beams being cast upon photoelectric cells

Figure 1.15 This Theremin was custom-made for Lucie Bigelow Rosen by Leon Theremin. (Thom Holmes)

Figure 1.16   An ensemble of cello Theremins, 1932. The monophonic instrument was played by pressing a finger to the plastic fingerboard to produce a note. A handle was used to adjust volume. Behind the performers are pictured several diamond-shaped loudspeakers.

to produce its electronic frequencies. Cowell used this device in a number of compositions during the 1930s.

In 1933 Varèse approached Theremin about constructing a new instrument for a new piece he was composing called *Ecuatorial*. Although written for a small ensemble consisting of baritone, organ, brass, and percussion instruments, Varèse wanted to add an electronic instrument with a pitch range that exceeded the high C on the normal piano by an octave and a fifth, something akin to the upper register of the violin. He had previously worked with an instrument known as the *Ondes Martenot* (see p. 25) as part of the 1929 staging of his massive orchestral work *Amériques* (1918–21) and was familiar with the limitations of that instrument. He asked Theremin to construct two instruments to meet his precise tonal and dynamic specifications. The instruments had to be able to play high, sliding pitches and sustain them for a long time.

Theremin responded by resurrecting an old idea from 1922—that of his "cello" or "fingerboard" Theremin. Using the same beat frequency principle as the space-controlled model, this Theremin was controlled by sliding the finger up and down a cylindrical fretboard about the size of that found on a cello. It was played upright, resting on the floor and positioned between the legs like a stringed instrument. The left hand picked the notes on the fretboard while the right hand controlled the volume with a lever. The specially designed cello Theremins were used for the premiere of *Ecuatorial* in New York in 1934. Overall, the work was greeted with favorable reviews, although the cello Theremins were variously described in the press as being "mere caterwauling" and "piercingly shrieking."[37]

Although by the 1940s the inventor of the Theremin had dropped out of sight, his famous instrument lived on. It gained a second life in the movies as a provocative element of soundtrack music. Composer Miklós Rózsa (1907–95) wanted to use a Theremin in his film music for Alfred Hitchcock's *Spellbound*, released in 1945. He first offered the job to Clara Rockmore, but the Theremin virtuoso declined the offer, in part because she was already committed to a concert tour, but also because she steadfastly refused to use her talents on the instrument for making "spooky noises."[38] Rockmore's refusal became the chance of a lifetime for a foot doctor from Hollywood named Dr. Samuel J. Hoffman (1904–68).

Trained as a violinist, Hoffman had continued to be active as a nightclub musician in a dance band even after opening his medical practice. In the mid-1930s, while living in New York, he acquired a Theremin in payment for a bad debt owed to him. He soon made the electronic instrument a part of his musical repertoire. Upon moving to Hollywood in 1941 he registered with the local musicians' union and, as a lark, listed the Theremin as one of his instruments. As he recalled later:

> When Miklós Rózsa thought of using a Theremin in his score for *Spellbound*
> he called the union to see if any Theremin players were available. I was the only
> one listed at that time who could read music. He came out to see me with a
> sketch of the part he wanted to write and was delighted when he discovered
> I could sight-read it. So the Theremin part went into the *Spellbound* score; the
> score won an Academy Award.[39]

This stroke of luck led to a long association of the Theremin with motion pictures, primarily through the inspired "spooky noises" that Hoffman was so masterful at creating. His respectable list of movie credits is spread equally among hit movies, near misses, and low-budget exploitation films. In addition to *Spellbound*, they include such diverse accomplishments as *The Lost Weekend* (1945), *Lady in the Dark* (1946), *The Fountainhead* (1949), *Rocketship X-M* (1950), *The Thing* (1951), *The Day the Earth Stood Still* (1951), *The Ten Commandments* (1956), and *Billy the Kid vs. Dracula* (1966).[40]

The design of electronic musical instruments began to liven up after the initial success of the Theremin in the 1920s. Many of these devices could rightfully be considered offspring of the Theremin, since the basic principles underlying them were borrowed from Leon Theremin.

The Theremin experienced another revival with the coming of the transistor age. Robert Moog (1934–2005), while still in graduate school at Cornell University, financed part of his education by running a business making transistorized Theremins out of his basement. Moog Music Co. continues to manufacture a solid-state Theremin line called the Etherwave and the instrument has gradually found its way into more recordings of contemporary music, particularly by rock groups such as the Pixies, Portishead, Blur, and noteworthy virtuoso Pamelia Kurstin. The use of a Theremin-like instrument on several Beach Boys recordings, including *Good Vibrations* (1966) is an interesting story about finding other ways to create a similar sound. The classical tradition of Theremin playing is being kept vital by Russian player Lydia Kavina, who happens to have been the grand-niece of the late Leon Theremin, from whom she first learned the instrument. Kavina is in demand as a concert soloist and particularly for providing virtuosic playing for movie soundtracks, including *Ed Wood* (1994) and *The Machinist* (2004).

The *Ondes Martenot*

The most successful offspring of the Theremin was the French-made *Ondes Martenot*, originally called the *Ondes musicales* ("musical waves"). This device was designed by musician Maurice Martenot (1898–1980). He wanted to invent an electronic musical instrument that could join the ranks of traditional symphonic instruments and be the focus of works written by leading composers. To accomplish this, he had to address two major obstacles that hindered the Theremin from becoming more widely accepted by musicians and composers. First, the Theremin didn't look like a musical instrument, but more like a radio; and, second, its space-controlled design was difficult and challenging for most people to master.

Martenot borrowed Theremin's principles for generating musical tones, but also stole a page from the Audion Piano by providing an instrument with a familiar keyboard. The cabinetry was also pleasing to the eye and looked at home in an orchestra.

The *Ondes Martenot* was the size of a small, upright keyboard instrument. It was housed in an elegant wooden cabinet fashionably tailored using an art deco motif, complete with matching loudspeakers.

The Theremin had existed in the public eye as a scientific curiosity before it was generally accepted as a serious musical instrument—a factor that Martenot believed probably stunted its acceptance as a legitimate instrument. To ensure the immediate success of his new instrument, Martenot commissioned an orchestral work to spotlight its musical qualities. The instrument was introduced to the world in Paris when Martenot himself played the solo part in the world premiere of Dimitri Levidis's (1886–1951) *Symphonic Poem for Solo Ondes Musicales and Orchestra* in May 1928. This very first piece used microtonal elements including quarter and eighth tones, an impressive beginning for an instrument that is still in active, albeit limited, use today.

The *Ondes Martenot* was more than a Theremin hidden inside a tasteful cabinet. Although it used the same beat frequency technology as the Theremin, Martenot designed it expressly for playing parts that could be transcribed for a keyboard. Like the Theremin, the *Ondes Martenot* was monophonic and was restricted to the playing of melodies, but it triggered notes in such a way that the musician could relate them to the chromatic scale. The original instrument played by Martenot at its Paris premiere controlled pitch by the lateral movement of a finger ring that was attached to a metal wire (see Figure 1.18). The ring was moved using the index finger of the right hand. This in turn adjusted a variable capacitor on the ribbon that changed the frequency of the tone over a seven-octave range. Sliding the ring to the left played lower notes; sliding it to the right played higher notes. The ribbon was ingeniously superimposed over a picture of a piano keyboard, and movements of the ring corresponded to notes of the scale and gradations in between. The left hand controlled volume with a pressure-sensitive key. This was unique in that, when the key was fully released, no sound was heard. As the player gradually depressed it, the volume increased. An appealing feature of the ribbon controller was the ability to produce minute fluctuations in pitch for vibrato effects by moving the finger back and forth ever so slightly. Later improvements in the design included a model with an organ-style keyboard, volume controls using either a knee lever or a foot pedal, and a small bank of expression keys to filter the tones that could be operated by the left hand.

Maurice Martenot succeeded in inspiring many leading composers to write music for his instrument and the *Ondes Martenot* met with unprecedented success for an electronic performance instrument. Following its impressive debut in 1928, the conductor Leopold Stokowski brought Martenot to the United States to perform the Levidis work with the Philadelphia Orchestra. This led to a tremendous flurry of composition for the device and the creation of a formalized training program and school for the instrument under the direction of Martenot in Paris. Many composers were drawn to the instrument for its flair in creating unusual harmonic effects, such as tolling bells or birdsong. Numerous works have also been written for ensembles consisting only of several *Ondes*

Figure 1.17 An ensemble of eight *Ondes Martenots*, a percussionist, and a pianist performing at the 1937 Paris World's Fair.

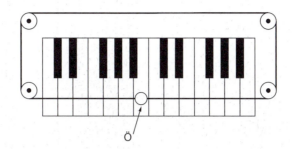

Figure 1.18   Ondes Martenot ring mechanism.

Figure 1.19   Performer and the original
Ondes Martenot showing keyboard template
and finger-ring controller.

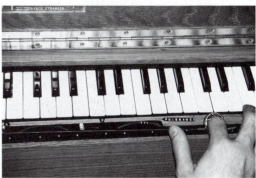

Figure 1.20   Ondes Martenot: right hand showing
view of finger-ring controller. (Thom Holmes)

Figure 1.21   Ondes Martenot: left-hand expression
controls. (Thom Holmes)

Figure 1.22   A keyboard model of the *Ondes
Martenot*. The left hand is positioned on the
expression controls. The index finger of the right
hand is inserted into the finger ring. Any individual
key could be jiggled laterally to produce vibrato.
(Thom Holmes)

Martenots. To date, more than 300 composers have contributed to this repertoire, which includes no fewer than 100 chamber works, 50 operas, 100 symphonic works, numerous ballets, and over 500 incidental scores for films and theater.[41]

Like the Theremin, the *Ondes Martenot* has been associated with several virtuosi performers. The first was Martenot's sister, Ginette Martenot. Perhaps the best-known *Ondes Martenot* performer was Jeanne Loriod (1928–2001), who from the age of 18 dedicated her career to the mastery of the instrument and the documentation of its written repertoire. She studied with Martenot himself, and recordings of her performances are commercially available. One of Loriod's most noted protégées is Valérie Hartmann-Claverie, who has been playing the *Ondes Martenot* with orchestras around the world since 1973.

Another keyboard-controlled beat frequency instrument was the *Sphärophon*, invented in 1924–25 by German Jörg Mager (1880–1939). Like Varèse and composer Charles Ives, Mager was an advocate of microtonal music and used the *Sphärophon* to subdivide the chromatic scale into additional pitches, making it a quarter-tone instrument. Although the *Sphärophon* was not widely used, Mager was commissioned in 1931 to provide a modified version that could produce electronic bell sounds for a production of the opera

ELECTRONIC MUSIC BEFORE 1945

LISTEN

1 *Risveglio dii una città* (1913) by Luigi Russolo
Mechanical noise-intoners

2 *Corale* (1921) by Luigi Russolo
Mechanical noise-intoners and orchestra

3 *Valse sentimentale* (Tchaikovsky) by Clara Rockmore (performance 1977)
Theremin

4 *Ecuatorial* (1933) by Edgard Varèse
Scored for chorus, small orchestra, organ, and two *Ondes Martenots*

5 *Langsames Stück und Rondo für Trautonium* (1935) by Paul Hindemith
Trautonium played by Oskar Sala

6 *Oraison* (1937) by Olivier Messaien
Ondes Martenot and orchestra

7 *Imaginary Landscape No. 1* (1939) by John Cage
Radios and turntables playing test signals

8 *Spellbound* (1944) by Miklós Rózsa
Musical score for the Alfred Hitchcock film, featuring Dr. Samuel J. Hoffman on Theremin

9 *Fantasia for Theremin, Oboe, String Quartet and Piano* (1944) by Bohuslav Martinů
Theremin, played by Lucie Bigelow Rosen when premiered in 1945

10 *Turangalîla-Symphonie* (1946–48) by Olivier Messaien
Ondes Martenot and orchestra

Parsifal at the Bayreuth festival in Germany. Mager also succeeded in producing a version of the instrument with as many as five keyboards—each dedicated to a different voice—which he called the *Partiturophon* (1935). Each of the closely spaced keyboards was monophonic but a polyphonic effect could be approximated by stretching the fingers to play more than one of the keyboards at the same time.

OTHER EARLY APPROACHES TO ELECTRONIC MUSIC

Electro-Mechanical Instruments

The early history of electronic musical instruments includes several inventions that used **electro-mechanical** means for generating tones. The earliest of these, like Cahill's Telharmonium, relied on raw voltage to amplify and project the sound without the miniaturizing benefits of vacuum tubes. A direct descendant of the Telharmonium was the Choralcelo, invented by Melvin Severy and George Sinclair in Arlington, Massachusetts, and first made public in 1909. This instrument most resembled a pipe organ, having two keyboards, organ-like stops, and a 32-note pedal board. The upper keyboard was a conventional piano, with hammered strings. The lower keyboard created organ-like tones using the tone wheel principle of the Telharmonium. The instrument had a third method of generating tones by using magnets to sympathetically vibrate a set of piano strings, creating an eerie drone. The timbre of the sound was modified using an ingenious set of mechanical filters consisting of resonators—wood, glass, and steel—through which the electrical output was driven. The addition of a paper roll made it possible to play previously recorded performances, much like a player piano. Six of these instruments were reportedly sold, some remaining in use for more than 30 years.[42]

In 1929, American inventor Laurens Hammond (1895–1973) demonstrated a new keyboard instrument that revived tone wheel technology yet again, only in a much more compact and self-contained design. Hammond's electro-mechanical method for generating musical tones was identical in principle to that used in the Telharmonium, only on a miniaturized scale due to the application of vacuum tube components. The instrument used 91 metal tone wheels each about the size of a quarter, all driven on a common rotating shaft.[43] By avoiding vacuum tubes to generate the tones, Hammond avoided the notoriously unstable nature of tube oscillators that made them difficult to keep in tune. Vacuum tubes were used in other components to manage the power, mix the tones, and amplify the sounds, making it possible to fit the complete instrument into a single cabinet no bigger than that of a common pipe organ manual. Hammond's design proved to be stable and produced a warm, instantly recognizable sound. It was built to mimic the functions of a pipe organ and had sliding tone filters—"drawbars"—reminiscent of organ stops, to selectively add and remove overtones from the sound. Some 5,000 Hammond electric organs were sold before 1940, with more than a third going straight into churches.[44] The Hammond model B3—introduced during the 1950s—remains one of the most sought-after older organs on the market and is highly prized by rock, rhythm-and-blues, and jazz musicians.

Another route taken in the development of early electronic musical instruments was the amplification and modification of conventional pianos through the addition of electrical components. The Crea-Tone (Simon Cooper, 1930) used electromagnets to induce the continuous vibration of some of the strings of an otherwise familiar piano, providing a sustained tone to which other more staccato notes could be played.[45] The idea of the magnetic **pickup**, so familiar on the electric guitar, was also applied quite early to piano strings. The pickup has the simple function of converting string vibrations into electrical energy. The resulting electrical signal, when amplified, reproduces the tone of the vibrating strings. Whereas the guitar pickup is not intended to touch the strings, some early electrified pianos used contact pickups that were fastened directly to a piano's soundboard. The Radiano (Frank Adsit, 1926) comprised a set of pickups that could be attached to any piano. It amplified the sound of the piano through the microphone input of a conventional radio set. The next generation of electrified pianos used proximity pickups and eliminated the soundboard entirely, providing a sound that was distinctively different from an acoustic piano. Various schemes were developed. The Neo-Bechstein (Oskar Vierling and Walter Nernst, 1929) divided the strings into groups of five, each with its own pickup. The Electronic Piano (Benjamin Miessner, 1930) was possibly the most elegant design of all, using an individual pickup for each string. Miessner found much success with this instrument and later produced several commercially successful electronic organs as well. The Wurlitzer Company licensed the pickup design of the Electronic Piano and used it in a smaller machine that replaced the strings with tuned metal reeds.

Electronic Tone Generation

By the 1920s, advances using the De Forest vacuum tube led to the development of radios, power amplification, and purely electronic means for producing musical tones. In the earliest such instruments, a vacuum tube could be dedicated to the task of playing a single note on the keyboard. An instrument of this type required one vacuum tube for each note and allowed more than one key to be played at the same time, providing true polyphony. The earliest such tube **oscillators** were notoriously hot, prone to burn out, and quickly became unstable and detuned. Even so, several early experimental instruments provided inventors with a body of experience for continually improving the development of purely electronic keyboard instruments. One early example was the Staccatone, created by Hugo Gernsback in 1923. This instrument used tube oscillators with an unadulterated sine wave tone. Its keyboard was no more than a series of on–off switches, giving the tones an abrupt staccato attack.[46] Gernsback invented an improved version called the Pianorad ("piano radio") in 1925, based on the same technology but with a more piano-like keyboard controller and the ability to sustain the sounds for any length of time. The tube oscillators of the Pianorad produced sounds that were nearly devoid of overtones, creating piercingly pure notes that were more reminiscent of the squeals from a radio than of musical sounds. R. C. Hitchcock developed an early "Radio Organ" for Westinghouse Electric in 1930, using vacuum tube oscillators and played using a three-octave keyboard similar to that of a pipe organ.

Another approach to electronic organ design combined the use of photoelectric sensors with vacuum tube oscillators. The basic principle is reminiscent of the tone wheel technology of the Telharmonium and Hammond organ. Sound was generated by beaming a light through the slits of a rotating disc onto a photoelectric cell. The rotation speed of the disc and the distance between the equidistant slits produced a prescribed frequency, or signal. The photoelectric cell converted the light signal into an electrical impulse equivalent to a musical tone and triggered a vacuum tube oscillator to produce an audible note. This principle was used on a variety of electronic instruments during the 1920s and 1930s, including the Cellulophone (Toulon and Bass, France, 1927), the Photo-Electric Organ (Free, United States, 1931), the Photona (Eremeef, United States, 1935), and the Light Tone Organ (Welte, Germany, 1936).

The most complex and successful electronic instruments to utilize the principle of "one vacuum tube per note" were developed by French inventors Edouard E. Coupleaux and Joseph A. Givelet during the 1930s. Their greatest improvement on earlier tube oscillator instruments was the introduction of controls over the tone quality of the notes. Even though the sine wave oscillators began with a simple, pure tone, additional circuitry was available for adding and subtracting overtones to produce a wide variety of tone color. The Coupleaux–Givelet organs were best known for their rich sound and chorus effects. Used extensively for radio broadcasts, these organs were large and hot and a typical model with three keyboards required more than 500 vacuum tubes to generate, filter, modify, and amplify tones.

The Hammond organization also experimented with electronic organs that used tube oscillators to generate notes instead of tone wheels. The most spectacular of these was the Novachord, introduced in 1939 (see Figure 1.23). The Novachord improved upon earlier tube oscillator organs by creating more notes on the keyboard with fewer tubes.

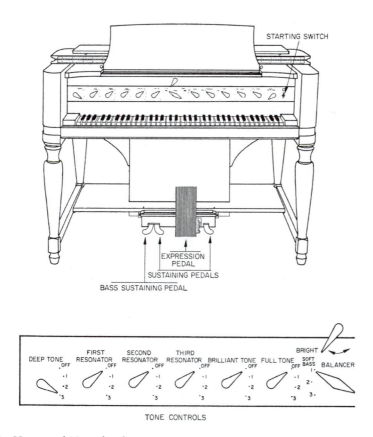

Figure 1.23 Hammond Novachord.

This was done by using a more complex tube oscillator and related circuitry that could electronically divide the basic waveform of an oscillator into other octaves. The Novachord, therefore, only needed 12 tube oscillators to service all 72 notes on its keyboard. The instrument was also known for its elaborate controls over the envelope of the sound and tone quality, reminiscent of the synthesizer technology that would become more prevalent in the 1960s. Even including the additional circuits required to process, divide, filter, and amplify its tones, the Novachord only had about 146 vacuum tubes, a stark contrast to the 500+ tubes of the Coupleaux–Givelet organ. Tone controls on the Novachord had imaginative and distinctive settings such as "deep," "brilliant," and "full" tone; "normal" and "small" vibrato; and "strong" and "soft" bass and percussion. Using combinations of these controls made it possible to imitate various orchestral instruments—another distinction of the Novachord as the forerunner of the modern synthesizer tuned with "presets" for specific sounds. Unfortunately, the Novachord proved to be unstable and unreliable in performance. About 1,100 Novachords were produced between 1939 and 1942. One could argue that it was, in fact, the first commercially available polyphonic synthesizer because its design was intrinsically suited for controlling tone color, filtering sounds, and generating a variety of attack and decay parameters using envelope generation.[47]

Some early electronic musical instruments departed radically from a piano or organ design. The Trautonium of Dr. Friedrich Trautwein (1888–1956) was developed in Germany between 1928 and 1930. The early evolution of this instrument was the result of a collaboration between Trautwein and composer Paul Hindemith (1895–1963). Oskar Sala (1910–2002), a composition student of Hindemith's at the time, recalled how the idea came about:

> I have no doubts now that he, the engineer [Trautwein], took the idea of an electrical string manual from the great composer and viola virtuoso not only because he wanted to show the experimentally interested professor that this could be done electronically, but also because the enlightening idea of an electronic string instrument had so far not been heard of.[48]

What Sala meant by an "electronic string instrument" was not an electric version of a cello, or viola, but a wire ("string") that was pressed by the finger to play a sound. The instrument had a fingerboard consisting of a metal plate about the width of a medium-sized keyboard instrument. Stretched only a few millimeters above the plate

Figure 1.24 The Westinghouse "Radio Organ" (1930) was an early electronic organ using vacuum tube oscillators.

was a wire. Pressing the wire with a finger so that it touched the plate closed a circuit and sent electricity to a neon-tube oscillator, producing a tone. The monophonic instrument spanned three octaves, with the pitch going up from left to right along the fingerboard. Volume was controlled by a foot pedal. The fingerboard was marked with the position of notes on the chromatic scale to make it easier for a musician to play. By 1934, Trautwein had added a second fingerboard so that two notes could be played at once. At the same time, he introduced an ingenious feature for manually presetting notes to be played. A rail was mounted just a few centimeters

Figure 1.25   Oskar Sala and the Mixtur-Trautonium. (Reiner Pfisterer)

above and running parallel to each of the two resistor wires. To this were attached 10–15 springy metal strips or "tongues" covered in leather, each of which could be slid to any position along the length of the wire. This enabled the musician to preset the location of notes to be played. Pressing a tongue was like pressing a key: it pushed the wire down so that it contacted the metal plate.[49]

The neon-tube oscillator produced a **sawtooth waveform** that was rich in harmonic sidebands. This waveform distinguished the sound of the Trautonium from that of the Theremin and *Ondes Martenot*, both of which used a beat frequency technology and produced waveforms with fewer harmonics. To take advantage of this unique characteristic of the neon-tube oscillators, Trautwein devised a set of filters, controlled by rotary dials, to adjust the amplitude of the harmonics in relation to the fundamental tone being played. This was an early experiment with **subtractive synthesis**—the careful reduction of sidebands to produce timbral changes in tone color.

Hindemith volunteered his composition students to assist with the construction of three instruments. Sala was the only one who jumped at the chance. "I had become a virtuoso on the soldering iron before becoming a virtuoso on the instrument," he recalled.[50] The German electronics manufacterer Telefunken, maker of the neon-tube oscillators used in the instrument, decided to manufacture and market a Trautonium for home use. The model featured a single fingerboard and a single pedal. Only 100 were built between 1932 and 1935.[51]

Hindemith composed a few more pieces for the instrument, most notably the *Concertino for Trautonium and String Orchestra* in 1931. But it was his student Oskar Sala who has been most closely associated with the instrument over the years, as both a composer and performer.

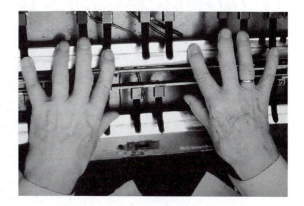

Figure 1.26   Oskar Sala demonstrating the string controls of the Mixtur-Trautonium. (Reiner Pfisterer)

After Trautwein's death in 1956, Sala assumed the role of keeper of the Trautonium and continued to make incremental enhancements to the instrument for many years. In 1952, he packaged it all together in a new version, which he introduced as the Mixtur-Trautonium.[52] Sala's primary improvement to the Trautonium was the expansion of harmonics available for the tones and improved controls. Sala's definition of a "mixtur" was a combination of four "subharmonics" or harmonics for a given master frequency. The warm, atmospheric sound of the Mixtur-Trautonium and touch-sensitive performance technique gained Sala some notice as a composer for dance and motion pictures. Among his accomplishments was the soundtrack he created for Alfred Hitchcock's 1963 horror film, *The Birds*, for which Sala created music as well as the menacing sound of the rampaging birds.

EARLY RECORDING TECHNOLOGY

The era of early electronic musical instruments was defined by the needs of the performance situation. All of the instruments described in this chapter were designed to be played in real time, often to the accompaniment of other instruments. The next era of electronic music was ushered in by the availability of the magnetic tape recorder, providing a means to record and manipulate sounds and opening up enormous new potential for the development of the medium.

Although tape recorders were not widely available until after World War II, experiments with audio recording technology closely paralleled those of even the earliest electronic musical instruments.

The *Phonautograph* by French inventor Edouard-Léon Scott (1817–79) (see Figure 1.27) is widely regarded as the first audio recorder, although it had no method for reproducing the sound. Scott made his first model in 1857. The Phonautograph detected

Figure 1.27   Scott's Phonautograph and an example of its paper recording (left).

Figure 1.29   The AEG Magnetophone. (AEG)

Figure 1.28   The Telegraphone. (Smithsonian Institution)

sound using a horn connected to a diaphragm. The diaphragm was connected to a stylus that vibrated to incoming sound waves. The recording consisted of a visual analog of a sound inscribed on a piece of paper. It was used in the scientific study of sound waves and their shapes. The principle of converting a sound into a physical impression using a stylus was key, however, to the development of the first "talking machine" by Thomas A. Edison (1847–1931) in 1876. Edison's first **Phonograph** inscribed a sound onto a sheet of tin foil wrapped around a rotating cylinder. The sound was played back using a stylus that amplified the vibrations recorded in the grooves of the tin foil.

Edison's breakthrough was soon followed by a myriad of competing mechanical sound recorders and playback machines. In 1887, Émile Berliner (1851–1929) introduced disc recording, the first examples of which consisted of glass discs coated with a thick fluid of ink or paint. Berliner called his first machine the **Gramophone** and imagined that it could be used to supply voices for dolls or to reproduce music. By 1896, windup mechanical turntables were widely available to play disc recordings and the Gramophone disc gradually displaced the Edison cylinder as the medium of choice for distributing popular recordings of music.

The first electrically activated audio recording technology was invented in Denmark by Valdemar Poulsen (1869–1942) in 1898. Called the Telegraphone, it was the first magnetic recorder and basal member of the family tree leading to magnetic tape recorders. The Telegraphone recorded sound on an uncoated steel wire as it rotated between the poles of an electromagnet. Poulsen described the device as an "apparatus for electromagnetically receiving, recording, reproducing, and distributing articulate speech," and envisioned it as a dictation machine. The Telegraphone could record for up to 30 minutes but its weak audio signal could only be heard using earphones because a practical means for amplifying electrical audio signals was not available at the time. Interestingly, in 1917, long after the rise and fall of the commercial version of the

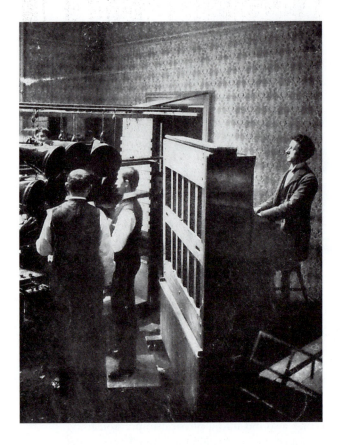

Figure 1.30
Early recording studio, *c.* 1910.
Without electronic amplification and
microphones, music was originally
recorded directly onto discs and
cylinders by projecting sound into a set
of horns. The horns, in turn, inscribed
the sound onto the recording medium
(e.g. wax cylinders or discs) by means
of a needle that vibrated in sympathy
with a membrane on the tip of the
horn. (Thom Holmes)

Telegraphone, Lee De Forest himself experimented with a version that was amplified
using his patented vacuum tubes. The patenting efforts of German Kurt Stille (1873–1957)
during the early 1920s kept the Telegraphone alive, resulting in incremental improvements to the technology, such as the replacement of steel wire with steel tape to increase
the surface area of the medium and to improve its fidelity.

Throughout the 1930s and 1940s, the two most practical and affordable audio recording mediums were those of acetate disc recording, primarily used in the music industry,
and **wire recording**, which found applications in office dictation machines, broadcasting
weather reports, home recorders, and military devices. It was during this time that the
development of the **magnetic tape recorder** took place, primarily in Germany. In
1928, engineer Fritz Pfleumer (1881–1945) patented a new recording medium that could
store electrical audio signals on paper or celluloid tape that had been coated with magnetic
(iron oxide) powder. German manufacturer Allgemeine Elektrizitätsgesellschaft (AEG)
began working with the technology in 1930, giving it the name *Magnetophone*. The first
commercial model was introduced in 1935, using coated paper tape at a cost-per-minute
that was seven times less than that of using steel tape. The earliest German tape recorders
had some kinks. The iron oxide powder was highly granular and much of it would scrape
off of the tape into a cloud of brown dust as the machine recorded or played sound.
As World War II approached, interest in magnetic tape recording waned outside of
Germany. The western Allies focused their engineers on making improvements to wire
recording technology.

At the end of World War II, the victorious Allies moved into Germany and were stunned to find that German magnetic tape recording machines were in wide abundance in military installations. The new generation of machines had overcome the limitations of earlier machines previously known to the West, including a much improved formula for the composition and magnetic coating of the paper tape medium. The audio fidelity was far superior to wire recorders and the West quickly adopted the magnetic tape medium.

By 1946, the United States held all patents on the AEG Magnetophone and licensed any American company that desired to build it. The first three American companies to make tape recorders included Magnecord, Rangertone, and the Ampex Electric Company. The first technical problem they faced was to replace the low-grade coated paper tape used by the Magnetophone with a higher-quality, more durable medium. This technical challenge was solved in 1948 by 3M (Minnesota Mining and Manufacturing Company) with the introduction of high-quality acetate magnetic tape, followed in 1953 by polyester tape. The medium of magnetic tape recording remained the most viable and affordable audio recording and editing medium for 40 years until the availability of affordable digital audio technologies in the 1990s.

The introduction of the magnetic tape recorder made possible a new era in the development of electronic music for it made possible the editing and manipulation of sounds as well as the performance of them, broadening the scope of the idiom beyond that of live performance.

LOOKING FORWARD

In the years leading up to World War II, Edgard Varèse continued his quest for an electronic musical instrument that would be obedient to his desires, a dream he had spoken of so often with his old mentor Busoni. While never suffering a deficit of ideas, he lacked the level of funding needed to make his grandest ambitions a reality. Beginning in 1927, Varèse devised a plan for the development of a laboratory in which to build sound synthesizing instruments and to train other musicians in their use. In 1927, Varèse's longtime friend René Bertrand invented an instrument known as the Dynaphone, and it was this electronic music device upon which Varèse conceived a master plan for the further development of such technology. In his own words, the objects of such an instrument would be:

- To obtain pure fundamentals.
- By means of loading the fundamentals with certain series of harmonics to obtain timbres which will produce new sounds.
- To speculate on the new sounds that the combination of two or more interfering Dynaphones would create if combined as one instrument.
- To increase the range of the instrument to reach the highest frequencies which no other instrument can give, together with adequate intensity.[53]

Varèse envisioned this project as applied research, marrying the engineering know-how of electrical engineers and acousticians with the practical application of the resulting technology by composers and musicians. It followed in Varèse's thinking that, "The practical result of our work will be a new instrument which will be adequate to the creative needs of musician and musicologist."[54] In actuality, the Dynaphone in its original form differed little in its beat frequency technology from the Theremin and *Ondes Martenot*, the latter being equally capable of making fine adjustments to tone color. What differed was that Varèse had an inside track with the instrument's inventor and found in the Dynaphone the potential to build future instruments with more capability.

Beginning in 1927 and for nearly ten years, Varèse approached such corporations as Western Electric and institutions including the Guggenheim Foundation with his proposal to fund the creation of a sound synthesis laboratory. Unfortunately for Varèse, such organizations neither understood nor could justify an endorsement of such ideas at such an early stage in the evolution of electronic music. Varèse himself only returned to electronic music after many years, when the availability of the tape recorder catapulted the field into the next stage of its development.

SUMMARY

- The first era of electronic music comprises the instruments and music created prior to 1945.

- In 1863, Hermann von Helmholtz published *On the Sensations of Tone as a Physiological Basis for the Theory of Music*, a classic work on acoustics and tone generation.

- The field of electronic music has often been led by composers and inventors with a need to invent a way to realize their musical visions.

- Two early electrical music devices, the Reis Telephone (1861) and Musical Telegraph (1874), were offspring of the new field of telecommunications.

- The first electronic music synthesizer was the massive Telharmonium patented by Thaddeus Cahill in 1896 and using a dynamo with rotating pitch shafts and tone wheels.

- Composer Feruccio Busoni published *Sketch of a New Aesthetic of Music* in 1907 and anticipated the use of electrical machines in the development of new music, revealing an important relationship between the inventor and the musician.

- Italian Futurist Luigi Russolo published *L'Arte dei rumori* (*The Art of Noise*) in 1913, a musical manifesto that encouraged the use of noise in music. Russolo and Piatti constructed mechanical noise-producing instruments for creating Futurist music, pre-dating the availability of audio recording technologies for the inclusion of noise in music by many years.

- Edgard Varèse was an experimental composer who anticipated the development of electronic musical instruments. In 1922 he spoke of the need for the collaboration of inventors and musicians and devoted much effort prior to World War II composing for available electronic musical instruments and seeking funds for research in the field.

- Electronic musical instruments invented prior to World War II were performance instruments designed to play live in real time.

- The first boom in electronic musical instrument development began in 1917 with the availability of the De Forest vacuum tube. The vacuum tube provided miniaturization of electrical circuits, amplification, and tone-generating capability.

- Electro-mechanical instruments used electrical means to amplify and modify mechanically produced tones. Examples include the tone wheel design of the Telharmonium and Hammond organ and the use of magnetic pickups to convert the vibrations of piano strings into electrically amplified sounds.

- Electronic tone generation was accomplished using vacuum tubes. The first such instruments used beat frequency technology and included the Theremin and *Ondes Martenot*. Another generation of instruments used multiple, tuned tube oscillators to reproduce tones, including the Coupleaux–Givelet organ (early 1930s) and the Hammond Novachord (1939). The Trautonium (1928) was a tube oscillator instrument that used a pressure-sensitive fingerboard instead of piano keys.

- The magnetic tape recording was invented in 1928 but was not widely available outside of Germany until 1945. The introduction of high-quality sound recording and editing ended the first era of live-performance electronic music and began the era of composing with recorded sounds.

Émile Berliner 35	Maurice Martenot 25
Feruccio Busoni 13	Fritz Pfleumer 36
John Cage 21	Valdemar Poulsen 35
Thaddeus Cahill 8	Francesco Pratella 14
Henry Cowell 23	Philip Reis 6
Lee De Forest 18	Luigi Russolo 14
Thomas A. Edison 35	Oskar Sala 28
Elisha Gray 6	Edouard-Léon Scott 34
G. P. Hachenburg 6	Kurt Stille 36
Hermann von Helmholtz 8	Leon Theremin 20
Paul Hindemith 28	Friedrich Trautwein 32
R. C. Hitchcock 30	Edgard Varèse 3, 4, 13
Filippo Marinetti 14	

KEY PEOPLE IN CHAPTER ONE

KEY TERMS IN CHAPTER ONE

amplitude 20	Phonautograph 34
dissonance 18	Phonograph 35
electroacoustic 16	photoelectric 23
electro-mechanical 29	pickup 30
electronic tone generation 30	polyphonic 6
envelope 6	sawtooth waveform 33
frequency 6	subtractive synthesis 33
Futurism 13	synthesizer 8
Futurist music 14	tape recorders 5
Gramophone 35	Telharmonium 8
hardwired 5	Theremin 20
heterodyning (beat frequency) 18	touch-sensitive 8
magnetic tape recorder 36	tone wheels 9
Magnetophone 36	tremolo 21
microtonal 13	vacuum tube 18
Musical Telegraphs 6	vibrato 21
Novachord 31	wire recording 36
Ondes Martenot 25	Westinghouse Radio Organ 30
oscillator 30	

MILESTONES

Electronic Music Before 1945

Technical and scientific	Year	Music and instruments
– Edouard-Léon Scott invented the Phonautograph, an early audio recorder.	1857	
	1861	– Philip Reis invented the Reis Telephone for electrically transmitting sound.
– Helmholtz published *On the Sensations of Tone as a Physiological Basis for the Theory of Music*, providing a scientific basis for electronic sound synthesis.	1863	
	1874	– Elisha Gray demonstrated the Musical Telegraph, a telegraph machine capable of playing two octaves of buzzing tones using a keyboard and vibrating metal reeds.
– Thomas A. Edison invented the Phonograph —a mechanical cylinder audio recorder and player.	1876	
– Émile Berliner invented the Gramophone, a mechanical disc audio recorder and player.	1887	

Technical and scientific	Year	Music and instruments
	1895	– Thaddeus Cahill patented the Telharmonium, an electro-mechanical keyboard instrument using rotating tone wheels to generate musical sounds.
– Valdemar Poulsen invented the Telegraphone, the first audio recording device using an electromagnetic principle.	1898	
– Lee De Forest invented the triode vacuum tube. By 1920, this type of vacuum tube would become the basis for a burgeoning electronic industrial revolution.	1906	– Cahill opened Telharmonic Hall in the heart of New York City.
	1907	– Feruccio Busoni published *Sketch of a New Aesthetic of Music* and suggested the promise of electrically produced music, mentioning Cahill's Telharmonium as an example.
	1911–14	– Proponents of Futurist music in Italy suggested that music should consist of everyday noises and proceeded to construct mechanical "noise-intoners" to demonstrate this new music.
– In an interview, composer Edgard Varèse stated that he was seeking "new mechanical mediums which will lend themselves to every expression of thought and keep up with thought," anticipating the marriage of technology and new music.	1915	– Lee De Forest invented the Audion Piano, the first musical instrument using his patented vacuum tube.
	1924	– Leon Theremin patented his invention, the Thereminovox, in the United States. It was a gesture-controlled electronic musical instrument using beat frequency technology. It became widely known as the Theremin.
– Fritz Pfleumer patented a new recording medium that could store electrical audio signals on paper or celluloid tape that had been coated with magnetic (iron oxide) powder.	1928	– Maurice Martenot invented the *Ondes Martenot*, a beat frequency-principle instrument with a fingerboard.
	1929	– Laurens Hammond invented the Hammond organ borrowing the tone wheel technology of Cahill's Telharmonium.

Technical and scientific	Year	Music and instruments
	1928–30	– Frederick Trautwein invented the Trautonium, an instrument using tube oscillators and a string fingerboard.
– The first commercially available magnetic tape recorder was introduced by AEG. It used paper tape.	1935	
	1939	– Hammond invented the Novachord, an electronic organ using tube oscillators.
– American companies Magnecord, Rangertone, and Ampex began making magnetic tape recorders.	1946	
– 3M produced the first acetate-based magnetic tape.	1948	

CHAPTER 2

Early Electronic Music in Europe

I noticed without surprise by recording the noise of things that one could perceive beyond sounds, the daily metaphors that they suggest to us.
—Pierre Schaeffer

Pierre Schaeffer operating the *Pupitre d'espace* (1951), the four rings of which could be used during a live performance to control the spatial distribution of electronically produced sounds using two front channels: one channel in the rear, and one overhead.

(1951 © Ina/Maurice Lecardent, Ina GRM Archives)

A convergence of new technologies and a general cultural backlash against Old World arts and values made conditions favorable for the rise of electronic music in the years following World War II. Musical ideas that met with punishing repression and indifference prior to the war became less odious to a new generation of listeners who embraced futuristic advances of the atomic age. Prior to World War II, electronic music was anchored down by a reliance on live performance. Only a few composers—Varèse and Cage among them—anticipated the importance of the recording medium to the growth of electronic music. This chapter traces a technological transition from the turntable to the magnetic tape recorder as well as the transformation of electronic music from a medium of live performance to that of recorded media. This important evolutionary stage of electronic music was rooted in Europe and marked the beginning of its second era of development.

BEFORE THE TAPE RECORDER

Prior to World War II, wire recorders and disc recorders were the only practical means for recording and playing sounds. Optical **sound-on-film** recording was another technology available in the 1930s. Lee De Forest, inventor of the Audion vacuum tube, was also the developer of one of the earliest optical sound technologies. The De Forest process, called Phonofilm, was introduced in 1919 about ten years before the widespread application of a variety of competing technologies for making movies talk. In the Phono-film process, audio signals were converted to electrical waveforms and photographically recorded on the edge of motion picture film. The soundtrack was made audible again by using a photoelectric cell to convert it during the playback of the motion picture. The quality of optically recorded sound was not substantively better than disc recordings of the time but the two-step recording and playback process and specialized equipment made sound-on-film less practical for composers than other technologies. Still, the art of sound splicing owes its beginnings to the movie industry, where optical sound was used to synchronize audio content with the moving picture. Some limited musical experiments with the direct creation of sounds using optical film recording had been done by John Whitney (1917–95) and James Whitney (1922–82) for their experimental films in 1940. Some composers, including John Cage, kept a watchful eye on all such audio recording technologies, hoping for a breakthrough that would make the capturing and editing of sounds possible for creating music. In 1937, Cage spoke of these technologies:

> Wherever we are, what we hear is mostly noise . . . We want to capture and control these sounds, to use them not as studio effects but as musical instruments. Every film studio has a library of "sound effects" recorded on film. With a film phonograph [sound-on-film] it is now possible to control the amplitude and frequency of any of these sounds to give it rhythms within or beyond the reach of imagination.[1]

Of the recording technologies available before World War II, the turntable had audio fidelity that was marginally superior to that of optical and wire recording. Table 2.1 compares the audio storage specifications of several competing technologies in 1930. Drawbacks of disc recording included a play-back time limited to a few minutes at a speed of 78 rpm and, for all practical purposes, no sound editing or mixing capability. Yet disc recorders were more widely available, less expensive, and more amenable to a trial and error process of sound assembly than both wire and optical recording. Despite the limitations of disc recording, or perhaps because "invention is the mother of necessity,"[2] several composers were nonetheless compelled to experiment with **turn-tablism**.

During the 1920s, turntables were often used onstage as part of performances, such as when composer Ottorino Respighi called for a disc recording of nightingales to be played during a performance of *The Pines of Rome* in 1924. Gramophones were a common household item and anybody who owned one was familiar with the amusing effect of letting a turntable wind down to a stop, gradually lowering the pitch of the recording as it did so. In 1930, inspired by the common gramophone, composers Paul Hindemith and Ernst Toch (1887–1964) found a new application for the turntable. Rather than using it to passively record the performance of other music, they experimented with the record player as the instrument itself. The occasion for their investigations was the 1930 Neue Musik festival of contemporary music in Berlin. Only a few weeks prior to

Table 2.1 Audio recording technologies, 1930

Technology	Typical media capacity	Frequency range[a]	Primary application	Editing
Phonograph cylinders (plastic)	8–9 minutes	100 Hz to 5,000 Hz[b]	Home recording and dictation	Playback and re-recording onto new cylinder
Gramophone discs (shellac)	4–5 minutes per side	80 Hz to 6,000 Hz	Commercial recordings of music and radio broadcasting	Playback and re-recording onto new disc
Wire recorders	60 minutes	200 Hz to 6,000 Hz	Home recording and dictation	Snipping the wire and tying or welding the loose ends together; or re-recording over an existing sound
Optical	5–10 minutes (early shorts) to full-length feature films	To 8,000 Hz	Motion picture soundtracks	Snipping the film and taping or gluing the loose ends together; the imprint of the audio signal was visible on the film and enabled accurate splicing

Notes

a The range of audio frequencies reproducible by an electrical audio device, expressed as a range from lowest to highest as measured in hertz (Hz). By comparison, magnetic tape media (*c.* 1950) and current digital media extended the frequency range of recorded media to the full span of human hearing, from about 20 Hz to 20,000 Hz.[3]

b Based on contemporary tests of an Edison Blue Amberol plastic cylinder conducted at Lawrence Berkeley National Laboratory, USA, and reported by V. Fadeyev, C. Haber, C. Maul, J. W. McBride, and M. Golden, "Reconstruction of Mechanically Recorded Sound from an Edison Cylinder using Three Dimensional Non-Contact Optical Surface Metrology" (LBNL-54927, April 20, 2004). Available online at http://repositories.cdlib.org/lbn/LBNL-54927/ (accessed April 29, 2007).

the festival, the composers were immersed in trial and error tests with microphones and disc cutters, producing what may have been the first music composed exclusively for the recording medium. It was the beginning of *Grammophonmusik*, the roots of turntablism. Their short program of *Originalwerke für Schallplatten*—original works for disc—included just five works lasting only a few minutes each. Hindemith named his two works *Trickaufnahmen* ("trick recordings") and the remaining three works by Toch were collectively named *Gesprochene Musik* ("spoken music").[4] The fundamental effect exploited by each man was the amusing effect of pre-recorded sounds being played back at the wrong speed, a trait of gramophone machines with which any owner of a hand-cranked model was already familiar. These short works were composed using a laborious multistep recording process. Equipped only with a microphone, disc lathe (recorder), and several playback turntables, the pieces were created by first recording a set of sounds onto one disc and then re-recording them onto a second disc as the first was played back, often at a different speed. In Hindemith's case, the *Trickaufnahmen* were devised for xylophone, voice, and cello, the latter being played at different speeds to change the pitch range of one of the parts. The several parts of Hindemith's piece may have required the playback of three discs at the same time, with the composer capturing the final "mix" by holding a microphone up to the sound. Hindemith was clearly intrigued by using the turntable to change the pitch of recorded sounds and mixing them to create new interactive rhythmic sequences. Toch's pieces used only voice and for these he employed a "four voice mixed choir."[5] Recordings of Toch's three examples of *Gesprochene Musik* have not survived, but one of the pieces, the charming *Fuge auf der Geographie* (*Geographical Fugue*), became Toch's most popular work and has since served to bring many a choral performance to a disarming conclusion. *Geographical Fugue* is essentially an exercise in tongue-twisting geographical names spoken to dramatic effect in various permutations of volume and pace. With such lines as, "Trinidad, and the big Mississippi," and "Nagasaki! Yokohama!" Toch's aim was to transform spoken word into rhythmic, musical sounds. His *Grammophonmusik* version used disc recordings to change the speed of the voices, a technique that had the unexpected consequence of changing some of the vowel sounds or **timbre** of the music. Together, Hindemith and Toch had discovered how to transform the gramophone into a sound-generating machine that could alter the pitch and color of a given recorded sound. What Hindemith and Toch recognized was that the mechanical traits that made machine music possible could also be explored for their own, inherently structural and musical qualities. Toch clearly explained this in a statement published at the time of the festival, saying that their purpose in working with *Grammophonmusik* was that of "exploiting the peculiarities of its [the gramophone's] function and by analyzing its formerly unrealized possibilities . . . thereby changing the machine's function and creating a characteristic music of its own."[6]

Very few composers immediately followed Hindemith and Toch in the exploration of *Grammophonmusik*, with the exception of Varèse, who by 1935 was experimenting with the playback of multiple turntables simultaneously at various speeds, and John Cage, who is well known for the turntable work *Imaginary Landscape No. 1* (1939).

Although in view of the *Grammophonmusik* of Hindemith and Toch it is a misnomer to call Cage's *Imaginary Landscape No.1* the first piece to be written specifically for a recording medium, the Cage work was certainly much better known and became part of a legacy of highly experimental works that greatly influenced music in the second half of the twentieth century. *Imaginary Landscape No.1* consisted of sounds produced

LISTENING GUIDE 2.1

Title: *Trickaufnahmen* [excerpt]

Artist: Paul Hindemith   **Year**: 1930   **Duration**: 01:02

Genre: Turntablism

Electronic Instrumentation: Turntables (recording and playback), recorded xylophone, and cello.

Background: One of the first works expressly composed with and for turntables, composer Paul Hindemith used speed changes to modify the natural pitch range of recorded snippets of xylophone and cello sounds.

	Listen For: Sped-up sounds and attempts to keep the three separately recorded parts synchronized. The piece maintains a pulse rhythm but the time signatures of the individual instrumental voices sometimes vary, creating a polyrhythmic effect. This short excerpt (about half of the complete work) is divided into six sections. These sections can be detected by listening for the cello "bass" line. The piece does not appear to repeat or loop sounds using a lock groove. Instead, each of the three parts was apparently recorded in entirety and then synchronized during playback in real time by adjusting the speeds of the turntables. This points out the technical challenges of working with analog technologies lacking the mechanics needed to synchronize the motors of individual components, a challenge that remained even with the advent of tape recorders and tape music in the 1950s.
0:00–0:10	After two initial beats of a tapping pulse rhythm, the sounds of all three instruments join in unison. The rhythm is halting and the parts slightly out of tune with one another. The xylophone track is sped up, the cello bass track is at normal speed, and a second cello track is sped up, giving it a strumming, guitar-like sound.
0:15–0:23	By the end of the first section, the xylophone has lost its synchronization with the accompanying cello bass line.
0:23–0:45	During four short sections, the tracks are synchronized better and a polyrhythmic effect is created as the xylophone plays double-time to the accompanying cello tracks. The xylophone plays up and down the scales.
0:46–1:02	The piece returns to a more synchronous rhythm for three successive passages followed by a short section for xylophone only.

Compare and Contrast

Symphonie pour un homme seul (1949–50) by Pierre Henry and Pierre Schaeffer
Williams Mix (1952) by John Cage
Demolition (1999) by Philip Jeck

by playing audio test recordings on variable-speed turntables with speed clutches in combination with cymbal and piano-string sounds. The waveform sounds on the recorded discs were originally electronically generated, giving the piece the distinctive charged energy of electronic music.

In using the disc recording medium, composers sought to liberate themselves from a dependence on the performance situation in order to create music. This early exploration of turntablism led directly to a creative outpouring of a newly conceived music of common noises that opened up the door to the second era of electronic music.

HALIM EL-DABH—ELECTRONIC MUSIC PIONEER

The musical career of Egyptian-born Halim El-Dabh (b. 1921) has spanned more than 60 years, during which he has become known as an influential composer, performer, ethnomusicologist, and educator. He arrived in the United States in 1950 after having received a Fulbright Scholarship to study music with Ernst Krenek at the University of New Mexico and was tutored by Aaron Copland, among others, for two summers at the Berkshire Music Center.

Equally important to El-Dabh's career were his early experiments with electronic music. El-Dabh composed one of the earliest known works of *musique concrète* in 1944, five years before Pierre Schaeffer would become famous for having coined that term to describe his experiments with recorded sound in Paris. While studying in Cairo, El-Dabh gained access to a magnetic wire sound recorder through the offices of Middle East Radio. He was allowed to borrow the wire recorder and, although it weighed 17 pounds and required a heavy microphone and power cable, El-Dabh took it into the streets to capture outside sounds. The primary subject of his recordings was a "pre-Islamic ritual" called a *zaar* ceremony, consisting of African-influenced vocal music and dances.[7] El-Dabh was fascinated by the possibilities of manipulating recorded sound for musical purposes but he had no models to go by. It seemed to him that the recording equipment from the radio station could open up the raw audio content of the *zaar* ceremony to further investigation, to unlock "the inner sound" that was contained within. "I just started playing around with the equipment at the station," explained El-Dabh, "including reverberation, echo chambers, voltage controls, and a re-recording room that had movable walls to create different kinds and amounts of reverb."[8] Using the equipment at his disposal, El-Dabh deconstructed the sound of the women's voices, concentrating in particular on the rhythm of the singing and overtones in the upper registers. "I concentrated on those high tones that reverberated and had different beats and clashes," explained the composer, "and started eliminating the fundamental tones, isolating the high overtones so that, in the finished recording, the voices are not really recognizable any more, only the high overtones, with their beats and clashes, may be heard."[9] Working in this way, isolated from the mainstream of contemporary music at the time, El-Dabh

Figure 2.1   Halim El-Dabh, early 1950s. (Halim El-Dabh)

independently discovered the potential of sound recordings as the raw material from which to compose music. The final piece was transferred to magnetic tape and lasted between 20 and 25 minutes. El-Dabh called the work *The Expression of Zaar* (1944) and it was first presented publicly during an art gallery event in Cairo.

MUSIQUE CONCRÈTE IN FRANCE

Pierre Schaeffer (1910–95) was a radio engineer, broadcaster, writer, and biographer. Pierre Henry (b. 1927) was a classically trained composer. Together, these two French collaborators fused an interest in new music with that of available recording technology to begin the second era of electronic music, that of the recorded sound. Building on precedents such as the *Grammophonmusik* of Hindemith and Toch, the turntablism of John Cage, and earlier predictions about machine music made by Busoni, Varèse, Cage, and others, Schaeffer and Henry pioneered the construction of music using sound recording tools, natural sounds, electronic signals, and instrumental sounds. The resulting form of music was called **musique concrète**, and the work of Schaeffer and Henry led to a growing institutional interest in electronic music and the establishment of electronic music studios around the world.

L'Objet Sonore—The Sound Object

Joining Schaeffer in his experiments with tape music was Abraham Moles (1922–92), a multidisciplinary theorist in information perception with degrees in engineering, philosophy, and psychology. Moles was fascinated by electronic music because it worked directly with the materials of sound production, providing composers with seemingly unfettered opportunities to forge sounds according to whatever psychological effect was prescribed. Moles viewed musical material as being "separable in experiments from the continuity of perception"[10] and therefore possible to examine as if one were dissecting any other natural phenomenon. Moles' approach to analyzing the psychological effects of musical sound began by objectifying the corporeal components of sound and, by implication, the audio materials that a composer could manipulate. Sound that existed apart from human perception was designated as *l'objet sonore* (**the sound object**). Music was regarded as a "sequence of sound objects" and experimental music could contain sounds that fell outside of what was normally considered harmonic or musical.

The sound object, according to Moles, contained three dimensions: amplitude (loudness); frequency (tone); and time (duration). These three dimensions of sound could be further articulated by examining their component parts, such as the attack, sustain, and decay characteristics of any sound and the harmonic relationships of tone combinations over time. For Moles, the impact of a piece of music does not lie solely in its inherent structure or sound choices; it is equally dependent on the way in which the work is perceived over time as it progresses. The technology of audio recording provided an excellent means to save and test the effects of various kinds of sounds. For the composer, the reduction of all sounds to these fundamental components was like leveling the playing field so that any conceivable sound could become a part of music. This is essentially the direction taken by Schaeffer and others who viewed electronic music as a valuable tool for shattering commonly accepted definitions of music, an understandable starting point for composers who found themselves immersed in a medium whose sound objects were not musical in a traditional sense.

The resourceful Schaeffer, energized by Moles' analysis of sound properties, drew these technical elements together into a strategy for the composer. He devised three *plans* for working with sounds:

1   The Harmonic Plan (*Plan harmonique*): the development of timbre (tone quality) as a function of the entire range of audible frequencies over time.
2   The Dynamic Plan (*Plan dynamique*): the development of dynamic aspects of sound (amplitude, envelope) with respect to time.
3   The Melodic Plan (*Plan mélodique*): the development of pitch and tone sequences over time.

Figure 2.2 is Moles' visualization of the amplitude (Dynamic Plan) and pitch (Melodic Plan) dimensions of the sound object.

The Harmonic Plan was illustrated in a separate figure, hinting at the challenges that Moles and Schaeffer faced in trying to create a taxonomy of musical sound material (see Figure 2.3).

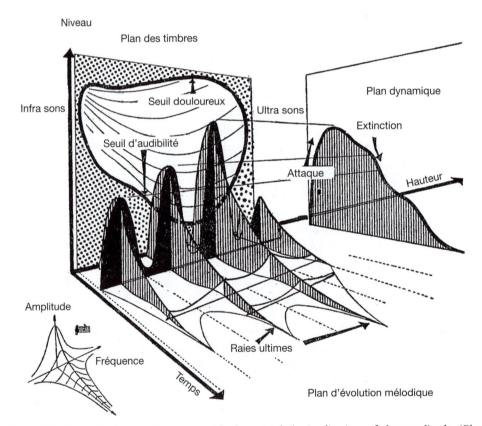

Figure 2.2 Sound in three dimensions: Abraham Moles' visualization of the amplitude (*Plan dynamique*) and pitch (*Plan mélodique*) dimensions of the sound object. (Moles, 1960)

Schaeffer's audio engineer Jacques Poullin went so far as to sketch a visual representation of the three-dimensional representation of a sound object using more conventional musical notation, as shown in Figure 2.4.

Poullin's sketch is also important because it represents an early attempt to notate the dymanic and attack characteristics of electronically manipulated sound—a challenge that would engage many composers over the years in their search for a nomenclature for documenting the audio traits of an electronic music work. Of his sketch that translates the given sound object onto a musical staff, Poullin freely admitted that it "becomes difficult to note all of its characters in only one figure," so he focused primarily on the fundamental or dominant frequencies of the tone.[11] Schaeffer, Poullin, and Moles all recognized the futility of trying to notate more than a few moments of music using their three-dimensional scheme, but the value of their approach to visualizing a sound object was nonetheless key to the ability to work with the raw material of musical sound on the basis of its constituent parts.

The idea of the sound object is critically important because it represented the appreciation of the traits that make up the composition of a sound. The accompanying diagrams represent only snapshot of a single moment in the span of a sound and presume that the sound object is accompanied by other transformative sounds before and after it. An approach such as this lent itself well to an approach to making music with technology, thrusting the composer into the role of chief engineer as well as musician.

Schaeffer had already composed several works for recorded media by the time he coined the term *musique concrète* in 1949.[12] The term has been somewhat misunderstood over the years and is commonly used to designate a work of electronic music composed for the recording media using electroacoustic or electronic sound sources. However, Schaeffer's original use of the term *concrète* was not intended to denote a kind of sound source at all but only the concept of the sound object as the driving principle behind the creation of the music. A *concrète* sound could come from any source, natural or electronic. In practice, *musique concrète* came to refer to any work that was conceived with the recording medium in mind, was composed directly on that medium, and was played through that medium as a finished piece.[13]

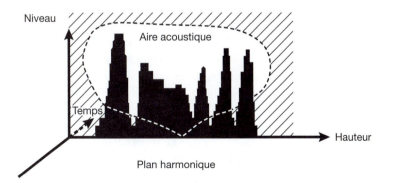

Figure 2.3 The *Plan harmonique*. Manually analyzing and illustrating even a single moment of sound became a challenge for Moles and Schaeffer in their attempts to create a taxonomy of musical sound material. (Moles, 1960)

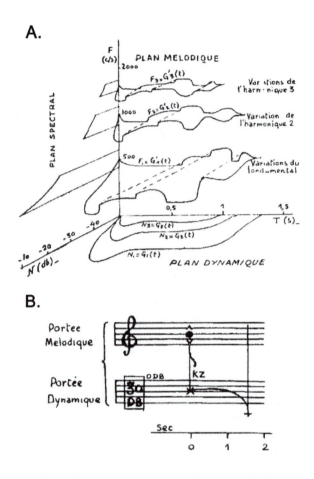

Figure 2.4   An attempt by audio engineer Jacques Poullin to visually depict the three-dimensional representation of a sound object using conventional musical notation. (Poullin, 1955)

Origins of *Musique Concrète*

Schaeffer graduated from the École Polytechnique in Paris in 1931 and continued his studies in the fields of electricity and telecommunications. He later accepted an apprenticeship as an engineer at the Paris facilities of French National Radio and Radiodiffusion-Television Françaises (RTF), which led to a full-time job as a technician and broadcaster.

RTF was at that time under the control of the German occupying forces. During World War II, Schaeffer led two lives. By day he worked as the director of a branch of RTF called the Studio d'Essai of the Radiodiffusion Nationale, which he had organized in 1943. His work there was devoted to experiments in radio production and musical acoustics. He also led a shadow life during the war as a member of the French resistance.

While employed at RTF Schaeffer had access to a wealth of radio broadcasting equipment, including phonograph turntables, mixers, microphones, and a direct-to-disc cutting lathe. He also had at his disposal a large archive of sound effects records owned by the studio and routinely used for radio productions. During 1944, he immersed himself in the production of an eight-part radio opera series called *La Coquille à planètes*.[14] Although an audio engineer by trade, Schaeffer had been raised in a musical family and was becoming acutely aware of the musical possibilities of audio recording techniques. For the opera production, he used a variety of non-musical sounds as part of the audio montage being broadcast over the radio. He undertook most of the technical work himself, learning how to work with turntable technology. In one part of the opera, Schaeffer combined noise and music in a more overt manner. He later explained that this experience in manipulating recorded sounds revealed "preoccupations which led to *musique concrète*."[15] Schaeffer was clearly immersed in a world of new discoveries while working on *La Coquille à planètes*:

> I was suddenly aware that the only mystery worthy of interest is concealed in the familiar trappings of triviality. And I noticed without surprise by recording the noise of things one could perceive beyond sounds, the daily metaphors that they suggest to us.[16]

After World War II, in 1947, Schaeffer met the audio engineer Jacques Poullin, who became his close collaborator on the design of specialized audio equipment for the radio studio. By January 1948, Schaeffer engaged himself in the production of a formidable set of five turntable compositions known collectively as the *Études de bruits* ("studies of noise"). After nearly a year of work on the material, the five pieces had their radio premiere on October 5, 1948.[17] These were the first completed works of *musique concrète*, a term that Schaeffer would coin in 1949.

The five pieces presented during the 1948 "concert of noises" were:

1   *Étude aux chemins de fer* (a montage of locomotive sounds recorded at a train depot).
2   *Étude aux tourniquets* (for xylophone, bells, and whistling toy tops called tourniquets or whirligigs).
3,4 *Étude au piano I* and *II* (both using piano material recorded for Schaeffer by Pierre Boulez).
5   *Étude aux casseroles* (using the sounds of spinning saucepan lids, boats, human voices, and other instruments).

Schaeffer composed the *Études de bruits* using only turntable technology and was faced with challenges similar to those of Hindemith and Toch some 18 years earlier. Schaeffer had the advantage, however, of being employed by a radio broadcasting station that gave him access to some mixing and filtering tools not normally found outside of a professionally equipped audio studio. Schaeffer used the following equipment to fashion his *Études de bruits*:

*   a disc-cutting lathe for making recordings of the final mixes;
*   four turntables;
*   a four-channel mixer;
*   microphones;
*   audio filters;

- a reverberation chamber;
- a portable recording unit;
- sound effects records from the radio station library and newly recorded sounds.

Schaeffer's list of recording and editing techniques for the *Études* reads like the lesson plan for an electronic music clinic. Remember that the year was 1948 and that the tape recorder was not yet in general use. Working only with a disc lathe to record sound was akin to working only with a film camera to edit a sequence of images: manipulation of the sequence of material was not possible except in real time during the recording of the content or the re-recording of previously made content while it was being played. Schaeffer edited different sounds together by playing them back and re-recording them directly onto disc masters. He played sounds in reverse. He created **lock grooves**— endless loops—with the disc cutter so that sounds would repeat. He played the sounds back at different speeds. He used volume control to modify the intensity and envelope of the sound, creating fades and balancing the amplitude levels of individual sound elements. He took some of the equipment outside of the studio to record natural sounds, including locomotives at the Batignolles train depot, amateur musicians, voices of friends, spinning saucepan lids, and piano music played for him by friends, including Pierre Boulez (b. 1925). Schaeffer combined sounds that he recorded himself with material from sound effects records and recordings of musical sounds from Bali and America.[18] The result was a tour de force of technical ingenuity and resourcefulness.

Historically, the *Études de bruits* introduced the world to the abstract plasticism of sounds plucked from the real world and woven together like so many swatches of multi-colored linen. Schaeffer did not merely offer a montage of sounds as if taken from a documentary film. He modified and structured them rhythmically and sonically as musical resources. Although Hindemith, Toch, and Cage had composed earlier works for the turntable medium, it was Schaeffer who generally gets credit for laying the groundwork for the emergence of electronic music composition—well-deserved praise for a man who in the end did not feel accomplished as a composer.

The significance of the *Études* to the second era of electronic music rests on four principles:

1   The act of composing music was realized through technological means, working directly with the recording medium.
2   Any and all manner of sounds could comprise the raw material of making the music. Many of the sound materials were of natural, not musical, origin.
3   The work could be replayed identically over and over again using mechanical means.
4   Presentation of the work did not require human performers.

Composing a work of *musique concrète* began with the sound material itself rather than with a mental schema, such as a score, laid out by the composer beforehand. *The material preceded the structure.* Sounds were then processed and edited by the composer until they were recorded in their final form. This approach to composition is nearly the opposite of that of traditional music, which begins abstractly by notating sound events on paper that are then only realized by a performer or group of musicians independently of the composing process. Not all tape compositions are composed in this manner, but it was the approach preferred by Schaeffer and which formed the basis for his discourse with sound objects.

The success of the *Études* attracted composer Pierre Henry to the studio and he joined Schaeffer and Poullin in their work in 1949. In 1951, after several more successful experimental works and broadcasts, the RTF provided funds for the creation of the first audio studio in the world devoted exclusively to the production of electronic music. This was the *Groupe de Recherches Musicales* (GRM), a collective of composers that became formally subsumed by RTF in 1958.

Henry's presence at the studio brought an immediate sense of musicality to the work of the studio. At the same time, Schaeffer's engineering mind was compelled to devise an empirical approach to making music from noise. Much like Russolo had done before him, he classified sound objects into several categories:

1   Living elements (including voices, animal sounds).
2   Noises.
3   Modified or "prepared" instruments.
4   Conventional instruments.

Symphonie pour un homme seul (*Symphony for a Man Alone*, 1949–50) was the first major collaboration between Schaeffer and Henry. Although the 12-movement work underwent many revisions over the years, the original recording, composed using only phonograph machines, was a striking and ambitious piece, even by today's standards. It was based primarily on two categories of sounds as defined by the composers:

1   Human sounds (breathing, vocal fragments, shouting, humming, whistling).
2   Non-human sounds (footsteps, knocking on doors, percussion, prepared piano, orchestral instruments).

As an approach to composing the work, these sounds were either modified using the technical resources that were at the composers' command or left alone and simply edited into intriguing patterns. The work freely employed spoken voice, broadcast music, prepared piano (an early approach to modifying the piano credited to Cage), and various mechanical or natural noises. Disc loops (repeating grooves) were effectively used to create rhythmic passages of spoken words. The piece was originally structured as a series of 22 movements or expositions on certain combinations of sounds. It grew in complexity from movement to movement, creating greater and greater abstractions of recorded sounds, until a finale of booming instrumental sounds brought it to a thundering close. It was highly charged and fraught with tension, a trademark of early *musique concrète*.

Tape recorders, audio signal generators, filters, and other audio equipment had become available to Schaeffer, Henry, and other composers at GRM, providing a much higher resolution audio recording medium than disc lathes and turntables. Schaeffer and Poullin also set to work on the design of several ingenious new tools for audio recording and editing. In addition to the requisite audio signal generators and filters, the studio was soon equipped with several unique sound processing devices:

- A three-track tape recorder.
- The *Morphophone*, a tape machine with ten heads for the playback of loops and the creation of echo effects.
- The *Tolana Phonogène*, a keyboard-operated tape machine designed to play loops. It had 24 preset speeds that could be triggered by the keyboard.

LISTENING GUIDE 2.2

Title: *Symphonie pour un homme seul:* Waltz

Artist: Pierre Henry and Pierre Schaeffer   **Year**: 1949–50   **Duration**: 0:56

Genre: *Musique concrète*

Electronic Instrumentation: Turntables (recording and playback), reverberation, pre-recorded sounds.

Background: This early work of *musique concrète* was composed using only pre-recorded sounds on disc. The disc tracks were edited and looped to create patterns and rhythms accentuating the dynamics of the recorded tracks. The piece was created through a process of recording and re-recording with turntables. This section is one of 12 parts. This early work of Schaeffer and Henry from Paris established much of the canon of sound editing techniques that were translated to tape composition beginning in 1950 and 1951.

	Listen For: Loops of pre-recorded sounds, repeating sections of sound, and sections of sounds played in reverse.
0:00–0:20	The piece begins with an alternating sequence of orchestral strings and voices (male and female), all treated with reverberation. This exchange includes shorter and shorter sequences.
0:21–0:48	The next section contains mixed sound of male and female voices and strings playing at the same time, and looping in short repeated sequences.
0:49–0:56	The piece ends with three short loops of the orchestral strings, the third of which audibly wobbles because of a manual speed adjustment.

Compare and Contrast
Williams Mix (1952) by John Cage
Fragment Opera (2001) by Marina Rosenfeld

- The *Sareg Phonogène*, a variable-speed version of the *Tolana Phonogène* tape loop machine.
- The *Potentiomètre d'espace*, a playback controller for distributing sound to four loudspeakers.[19]

The RTF studio attracted much attention through its ambitious stagings of electronic music and collaborations with performance troupes. In 1953, Schaeffer and Henry produced *Voile d'Orphée*, a "concrete opera." The work combined traditionally sung arias with *musique concrète* played through loudspeakers. The tape sounds of sweeping electronic tones and distorted human voices were mixed with scored music being played by a live orchestra. The performance created an uproar at the annual Donaueschingen festival in Germany. A new version of *Symphonie pour un homme seul* was produced in 1955 as the basis for a ballet by the choreographer Maurice Béjart (1927–2007). Béjart and Henry continued to collaborate for many years afterward.

In the early 1950s, Schaeffer began to present lecture-demonstrations of the group's work, and during the next few years many composers visited to try their hand at tape composition. Among these were Pierre Boulez (who had already assisted Schaeffer by providing piano fragments for two works), Karlheinz Stockhausen (1928–2007), Marius Constant (1925–2004), Darius Milhaud (1892–1974), and Olivier Messiaen (1908–92).

Schaeffer and Moles developed one of the first formal aesthetic handbooks for electronic music. In it, they catalogued sounds, described the various tape editing techniques that formed the basis of *musique concrète*, and tried to establish a philosophical basis for the new medium. They touched upon the major themes that continue to underscore the essence of the electronic music medium: the permanency of recorded work; the ability to reproduce music without the participation of performers; and the ability to manipulate the space and time components of the material. In 1952, Schaeffer published a treatise on the treatment of "sound objects," classifying them according to seven values of sounds that govern the creation of electronic music:

Figure 2.5   The GRM Paris Studio, *c.* 1960: François Bayle, Pierre Schaeffer, and Bernard Parmegiani. (Laszlo Ruszka, Ina C 1030)

- Mass: organization of the sound in a spectral dimension.
- Dynamics: measurable values of the various components of the sound.
- Tone quality/timbre: particular qualities and "color" of the sound.
- Melodic profile: temporal evolution of the total spectrum of the sound.
- Profile of mass: temporal evolution of the spectral components of the sound mass.
- Grain: analysis of the irregularities of the surface of the sound.
- Pace: analysis of the amplitude dynamics of the sound.[20]

Figure 2.6   The RTF/GRM Studio *Phonogène*, a keyboard-operated tape machine designed to play tape loops. (1967 © Ina/Laszlo Ruszka, Ina GRM Archives)

Schaeffer further divided these characteristics into about 50 "points of morphological description," approaching his own form of **serialism** for electroacoustic sounds that might also include musical tones.

Pierre Henry became the most consistently accomplished and prolific composer associated with the RTF studio. Still at work today, Henry is the veritable Debussy of electronic music—a central figure and the most influential of French composers in this medium. By 1954 he had composed no fewer than 44 pieces, most as solo works. He composed at RTF until 1958, when he left to start his own studio, the Studio Apsome, with Maurice Béjart. He continued in the tradition of *musique concrète* but gradually began to bring more lyricism and dynamic variety to a medium that had been characterized by extremities of contrast and special effects. One of his best-known works, *Le Voyage* (1961–62), consists largely of processed feedback. *Variations pour une porte et un soupir* (*Variations for a Door and a Sigh*, 1963) is among the most mature pieces of *musique concrète* ever realized.

Henry's colleague, Maurice Béjart, choreographed a ballet for a performance version of *Variations pour une porte et un soupir*. He described the music and the dance as "a cyclical work which closes in on itself; unfolding, development, exhaustion and destruction, evoking the rhythm of a day or of a life."[21] For each of the 25 parts of the dance version, the dancers drew lots prior to each performance to determine who would dance which parts. A certain number of dancers was prescribed for each part. The dancing was improvised but inspired by the names of the different parts of the work: Slumber, Hesitation, Awakening, Yawning, Gymnastics, Waves, Snoring, Death, and so forth. A blackboard was used to inform the audience ahead of time as to which dancers had drawn which parts for a given performance. Béjart explained his rationale for working this way:

> The dancers draw lots for their numbers on stage, in front of the audience, thus renewing each evening the cyclical ritual of life with its arbitrary course in which the human being and anguish swirl around in the multiple stages of an absurd theater.[22]

Figure 2.7
The RTF/GRM Studio *Magnétophone*, a six-track tape recorder. (1962 © ORTF, Ina GRM Archives)

Henry is a composer rather than an engineer. He works with the emotional content of music, composing with an acute instinct for the communicating power of musical and non-musical sounds. Whereas the sounds themselves were the starting point for Schaeffer, Henry's compositions begin with a structure or form:

> One of course has to compose with a direction, a lucid idea. One has to have in mind a certain construction, a form. But that form differs according to the theme, to the character of the work and of course according to the material. A work like Le Voyage has a form, another like La Porte another one. And another work that requires a voice or chanting . . . every work has its form, but this form is there in the art of creation. I think that from the beginning of my work I have been more original in my form than in my material.[23]

Henry has remained a vital composer of electronic music for over 30 years. Many of his tape pieces have been written for live performance with singers, orchestras, or dance ensembles. In 1975 he composed a work called *Futuriste* (1975) to honor Luigi Russolo, which used a newly constructed set of mechanical *Intonarumori* and was accompanied by a montage of recorded noises.

During the 1990s, Henry returned to some of the ideas that he first explored while at the RTF studio. Looking back, he underscores the emotional and symbolic nature of the sounds with which he works:

> My sounds are sometimes ideograms. The sounds need to disclose an idea, a symbol . . . I often very much like a psychological approach in my work, I want it to be a psychological action, with a dramatic or poetic construction or association of timbre or, in relation to painting, of color. Sounds are everywhere. They do not have to come from a library, a museum. The grand richness of a sound palette basically determines the atmosphere. At the moment I try to manufacture a certain *tablature de serie*. I won't talk about it. I almost become a late serialist. After a big vehement expressive period, post-romantic, I think that now I'm going into a period of pure ideas. It all reminds me very much of my work of the '50s.[24]

Pierre Schaeffer gradually withdrew from composing at the RTF studio as more musically educated composers arrived. Instead, he found himself in a pitched philosophical battle with the Studio for Electronic Music in Cologne, where Herbert Eimert (1897–1972) and Werner Meyer-Eppler (1913–55) were lecturing about the purity of their serial approach to composing music using only electronic signals (see p. 63).

Interestingly, Schaeffer questioned whether much of his own *musique concrète* work was acceptable as music at all:

> I fought like a demon throughout all the years of discovery and exploration in *musique concrète*. I fought against electronic music, which was another approach, a systemic approach, when I preferred an experimental approach actually working directly, empirically with sound. But at the same time, as I defended the music I was working on, I was personally horrified at what I was

doing. I felt extremely guilty. As my father, the violinist, used to say, indulgently, "What are you up to, my little boy? When are you going to make music?" And I used to say, "I'm doing what I can, but I can't do that." I was always deeply unhappy at what I was doing. I was happy at overcoming great difficulties—my first difficulties with the turntables when I was working on *Symphonie pour un homme seul*, my first difficulties with the tape recorders when I was doing *Étude aux objets*—that was good work, I did what I set out to do. My work on the Solfège—it's not that I disown everything I did—it was a lot of hard work. But each time I was to experience the disappointment of not arriving at music. I couldn't get to music, what I call music. I think of myself as an explorer struggling to find a way through in the far north, but I wasn't finding a way through.[25]

After kick-starting the RTF studio, Schaeffer pulled back from composition and was content to observe the development of the medium at arm's length while he served as a guiding influence. Not the least of his achievements was bringing several noted composers to the studio, including Luc Ferrari (1929–2005), Iannis Xenakis (1922–2001), and Edgard Varèse, composers whose contributions to modern music are forever linked to the pioneering work of Pierre Schaeffer.

EARLY ELECTRONIC MUSIC IN EUROPE

1 *Études de bruits* (1948) by Pierre Schaeffer
Early *musique concrète* using turntables (Paris)

2 *Symphonie pour un homme seul* (1949–50) by Pierre Schaeffer and Pierre Henry
Early *musique concrète* using magnetic tape (Paris)

3 *Klangstudie II* (Tchaikovsky) by Herbert Eimert
Early *elektronische Musik* using magnetic tape (Cologne)

4 *Studie I* (1953) by Karlheinz Stockhausen
For sine waves (Cologne)

5 *Glissandi* (1955) by György Ligeti
Produced in Cologne

6 *Scambi* (1957) by Henri Pousseur
Produced in Milan

7 *Diamorphoses* (1957) by Iannis Xenakis
Produced in Paris

8 *Thema–Omaggio a Joyce* (1958) by Luciano Berio
Early text-composition piece (Milan)

9 *Whirling* (1958) by Tom Dissevelt
Early electronic pop music (Utrecht)

10 *Kontakte* (1959–60) by Karlheinz Stockhausen
Cologne

ELEKTRONISCHE MUSIK IN GERMANY

The French jumped into electronic music headfirst. The Germans went in one toe at a time, writing about it first, acting it out later. In 1949, Dr. Werner Meyer-Eppler, a German physicist and information theorist, published an important book, *Elektronische Klangerzeugung: Elektronische Musik und synthetische Sprache*, outlining the development of electronic music technology. At the same time, composer and musicologist Herbert Eimert became interested in electronic musical instruments as a means of extending the compositional theories of Anton Webern and other serialists. The link between these two men was a sound engineer named Robert Beyer (1901–89), who collaborated with Meyer-Eppler in 1950 to present a series of lectures on the possibilities of what they termed **elektronische Musik** (electronic music). These demonstrations resulted in a program that Meyer-Eppler, Beyer, and Eimert organized for *Nordwestdeutscher Rundfunk* (Northwest German Broadcasting, or NWDR) in Cologne on October 18, 1951. That event marked the government broadcasting system's commitment to sponsor an electronic music studio under the direction of Eimert. In 1956, with the split of NWDR into Westdeutscher Rundfunk (West German Broadcasting, or WDR) and Norddeutscher Rundfunk (North German Broadcasting, or NDR), the electronic music studios remained with WDR.

The animosity that existed between the NWDR studio in Cologne and the RTF studio in Paris was tangible. Dutch composer Konrad Boehmer (b. 1941) worked in the German studio at the time. "You could say that in the '50s, you had two types of Cold War," explained Boehmer. "One between the Soviet Union and the United States and one between the Cologne studio and the French studio. They disgusted each other. The aesthetic starting points of Schaeffer were completely different from Eimert's views."[26]

The roots of this dislike first sprung from the French, with memories of World War II still fresh in their minds. Pierre Schaeffer poignantly recalled:

> After the war, in the '45 to '48 period, we had driven back the German invasion but we hadn't driven back the invasion of Austrian music, 12-tone music. We had liberated ourselves politically, but music was still under an occupying foreign power, the music of the Vienna school.[27]

Schaeffer was reacting to the potent drawing power of serialism following World War II.

A slight digression into a discussion of serialism is necessary here so that the context within which early electronic music was developed in Germany can be fully understood. Serialism is another name for **12-tone music**, an outgrowth of the work of composer Arnold Schoenberg (1874–1951). Schoenberg composed his last piece of music to use a major or minor key signature, the *String Quartet No. 2 in F-sharp Minor*, in 1907, and turned all of his attention to developing what he called 12-tone music. By the 1920s, Schoenberg had refined his technique so that it focused on a basic characteristic of the equal-temperament scale that had previously been avoided. In his system, the smallest atomic unit of the scale was not the chord, as had been previously practiced, but an individual note. Thus he discarded the time-honored rules governing tonal harmony and key relationships. Schoenberg and his followers Alban Berg (1885–1935) and Anton Webern (1883–1945) began to compose music based on the relationships of the notes to one another, regardless of key. Notes were free to be themselves without respect to traditional harmony. Schoenberg devised the following rules that could be applied to any adjacent set of 12 notes (e.g. any series of black and white keys on the piano):

- The 12 notes must be arranged in a definite order (the tone row).
- Each composition is created around its own tone row.
- The 12 tones can be used in a melody in any order, provided that no tones are repeated before any others are used.
- Each tone is given equal importance.
- The tone row may be inverted or reversed.[28]

Music composed using this 12-tone system was called **atonal music** because it lacked a tonal center or key. With its emphasis on the tone row, this music avoided the use of familiar chord and melody structures, and employed a highly organized, often mathematical approach to building a piece of music from sequences of notes.

Webern extended Schoenberg's principles beyond the tone row to the combination of instruments that he would allow to play at the same time, giving him control over both the notes and the tone color. Webern's music is austere and threadbare—a clothes-line without the clothes. He exploited the most radical portions of Schoenberg's doctrine, and suppressed all repetition in his work, feeling that this led to a continually renewable source of creativity. In *Symphony* (1928) for chamber orchestra, the brief theme consisted of a seemingly disconnected sequence of tones that bore little relationship to one another. Webern allowed each instrument to play one note in turn but they could not play another until all of the other instruments had sounded.

In serialist music there is a nascent tendency toward time compression that Webern took to extremes. His works were shorter than short. The longest of his *Five Pieces for Orchestra* (1911–13) was only a minute. His life's output consisted of only 31 works and it only requires about three hours to play them all back-to-back. "This is not much to show for a creative activity that extended over thirty-five years," remarked music historian Joseph Machlis, "but the music is so carefully calculated that it impresses one as having been written at the rate of a few notes a day."[29]

Webern moved toward the complete control of all tonal elements of a work, applying strict rules to the designation of pitch, timbre, and rhythm. Those that followed him—most notably Pierre Boulez and Karlheinz Stockhausen—extended his ideas even further by seeking the total "serialization" of a piece of music, applying his technique not only to pitches, timbres, and rhythms, but to dynamics, densities, and amplitude as well.

Serialism as a composition technique was by no means restricted to the work of German composers; nor was it originally intended for electronic media. But under the auspices of Meyer-Eppler and Eimert at the Cologne studio, serialism briefly became the grand experiment on which their electronic music would hinge.

Meyer-Eppler and Eimert had little respect for *musique concrète*, which the Germans characterized as nothing more than "fashionable and surrealistic." Eimert was determined not to go down the same path as the French, whose music he thought was composed of "any incidental manipulations or distortions haphazardly put together for radio, film or theatre music."[30] Mole's conception of the sound object, although disciplined and well respected, did not translate easily to the art of composition. The French, in turn, denigrated Meyer-Eppler's early electronic music as consisting of nothing more than elementary laboratory experiments carried out on the smallest of scales.[31]

Whatever their differences, both the French and the German pioneers agreed that electronically created music was a unique and significant development. As Schaeffer wrote in 1952:

> Photography, whether the fact be denied or admitted, has completely upset painting, just as the recording of sound is about to upset music . . . For all that, traditional music is not denied any more than the theatre is supplanted by the cinema. Something new has been added, a new art of sound. Am I wrong in still calling it music?[32]

Eimert wrote with clarity about the same topic in the very first article of the inaugural issue of *die Reihe*, a German journal devoted to contemporary music:

> Electronic music is, and remains, part of our music and is a great deal more than mere "technology." But the fact that it cannot be expected either to take over or to imitate the functions of traditional music is clearly shown by the unequivocal difference of its material from that of traditional music. We prefer to see its possibilities as the potentialities of sound itself.[33]

These statements are as relevant today as they were in the early 1950s, the only difference being that the technological tools to realize such music have evolved.

If there was a galvanizing moment in the early history of electronic music, it may have been a demonstration at the summer school of the Darmstadt music festival in 1952. Prior to this, the *elektronische Musik* work of Meyer-Eppler and Beyer at the NWDR had not yet become widely known. Meyer-Eppler had previously lectured about "new methods of electronic tone generation" to an audience of engineers and scientists, but it was not until the Darmstadt summer school that he demonstrated some tangible results to an audience of composers and musicians. Italian composer Bruno Maderna worked with Meyer-Eppler to realize a work for this demonstration. Presented on tape, *Musica su due Dimensioni (Music in Two Dimensions)* was scored for flute, cymbals, and tape and was described as a "first attempt to combine the past possibilities of mechanical instrumental music with the new possibilities of electronic tone generation." In performance, a flutist played to the accompaniment of electronic tones presented on tape. The musical content clearly leaned toward the tradition of art music and thus differentiated itself from the *musique concrète* experiments coming out of Paris. In the audience for this demonstration were several twenty-something composers, including Pierre Boulez, Karel Goeyvaerts, Bengt Hambraeus, Giselher Klebe, Gottfried Michael Koenig, and Karlheinz Stockhausen.[34] Their reaction was an enthusiastic mixture of excitement over the implications for new music and disquiet over how best to get engaged in such a challenging new endeavor. Another Darmstadt participant, Italian musician and composer Teresa Rampazzi, was attending as a chorus singer. She recalled a moment when Herbert Eimert of the Cologne contingent stepped out on stage and demonstrated an audio oscillator, an event that introduced many musicians for the first time to the equipment needed to generate tones electronically. "Musicians looked at it suspiciously and did not attach much significance to it," said Rampazzi. "For me, that little, tricky object could certainly grow, multiply, shock the world that is the musical world."[35]

Figure 2.8 A section of the WDR Studio for Electronic Music, Cologne, in 1966, when Stockhausen was composing *Hymnen*. From left: corner of a four-track tape recorder; mixing console; mono tape recorder; *Springer* (in front of the mono tape recorder) with rotating head for suspending sounds; board with six roller guides for long tape loops; switching board with three sliding faders; sound meter; large stopwatch; second mono tape recorder; nine-octave filter; two Albis filters; portable Telefunken M5 tape recorder. (Stockhausen Verlag)

The NWDR contingent of composers viewed serialism as the focal point of their first electronic music efforts and equipped their studio accordingly. Whereas the early equipment found in the French studio was intended to record, manipulate, and process sounds of all kinds—ambient noise effects included—the German studio initially leaned toward the use of tone-generating devices and filters, reflecting the German interest in working directly with the physics of musical tone production. Among the tools at their disposal were several tone-generating electronic musical instruments. One such instrument was the Monochord—an updated version of the monophonic Trautonium built especially for the Cologne studio by Friedrich Trautwein. The NWDR also had a *Melochord*, originally built by Harald Bode (1909–87) in 1947 for Meyer-Eppler to use during his physics lectures and demonstrations. The Melochord had two monophonic tone-generating systems that were separately controlled using a split, five-octave keyboard for which the upper three octaves could be assigned to one tone generator and the lower two octaves to another. Two notes could be played at a time. It also had controls for shaping the attack, sustain, and decay envelopes of the sound. In 1953, the NWDR studio commissioned Bode to build a second Melochord for them. The new model had two separate keyboards. Another new feature was the ability to control the filter from the keyboard, adjusting the timbre of the sound. One could, for example, maintain a steady pitch and only change the tone color.[36]

Engineers were often the unheralded geniuses behind most of the classic electronic music studios: GRM had Jacques Poullin, the NWDR Fritz Enkel (1908–59). As the work of the Cologne studio began to reach beyond the generation of music using only pure electronic tones, Enkel was instrumental in engineering a control console for mixing and recording other numerous sound sources and audio processing devices, including:

- audio oscillators for generating **sine** and **sawtooth waveforms**;
- a variable-speed tape recorder;
- a four-track tape recorder, among the first in use anywhere in the world;
- audio filters, including **band-pass filters**;
- a **ring modulator**;
- a **white noise** generator.

The first musical output of the Cologne studio was by Eimert with the assistance of Beyer, whose task was largely that of editing tape. The studio bore little resemblance to a place to create music: "The equipment with its arrangement of different electro-acoustic procedures outwardly resembles more a research laboratory."[37] Eimert carefully controlled the first output of the studio to ensure that nothing frivolous or "fashionable" was going on there. Exercising tight control over every aspect of the sound, Eimert and Beyer constructed their earliest works by additive and subtractive synthesis, using sine

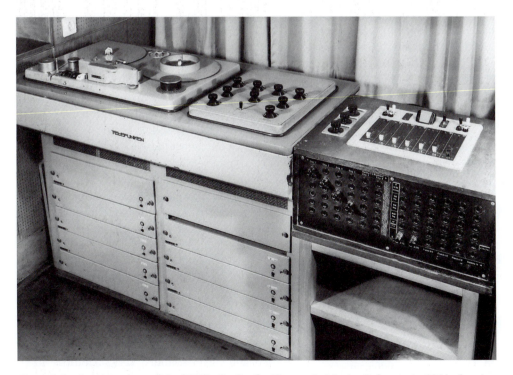

Figure 2.9   Another view of the WDR Studio for Electronic Music, Cologne, in 1966, showing audio filtering and recording equipment. (Stockhausen Verlag)

waves as their primary tonal constituent. Eimert likened his group to visual artists who had to first learn the traditional techniques of oil painting before breaking the rules: "The work of composition begins first with the mastering of the 'material,' in other words, the given material itself must suggest a suitable and direct method of erecting and working on it."[38]

The Melochord was capable of generating stable and relatively unadorned sine waves, making it a valuable tool for Eimert. Composer Konrad Boehmer, who was invited by Eimert to join the studio in the late 1950s, recalled that in order to use the Melochord for exercises in **additive synthesis** they "had to take every sound from the keyboard, put it on a tape and then start the synchronization and the montage work."[39]

The availability of tone and white noise generators greatly influenced the nature of early examples of *elektronische Musik*. The ability to work with pure sine tones led naturally to experiments with tone mixtures without a dominating, fundamental frequency. The use of white noise and filters added to the repertoire of tones that composers could use for composing with a variety of harmonically related or dissonant sounds. The precision required by serialism was complemented by the nature of early electronic music sound sources, which were largely a collection of engineering devices with precise switches and dials that could be set to replicate a sequence of audio elements prescribed by the composer as a score.

Eimert's focus on serialist electronic music compositions dominated the earliest work at NWDR, resulting in many experiments dominated by a rules-based selection of tone rows and patterns using little more than sine wave generators as the principal source of sounds. As a listening experience, however, the differences between *elektronische Musik* and *musique concrète* began to dissolve as early as 1952. Within a year, the work of some of the Cologne composers was veering away from simple tone exercises into the more broadly challenging possibilities offered by electronic music. The slippery slope away from serialist composition began with the use of echo and reverberation and quickly radiated into a plethora of styles combining approaches used by both the French and the Germans. Boehmer noted:

Though it may be true that the (self-nominated) "spokesman" of the Cologne School tried to give the impression of an absolute homogenous stylistic and technical evolution within the WDR studio, the compositions which were realized between 1952 and about 1958 manifest considerable aesthetic and methodological differences.[40]

Figure 2.10   Herbert Eimert and engineer Leopold von Knobelsdorff in the early Cologne studio. (Westdeutscher Rundfunk)

In spite of whatever serialist techniques may have been applied to the composition of a piece, the audio results were often indistinguishable from works created more directly with the sound medium, as in *musique concrète*. The piece *Klang im unbegrenzten Raum* (1952) by Eimert and Beyer sounded very "acoustic" in its spatial movement of sound, reverberating depths, and fuzzy tones. Eimert's *Klangstudie I* (1952) bore little

LISTENING GUIDE 2.3

Title: *Scambi*

Artist: Henri Pousseur   **Year**: 1957–58   **Duration**: 06:34

Genre: Tape composition

Electronic Instrumentation: White noise generator, frequency filter, amplitude modulator, reverberation, and magnetic tape.

Background: *Scambi* ("Exchanges") is an early example of tape music from the RAI Studio di Fonologia Musicale in Milan. Pousseur intended to create a work lacking in periodic rhythm but composed of "structures which would allow the listener some freedom of perception."* The composer realized the entire piece using filtered white noise. The filtering was accomplished in combination with an adjustable amplitude modulator, allowing the composer to specify precise settings on the filter (e.g. frequency band range) as well as the attack and decay characteristics of the processed sound. Pousseur wrote a *technical score* dividing the work into 32 sequences, for which he specified various combinations of four parameters: relative pitch (low to high band pass); speed (slow or fast); homogeneity of the sound material (degrees of reverberation); and the degree to which a sound was continuous or contained pauses. The composition process was complicated, beginning with the recording of 45 tracks of source material onto tape loops, the sounds of which were subsequently modified by filtering, editing, reversal, adding reverberation, and other techniques until the composer assembled his final realization, without cutting the tape, by mixing the final stereo tracks in real time. The technical score was not entirely prescriptive and allowed for individual choice, or a "web of possibilities," in realizing the piece. Several others have created versions of *Scambi*, including Luciano Berio.

	Listen For: Pousseur's manipulation of his four parameters of the sound: relative pitch, speed, homogeneity (degrees of reverberation), and the continuous or discontinuous passage of individual sounds. Overall, the piece is constructed of sections representing average variations on pitch (high, low) and speed (fast, slow).
0:00–0:15	The piece opens with a short sequence of bursting sounds moving from high-fast to high-slow.
0:15–2:00	The volume increases sharply as the piece moves into a longer section, moving from high-fast to low-fast. Two distinct tracks are mixed, each having contrasting parameters. Drenching reverberation is added at about the 55-second mark.
2:00–4:00	This section settles into an exploration of low-slow and low-fast parameters. Note the sloping attack of some sounds that reveals the use of tape reversal. By about 3:00, pauses become longer and more pronounced as a textural component.
4:00–6:10	The density, thickness, and complexity of the sound increases, exploring alternating combinations of slow-fast and low-high sections.
6:10–6:34	The sound thins out and concludes with a high-slow passage before stopping.

Compare and Contrast
Transicion I (1958) by Mauricio Kagel
Studie II (1953) by Karlheinz Stockhausen
Projection Esemplastic for White Noise (1964) by Joji Yuasa
Paris Hiss (1996) by Francisco Lopez

Note: *Henri Pousseur, "Scambi," *Gravesaner Blätter* 13 (1959), 36–47 (German) and 48–54 (English).

resemblance to serialism, with its repeating sweeps of the sound spectra and dramatic subplots of clangorous noises that appear and disappear into washes of echo frizz.

The electronic music tools available at NWDR changed little during the 1950s. Stockhausen and other composers who later worked there—including guests Henri Pousseur (1929–2009), Györgi Ligeti (1923–2006), Cornelius Cardew (1936–81), and Mauricio Kagel (1931–2008)—began to push the technical limits of the studio, devising an engineering bag of tricks to realize their musical ideas. Stockhausen was clearly at the forefront of this innovation, inspired and propelled by the competitive nature of the field at the time.

Stockhausen's Early Work

Buried in the visitors' log of Schaeffer's French GRM studio for 1952 are several entries for a 24-year-old composer from Germany. The young man was living in Paris while studying with Olivier Messiaen. After meeting Pierre Schaeffer, he was granted a few hours of supervised studio time each week at the GRM. Thus began Karlheinz Stockhausen's apprenticeship in tape editing and electronic music:

> First, I recorded six sounds of variously prepared low piano strings struck with an iron beater, using a tape speed of 76.2 centimeters per second. After that, I copied each sound many times and, with scissors, cut off the attack of each sound. A few centimeters of the continuation [remaining sound], which was, briefly, quite steady dynamically, were used. Several of these pieces were spliced together to form a tape loop, which was then transposed to certain pitches using a transposition machine [one of the *Phonogènes*]. A few minutes of each transposition were then recorded on separate tapes.[41]

After making those recordings, Stockhausen began to splice in sections of silent leader tape at regular intervals throughout the piece. His plan was to break up the continuous tones with patches of silence to create a rhythmic pattern. The few hours of supervised studio time that was granted Stockhausen each week was not enough to finish editing the work. Stockhausen created a makeshift editing bench at his student hostel by pounding several nails into the top of his desk. These served as spokes for the tape reels containing his raw sound files. He edited without being able to listen to the result, calculating the length of his leader insertions down to the millimeter. This was done on two separate reels of tape. Back in the studio, he synchronized the start of the tapes and played them back so that he could mix the result onto a third tape to create the final mix. The result was not what he had expected. As he listened to the juxtaposed tracks, Stockhausen became "increasingly pale and helpless. I had imagined something completely different! On the following day, the sorcery despairingly continued. I changed my series, chose other sequences, cut other lengths, spliced different progressions, and hoped afresh for a miracle in sound."[42]

The result was a brief but striking monophonic piece called *Étude*—a progression of atomized bursts of sound that dramatically transformed the sound of the piano. It was not much more than an exercise and lasted a slight 3′ 15″. But Stockhausen was affected for life by the creation of this simple tape piece. He found that it stimulated his most creative and obsessive forces, taking him inside the molecular structure of sound. It was a place he liked to be, in a zone of his own. This is what he would come to call the "unified time domain"[43]—a personal realization inspired by his experience with tape composition. In this domain, space and time became part of the material substances of music. This was because the physical nature of the tape medium could be related directly to time—the duration of a given recorded sound when played back. The technical instrumentation and editing techniques of electronic music permitted Stockhausen to gain control over all of the constituent parts of musical sound:

> The ranges of perception are ranges of time, and the time is subdivided by us, by the construction of our bodies and by our organs of perception. And since these modern means have become available, to change the time of perception continuously, from one range to another, from a rhythm into a pitch, or a tone or noise into a formal structure, the composer can now work within a unified time domain. And that completely changes the traditional concept of how to compose and think music, because previously they were all in separate boxes: harmony and melody in one box, rhythm and meter in another, then periods, phrasing, larger formal entities in another, while in the timbre field we had only names of instruments, no unity of reference at all.[44]

Stockhausen left Paris and returned to the Cologne studio fortified by these personal discoveries in music and sound. The lessons learned would forever permeate his music.

The first live concert of tape music from the Cologne studio was given on October 19, 1954 in a small transmission hall of the radio station. The works were played over loudspeakers. Among the pieces were Stockhausen's *Studie I* (1953) and *Studie II* (1954).

Studie I is among the first works of electronic music composed entirely for sine waves. Although the means for creating *Studie I* are readily available today using computer synthesis, its composition in 1953 required much manual intervention and ingenuity by Stockhausen. *Studie I* was a completely serialized composition in which the composer applied the mathematical analysis of tones and timbres to the way in which he generated, shaped, and edited sounds for a tape composition. With electronic tone generators and tape recorders at his disposal, Stockhausen felt that it was possible to "compose, in the true sense of the word, the timbres in music," allowing him to synthesize from base elements such as sine waves the structure of a composition, its tone selection, and all of the audio dynamics such as amplitude, attack, duration, and the timbre of the sounds.[45] He approached the composition by first recording a series of electronic tones that met certain pitch and timbral requirements that he prescribed and then using serial techniques to devise an organizational plan that determined the order and duration of the sounds as he edited them together.

Stockhausen's approach to composing *Studie I* is a good example of the application of serial technique to the tape composition and also illustrates the discipline shown by classically trained composers in creating music with the new medium. Stockhausen specified the tones for *Studie I* using a set of frequency ratios to multiply a starting frequency of 1,920 Hz, which is at about the center of the frequency range of the human voice. He used the following five ratios applied to 1,920 to obtain a progression of six successive frequencies below 1,920 Hz:

Calculation		Resulting frequency
(1,920/12) × 5	=	800 Hz
(800/4) × 5	=	1,000 Hz
(1,000/8) × 5	=	625 Hz
(625/5) × 12	=	1,500 Hz
(1,500/5) × 4	=	1,200 Hz

Stockhausen next devised a set of similar frequency ratios above 1,920 Hz to establish a complementary series of tones in the higher register. All of the resulting frequency values were further divided by the same set of ratios, giving the composer a broad palette of tones with which to work. This set of frequencies was then subjected to a series of additional calculations to determine which tones would be combined with other tones to produce timbral effects. Each of the values equated to a frequency that could be set on an electronic audio oscillator. Stockhausen recorded each singly and then mixed individual tones according to his prescribed plan. Unlike the chance composition of John Cage in which the act of composition was disconnected by choice from its performance, Stockhausen's sound choices for *Studie I* were ultimately and irrevocably governed by the composer's own subjective requirement to avoid all octaves, unisons, and "symmetrical and monotonous" sequences.[46]

The resulting mixture of sine waves produced overtones and sidebands that did not exist in the individual tones but only as a result of the additive synthesis of compound waves from single sine waves. The application of reverberation to the tones combined with their often sharp attacks and rounded sonorities gave the music a strikingly bell-like sound. Tone groups overlapped in sequence, providing harmonic as well as slightly detuned sounds and an overall sense of suspended motion. Another technique explored by Stockhausen and other early electronic music composers was the variability of the speed of recorded sound.

For *Studie II*, Stockhausen extended his experiments with sine waves begun on *Studie I* by exploring the use of attack and decay characteristics as elements of composition. *Studie II* is one of the first post-war tape works to have a written score, albeit a graphic one in which overlapping translucent geometric shapes are used to denote the occurrence of a tone of a given amplitude in a given frequency with specific attack and decay characteristics (see Figure 2.11). For *Studie II*, Stockhausen defined a set of frequencies based on the same ratio, resulting in an 81-tone scale of tones divided into one-tenth octave steps. The loudness and attack characteristics of the tones were divided into five stages. Tones based on such equal divisions of the frequency spectrum proved to be more harmonic when mixed. Stockhausen recorded short passages of the given tones and spliced them together in a loop that could be played repeatedly. These loops were then played through a reverberation system and then recorded to provide the final material with which the composer worked. Stockhausen's extensive use of reverberation added body and a noise quality to the sounds that embellished the raw sine tones. Using serial techniques to determine how to edit the material together, Stockhausen varied the attack characteristics and then also played some of the sounds backward to create a ramping decay that would abruptly cut off. His application of attack and decay characteristics in five prescribed stages of amplitude resulted in passages that were highly articulated by cascading, irregular rhythms. "Rhythm is involved immediately," explained Stockhausen,

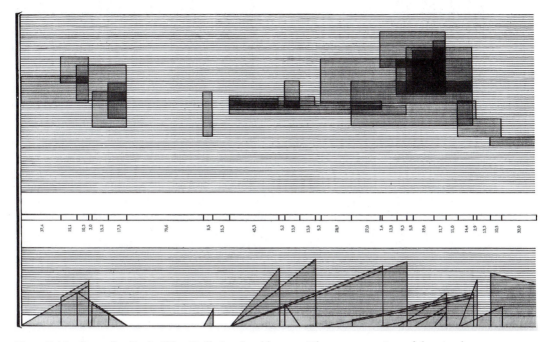

Figure 2.11   Score for *Studie II* by Karlheinz Stockhausen. The upper portion of the visual score denoted frequency ranges and durations; the lower portion specified envelopes of the prescribed sine tones. (Stockhausen Verlag)

"insofar as we subdivide the overall dynamic curve of a sound; and we have then to say when the envelope falls in amplitude, when it's raised again, etc."[47] *Studie I* and *Studie II* played a significant role in the early formulation of electronic music, exploring additive synthesis, the modification of purely electronic sounds, the use of tape reversal, exploration of reverb and noise spectra, and the prescription of most sound parameters through a score or plan for the pitch, loudness, duration, occurrence, and envelope of all sound elements. Stockhausen's work was a blueprint for future composers in taming the seemingly infinite spectrum of all possible sounds through carefully conceived plans for the technical manipulation and definition of a given work.

Like other composers engaged in early experiments with tape composition, Stockhausen soon found himself immersed in a medium so rich with sonic possibilities that it was difficult to know where to begin. These ideas were forming around 1957 when he wrote an influential article called ". . . how time passes . . ." for the journal *die Reihe*.[48] In this article, Stockhausen approached music as an acoustical phenomenon with its own "order relationships in time." He objectified musical sound and used largely mathematical and acoustical terms to describe the elements of musical material and structure. This thinking led the composer naturally to the further exploration of electronic music. Looking back in 1971, Stockhausen explained the way in which he had distilled the composition of electronic music into four guiding principles:

1   Unified time structuring—the modification of frequency, timbral, and dynamic elements of a sound through speed changes to the tape medium.

LISTENING GUIDE 2.4

Title: *Studie II*

Artist: Karlheinz Stockhausen   **Year**: 1953   **Duration**: 3:10

Genre: *Elektronische Musik*

Electronic Instrumentation: Sine wave generators, filters, amplitude modulators, and reverberation.

Background: An early tape work applying serial composition concepts to electronically generated sounds. Stockhausen used only sine wave generators as his source material and devised a score that explored a sequence of many possible pitch ranges and attack and decay characteristics (see main text). *Studie II* was one of the first pieces of electronic music to have a printed score. The score was partly technical—numerically specifying frequency and attack characteristics—and partly graphic, depicting the desired overlap and ramping characteristics of the waveforms.

	Listen For: The richness of tones derived from simple sine waves, the dramatic use of silence, and the statistically explicit exploration of attack and decay characteristics as the piece progresses.
0:00–0:27	The piece opens by running through a sequence of sharply defined tones, given a bell-like quality though the use of reverberation. The attack and decay characteristics are sharp. The tones are short. Individual tones do not overlap. There is no perceivable rhythm, but a kind of organic, breath-like quality to the flow of sounds. Silence already plays a role as a palpable element of the music.
0:30–1:30	The duration of the tones becomes generally longer at first. A sequence of bursts contrasts short and long sounds and the volume of some tones becomes distinctly louder than others. The work introduces more variety in the attack characteristics of the tones, producing a long, ramping buildup in some tones that is noticeably longer than the parts of the tones that are sustained and decayed.
1:30–1:50	The piece returns to a rapid-fire sequence of short tones with sharp attacks and decays, signifying a transition to the next section.
1:50–3:10	Up until this point in the piece, tones have not overlapped, but were constructed (through tape editing) as a linear sequence of discrete sounds. During this section, mixing was used in places to combine as many as six tones at once. The music continues to explore the effect of slowly attacking sounds, only now they are layered through multitracking. The decay portion of some tones also begins to dissipate more slowly. The thick textures that began this section gradually thin to a few lower frequency tones punctuated by silence.

Compare and Contrast
Study I: Music for Sine Wave by Proportion of Prime Number (1955) by Toshiro Mayuzumi
I of IV (1966) by Pauline Oliveros

2   Splitting of the sound—the ability to inde-
    pendently manipulate the smaller elements of
    a synthetically produced sound, for example
    changing any individually generated tones
    that are joined to make a combined sound.
3   Multilayered spatial composition—the control
    of amplitude and the placement of sounds
    (using loudspeakers) in the listening hall.
4   Equality of tone and noise—providing the
    means to control the spectrum of audio
    possibilities between tone and noise. While
    Stockhausen claimed on one hand that "any
    noise is musical material," he has also said that
    "you cannot just use any tone in any interval
    relationship." Considered from the standpoint
    of electronic music composition, he preferred
    to construct noise sounds synthetically over
    letting natural sounds just be themselves.[49]

Figure 2.12   Karlheinz Stockhausen, 1956.
(Stockhausen Verlag)

Around the time that Stockhausen was formu-
lating these criteria for electronic music, the nature
of his work began to change dramatically. After
completing the two electronic *Studien*, he returned
to instrumental writing for about a year, complet-
ing several atonal works for piano and woodwinds, as well as the ambitious orchestral
work *Gruppen*, written for three complete orchestral groups stationed at three posts around
the audience so that the sounds of each ensemble were physically segregated in the listening
space. By the time Stockhausen embarked on the creation of the electronic work *Gesang
der Jünglinge* (*Song of the Youths*, 1955–56), his views on the control of the dynamic elements
of electronic music had broadened considerably.

   Gesang der Jünglinge was begun three years before Varèse completed *Poème électronique*.
Like the Varèse work, *Gesang der Jünglinge* was produced using a host of electronic music
production techniques cultivated earlier at the RTF and NWDR studios. Stockhausen's
approach was to fuse the sonic components of recorded passages of a youth choir with
equivalent tones and timbres produced electronically. Stylistically, Stockhausen avoided
the choppy, sharply contrasting effects that were so evident in many early magnetic tape
pieces, instead weaving his sound sources together into a single, fluid musical element.
He practiced his newly formed principles of electronic music composition, setting forth
a plan that required the modification of the "speed, length, loudness, softness, density
and complexity, the width and narrowness of pitch intervals and differentiations of
timbre" in an exact and precise manner.[50] The piece was painstakingly sculpted from a
visual score specifying the placement of sounds and their dynamic elements over the
course of the work (see Figure 2.13). At 13′ 14″ long, *Gesang der Jünglinge* was longer
than any previous work realized at the Cologne studio. The result was an astonishingly
beautiful and haunting work of sweeping tones and voices. The text, taken from the
Book of Daniel, was sung by a boys' choir as single syllables and whole words. The words

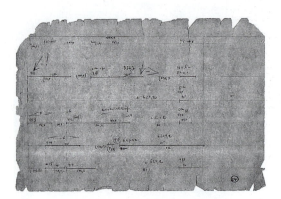

Figure 2.13 Sketch for Stockhausen's *Gesang der Jünglinge*, 1956. (Stockhausen Verlag)

were sometimes revealed as comprehensible language and at other times merely as "pure sound values."[51]

Stockhausen's assimilation of a boy's singing voice into the work was the result of meticulous preparation on his part. He wanted the sung parts to closely match the electronically produced tones of the piece. His composition notes from the time explain how he made this happen:

Fifty-two pieces of paper with graphically notated melodies which were sung by the boy, Josef Protschka, during the recording of the individual layers. Stockhausen also produced these melodies as sine tones on tape loops for the circa 3-hour recording sessions. The boy listened to these melodies over earphones and then tried to sing them. Stockhausen chose the best result from each series of attempts for the subsequent synchronization of the layers.[52]

Gesang der Jünglinge is historically important for several reasons. Although Varèse's familiar *Poème électronique* became more widely known, *Gesang der Jünglinge* shared with it the distinction of marking a transition from the mutually exclusive aesthetic approaches of the Paris and Cologne studios to a more broadly stylistic and open-minded period of electronic music composition. The maturity of Stockhausen's approach to composing the work, blending acoustic and electronic sounds as equivocal raw materials, signified a maturing of the medium. The work successfully cast off the cloak of novelty and audio experiments that had preoccupied so many tape compositions until that time. Stockhausen's concept of "composing the sound"—splitting it, making the changing parameters of sound part of the theme of the work—was at the heart of *Gesang der Jünglinge*. Rhythmic structures were only nominally present, no formal repetition of motifs existed in the work, and its theme was the continuous evolution of sound shapes and dynamics rather than a pattern of tones, chords, and other familiar musical elements.

The composer's newly formed interest in the spatial deployment of sound, as nurtured during the production of *Gruppen* the year before, was another important milestone for this work:

This is a new way of experiencing musical speech, but another feature of the composition is equally essential: here for the first time the direction and movement of sounds in space was shaped by the composer and made available as a new dimension in musical experience.[53]

Gesang der Jünglinge was composed on five tracks. During its performance, five loudspeakers were placed so that they surrounded the audience. The listener was in the eye of the sonic storm, with music emanating from every side and rotating in various directions. During the late 1950s, Stockhausen continued to refine the spatial projection of his music both on his recordings and in the performance space. *Kontakte* (1958) was a piece for four-track tape. While recording this work in the studio, Stockhausen wanted to create the effect of sounds spinning around the listener at various speeds. To achieve this effect, he mounted a loudspeaker on a manually rotated platform and set up four microphones—one for each tape track—around the platform. Whatever sound he played through the rotating loudspeaker was then recorded onto four individual tape tracks. The loudspeaker could be cranked to spin at any rate up to about four revolutions per second and each microphone would catch the sound slightly behind the one before it. When the resulting four-track tape was played in an auditorium—with a speaker for each channel positioned in the four corners of the space—the sound spun around the audience from speaker to speaker. This dizzying effect only worked, of course, if the speakers were hooked up in the same order as the microphones that recorded the sound. This was a favorite technique of Stockhausen's, who personally manned the mixing board during his live performances. He was still using this technique in compositions during the late 1960s. The recorded version of *Kontakte* was mixed down to two stereo channels, but the effect was still quite potent, especially when experienced on headphones. Stockhausen was experimenting with such spatial projections of sound on stereo recordings nearly ten years before rock artists such as Pink Floyd, The Beatles, and Jimi Hendrix would popularize the same technique.

Stockhausen also used a specialized tape recorder called the *Springer*. Originally developed to lengthen or shorten radio broadcasts, it used a rotating matrix of four to six playback heads that spun in the opposite direction to the tape transport. As the tape passed the rotating playback array, one of the playback heads was in contact with it at

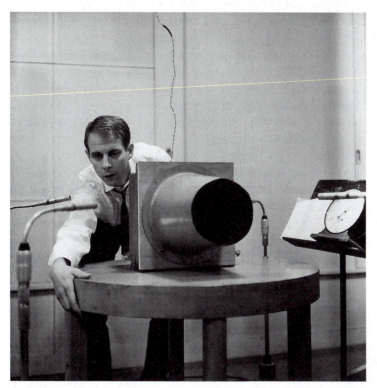

Figure 2.14
Stockhausen built this rotating speaker table in 1958 to create a spinning sound effect using multiple tape tracks. Microphones fixed around the turntable recorded the output of the loudspeaker on separate tracks as the speaker rotated. In a multi-track surround-sound performance, the resulting sounds would rotate around the audience. (Stockhausen Verlag)

all times. The output was equal to the sum of the rotating heads. The speed of the rotating heads could be adjusted within a variable playback speed range from −30 percent to +50 percent.[54] Stockhausen employed a *Springer* with a rotating six-part playback head, using it to provide the disorienting effect of gradually speeding up or slowing down the tempo of a recorded sound without changing its pitch. He frequently used this technique in his major works of the mid-1960s, especially *Hymnen* (1966–67).

Stockhausen succeeded Eimert as director of the Cologne studio in 1963. The electronic music studio of the WDR has a long history. Over the years it has been moved and upgraded with new equipment, particularly synthesizers. During the 1970s, a British-made EMS Synthi 100 analog modular synthesizer with a digital sequencer was added to the studio along with an EMS Vocoder and E-mu Emulator digital sampler. Other composers who realized works there included Krenek (*Pfingstoratorium-Spiritus Intelligentiae*, 1956), Ligeti (*Glissandi*, 1957; *Artikulation*, 1958), Cardew (*1st and 2nd Exercises*, 1958), Kagel (*Transición I*, 1958–60; *Acoustica*, 1969), and Gehlhaar (*Tanz I–V*, 1975). Stockhausen himself was artistic director of the studio until 1977. Stockhausen was informed in 2000 that the building housing the studio had been sold and that the studio was going to be closed down. Much of its equipment was to be scrapped. When asked most recently about whether he had met with any success in keeping the WDR studio intact, the composer simply told me, "No progress. It will be closed!"[55]

ELECTRONIC MUSIC IN ITALY

Interest in electronic music grew rapidly after the establishment of the Paris and Cologne studios. So, too, did the aesthetic choices being made by composers in the new medium. All were faced with a common challenge—that of transforming the artistically neutral technology of audio recording and processing equipment into expressive content. This required the "apparatus" to be "filled with a content that hardly can be offered by a purely musical means." The implication was that there was an essential dependency in electronic music on "external elements, both as references and subjects."[56] Electronic music provided a clean slate of possibilities and made the choice of which sounds to eliminate as important as that of which sounds to include. There was much energy spent by composers and critics during the early days of electronic music assessing its value and aesthetic appeal as music, a debate now not inflicted on twenty-first-century composers whose adoption of technology is second nature. Following the initial debates over *musique concrète* and *elektronische Musik*, the choices made by composers for creating electronic music broadened considerably.

A third state-sponsored studio for the research and production of electronic music was founded in Milan in 1955. Radio Audizioni Italiane (RAI), the Italian public broadcasting network, opened the *Studio di Fonologia Musicale* under the artistic direction of composers Luciano Berio (1925–2003) and Bruno Maderna (1920–73). Berio's interest in electronic music went back to 1952, when he attended one of the first tape concerts given by Otto Luening and Vladimir Ussachevsky of Columbia University (see Chapter 3, p. 111). Maderna had already composed some works of tape music at the Cologne studio. The technical director of the studio was Alfredo Lietti and the chief technician was Marino Zuccheri.

The RAI studio was one of the best-equipped European studios for many years. One reason for this was that Berio and Maderna kept an open mind about the music that would be produced under its roof. They did not align themselves aesthetically with either the *musique concrète* approach taken in Paris or the serialist, rules-based composing style of Cologne. "Bruno and I immediately agreed," explained Berio, "that our work should not be directed in a systematic way, either toward recording acoustic sounds or toward a systematic serialism based on discrete pitches."[57] As a consequence, Lietti filled the Italian studio with equipment that appealed to a wide spectrum of compositional needs. The box on p. 78 provides a summary of the various sound-generating, processing, and recording devices found in the RAI studio.

Berio's work at the RAI studio came just before he gained much wider recognition as a leading composer and popular figure in contemporary music. By 1962 he had moved to America, first to teach at Mills College and then to join the faculty of the Juilliard School of Music where he founded the Juilliard Ensemble, an ensemble dedicated to the performance of contemporary music. His later work was known for its novel combinations of instrumental and vocal material and dramatic stage settings where theater, politics, and dialog often blended with his music. The roots of many of these ideas can be heard in Berio's electronic music from Milan.

Berio completed less than a dozen solo tape pieces in the Milan studio, beginning with *Mutazioni* (1955) and ending with *Visage* (1961). During this period, he continued to write music for instrumental ensembles and vocalists as well as magnetic tape, providing a rich cross-pollenization of ideas and techniques. *Momenti* (1960) engaged 92 sound frequencies moving continually over the sound spectrum. *Différences* (1958–60) for five instrumentalists and tape combined a score for flute, clarinet, viola, cello, and harp played live to taped sounds played by the same musicians. During the performance of this work, the four-track tape of the instruments was integrated with that of the live musicians, subtly expanding the listening horizon beyond that which could be followed on stage.

One hallmark of the Milan studio was the use of speech as sound material. Berio was at the forefront of this experimentation. *Thema–Omaggio a Joyce* (1958) derives all of its source material from a single spoken passage from the beginning of chapter 11 of James Joyce's novel *Ulysses*. The passage was read on tape in English, Italian, and French by mezzo-soprano Cathy Berberian (1925–83), who was married to Berio from 1950 to 1966. *Thema–Omaggio a Joyce* is remarkable for the gradual transformation of spoken language into increasingly rhythmic, abstract musical material (see Figure 2.16). Berio

Figure 2.15 RAI Milan Studio, 1960: technician Marino Zuccheri (left) and composer Luigi Nono. (Fondazione Archivio LN)

ELECTRONIC MUSIC EQUIPMENT OF THE STUDIO DI FONOLOGIA MUSICALE (MILAN, *c.* 1960)*

Sound Generators

   9 sine wave oscillators
   1 white noise generator
   1 pulse generator

Sound Modifiers

   Chamber, tape, and plate reverberation units
   Octave filter
   High-pass filter (6 cutoff frequencies)
   Low-pass filter (6 cutoff frequencies)
   Variable band-pass filter
   Third-octave filter
   Spectrum analyzer
   Ring and amplitude modulators
   Variable-speed tape machine
   Springer time regulator
   Amplitude filter

Recording and Reproduction Equipment

   Microphones
   Mixing console
   Amplifiers and loudspeakers for four-channel sound monitoring
   6 monophonic tape recorders
   2 two-channel tape recorders
   2 four-channel tape recorders

*As cataloged in *Répertoire international des musiques expérimentales* (Paris, GRM, 1962).[58]

INNOVATION

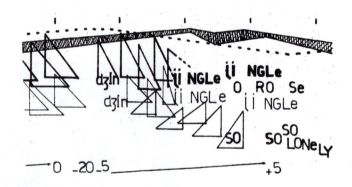

Figure 2.16   Portion of the score for Berio's tape piece, *Thema–Omaggio a Joyce*, which is comprised entirely of modified vocal sounds. The visual plan denoted words to be sung, pitch, duration, and the envelopes of the sounds, but only roughly approximated the end result that would be edited together using tape. (Turnabout Records TV 34046S, 1966)

achieved these results through many hours of tedious tape editing, copying and recopying of sounds, speed changes, and other effects, completely transforming the sound. About the process, Berio said, "I was interested in constant and controlled transformation from discontinuous to continuous patterns, from periodic to non-periodic events, from sounds to noise, from perceived words to perceived musical structures, and from syllabic to a phonetic view of the text."[59] Spanning only 6′ 23″, *Thema–Omaggio a Joyce* remains one of the most remarkable examples of classic electronic music because of its achievement as a work using tape manipulation and for its timeless qualities as an evocative piece of music.

Berio's final tape piece from the Milan studio was *Visage* (1961), a much longer work at 21′ 4″ that also used the voice of Cathy Berberian as its sound material. Built primarily upon the utterance of a single word—*parole*, which means "word" in English— the piece also comprised unintelligible vocalizations, laughing, crying, and hauntingly visceral utterances with electronically produced sounds to paint a dramatic sound story. At the conclusion of his immersive period of experimentation with tape music, Berio wrote:

> I regard the experience of electronic music as very important precisely because rather than opening the door to the discovery of "new" sounds it proved the possibility of a definite outcome of dualistic conceptions of musical materials and gives the composer the practical means of integrating in a musical thought a larger domain of sound phenomena viewed as segments of the sound continuum.[60]

Following Milan, Berio did not return to the production of purely electronic music but often incorporated electronic elements into his works for vocalists and instrumentalists, one of the last of which was *Altra voce* (1999) for mezzo-soprano, alto flute, and live electronics.

Thema–Omaggio a Joyce and *Visage* demonstrated the potential of using speech sounds and vocal patterns as source material for composing electronic music. Several composers at other studios immediately followed in Berio's path, producing such works as *U 47* (1960) by Jean Baronnet and Françoise Dufrene and *Trois visages de Liège* (1961) by Henri Pousseur, each of which manipulated vocal sounds as a key source of material. These early works for vocal sounds marked the beginning of an entire genre of electronic music now known as **text-sound composition**.

The open-minded atmosphere of the Milan studio attracted many other composers. Among them were Luigi Nono (1924–90) and John Cage, both of whom used unorthodox approaches to composing that were welcomed at the Studio di Fonologia in 1958. The Milan studio was perhaps the most important of the early European studios because of its excellent facilities, willingness to reach out to other composers, and lack of dogma.

The Milan studio represented a trend away from the two previously established European schools of thought regarding electronic music—the pure electronic approach of the WDR in Cologne and the manipulation of natural sounds of the GRM in Paris. Composers interested in exploring aesthetic paths of their own, with little interference, turned to Milan and other like-minded studios that began to crop up during the early 1960s. Three small, privately funded studios in Italy followed the general direction of the RAI. Pietro Grossi (1917–2002) founded the *S 2F M* studio in 1963 in Florence,

LISTENING GUIDE 2.5

Title: *Thema–Omaggio a Joyce*

Artist: Luciano Berio   **Year**: 1958   **Duration**: 6:21

Genre: Tape composition

Electronic Instrumentation: Tape composition using only vocal sounds as source material.

Background: Berio's graphic score for the piece adapted words from James Joyce's *Ulysses*, spoken and sung by vocalist Cathy Berberian. The score indicated which words to be spoken, their relative pitch and their duration. Berio then applied tape editing and mixing techniques to modify the sounds electronically, paying particular attention to the envelopes—attack, sustain, and decay characteristics—of the result. The work was composed at the RAI Studio di Fonologia Musicale in Milan, which was equipped with an amplitude modulator for modifying the envelope of a recorded sound. The piece has no regular meter or rhythmic structure, includes many moments of silence, and is generally constructed to mimic the cadence of speech.

	Listen For: A large repertoire of tape composition techniques, including speed variations, editing, sound reversal, amplitude modulation, and sound modification.
0:00–0:25	The piece begins with a sequence of phrases that become the source material for much of the first part of the work. The words are recognizable at this stage, treated with reverberation and spoken in a fairly normal cadence, although a hint of what is to come can be heard at about 0:22 as the voice is double-tracked with the same passage played in reverse.
0:26–1:00	The texture of the piece thickens suddenly with an explosion of single words, some processed and played in reverse, presented in rapid succession. Tape loops are used to create a rapid repetition of certain words. In some cases, such as the repetition of the word "Bloomie" beginning at about 0:48 seconds, Berio consciously creates a kind of reverse echo effect in which, instead of diminishing with each repetition, the sound of the word "Bloomie" becomes louder and more distinct.
1:01–3:20	Silence followed by a section in which passages of voice in the natural tonal range are contrasted with extremely rapid repetitions forming high-pitched, bird-like sounds. During this section, the sound of the voice is almost entirely abstracted, acting as raw sound material, with few distinguishable words. Single words and parts of words make up much of this section.
3:21–4:00	During this section, the voice is further modulated to create pitch-like electronic tones and effects. Stereo channels are used to produce interesting spatial effects in the distribution of sounds within the listening field.
4:01–4:48	The texture thickens and thins, beginning with an accumulation of processed vocal sounds that are multitracked to form a barrage of noisy sounds. Wobbly speed variations were created by hand-turning the reels of the tape machine. The barrage subsides, to be replaced by another sequence of high-pitched, bird-like sounds—rapidly repeated loops of voice played at high speed.
4:49–6:21	A passage of multitracked, slowly descending vocal sounds begins the final section of the work. Lengthy passages of silence are contrasted with highly processed, discontinuous vocal sounds. At about 5:15, whole words and phrases become distinguishable again, and one has the impression that the composer is now making clear the source material from which abstracted sounds were earlier derived. After the word "war" is clearly spoken, the piece fades to a provocative silence.

Compare and Contrast

Incantation for Tape (1953) by Otto Luening and Vladimir Ussachevsky

Emily (2004) by Robin Rimbaud

Enore Zaffiri (b. 1928) founded the *Studio di Musica Elettronica di Torino* (SMET) in 1964 in Turin, and Teresa Rampazzi (1914–2001) established the *Nuove Proposte Sonore* (NPS) in Padua. The work of these studios was quite varied and often associated with exhibitions and the work of visual artists, showing the growing consolidation of efforts by avant-garde artists in a variety of media. Grossi's work was more pragmatic and experimental, like his American contemporaries, in exploring the acoustic properties and relationships of electronically generated sounds. He was an important instructor in such techniques at the Italian Conservatory of Music in Florence, establishing one of the first university courses in electronic music anywhere. Grossi also experimented with **computer music** as early as 1967.[61]

The work of Zaffiri in Turin followed closely on the heels of Grossi. He took a systematic, research-based approach to applying technology to the composition of art music, developing a college curriculum around this approach and composing many classically structured pieces that could be performed live.

LISTENING GUIDE 2.6

Title: *Duodeno normale*

Artist: Teresa Rampazzi   **Year**: 1970   **Duration**: 1:27

Genre: Tape composition

Electronic Instrumentation: Oscillators, reverberation, and sound processing.

Background: Composed for a television documentary that pictured an exploration of the human body through the use of the endoscope. Rampazzi and her colleagues were asked to compose fitting electronic accompaniment for a variety of organs, such as the stomach and various sections of the intestines. This piece was composed for the small section of intestine just following the stomach. The music reveals Rampazzi's stylistic tendency to create a pulsing, drone-like sequence of harmonizing electronic tones, a style that preceded many later experiments in trance, ambient, and drone music.

	Listen For: Simple, pulsing tones and textures, played manually using audio oscillators.
0:00–0:54	The piece begins with a drone consisting of two continuous tones: a low-pitched buzz from a sawtooth wave accompanied by a pulsating higher-pitched tone. The drone is joined at the 11-second mark by a high-pitched ringing tone played on a second oscillator. This ringing tone is repeated every 5–8 seconds and sustained for two or more seconds each time. The irregular timing of the tone suggests that Rampazzi was manually playing it by turning the dial of an oscillator.
0:55–1:27	The lower-pitched buzzing drone drops to a lower volume as the higher-pitched pulsating drone increases in volume and becomes the center of attention. The ringing tone appears again at 1:07 and is sustained for the duration of the piece, creating a three-part drone. The drones fade out, beginning with the lower buzzing tone.

Compare and Contrast

Vibrations composées – Rosace 3 (1973) by François Bayle
A Chance to Cut is a Chance to Cure (2001) by Matmos (a soundtrack to a surgical video)

Figure 2.17   Studio of the Italian electronic music collective, Nuove Proposte Sonore, led by Teresa Rampazzi, 1968.

Rampazzi is yet another female pioneer of electronic music whose work should be more widely known than it is. Italy's answer to Delia Derbyshire, Rampazzi was a pianist and performer of avant–garde music in the 1950s, having taken part in performances with Cage and others. She was exposed to electronic music early, "exactly at its birth" as she once said, during a concert of recorded tape music in Darmstadt in 1952.[62] She organized a concert of electronic music in 1963 and next founded her private studio, NPS, with visual artist Ennio Chiggio. Equipped with little more than an audio oscillator and monophonic tape recorder, they began to explore the development of organically complex collage pieces and experimental music. Unlike Pietro and Zaffiri, whose work took a structured, systematic approach, Rampazzi's music more freely explored sound densities, drones, textures, and the possibilities of treating sound sources through many variations. Her legacy of music, composed primarily between 1960 and 1980, is surprisingly timeless stylistically, sounding entirely contemporary in its contemplations of slowly changing sonorities and timbres. She was clearly practicing a music of slow transformations, not unlike Xenakis, in works such as *With a Light Pen* (1976) and *Atmen Noch* (1980). Her earliest works often integrated environmental sounds with voices and undulating electronic patterns to create organically structured soundscapes. Although not intended for commercial broadcast, Rampazzi's work in many ways paralleled the sonic experiments taking place in the UK at the BBC Radiophonic Workshop (see below) and Pauline Oliveros in San Francisco (see Chapter 3). Rampazzi founded the NPS, an experimental music collective, in the late 1960s and was one of the founders and key composers associated with the *Centro di Sonologia Computazionale* at the University of Padua, a computer music research center beginning in the early 1970s.

THE UNITED KINGDOM AND THE BBC RADIOPHONIC WORKSHOP

In London, the British Broadcasting Corporation (BBC) established the *BBC Radiophonic Workshop* in 1958 for the production of sound effects and electronic music for radio and television productions. The studio was in operation until 1998. In its heyday, from 1958 to the middle 1970s, the Workshop was a hotbed of ingenuity and innovation in the development of electronic music and techniques. Because the primary role of the Workshop was to create music and sound effects for mass consumption, its output was influential in shaping the public's acceptance of electronic music. It was responsible for creating everything from atmospheric background music to special effects, advertising jingles, and catchy program themes. The wide exposure of its music provided impetus for the assimilation of electronic music in popular music and media.

The idea for the Workshop was proposed in 1956 by Brian George, chief of program operations at the BBC. The idea came in response to a report by a member of his engineering staff on the technical innovations taking place in the creation of *musique concrète* in France and *elektronische Musik* in Germany, both sponsored by nationalized radio corporations. The proposal recommended the establishment of a small operation to be maintained by four employees to create the sounds and maintain the equipment. Those who described the operation were careful to keep it grounded in reality by not suggesting that it be staffed by any musicians, just engineers, "tape editors and devisors of special effects."[63] After more than a year of dragging its feet over details, the BBC finally opened the Radiophonic Workshop in the Spring of 1958.

Daphne Oram (1925–2003) was among the first staff members. She was a classically trained musician as well as an experienced BBC studio manager and engineer. Oram had, essentially, schooled herself in the techniques of creating tape music by visiting Schaeffer at the RTF in Paris. Even before the Workshop opened, Oram had distinguished herself by composing the music for an original television drama, *Amphitryon 38*, in 1957, the first piece of electronic music composed for a television program in the United Kingdom. Having no dedicated studio facilities in which to create this work, Oram composed after hours by wrangling the equipment she needed from various studios in the building. The tape piece was composed entirely between midnight and 4 a.m. once the other studios had gone off the air for the night. "I could not, of course, use the very special equipment I needed," explained Oram. "So, I evolved techniques, akin to Cologne and Paris, which could be achieved with the normal broadcasting equipment I had available."[64] Oram composed her landmark work using several sine wave generators, a tape recorder, and homemade audio filters. The excitement over Oram's electronic music generated much demand for her services even before the Workshop officially began operation. But her personal musical ambitions led to a quick departure from the Workshop in 1959 over artistic differences. The BBC viewed the Workshop primarily as a special effects factory, whereas Oram sought to establish an experimental laboratory for making exclusively musical works like her peers in France, Germany, and the United States. In 1959, Oram established her own independent production company to produce a broader, more diverse range of sonic experiments for music, television, and motion pictures. Among her projects was the invention of an early synthesizer that produced electronic sounds by optically scanning hand-drawn images on sprocketed loops of clear 35mm film. The *Oramics machine*, as she called it, included ten such film loops that could be synchronously programmed, each equivalent to a recording track with added control functions. Some of the loops controlled the waveform, duration, and vibrato while others controlled timbre, amplitude, and pitch. The sprocketed loops rotated over a bank of photocells. The opaque images on the loops modulated a stream of light that was then transformed into voltages by the photocells. The voltages then triggered sound-generating oscillators, filters, and envelope shapers to create the music. Introduced in 1962, the Oramics machine was extraordinarily complicated to use. Oram was continually making improvements. Only a handful of composers used the instrument before it was overshadowed by a new generation of easier-to-use voltage-controlled synthesizers, such as those made by Robert Moog. But Oram continued to produce music using the Oramics instrument, found success as an independent composer of electronic music, and was working on a digital version of Oramics before she was slowed by a severe stroke in the 1990s. Some of her final

LISTENING GUIDE 2.7

Title: *Four Aspects*

Artist: Daphne Oram   **Year**: 1960   **Duration**: 8:15

Genre: Tape composition

Electronic Instrumentation: Tone generators, feedback, tape manipulation.

Background: This piece was composed in 1960, shortly after Oram left the BBC Radiophonic Workshop. It demonstrates her interest in creating works that were longer than the short snippets of music that she had produced for radio and television themes. The piece was patiently crafted and is strikingly harmonic, exploring a rich tone field that lacked the herky-jerky nature of other tape music of the time.

	Listen For: Development of musical chords and harmonic fields from monophonic tone generators, combined during mixing, developing slowly and gradually using filtering and loops.
0:00–2:15	The piece opens with a regular rhythm and eight-bar musical structure, organized through the use of tape loops and percussive sounds. Oram introduces a melody consisting of ten notes that becomes a recurring motif for the piece. The notes are produced electronically, presumably using a keyboard-controlled oscillator. Each note in the motif has a dreamy, soft attack, sustains for a long time and diminishes while the next note begins. The tones are treated with abundant reverberation. Shadows of the motif begin out of phase with the original, producing a kind of shifting harmony based on whatever notes are cued up at the time. After about 2:00, the interlocking melodies gradually fall out of phase and sound more dissonant, largely because of the introduction of echo.
2:16–3:35	This section comprises a noisy accumulation of harmonic elements that multiply and clash through the use of excessive echo. The harmonic elements disappear as sidebands of noise increase in volume. The section culminates in a dense cacophony of noise.
3:36–5:50	The noisy conclusion of the previous section gives way to a more clustered presentation of dissonant tone blocks, bell-like sounds, and quiet, reverberating sine waves. At about 4:15, a periodic rhythm begins to take shape through the alternative beats of tone clusters, played using tape loops. At about 4:35, the melody from part one is repeated. The melody is joined by a second, out of sync repetition of the motif, and a recurring line of bell-like sounds, reminiscent of Varèse's *Poème électronique*.
5:50–8:15	The final section begins with a variation on the original melodic motif, this time slowed down with some parts that appear to be transposed and other parts played in reverse. Oram has synchronized these elements so that they change in a uniform manner as a sequence of chords, undulating and changing in unison until the work fades.

Compare and Contrast

Poème électronique (1958) by Edgard Varèse

On the Other Ocean (1977) by David Behrman

projects included outdoor **sound installations**.[65] Even though the Oramics instrument was not widely adopted, Oram had succeeded in transcending one of the major obstacles to composing electronic music at the time—writing or notating ideas for synthetic sounds that could be faithfully reproduced by a sound-generating instrument. The significance and originality of her contribution was on a par with contemporary attempts at the Columbia–Princeton Electronic Music Center in New York (see Chapter 3) and Siemens Corporation in Munich to pre-program electronic music sequences using punched paper tape as a control medium. Oram's work was unique, however, in combining the concept of the graphic score—which had been pioneered by such composers as Stockhausen, Varèse, and Xenakis—with a direct means for converting drawn images into electronically generated musical sound. To understand how revolutionary this was, the rest of the world of electronic music instruments did not truly catch up with Oram until the introduction of interactive computer composition in the early 1980s. It was during that time, some 20 years later, that instruments such as the Fairlight Computer Music Instrument provided a means for drawing and editing wave shapes by hand, a routine feature of many software-based synthesizer programs produced since 1990. Oram was an important pioneer during the formative years of European electronic music and a key influence, especially in the United Kingdom.

Back at the Workshop, efforts were mobilized to assemble a studio full of the proper equipment to make electronic music. It was initially equipped with cast-off tape recorders, microphones, and mixing panels from other BBC facilities. Initially, the organization was only given an outlay of £1,900 to buy new equipment, which was

Figure 2.18   Electronic music pioneer Daphne Oram left the BBC Radiophonic Workshop in 1959 to develop her own graphically controlled synthesizer, which she called Oramics. Oram was one of the first women to operate her own electronic music production business. (Ray White)

equivalent to about 5,300 US dollars at the time. The latest rage in the production of tape music was the use of tape loops for creating repeating sound patterns, and the Workshop composers were well equipped with tape recorders to exploit this technique. Among the new equipment purchased were a few basic items for creating tape music: two variable speed tape recorders, an audio oscillator, an audio wave converter, one variable voice frequency filter and two transcription turntables used for both recording and playback on disc.[66]

Until the availability of commercially available music synthesizers in the late 1960s, the engineering of musical equipment at the Workshop was largely a do-it-yourself affair by some of the cleverest engineers in the business. Dave Young, who joined the operation in 1963, invented many of the engineering marvels of the early Workshop years. He was previously experienced with communication electronics during World War II and had built several Hammond-style electronic organs. He brought enormous ingenuity to the Workshop and nearly always found a technical means to fulfill the wishes of the resident composers.[67]

Off-the-shelf electronic music products gradually supplemented the innovative equipment devised during the early years of the Workshop. Following are some examples of audio equipment, inventions, and instruments used during the two most fruitful decades of the Workshop's existence: the emerging years from 1957 to 1965 and the early synthesizer years from 1965 to 1975.

Workshop Emerging Years, 1957–65

- **Tape machines**. Six Philips tape recorders were acquired, and fitted with remote control switches for triggering the mixing desk from the tape recorder. Three of these machines were aligned so that a single reel of tape could be passed through the recording and playback heads of each machine, providing many options for creating overdubs, echo, and tape delay in real time, all activated by a single switch.
- **Keyboard-controlled oscillators**. Two small "keying units" were devised to control the sound generation of oscillator banks. One unit controlled nine oscillators (the "Jason Unit"), the other 12. Each was also fitted with adjustable timing circuits for modifying the attack and decay characteristics of the sound. Composer Delia Derbyshire used the 12-oscillator unit to realize her famous electronic version of the *Doctor Who* theme in 1962.
- **The wobbulator**. Like many pieces of audio equipment in the early days of tape music, many of the most useful sound-producing devices were originally designed for engineering tests. Radio stations naturally had many such devices, including wave-generating oscillators for testing signals and frequency ranges. The wobbulator was an audio oscillator whose tone could be continuously varied by a second oscillator. The effect was that of a smoothly sweeping wave of sound modulated across a wide frequency range.
- **Reverberation room**. Originally, reverb effects for the Workshop were recorded using an actual room rather than artificially by means such as spring reverberation. This was a familiar technique first developed for radio broadcasts. A room located in the basement of the studio building provided a resonant chamber to produce reverberation. The walls were smoothly painted to enhance their reflective quality. Reverb was recorded by having a microphone at one end of the room and a speaker

with amplifier at the other end. Live or recorded sound could be fed through the speaker and picked up by the mike at the other end of the room, thus modified slightly by the ambient effect of the room itself. The amount of reverberation depth was slight and also fixed, but noticeably different from an unaltered sound.

- **Artificial reverberation unit**. This machine produced echo effects by means of a rotating drum coated with magnetic oxide—similar to magnetic tape—and multiple playback heads that read the recorded sound signal from the drum. The frequency of the repeated sounds (echoes) was varied by turning the individual playback heads on and off.[68]

- **Crystal Palace**. Invented by Dave Young, this was a combination mixer and cross-fading device that could manage audio input from up to 16 sources and provide a variable mix to four outputs. When connected to tone generators, the effect was that of producing a dense, heavily layered organ-like sound. The circuits were housed in a clear, acrylic box, hence the name "Crystal Palace."

- **Programme effects units**. In 1961 the BBC upgraded several aspects of the Radiophonic Workshop, providing a new studio, custom-made mixing console, a panel of sound filtering controls that were called "programme effects units," and remote controls for triggering playback and recording of the tape machines from another room.

Early Synthesizer Years, 1965–75

The daily production needs of the BBC required that the Workshop staff produce original electronic music and effects quickly and efficiently. This was not easy when everything had to be done, essentially, by hand, from the twiddling of dials on an oscillator to the editing of magnetic tape with a razor blade. Every sound, edit, and mix of an electronic work had to be painstakingly crafted and it might require days to produce even a few seconds of sound. As a result, the Workshop was always on the lookout for means of automating or improving the efficiency of the process. By 1967, plans were laid to build an extravagant switching panel that could manipulate up to 50 sound inputs, provide sequence control, and individually manipulate the envelope characteristics of each sound.[69] These plans became unnecessary, however, with the commercial availability of several early voltage-controlled synthesizers. These instruments promised the diversity of sound sources, treatments, and control that would make music-making a much more efficient process. Although the Workshop carefully considered the American-made Moog Synthesizer, it ultimately selected a British company, Electronic Musical Instruments (EMS), as the provider of its first synthesizers. Here is a rundown of the analog synthesizers found at the Workshop from the late 1960s to mid-1970s:

- **EMS VCS3**. Two of these desktop, voltage-controlled monophonic synthesizers were purchased between 1969 and 1971. Each was more compact than the studio version of the Moog Synthesizer because the EMS models used a small, 16-pin matrix for connecting components, in contrast to the large phono-cable design of the Moog that resembled a telephone switchboard. The VCS3 contained three solid-state oscillators, a ring modulator, envelope shaper, voltage-controlled filter, an internal spring reverb unit, white noise generator, a joystick controller for mixing signals, and a keyboard.

- **EMS Synthi A**. This was a compact version of the VCS3 built into a handy briefcase, with a touch-sensitive keyboard and the same 16-pin programming matrix.
- **EMS Synthi 100—the Delaware**. Acquired in 1971, this was a large-scale modular monophonic synthesizer using the same principles as the VCS3, but greatly expanded. More intimidating to the musicians, it took some adjustment to learn how to control its 12 oscillators and ancillary controls, two keyboards (allowing two notes at a time), multiple pin-matrix panels, and various modulating controls. It included an impressive 256-event sequencer, one of the most elaborate of the time, which made possible the programming of long musical sequences.
- **ARP Odyssey**. The Workshop acquired an ARP Odyssey in 1972—a portable, monophonic keyboard-based instrument with a pitchbending rotary dial.
- **Polyphonic synthesizers**. A host of polyphonic synthesizers became available during the mid-1970s and several found their way into the Workshop. Among them were Sequential Circuits Prophet 5, Oberheim OBX8, and several Yamaha keyboards including the CS15 and CS40M (both duophonic).

The gradual changeover to synthesizers also signaled a transition from the tape-editing days of the early Workshop to the making of more purely musical sounds that could be programmed, organized, and played in real time. As a result, the music of the 1970s' Workshop relied less on the manipulation and editing of natural sounds than it did on synthesized music.

The void left by the early departure of Daphne Oram was capably filled by a fresh crew of composers and engineers. John Baker (1937–97) joined in 1960 and had studied composition at the Royal Academy of Music and worked largely in jazz and electronic music. He was adept at incorporating concrete sounds into his music and effects and was responsible for a host of themes and sound effects for many popular programs. Brian Hodgson (b. 1938) was responsible for many of the sound effects associated with the television show *Doctor Who* from 1963 to 1972, creating some of the "special sounds" that remained with the program for several decades.

Delia Derbyshire (1937–2001) joined in 1962 and was a musician with a degree in mathematics from Cambridge. She was the most prominent of numerous women composers employed by the Workshop over the years. Derbyshire is perhaps best known for her electronic realization of Ron Grainer's theme music to *Doctor Who*, a long-running British science fiction television series. But her other works were numerous, inventive, and far ahead of their time stylistically. Like many of the Workshop composers, Derbyshire became skilled at mixing pieces in real time using multiple tape loops and tape recorders. She is thought to have produced the longest single tape loop at the Workshop. "It went

Figure 2.19   BBC Radiophonic Workshop composer Delia Derbyshire, 1965. (Ray White)

out through the double doors and then through the next pair, just opposite the ladies toilet and reception," explained Derbyshire with delight. "The longest corridor in London, with the longest tape loop!"[70] She was a clever programmer of rhythmic sequences and several of her experiments of the late 1960s and early 1970s sound as fresh and contemporary as the latest electronica. Derbyshire also worked outside of the Workshop, and by the mid–1960s had forged relationships with other figures in the experimental and rock music scene. An early side project developed in 1966 when she collaborated with composer Brian Hodgson and the founder of EMS to form an organization called Unit Delta Plus to promote the development of electronic music. Derbyshire's tape work was featured at the *The Million Volt Sound and Light Rave*, one of the UK's early

Figure 2.20   BBC Radiophonic Workshop composer Brian Hodgson and the 12-oscillator "keying unit" used by Derbyshire in the composition of the *Doctor Who* theme. (Ray White)

electronic music festivals that also featured tape music by Paul McCartney. She developed associations with members of The Beatles and Yoko Ono, providing a soundtrack for one of Ono's performance films.[71] Derbyshire discussed a collaboration, never realized, with The Beatles around the time when they were first experimenting with tape loops. She formed the experimental electronic group White Noise in 1969 with fellow musician David Vorhaus to explore a less commercial approach to creating electronic music. Derbyshire left the Workshop in 1973 and continued to have a fruitful career as an influential electronic music composer.

David Cain (b. 1941) was educated at Imperial College where he earned a degree in mathematics. He became a studio manager at the BBC in 1963 and officially joined the composing staff of the Radiophonic Workshop in 1967, at first composing jingles and then moving on to create remarkable background music for radio dramas, including BBC productions of *The War of the Worlds* (1967) and *The Hobbit* (1968).

As discussed above, Oram and Derbyshire were two of the earliest and most notable women composers of this period of electronic music. The Workshop, although always largely male-dominated in its attitudes toward composers and engineers, nonetheless provided opportunities for many pioneering female electronic musicians. In addition to Oram and Derbyshire were Maddalena Fagandini, Elizabeth Parker, and Glynis Jones.

The pre-synthesizer era of the BBC Radiophonic Workshop, with its composers engaged in the daily, tactile practice of creating electronic music from the most rudimentary of building blocks, produced accessible music, consumed by millions of television viewers, and was probably the single most important force in bringing the sound of electronic music into the popular music mainstream.

Electronic music in the UK was well represented by the output of the Workshop, but it should also be noted that the 1960s was also a time of widespread experimentation with music in other sectors. Lily Greenham (1924–2001) was a Danish-born poet and artist who explored the possibilities of combining poetry and electronic sound modification. Based in London beginning in the early 1970s, Greenham's text-sound compositions began with fragments of spoken word that she then edited and treated electronically to create abstract textures, rhythms, and soundscapes. In 1974, she completed the work *Relativity* as a guest at the BBC Radiophonic Workshop. Hugh Davies (1943–2005) was a younger British composer who studied and worked with Karlheinz Stockhausen in Germany from 1964 to 1966 before embarking on his own inventive path in experimental music. Among his achievements was the formation in 1968, with guitarist Derek Bailey and saxophonist Evan Parker, of the live electronic music group the *Music Improvisation Company*, an innovative experiment in improvisational music. Davies was also an educator, a hacker of homemade electronic instruments, and researcher who documented the early history of electronic music.

OTHER EUROPEAN STUDIOS

By the early 1960s, Europe was a hotbed of electronic music activity and many studios, both privately and institutionally sponsored, arose in a number of countries (Table 2.2). Each expansion of the field encouraged new ideas and new applications of electronically produced music. At the same time that composers in Paris, Cologne, and Milan were producing electronic music of an experimental nature, so, too, were others beginning to test the potential of tape composition in producing pop music, jazz, soundtracks, and music for dance.

Philips' Research Laboratories established the *Center for Electronic Music* in Eindhoven in 1956. This is the studio where Varèse created *Poème électronique* in 1958, but it also served as the launching pad for the playfully composed space-age pop songs of Tom Dissevelt (see pp. 456–8). In Norway, composers at the *Norsk Rikskringkasting* (Norse Broadcasting) studio, including Arne Nordheim (1931–2010), Alfred Janson (b. 1937), and Bjorn Fongaard (1920–80), experimented broadly with the combination of orchestra, vocalists, and magnetic tape in live performance. Swedish composer Karl-Birger Blomdahl (1916–68) spent two years developing his science fiction opera *Aniara* (1959), which included portions of tape music produced with the help of the electronic music studios of Swedish Radio.

Figure 2.21 Dick Raaijmakers in the Philips Research Laboratories, *c.* 1958. (Philips International BV, Eindhoven)

Another well-equipped European electronic music studio was the Studio für Elektronische Musik in Munich, established by the Siemens Corporation in 1956.

The studio was originally organized in Gauting under the direction of composer Carl Orff (1895–1982) to produce a promotional soundtrack for an industrial film about the Siemens Corporation. The electronics firm spared no expense in creating a state-of-the-art studio. The audio laboratory included a **vocoder**, a paper tape reader for setting the pitch, duration, and timbre of a bank of multiple sine wave oscillators, a sawtooth oscillator, reverberation unit, and mixing console. The successful completion of the

Figure 2.22   The Research Laboratories operated by Philips, 1958. (Philips International BV, Eindhoven)

film led Siemens to establish a permanent studio in Munich in 1960, where it became a regular stopover for visiting composers. Upon its move, a control room was added to the studio as well as a unique optical scanner for converting graphical scores into sound-generating signals. Siemens gave up the studio in 1963 and transferred it to the Staatliche Hochschule für Gestaltung, a national university of the arts and sciences where it was operated using the original Siemens equipment until 1966. At the peak of its popularity, the studio occupied six rooms and the paper tape sequencing equipment was expanded to control 20 sine wave oscillators. The Siemens laboratory was a precursor of the modern synthesizer in providing the composer with a way to store programmed sound sequences. The use of paper tape as a programming medium and its integrated controls paralleled similar work being done by RCA at the *Columbia–Princeton Electronic Music Center* in New York (see Chapter 6, pp. 176–90). Like the BBC Radiophonic Workshop, Siemens had primarily intended its studio to be used for making commercial music for radio and television. In addition, the studio did host from time to time a number of well-known composers including Mauricio Kagel, György Ligeti, and Iannis Xenakis.

The second era in the development of electronic music had its origins in post-World War II Europe. In only 15 short years, from 1945 to 1960, electronic music evolved from being a strictly experimental medium to being a viable new genre that widely influenced the creation of music for records, stage, screen, radio, and television media. While the importance of its European roots cannot be overestimated, electronic music also had proponents in North America who furthered the genre both technically and aesthetically. These developments will be explored in the next chapter.

Table 2.2   **Key European electronic music studios, 1948–67***

Studio location	Affiliation	Year established	Sample of works completed
Paris, France: Groupe de Recherches Musicales (GRM)	Office of French National Radio-Television (ORTF)	1948	*Étude aux chemin de fer* (Schaeffer, 1948; the first work of *musique concrète* logged at the Paris studio, which was one of five parts of the work *Études de bruits*); *Symphonie pour un homme seul* (Henry and Schaeffer, 1949–50); *Le Microphone bien tempéré* (Henry, 1950–51); *Étude I sur un son* (Boulez, 1952); *Timbres-durées* (Messiaen, 1952); *Étude* (Stockhausen, 1952); *Le Voile d'Orphee* (Henry, 1953); *La Rivière endormie* (Milhaud, 1954); *Déserts* (Varèse, 1954); *Pau-Amma* (Arthuys, 1955); *Nature morte au Vibraphone* (Arthuys, 1956); *Étude II* (Philippot, 1956); *Trois aspects sentimentaux* (Sauguet, 1957); *Étude aux accidents* (Ferrari, 1958); *Étude aux allures* (Schaeffer, 1958); *Continuo* (Ferrari and Schaeffer, 1958); *Diamorphoses* (Xenakis, 1957–58); *Concret P. H.* (Xenakis, 1958); *La Voix* (Baronnet, 1958); *Visage V* (Ferrari, 1958–59); *Texte II* (Boucourechliev, 1959); *Étude aux objets* (Schaeffer, 1959); *Orient–Occident* (Xenakis, 1960); *Dahovi* (Malec, 1961); *Collage I* (Carson, 1962); *Bohor* (Xenakis, 1962); *Mensonges* (Bayle, 1963); *Times Five* (Brown, 1963); *Tournoi* (Bayle, 1964); *Laborintus II* (Berio, 1965); *Deux poémes* (Tamba, 1966)
Cologne, Germany: Studio for Electronic Music	West German National Radio (WDR)	1951	*Klang im unbegrenzten Raum* (Beyer and Eimert, 1951–52); *Klangstudie I* (Beyer and Eimert, 1952); *Struktur 8* (Eimert, 1953); *Studie I* (Stockhausen, 1953); *Seismogramme I und II* (Pousseur, 1954); *Klangfiguren II* (Koenig, 1955–56); *Gesang der Jünglinge* (Stockhausen, 1955–56); *Fünf Stücke* (Eimert 1955–56); *Pfingstoratorium—Spiritus Intelligentiae* (Krenek, 1956); *Glissandi* (Ligeti, 1957); *Audiogramme* (Nilsson, 1955 and 1957); *Artikulation* (Ligeti, 1958); *1st and 2nd Exercises* (Cardew, 1958); *Transición I* (Kagel, 1958–60); *Kontakte* (Stockhausen, 1959–60); *Position* (Boehmer, 1961–62); *Sechs Studien* (Eimert, 1962); *Mikrophonie I* (Stockhausen, 1964); *Mixtur* (Stockhausen, 1964–65); *Mikrophonie II* (Stockhausen, 1965); *Hymnen* (Stockhausen, 1966–67)
Geneva, Switzerland: Studio de Phonologie de Radio Geneva	Centre de Recherches Sonores, Swiss National Radio	1951	*Musique de film* (Christen, 1951–52); *Vérité garantie* (Sassi, 1956); *C'est arrivé l'année prochaine* (Zumbach, 1958); *Éclipses* (Kaegi, 1964)
Copenhagen, Denmark: Danmarks Radio	Denmark National Radio	1953	*En dag pa Dyrehavsbakken* (Pade, 1953–55); *Glasperlespil II* (Pade, 1958); *Dommen* (Norgard, 1961–62); *Ave* (Pedersen, 1963); *Pastorale No. 5* (Schultz, 1963)
Milan, Italy: Studio di Fonologia Musicale	Italian National Radio (RAI)	1953	*Mimusique n. 1* (Berio, 1953); *Notturno* (Maderna, 1955); *Étude 1* (Boucourechliev, 1956); *Scambi* (Pousseur, 1957); *Thema–Omaggio a Joyce* (Berio, 1958); *Continuo* (Maderna, 1958); *Fontana Mix* (Cage, 1958–59); *Momenti* (Berio, 1960); *Intolleranza* (Nono, 1960); *Visage* (Berio, 1961); *Music for Vibraphones* (Hassell, 1965)
London, England: BBC Radiophonic Workshop	British Broadcasting Corporation (BBC)	1956	*The Disagreeable Oyster* (Briscoe, 1959); *Opium* (Almuro, 1959); *Anathema, for Reciter and Tape* (Wilkinson, 1962); *A Round of Silence* (Smalley, 1963).
Eindhoven, Netherlands: Center for Electronic Music (Philips Research Laboratories)	Philips Electric	1956	*Variations électronique* (Badings, 1957); *Whirling* (Dissevelt, 1958); *Poéme électronique* (Varèse, 1958); *Electronic Ballet Music III* (Badings, 1959); *Contrasts* (Raaijmakers, 1959); *Pianoforte* (Raaijmakers, 1960)

Table 2.2   (continued)

Studio location	Affiliation	Year established	Sample of works completed
Munich, Germany: Studio für Elektronische Musik	Siemens Corporation	1957	*Studie für elektronische Klänge* (Riedl, 1959); *Klänge unterwegs* (Brün, 1961); *Antithese* (Kagel, 1962); *Rota II* (Hambraeus, 1963); *Imaginary Landscape No. 3* (Cage, realized by Kagel, 1964); *Heterophony* (Antoniou, 1966)
Warsaw, Poland: Studio Eksperymentalne	Polish National Radio	1957	*Campi integrati* (Evangelisti, 1959); *Passacalia na 40 z 5* (Dobrowalski, 1960); *Brygaa smierci* (Penderecki, 1963); *Assemblage I–III* (Schaeffer, 1966)
Stockholm, Sweden: Elektronmusikstudion (EMS)	Swedish National Radio	1957	*Reaktion* (Hambraeus, 1958); *Aniara* (Blomdahl, 1959); *Semikolon* (Bodin, 1965); *Skorpionen* (Nilsson, 1965).
Paris, France: Studio Apsome	Private (Pierre Henry)	1958	*Arcane II* (Henry, 1958); *Orphée* (Henry, 1958); *U 47* (Baronnet and Dufréne 1960); *Le Voyage* (Henry, 1961–62); *Musique pour les évangiles* (Henry, 1965); *L'Agression* (Henry, 1967)
Berlin, Germany: Oskar Sala Elektronisches Studio	Private (Oskar Sala)	1958	*Forschung und Leben* (Sala, 1958); *Der Meisterdieb* (Sandloff, 1958); *Kompositionen für MTR und Tonband* (Genzmer, 1959); *Die Grasharfe* (Sala and Sandloff, 1959); *Electronics* (Gassmann and Sala, 1958–60); *Korallen* (Sala, 1964); *Mixturen* (Sala, 1966)
Rome, Italy: Electronic Music Studio	American Academy	1958	*Dynamophonic Suite* (Luening, 1958); *Duo for Clarinet and Recorded Clarinet* (Smith, 1961); *Concert Music for Tape and Jazz Ensemble* (Eaton, 1964); *Roma: A Theater Piece in Open Style for Improvisation Ensemble and Tape* (Austin, 1965); *Watercolormusic* (Curran, 1966)
Bratislava, Czechoslovakia: Zvukove Pracovisko	Czechoslovak National Television	1961	*65 Milionov* (Zeljenka, 1961); *Russiches Wunder* (Dessau, 1962); *Vzbura na ulici Sycamore* (Berger, 1963)
Utrecht, Netherlands: Studio voor Elektronische Muziek (STEM)	University of Utrecht	1961	*Intersection for Tape and Orchestra* (Dissevelt, 1961); *Crystal Diode 1* (Raaijmakers, 1961); *Herakles* (Kox, 1961); *Alchemie 1961* (Boerman, 1961); *3 Lucebert Songs* (Badings, 1963); *Fantasy in Orbit* (Dissevelt, 1963–64); *Toccatas I and II* (Badings, 1964); *Tremens* (Kagel, 1966); *Mémories* (Shinohara, 1966); *Terminus II* (Koenig, 1966–67)
Oslo, Norway: Norsk Rikskringkasting	Norse National Radio (NRK)	1961	*Epitaffio* (Nordheim, 1963); *Response I* (Nordheim, 1966)
Moscow, Russia: Eksperimentalnaya Studiya Elektronnoi Muzyki	Private (Muzei A. N. Skryabina)	1961	*Metchte Navstrechu* (Artem'ev, 1961); *Sl'ezy* (Nemtin, 1961); *Na Otdykhe* (Kreichi, 1961); *Prelyudiya* (Kreichi, 1964)
Gent, Belgium: Electronic Music Studio	Institut voor Psychoakoestiek en Elektronische Muziek (IPEM)	1962	*Escurial* (de Meester, 1963 for television); *Endomorfiel* (Goethals, 1964); *Stuk voor piano en geluidsband* (Goeyvaerts, 1964); *Votre Faust* (Pousseur, 1965–66); *Ouverture* (Buckinxc, 1966)
Berlin, Germany: Experimentalistudio für Künstliche Klang und Gerauscherzeugung; Laboratorium für Akustisch-Musikalische Grenzprobleme	East German National Radio (RFZ)	1962	*Der faule Zauberer* (Kurth, 1963); *Amarillo Luna* (Kubiczek, 1963); *Quartet für elektronische Klänge* (Wehding, 1963); *Variationen* (Hohensee, 1965); *Zoologischer Garten* (Rzewski, 1965)

Note: *Studios listed include key private and institutional facilities that were used by more than one composer. Excludes private studios used by only one individual.

SUMMARY

- Prior to World War II, experiments with recorded sound were conducted by composers using turntable technology. Hindemith and Toch may have been the first composers to create works specifically for recorded media (1930).

- *Musique concrète* was the name given to early electronic music developed in France by Pierre Schaeffer (1949). In *musique concrète*, sound material primarily consisted of recorded natural sounds that were composed using the medium itself. Schaeffer created his first *musique concrète* using turntables, microphones, and disc lathes for recording and playing back sounds.

- The availability of the magnetic tape recorder following World War II made the creation of electronic music more feasible and resulted in several parallel developments in France, Germany, Italy, and other European countries.

- The Groupe de Recherches Musicales (GRM) was founded in 1951 in Paris by Radiodiffusion-Television Françaises (RTF), the French national broadcasting service. It was the first state-sponsored electronic music studio.

- In late 1951, Nordwestdeutscher Rundfunk (NWDR) established an electronic music studio in Cologne under the direction of Dr. Werner Meyer-Eppler and Herbert Eimert. Their work was initially focused on a form of serialism produced as *elektronische Musik.*

- The aesthetic approaches to electronic music by the Paris and Cologne studios were initially distinct, the French using only recorded natural sounds as source material and the Germans using only electronically generated tones. This distinction quickly dissolved as an influx of composers to both studios quickly began to assert their own ideas about the composition and content of their experimental music.

- Along with Varèse's *Poème électronique* (1958), Stockhausen's *Gesang der Jünglinge* (1955–56) marked an important transition from the mutually exclusive aesthetic approaches of the Paris and Cologne studios to a more broadly stylistic and open-minded period of electronic music composition.

- The Studio di Fonologia Musicale in Milan encouraged much experimentation in the composition of electronic music and was noted for Berio's important contributions to text-sound composition using the human voice.

- The BBC Radiophonic Workshop was the United Kingdom's leading laboratory for the development of electronic music. Through its production of electronic music for commercial radio and television programs, the Workshop helped popularize electronic music with the general listening public, leading to its increased use in popular music and jazz.

- Other notable early European studios for electronic music were created in Eindhoven, Stockholm, London, and Munich.

KEY PEOPLE IN CHAPTER TWO

KEY TERMS IN CHAPTER TWO

MILESTONES

Early Electronic Music of Europe

Technical and scientific	Year	Music and instruments
– Lee De Forest perfected Phonofilm, an optical sound-on-film process.	1919	
	1922	– John and James Whitney created music directly on optical recording film.
	1930	– Paul Hindemith and Ernst Toch used the turntable as an instrument to create music.
	1939	– John Cage produced *Imaginary Landscape No. 1* for turntables and radios.
	1948	– Pierre Schaeffer premiered *Études de bruits*, five formative turntable compositions for recorded sound.
	1949	– Schaeffer coined the term *musique concrète* to describe the approach to electronic music of the Paris studio.
– Magnetic tape recorders became available to composers in Paris and Germany.	1950	– Herbert Eimert and Werner Meyer-Eppler coined the term *elektronische Musik* to describe the approach to electronic music of the Cologne studio. – *Symphonie pour un homme seul* was completed by Schaeffer and Henry.
– The Groupe de Recherches Musicales (GRM) electronic music studio was established in Paris by French public broadcasting. – The Nordwestdeutscher Rundfunk (NWDR) electronic music studio was established in Cologne by German public broadcasting.	1951	
	1953–54	– Karlheinz Stockhausen composed *Studie I* and *Studie II* using sine waves as primary souce material. *Studie II* had a visual score. – The *concrète* opera *Voile d'Orphée* was completed by Schaeffer and Henry.
– The Radio Audizioni Italiane (RAI) electronic music studio was established in Milan by Italian public broadcasting.	1955	
– Philips Research Laboratories established an electronic music studio in Eindhoven.	1956	– Stockhausen completed *Gesang der Jünglinge*.
– The BBC established the BBC Radiophonic Workshop.	1957	
	1958	– Luciano Berio completed the tape piece *Thema–Omaggio a Joyce*, an early text-sound composition. – Varèse composed *Poème électronique* in the Philips studio.

CHAPTER 3

Early Electronic Music in the United States and Latin America

I was at a concert of electronic music in Cologne and I noticed that, even though it was the most recent electronic music, the audience was all falling asleep. No matter how interesting the music was, the audience couldn't stay awake. That was because the music was coming out of loudspeakers.
—John Cage

David Tudor and Gordon Mumma performing *Mesa* in 1966. (Gordon Mumma)

Electronic music activity in the United States during the early 1950s was neither organized nor institutional. Experimentation with tape composition took place through the efforts of individual composers working on a makeshift basis without state support. Such fragmented efforts lacked the cohesion, doctrine, and financial support of their European counterparts but in many ways the musical results were more diverse, ranging from works that were radically experimental to special effects for popular motion pictures and works that combined the use of taped sounds with live instrumentalists performing on stage. The first electronic music composers in North America did not adhere to any rigid schools of thought regarding the aesthetics of the medium and viewed with mixed skepticism and amusement the aesthetic wars taking place between the French and the Germans. This chapter traces the works of early experimenters with tape music in North America leading up to the establishment of the first well-funded institutional studios such as the Columbia–Princeton Electronic Music Center in New York.

LOUIS AND BEBE BARRON

The first piece of electronic music for magnetic tape composed in America was most likely a little work called *Heavenly Menagerie* by Louis (1920–89) and Bebe Barron (1927–2008). Bebe dated the work to 1950, about the time that she and her husband acquired their first tape recording equipment.[1]

The Barrons were musically inclined and creatively blessed. She had studied music with Wallingford Rieger and Henry Cowell. He had studied music at the University of Chicago and also had a knack for working with a soldering gun and electrical gear. Having just married and moved to New York in 1948, the couple decided to try their hand at the business of music recording. They started their enterprise mostly because it seemed like an interesting thing to do. They didn't really expect great success:

> We had to earn a living somehow so we opened a recording studio that catered to the avant-garde. We had some pretty good equipment, considering. A lot of it we built ourselves. Then the commercial equipment began to come onto the market. We were able to purchase some of it. We had a really thriving recording business. There was nobody who was competition. So, we did all right.[2]

New York City in the early 1950s was the base of operations for America's experimental in art culture—avant-garde music, film, painting, dance, and writing all thrived in the growing bohemian atmosphere of Greenwich Village. The Barrons were at the epicenter of the post-war American cultural revolution and were soon collaborating with many rising composers and filmmakers. They were in a unique position to do so because the Barrons had assembled the first electronic music studio in America. "The only people that I knew who were working before us were Schaeffer and Henry in France," explained Bebe.[3] *Heavenly Menagerie* was a purely electronic work that grew out of the Barrons' interest in avant-garde music.

One reason for the Barrons' early success with their electronic music studio was that they had a short-lived monopoly on tape recording equipment. Just after World War II, when the secrets of the tape recorder were just being distributed in the United States, Bebe and Louis had two family connections that proved to be instrumental in getting them into the business of electronic music. The first was a link to the man who invented the Stancil-Hoffman tape recorder, one of the first American-made magnetic tape recorders to be manufactured following World War II. The other connection was a cousin working for the Minnesota Mining and Manufacturing Company (3M). The Barrons had a Stancil-Hoffman tape recorder custom-made for them and through their cousin they were able to obtain some of the earliest batches of magnetic recording tape developed by 3M. By the early 1950s, the Barrons' studio at 9 West 8th Street in Greenwich Village was a well-equipped, if not entirely orthodox, hub of electronic music gear. Bebe recalled:

> We were using the same equipment that the classic electronic music studios were using, although we were more limited because, number one, we were considerably earlier than most of them and we had to make a lot—in fact almost all—of our own equipment. We were also limited financially because we were trying to support ourselves. We didn't have an institution behind us.
>
> We built this monstrous big speaker and it sounded wonderful. It had a very heavy bass, which I always loved. That was the speaker we worked with. I believe it was one of those big old theater speakers. We built the encasing out of fiberglass. We had electronic oscillators that we built ourselves. We had one that produced sine and sawtooth waves and one that produced sine and square waves. We had a filter that we built; a spring reverberator; several tape recorders. The Stancil-Hoffmann was built primarily for playing loops, which we had just discovered and were wildly excited about. We had a setting on the front of the machine that enabled us to play loops very easily.[4]

In their partnership Louis did most of the circuitry design and Bebe did much of the composing and production. Both became adept at soldering circuits and editing tape. They were both influenced by mathematician Norbert Weiner's book, *Cybernetics: Or, Control and Communication in the Animal and the Machine* (1948), and this carried over into their approach to circuit design:

> We never considered what we did at that point, [to be] composing music. It really wasn't at all like music because we were not concerned with note-by-note composition. What we did was build certain kinds of simple circuits that had a peculiar sort of nervous system, shall we say. They had characteristics that would keep repeating themselves.[5]

The Barrons met composer John Cage at a monthly gathering of the Artists' Club on 8th Street in New York City, where participants took turns explaining their work and projects to others. Cage had conceived a work for magnetic tape and saw in the Barrons an opportunity to establish a working relationship with a well-equipped sound studio. David Tudor (1926–96), composer and longtime Cage collaborator, later recalled:

> In those days one did not have easy access to electronics, so John Cage tried to find something like we now would call a grant situation and a friend of ours [Paul Williams] gave us $5,000 to start experimenting with magnetic tape so we could use an electronic studio and pay an engineer [the Barrons].[6]

Figure 3.1   Louis and Bebe Barron in their Greenwich Village electronic music studio, 1956. The studio was equipped to record electronic sounds onto magnetic tape and synchronize them to motion picture images using 16 mm magnetic film recorders. (Bebe Barron)

Figure 3.2   Second view of the Barrons' electronic music studio in New York City. The workbench in the foreground was used by the couple to make circuits for generating electronic sounds for such films as *Forbidden Planet*. (Bebe Barron)

In 1951, Cage organized the *Project of Music for Magnetic Tape*. He and fellow composers Earle Brown (1926–2002), Morton Feldman (1926–87), Christian Wolff (b. 1934), and David Tudor all began to explore the tape medium with the technical assistance and studio facilities of Louis and Bebe Barron.

JOHN CAGE AND THE PROJECT OF MUSIC FOR MAGNETIC TAPE

By 1950, while many of his contemporaries, particularly in Europe, were exploring serialism as a means for determining every aspect of written music, Cage was investigating **chance operations** as a way to create music for which the outcome was not preconceived—composition that was indeterminate of its performance. Although polar opposites in most every respect, serialism and chance music begin with a similar motivation—that of disengaging a composer from their natural instinct for making pretty music. Serialism subverts convention through an elaborate set of rules for choosing which notes and dynamics occur in a series—but the sound themselves are all part of the accepted musical scale. Cage also wanted to remove the composer's taste in entirety from the process of composition. He opened his ears to any and all possible sounds, pitched and unpitched. His method of composing removed not only his taste from the outcome, but also the minutest degree of control or personal choice over the music. In about 1950, he

LISTENING GUIDE 3.1

Title: *Forbidden Planet: Overture* (reprise)

Artist: Bebe and Louis Barron   **Year**: 1956   **Duration**: 2:16

Genre: Soundtrack

Electronic Instrumentation: Oscillators, reverberation, tape manipulation, and homemade audio signal generators.

Background: Bebe and Louis Barron produced electronic music for film and television from their private studio in New York City. Their music was more atmospheric than rhythmic, due in part to the difficulty of manually synchronizing the output of multiple tape recorders during their mixdowns. Much of their equipment was built by hand, including audio oscillators, a filter, spring reverberation, and sound-producing circuits that they soldered themselves (see main text). Many of their composition techniques took advantage of tape loops for repeating patterns, tape echo, and reverberation, all of which are evident in this part of their famous electronic score for the motion picture *Forbidden Planet*—the first feature film score produced entirely using electronic music.

	Listen For: The use of echo and repeated sound patterns (tape loops) to provide form and structure to the piece as well as electronic tones played manually to give the music an organic feeling.
0:00–0:30	A short loop with a repeated bass rhythm and bubbly sounds begins the piece. After a few seconds these serene pulses are joined by one, then two, and three manually played tone generators producing harmonizing, unbroken flute-like tones. At about 0:20, one of the tones begins to waver and another becomes louder as it descends in tone. Notice the pronounced use of reverb, especially for the bubbling sounds that continue during this passage. The sounds become darker and more intense.
0:30–1:10	The calm is suddenly broken by a loud, intense, deep vibrating tone with the qualities of a sawtooth wave. Note the heavy use of echo to extend the effect of the tone sequence. The section becomes thickly layered using loops, more echo, and siren-like tones that rise and fall threateningly.
1:11–2:05	Calm is restored momentarily as the density of the sound is reduced to two harmonizing tones, followed by the signature *Forbidden Planet* sound of descending sine waves treated with heavy vibrato (used in accompaniment to images of a slowly approaching spacecraft) and a loud, booming drone that dominates this section of the work. Six to eight tracks of independently recorded tones can be heard during this passage.
2:06–2:16	The *Overture* ends as it began, with a short loop with a repeated bass rhythm and bubbly sounds.

Compare and Contrast

Klangstudies II (1952) by Herbert Eimert and Robert Beyer
Sorcerer: Main Title (1977) by Tangerine Dream
Fantasy in Orbit (1963) by Tom Dissevelt

established his own rules for doing so based on chance operations derived from the *I Ching*—the ancient Chinese *Book of Changes* that provided a methodology for choosing random number sequences.

Cage developed various schemes for composing with chance operations. He sometimes decided on the instrumentation for a piece ahead of time—such as prepared piano, strings, or radio sounds—although some works were also written for any number and kind of unspecified instruments. He then used random numbers to denote choices for any decision that had to be made regarding the characteristics of the sound, such as pitch, amplitude, duration, timbre, and envelope. Individual performances might also vary because his works often had interchangeable parts. In 1952, after establishing the Project of Music for Magnetic Tape, Cage was eager to combine his interest in chance operations with a music that could consist of many kinds of recorded sounds. Cage's interest in composing with the recording medium dated back to *Imaginary Landscape No. 1* in 1939, conceived for a small percussion ensemble and turntables playing recordings of electronic test patterns: "*Imaginary Landscape No. 1* used records of constant or variable frequency. We had clutches on those machines that allowed us to produce slides. You didn't shift from 33⅓ to 45 rpm, for instance, but you could go gradually through the whole thing."[7] Working with the Barrons gave Cage immediate and unfettered access to the kinds of equipment to which few composers had access in America in 1952.

Cage and the Barrons completed their first tape project, with the help of David Tudor, in January 1952. The piece was called *Imaginary Landscape No. 5* and although it used magnetic tape as the composing medium all of the sounds were copied from phonograph records. The score called for "making a recording on tape, using as material any 42 phonographic records."[8] Composed using the *I Ching*, the score was written on block paper where each square represented three inches of tape. Chance operations denoted the duration and amplitude of the recorded blocks of sound but not which specific phonograph records should be used. Cage chose as his source material a collection of mostly jazz recordings and the result was a collage of fragments lasting four minutes.

Having become familiar with the tape medium through *Imaginary Landscape No. 5*, Cage chose as his next project a work that would more fully explore the potential of using tape splicing techniques to control dynamic aspects of recorded sound. The money they had been granted was not going to last forever, so Cage determined that it would be best spent focusing on one ambitious undertaking. He called it *Williams Mix*, after their benefactor Paul Williams. Tudor recalled that, after *Imaginary Landscape No. 5*, Cage realized that "experimentation takes a great deal of money, so he decided that in order to have a result, they should make a project which would enable one to experience things to the greatest depth possible."[9]

The novelty of *Williams Mix* was that Cage relied on tape splicing techniques as a major compositional element of the piece rather than merely as a device for hiding transitions from one recorded sound to another. Instead of using sounds from previously recorded phonograph records as source material, Cage commissioned the Barrons to make an extensive set of field recordings with their tape recording equipment. *Williams Mix* consisted of hundreds of taped sounds edited together using unusual splices to change the envelope of the sounds. The score was a daunting 192-page graphical composition (see Figure 3.3). Cage conceived the work for eight tracks of magnetic tape played simultaneously. "Each page has two systems comprising eight lines each," wrote the composer. "These eight lines are eight tracks of tape and they are pictured full-size so that the score constitutes a pattern for the cutting of tape and its splicing."[10] The work was begun in May 1952 and took the better part of nine months to complete. The completed work is only 4′ 15″ long.

The score required sound recordings made in six categories: city sounds, country sounds, electronic sounds, manually produced sounds (including musical instruments), wind-produced sounds, and small sounds requiring amplification to be heard. The Barrons were given the assignment of recording literally hundreds of sounds in the six categories required by the score. As Bebe Barron explained:

> It sounds like an easy assignment, but in those days, to record country sounds, small sounds, and so forth, it was a major assignment because we were in no way prepared to go out into the country. We did a couple of times and we took our most portable equipment with us, which was in no way portable.[11]

By Cage's account, the Barrons recorded between 500 and 600 sounds, although Bebe Barron's recollection is that it was somewhat fewer than that.[12] The resulting eight tapes were assembled over a nine-month period by a team consisting at times of Cage,

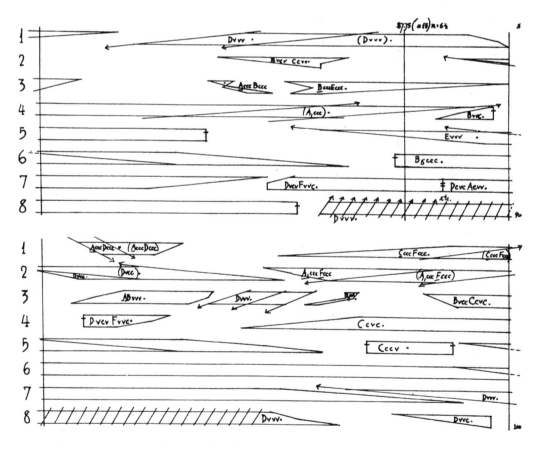

Figure 3.3 The score for *Williams Mix* by John Cage was actually a plan for making various kinds of tape splices. (Edition Peters)

Tudor, and the Barrons at their Greenwich Village studio, but also at various other places, including Cage's apartment. The splicing job was so laborious that any friend who happened to be in town or visiting was recruited to make a contribution. It required hundreds of *I Ching* operations to determine the various parameters that governed the assembly. The nature of each splice was determined by chance from a number of predetermined choices. However, one choice required the editor to freely make a splice in whatever pattern he or she wished, however irregular or unconventional.[13]

> We cut the tape into wild shapes. It was a tremendous editing job. We were obviously shaping the envelopes and we were putting tapes together so you could not discern where one piece of tape ended and the next one began, even though it may have been a totally different category.[14]

The piece received its first public performance in 1953 at the Festival of Contemporary Arts, University of Illinois. Cage was not unaware of the impact of his unconventional approach to splicing sounds on tape. In 1958, he wrote:

> The chief technical contribution of my work with tape is in the method of splicing, that is, of cutting the material in a way that affects the attack and decay of sounds recorded. By this method, I have attempted to mitigate the purely mechanical effect of electronic vibration in order to heighten the unique element of individual sounds, releasing their delicacy, strength, and special characteristics, and also to introduce at times complete transformation of the original materials to create new ones.[15]

One can imagine that a piece as radically experimental as *Williams Mix* was met with mixed reactions by other composers and the music-going public. One recorded performance of *Williams Mix* at Town Hall in New York in 1958 plainly reveals that the work was met with equal amounts of applause and verbal invective.

By 1954 the Project of Music for Magnetic Tape had run its course, largely because the participants became disenchanted with the restrictions of formal tape composition. Under the umbrella of the project, Cage and Tudor had produced *Williams Mix*, as well as *Imaginary Landscape No. 5*; Brown created *Octet I* (1953); Feldman composed *Intersection* (1953); and Wolff created *For Magnetic Tape* (1953).[16] After this, Brown, Feldman, and Wolff returned to experimental music using acoustic instruments, while Cage and Tudor continued to work with tape to some extent but also with the application of electronic music in live performance.

By 1954, the Barrons had established themselves as important providers of electronic music and sound effects for film. They collaborated with such celebrated avant-garde filmmakers as Maya Deren and Ian Hugo, who was married to the writer Anaïs Nin. The Barrons scored three of Hugo's films based on Nin's writings, including *Bells of Atlantis* (1952). For Deren, they assisted in the audio production of the soundtrack for *The Very Eye of Night* (1959) featuring the music of Teiji Ito. A few years later, when Madison Avenue became interested in using electronic music in commercial advertisements, the Barrons were one of the only options in town. They were competing with other private New York studios, particularly those of Raymond Scott (1908–94) and Eric Siday (1905–76).

LISTENING GUIDE 3.2

Title: *Williams Mix* (excerpt)

Artist: John Cage   **Year**: 1952   **Duration**: 3:00

Genre: Tape composition

Electronic Instrumentation: Tape composition using recordings of natural sounds as source material.

Background: *Williams Mix* consists of hundreds of taped sounds edited together using unusual tape splices to modify the attack and decay characteristics of the sounds. It was realized as eight tracks of tape edited to splicing instructions determined by chance and documented in a 192-page graphic technical score (see main text). Sounds were collected in six categories: city sounds, country sounds, electronic sounds, manually produced sounds (including musical instruments), wind-produced sounds, and amplified small sounds. The piece took several people nine months to edit. The eight tracks were mixed down to a two-track stereo mix.

	Listen For: Sounds from the six categories and the variety of envelope characteristics of the sounds as determined by the splicing methods.
0:00–3:00	Because the piece was realized using chance operations, it contains no discernible pattern or structure. Sounds occur without any special intent to build form, drama, or expression, representing only themselves—sounds for the sake of sounds. In the course of the piece one can detect the sound of frogs at various speeds (1:28), voices sped up (0:30; 2:43), a piano (0:33), blasts of white noise (2:53), electronic oscillations (0:41; 1:14), ambient sounds (1:09), musical sounds at various speeds (0:45; 1:21), and occasional moments of silence (2:00). The sound is broken up or chunked because of the many randomly applied tape splicing techniques to cut from one sound to another. In the most extreme cases, one sound cuts directly into another using a vertical cut (2:44) and these transitions are so rapid that it results in a stuttering effect. Other times, the cuts produce a more gradual fade into a sound or fade out from a sound (0:12; 1:53), effectively creating a sense of pace in the form of a passing sequence of momentary fluctuations in amplitude or intensity.

Compare and Contrast
For Magnetic Tape (1953) by Christian Wolff
Intersection (1953) by Morton Feldman
Super Digital (2000) by Tetsu Inoue

The most celebrated output of the Barrons' studio remains the soundtrack to the science fiction movie *Forbidden Planet* (1956). Many previous movies—including *Spellbound* and *The Day the Earth Stood Still*—had used electronic musical instruments such as the Theremin as part of their scores, but *Forbidden Planet* was the first score for a major motion picture consisting entirely of electronic music. The producers of the film had not originally intended to use so much electronic music and had considered hiring Harry Partch (1901–74) to do most of the score. As Bebe Barron explained:

> We were hired originally to do 20 minutes of scoring. After they heard the 20 minutes of sample scoring that we did they got very enthusiastic about it. We were then assigned about an hour and ten minutes of scoring. They gave us a work print of the film. We took it to New York and worked there.

This in itself was unheard of, because most film scores were made in Hollywood at the time. The studio had wanted to move the Barrons and their equipment to the West Coast, but the couple would not be uprooted.[17]

The Barrons developed a method of working that was the organic equivalent of the simple circuits that they were building. Mixdowns of multiple tracks were accomplished using multiple tape recorders. They would manually synchronize the starting points of the two tapes that were to be mixed, count "one-two-three-go," and then push the playback buttons simultaneously. The output of each machine was fed into a third tape recorder that would record the two tracks as a mix onto one tape. Precise synchronization was not vital for their style of atmospheric music: "That was close enough sync for us. If it was a little bit out of sync, it usually enhanced the music. We were loose in our requirements."[18]

The sounds themselves were generated from homemade circuits. As Bebe Barron recalled:

> With *Forbidden Planet*, we built a circuit for every character. Then we would vary these circuits accordingly. We would consider them as actors. They were like *leitmotifs*. Whenever one character was on screen and another would appear, you would get the motif of both characters working. Of course, the form of the music was dictated by the film.[19]

The sound circuits they built tended to burn out eventually, never to be revived. They never knew how long one might last, so they made a habit of recording everything and then piecing it together using their tape recorders. About the life of their circuits, Barron recalled, "No matter what we did, we could never reconstruct them. They just seemed to have a life span of their own . . . We never could predict the movement of them, the patterns of them. It really wasn't like composing music at all."[20]

The Barrons edited the entire score of *Forbidden Planet* themselves. The music and sound effects were so stunning that, during a preview of the movie, the audience broke out in spontaneous applause after the energizing sounds of the spaceship landing on the planet Altair IV. An interesting bit of trivia involves the screen credit for the Barrons. It was originally to read, "Electronic Music by Louis and Bebe Barron." At the last minute, a contract lawyer became fearful that the musicians' union would be in an uproar if they called the score "music." The credit was changed to the more neutral, "Electronic Tonalities by Louis and Bebe Barron."[21]

John Cage and the Advocacy of Chance

A first impression upon learning that John Cage composed music using chance operations is that the result must have been chaotic, noisy, and disorganized. Although some of Cage's music might certainly be described as lacking conventional musical structure and harmony—particularly when electronic sounds were incorporated into the mix—much of the composer's music for conventional instruments produces the opposite effect: restive, harmonic, and unpredictable. Cage described many of his compositions as being *indeterminate* of their performance. What the composer meant by this was that, while the composition process itself was dictated by chance operations, the performance itself was not; the score was created using a system for making chance decisions about notes, duration, amplitude, timbre, and other possible dynamics, but the outcome was determined once the score was being followed. Of course, many of Cage's works, particularly for live electronic performances, did indeed involve a degree of improvisation and on-the-fly decision-making by the performers, but even this aspect of his music was sometimes orchestrated through a carefully plotted sequence of decision points determined ahead of time by chance. Cage originally made his "chance" decisions by tossing yarrow sticks or coins, according to practices described in the *I Ching*. He later found a more productive way of deriving lists of random numbers through the use of computers. In the late 1960s, a friend of his at Bell Labs wrote a program that printed out a long list of randomly generated numbers. The printout was several inches thick and was produced using a large IBM computer that was programmed using keypunch cards. Cage used this list for several years. He kept the edge-worn printout on his work table, consulting it regularly, crossing off numbers as he used them, continuing page after page. He told me that, when the list began to run short, he asked his friend Paul Zukofsky, who had connections at Bell Labs, if he could replenish his supply of numbers by having the program run again. That was so many years later that the keypunch-card computer had since become obsolete and was no longer manufactured. After some scrambling at Bell Labs, one old but operational IBM mainframe of the correct vintage was found and a new printout was made for the composer. Cage had a million new numbers again. But the new printout came with the implicit warning that he had better find another source of random numbers for the next time around. He was able to do this with microcomputers by about 1984. He also found that the computers at IRCAM could assist him in this way as well. "I was delighted when I got to IRCAM," he told me, "to discover that I didn't need my printout because they have it in their computer there. You can have the I Ching whenever you want it!"[22]

CAGE IN MILAN

Following *Williams Mix*, Cage immediately returned to composing for instruments and further developing his use of chance operations. Except for an unfinished magnetic tape piece (1952), he did not work again directly with magnetic tape composition until 1958 and the creation of *Fontana Mix*. The occasion was a visit to Italy that brought him an invitation from Berio and Maderna to work in the *Studio di Fonologia Musicale* in Milan. The actual reason for his visit to Italy was to compete on a popular television quiz show, *Lascia o raddoppia (Double or Nothing)*, where Cage was quizzed on his extensive knowledge of mushrooms. During five appearances on the program he won the equivalent of $6,000 by correctly answering questions put before him. The award money represented a turning point in the composer's financial situation:

> After the work in Milan, where I won the "Lascia o Raddoppia" prize, that was the first time I had any money to speak of. Otherwise I was as poor as a church-mouse and I was nearly 50 years old. Through the money I made there, and then through the invitation from Richard Winslow to become a fellow in the Center for Advanced Studies at Wesleyan, everything began to change and it was at that moment that Peters decided to be the exclusive publisher of my music. So everything came together at that point. I used the fellowship at Wesleyan to prepare fair copies of much of the music that I didn't have good copies of.

Everything began to change. People, for instance, who didn't like my music could say they liked my writing [his book of essays, *Silence*, was published in 1961]—and vice versa.[23]

Fontana Mix, named after Cage's landlady in Milan, Signora Fontana, was completed at the Studio di Fonologia Musicale in November 1958. *Fontana Mix* was scored for any number of tracks of magnetic tape, for any number of players, or any kind and number of instruments. Its duration was unspecified and the composition was indeterminate of its performance, meaning that each realization of the work would be different. Cage had previously explored a number of novel scoring techniques for emphasizing the chance routines behind his composition methods. For example, notes for *Music for Piano 1* (1952) corresponded to imperfections in the paper upon which the piece was written. The *Concerto for Piano and Orchestra* (1957–58) had no overall score but explicit written instructions for orchestral parts in which notes were provided in three different sizes; the size could refer to the duration or amplitude of the note or both, a determination made by the performer. The score for *Winter Music* (1957) consisted of 20 unnumbered pages plus pages with performance instructions. The 20 pages were used in part or in whole by as many as 20 pianists and the individual performers were required to make decisions regarding the length of the program. *Fontana Mix* was his first magnetic tape piece to fully explore Cage's chance composition technique.

The score for *Fontana Mix* was itself an experiment (see Figure 3.5). It consisted of several transparent plastic sheets that were imprinted with geometric images. One sheet included a grid upon which the other transparencies were laid according to Cage's instructions. There were ten transparencies with points, ten with curves (six each), and a transparency with an even line. The parameters of the sound events were determined by laying these sheets on top of one another and interpreting the intersection of the graphic elements. For example, the height of a curve on the grid determined the amplitude of the sound. The duration of a sound would be determined by the point at which a curve first touched the grid and then left it. Spaces in between the intersection would mark silence. The relationship of sound and silence was thus spatially defined.

The source material for *Fontana Mix*, as first realized by Cage, contained a similarly eclectic blend of noise sounds, outdoor sounds, recorded music, and electronic effects made available at the Milan studio. Cage also included silence as a component of the mix and the whole was pieced together using chance operations to determine the sequence of the edit.

From his work in Milan, Cage created a version of *Fontana Mix* for two tapes that was also released on record. It was 11′ 39″ long. The work was stunningly experimental and reinforced the American composer's reputation as chief advocate of the most avant-garde reaches of contemporary music at the time.

Fontana Mix was effectively the last major composition by Cage for magnetic tape alone. The taped sounds of *Fontana Mix* were redeployed by the composer in several live performance works,

Figure 3.4 John Cage performing *Water Walk* on Italian television, 1959. (John Cage Trust)

Figure 3.5
Score of *Fontana Mix*.
(Edition Peters)

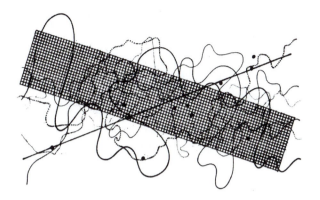

including *Water Walk* (1959), *Sounds of Venice* (1959), and *Theater Piece* (1960). Cage continue to explore the use of electronic media throughout his long career, particularly in collaboration with the Merce Cunningham Dance Company, for which he was a musical advisor for over 40 years. But rather than compose for recorded media alone, Cage extended the use of electronics to live performances, many of which were then recorded. Having the Merce Cunningham Dance Company to work with was probably responsible for maintaining Cage's interest in electronic music for he disliked the typical format of magnetic tape concerts at the time. Cage later remarked:

> I was at a concert of electronic music in Cologne [1952] and I noticed that, even though it was the most recent electronic music, the audience was all falling asleep. No matter how interesting the music was, the audience couldn't stay awake. That was because the music was coming out of loudspeakers.[24]

Cage's longtime musical collaborators in live electronic music included David Tudor, Gordon Mumma (b. 1935), David Behrman (b. 1937), and Takehisa Kosugi (b. 1938), all of whom figure importantly in the later history of live electronic music performance (Chapter 13).

A point is worth mentioning here about the apparent contradiction between "chance music" with indeterminate outcomes and the recording of such works. A magnetic tape composition, no matter how the material was conceived, remains forever fixed as a recorded performance in time. Cage was conflicted over this, because chance music should be just that: indeterminate of its performance. He once told the author:

> Everyone now knows that there's a contradiction between the use of chance operations and the making of a record. I mean not only myself, but I see no reason for living without contradictions. But I do think that one can live without recordings. And I do that. I don't play them, except when I use them in a live performance . . . I still believe that's true; that if you want music to come alive, that you must not *can* it.[25]

Having been Cage's discographer, the author can attest to the fact that the composer did not even own a record player.

LISTEN

EARLY ELECTRONIC MUSIC IN THE UNITED STATES

1   *Heavenly Menagerie* (1950) by Louis and Bebe Barron
Early tape composition (New York)

2   *Williams Mix* (1952) by John Cage
Produced at the Barrons' studio (New York)

3   *Fantasy in Space* (1952) by Otto Luening
Produced at the Columbia Tape Music Center (New York)

4   *Sonic Contours* (1952) by Vladimir Ussachevsky
Produced at the Columbia Tape Music Center (New York)

5   *Intersection* (1953) by Morton Feldman
Produced at the Barrons' studio (New York)

6   *A Poem in Cycles and Bells* (1954) by Luening and Ussachevsky
One of the first works for tape and live orchestra (New York)

7   *Forbidden Planet* (1956) by Louis and Bebe Barron
Soundtrack for the motion picture of the same name (New York)

8   *Linear Contrasts* (1958) by Ussachevsky
Early tape work using the RCA Music Synthesizer (New York)

9   *Stereo Electronic Music No. 1* (1960) by Bülent Arel
An RCA synthesizer piece by Turkish composer Arel (New York)

10   *Music from the Venezia Space Theater* (1964) by Gordon Mumma
Representative of the electronic music produced by Gordon Mumma and
Robert Ashley for Milton Cohen's Space Theater (Ann Arbor)

THE COLUMBIA–PRINCETON ELECTRONIC MUSIC CENTER

Another important thread in the storyline of early tape music in the United States took place in academic circles. In 1951, around the same time that Cage was getting acquainted with the Barrons, composers Otto Luening (1900–96) and Vladimir Ussachevsky (1911–90) were both music instructors at Columbia University in New York City. The music department had acquired some tape equipment for the recording of music performances, including a dual-speed Ampex 400 tape recorder that could run at 7.5 and 15 inches per second, a Magnecord tape recorder borrowed from a radio store, and a Western Electric 369 microphone. A young engineer at the school named Peter Mauzey (b. 1930), who provided the composers with technical help, also built a circuit for creating reverberation.

Luening and Ussachevsky began a long-standing partnership as collaborators and caretakers of what was initially called the Columbia Tape Music Center (in 1958 it became the *Columbia–Princeton Electronic Music Center*). There was no permanent studio at first; the two men moved the portable equipment from one location to another in the trunk of Ussachevsky's car. There had been enough interest in their experiments to generate several commissions during 1952 and 1953 and, during August of 1952, the composers set up shop in the corner of a renovated carriage barn at Bennington College in Vermont. That fall, they moved for two weeks into composer Henry Cowell's cottage in Shady, New York, and completed several short works for a Leopold Stokowski concert to be held at the Museum of Modern Art (MoMA) in Manhattan. From there the portable studio landed for a short time in the Ussachevsky living room in New York and then the sound studio in the basement of conductor Arturo Toscanini's posh Riverdale home. Luening mixed his piece *Invention in Twelve Tones* (1952) using the far superior collection of tape recorders at the Union Theological Seminary in New York.[26] Finally, after many months of nomadic existence, the Tape Center landed in a room at the Columbia music department.

Luening's and Ussachevsky's earliest experiments, like those of the Paris studio, did not make use of any electronically produced sounds. They had no oscillators or other signal-generating equipment. Instead, the two composers turned to the manipulation of recorded instrumental sounds. This was an important decision for them to make. Explained Luening:

> We had a choice of working with natural and "non-musical" sounds like subway noise and sneezes and coughs, or widening the sound spectrum of existing instruments and bringing out new resonances from the existing world of instruments and voices. We chose the latter.[27]

Luening and Ussachevsky composed their first pieces using only tape manipulations (speed changes, reverse sounds, splicing) and reverb using Mauzey's black box. Luening first worked with flute sounds and Ussachevsky the sounds of the piano.

The first public recital of their tape music took place at a Composers Forum recital organized by Ussachevsky on May 9, 1952.[28] Among the works premiered was Ussachevsky's *Sonic Contours*, featuring the electronically modified sounds of the piano. This raised some eyebrows and the word began to spread about tape music being created at Columbia University.

Figure 3.6
Otto Luening and
Vladimir Ussachevsky in
the Columbia–Princeton
Electronic Music Center,
c. 1960. (Columbia University
Computer Music Center)

When invited to present some electronic music at the MoMA in the fall of 1952, Luening and Ussachevsky set to work on completing several foundational works of tape music. The concert took place on October 28, 1952 and featured *Sonic Contours* by Ussachevsky as well as several new works by Luening, including *Fantasy in Space* (1952), *Low Speed* (1952), and *Invention in Twelve Tones* (1952). Both composers experimented with altering the nature of the sounds through tape speed changes. Luening also employed some 12-tone composition techniques in his work and used multiple tracking to superimpose separate tracks of flute sounds to create the effect of slightly wavering frequencies. *Low Speed* used these techniques to synthesize overtones from flute sounds in much the same manner as could also be done using sine wave oscillators. Together, these works demonstrated the potential of using the familiar sounds of classical musical instruments to generate new, unfamiliar tonalities.

The public and professional reaction to the concert was a mixture of politely nodding heads and astonishment. This soon led to enthusiasm as reports from the press emerged. A reporter from the *New York Herald Tribune* wrote, "It has been a long time in coming, but music and the machine are now wed. . . . The result is as nothing encountered before. . . . It is something entirely new."[29]

The MoMA concert catapulted Luening and Ussachevsky into the public eye. They were featured on television, including a live appearance on NBC's *Today* show. The two men became America's spokesmen for electronic music. After three more years of composing, lecturing, demonstrating, and performing their work, they received a grant from the Rockefeller Foundation to study the field of electronic music in Europe and America and to respond with a plan for establishing an electronic music center in the United States.

In their travels in Europe, Luening and Ussachevsky visited the GRM studio in Paris, WDR in Cologne, and several others. They had never seen so much audio equipment before and sought technical advice from anyone who would give it. They endured Schaeffer's intellectual browbeating about a new aesthetic, which Luening later called the "aesthetic of an engineer."[30] Eimert proselytized about the purity of German electronic music, and Stockhausen decided against letting them look over his shoulder while he worked, because, he said, any fool could make electronic music; it was just a matter of knowing the electrical permutations and algorithms.[31]

Luening and Ussachevsky were intellectually and physically exhausted after their trip. Not only was post-war Europe a completely changed place from the Europe that the two of them had previously known, but now the rise of electronic technology was beckoning in a radical new stage in the history of music. On the flight home, their minds darted back to the sophisticated tape machines, audio generators, filters, and other gear that they had seen in European studios. They were already making a wish list when they arrived back in the States.

Upon their return, they were pleasantly surprised to hear about a new electronic music "synthesizer" that had been developed at the Radio Corporation of America's (RCA) David Sarnoff Laboratories in Princeton, New Jersey. This most propitious announcement could not have been better timed for them. The two composers immediately arranged for a demonstration and saw an opportunity to establish a modern, fully equipped electronic music studio at Columbia University with this synthesizer at its core.

The RCA device was called the Olson–Belar Sound Synthesizer and later simply the *RCA Electronic Music Synthesizer*. It was named after its inventors, Harry F. Olson (1901–82) and Herbert F. Belar, senior engineers at RCA. Introduced to the public in 1955, the device was the first sound synthesizer in the modern sense. It was comprised of integrated components that could generate, modify, process, record, and present complex sonorities intended for musical applications. Built with the knowledge of rudimentary computer controls, it was one of the first examples of a computer-operated instrument, although totally analog in its sound-generating capability. See Chapter 6 for a detailed description of the specifications and capabilities of the instrument.

The RCA Electronic Music Synthesizer was formally unveiled to the public on January 31, 1955 by Brigadier General David Sarnoff himself, chairman of the board of RCA, who in his opening statement shared a view once expressed by Busoni. "[It] must occur to you," said Sarnoff, "that the day is here when the engineer and the artist should join forces and seek to understand the terminology and problems of each other in order to advance together."[32]

Early hopes for the RCA Electronic Music Synthesizer focused on its ability to imitate and play the sounds of existing musical instruments—without needing musicians:

> If a composer has in mind what he wants to achieve, the effects can be obtained by means of the electronic music synthesizer, regardless of whether he can play a musical instrument or not. The composer or musician can produce the sound of any existing musical instrument as well as other sounds, regardless of whether they have ever existed.[33]

The reaction of musicians and music unions to such an idea has been a recurring issue in the history of electronic music. Years later, in 1967, Olson qualified his statement about replacing musicians because it had become increasingly unfashionable to suggest such a thing. "Electronic music does not displace or supplant anything or anyone," explained Olson. "The idea is to supplement conventional music."[34]

Another application of the synthesizer suggested by Olson was the automated composition of popular music for radio and television commercials. For this pedestrian application, Olson developed the "electronic music composing machine," a component that could be programmed to compose music in any style that could be defined in binary code: "The electronic music composing machine, which has been developed as an aid to music composition, depends upon a random selection of notes weighed by a probability based upon preceding events."[35] Olson was drawing upon mathematical relationships that exist between notes and rhythms in a music composition and the probability that only certain notes are likely to follow certain other notes. Olson's composing machine used random probability calculations to pick notes and create a chord sequence. There was clearly a hope at RCA that, by coupling the RCA Electronic Music Synthesizer with the Electronic Music Composing Machine, the equipment could be commanded at the push of a button to churn out song after song like a sonic sausage factory. Apparently none of those hopes was realized, but the instrument soon became the focus of Luening and Ussachevsky's quest to equip an electronic music studio.

Luening and Ussachevsky immediately saw the musical value of the RCA Electronic Music Synthesizer as an instrument capable of generating new and unlikely sounds and patterns. Its control features, which included a paper tape drive for storing and playing a sequence of tones, surpassed any such capability they had seen in Europe. Having 12 separate audio frequency sources, the RCA Electronic Music Synthesizer provided a full complement of tone generators equal to or greater than most they had observed in their travels. Having only previously worked with a hodgepodge assembly of tape recorders and special effects boxes, Luening and Ussachevsky suddenly found themselves on the threshold of establishing perhaps the most advanced electronic music studio in the world. This one device took care of their entire wish-list of components that they had developed on their travels.

Discovering that composer Milton Babbitt (1916–2011), then at Princeton University, was also interested in experimenting with the synthesizer, Luening and Ussachevsky joined forces with him to lobby for some time on the machine. For the next three years the trio made regular trips to the Sarnoff labs to develop new musical material.

In 1957, Luening and Ussachevsky completed a 155-page report on their findings in the electronic music field to fulfill their initial Rockefeller Foundation grant. In it they recommended the establishment of the Columbia–Princeton Electronic Music Center, which would become the first institutionally sponsored studio in the United States. The result was an additional grant from the foundation for $175,000 to be paid to both Columbia and Princeton universities over a five-year period. In cooperation, RCA first rented their synthesizer to them, and in 1959 gave an improved version (then called the RCA Mark II) to the center on permanent loan. The operational committee of the center included Luening and Ussachevsky from Columbia and Milton Babbitt and Roger Sessions (1896–1985) from Princeton, with Ussachevsky as chairman. The center was established in New York City and consisted of three studios: one for the RCA Mark II and related recording equipment and two other studios equipped in a more traditional manner with audio oscillators, mixers, reverberation, and other familiar tape composition tools.

Luening and Ussachevsky became well known for their experiments with tape composition. Together with Babbitt and Sessions, they were the guiding lights behind the Columbia–Princeton Electronic Music Center and continued their work using equipment such as the RCA Mark I and II synthesizers. Sticking close to the classical tradition, these men often explored modern elements of music using electronics in combination with traditional instruments. Some of their most important achievements prior to availability of the RCA synthesizer centered on the synchronization of live performers with electronic music played on tape. In 1954, Luening and Ussachevsky composed *A Poem in Cycles and Bells* (1954) for tape recorder and orchestra, which was, along with Varèse's *Déserts* of the same year, among the first works to synchronize the live performance of a symphony orchestra with tape music. This approach became the standard operating procedure for combining the live performance of an ensemble of musicians with electronic music until the availability of portable synthesizers in the late 1960s.

The availability of the RCA synthesizer at Columbia by the late 1950s attracted many composers who wanted to experiment with electronic music. The machine was particularly well suited for highly organized and structured works due to the laborious but meticulous method of entering commands using a paper tape reader. While the catalog of works composed using the synthesizer would grow impressively during the 1960s, some early experiments were completed with the Mark II during 1958 and 1959,

LISTENING GUIDE 3.3

Title: *Linear Contrasts*

Artist: Vladimir Ussachevsky   **Year**: 1958   **Duration**: 3:46

Genre: Tape composition

Electronic Instrumentation: Tape recorders, audio oscillators, filters, reverberation, piano, and harpsichord.

Background: As one of the founders and early directors of the Columbia–Princeton Electronic Music Studio, Ussachevsky was one of the first American maestros of tape music. This piece, composed before the availability of the RCA Music Synthesizer at the studio, is a mature piece of tape music incorporating all of the tricks in the book, from modified natural sounds to modulated white noise, echo, and the spatial movement of the sound between the two tracks.

	Listen For: The blend of concrete and electronic sounds, examples of modification through tape composition techniques, and the spatial distribution of sounds. The piece is composed of parts comprising different sound textures and rhythms.
0:00–1:15	The piece opens with a sound reminiscent of ocean waves and wind, which drifts from right to left and back again. This was produced using filtered white noise and hand-mixed to create the spatial drifting effect. The ocean/wind sounds continue throughout the piece at varying levels of intensity. At 0:14, the first sound of a slow rhythmic pulse is heard. The throbbing beat was produced using a piano and a harpsichord, recorded separately, and then mixed by hand to adjust the levels of each instrument at any given beat.
1:16–3:00	This section begins with several short phrases and beats of the keyboard instruments, one after another, each diminishing gradually over the course of five or six repetitions, suggesting the use of a tape loop or a tape delay in which the same signal is repeatedly re-recorded, producing successively diminishing amplitudes. During this sequence, some of the loops play at the same time until a heavily layered cacophony results at about 2:55. Note the wobbling sound of some of the instrumental beats; this could have been created manually by the composer by manipulating the variable playback speed of the loops or the wobbling might simply be an artifact of misaligned tape loops traveling unevenly over the heads of the tape recorder.
3:01–3:46	The rhythm drops out and the piece concludes with a passage of quiet, extended tones, filtered and treated with reverberation, producing a hollow, metallic sound.

Compare and Contrast

Prélude (1958) by François-Bernard Mâche

Violostries I (1962) by Bernard Parmegiani

Sculptor (2001) by Curtis Roads

including *Mathematics* (1957) by Luening and Ussachevsky and *Linear Contrasts* (1958) by Ussachevsky.

THE COOPERATIVE STUDIO FOR ELECTRONIC MUSIC

Gordon Mumma (b. 1935) and Robert Ashley (b. 1930), working independently of John Cage and the Columbia group of tape composers, founded their own tape music studio in Ann Arbor, Michigan, and by 1958 were producing weekly performances of live electronic music using homemade instruments.

In 1947, when he was just 12 years old, Gordon Mumma took apart one of his father's record players and rebuilt it "so that it played records both forwards and backwards, and by attaching a rubber band around one of the gears I could vary the speed of playback."[36] In 1949, he learned about the latest audio recording technology of the time from a neighbor who had in his basement a large studio for making 78 rpm records. While studying at the University of Michigan in Ann Arbor in 1953, he was asked to compose music for the theater department. They had some of the first tape recorders Mumma had seen, and he proceeded to take them apart to see how they worked. Around 1955, after he had dropped out of college, Mumma had learned enough about electronics to begin designing his own circuits for making electronic music. "Motivated further by broadcasts of *musique concrète* from France and the early recordings of Les Paul and Mary Ford,"[37] making circuits and exploring electronic music became a "non-stop activity."[38] These were his first steps toward a long and distinguished career as a composer, performer, and circuit designer in the field of electronic music.

Robert Ashley was born in Ann Arbor, Michigan, and was educated at the University of Michigan and the Manhattan School of Music. As a graduate music student in Ann Arbor, he also took some courses and worked for three years at the university's Speech Research Laboratory, where he could get access to the latest acoustic technology: "The materials of that science were the same materials that interested me in music. It was the same technology that you would find inside an electronic music studio." Although Ashley was not formally enrolled in the acoustic-research program, the head of the department offered him a doctorate if Ashley would stay on. He declined because he was most interested in music.[39]

Figure 3.7 Gordon Mumma and Robert Ashley, in Ashley's home in Ann Arbor, where his half of the Cooperative Studio for Electronic Music was located, 1960.
(Gordon Mumma)

Mumma and Ashley knew each other from their student years, both having been a part of Ross Lee Finney's graduate composition seminars. But it was through a sculptor named Milton Cohen that the two began working together. In 1957, Cohen had constructed his "Space Theater"—a loft designed for performances of projected images and music in Ann Arbor. He asked Ashley and Mumma to produce electronic music for the events.

This collaboration between Ashley and Mumma led to the creation of the *Cooperative*

Studio for Electronic Music in 1958. The "studio" consisted of rooms set aside for electronic music equipment in each of their two homes. Ashley's room was about as big as a small bathroom. Each composer had his own equipment but shared resources as needed. They had about a half-dozen tape recorders between them, as well as oscillators, filters, mixers, and other audio processing circuits, many that they devised and built themselves. Mumma and Ashley were serious tinkerers in electronics.

The Space Theater was a loft converted by architect Harold Borkin (b. 1934) so that it could serve as a multimedia performance space. Borkin created a domelike effect in the loft by covering the corners of the ceiling with white reflective panels. People sat on the floor or lay down on pillows to experience the performances. Ashley explained:

Figure 3.8   View from inside Milton Cohen's Space Theater in Ann Arbor, *c.* 1960. The Space Theater was the site of weekly live electronic music and light performances by Mumma, Ashley, and others. (Gordon Mumma)

> It basically consisted of a huge pile of various kinds of projection equipment and mirrors that rotated to put light projections all around the room. Milton wanted to have live electronic music with those performances. He asked Gordon and me to work with him. We transformed his loft, the Space Theater, into a light projection and electronic music theater.[40]

The group produced live multimedia performances twice a week for seven years, from 1957 to 1964, always to capacity audiences of about 40 people. Because it was before the time of commercial electronic musical instruments and synthesizers, the music was created using instruments and equipment designed and built by Ashley and Mumma.

The following "script" was typical of the "simple, but dramatic" performance pieces presented at the Space Theater, this one being conceived by Ashley:

- Milton and his wife entered in white formal dress, as if at a wedding.
- There was an extended rubbing together of stones.
- A man was dragged on his back (by a rope) through the performance space.
- There were four steel wires drawn from the four lower corners of the space, meeting at its apex, with steel rings to be "thrown" on the wires toward the apex. All of this was treated with "enormous amplification of the wires—a kind of thunder and lightning effect."[41]

Mumma's effect of the amplified wires was later used in one section of his electronic theater composition *Megaton for William Burroughs*, and his film score *Truro Synodicle* of 1962.

In the world of the Space Theater, every theatrical piece was also conceived with an electronic music component. Every performance was live. Mumma and Ashley would make use of tapes they had composed in their home studios, but these were always

Table 3.1 **Key North American electronic music studios, 1948–67***

Studio location	Affiliation	Year established	Sample of works completed
New York: Louis and Bebe Barron Studio	Private (Louis and Bebe Barron)	1948	*Heavenly Menagerie* (Barron, 1951); *Imaginary Landscape No. 5* (Cage, 1951–52); *Williams Mix* (Cage, 1952); *The Bells of Atlantis* (Barron, 1952); *For Magnetic Tape* (Wolff, 1952–53); *Forbidden Planet* (Barron, 1956); *Visit to a Small Planet* (Barron, 1957).
New York: The Columbia–Princeton Electronic Music Center	Columbia and Princeton Universities	Tape Center, 1951; Electronic Music Center, 1958	*Transposition, Reverberation, Experiment, Composition* (Ussachevsky, 1951–52); *Sonic Contours* (Ussachevsky, 1952); *Invention in 12 Notes* (Luening, 1952); *Fantasy in Space* (Luening, 1952); *Incantation* (Luening and Ussachevsky, 1953); *Metamorphoses* (Ussachevsky, 1957); *Waka* (Toyama, 1959); *Consort for Voice and Instruments* (Wuorinen, 1960); *Electronic Music No. 1* (Arel, 1960); *Electronic Fanfare* (El-Dabh and Luening, 1960); *Electronic Study No. 1* (Davidovsky, 1960); *Composition for Synthesizer* (Babbitt, 1960–61); *Study in Synthesized Sounds* (Luening, 1961); *Electronic Setting* (Powell, 1961); *Déserts* (Varèse, 1960–61); *Electronic Study No. 2* (Davidovsky, 1962); *Electronic Study No. 2* (Whittenberg, 1962); *Laborintus II* (Berio, 1962); *Synthesis, for Orchestra and Tape* (Luening, 1962); *Triad* (Sender, 1962); *Ensembles for Synthesizer* (Babbitt, 1961–63); *Dialogues for Piano and Two Loudspeakers* (Carlos, 1963); *Synchronisms No. 1* (Davidovsky, 1963); *Composition for Four Loudspeakers* (Carlos, 1963); *Intersections, for Tape Recorder and Orchestra* (Maginnis, 1963); *Rhapsody* (Mimaroglu, 1963); *No Exit* (Ussachevsky, 1963); *Philomel* (Babbitt, 1963–64); *Vocalise* (Avni, 1964); *Variations, for Flute and Electronic Sounds* (Carlos, 1964); *Nocturne, for Strings and Tape* (Mimaraglu, 1964); *Study No. 3* (Appleton, 1965); *Infantasy* (Appleton, 1965); *Orchestral and Electronic Exchanges* (Wuorinen, 1965); *Animus I, for Trombone and Tape* (Drickman, 1966); *Composition for Two Speakers* (Howe, 1965–66); *The C (S) for ONCE, for Eleven Players and Three Tape Recorders* (Oliveros, 1966); *Reciprocals, for Converted Digital Tape and Two Percussionists* (Dodge, 1967); *Animus II* (Druckman, 1967).
Ontario, Canada: Elmus Lab	National Research Council	1955	*Dripsody* (Le Caine, 1955); *Invocation* (Le Caine, 1956); *Electronic Composition No. 1* (Anhalt, 1959).
Murray Hill, New Jersey: Bell Telephone Laboratories	Bell Telephone	1957	*In the Silver Scale* (Guttman, 1957); *Pitch Variations* (Guttman, 1957); *Stochatta* (Pierce, 1959); *May Carl I* (Mathews, 1959); *Five Stochastic Studies* (Tenney, 1962); *Composition No. 3— Music for the IBM 7090* (Strang, 1963); *Composition* (Risset, 1965); *Swansong* (Mathews, 1966).

Table 3.1   (continued)*

Studio location	Affiliation	Year established	Sample of works completed
Ann Arbor, Michigan: The Cooperative Studio for Electronic Music	Private (Gordon Mumma; Robert Ashley)	1958	*The Bald Soprano* (Mumma, 1958); *The Image in Time* (Ashley, 1958); *Mirrors for Milton Cohen* (Mumma, 1960–61); *Big Danger in Five Parts* (Ashley, 1961); *Music for Everybody* (Krumm, 1962); *The Wolfman* (Ashley, 1964); *The Dresden Interleaf* (Mumma, 1965); *Horn* (Mumma, 1965).
Ontario, Canada: University of Toronto Electronic Music Studio	University of Toronto	1959	*Étude No. 1* (Schaeffer,1959); *Composition for Flute and Tape Recorder* (Aitken, 1963); *Sequence Arrangement No. 1* (Hassell, 1964); *Three Études for Hugh Le Caine* (Cross, 1965); *Pictures from the Old Testament* (Pederson, 1965); *Alchemy* (Charpentier, 1966); *I of IV* (Oliveros, 1966).
Urbana, Illinois: University of Illinois Experimental Music Studio	University of Illinois	1959	*Three Electronic Studies* (Hoffman and Shallenberg, 1959); *Collage No. 1* (Tenney, 1961); *Amplification* (Hiller, 1962); *Seven Electronic Studies* (Hiller, 1962–63); *Computer Cantata* (Baker and Hiller, 1963); *Antiphone* (Gaburo, 1963); *Futility* (Brün, 1964); *Machine Music* (Hiller, 1964); *27' 10.554" for a Percussionist* (Cage, realized by Neuhaus, 1965); *Tape Piece Using Trombone Sounds* (Lewis and Powell, 1965); *Adjacencies* (Amacher, 1965); *Algorithms I and II* (Hiller, 1966).
San Francisco, California: The San Francisco Tape Music Center	Private through 1966; later affiliated with Mills College	1961	*Soundblocks* (Subotnick, 1959); *Kronos* (Sender, 1960); *Mescalin Mix* (Riley, 1961); *Time Perspectives* (Oliveros, 1961); *M-Mix* (Riley, 1961); *In C* (Riley, 1961); *Interstices* (Sender, 1963); *Seven Passages for Dancer* (Oliveros, 1963); *Three Electronic Dances* (Martirano, 1963); *Play! No. 2, for Orchestra and Tape* (Subotnick, 1964); *Light Piece for David Tudor, for Electronically Modified Piano, Light, Film, and Tape* (Oliveros, 1965); *In the Garden, for Projection and Tape* (Sender, 1965); *Antiphonies I* (Shapiro, 1965); *Mnemonics II, III, V, VII* (Oliveros, 1965); *Flight* (Maginnis, 1965); *Catharsis* (Austin, 1965); *Banger* (Jepson, 1966); *Beautiful Soop* (Oliveros, 1967).
Waltham, Massachusetts: Brandeis University Electronic Music Studio	Brandeis University	1961	*Perspectives* (Shirley, 1962*); Étude No. 1* (Hughes, 1962); *UCLA* (Subotnick, 1964); *Piece One* (Adamis, 1964); *Milwaukee Combination* (Behrman, 1964); *Mix No. 2* (Gnazzo, 1964); *Rozart Mix for Magnetic Tape* (Cage, 1965); *Elegy for Albert Anastasia* (Lucier, 1965); *Quintona* (Krenek, 1965); *Music for Solo Performer* (Lucier, 1965); *Tonegroups I* (Epstein, 1965); *Medeighnia's* (Lentz, 1965); *From My First Book of Dreams*—live electronic music (Lucier, 1965); *Whistlers* (Lucier, 1966–67).
Trumansburg, New York: Electronic Music Studio	Independent Electronic Music Center (Robert Moog)	1964	*Jazz Images* (Deutsch, 1964); *Concrete Piece* (Morris, 1965); *Fantasy of Echoes* (Robb, 1965); *Approach* (Perry 1965); *Filmusic* (Weidenaar, 1966); *Reconnaissance* (Erb, 1967).

Note: *Studios listed include key private and institutional facilities that were used by more than one composer. Excludes private studios used by only one individual.

combined with live electronics. Most of the performances were about an hour and a half in duration, much longer than most tape compositions at the time.

Mumma and Ashley, along with Cage, represented a kind of outreach in the 1950s' world of electronic music. This choice was made largely out of necessity. Without the kind of institutional support provided to their European counterparts or even their counterparts at the Columbia–Princeton studio, Mumma and Ashley, and Cage working with David Tudor transformed electronic music into a live performance medium. What began as an experiment soon established these performers as the forerunners of a widely respected school of live performance artists, the impact of which is explored in Chapter 13.

The swansong for the Space Theater came in 1964. Italian composer Luigi Nono invited Milton Cohen and the Space Theater troupe to perform during the music portion of the annual Venice Biennale performing arts festival. Ashley designed four pieces in the four-part manner of the Space Theater performances, and a number of Ann Arbor people came along to help out. Their performance space was a loft above the old Teatro La Fenice opera house. The group performed daily for five days. The event was a great success, except that they had trouble getting paid. The growing differences between the American and European avant-garde were punctuated one day by a conversation over lunch, which Ashley recalled:

> We were taken to lunch by Nono in a beautiful restaurant on the Grand Canal (where Nono was addressed by the restaurant workers as "Maestro"). It was the best lunch anyone had ever had. After the lunch, over coffee, Nono said to me, "May I ask you an important question?" Of course. "Is John Cage serious?" I said I thought so.[42]

Before the Ann Arbor group departed Venice for home, Cohen quietly announced to his friends that he was done with the Space Theater and was going to return to sculpture. "Who could blame him?" said Ashley. At the time of this writing, the only commercially available recording of music composed for the Space Theater is one of Gordon Mumma's compositions—an excerpt from the Venice production called *Music from the Venezia Space Theater* (1964).

The Cooperative Studio for Electronic Music came to an end in 1967 when both Mumma and Ashley moved on from Ann Arbor to continue their musical work elsewhere. In the nine years that they maintained their home studios, they completed more than 75 tape compositions. Mumma joined Cage and Tudor from 1966 to 1974 to produce music for the Merce Cunningham Dance Company. Ashley established an electronic music studio at Mills College and continued to compose in electronic music and mixed media. The works of each of these composers are discussed in Chapter 12. Table 3.1 lists the major North American studios in operation from 1948 to 1967, together with some of the works completed there.

ROOTS OF COMPUTER MUSIC

Computer music is the subject of Part III of this book, although some important origins are worth noting here as part of the overall picture of electronic music in 1950s' America.

In 1955, the term "computer music" had a different connotation from today. Rather than describing music whose sounds were electronically generated, computer music in 1955 referred to the use of a computer to compose music. Among several early experiments in this field was the work conducted by composer Lejaren Hiller (1924–94) at the University of Illinois and his collaborator, Leonard Isaacson, a mathematician with the Standard Oil Company.

Hiller and Isaacson viewed music as a form of information that could be managed by a computer. Working at the University of Illinois, they gained access to *ILLIAC I* (Illinois Automatic Computer)—an early mainframe computer built in 1952, and the first such device owned entirely by an educational institution. This massive machine had 2,800 vacuum tubes and weighed five tons. The ILLIAC was programmed by using codes punched onto Teletype paper tape. Other early computers used input from punched cards and magnetic tape.

Hiller and Isaacson set out to determine just how to compose music using a computer. Being the first to explore the compositional capabilities of computers to produce a fully formed musical score, the team faced many obstacles requiring original research. "Technical decisions of many types," wrote Hiller, "would necessarily outweigh in importance subtler aesthetic considerations."[43] Accordingly, they divided their work into several stages of development:

1   Select a simple, polyphonic style of music composition suitable for computer programming. A form of strict counterpoint was chosen as a suitable match for the project.
2   Determine how to code such musical information and demonstrate that "standard musical techniques could be handled by computer programming," the result being conventional musical output that any musician could read.
3   Demonstrate that a computer could also produce "novel musical structures" and code elements such as dynamics and rhythm.
4   Show that computers might be useful to composers of contemporary music intent on developing new "species" of music with unconventional musical elements.[44]

The result of their efforts was the score for the *Illiac Suite for String Quartet* (1957), the first fully developed piece of music composed with the aid of a computer. The four movements of the work chronicled the four experimental stages of development undertaken by the composers. In the first movement, the music began with a single line of notes and moved progressively through the addition of two and four parts. The second movement more fully explored conventional rules of counterpoint. In the third movement, the piece adopted some twentieth-century composition techniques, applying new harmonies, varying rhythmic structures, and passages engaged in serialism. The final movement was more purely mathematical in origin, forming the basic of a "stochastic" musical approach in which the computer helped select notes based on probability factors and weighted frequency distributions.[45]

Hiller continued to work in computer composition at the University of Illinois, switching to an IBM 7094 computer in 1962 and working with a music program called *MUSICOMP*, a more widely used music composition program. He also tutored other composers in the use of computers for making music, including James Tenney, a prominent researcher and composer at Bell Labs during the 1960s.

Experiments with computer composition techniques were occurring elsewhere during the late 1950s, among them being the work of Iannis Xenakis in Paris. Beginning in 1956, Xenakis experimented with writing computer programs that also used probability factors to aid in the composition of music. Unlike Hiller and Isaacson, Xenakis's early experiments did not result in the computer itself composing music. Instead, he used the machine to calculate values for the complex parameters of scores for various sizes of instrumental groups. Works he composed using this approach included *Atrées (Law of Necessity)* (1960) for 11 musicians, *ST/10* (1962) for 10 musicians (1962), *ST/48* (1962) for 48 musicians, and *Morsima-Amorsima* (1962) for piano, violin, and contrabass.

Early work in the computer generation of sound also had its roots in the United States by the late 1950s. In 1956, two computer engineers at the Burroughs Corporation, Martin L. Klein and Douglas Bolitho, programmed a *Datatron* computer to automatically compose popular songs. Affectionately nicknamed "Push-Button Bertha," the unit reportedly composed some 4,000 pop songs after being fed the characteristics of 100 that were then popular. More significantly, in 1957 a researcher at Bell Labs named Max Mathews (1926–2011) successfully demonstrated the computer generation of sound for the first time using a **digital-to-analog converter (DAC)**. For Mathews, this was the beginning of a long association with computer music (see Chapter 9, pp. 273–5).

By the end of the 1950s, the United States had become an influential force in the development of electronic music. Even with little institutional support, composers such as Cage, Louis and Bebe Barron, Luening, and Ussachevsky engaged themselves in earnest experiments with tape music as soon as tape recorders were available to them. Mumma and Ashley developed their own electronic music equipment and experimented regularly with live performance, as did Cage and Tudor. With the establishment of the Columbia–Princeton Electronic Music Center in 1958, the world took notice and composers from several countries began to visit the United States to work with the RCA Electronic Music Synthesizer.

As the 1950s came to a close, the scale and diversity of electronic music works being created on American soil was impressive. In 1960, Luening and Ussachevsky produced the massive *Concerted Piece* for tape recorder and symphony orchestra, the composition and premiere performance being commissioned by Leonard Bernstein and the New York Philharmonic Orchestra. The performance was televised for a youth concert and followed by four appearances at Carnegie Hall and a CBS television broadcast. In 1961, the international repertoire represented by the Columbia–Princeton Electronic Music Center was evident in the program for its first two public performances in 1961, wherein works were presented by composers including Halim El-Dabh (Egypt), Bülent Arel (Turkey), and Mario Davidovsky (Argentina), as well as Luening, Ussachevsky, Babbitt, and Wuorinen from the United States. Even Edgard Varèse, at age 77, worked at the Columbia–Princeton center for a time as he created a revised, and definitive, version of *Déserts* (1954/1960), one of the first works pairing live instrumentalists with taped sounds in performance.

The practice of electronic music grew rapidly in the United States during the early 1960s. The *San Francisco Tape Music Center*—home to composers Terry Riley (b. 1935) and Pauline Oliveros (b. 1932) among others—was established in 1961 as a private cooperative of musicians similar to what Mumma and Ashley had done in Ann Arbor (see Chapter 12, pp. 392–5). Technical developments were also under way in the

LISTENING GUIDE 3.4

Title: *Postlude* from *Music for a Sacred Service*

Artist: Bülent Arel   **Year**: 1961   **Duration**: 3:54

Genre: Tape composition

Electronic Instrumentation: Sine, square, and sawtooth wave oscillators, filters, frequency shifter, tape editing.

Background: This piece was composed by Turkish composer Arel working at the Columbia–Princeton Electronic Music Center in New York. Although the work does not specifically use the RCA Electronic Music Synthesizer, the composer employed many of the other traditional tape music facilities of the studio. The work could be called melodic but atonal. It was composed prior to the availability of voltage-controlled synthesizers, such as the Moog and Buchla, yet shows a remarkable alacrity for precision and texture. The work was a labor of love—and many hours of editing tape to create the flow of cascading patterns and transitions that make it remarkable. The cascading sounds that make up much of the work were created using an electronic switch and a frequency shifter in tandem. The switch allowed the shifting between two audio oscillator inputs. The output of one switch was fed into a frequency shifter (changing the fundamental tone and subharmonics of the audio signal) then into the second switch. Arel recorded sequences of rapidly ascending and descending tones and edited them to create the layered textures in this piece. Building the piece in this way—using a few core sequences that could be modified plus some additional passages that had been recorded during his experiments—was an economical way to build the piece and reduce the amount of tape editing.

Listen For: Variation in tonal textures, multitrack recording, tape editing.

0:00–1:05	The basic tonal material is introduced during this section: short tones that cascade up and down the scale; soft, sustained tones; shadow tones that lurk in the background, providing harmonic continuity; and occasional bubbling sounds. The characteristic bell-like sounds have soft attacks and gently reverberate.
1:06–2:55	By about this juncture, the piece has developed two distinct personalities. The first is a gentler part, which predominates the left channel, dominated by short, sustained tones in the mid-range, a hollow-sounding drone that shadows the individual tones, and a repeating pattern of five notes, probably a tape loop, that appears occasionally to provide an underlying, sporadic rhythm. The loop can be heard clearly at about 1:31 and continues for much of the piece.
	The second personality of the piece predominates the right channel and consists of variations on the technique of rapidly cascading tones heard at the opening of the piece. There appear to be two distinct sequences of cascading sounds that are repeated and layered to produce the body of this section. Once "programmed" using the settings on the analog switches and frequency shifter, Arel probably recorded several versions of each and then selectively filtered and processed the sound to ensure that none of the sequences sounded exactly the same. What remains the same, however, are the lengths of core sequences. There are at least two. The first is about 15 seconds long and is heard for the first time beginning at 1:06. It reappears at 1:56 in a modified form and is somewhat obscured by another parallel sequence. The second core sequence is first heard at 1:19 and lasts about ten seconds. It is sharper and much louder. The second core sequence repeats at least two more times, beginning at 1:45 and 2:36 respectively. By the end of this section, Arel has pulled out all the stops and layered many copies of these core sequences with "spare parts"—other recordings of the cascading tones not used until now.
2:56–3:54	The texture of the piece ebbs for a moment then resumes a purer, less noisy version of the manic cascading sounds of the previous section. The quieter tones and looped five-note pattern that dominate the left channel continue. The piece ends suddenly with a three-second cascade of ascending and descending notes beginning at 3:50.

Compare and Contrast

Leyla and the Poet (1959) by Halim El-Dabh
Dance Piece No. 3 (1969) by Alice Shields
A Sky of Cloudless Sulphur: Dance (1978) by Morton Subotnick

development of voltage-controlled synthesizers, particularly in San Francisco where Donald Buchla (b. 1937) created his first instruments, and Trumansburg, New York, home of Robert Moog (see Chapter 8).

ELECTRONIC MUSIC IN LATIN AMERICA

The history of electronic music in Central America, South America, and Cuba has its origins in the earliest days of tape music. The exploratory works from these regions suffered for many years from little documentation and a lack of institutional support for the preservation of recordings. American composer Gordon Mumma, who knew and worked with many of these artists in the 1960s, did much to recount its early history in an article written in 1986.[46] A more recent effort was undertaken by composer Ricardo Dal Farra, an Argentinian composer and educator. This work culminated in the curation of over 200 electronic works and an archive of more than 1,700 compositions by 390 composers dating from the early 1950s to the present.[47] Locating and preserving most of these works was accomplished by establishing personal contact with the composers or their estates and undertaking efforts to restore magnetic tape recordings that had been stored for many years.

The most familiar Latin American composers are those who left their home countries and made their reputations in Europe or the United States. Argentinian Mauricio Kagel and Mario Davidovsky are two of the most notable. But for every famous expatriate there were dozens of other pioneers of electronic music whose work never became known outside of Latin America. What emerges is an impression of a vibrant musical culture that embraced electronic music and found its own voice. Latin American composers were as excited, engaged, and innovative in the exploration of the potential of electronic music as their counterparts in North America, Europe, and Asia.

The early days of Latin American electronic music were marked by two general trends regarding access and practice. Numerous composers were studying music and composition abroad and had the opportunity to access electronic music facilities in their host cities, specifically New York, Cologne, Milan, and Paris. Another group of composers established the first studios to be found in their home nations and explored the techniques of creating tape music within the context of their culture. By the early 1960s, the flavor and content of Latin electronic music had become to some extent an interesting amalgam of styles invented at home and learned abroad. There is a clear analogy to the evolution of Latin jazz that infuses an essentially American idiom with instruments, rhythms, and forms all its own.

For those composers working abroad, each situation provided a unique learning environment. Latin American composers visiting New York were working in the midst of two contrasting schools of thought—the systematic, often serial approach used by the Columbia–Princeton Electronic Music Center and its mammoth analog, programmable synthesizer, and the contrasting, do-it-yourself affinities of the downtown school of chance composition represented by John Cage. In Paris, composers became immersed in the pedagogy of Pierre Schaeffer and the GRM, where *musique concrète* was the big game in town. In Cologne, visiting composers learned to construct highly logical pieces of purely electronic sounds, although this stricture was waning by the end of the 1950s. The Milan studio of the RAI was open to everything, and to some extent was the most clearly democratic, or anarchic as the case may be, of the various schools of electronic music thought.

During the formative years of electronic music development in the 1950s, there was a tendency for works from all over the world to share a common vocabulary of sound and techniques. By about 1960, it was truly difficult to distinguish tape music stylistically from one country or another. There was an inclination to imitate because so many practitioners were working with so few technical options. In the case of Japan, for example, the first Japanese composers who learned the art of electronic music were taught by people from the Cologne school, so it is not surprising that their first works sounded quite like those of their European counterparts. Latin American electronic music was no different. But after experiencing a brief period of imitation during the late 1950s and early 1960s, Latin composers effectively subsumed the basic techniques of tape music and broadened the content of their works to better reflect aspects of their own lands. Examining works of many composers can make the case, but one simple example will suffice. Cuban composer Juan Blanco's (1919–2008) earliest works of electronic music were composed using only tape recorders, recorded sounds, and tone generators. *Ensamble VI* and *Estructuras*, both from 1963, are impossible to differentiate from tape music composed even four or five years earlier in France, Germany, Italy, or Japan. The music consisted primarily of textural extremes, echo, banging inside a piano, and sweeping amplitude changes. Within a few years, however, Blanco was composing larger works for voice, orchestra, and electronic sounds that bore the mark of Cuban music, voices, and rhythms. *La Partida Viviente* (1967) was a tape piece featuring orchestra, a Cuban-Spanish speaking narrator, and actors. This approach became his trademark and he went on to produce numerous works with electronics, including those intended for public performance and national events. Through the years, Blanco's works were more distinctly Cuban in identity, assimilating electronics more as a tool than a preoccupation. Much the same can be said for the way in which the electronic music of Latin American composers from many countries succeeded in creating a diverse approach to this new media that mirrored the cultural wealth and influences of South and Central America and Cuba.

Soon after tape music had become available to Latin composers, it was being used as a component of larger works for outdoor events, theater, and concerts involving orchestral players and singers. This development can be seen in nearly every Latin American country. Early works of this nature included *Música para la Torre* (Argentina, Kagel, 1953) for a sound installation; *La Llorona* (Mexico, Mabarak, 1961) for strings, small ballet orchestra, piano, percussion and oscillator; *Contrastes* (Guatemala, Orellana, 1963) for ballet orchestra and tape; *Música para el Quinto Desfile Gimnástico Deportivo* (Cuba, Blanco, 1965) for orchestra and tape; *Dissolução* (Brazil, Antunes, 1966) for string orchestra and tape; *Hecho 2* (Uruguay, Aharonián, 1966); *Alfa-Omega* (Peru, Bolaños, 1967) for two narrators, choir, dancers, instruments, tape and light projections; and *Mística No. 3* (Bolivia, Villalpando, 1970) for double string quartet, horns, flute, double bass and tape.

Latin culture itself is a blend of many influences with strong European and African ties infused by the art and music of indigenous traditions. It is perhaps not surprising that electronic music would be embraced so readily in this region of the world and integrated into many streams of academic musical experiments as well as broader productions intended for widespread public consumption.

The First Inter-American Experimental Music Encounter, Argentina

By the mid-1960s, the avant-garde music of Latin American composers was also becoming more widely known around the world. This attracted musicians from North America and Europe to visit and perform in Latin countries, creating an exchange of ideas, methods and influences. An example of one such opportunity was a festival of avant-garde music held in connection with the Third Inter-American Biennial of Art in Córdoba, Argentina in October 1966, organized by Argentinian composer Horacio Vaggione (b. 1943), founder of an electronic music studio at the College of Fine Arts of the University of Córdoba. Over four nights of concerts, Argentinian audiences witnessed performances by a gathering of some of the world's most notable electronic and avant-garde composers from the United States, including Herbert Brün, Christian Wolff, John Cage, Lejaren Hiller, Gordon Mumma, Ernst Krenek, Morton Feldman, and Earle Brown. South American composers were also well represented, including several composers associated with electronic music, such as Mario Davidovsky, Horacio Vaggione, Carlos Ferpozzi, Miguel Angel Rondano, Hilda Dianda, Francisco Kröpfl, Mauricio Kagel, and Virgilio Tosco from Argentina; Jose Vicente Asuar from Chile; and César Bolaños from Peru. This Pan-American showcase was an important factor in stimulating greater interest in electronic music in South America. Many of the works performed during the festival involved some form of pre-recorded electronic music, often presented in combination with live instrumentalists and vocalists. Some of the key electronic works of Latin American composers featured during the festival were:[48]

Edgardo Cantón, *Voix Inouies*, for modulated voice on tape (1966)
Mario Davidovsky, *Electronic Study No. 3 (Hommage á Edgard Varèse)* (1966)
José Vicente Asuar, *Prelude: The Night*, for tape (1961)
Graciela Castillo, *Concretion*, for tape (1966)
Pedro Echarte, *Treno*, for tape (1965)
Nelly Moretto, *Composition 9b*, for tape (1966)
Aurelio de la Vega, *Interpolation*, for solo clarinet and pre-recorded sounds (1965)
Hilda Dianda, *A 7*, for cello and six-channel tape of pre-recorded cello sounds (1966)
Alcides Lanza, *Plectros II*, for modulated piano sounds on tape (1966)
César Bolaños, *Intensity and Height*, for tape (1964)
Francisco Kröpfl, *Dialogues I–II*, for tape (1966)
Horatio Vaggione, *Sonata IV*, for piano and tape (1965).

Argentina

Composers from Argentina played a central role in the development of electronic music in Latin America. It was home to perhaps twice as many active composers of tape music as the next ranking country, Brazil. Some of its composers and their works are more widely known because they were among the first Latin composers to study and compose abroad. It was also home to the two most influential educational centers and studios in South America. The *Estudio de Fonologia Musical* was founded in 1958 at the University of Buenos Aires by composers Francisco Kröpfl (b. 1931) and Fausto Maranca. The *Centro Latinoamericano de Altos Estudios Musicales* (CLAEM) at the Torcuato Di Tella

Institute in Buenos Aires was founded in 1962 by composer Alberto Ginastera (1916–83). CLAEM was perhaps the best organized and funded institutional studio in Latin America and provided scholarships and residences for composers from many Latin American countries to learn the art of electronic music making in its studios. Both organizations were defunct by the early 1970s, but their legacy and mission, not to mention some staff and equipment, were inherited by the *Laboratorio de Investigación y Producción Musical* (LIPM), a government-sponsored studio that is part of the Buenos Aires Recoleta Cultural Center and that is still active today.

One of the most influential Argentinian composers of experimental music was Mauricio Kagel (1931–2008). Although he permanently immigrated to Germany in 1957, he is credited with having produced the first works of electronic music in South America between 1950 and 1953. Some of these early studies were carried out using disc turntables, much like Schaeffer in Paris.[49] In 1953–54, Kagel completed a lengthy electronic music installation for an industrial exhibit in Buenos Aires. Lasting nearly 110 minutes, the work *Música para la Torre* (*Tower Music*) combined lighting effects with a backdrop of electroacoustic music on tape projected from a tower. This was not only one of the longest electronic works composed by that time in any country, but also an

Figure 3.9 Argentinian composer Mauricio Kagel, pictured in 1958, was one of the first Latin American composers to experiment with electronic music.

Figure 3.10   The Centro Latinoamericano de Altos Estudios Musicales (CLAEM) at the Torcuato Di Tella Institute in Buenos Aires was founded in 1962 by composer Alberto Ginastera. The panel above the control bench was a touch-controlled patch bay for controlling sound generators.

early example of a **sound installation**. In 1957, the young composer was persuaded by Pierre Boulez to study in Cologne, which is where the Argentinian lived for the rest of his life. Kagel's stature as a significant composer of electronic music was established in 1957 with *Transicion I* for electronic sounds (1958), followed by *Transicion II* (1958–59) for piano, percussion, and two tapes. Clearly influenced by the Cologne school of serialism, Kagel's *Transicions* were each characterized by an exploration of the many aural possibilities of his sound sources set to an arrhythmic, seemingly formless sequence of sonic exclamations without pattern. These works were similar in effect to some of Stockhausen's instrumental pieces of the same period, but radically different from the German's evolving approach to tape composition. The formless nature of Kagel's electronic works were more closely affiliated with Cage's indeterminate work, as was his urge to satirize the performance act itself. *Transicion II*, with its heavy reliance on instrumental piano sounds, also indicated that Kagel was slowly transitioning away from heavily electronic works to experimental works for acoustic instruments. By 1963, Kagel had nearly exhausted his interest in composing electronic works but remained interested in the spatial projection of music and the incorporation of noise elements in his works, attributes associated with his experiments with tape, sound processing, and the amplified projection of electronic music.

In 1960, after studying with Americans Aaron Copland and Milton Babbitt, Argentinian Mario Davidovsky (b. 1934) took up residence in New York and composed his first electronic tape pieces at the Columbia–Princeton Electronic Music Center. His early works included *Electronic Study No. 1* (1960) and *Electronic Study No. 2* (1962), after which he began a series of individual works that he called *Synchronisms*, which often combined the use of live instrumentalists and accompanying taped sounds. Twelve *Synchronisms* were composed in all, spanning the years 1962 to 2006. Davidovsky was awarded the Pulitzer Prize in 1971 for *Synchronisms No. 6* (1970), written for piano and electronic sound. His work is characterized by the interaction of virtuoso musicians with a counterpoint of electronically generated sounds covering a broad tonal and timbral spectrum. Davidovsky remained in the United States and became Varèse's assistant at the Columbia studio until the elder composer's death in 1965. The Argentinian was also director of the Columbia–Princeton Electronic Music Center from 1981 to 1993, although by that time he was composing primarily for non-electronic musical instruments again.

Argentinian composer Hilda Dianda (b. 1925) completed works of purely electronic music while at the RAI in Milan, including *Dos Estudios en Oposición* (1959). While in California in the mid-1960s, Dianda explored the electroacoustic possibilities of live performance pieces combining tape and musicians. Her piece *A7* (1964) for cello and tape included a cello part played live to three separate tracks of cello sounds that were modified using tape treatment and editing techniques. Dianda returned to Argentina and continued working in electronic music development.

Two other Argentinian composers, Tirso de Olazábal (1924–60) and Edgardo Cantón (b. 1934) worked in the GRM studios in Paris, the latter producing numerous electronic works including *Promenade* (1963) and *2 Times* (1963), each comprising tape music for ballet.

Another noteworthy Argentinian who experimented with tape music in the early 1960s was Guillermo Gregorio (b. 1941). Now better known as a clarinettist, alto saxophonist and bandleader, Gregorio took a detour from the performance of jazz while still in his early twenties to experiment with tape collages and performance art involving electronic music. From about 1963 to 1965, working in his home studio, Gregorio developed improvisational solo works using overdubs and tape recorder techniques. Works such as *Campanitas* (Little Bells, 1963–64), *Elastikon* (1964), and *Clarinete* (1964–65) featured the amplified sounds of resonating objects, acoustic instruments, voices, and noises blended and edited into jarring soundscapes that echoed the work of European *musique concrète* yet anticipated the integration of jazz and electronic music that was yet to come.

Brazil

Electronic music in Brazil had its beginning with the work of Reginaldo Carvalho (b. 1932), who created his first tape piece *Sibemol* (1956) in his private studio in Rio de Janeiro, which he called the *Estudio de Experiencias Musicais*.[50] His pieces were electro-acoustic in nature, mixing processed natural sounds with electronic sounds. Prior to creating these works in Brazil, Carvalho had studied composition in Paris and worked for a short time under Pierre Schaeffer at the GRM, learning the techniques of *musique concrète*. In 1966, Carvalho was named director of the Conservatorio Nacional de Canto Orfeonico (National Conservatory of Choral Singing) in Rio and established the Villa-Lobos Institute for exploring new music. He recruited the young electronic music composer Jorge Antunes (b. 1942) to join the teaching staff and establish the *Laboratorio de Arte Integral* (Integral Art Laboratory) to advance the practice of electronic music and multimedia art.

Antunes is one of the most interesting and influential Brazilian composers from the classic era of tape music. A physicist and musician, by 1961 he had built several components for making electronic music, including a sawtooth oscillator, a spring-reverb device, a frequency filter, and a Theremin. His first tape pieces were created in a bare-bones home studio with the help of a tape recorder, a single oscillator, and a piano. Antunes is credited with composing the first Brazilian work consisting only of electronic

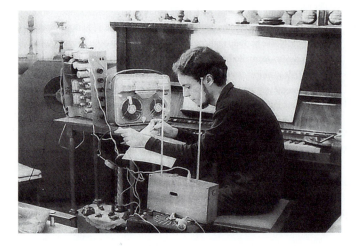

Figure 3.11   Brazilian electronic music composer Jorge Antunes in his home studio, 1962.

tones in 1962, when he realized the piece *Valsa Sideral*. Antunes' knack for combining disparate media materials into expressive works led him into multimedia production by the mid-1960s. He dabbled in special stagings of his works in the spirit of Cage's so-called performance pieces and "happenings" in the United States, in which performers and audience members became part of the same interactive experience. For *Ambiente I* (1965), Antunes played a tape of electronic music but provided other tactile performance elements including changing lights, moving and stationary objects, "incense and food."[51] From there, Antunes graduated to producing more fully developed works for orchestra and electronic music on tape. He received a scholarship to study at CLAEM in 1969 and 1970, where he continued his work in electronic music.[52] Despite his stature as an accomplished electronic musician, he was not able to release a commercial recording of his music until 1973.

Cuba

Juan Blanco was a seminal figure in Cuban avant-garde music. Like the older Varèse, Blanco had dreamed of creating new sounds with electronic instruments long before the means were available. He reportedly conceived the idea of an automated sound storage and playback instrument—conceptually much like the Mellotron—in 1942, prior to the practical means for creating such an instrument existed. By about 1960, he had read Pierre Schaeffer's book *A la recherche d'une musique concrète* and was anxious to try his hand at producing tape music. This book proved to be his only real schooling in the techniques of electronic music because he was unable to leave Cuba to visit the various institutions of electronic music development in person. He equipped himself with three cheap tape recorders from a department store, a single audio oscillator, and a microphone and began experimenting. He duplicated many of the techniques that he had read about—tape reversal, microphone feedback, speed changes, re-recording and layering sounds from one machine to another, and tape splicing. Lacking a tape machine with variable speed control, like those in the Paris and German studios, he applied pressure with his fingers to manually alter the preset speeds of his tape machines. His first work was 5′ 30″ long, called *Música para Danza*, completed in 1961, and was probably the first work of electronic music composed in Cuba. Even this short work, with rhythms reminiscent of Cuban mambos, hinted at Blanco's interest in fusing elements of Cuban music with experimental sounds. His next few works were less Cuban in influence and explored the wide world of sounds around him. Blanco was evidently hearing a lot of outside music and his own works from 1961 to 1964 could be considered studies of these techniques. His pieces ran the gamut from industrial noise and machinery rhythms (*Interludio con Máquinas*, 1963) to electronically treated recordings of prepared piano (*Ensample V* and *VI*, 1963), with additional studies of pure electronic tones.[53]

Blanco returned to his Cuban roots in works beginning in the mid-1960s, finding ways to incorporate elements of Cuban popular music and dance into his electronic works. He was at the forefront of a revolution in Cuban music that embraced popular, jazz, and avant-garde artists. Blanco was in demand

Figure 3.12   Cuban electronic music composer Juan Blanco, pictured *c.* 1975, fused elements of Cuban music with experimental sounds.

as a composer for film as well as large public events and he generally found ways in which to integrate his know-how with electronic music into each of these multi-media productions. His electronic music was used for several large-scale exhibitions and public spaces, including a gymnastics competition in 1965, a hospital in Havana, and an installation of sound art for Cuban pavilions at world expositions in Montreal (1967) and Osaka (1970). His performance pieces continued to grow in complexity and elements, often using live actors, choirs, instrumentalists, and elaborate staging in combination with music on magnetic tape. In 1969, Blanco staged *Contrapunto Espacial III* at the Garcia Lorca Opera House in Havana. The avant-garde production required two dozen instrumental groups scattered throughout the theater, actors, two magnetic tapes, and a saxophone soloist (a young Paquito D'Rivera). The atonal music and actors illustrated the evolution of various social stages in human development, from primitive life to modern life. The tapes provided sound effects. At regular intervals during the piece, just at the conclusion of another stage of human development, a booming voice of authority would declare "No!" from a large loudspeaker at center stage. The actors, led by the refrains of a solo saxophonist, eventually revolt. In Communist Cuba, this public expression of political freedom did not go down very well. The work was banned.[54]

Blanco continued to work in the electronic music medium, began teaching the art of electronic music production, and established a studio to aid budding artists.

There is a scarcity of prominent women composers from the early period of Latin American electronic music, with the notable exception of Jacqueline Nova (Sondag) (1935–75). Nova was born in Belgium and relocated to Colombia with her family. Raised primarily in Bogotá, she studied piano and classical music composition, earning a Masters degree from the National Conservatory of Music in 1967. Nova had already composed more than 25 instrumental and vocal works by this time, often exploring trends in aleatory composition. She was granted a scholarship to study electronic music in Buenos Aires in 1967 and embarked on a brief but highly productive exploration of multimedia pieces before her untimely death from cancer in 1975. Her first electronic

Figure 3.13   Colombian electronic music composer Jacqueline Nova, *c.* 1967.

piece, *Resonancias 1* for prepared piano and electronic sonorities, was completed in 1968. Her mixed media work became increasingly daring and experimental, combining traditional instruments with pre-recorded materials, including radio signals, modulated voices, and electronic sound distortion. Among her most noted works were *Oposición-fusión* (1968) for electronic sounds; *Espacios* (1969), a stage work for taped sounds, light projections, voice, and movement; *LM-A 11* (1969), combining tape with strings, voices, and percussion; and *Creación de la Tierra* (1969), comprising only electronically modified and edited voices. Her last works included an electroacoustic sound installation for *Las Camas*, an exhibit of modern sculpture by artist Feliza Bursztyn. The style of her electronic music reflected the influence of European know-how in the production of electronic music but also echoed the work of American avant-gardists such as Cage, Tudor, Oliveros, and others who produced multimedia performance pieces incorporating electronic music.

Table 3.2 comprises a list of representative composers and their works from the developmental years of Latin American electronic music.

SUMMARY

- The development of electronic music in the United States in the early 1950s was largely the effort of independent artists working without institutional support.

- The first piece of electronic music for magnetic tape composed in America was *Heavenly Menagerie* (1950) by Louis and Bebe Barron, who had one of the first well-equipped private studios.

- In 1951, Cage organized the Project of Music for Magnetic Tape in New York. The group worked with the Barrons as technical advisors and comprised composers Cage, David Tudor, Morton Feldman, Earl Brown, and Christian Wolff.

- *Williams Mix* (1952) by Cage used chance operations to determine the way in which a variety of recorded sounds would be edited together using magnetic tape. He further extended the application of chance operations to the creation of *Fontana Mix* (1958), a work scored for any number of tracks of magnetic tape, for any number of players, or any kind and number of instruments, and whose composition was indeterminate of its performance. After completing these works for magnetic tape, he concentrated his efforts in electronic music on live performance using mixed media.

- In 1951, Luening and Ussachevsky began a long-standing partnership as collaborators and caretakers of what was initially called the Columbia Tape Music Center, a collection of audio recording equipment borrowed from Columbia University.

- The first public recital of tape music from Columbia Tape Music Center took place at a Composers Forum recital organized by Ussachevsky in 1952. Among the works

Table 3.2 Early electronic music in Latin America

Country	Composer	Affiliation	Representative work(s)
Argentina	Maurico Kagel	Private studio and WDR (Cologne)	Música para la Torre (1953); Transición I (1958)
	Tirso de Olazábal	GRM (Paris)	Estudio para Percussion (1957)
	Hilda Dianda	RAI (Milan)	Dos Estudios en Oposición (1959)
	Francisco Kröpfl	Estudio de Fonología Musical	Ejercicio de Texturas (1960); Ejercicio con Impulsos (1960)
	César Franchisena	National University of Córdoba	Numancia (1960)
	Mario Davidovsky	Columbia–Princeton Electronic Music Center (New York)	Synchronisms No. 1–6 (1962–70)
	Horacio Vaggione	Private studio	Música Electrónica I (1961)
Bolivia	Alberto Villalpando	CLAEM	La Muerte (1964); Mística No. 3 (1970)
Brazil	Reginaldo Carvalho	Private studio, Estudio de Experiencias Musicais	Sibemol (1956); Troço II (1957); Estudo I (1958); Dissolução (1966)
Chile	León Schidlowsky	Private studio	Nacimiento (1956)
	Juan Amenábar	Taller Experimental de Sonido	Los Peces (1953–57); Feed-Back (1964); Klesis (1968)
	José Vicente Asuar	Taller Experimental de Sonido	Variaciones Espectrales (1959)
Colombia	Fabio Gonzáles-Zuleta	Studios of the National Radio of Colombia (Bogotà)	Ensayo Electrónico (1965)
	Jacqueline Nova Sondag	CLAEM	Resonancias 1 (1968); Oposición-fusión (1968); Luz-sonido-movimiento (1969); LM-A 11 (1969)
Cuba	Juan Blanco	Private studio	Música para danza (1961); Estudio I (1961–62); Ensamble VI (1963); Interludio con Máquinas (1963); Contrapunto Espacial III (1969)
	Aurello de la Vega	Private studio	Interpolation (1965); Para-Tangents (1971)
Guatemala	Joaquín Orellana	Private studio and CLAEM	Contrastes (1963); Metéora (1968)
Mexico	Carlos Jiménez Mabarak	Private studio	El paraíso de los ahogados (1960); La llorona (1961)
	Héctor Quintanar	Private studio	Aclamaciones (1967); Sideral I (1968)
Peru	César Bolaños	CLAEM (Buenos Aires); private studio	Intensidad y Altura (1963); Interpolaciones (1966); Alfa-Omega (1967)
	Edgar Valcárcel	Columbia–Princeton Electronic Music Center (New York)	Invención (1967); Canto Coral a Tupac Amaru (1968)
Uruguay	Conrado Silva	Private studio	Musik für zehn Kofferradiogeräte (1964)
	Coriún Aharonián	Private studio and CLAEM (Buenos Aires)	Hecho 2 (1966); Música para aluminios (1967)
Venezuela	Alfredo del Mónaco	Estudio de Fonología Musical of the Instituto Nacional de Cultura y Bellas Artes (INCIBA) and Columbia–Princeton Electronic Music Center (New York)	Cromofonías I (1966–67); Estudio electrónico I (1967–68); Metagrama (1969–70); Syntagma [A] (1971–72)

premiered was Ussachevsky's *Sonic Contours*, featuring the electronically modified sounds of the piano. This was followed by a much-publicized concert at the Museum of Modern Art in the fall of 1952 featuring works by both composers. Luening used tape manipulation to modify the sound of the flute, which figured prominently in works such as *Fantasy in Space* (1952), *Low Speed* (1952), and *Invention in Twelve Tones* (1952).

• The RCA Electronic Music Synthesizer was publicly unveiled in January, 1955. It was the first sound synthesizer in the modern era and was comprised of integrated components that could generate, modify, process, record, and present complex sonorities intended for musical applications. Luening and Ussachevsky, along with Milton Babbit, began working experimentally with the machine in the composition of electronic music.

• The Columbia–Princeton Electronic Music Center was founded in 1958 with the help of a Rockefeller grant. By agreement with RCA, the Center became the new home of the RCA Electronic Music Synthesizer.

• Mumma and Ashley founded the Cooperative Studio for Electronic Music in 1958 in Ann Arbor. The composers built their own sound-generating circuits and produced live multimedia performances twice a week for seven years at Milton Cohen's Space Theater.

• Hiller and Isaacson experimented with the composition of music using a computer, producing the *Illiac Suite for String Quartet* in 1957.

• The history of electronic music in Central America, South America, and Cuba has its origins in the earliest days of tape music. With roots in the mid-1950s and the work of Mauricio Kagel, the practice of tape composition grew widely throughout Latin America during the early 1960s, encompassing work in more than a dozen countries led by artists in Argentina, Brazil, Columbia, and Cuba.

KEY PEOPLE IN CHAPTER THREE

Bell Labs   107

Centro Latinoamericano de Altos
    Estudios Musicales (CLAEM)   126

chance operations   100

Columbia Tape Music Center   110

Columbia–Princeton Electronic Music
    Center (1958+)   110

Cooperative Studio for Electronic
    Music   116

Datatron "Push-Button Bertha"
    122

digital-to-analog converter   122

Estudio de Fonologia Musical   126

First Inter-American Experimental
    Music Encounter, The   126

ILLIAC I   121

Laboratorio de Investigación y
    Producción Musical (LIPM)   127

Project of Music for Magnetic
    Tape   100

RCA Electronic Music Synthesizer
    113

San Francisco Tape Music Center
    122

sound installation   128

Studio di Fonologia Musicale   107

MILESTONES

Early Electronic Music of the United States

Technical and scientific	Year	Music and instruments
	1950	– Louis and Bebe Barron composed *Heavenly Menagerie*, the first known magnetic tape composition produced in the United States.
– John Cage organized the Project of Music for Magnetic Tape.	1951	
– Otto Luening and Vladimir Ussachevsky established the Columbia Tape Music Center. – In October, Luening and Ussachevsky produced a concert of their tape music for the Museum of Modern Art (New York).	1952	– Cage completed *Imaginary Landscape No. 5*, composed on tape using pre-recorded sounds from phonograph records. Next, he completed *Williams Mix* using a variety of newly recorded natural sounds and having a graphic score specifying tape editing instructions. – Luening completed *Invention in Twelve Tones* using tape manipulation of flute sounds.
	1954	– Luening and Ussachevsky completed *A Poem in Cycles and Bells* for tape recorder and orchestra.
– The RCA Mark I Electronic Music Synthesizer unveiled.	1955	– Lejaren Hiller and Leonard Isaacson programmed the ILLIAC I computer at the University of Illinois to compose sheet music.
– A Burroughs Datatron computer nicknamed "Push-Button Bertha" was programmed to compose pop songs.	1956	– The Barrons completed the electronic score for the motion picture *Forbidden Planet*.

Technical and scientific	Year	Music and instruments
– Luening, Ussachevky, Milton Babbit, and Roger Sessions established the Columbia–Princeton Electronic Music Center at Columbia University. – Max Mathews of Bell Labs generated sound with a computer using a digital-to-analog converter.	1957	– Luening completed the tape piece *Mathematics* using the RCA Electronic Music Synthesizer. – Gordon Mumma and Robert Ashley began to produce music for Milton Cohen's Space Theater (Ann Arbor). – Hiller and Isaacson completed the *Illiac Suite for String Quartet*, an early work composed with computer assistance for conventional instruments.
– Mumma and Ashley established the Cooperative Studio for Electronic Music (Ann Arbor).	1958	– Cage completed *Fontana Mix* in Milan.
– RCA donated the Mark II Electronic Music Synthesizer to the Columbia–Princeton Electronic Music Center.	1959	

CHAPTER 4

Early Electronic Music in Japan, Southeast Asia, and China

How thirsty were we for free soaring of an artist's soul without being restricted by the conventional conditions of the materials or the boundary of human performance.
—Toshiro Mayuzumi[1]

Jikken Kobo experimental performance group, 1957.
(Kiyoji Otsuji, courtesy of Taka Ishii Gallery)

The development and radiation of electronic music worldwide occurred rapidly following the establishment of the Paris and Cologne studios in Europe. Some of the most interesting and dedicated efforts occurred in Japan, where institutional sponsorship enabled composers to experiment with the latest audio recording and processing equipment. Although initially influenced by exposure to French and German electronic music, these efforts gradually became independent and blended elements of Asian music with Western-influenced theories of composition. This chapter explores the early electronic music of Japan and the work of its early proponents.

The evolution of electronic music in Japan was significant because it represented the first infusion of Asian culture into the new genre. The development of tape music in Japan also marked the beginning the nation's fascination with electronic instrumentation and the eventual domination of Japanese industry in the development of music synthesizers and other music technology.

The story of early Japanese electronic music began in relative isolation following World War II. As in the West, where composers such as Varèse and Cage had anticipated the use of musical technology, there were a few Japanese composers who anticipated the development of synthetic means for creating music. As early as 1948, composer Toru Takemitsu (1930–96) conceived a music in which he could use technology to "bring noise into tempered musical tones" and noted that Schaeffer had apparently thought of the same thing at about the same time in Paris when he developed *musique concrète*.[2] Composer Minao Shibata (1916–96) wrote in 1949 that "Someday, in the near future, a musical instrument with very high performance will be developed, in which advanced science technology and industrial power are highly utilized. We will be able to synthesize any kind of sound waves with the instrument."[3] Although electronic musical instruments such as the *Ondes Martenot*, Theremin, and Trautonium were little known in Japan until the 1950s, a few composers including Shibata had heard about them.

THE SONY TAPE RECORDER AND EARLY TAPE MUSIC

The technological means for creating electronic music in Japan were first provided by the *Tokyo Tsushin Kogyo KK* (Tokyo Telecommunications Engineering Corporation), an electronics firm founded by engineer Masaru Ibuka and physicist Akio Morita in 1946 to manufacture telephones and amplified megaphones. In 1950, this small firm developed Japan's first magnetic tape recorder, known as the G-Type for "government unit" because it became a popular recording device for use in courtrooms and government offices. This same firm released a home model tape recorder, the Type-H, in 1951 and, after becoming Japan's first licensee to manufacture transistors in 1954, changed its name to *Sony*.

Independently of the rise of Sony, an interdisciplinary group of Japanese poets, painters, and

Figure 4.1   Sony G-Type tape recorder. (Sony)

musicians formed a loosely knit collective called the *Jikken Kobo* (Experimental Workshop) to collaborate on multimedia projects. Beginning in 1951, the group was active for about seven years and included such musicians as Takemitsu, Kuniharu Akiyama (1929–96), Joji Yuasa (b. 1929), Kazuo Satoh (b. 1926), Hiroyoshi Suzuki (b. 1931), and Takahiro Sonoda (1928–2004). Soon after their founding, Jikken Kobo was drawn into the world of electronic music by Tokyo Tsushin Kogyo (Sony). Ibuka and Morita of Tokyo Tsushin Kogyo were well aware that the tape recorder had musical applications. To illustrate the usefulness of its G-Type machine in the arts, Sony hired composer Takemitsu on a part-time basis to compose music on tape. This led to a mutually beneficial relationship between Jikken Kobo and Sony, wherein the arts collective was provided with access to the latest tape recording and audio visual technology in exchange for the development of music and projection art for demonstration purposes. This led in some cases to concerts sponsored and presented by Sony.[4] Sony continued its supportive relationship with Jikken Kobo until 1960, donating the studio to the Sogetsu Art Center, which continued to provide facilities for the composers until 1966.

Although Takemitsu was apparently one of the first Japanese composers to work with a tape recorder, credit for having completed the first Japanese tape music compositions goes to Akiyama, who produced *Toraware no Onna* (*Imprisoned Woman*) and *Piece B* in 1951. Yuasa was also active early on and worked with tape music and slide projections using a machine produced by Sony that allowed for the synchronization of tape music and slides. A concert using this device was given in 1955. Despite these efforts, the earliest tape music of Jikken Kobo went largely unnoticed.

Japanese post-war composers including Shibata, Takemitsu, and the Jikken Kobo group had heard about *musique concrète* from Paris, but the actual recordings of this electronic music were not available in Japan until 1957. The initial exposure of Japanese musicians to *musique concrète* came by way of composer Toshiro Mayuzumi (1929–97), who had attended a concert of Schaeffer's electronic music while studying in Paris in 1952.[5] Upon his return to Japan, Mayuzumi completed *Les Œuvres pour musique concrète x, y, z* (1953)—the first tape composition by a Japanese composer to gain wide exposure in Japan when it was publicly broadcast by radio station *JOQR* (Nippon Cultural Broadcasting) on November 27, 1953. Mayuzumi effectively used *Les Œuvres pour musique concrète x, y, z* to convey the basic electronic music techniques used by his European counterparts. His only available equipment included audio oscillators and tape recorders.

Japanese composers who anticipated an opportunity to work in tape composition were initially surprised by what they heard in Mayuzumi's version of *musique concrète*. Takemitsu and others had imagined a more organized approach to composing, with

Figure 4.2 Some of the first electronic music composed in Japan was influenced by serial composition techniques being practiced in Germany. Composer Minao Shibata was experimenting with 12-tone rows in 1955, as evidenced by this extract from the score manuscript and its transcription. (After Koichi Fujii, 2004)

sounds rather than the apparently formless, unwritten results heard in *Les Œuvres pour musique concrète x, y, z*. "I experienced a kind of shock," explained Takemitsu. "I thought it was quite different from what I had imagined ... I had the same impression of Schaeffer's works long after [hearing Mayuzumi's]."[6]

Despite the puzzlement of some Japanese composers over *musique concrète*, there remained a keen interest in Japan in the new medium of tape composition and other Western music theory. Serialism was of special interest and evidence of its use in the organization of electronic sounds is found as early as Mayuzumi's *Les Œuvres pour musique concrète x, y, z*, in which 12-tone techniques were used to compose a short passage of cello music for part *z*. By 1956, Shibata was also using serialist techniques to plan electronic music (see Figure 4.2).[7]

ESTABLISHMENT OF THE NHK STUDIO

The German approach known as *elektronische Musik* quickly took hold in Japan, forming an active interchange of ideas between the two countries as early as 1954. It was about this time that staff members of the *Nippon Hōsō Kyōkai* (NHK, Japanese Broadcasting Corporation), took an interest in the potential of tape composition for the creation of **radiophonic** effects and music. Members of the NHK staff translated a handbook from the NWDR Cologne studio into Japanese, and this document reportedly became their blueprint for the creation of their own electronic music studio. Composer Makato Moroi (b. 1930) visited Cologne in 1955 to view the German studio first-hand. Upon his return, he worked with fellow experimenter Mayuzumi to guide NHK into the establishment of an electronic music studio. Founded by a coalition of NHK radio producers, engineers, and composers, the studio's founding director was Wataru Uenami and the first composers associated with the studio included Mayuzumi, Shibata, Yuasa, Moroi, and Ichiyanagi. Takemitsu also became a regular user of the studio by the late 1950s.

The original NHK studio was equipped much like the Cologne studio and featured a wealth of tone-generating, audio processing, and recording equipment (see Figure 4.4). Among the electronic musical instruments and components in the studio were an *Ondes Martenot*, Monochord (sawtooth wave generator), and Melochord, six stepped and three continuously variable sine wave oscillators, two tape recorders, two ring modulators, thirty-two band-pass filters, and two mixers (eight- and four-channel), among other equipment.

The first pieces completed at the NHK studio acknowledged the influence of the German studios and had an inherently mathematical structure. Mayuzumi completed three early works at the studio, all based on the process used by Karlheinz Stockhausen to compose *Studie I*: *Music for Sine Wave by Proportion of Prime Number* (1955), *Music for Modulated Wave by Proportion of Prime Number* (1955), and *Invention for Square Wave and Sawtooth Wave* (1955), using the various tone-generating capabilities of the studio and each being about five minutes long. Shibata composed *Musique Concrète for Stereophonic Broadcast* (1955) at about the same time—a much longer work lasting 20 minutes, and the first stereo piece composed at the NHK studio.

By the mid-1950s, the NHK studio was one of the world's leading electronic music facilities. Together with the Sony studio and highly visible Jikken Kobo group, Japan nurtured an increasingly influential and productive body of electronic music composers. Public performances, both on stage and by broadcast, were frequently sponsored by NHK or Jikken Kobo/Sony, providing the Japanese audience with much exposure to new music in much the same way RTF and WDR did in their respective countries. The culmination of this early period of development of Japanese electronic music is considered by some to be the completion of *Shichi no Variation* (*7 Variations*) (1956) by Moroi and Mayuzumi.[8] This was a strictly serial piece based on the composition process used by Stockhausen for *Studie II*, in which all parameters of the sound, including envelopes, were determined by using serial formulae. The work was scored graphically and used seven mixtures of sine waves instead of five as in *Studie II*. The serial nature of the composition, in which a given tone mixture cannot

Figure 4.3   NHK Electronic Music Studio, 1960. (NHK)

be repeated until all others have been played, is clearly seen in the scoring of the two-voice part from variation two shown in Figure 4.5.

The use of filtered bands of white noise in *Shichi no Variation* (*7 Variations*) was also scored using serial techniques, as can be seen in the portion of a two-voice part from the seventh variation in Figure 4.6.

By the 1960s, Japanese electronics manufacturers were forging ahead as innovative developers of tape recorders, musical instruments, and audio equipment. It was perhaps no great surprise that Stockhausen himself visited Japan in 1966 to create a new kind of electronic music using the excellent facilities of NHK. It was in the Tokyo broadcaster's electronic music studio that Stockhausen spent four months creating *Telemusik* (1966)— a foundational brew of world music combining the taped sounds of folk music from many industrialized and non-industrialized countries and electronically generated sounds. This piece was developed on a six-track tape recorder at the NHK studio, the only one of its kind in an electronic music studio at the time.

During the late 1950s, much Japanese electronic music bore a close resemblance to that of the European and American music that originally inspired it. By this time there was a growing movement among Japanese composers to introduce elements of Japanese music into their tape works. Mayuzumi did this in 1959 with the electronic work *Campanology*, which combined the resonant sounds of Asian temple bells, recorded at

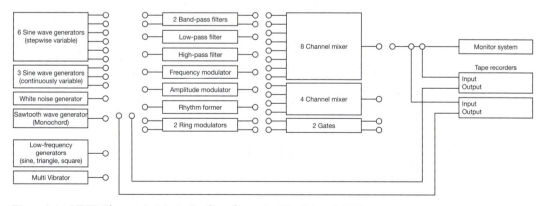

Figure 4.4   NHK Electronic Music Studio schematic. (After Takatsuji, 1956)

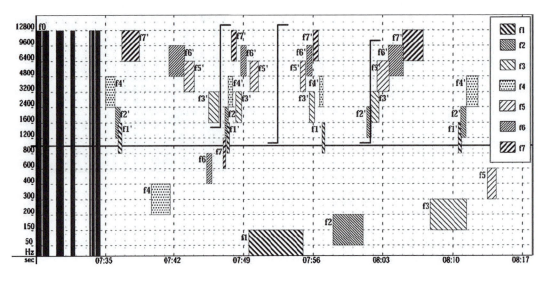

Figure 4.5 Excerpt from the visual score for *Shichi no Variation* (*7 Variations*) (1956) by Moroi and Mayuzumi—a serial composition for sine waves. This view of the graphic transcription of the second variation clearly shows how each of the seven defined tone mixtures was played before any could be repeated. (C. F. Peters)

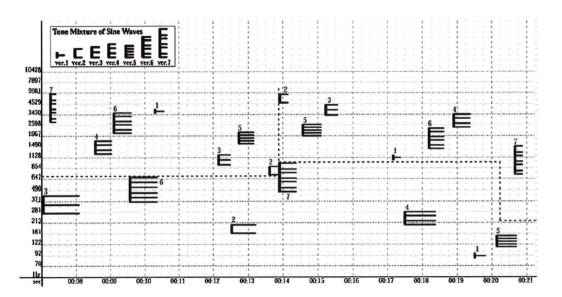

Figure 4.6 The seventh variation of *Shichi no Variation* (*7 Variations*) (1956) by Moroi and Mayuzumi used serial techniques to organize sections of filtered white noise, all of which were graphically transcribed as seen in this extract from the score. (C. F. Peters)

temples throughout Japan, and Western church bells with electronic tones to produce synthetically complex melodies. In 1961, Joji Yuasa recorded *Aoi No Ue*, a title borrowed from a fifteenth-century Noh play. The piece was operatic in scope and fused elements of traditional Japanese vocal chants and electroacoustic sounds such as snippets of birdsong, dripping water, tinkling glasses, a distorted vibraphone, and electronic tones. Traditional instruments such as the Noh flute and two-sided drum were produced synthetically using sine waves, click filters, and reverberation.[9] The result was a mesmerizing 30 minutes of sonic storytelling that combined techniques of Western electronic music making with recognizable sounds from Japanese culture.[10] Other experiments included the exploration of interminacy and chance music, influenced by American John Cage, who in turn had been inspired by Japanese Zen Buddhist philosophy. Toshi Ichiyanagi (b. 1933) produced *Parallel Music* (1962) using this approach. The tape piece featured a variety of electronic sound sources that appear disconnected. The only link between the sources was the way in which rules of chance were used to determine which sounds would be played when, the results for each individual source then being played at the same, or parallel time.

The direction of early electronic music in Japan was shaped by only a few composers whose determination to experiment ran contrary to other accepted forms of music in their culture. Often marginalized as mere program music for television, film, and stage productions, electronic music in Japan did not achieve its status as a serious and vital musical genre until well after the 1970s and the work of a new generation of composers working independently of institutions and studios.[11] To some extent, early Japanese electronic music practitioners painted themselves into an artistic corner, falling victim to artistic pressures in post-war Japan to assimilate Western musical styles. While this factor may have stifled the aesthetic development of early electronic music as an expression of a uniquely Japanese style, there is no denying the importance of the NHK studio in nurturing the genre since the inception of the studio in 1954 (see Table 4.1). The emergence of Japanese electronic music onto the world stage was greatly furthered by works commissioned for *Expo '70*, the World's Fair at Osaka in 1970. At least 20 Japanese composers received commissions to produce new music for a variety of pavilions at the fair, forming a competition resulting in many spectacular presentations.[12] Many of these works were electronic in nature and provided an opportunity for Japanese composers to work with some of their Western counterparts. As might be expected, the studios of the NHK figured prominently in the development of original tape music for many of these pieces.

Stockhausen visited Japan in 1966 at the invitation of the NHK studios and was commissioned to compose two works, one of which was the electronic piece *Telemusik*. Comprised of five recorded tracks, the work consisted of recorded fragments of ethnic world music combined with electronic sounds, often blended and modulated to produce new sonorities. For live performances, Stockhausen produced spatial projections of the music through the use of a panoramic mixing console to sweep the sound around the listening space. He used a specially constructed six-channel tape machine at the NHK studios to compose the work and collaborated closely with his Japanese colleagues, transforming his residency into a valuable workshop of techniques for the local composers. Yuasa was inspired by this experience to compose his work *Icon on the Source of White Noise* (1967), employing filtered white noise and exploring the spatial projection of electronic music as a means for creating live performances.[13]

Table 4.1   **Key Japanese electronic music studios, 1948–67***

Studio location	Affiliation	Year established	Sample of works completed
Tokyo, Japan: Electronic Music Studio	Sony Corporation	1951	*Toraware no Onna* (Akiyama, 1951); *Another World* (Yuasa, 1953); *Relief Statique* (Takemitsu, 1954); *Sky, Horse, Death* (Takemitsu, 1958).
Tokyo, Japan: Electronic Music Studio	Nippon Hōsō Kyōkai (NHK, Japanese Broadcasting Corporation)	1954	*Music for Sine Wave by Proportion of Prime Numbers* (Mayuzumi, 1955); *Musique Concrète for Stereophonic Broadcast* (Shibata, 1955); *Shichi no Variation* (*7 Variations*) (Moroi and Mayuzumi, 1956); *Otoko no shi* (*Death of a Man*) (Takemitsu, 1957); *Ondine* (Miyoshi, 1959); *A Red Cocoon* (Moroi, 1960); *Phonogène* (Takahashi, 1962); *Parallel Music* (Ichiyanagi, 1962); *Telemusik* (Stockhausen, 1966); *Comet Ikeya* (Yuasa, 1966).
Tokyo, Japan: Electronic Music Studio	Sogetsu Art Center (formerly the Sony studio)	1960	*Hi Ho 19* (Akiyama, 1960); *Water Music* (Takemitsu, 1960); *Aoi no Ue* (Yuasa, 1961); *Time* (Takahashi, 1962); *Mixture* (Ichiyanagi, 1963); *Music for Strings No. 2* (Ichiyanagi, 1966).

Note: *Studios listed include key private and institutional facilities that were used by more than one composer. Excludes private studios used by only one individual.

Expo '70 proved to be the catalyst for a generation of Japanese electronic musicians who sought to develop a style of music that was clearly distinguishable from the music of Europe and America. This evolution in Japanese electronic music coincided with the establishment of several university-based electronic music studios, notably at the Tokyo University of Fine Art and Music (1966), the College of Art and Technology of Kyushu (1967), Osaka Art University (1969), Aichi Prefectural Art University (1971), Tokyo Gakugei University (1972), and the Kunitachi College of Music (1974).[14] The availability of institutional studios made it possible for young composers to remain in Japan to learn the techniques of electronic music rather than study abroad. As a result, a more uniquely Japanese style of new music began to emerge. Interestingly, by the late 1970s, Japan had also overtaken the West in becoming the leading supplier of commercially available electronic music instruments, a factor that influenced the creation of many private studios and the appearance of several popular electronic musicians such as Isao Tomita (b. 1932), Kitaro (b. 1953), and Ryuichi Sakamoto (b. 1952).

Japanese Electronic Music Beyond the Studio

The work of composer Takehisa Kosugi (b. 1938) represented a transition from the tape music studio of the 1950s to live, improvised, and experimental composition that took shape in the 1960s. Trained as a violinist, Kosugi graduated from the Tokyo University of Arts in 1962. As a follower of the music of John Cage, Kosugi and his colleagues represented a decided break from the German-influenced work of the NHK studio and even Jikken Kobo. In 1961, Kosugi co-founded Group Ongaku, an avant-garde performing ensemble, with several other Japanese experimenters, including Toshi Ichiyanagi, Yasunao Tone (b. 1935), and Yuji Takahashi (b. 1938), all to become well-known leaders of the then fledgling Japanese experimental music movement. The group gave its first public performance in Japan in 1961 and, during the course of their short two-year tenure, introduced Japanese audiences to Asian premieres of musical works by such composers as John Cage, Christian Wolff, and Morton Feldman. These performances sparked interest in electronic and experimental music in Japan, provided a new audience for Western electronic music composers, and inspired a new generation of Japanese composers.

Kosugi, Tone, and Yoko Ono (b. 1933) also became associated with the *Fluxus*—a loose collective of experimental artists from many cultures spawned by the teaching work of John Cage at New York's New School for Social Research (1957–59) and officially considered a performance art "movement" in 1962 under the guidance of artist and organizer George Maciunas (1931–78). Fluxus was known for its live, improvisatory, and multimedia "happenings," of which Kosugi, Tone, and Ono were frequently a part. Much of the Fluxus music was task-oriented, providing seemingly simple instructions to be followed by the performer, such as *Watch a flower until one of them falls or until all of them fall* (Kosugi, 1964),[15] or *Cut a hole in a bag filled with seeds of any kind and place the bag where there is wind* (Ono, 1961).[16] Kosugi's piece *Anima 7* (1964) required the artist to simply perform "any action as slowly as possible."[17] Instructions such as these shifted the focus of the performer to the action rather than the musical result, which was Kosugi's way of introducing a new sense of discovery to the experience of music.

Whereas much of the earliest Japanese electronic music was formed around Western musical ideas, Kosugi's work consistently embodied Japanese sensibilities toward a unity of time, space, and the physicality of being. *Anima 7* drew in upon itself by accentuating the passing of time and its relation to the physical actions of the performer. Kosugi's earlier works, such as *Anima 1* (1961) and *Anima 2* (1962), required one to become wrapped up in string or to be sealed inside a large zippered bag, both pieces being immersed in a physical act not normally associated with music or performance. Kosugi's concept of "multimedia" involved more than the listening experience. "Rather than placing the focus on sound," Kosugi explained, "what I'm trying to do is capture a more diverse side of the media and the varied state of the situation or setting that surrounds the sound . . . What I'm after is not merely sound, but the waves themselves."[18] Kosugi's *Catch Wave* (1969) embodied this philosophy in literal terms by staging a game of catch with two sine wave generators emitting **ultrasonic** frequency tones outside of the range of human hearing. During the game of catch, the signals became sporadically joined, modulating into an audible frequency—the same principle of heterodyning used in the Theremin.

EARLY ELECTRONIC MUSIC IN SOUTHEAST ASIA AND CHINA

Electronic music took root in Japan soon after its appearance in Europe and America, but was much slower to develop in other Asian countries. This was primarily due to economic and political conditions that deflected the influence of Western culture and provided little in the way of institutional support for the creation of music laboratories. Most of the Asian electronic music created by 1970 had been realized by Japanese composers or others working in Western countries. Indonesian composer Slamet Sjukur (b. 1935) is mostly known for his work in chamber, vocal, and dance music. In 1963, while working at the GRM studio with Schaeffer, he composed electronic music for the ballet *Latigrak*, which premiered in Paris. He did not compose a second work of purely electronic music until 20 years later, although he continued to incorporate aspects of electronics in his multimedia stage productions.[19] In addition, there were Asian composers who emulated the modernism of Westerners such as Cage, Varèse, and Xenakis, but did not dabble directly in electronic music. The Philippine composer José Maceda (1917–2004) admired Varèse and worked in the Paris GRM studio in 1958–59 with Pierre Schaeffer. While there he also met Stockhausen, Boulez, and Xenakis, but did not add a work of tape music to his long list of interesting creations. Instead, using his training as an ethnomusicologist, Maceda organized a series of participatory, ritualized musical concert events leveraging audio technology to create a collective, urban listening experience. His audio material consisted of fragments of Philippine village music curated as part of his ethnomusical studies. *Cassette 100* (1971) was for 100 audience members and cassette players. For *Ugnayan* (1974), Maceda recruited 20 radio stations to simultaneously broadcast different fragments of his village music recordings.[20] For this work, he encouraged listeners to tune in with portable radios and create a mix of their own by experiencing the broadcasts of several stations at once, a brilliant real-time experiment in *musique concrète*.

Interestingly, when electronic music did finally take root in China and Southeast Asia in the 1970s, it eschewed the imitative quality of the first electronic music in Japan and succeeded in blending the techniques and musical ideas of Western composers with local music traditions.

Indonesia

Sjukur was the first Indonesian composer to dabble in electronic music before the introduction of synthesizer. The availability of more affordable electronic instruments such as synthesizers in the 1970s led to the exploration of electronic music by several other Indonesian composers. Interestingly, much of the work of these artists embraced elements of their indigenous music and instruments, even adopting traditional Indonesian musical scales, such as the pentatonic scale associated with gamelan music. Tape works from this era include *Batas Echo* (1978) by Harry Ruesli (1951–2004), better known for his work as a rock musician and activist, and *Kemelut* (1979) by Otto Sidharta (b. 1955), a concrete piece using the sounds of water as raw material. Much of Sidharta's work over the years has continued to explore the possibilities of combining electronic music with environmental sounds.

Many of the composers associated with the development of electronic music in Indonesia are better known for their work with the development of traditional music and education. Sapto Raharjo (1955–2009) learned to play gamelan and studied Javanese dance as a teen. He is best known as a supporter of contemporary gamelan music. Raharjo was devoted to modernizing the canon for gamelan and credited with combining the gamelan with electronic music to extend the possibilities of traditional Javanese instruments. His first work combining synthesizer with gamelan was *Yogya Harmony 78* (1978). Much of his subsequent work combined synthesizer with a variety of Indonesian and Western instruments. In 1987 he produced a performance blending many musical styles, billing it as *Gamelan Meets Synthesizer Meets Art Rock*, in his home of Jakarta.

China

Electronic music arrived even later in China and virtually did not exist before experiments with synthesizers at the Beijing Conservatory of Music in 1984. The Conservatory sponsored the first concert of electronic music by Chinese composers in the same year. Composers who were represented included Tan Dun, Zhu Shi-rui, and Zhou Long, and most of the music was produced using synthesizers and prerecorded sounds.[21] This early work led to the establishment of several university programs and studios devoted to electronic music, the most important of which has been the *Center of Electroacoustic Music of China* at the Central Conservatory of Music in Beijing, founded in 1993. Several of the key educators and composers associated with Chinese electronic music, including Yuanlin Chen (b. 1957) and Zhang Xiaofu (b. 1954), have studied abroad in the United States and Europe. Zhang is one of the best-known figures in Chinese electronic music. He did advanced studies in Paris during the early 1990s, learning the latest electronic music technology at the GRM studios founded by Schaeffer. As a result of his academic links, Zhang has succeeded in developing an active exchange program for composers living in China and Europe and has sponsored several international conferences for electronic music in Beijing. His works embrace elements of Asian and Western culture.

EARLY ELECTRONIC MUSIC IN JAPAN

1 *Toraware no Onna* (*Imprisoned Woman*) by Kuniharu Akiyama
   The first work of tape music completed in Japan

2 *Les Œuvres pour musique concrète x, y, z* (1953) by Toshiro Mayuzumi
   The first piece of Japanese tape music broadcast over the radio in Japan

3 *Another World* (1953) by Joji Yuasa
   Tape music and accompanying slide projection (performed live in 1955)

4 *Studie I: Music for Sine Wave by Proportion of Prime Number* (1955) by Toshiro Mayuzumi
   Produced at the electronic music studio of NHK (Tokyo)

5 *Musique Concrète for Stereophonic Broadcast* (1955) by Minao Shibata
   The first stereo tape piece completed at the NHK studio (Tokyo)

6 *Relief Statique* (1956) by Toru Takemitsu
   Completed at the Sony studios of Jikken Kobo

7 *Shichi no Variation* (*7 Variations*) (1956) by Makato Moroi and Toshiro Mayuzumi
   Completed at the NHK studio

8 *Otoko no shi* (*Death of a Man*) by Toru Takemitsu
   Completed at the NHK studio

9 *Sky, Horse, Death* (1958) by Toru Takemitsu
   Completed at the Sony studios of Jikken Kobo

10 *Ondine* (1959) by Akira Miyoshi
   Electronic music to accompany a stage production

LISTEN

SUMMARY

- Electronic music in Japan was initially inspired by works coming out of the Paris and Cologne studios; it represented the first infusion of Asian culture into the new genre.

- Japanese composers Takemitsu and Shibata anticipated the use of electronics to produce music as early as 1948.

- In 1951, the Tokyo Telecommunications Engineering Corporation—now Sony—provided early tape recorders and studio facilities to composers associated with the Jikken Kobo (Experimental Workshop).

- The first completed examples of Japanese tape music were *Toraware No Onna* (*Imprisoned Woman*) and *Piece B* by Akiyama in 1951.

- The Nippon Hōsō Kyōkai (NHK) electronic music studio was founded by composers Moroi and Mayuzumi and a coalition of NHK radio producers and engineers in 1954. The studio design and equipment was modeled after the WDR studio in Cologne.

- The first wave of Japanese electronic music was largely based on serial composition techniques first tried by German composers including Stockhausen.

- Electronic music was much slower to take root in Asian countries other than Japan. When it did in China and Southeast Asia in the 1970s, it eschewed the imitative quality of the first electronic music in Japan and succeeded in blending the techniques and musical ideas of Western composers with local music traditions.

MILESTONES

Early Electronic Music of Japan

Technical and scientific	Year	Music and instruments
– Masaru Ibuka and physicist Akio Morita founded Tokyo Tsushin Kogyo KK, an electronics manufacturing firm.	1946	
	1948–49	– Composers Toru Takemitsu and Minao Shibata independently wrote about the possible use of electronic technology to produce music.
– Tokyo Tsushin Kogyo KK produced Japan's first magnetic tape recorder, the "G-Type."	1950	
– Jikken Kobo (Experimental Workshop) established by a cooperative of musicians and other artists. – Tokyo Tsushin Kogyo KK provided Jikken Kobo with recording equipment to produce electronic music experiments.	1951	– Kuniharu Akiyama produced *Toraware no Onna* (*Imprisoned Woman*) and *Piece B*, the first works of tape music completed in Japan.
	1953	– The tape piece *Les Œuvres pour musique concrète x, y, z* by Toshiro Mayuzumi was broadcast over Japan public radio.
– NHK (Japanese Broadcasting Corporation) established its electronic music studio in Tokyo. – Tokyo Tsushin Kogyo KK changed it name to Sony.	1954	
	1955	– Makato Moroi visited Cologne to study the plan of the Cologne electronic music studio at WDR. – Mayuzumi completed three electronic works at the NHK studio: *Music for Sine Wave by Proportion of Prime Number* (1955), *Music for Modulated Wave by Proportion of Prime Number* (1955), and *Invention for Square Wave and Sawtooth Wave* (1955), using serialist techniques modeled after Stockhausen.
	1956	– Moroi and Mayuzumi completed *Shichi no Variation* (*7 Variations*), marking a high point in the Japanese serialist approach to composing with electronic tones.

PART II

Analog Synthesis and Instruments

CHAPTER 5

Tape Composition and Fundamental Concepts of Electronic Music

I think of the delay system as a time machine, because first you have to be present to make a sound and play it. Then it's recorded and played back in the future, so that what the future is essentially dealing with is really the past. So it sort of expands your sense of time.[1]
—Pauline Oliveros

Pauline Oliveros at the San Francisco Tape Music Center, 1965.
(John Bischoff, Mills College Center for Contemporary Music)

In 1966 the magnetic tape studio still represented the leading edge in electronic music technology. Just 18 short years after the establishment of the first major electronic music studio in Paris, there were at least 560 documented institutional and private tape studios in the world.[2] Of these, only 40 percent were sponsored by institutions and corporations, the rest being privately equipped and operated as a result of the increasing affordability of tape recorders, mixers, microphones, oscillators, and other basic tools of the trade. The year 1966 was pivotal because it marked the point at which the earliest analog music synthesizers were becoming known—a new trend in musical technology that would temporarily drive electronic musicians back to the confines of institutional studios, which were among the earliest adopters of the new and expensive equipment. The first synthesizers were not designed as performance instruments for making live music but rather as sophisticated, modular alternatives for producing electronic sounds for the tape studio. The development of analog synthesizers is the topic of the next chapter. Before leaping into the history of yet another episode in the evolution of music technology, this chapter pauses to assess the imprint made by early tape composition on the development of the electronic music field even to this day.

In spite of the numerous successive waves of music technology development, many of the basic aesthetic concepts and artistic choices that were invented by early composers of tape music remain at the core of electronic music still being produced today. These traits of electronic music can be traced not only to the exigencies of the tape medium itself, but also to the underlying principles that make electronic music different from music composed and performed for acoustic instruments. This chapter explores the characteristics that differentiate electronic music from other kinds of music and examines the roots of the aesthetic choices, effects, and techniques of electronic music that are descended from the early days of tape composition.

SEVEN FUNDAMENTAL TRAITS OF ELECTRONIC MUSIC

The emergence of electronic music in the 1950s was yet another example of the ability of musical culture to reinvent itself through new approaches to instrumentation, style, and structure. Writing in the first issue of the contemporary music journal *die Reihe*, musicologist H. H. Stuckenschmidt (1901–88) characterized electronic music as the Third Stage in the aesthetic history of music, the first two being the invention of vocal music and instrumental music:

> Music has developed further and further away from its human origins; now, at what we define as its Third Stage, the Electronic, we are astonished and not without pride, to have before us an art, totally controlled by the spirit of man, in a way not previously imaginable.[3]

Early practitioners of electronic music, regardless of their school of thought toward composing music, uniformly recognized several key aspects of electronic music that distinguished it from making music in a traditional way. These guiding principles can be divided into seven traits:

1   **The sound resources available to electronic music are unlimited**. New sounds can be constructed from the raw material of electronic waveforms. The composer not only creates the music, but composes the very sounds themselves. Eimert explained the innate potential of electronic music in the following way:

> The composer, in view of the fact that he is no longer operating within a strictly ordained tonal system, finds himself confronting a completely new situation. He sees himself commanding a realm of sound in which the musical material appears for the first time as a malleable continuum of every known and unknown, every conceivable and possible sound. This demands a way of thinking in new dimensions, a kind of mental adjustment to the thinking proper to the materials of electronic sound.[4]

The composer can invent sounds that do not exist in nature or radically transform natural sounds into new instruments. For *Thema–Omaggio a Joyce*, Berio used tape manipulation to transform the spoken voice into a myriad of sound patterns eerily laced with the tonalities of human communication. In the piece *Luna* (1984), Wendy Carlos (b. 1939) modeled a digital instrument, the voice of which could be modified in real time as it played a theme, metamorphosing from the sound of a violin to a clarinet to a trumpet and ending with a cello sound. This sound wasn't possible in the world outside of the computer, but became possible with her library of "real-world orchestral replicas" that the GDS and Synergy synthesizers allowed.[5] For *Beauty in the Beast* (1986), Carlos took this experimentation a step further by "designing instrumental timbres that can't exist at all, extrapolated from the ones that do exist."[6]

2   **Electronic music can expand the perception of tonality**. On one hand, the invention of new pitch systems is made easier with electronic musical instruments. Microtonal music is more easily engineered by a composer who can subdivide an octave using software and a digital music keyboard than by a piano builder. On the other hand, electronic music also stretches the concept of pitch in the opposite direction, toward less defined tonality into the realm of noise. All sounds may be considered equally important increments on the electromagnetic spectrum. Varèse sensed this early on and introduced controlled instances of noise in his instrumental and electronic music. Cage accepted the value of all sounds without question and let them be themselves:

> Noises are as useful to new music as so-called musical tones, for the simple reason that they are sounds. This decision alters the view of history, so that one is no longer concerned with tonality or atonality, Schoenberg or Stravinsky (the twelve tones or the twelve expressed as seven plus five), nor with consonance and dissonance, but rather with Edgard Varèse who fathered forth noise into twentieth-century music. But it is clear that ways must be discovered that allow noises and tones to be just noises and tones, not exponents subservient to Varèse's imagination.[7]

3   **Electronic music exists in a state of actualization**. Igor Stravinsky (1882–1971) wrote that "it is necessary to distinguish two moments, or rather two states of music: potential music and actual music . . . It exists as a score, unrealized, and as a performance."[8]

In the world of electronic music there are many works that cannot be accurately transcribed and reproduced from a printed score. The underlying reason for this is that electronic music is a medium in which the composer directly creates the performance either as a recording or a live performance. There is rarely a need for somebody else to interpret or read a score other than the composer. Many works are realized directly only one time using electronic media for the purpose of creating a recording. This is not to deny attempts made by composers to score electronic music. But scoring often results in a composer devising a unique form of notation to define the elements of a work that is especially suited to whatever sound-generating technology is available to them. For *Studie II*, Stockhausen developed a graphical score using geometric shapes representing the pitch and dynamic components of the sine waves used to create the piece. In this case, specific pitches and dynamics were determined with such precision that an accurate reproduction is possible using other media. One such faithful realization of *Studie II* was completed 52 years after the original in 2006 by German composer Georg Hajdu using the graphical programming language *Max/MSP* for laptop computer. The work *Game* (1975) by Carl Michaelson was written for two flutes and ring modulator; the flutists perform notes prescribed using a conventional score and their output is miked and modulated using a ring modulator with settings noted by the composer. There is no standardization for the creation of a score for electronic music. The scores for many electronic works consist of written instructions and vary widely depending on the needs of the composer. *I Am Sitting in a Room* (1969) by Alvin Lucier (b. 1931) was an experiment in the degenerative effects of recording and re-recording the same sound using a microphone and two tape recorders. The basic sound material was a written text passage provided by the composer. The instructions consisted of the procedural steps needed to record and re-record the sound "through many generations" and instructions for splicing them "together in chronological order" to "make a tape composition the length of which is determined by the length of the original statement and the number of generations recorded."[9] But even such a seemingly straightforward set of instructions will have widely varying results depending on the acoustical properties of the room in which the piece is recorded, the fidelity of the tape recording equipment, and the number of generations of the passage recorded. Originally intended as a recorded tape piece, a live, real-time realization was performed in 2000 by Christopher Burns using a program called *Pure Data* (*Pd*) for the creation of interactive computer music. In his interpretation, Burns chose not to fix the duration of the performance ahead of time because he was "unsure of how quickly the process would unfold when the intended performance space was filled with an audience."[10]

Experiencing electronic music is a part of its actualization. The term **realization** was adopted by electronic music pioneers to describe the act of assembling a finished work. A work of electronic music is not real—does not exist—until a performance is realized, or played in real time.

Other than assisting the composer in making notes for the realization of a work, reasons for creating or publishing a score include providing an example that might be instructional for others, copyrighting a work, and providing instructions for instrumentalists when a work can be performed live.

4   **Electronic music has a special relationship with the temporal nature of music.**
"Music presupposes before all else a certain organization in time, a chronomony."[11]

The plastic nature of electronic music allows the composer to record all of the values associated with a sound (e.g. pitch, timbre, envelope) in a form that can be shifted and reorganized in time. The ability to modify the time or duration of a sound is one of its most fundamental characteristics. Traditional instrumental music, once recorded, benefits from a similar control over the manipulation of a real-time performance. The equivalency between space and time that Cage attributed to the coming of magnetic tape recording—and which can be extended to any form of analog or digital sound recording, MIDI control signals, or even a performance sequence outlined in *Max/MSP*—has the liberating effect of allowing the composer to place a sound at any point in time at any tempo.

5   **In electronic music, sound itself becomes the material of composition**. The ability to get inside the physics of a sound and directly manipulate its characteristics provides an entirely new resource for composing music. The unifying physics behind all sounds—pitched and unpitched alike—allow a composer to treat all sounds as being materially equal.

6   **Electronic music does not breathe: it is not affected by the limitations of human performance**. As Robert Ashley learned about electronic music early on, "It can go on as long as the electricity comes out of the wall."[12] The ability to sustain or repeat sounds for long periods of time—much longer than would be practical for live instrumentalists—is a natural resource of electronic music. In contrast to its sustainability, electronic music can play rhythms too complex and rapid for any person to perform. The composer is freed from the physical limitations of human performance and can construct new sounds and performances of an intricacy that can only exist when played by a machine.

7   **Electronic music often lacks a point of comparison with the natural world of sounds, providing a largely mental and imaginative experience**. Hearing is a "distance" sense, as opposed to the "proximal" senses of touch and taste. The essence of electronic music is its disassociation with the natural world. Listening engages the intellect and imagination to interpret what is heard, providing "only indirect knowledge of what matters—requiring interpretations from knowledge and assumptions, so you can read meaning into the object world."[13] Having little basis in the object world, electronic music becomes the pulse of an intimate and personal reality for the listener. Its source is mysterious. "It is thought, imagined and engraved in memory. It's a music of memory."[14] In these ways, the human being becomes the living modulator of the machine product; the circuitry dissolves into the spirit of humanness that envelops it.

TAPE COMPOSITION METHODS AND TECHNIQUES

Until the arrival of the magnetic **reel-to-reel tape recorder**, electronic music had only been a live performance medium using instruments such as the Theremin, *Ondes Martenot*, or the humble turntable. The tape recorder transformed the field of electronic music overnight by making it a composer's medium. Most classical music composition for the Theremin and *Ondes Martenot* came to a halt during the 1950s as composers turned to the tape medium to explore new sonic possibilities. The early practitioners of tape music sought new sounds, structures, and tonalities by working directly with the raw materials of sound.

Composing with Tape

For the early adapters of magnetic tape composition—Schaeffer, Henry, Cage, Luening, Ussachevsky, and Varèse—the medium had the liberating effect of separating the creation of music from the traditional practice of scoring and notating parts. John Cage put it plainly when he told the author:

> It made one aware that there was an equivalence between space and time, because the tape you could see existed in space, whereas the sounds existed in time. That immediately changed the notation of music. We didn't have to bother with counting one-two-three-four anymore. We could if we wanted to, but we didn't have to. We could put a sound at any point in time.[15]

To understand what Cage meant you may have had to visit an electronic music studio. There was usually a rack from which hung pieces of tape that had not yet been spliced together. Holding a strip of magnetic tape in one's hand was equivalent to seeing and touching sound. You could manipulate this normally elusive phenomenon in ways that were previously unavailable to composers. It was a technological, psychological, and social breakthrough without parallel for music.

Karlheinz Stockhausen had a similar revelation about the materiality of time when using the magnetic tape medium. By speeding up or slowing down a sound—even a conventionally musical sound—all of the characteristics comprising the physics of a sound could be leveled by the hammer of technology. Rhythm once organized in familiar meters could be sped up or slowed down beyond the point of recognition. Such elements as the timbre of chosen instruments, harmony, and melody could each be transformed uniformly and unequivocally by so many inches-per-second of tape running on a variable-speed tape recorder. Chords could be sped up to become beats and rhythms. Rhythms could be slowed down to become drones. The components of a musical work were all reduced to the common denominator of vibration. This was the unified field theory of serialism "in which duration, pitch and color were aspects of the same thing."[16] Stockhausen called it the "unified time domain."[17] These insights were shared by many other composers who first worked with magnetic tape in Paris, Cologne, Milan, New York, and other early studios.

Even though the practice of composing with magnetic tape is obsolete today, many of the most fundamental effects associated with electronic music originated with the pioneers who learned how to push the limitations of this fragile medium. The state of the art may have shifted from magnetic tape to digital media but the basic concepts of sound manipulation born over 50 years ago still apply. Most of these techniques are still fundamental to the recording and manipulation of sounds using digital media and software. In fact, most software designed for the editing and processing of sounds continues to borrow its lexicon of terms and controls from the world of magnetic tape, where the concepts of Record, Play, Fast Forward, Rewind, and Pause were first applied.

Tape Splicing

The cutting and splicing of magnetic tape is, in effect, no different from moving sound around in time and space. A magnetic tape recording is linear in that the signal is recorded from the start of the tape to its end

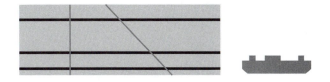

Figure 5.1   Splicing block.

as it passes across the recording head of the tape recorder. The recording head instills an electromagnetic imprint of the audio signal onto the iron oxide coating of the tape. This imprint is not permanently fixed and can be recorded over or disturbed by bringing it into close proximity with any strong magnetic field such as that of a loudspeaker. A recorded sound is played by passing the taped signal across a playback head that translates the magnetic imprint into an audible sound. The magnetic tape recording process is **analog**, meaning that no digitization of the signal is used to record or playback sounds.

Tape editing or **splicing** allows a sound that occurred at one time or location in a recording to be moved to another, changing the linear sequence of the original recording. Conceptually, splicing relies on the linear nature of the tape medium in which one sound follows another, unlike the random access nature of digital media other than digital tape.

The mechanics of magnetic tape splicing are simple. Tape is placed on open reels, mounted on a tape recorder, and manually moved across the playback head to locate a point in the sound where an edit is to occur. Locating a sound on tape can be likened to the manual spinning of a vinyl record by a DJ to cue up a particular point in a recording. The composer's only other tools are a ruler to "measure" time in inches or centimeters of tape, a razor blade, a **splicing block** (see Figure 5.1), and splicing tape or glue to join two ends of tape to form a permanent edit. The splicing block is a rectangular aluminum block with a slot to securely hold a length of magnetic tape. It is made of aluminum to avoid magnetization of the block that could add noise to the splice. The splicing block has two narrow channels across the width of the tape to guide a razor blade while the tape is cut. One slot is perpendicular to the tape and the other angled to provide a diagonal cut. A diagonal cut is potentially stronger because the joint between the two pieces of tape is longer and more gradual than a simple vertical cut. A vertical cut is also more likely to cause an audible popping sound when the edit is played back. To splice magnetic tape together, the end of each piece of tape is mounted on the splicing block and then trimmed with a razor blade using one of the cutting channels as a guide. Using the cutting channels ensures that the two lengths of tape to be joined are trimmed at precisely the same angle. The ends of tapes are then inserted into the splicing block channel and butted up against each other in the track of the splicing block and joined with splicing tape.

From this limited technology arose various philosophies about splicing tape. The object was first and foremost to create an absolutely silent cut. The slightest misadventure with matching up the two ends of tape, a bubble in the splicing tape, or dust in the adhesive of the splicing tape could result in an audible pop in the edited sound. Various tricks of the trade came about because of this, including the "hourglass" splice, which reduced the width of the tape at the point of a splice, providing less surface area for

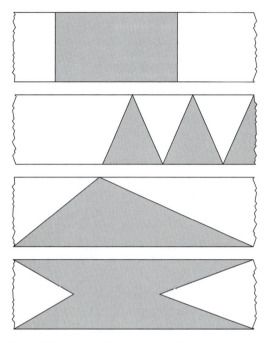

Figure 5.2   Examples of tape splicing techniques, each having a different effect on the transition of one sound to another.

noise during the transition from one piece of tape to the next. Unfortunately, this method could momentarily reduce the amplitude of the signal at the point of the splice—an effect that was sometimes audible.

Splicing could be used in a limited way to change the attack and decay patterns of recorded sounds (see Figure 5.2). A long, angled splice of several inches would create a perceptible dissolve from one sound to the next. Cutting periodic segments of blank tape—or **leader tape**, the non-magnetic protective tape at the beginning or end of a reel—into a passage of continuous sound could induce a rhythmic or pulsing effect. Cuts made at right angles created a sharper, percussive jump from sound to sound. Cage experimented with radically extreme splices when he produced *Williams Mix* (1952), using the shape and angle of splices to alter the slope of attack and decay of recorded sounds. Morton Feldman used leader tape to space the sequence of sounds that he pre-recorded for assembling *Intersection* (1953).

In practice, composers in the classic tape studio followed a three-step process for composing with tape. The first step involved *the recording of raw material*—sounds developed by whatever means and recorded onto magnetic tape. The second step involved listening to the tapes and *extracting sections of sound to be used in the final assembly* of the piece. These sounds were literally spliced out of the original tape, labeled, and stored for easy access, often on a wall rack where the pieces of tape could be hung. The third step was *assembling the chosen segments of tape into the desired sequence* using a splicing block and splicing tape. Barring any additional remixing or modification, the final edited sequence comprised the master tape of the work.

Degeneration of a Recorded Signal

The fidelity of a magnetic tape recording will degenerate with each successive copy of the original or master. This is due to noise introduced in the recording process and the inability of the tape machine and tape medium to respond equally well to all frequencies of sound. Master or first-generation tapes include the least amount of noise. All other factors being equal, recordings made at a higher tape transport speed with have improved fidelity because the denseness of the incoming signal will be extended over a longer length of tape, raising the threshold of frequency and dynamic response at the point where the tape meets the record head. While high-speed recording and dubbing can improve the fidelity of copies, some level of noise is always going to creep into a copy of a tape. Until the introduction of digital recording—which allows for the making of copies that are as good as the master—composers needed to be mindful of noise as a necessary evil of the magnetic tape composition process.

CLASSIC TAPE COMPOSITION TECHNIQUES

1 *Intersection* (1953) by Morton Feldman
  Feldman used leader tape to add patches of silence required by his piece

2 *I Am Sitting in a Room* (1969) by Alvin Lucier
  An experiment in the degeneration of magnetic tape sounds

3 *Discreet Music* (1975) by Brian Eno
  Used tape delay with multiple tape recorders

4 *Invention in Twelve Tones* (1952) by Otto Luening
  Used tape echo

5 *Beautiful Soop* (1967) by Pauline Oliveros
  Used multiple tape echo signals

6 *Le Microphone bien tempéré* (1950–52) by Pierre Henry
  Used reverberation

7 *Music for the Gift* (1963) by Terry Riley
  One of the first uses of tape delay with multiple tape recorders

8 *I of IV* (1966) by Pauline Oliveros
  Combined multiple tape delay system with the gradual degeneration of the audio signal

9 *Cinq études de bruits: Étude violette* (1948) by Pierre Schaeffer
  Early application of backwards sounds using a turntable

10 *Glissandi* (1957) by György Ligeti
  Extensive use of tape speed variation and backwards sounds

LISTEN

Some composers have used the degenerating effect of tape copying as an element in their compositions. This effect was the underlying idea behind Brian Eno's (b. 1948) *Discreet Music* (1975), in which two short melodic lines played on a synthesizer were recorded onto a long loop of tape that was channeled through two tape recorders. The recording made on the first machine was then played on the second machine, the output of which was then played back into the recording input of the first machine. In this way the first tape recorder continued to make successively degenerating copies of the original recording. Once set in motion, Eno did little to modify the sound other than "occasionally altering the timbre of the synthesizer's output by means of a graphic equalizer."[18]

The crowning achievement in the use of tape degeneration in electronic music was *I Am Sitting in a Room* (1970) by Alvin Lucier, completed five years prior to *Discreet Music*. The score for the piece, described earlier in this chapter, was devised after an evening of acoustical experimentation by the composer. Lucier explained the genesis of the piece as follows:

> I had heard that Bose had tested his loudspeakers by doing some kind of a
> cycling process to see where the frequencies were. I tried it out in *I Am Sitting in*

> *a Room*. I did it one night in an apartment that I was in. I thought up that text right there that night. I wrote it down, without much editing, and then with a pair of tape recorders, a KLH loudspeaker, and an amplifier I just made that piece. I set up the two tape recorders outside the apartment so there wouldn't be any noise from the machinery. I sat inside with a microphone and spoke the text two or three times to get the volume right. Then I put the loudspeaker up where I had been sitting so that the speaker became my voice. The evening was spent with these machines and I would play back the original text recording through the speaker into the microphone to a second machine. I would check that to make sure that the volume was all right. Then I rewound that, spliced it onto the first machine, and played that back. I spliced it 16 times. It took me all night. So the final product is that tape.[19]

In this work, the acoustics of the room provided a natural filter for the sound that was being "heard" by the microphone, accentuating certain frequencies and dampening others. As the piece progressed, only the sharpest characteristics of the sound continued to propagate during each successive generation of recordings, eventually disintegrating into an unintelligible, pulsating set of modulations. It was the aural equivalent of the visual degeneration that takes place when you make successive photocopies of photocopies.

Tape Echo, Reverberation, Loops, and Delay

The tape recorder made possible several basic techniques for repeating sounds that have been popular since the earliest experiments with tape composition. Echo, delay, and tape loops are among the effects that persist conceptually in the manipulation of sound by digital systems today.

Echo is the repetition of a single sound that gradually decays in amplitude and clarity with each successive repetition until it fades away. This was first achieved using tape recorders equipped with three "heads"—the erase, recording, and playback heads—across which magnetic tape was transported to erase, record, or play sounds.

To create echo with a tape recorder, the playback output signal of the machine was fed back into the input, or record head, of the same machine (see Figure 5.3). In this configuration, the tape recorder was simultaneously recording and then playing back the sound just recorded. The distance that the tape must travel from the record head to the playback head, and the speed of the tape transport, determined the length of the delay. Continuing in this manner without interruption created the echo effect and the signal degenerated in strength, or amplitude, with each successive echo. The strength or persistence of the echo—how many repetitions were possible—was determined by the amplitude of the playback signal being fed back into the recorder. The stronger the signal, the longer the sequence of repeats. Turning up the playback to the point of distortion produced echo "frizz"—echoes that eventually became stronger than the source signal and produced a **white noise** effect.

Tape echo quickly became a staple effect of electronic music composition. While the French and German schools used echo only sparingly in their earliest works, perhaps because they had so many other audio resources at their disposal, the effect was popular with composers working in America who had little more than tape recorders with which

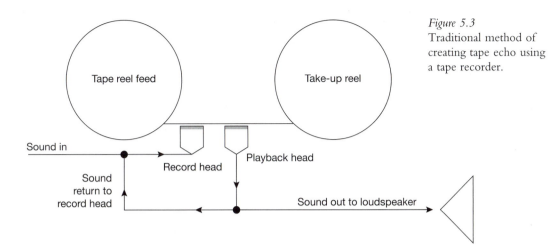

Figure 5.3
Traditional method of creating tape echo using a tape recorder.

to work. In New York, Otto Luening utilized echo as an important structural element in his early works that modified the sound of the flute, such as *Low Speed* (1952) and *Invention in Twelve Tones* (1952).

By the 1960s, a variety of dedicated black box devices were manufactured to produce echo. Designed primarily for use by performing musicians such as rock artists, products such as the Echoplex were essentially tape recorders dedicated to the creation of echo. Inside such a device was a loop of magnetic tape along with the requisite erase, record, and playback heads. The sound to be enhanced with echo was patched in using a guitar cable. One advantage of these dedicated devices was that the distance between the record and playback heads could be adjusted to increase the length of time between echoes.

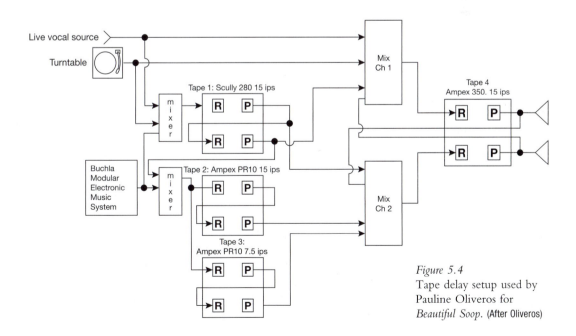

Figure 5.4
Tape delay setup used by Pauline Oliveros for *Beautiful Soop*. (After Oliveros)

Such analog echo devices have since been replaced by software programs and digital effects units that model their audio processing after the most familiar and interesting tape echo boxes of the past.

Composer Pauline Oliveros used tape echo as the structural process behind many of her groundbreaking works. In *Beautiful Soop* (1967), she used three different brands of tape recorders to create multiple echo effects simultaneously from the same input signal, exploiting the different distances between the record and playback heads of the different machines (see Figure 5.4). She described this complex circuit:

> With all the feedback loops in operation there is a shimmering effect on attacks, and interesting timbre changes on sustained sounds. Because every delay line was controlled by a separate mixing pot, as much or as little feedback [echo] as designed was introduced, and each delay line could be treated as a separate source. By sending delay lines to various modifying devices, a large number of variations could occur.[20]

The work combined fragments of Lewis Carroll verse recited by several people with synthesized tones, creating a dialog between the spoken word and synthetically produced music. Echo was liberally applied simultaneously to all of the material using three tape recorders, resulting in echo effects that were at times distinct but also multilayered and complex.

Reverberation is sometimes confused with echo and, although technically the two effects are based on a similar psychoacoustic phenomenon, reverberation is generally defined as minute or fractional time delays in the perception of sound waves as they bounce back from reflective surfaces of varying distances in the listening environment. Reverberation occurs naturally in any environment and is most obvious when experiencing the ambient characteristics of concert halls, sports arenas, and outdoor stadiums. Reverberation effects were created in the classic tape studio by mixing the source signal with ghost frequencies of itself. Before the advent of digital delay systems, this was commonly done using a simple physical device known as *spring reverberation*. The source signal was run through a metal coil and detected by a **pickup** at the other end. In traveling through the coil, the sound signal was delayed just slightly enough to create an artificially produced ghost sound when recombined with the undelayed source signal. The thickness of the wire and tightness of the coil affected the degree of reverberation that could be generated and the more sophisticated units had several options depending on the degree of reflectiveness desired.

Reverb was one of the most-used audio processing effects during the formative years of the Paris and Cologne studios. It was used in many early disc and tape works by Pierre Schaeffer and Pierre Henry in Paris, including their collaboration *Symphonie pour un homme seul* (1950) and Henry's first solo work of *musique concrète*, *Le Microphone bien tempéré* (1950–52), in which the composer used reverb and other effects to modify the sound of a piano in 16 short movements.

A length of tape can be spliced end to end to form a **tape loop**. The idea of tape loops pre-dated the use of magnetic tape and was borrowed from the lock grooves created by early turntablists, including Paul Hindemith and Pierre Schaeffer. Unlike echo, in which each repetition of an initial sound becomes weaker until it diminishes entirely, the sound repeated by a tape loop does not weaken.

Figure 5.5
Vladimir Ussachevsky with a specially designed tape loop feeding device for a tape recorder, 1965. (Columbia University Computer Music Center)

The rate at which a tape loop repeats is determined by the length of the loop and the playback speed of the tape machine. Digital **sampling** essentially mimics the creation of a loop, resulting in a sound that can be played by itself or "looped" in a repeating pattern. Digital samplers can be set to repeat a sound at the same volume in a looping cycle or allow it to diminish for an echo effect, blurring the line between what once were separate techniques in the analog world of tape machines.

Tape delay is an extended form of tape echo in which the time between repetitions is lengthened well beyond what can be normally achieved on a single tape recorder. This was most often done by using two or more widely spaced tape recorders through which a single length of magnetic tape was threaded. A sound was recorded on the first machine and played-back on the second, creating a long delay between the first occurrence of the sound and its repetition on the second machine. If the sound being played back on the second machine was simultaneously recorded by the first machine, an extended echo effect was created with long delays between successive, degenerating repetitions.

Tape delay has been used extensively by several composers. Its origins go back to the composers associated with the San Francisco Tape Music Center in 1960.[21] Terry Riley may have been the very first to compose a piece using this technique when he created *Music for the Gift* in 1963, possibly the first work to use the technique of a long tape loop fed through two widely separated tape machines. Riley was in Paris working with jazz musician Chet Baker's group when he got the idea:

> The accumulation technique hadn't been invented yet and it got invented during this session. I was asking the engineer, describing to him the kind of sound I had worked with in *Mescalin Mix* [an earlier tape composition]. I wanted this kind of long, repeated loop and I said "can you create something like that?" He got it by stringing the tape between two tape recorders and feeding the signal from

the second machine back to the first to recycle along with the new incoming signals. By varying the intensity of the feedback you could form the sound either into a single image without delay or increase the intensity until it became a dense chaotic kind of sound . . . The engineer was the first to create this technique that I know of. This began my obsession with time-lag accumulation feed-back.[22]

Oliveros's piece *I of IV* (1966) made extensive use of accumulative tape delay and degeneration of the repeating signal. Like Riley, Oliveros did this by threading one reel of tape through two tape recorders. The sound was recorded on the first machine, played back on the second, and fed back to the first machine to be recorded again. The distance between the two machines caused a lag of about eight seconds, a fairly long delay. The music was further layered by splitting the output signal and playing one version of the output directly, without delay, and then applying echo to the other output.

I of IV was made in July 1966, at the University of Toronto Electronic Music Studio. It was produced in real time, without edits, using a sound processing technique that Oliveros called the amplification of "combination tones and tape repetition." She explained:

The combination tone technique was one which I developed in 1965 at the San Francisco Tape Music Center. The equipment consisted of 12 sine tone square wave generators connected to an organ keyboard, 2 line amplifiers, mixer, Hammond spring-type reverb and 2 stereo tape recorders. 11 generators were set to operate above 20,000 Hz, and one generator at below 1 Hz. The keyboard output was routed to the line amplifiers, reverb, and then to channel A of recorder 1. The tape was threaded from recorder 1 to recorder 2. Recorder 2 was on playback only. Recorder 2 provided playback repetition approximately 8 seconds later. Recorder 1 channel A was routed to recorder 1 channel B and recorder 1 channel B to recorder 1 channel A in a double feedback loop. Recorder 2 channel A was routed to recorder 1 channel A, and recorder 2 channel B was routed to recorder 1 channel B. The tape repetition contributed timbre and dynamic changes to steady state sounds. The combination tones produced by the 11 generators and the bias frequencies of the tape recorders were pulse modulated by the sub-audio generator.[23]

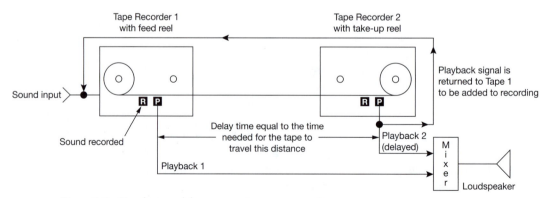

Figure 5.6   Simple tape delay setup using tape recorders.

LISTENING GUIDE 5.1

Title: *I of IV* (excerpt)

Artist: Pauline Oliveros   **Year**: 1966   **Duration**: 3:00

Genre: Tape composition using real-time tape delay

Electronic Instrumentation: Twelve sine wave oscillators (keyboard controlled), two tape recorders, two line amplifiers, mixer, spring-reverberation.

Background: This piece is built around a performance process that is conducted in real time. Therefore, the technique for creating this work is essentially that of live electronic music. Realized in the studios of the University of Toronto, where Oliveros was visiting, it is based on real-time tape manipulation and audio processing techniques first developed at the composer's home base, the San Francisco Tape Music Center. The main text of this chapter includes a detailed description of the composer's step-by-step process. In short, the work was created by recording a mix of 12 sine tones using the first tape machine and playing the sounds back on the second machine using a long tape loop and a time lag of about eight seconds. In addition, another version of the tones bypassed the delay entirely and is heard using echo effects. These outputs—tape delay and echo-treated sine waves—are combined by the composer in a real-time mix.

	Listen For: Accumulative tape delay and gradual degeneration of a repeating audio signal. Imagine the process of creating this work in real time.
0:00–1:20	The piece begins with an intense buzzing of multi-layered sound waves; after eight seconds you can hear a slight bump in the sound indicating that the tape delay system has begun. From this point onward, the composer continually adjusts the modulation, filtering, and mixing of the sine tones as the sound is recorded on a tape loop and fed to the playback head of the second machine. Oliveros is mixing the results to produce the sound that you hear, all in real time. For about the first minute, the buzzing sound dominates the mix. At about 60 seconds, Oliveros begins to adjust the sine wave tones to higher, more harmonic pitches and the buzzing sound gradually diminishes. She creates a mix of wavering, continuous tones accented by short, fuzzy bursts. The long, continuous tones blend into the background of the tape delay sequence, providing a droning effect that effectively masks the eight-second cycle of repetition. The long tones blend and interfere with one another, creating interesting beat frequency effects. The short, fuzzy bursts provide accents to the droning sounds, giving the music intermittent rhythmic moments. Notice how the composer selectively builds layers of new sounds on sounds that are repeating, forming complex rhythms and textures.
1:21–3:00	Beginning at about 1:21, you can hear the entrance of sine tones that bypass the tape delay and are being played by the composer using tape echo. These echoing tones, at first very clear and distinct, become a part of the tape delay mix and gradually diminish. For the remainder of the work beyond this excerpt, the composer continues to explore various combinations of sine tones, tape delay, and echo effects, gradually shifting the nature of the mix and fully exploring the timbral changes introduced by the effects of sound accumulation and degeneration.

Compare and Contrast

Discreet Music (1975) by Brian Eno
Erosphere (1981) by François Bayle
Live Echo (2007) by Susumu Yokota

FROM TAPE RECORDERS TO LAPTOPS—THE EVOLUTION OF *FONTANA MIX*

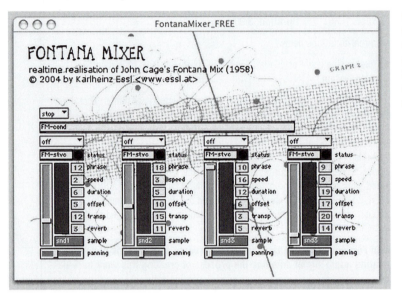

Figure 5.7
FontanaMixer, a real-time software performance program based on John Cage's score for *Fontana Mix*. (Karlheinz Essl)

The 1958 tape piece *Fontana Mix* by John Cage was a work whose composition was indeterminate—unfixed—in relationship to its performance. Cage accomplished this by introducing a randomization process to formulate each performance from a set of provided compositional materials. The score consisted of 10 sheets of paper and 12 transparencies. The sheets of paper had drawings of six curved lines differentiated by thickness and texture. Ten of the transparencies had randomly distributed points, the number of points per transparency being 7, 12, 13, 17, 18, 19, 22, 26, 29, and 30. Another transparency had a grid measuring two by ten inches and the tenth transparency contained a 10¾-inch straight line. The work was intended to be performed by "any kind and number of instruments."[24] The score materials were used to determine the parameters of each available instrumental part through a set of instructions: "Place a sheet with points over a drawing with curves (in any position). Over these place the graph. Use the straight line to connect a point within the graph with one outside."[25] Among Cage's additional instructions, all originally dictated by chance operations, was the selection of six elements (e.g. sound sources or a dynamic element such as amplitude) and up to 20 values that could be assigned to each of the six elements. Cage expressly stated that the composition was not "limited to tape music but may be used freely for instrumental, vocal, and theatrical purposes."[26] The composer also encouraged others to consider as an option the distribution of the sound in space.

For his first realization of the work, Cage created four monophonic tracks of magnetic tape music. Each of the four parts required a separate interpretation of the score and he drew from a variety of concrete sound sources for the audio material as he had been done for the earlier *Williams Mix*. The selection, duration, and editing sequence for each tape was based on the pattern of intersecting dots and lines rendered by each interpretation of the score.

INNOVATION

Cage's imaginative graphical score for *Fontana Mix* has been interpreted by many artists over the years. Most recently, two composers working independently have created computer versions of *Fontana Mix*. Canadian Matt Rogalsky (b. 1966) created *FontanaMixer* in 2002, an application for electronically generating a graphical score for *Fontana Mix* using a digital representation of Cage's graphical score (see Figures 5.7 and 5.8). Anyone can download the program and make up their own version of the work (http://royallyvague.com/fontananet). Rogalsky also developed *FontanaNet* (2002), a shared laptop version of the work that can be performed in real time by several interacting performers. Several players interact with a central computer that serves as the server for the work. Developed using the software tool *SuperCollider*, 20 different sampled sound sources are shared by the performers who then make changes to audio parameters as they each interpret a version of the score.

Performers act by (1) using the top two rows of keys on the laptop to select a sound sample; (2) pressing the spacebar to start the selected sound sample; and (3) pressing one of the z, x, c, v, or b keys to activate one of five dynamic settings including amplitude, pan speed, sample playback speed, high-pass filter cutoff frequency, or amplitude modulation depth, and then using a Wacom tablet to modify the values for the chosen dynamic parameter. Rogalsky also took into consideration the distribution of the sounds in space, explaining that "Each version of the sound travels independently around the circle of loudspeakers. They kind of wander around."[27]

Yet another laptop version of *Fontana Mix* was developed by Austrian composer Karlheinz Essl (b. 1960) in 2004. Essl's version, also called *FontanaMixer*, is a completely self-generating sound environment that the composer programmed using *Max/MSP*. Adhering to Cage's instructions, and providing four sound channels as in Cage's four-track tape version, Essl's program uses chance-based operations to assign values to each of six possible parameters affecting the sound source. The audio sources become highly modified using granular synthesis techniques. Essl's *FontanaMixer* (www.essl.at/works/fontana-mixer.html#english) is provided with four sound sources including the voice of John Cage and nature sounds, but the user is invited to replace any of the given sources with audio tracks of their own.

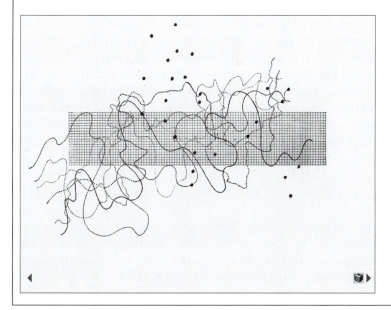

Figure 5.8
Matt Rogalsky's
FontanaMixer
program generates
individualized scores
for the performance of
Cage's *Fontana Mix*.
(Matt Rogalsky)

Oliveros's widely heard recording of *I of IV* in 1967 occupied the entire side of a CBS-Odyssey record album of electronic music. This recording can be credited with seeding the musical world with the idea of tape delay (see Figure 5.6) and has been often repeated by experimental composers, including Eno on *Discreet Music* and some related work for guitar by Robert Fripp. Fripp's real-time performances using dual tape recorders and a feedback delay system—dubbed *Frippertronics* by his friends—led Fripp and Eno to collaborate on the recordings *No Pussyfooting* (1972) and *Evening Star* (1974), each of which combined elements of rock music with Fripp's distinctive tape delay style of guitar playing.

Another Oliveros piece—*C(s) for Once* (1966)—used three tape recorders with one tape threaded through all three to affect the sounds being played of live voices, flutes, trumpets, and organ. Another notable work whose performance depended on a tape recorder was *Mugic* (1973), by Charles Amirkhanian. In this piece, the composer threaded a single reel of magnetic tape through the record and playback heads of three tape recorders. Spoken words were recorded on tape machine 1 and played back as a delayed signal on machines 2 and 3. Then, taking a page from Lucier's book, Amirkhanian also used a microphone to pick up the acoustic resonance of the sounds being played in the room so that the clarity of the dialog and playback signal gradually deteriorated as the piece continued.

Tape Reversal: Playing Sounds Backwards

The idea of playing recorded sounds in reverse—**tape reversal**—was another technique borrowed from turntablism. Pierre Schaeffer was one of the first composers to record a turntable piece that included an extended section of backwards sounds. About one minute into the short *Cinq études de bruits: Étude violette* (1948) there was a 35-second section consisting primarily of slowly advancing piano notes and chords played in reverse. This type of effect was evidently unwieldy to achieve with a turntable, for reverse sounds were not used in very many of the early *musique concrète* works created with discs. The introduction of the tape recorder greatly simplified the ability to play recorded sounds backwards while also extending the duration of a reversed sound to virtually the entire length of a tape if desired. On a monophonic, **full-track**, tape recorder capable of recording only one track in one direction across the entire width of the magnetic tape, playing a sound in reverse was as simple as flipping the tape over and playing the tape upside down. Later recorders that were capable of recording two tracks—**half-track stereo**—in one direction could also play sounds in reverse if the tape was flipped over, but tracks would be transposed from the left to the right and vice versa. The most common commercially available tape recorders of the 1960s and 1970s recorded stereo tracks on both sides of a tape, therefore having two quarter tracks running in either direction. Although trickier to play sounds in reverse on such a machine, it could be accomplished by changing the way that the tape was threaded around the capstan. That trick only worked if the tape recorder was equipped with three drive motors—one for the supply reel, one for the take-up reel, and one for the capstan. Threading the tape behind the capstan and pinch roller had the effect of reversing the direction of the tension-activated supply and take-up reel motors, causing the supply reel to take up the tape, the result being that the recording traveled backward across the playback head. Of course, the most manageable method of working with reversed sounds was simply to snip out a length of recorded tape and splice it back into the piece backwards.

The most distinctive change to a sound when it is reversed is that its envelope characteristics also become reversed. Whereas a sound may have previously ramped up from a low volume and concluded with a bang, it did the opposite when reversed, beginning with a bang and subsiding as a fade-out. Playing the sound of the voice in reverse has the effect of turning something familiar into the unfamiliar and has been the source of much experimentation in electronic music. Reversing sounds quickly became a popular technique in tape composition and an indispensable tool for the composer who wanted to modify sounds without quite changing them altogether. Early works from all of the major electronic music studios of Europe, the United States, and Japan all made use of this technique. Playing sounds in reverse, like echo and reverberation, became one of the most familiar electronic music techniques and persists as a valued resource today of digital sound editing systems.

Tape Speed Manipulation

Another classic tape music technique was the effect of playing a sound at a speed other than that at which it was recorded, or **tape speed manipulation**. Tape recorders usually had two or three standard tape transport speeds: 7.5 inches (19 cm) per second, 15 inches (38 cm) per second, and 30 inches (76 cm) per second on professional machines. Using a faster tape speed resulted in higher fidelity because more magnetic particles were being devoted to recording a given sound than if the tape was running more slowly. Tape transport speed was controlled by a **capstan**—a tiny rotating, motor-driven spindle that pinched the tape against a rubber roller and pulled it from the supply reel to the take-up reel. Changing the diameter of the capstan would change the transport speed.

The setting for the fixed speeds used on tape recorders were not arrived at by accident. Note that each of the speeds was twice as fast as the speed before it. In musical terms, these speeds were exactly one octave apart. If a note recorded at 15 inches per second (ips) was played at 30 ips, it would have been one octave higher. Greater extremes in octave ranges could be achieved by re-recording sounds multiple times at different speeds to multiply the effect of octave changes. Composers purposefully recorded sounds at speeds other than the final playback speed of the master so that they could transpose the sounds up or down in the frequency range.

Changing the playback speed of a sound modified its pitch and duration. While the dominant pitch of a sound would change by an octave if the speed were shifted up or down, the tempo of the sound and its timbre were also transformed, often with unexpected results.

While most tape machines had specific speed settings, it was sometimes desirable to provide variable speed control through a continuous range of speeds without graduated increments. Some special purpose tape recorders were capable of varying the speed on a sliding scale between the standard settings, allowing one to gradually shift speed in smaller increments than simple octave steps. If working without a variable-speed tape recorder, a makeshift method of adding slight increases in transport speed and pitch could be accomplished by wrapping the capstan with one or more layers of splicing tape. By the 1970s, some commercially available reel-to-reel tape recorders came equipped with variable-speed capstans, or *varispeed*, which allowed speed to be varied over a continuous range.

Glissandi (1957) by György Ligeti was a short work of electronic music that used the techniques of tape reversal and variable speed changes as its chief structural guideposts. This work and *Artikulation* (1958) comprise the composer's only completed electronic works. As a young composer, Ligeti had little first-hand knowledge of contemporary music outside of Soviet-controlled Hungary where he lived. After reportedly hearing a radio concert of Stockhausen's *Gesang der Jünglinge* (1956), he began a correspondence with Stockhausen that led to his invitation to work at the studios of the WDR, which he did in 1957.[28] *Glissandi* was Ligeti's first completed electronic music composition and for many years he was reluctant to release it publicly because he considered it to be more of a test piece than a fully realized work. "*Glissandi* is a weak piece, concerning both the sound and form," declared Ligeti many years later. "It has a primitive, almost schematic, form."[29] Ligeti is known for his highly organized and mathematical approach to composition, an instinct that he shared with the Cologne school of electronic music. Although *Glissandi* did not embody the fully-formed serialism of Stockhausen's *Studie I* and *Studie II*, it is clear from analyzing the work and Ligeti's notes that he gave much thought to its structural plan.

Ligeti made use of several key pieces of equipment at the Cologne studio when composing *Glissandi*. Chief among these was a sine wave generator with a rotary dial for varying the pitch manually, reverberation, a variable-speed tape recorder, and filter banks. The audio filters found at the Cologne studio were some of the most advanced in any electronic music studio of the time and provided the composer with a fine degree of control over audio frequencies across the spectrum.

Glissandi had a planned structure that was more well-defined than might be evident upon first hearing the recording. The entire piece was 7′ 44″ long. Consisting of a sequence of rising and falling sine waves, glissandi made up the major tonal material of the piece. Some of the glissandi were created by manually adjusting the dial of a sine wave generator, while others appear to have been created using variable speed changes on a tape recorder. The basic sound material lasted 3′ 52″, after which, at the precise middle of the work, the first half of the piece was played entirely in reverse. In addition to playing the material in reverse, the second half of the piece also included an overdub of the first half played normally, but highly filtered so that only small particles of the sound were audible. The mirror-like structure of the work was carefully timed and added to the listening experience. For example, one could listen to a sound that occurred 25 seconds from the beginning of the work and then hear the same passage in reverse precisely 25 seconds before the end of the work. Ligeti did not evidently apply serial techniques to select the tones for the piece, but his organizational scheme was clearly symmetrical. The composer's sketches for the first half of the piece consisted of several sections of approximate durations labeled with Roman numerals (Table 5.1).

Table 5.1   A sketch from the first section of Ligeti's *Glissandi*[30]

Section	I	II	IIIA	IIIB	IIIC	IIID
Duration (seconds)	40–50	40–45	24	20	17	15

Detailed analysis of the recording by musicologist Benjamin Robert Levy revealed subsections within Ligeti's major sections (Table 5.2).

Table 5.2 A sketch from Ligeti's *Glissandi* showing subsections[31]

Subsection	IIIe	IIIf	IIIg	IIIh	IIIi	IIIj	IIIk	IIIl	IIIm	IIIn	IIIo
Duration (seconds)	12	11	9.5	8	7	6	5	4	3	2	1

Furthermore, Levy discovered that the succession of durations for some of the sections closely corresponded to a **Fibonacci series** of numbers—a sequence in which each new value in a series is simply the sum of the two before it. "Beginning with Roman numeral III, the subdivisions steadily decrease in length, and the rate at which they do so is determined by a Fibonacci-like series. Examining the differences in duration between sections yields the following arrangement" (see Figure 5.9).[32]

Note how the Fibonacci series is revealed if, reading Levy's diagram from right to left, one adds the duration of a sequence and the difference between it and the successive sequence, the result being equal to the duration of the next sequence in the row.

Aesthetically, *Glissandi* was an exercise in the exponential concretion and expansion of sonic textures. Using only pure sine waves as source material, the rich overtones and brushes of noise were the result of Ligeti's methodical combinations of groups of sliding tones. It was an atmospheric music of sweeping sonic textures, a characteristic that Ligeti would further explore in his long history as a composer of instrumental music. His experience in Cologne made an indelible impression on Ligeti, so much so that he has often been described as a composer who brought the textures of electronic music to works for orchestra. The influence of his experience with electronic music fundamentally changed Ligeti's approach to composing music for orchestra.

The methods and techniques associated with composing music for tape laid the groundwork for the development of all future electronic music. When digital media and sound editing software began to replace the tape recorder and splicing block during the 1980s, many familiar techniques associated with tape editing were transferred to the toolkits of computer programs designed for organizing, synthesizing, and editing music. Part III, Digital Synthesis and Computer Music, discusses the evolution of digital music development and the extension of traditional analog audio processing techniques to the computer electronic music studio.

Grouping			1	1			3	2
Difference		4	3	2	2	2	1.5	1.5
Duration	24	20	17	15	13	11	9.5	8

								8
1	1	1	1	1	1	1	1	
7	6	5	4	3	2	1	0	

Figure 5.9
A sketch from Ligeti's *Glissandi* showing Fibonacci-like series.
(After Levy, 2006)

SUMMARY

- Many of the basic aesthetic concepts and artistic choices invented by early composers of tape music remain at the core of electronic music still being produced today.

- The seven fundamental traits of electronic music are:
  1 The sound resources available to electronic music are unlimited.
  2 Electronic music can expand the perception of tonality.
  3 Electronic music exists in a state of actualization.
  4 Electronic music has a special relationship with the temporal nature of music.
  5 In electronic music, sound itself becomes the material of composition.
  6 Electronic music does not breathe—it is not affected by the limitations of human performance.
  7 Electronic music often lacks a point of comparison with the natural world of sounds, providing a largely mental and imaginative experience.

- Many modern practices and techniques found in modern electronic music had their origins in the classic tape studio.

- Classic tape techniques that have successfully transferred to the tapeless digital domain include editing (cutting and pasting of sounds), tape echo, reverberation, sound loops, delay, reversal of sounds, and tape speed manipulation.

CHAPTER 6

Early Synthesizers and Experimenters

Vladimir [Ussachevsky] often discussed with me how important he felt it was that composers in an electronic music center take the lead in imagining what they would like, as he did, and then involve the creative capacity of engineers on staff to realize that musical goal. The engineers at the Center, often of enormous talent, were there to await his directives.
—Alice Shields, commenting on the Columbia–Princeton Electronic Music Center

Columbia–Princeton Electronic Music Center, 1958, and the RCA Mark II Electronic Music Synthesizer. Pictured from left to right are Milton Babbitt, engineer Peter Mauzey, and Vladimir Ussachevsky. (Columbia University Computer Music Center)

Electronic music studios arose during a dramatic time of transition in the field of electronic audio technology. The coming of the transistor and especially its rapid adoption by American and Japanese manufacturers of radios, stereos, and tape recorders effectively brought the reign of the vacuum to an end by the early 1960s. Transistors were the building blocks of electrical circuitry and the first stage in the evolution of increasingly small, efficient, and versatile integrated circuits that now make up the essence of computers and most other electronic devices. Transistors can have many functions but are primarily used for amplifying signals and switching control signals. The first practical transistor was developed at Bell Labs in 1947 and was in widespread production and use by the early 1950s. Transistors had several advantages over their vacuum tube predecessors, including small size, durability, low power consumption, and a highly automated manufacturing process. Transistors could withstand shock and did not require a warm-up period like vacuum tubes. All of these factors made transistors ideally suited for use in commercial audio products, including those components commonly found in the electronic music studio.

Hobbyists took up electrical projects in increasing numbers as retail stores such as Radio Shack, Lafayette, and Heathkit competed vigorously for their business. Magazines such as *Popular Electronics* were brimming over with projects for self-taught gadget makers. One of the consequences of this Renaissance of inventing was a new generation of amateur and professional engineers who turned their attention to improving the state of electronic musical instruments. Robert Moog, Donald Buchla, Hugh Le Caine, and Raymond Scott were all a part of this new wave of inventors.

This chapter traces the development of the analog synthesizer and the building blocks of electronic music components leading to the rise of the voltage-controlled synthesizer in the 1960s.

SYNTHESIZER PREDECESSORS

The idea of the **synthesizer** is as old as Cahill's Telharmonium. The American inventor goes on record as the first to use the term for a musical instrument when, in 1896, he used it to describe his power-hungry dynamo. Cahill's idea was virtually the same as those of later inventors: use a combination of tone-generating and modulating devices to build sounds from their component parts.

During the 1950s, the best-executed design of a complete music synthesizer from the age of vacuum tubes was the RCA Mark II Electronic Music Synthesizer housed at the Columbia–Princeton Electronic Music Center from 1958. Although large, cumbersome, and difficult to master, the RCA synthesizer was a serviceable if not elegant solution for creating music electronically with the most advanced analog technology of its time. Although overshadowed after only a few years by increasingly successful experiments with computer synthesis at Bell Labs and the rise of the Moog and Buchla analog synthesizers, the RCA Mark II provided valuable insight into the problems facing composers and engineers alike in building more advanced electronic musical instruments.

RCA Electronic Music Synthesizer

The early history and origins of the Columbia–Princeton Electronic Music Center (see Chapter 3, pp. 110–16) form a story of intersecting desires of engineers and composers working at RCA, Princeton University, and Columbia University to establish a studio with the RCA Mark II Electronic Music Synthesizer at its core. About eight years before, the inventors of the RCA synthesizer, Harry F. Olson and Herbert F. Belar, originally embarked on the experimental development of a machine to compose songs. Using statistical analysis as the basis of their approach, the two analyzed the melodies of Stephen Foster songs with the intent of creating a machine that could synthesize new songs based on such parameters. The machine they built and tested as early as 1950 was a rudimentary form of analog computer dedicated to the input of data for the creation of songs.[1] The *Olson–Belar "electronic music composing machine"* was distinguished from other early large-scale computers because it could produce audio output from pre-programmed routines, perhaps its most significant achievement when viewed in retrospect. It was also dedicated to one task—that of composing music—unlike a general-purpose computer.

The Olson–Belar composing machine was based on information theory and developed as an aid to the composer. The machine created music based on the random selection of notes that were weighted by "a probability based upon preceding events."[2] Analysis of 11 Stephen Foster songs was carried out to determine the relative frequency of notes, patterns of note repetition, and rhythms of the songs, producing tables used to regulate the computing functions of the machine.[3] The "preceding events" were patterns of two and three notes that the engineers entered into a table to regulate the probability factors associated with selecting the next note. The frequency count of notes found in such Foster chestnuts as *Old Folks at Home, Oh Susannah, My Old Kentucky Home*, and other songs were all transposed to the key of D major for the purpose of engineering new songs with a manageable number of 12 notes. Minimizing the complexity of the note choices was important because the selection and synthesizing of pitches was all done mechanically using hardwired rotary stepper switches and relays. Table 6.1 shows the results of the initial frequency analysis of the songs.

Further analysis was conducted to determine the likelihood of one note following another in a Foster melody, the result being additional tables representing two-note and three-note sequences. Table 6.2 shows the values for the two-note sequences determined by the engineers.

In this analysis, probability was divided into sixteenths. The number 16 was chosen because it matched the number of mechanical relay channels in the output of the machine. In Table 6.2 for two-note sequences, the first two-note sequence tabulated was B_3 and there were 16 chances in 16 (100 percent certainty) that the note D_4 would follow B_3. In the third line of the table, for note D_4, there was one chance in 16 that the note B_3 would follow D_4, two chances in 16 that note D_4 would follow D_4, and so on. Regulating the selection of notes and rhythms were two random number generators. The values tabulated for the probability of notes were translated into pitch choices and the likelihood of their occurrence following any other note. A rotary stepper switch with 50 positions—one for each possible two- or three-note sequence tabulated by the

Table 6.1 **Relative frequency of the notes in 11 Stephen Foster songs (after Olson)**

Note	B_3	$C_4^\#$	D_4	E_4	$F_4^\#$	G_4	$G_4^\#$	A_4	B_4	$C_5^\#$	D_5	E_5
Relative frequency	17	18	58	26	38	23	17	67	42	29	30	17

Source: After Olson and Belar (1950).

Table 6.2 Probability of the notes following a two-note sequence in 11 Stephen Foster songs*

Note	B_3	$C^{\#}_4$	D_4	E_4	$F^{\#}_4$	G_4	$G^{\#}_4$	A_4	B_4	$C^{\#}_5$	D_5	E_5
B_3			16									
$C^{\#}_4$			16									
D_4	1	1	2	5	3	1		1		1	1	
E_4		1	6	3	4			1			1	
$F^{\#}_4$			2	4	5	2		2	1			
G_4					4	3		6	3			
$G^{\#}_4$								16				
A_4		1			5	1	1	4	3		1	
B_4		1			1	1		9	2		2	
$C^{\#}_5$									8		8	
D_5								4	7	3	1	1
E_5								6		10		

Note: *The probability of the note following the preceding note is expressed in sixteenths.

Source: After Olson and Belar (1950).

engineers—responded to the output of the random number generators for rhythm and pitch and hardwired probability circuits to send an electrical signal to the tone-synthesizing component. The output could be recorded onto magnetic tape or monitored by loudspeaker. Tones were created using vibrating tuning forks amplified by contact pick-ups. A schematic for the Olson–Belar music composing machine is found in Figure 6.1.

However grand the intention, the aesthetic range of the resulting music was limited to the tonal structures and rhythms associated with 11 songs by Stephen Foster. Any wider application of the machine to the creation of more complex music was deemed impractical so the composing machine was essentially dead on arrival as far as the practiced composer was concerned. Olson would later write that "the creative process of the composer is not fully understood because the ability to create is a gift."[4] There is no doubt, however, that this early work of Olson and Belar did much to advance their understanding of electronic music composition and led directly to the invention of the *RCA Electronic Music Synthesizer*.

In engineering the RCA synthesizer, Olson and Belar shifted their attention from developing automated composing schema to more fully exploring the sound-generating and modification characteristics of the synthesizer. Their stated purpose was to provide a means for pre-programming all of the basic properties of musical tone, including pitch, amplitude, envelope, timbre, vibrato, **portamento**, and modifications such as frequency filtering and reverberation. Unlike the composing machine, the RCA synthesizer did not compose music but was managed by a composer who pre-programmed the machine's operation using a punched paper input device.

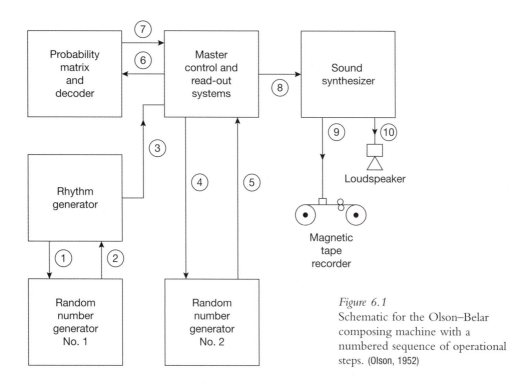

Figure 6.1
Schematic for the Olson–Belar composing machine with a numbered sequence of operational steps. (Olson, 1952)

The first RCA Electronic Music Synthesizer, also known as the Mark I, was unveiled in 1955 and housed at Princeton University where the technical staff sought the assistance of composers from the music departments of Princeton and Columbia universities. The synthesizer was designed to produce two channels of output that could be played on loudspeakers or recorded directly onto disc using a turntable lathe. Sound was generated using a bank of tuning fork oscillators amplified with pickups to produce **sine waves**—a technology borrowed from the Olson–Belar music composition machine.

In 1958, RCA created an improved version of the synthesizer called the Mark II, adding two more channels, a second punched paper input device, additional audio oscillators, and several additional means for modifying sound, including high- and low-pass filters. The original 12 tuning fork oscillators of the Mark I were supplemented by a noise generator as well as two banks of vacuum tube oscillators that could be variably tuned to nearly any pitch within the range of normal human hearing, from about 8,000 to 16,000 Hz. The expanded tone-generating capabilities of the Mark II were impressive and covered a ten-octave range. The tuning fork oscillators provided a master octave comprised of sine waves. The new electronic oscillators could produce **sawtooth** and **triangular waves** and a noise generator was also available for producing white noise and other audio signals with a randomized arrangement of harmonics. A **frequency shifter**, or octaver, was available as a secondary step in the synthesis of basic tones. This device was controlled by the paper tape reader. The device took a designated sine wave frequency and through a hardwired process of frequency division and multiplication added harmonics to produce a sawtooth wave composed of all even and odd harmonics. Other available modifications to the electronic source signal included the modulation of vibrato and tremolo, and a "portamento glider" that created a sliding transition from one frequency to another. A timbre modifier allowed the composer a limited amount of control over the accentuation of individual components of the overtone structure of a sound. The **envelope** characteristics of a sound could be applied to the **attack**, **duration**, and **decay** characteristics of a sound. Finally, artificial reverberation could be added to the synthesized sound and the system included a way of mixing signals for the desired balance of audio components prior to recording on magnetic tape.

The Mark II was rented for a nominal fee to Columbia and Princeton Universities and installed on the Columbia campus with the founding of the Columbia–Princeton Electronic Music Center. The Mark II is the RCA synthesizer most closely associated with the output of the studio and was actively used throughout the 1960s, eventually being superseded by voltage-controlled analog synthesizers and computer music systems. A schematic of one stage in the development of the Mark II is shown in Figure 6.2 and a diagram of the components of the synthesizer in Figure 6.3.

Of importance to the composer was the way in which sounds were specified using the RCA Electronic Music Synthesizer. The machine was equipped with a punched paper tape input device (shown by "coded paper record" on the accompanying schematic). Working directly at the console of the synthesizer, using a Teletype-like keyboard, the machine was programmed by punching holes directly onto a 15 inch (38 cm)-wide roll of perforated paper that ran at a speed of about 4 inches (10 cm) per second. Using this mechanism, the composer could enter binary codes controlling five elements for each of the two channels: frequency, octave, envelope, timbre, and volume. A piece was entered onto the punched paper tape one row at a time, presupposing a plan that was prescribed ahead of time using a worksheet (see Figure 6.4) for transposing musical notation to codes on the punched paper tape. All of this was done manually, requiring much patience and precision, but saved time by generating, without tape editing, some of the effects normally accomplished with a razor blade and splicing tape. The punched paper settings for each channel occupied one half of the width of the paper roll, providing 36 possible columns of settings for two channels. A diagram of a sample paper record, shown in Figure 6.5, denotes the number of possible settings per row for each element of a tone.

The paper punch recorder was also a reader. Below the paper was a relay tree of hardwired contact points for each possible position of a punched hole on a row. Above the paper was a series of metal brushes corresponding to the relay tree below. As the paper roll was set into motion, the brushes made contact with the relay tree whenever there was a punched hole in the paper. This contact closed a circuit, sending an electrical pulse along the relay tree to each of several separate, hardwired switches that would activate the designated frequency, octave, envelope, timbre, and volume. The paper roll contained 36 columns of possible instructions per row, 18 for each of the two channels. Olson and Belar intended the punched paper reader to allow a composer to transcribe an entire composition to a machine-readable record. The result was a permanent program or document of a piece of music that could be run through the synthesizer for playback, modification, and recording of the sounds. Even when operated at its slowest speed, however, a single, continuous roll of punched paper could only reproduce four minutes of music at the most, necessitating the construction of longer works as a sequence of smaller parts that would be joined using the facilities of the associated tape recording machines.

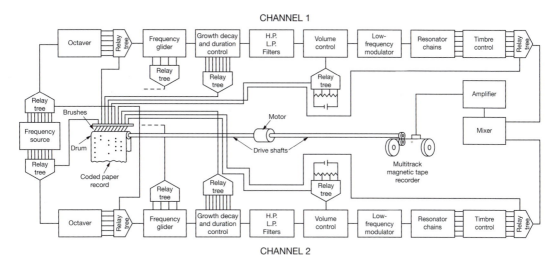

Figure 6.2 Schematic for the Olson–Belar RCA Mark II Electronic Music Synthesizer. (Olson, 1967)

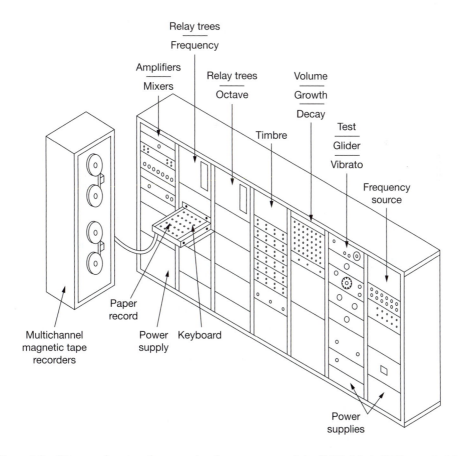

Figure 6.3 Diagram showing the operational components of the RCA Mark II Electronic Music Synthesizer. (Olson, 1967)

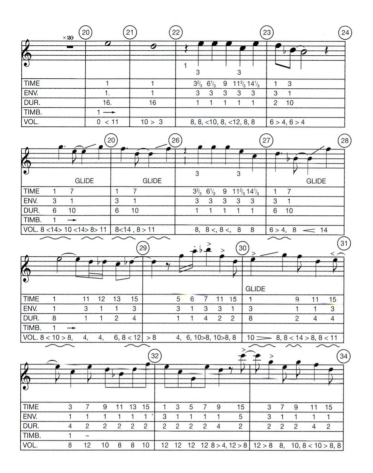

Figure 6.4
Composers using the RCA Mark II employed a worksheet to transcribe a musical score to codes for the punched paper tape input device of the synthesizer. (Olson, 1967)

While it was possible to construct a piece of music by merely recording, in real time, the output of the punched paper reader, this was not generally the approach taken at the studio. In practice, composers generally used the RCA synthesizer to create individual layers and sections of a work, often produced out of sequence, for later modification and assembly using the extensive modulation, mixing, and tape recording facilities of the studio. The sound palette for a work was also not limited to the output of the synthesizer's tone generators. Natural sounds could be input, modified, and recorded using a microphone in the studio and pre-recorded tapes of other sounds could be modified and added through the studio's tape recording facilities.

The original Mark I RCA Music Synthesizer was not equipped with a tape recorder but rather an elaborate disc-cutting lathe and playback turntable for recording purposes. Using that system, the composer could record any audio output on a disc and then combine it with other sequences being played in real time onto a new disc. Working with disc recording limited the composers to short passages of sound recording and introduced a level of mechanical dexterity and timing that made it difficult for anyone to capture and manipulate sound output. Working closely with RCA, Milton Babbitt succeeded in having the disc lathe replaced with a multitrack tape recording system in 1959.

Figure 6.5
Diagram showing the layout
of the punched paper tape used
to program the RCA Mark II.
(Olson, 1967)

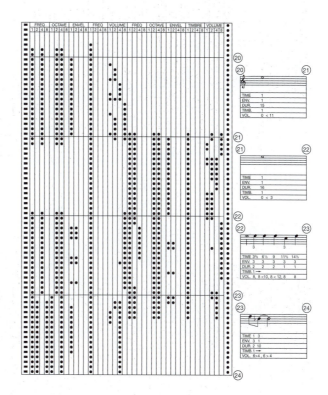

Multitracking became a useful technique for composers who wanted to write music for more voices than the synthesizer was capable of accommodating in a single pass of the punched paper reader. Each channel of the tape recorder could record up to seven individual tone sequences, providing up to 49 tone sequences per tape through a process of overdubbing and synchronization of the paper reader for each pass. The process could be repeated again for a tape containing 49 tone sequences, multiplying the total number of available simultaneous note sequences to as many as 343 (49 × 7 tracks).

The combination of punched paper reader and multitrack recording made the RCA synthesizer ideally suited to Babbitt's 12-tone experiments. Babbitt, the son of a mathematician and advocate of serial composition, found in the RCA synthesizer the perfect laboratory with which to experiment with the total serialization of all aspects of a piece—the pitch, amplitude, envelope, timbre, rhythm, and pitch relationships in time. Babbitt completed several extended 12-tone works with the RCA synthesizer, including *Ensembles for Synthesizer* (1961–63), *Philomel* (1963–64) for soprano, recorded soprano, and synthesized accompaniment, and *Composition for Synthesizer* (1964). Such a purist was Babbitt that most of these works were completed using only those audio-generating parameters found on the punched paper score, purposefully avoiding "any further mutations or modifications" that could have been made using the extended audio processing modules of the synthesizer.[5] The resulting music was complex and arithmetic, and was comprised of complicated intersections of tone sequences, sparsely orchestrated harmonies, and carefully predetermined spasms of rhythms. Because Babbitt did not modify the sounds with reverberation, vibrato, or tape editing tricks, his works were an exercise in

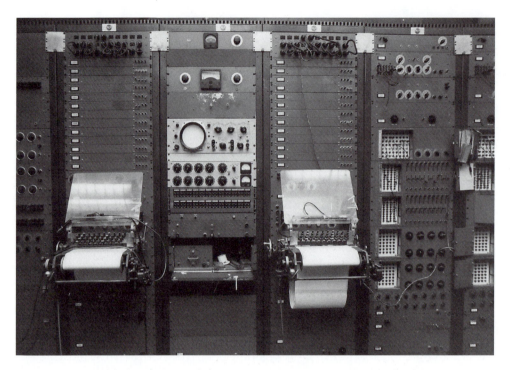

Figure 6.6   RCA Mark II front panel showing two punched paper recorder/readers.
(Columbia University Computer Music Center)

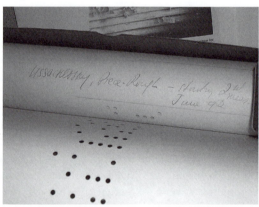

Figure 6.8   Sample punched paper roll created by
Vladimir Ussachevsky and marked "Piece-Rough,"
c. 1960. (Thom Holmes)

Figure 6.7   Punched paper recorder/reader
of the RCA Mark II. (Thom Holmes)

Figure 6.9 The RCA Mark II Electronic Music Synthesizer today at Columbia University. It rests in the same location in which it was originally installed in 1958. Although not currently operational, there are plans to restore the instrument. (Thom Holmes)

Figure 6.10 Close-up of the front panel of the RCA Mark II as it is today at Columbia University. (Thom Holmes)

Figure 6.11 Close-up of the rear panel housing circuits and vacuum tubes for one of the "resonator" modules of the RCA Mark II. (Thom Holmes)

purely abstract tones, a purpose for which the RCA synthesizer was ideally suited. In contrast to Stockhausen, whose early serial compositions for sine waves were always colored psychologically by carefully metered tape effects, reverberation, and speed shifts, Babbitt's works were stripped of such emotional content as anticipation, resolve, and acoustically familiar reverberations, resulting in a listening experience that was fascinating because of its austere complexity as well as its disassociation from human experience.

The RCA Mark II Electronic Music Synthesizer weighed about 3 tons, stood 7 feet tall, was 20 feet long, contained 1,700 vacuum tubes, and was the centerpiece of the studio in which it was housed. To the untrained eye the machine most closely resembled a mainframe computer. This was not surprising, because its electronics consisted of vacuum tube components and hardwired circuits used for the first, analog, general-purpose computers. The studio and its equipment continued to evolve. During the early 1960s, the punched paper reader was replaced with a somewhat more flexible optical recognition system that responded to ink marks on paper rather than hole punches. With the availability of commercial analog synthesizers by 1965, the RCA synthesizer was supplemented with the modular, solid-state Buchla synthesizer, Ampex tape recorders, and expansion of the studio's workspace to include several individual workstations for composers. By 1969, the RCA synthesizer was much less used and was all but supplanted by four similarly equipped studios featuring Buchla synthesizers, individual wave generators, four-track and two-track tape recorders, and a central mixing console. The mixing console connected all of the studios, allowing up to 24 individual inputs from the satellite studios.[6] Milton Babbitt was probably the last serious advocate of the RCA synthesizer and reportedly still favored it for his electronic works as late as 1972.[7]

Another electronic piece composed later in the life of the RCA synthesizer was *Time's Encomium* (1968–69) by Charles Wuorinen (b. 1938). This work also has the distinction of being the first electronic work to win the Pulitzer Prize for music. Wuorinen's stated goal was to explore the "precise temporal control" such as note-to-note distances and absolute time values that could be assigned by the synthesizer, mapping a sequence of pitch and time relationships.[8] Like Babbitt, Wuorinen chose only the purest, most unadulterated tones of the RCA synthesizer for the first 15 minutes of the work. For the second half, he reworked the recorded tone patterns from the first half using the sound processing and tape facilities of the studio.

As a technological marvel, the Olson–Belar RCA Electronic Music Synthesizer was well suited for the composition of 12-tone music but its elaborate punched paper input system was of little value to most composers working in the Columbia–Princeton Electronic Music Center. Alice Shields (b. 1943), whose tenure at the studio began in 1963 as an assistant to Ussachevsky, was one such composer:

> No one, to my knowledge, composed a piece on the RCA (which arrived at the studio around 1959), but Milton Babbitt and Charles Wuorinen. I had little interest in it, as the timbres were very limited, and the key-punch mechanism was so inferior to music notation for live instruments whose timbres were not at all limited. My interest was, and largely still is, in "concrete" or sampled sounds as sources for electronic manipulation and transformation.[9]

The output of the Columbia–Princeton Electronic Music Center varied considerably with the taste and inclination of each visiting composer. Internationally known composers were often invited to use the center. In the first two years, it sponsored work by such composers as Michiko Toyama (b. 1913) from Japan, Mario Davidovsky from Argentina, Halim El-Dabh (b. 1921) from Egypt, Bülent Arel (1919–90) from Turkey, and Charles Wuorinen from the United States. The center drew on this body of work when it presented its first public concerts on May 10, 1961, in the McMillan Theater of Columbia University. The program consisted of seven works, six of which were later released on a Columbia record album. These works were tape pieces alone or involved the interaction of live musicians with tapes of synthesized sounds. Aside from the use of the RCA synthesizer and the center for 12-tone composition, many prominent and up-and-coming composers contributed to the studio's growing repertoire of adventurous works using a wide variety of compositional approaches. Edgard Varèse himself used the studio in 1960 and 1961 to revise the tape parts to *Déserts* with the assistance of Max Mathews and Bülent Arel.[10] Hundreds of composers passed through the center to take a closer look and often work in the studio. Babbitt remarked that the center was instrumental in helping people to better understand what electronic music was about and to "disabuse them of the notion that it's a particular kind of music." Babbitt recalled that Stravinsky "had a heart attack there, he got so excited."[11] In addition to Ussachevsky, Babbitt, Luening, Varèse, Arel, and Mathews, other noted composers who used the center included Tzvi Avni (b. 1927), Luciano Berio, Wendy Carlos, Mario Davidovsky, Charles Dodge (b. 1942), Jacob Druckman (1928–96), Halim El-Dabh, Ross Lee Finney (1906–97), Malcolm Goldstein (b. 1936), Andres Lewin-Richter (b. 1937), İlhan Mimaroğlu (b. 1926), Jon Appleton (b. 1939), Pauline Oliveros, Alwin Nikolais (1910–93), Mel Powell (1923–98), William Overton Smith (b. 1926), and Charles Wuorinen. More electronic music was released on record from this single studio than from any other in North America.

Wendy Carlos, a graduate student at Columbia at the time, ran tape machines for the premiere of Babbitt's *Philomel* in 1964.[12] Carlos's own *Variations for Flute and Electronic Sound* (1964) was written for a flutist accompanied by magnetic tape. The work consisted of a "strictly organized set of six variations on an eleven bar theme stated at the outset by the flute."[13] Mimaroğlu's *Le Tombeau d'Edgar Poe* (1964) used as its only sound source a recorded reading of the Mallarmé poem, utilizing the full spectrum of studio editing techniques and effects to modify and transform the sound. Davidovsky's *Electronic Study No. 1* (1960) used the purely electronic sound sources of sine waves, square waves, and white noise modified through the use of filters and reverberation, then layered five times, inverted, and transposed to change their amplitude and density. *Animus I* (1966) by Jacob Druckman employed a live trombonist who traded passages with a tape of electronic sounds, eventually being driven off the stage by the ensuing pandemonium; it concluded with the musician returning for an uneasy truce with the tape recorder.

One of the most influential composers associated with the early years of the studio was Halim El-Dabh, who worked there from 1959 to 1961. By the time Otto Luening and Vladimir Ussachevsky became acquainted with Halim El-Dabh's music in 1955, the Egyptian composer had been dabbling in electronic music for more than ten years. El-Dabh's musical style was unlike the mathematically derived compositions of Babbitt and other serial composers working at the center. Although El-Dabh soon moved on from the studio to begin a long and distinguished career as an ethnomusicologist and composer, his early tape piece *Leiyla and the Poet* (1961) became something of a cult favorite with up-and-coming composers who heard it on a recording released in 1964.[14] El-Dabh's seamless blending of vocal sounds, electronic tones, and tape manipulation such as speed transposition gave the short work—part of a longer multipart electronic opera—an unearthly quality that influenced many young composers working at the time. His approach to composing electronic music was one of immersion in the sound. While at Columbia, he made full use of all ten Ampex tape recorders available to him, often working throughout the night and sleeping on Ussachevsky's cot in a back room at the studio. "I always like the idea of solid noise, and I felt like a sculptor who was chiseling the sound away," revealed El-Dabh. Some of his material consisted of loops that were so long that they had to be run out of the room and back.[15] The roster of people who acknowledge the importance of El-Dabh's recording to their work ranges widely from Neil Rolnick to Charles Amirkhanian, Alice Shields, and rock musician Frank Zappa.[16] *Leiyla and the Poet* had a certain degree of crossover appeal to other genres of music and was the obvious and imitated source of the song *Leiyla* (1967) by the Los Angeles-based rock band The West Coast Pop Art Experimental Band, two members of which were the sons of composer Roy Harris.

The Columbia–Princeton Electronic Music Center and the Olson–Belar RCA synthesizer were groundbreaking in many respects. The synthesizer, although bearing tone-generating capabilities limited to the 12-tone scale, radically modernized the degree of control given the composer over the synthesized result. The punched paper recorder/reader was a precursor of machine-controlled input devices that would become available on large-scale computer music systems during the 1960s and provided unprecedented control over the basic audio parameters of musical sounds. The modular design of the audio signal processing components of the RCA synthesizer would be duplicated more efficiently in commercially available voltage-controlled synthesizers of Buchla and Moog in the mid-1960s. The multitrack tape recorder anticipated the widespread availability of overdubbing in commercial recording studios.

It would be unfair to assign total credit for the success of the Columbia–Princeton Electronic Music Center to the technological feats of programmability, modularity, and mixing/recording capabilities of the RCA synthesizer. This was a studio with a list of completed works that rivaled in number those produced in the public broadcasting facilities of Paris and Cologne radio; a reported 225 works were produced at the Columbia–Princeton studio in its first decade of operation.[17] The majority were produced using ancillary audio processing equipment at the center rather than the RCA synthesizer and most works could be described as using concrete or electroacoustic sources rather than the 12-tone system embodied by the synthesizer proper. Shields elaborated on the RCA synthesizer and the body of works created at the studio:

> The machine was always very delicate, with its punch keys and little telephone cables, and looked somewhat decayed and disheveled even when I arrived in 1963 at the Center. One of the reasons it was so little used was indeed its delicacy, and that I believe in Vladimir's mind it had to be preserved in as intact a state as possible for the use of Milton Babbitt . . . Still another reason it wasn't attractive to most composers was that it allowed only the tempered scale, and in the 1960s all the conflagration of wild experimentation and newness was in almost anything but the tempered scale. The RCA was obviously designed by engineers, not composers. But it was always interesting to visiting groups who I would take around the Center and demonstrate various pieces of equipment and

Figure 6.12
Alice Shields at the Columbia–
Princeton Electronic Music
Center, 1970. (Alice Shields)

play compositions made at the Center. When I brought them in front of the RCA, they would always take a deep breath of satisfaction, impressed, when they saw the huge metal box with its key-punches and telephone wires . . . But it was at the least a good visual advertisement for the Center, in addition to providing Milton with a device well suited to his compositional concerns.[18]

Babbitt also found the RCA synthesizer to be unreliable:

It was not a comfortable device . . . You never knew when you walked in that studio whether you were going to get a minute of music, no music, two seconds of music. You just didn't know what you were going to get. You never knew what was going to go wrong. You never knew what was going to blow.[19]

Behind the technical achievements of the center was a joint venture between two noted university music schools that opened the facilities to established composers and students alike. Ussachevsky, who held degrees in engineering and music, was not only an able administrator but prescribed the functional requirements for many of the ancillary audio processing devices created by Peter Mauzey, James Seawright, Virgilio de Carvalho, John Bittner, and other technicians working at the center.[20]

The Columbia–Princeton Electronic Music Center was the first notable university-based electronic music studio in North America, a trend that shifted activity in the field away from commercial studios or broadcasting establishments to educational institutions. The result was greater access to equipment and a nurturing environment in which to learn the art of electronic music. Significantly, the center became one of the first studios to provide opportunities for women and people from a wide variety of ethnic and racial backgrounds. Among the earliest practitioners in the studio were the Egyptian composer Halim El-Dabh (1959), the Japanese woman composer Michiko Toyama (1959), and American women Alice Shields and Pril Smiley (from about 1963 to the mid-1990s), Pauline Oliveros (1966), and Ann MacMillan (from the late 1960s to 1970s). Alice Shields credits Vladimir Ussachevsky with encouraging women composers to work at the studio.

Shields and Pril Smiley (b. 1943) in particular had pivotal roles at the center, assisting in the technical management of the studio while also composing and teaching others in the use of the facilities. El-Dabh, Shields, and Smiley remain active in music to this day, having had the opportunity to explore the outer reaches of music as part of their early experiences at the Columbia–Princeton Electronic Music Center.

The Columbia–Princeton Electronic Music Center is still in operation although the RCA synthesizer is no longer operable and has been relegated to the status of a museum display. Before Shields left the center in 1996, she brought back fellow alumni Wendy Carlos to help label and archive the vast store of handmade electronic processors, mixing boards, tape recorders, and other valued gear that was no longer in active use.

The Siemens Studio für Elektronische Musik

In 1955, about the same time that Olson and Belar were unveiling the RCA Mark I Electronic Music Synthesizer in the United States, German electronics manufacturer Siemens established an audio laboratory in its Munich facilities to produce electronic music for its promotional films. Siemens engineers Helmut Klein, Alexander Schaaf, and Hans Joachim Neumann were charged with assembling the components for the studio and providing a means for controlling the composition, synthesis, and recording of music (see Figure 6.13). The team was well acquainted with the application of electronic technology for telecommunications applications. Klein had previously worked on the

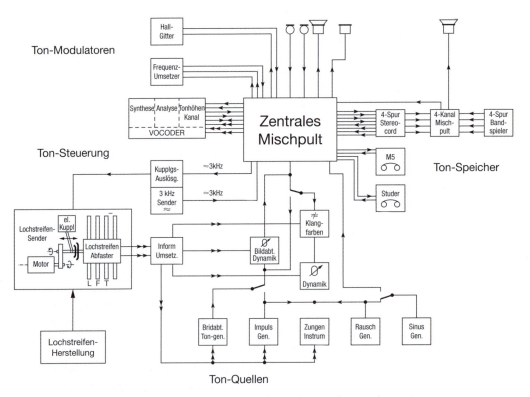

Figure 6.13   Schematic of the Siemens Studio für Elektronische Musik, 1960. (Siemens)

development of the Siemens **vocoder** (voice encoder–decoder)—a voice synthesis system used to mimic the human voice based on earlier patents at Bell Labs. Schaaf had the design of a loudspeaker system to his credit and Neumann was a recent university graduate with experience in the analysis of sound spectra.[21] The group then contracted composer Josef Anton Riedl (b. 1929) to serve as artistic director and conductor of music projects because of his familiarity with the development of music for films.

Under the guidance of Riedl, the laboratory took shape so that by 1956 the engineering staff was making progress in integrating an assemblage of otherwise individual components, not all of which were originally intended for music production. Equipment found in the *Siemens Studio für Elektronische Musik* (Siemens Studio for Electronic Music) included a vocoder, an electrically amplified reed instrument known as the Hohnerola, a preset sawtooth wave generator with 84 tone gradations, four variable-controlled sine wave generators, 20 special purpose sine wave generators, each with fixed settings of 15–160 Hz, 150–1,600 Hz and 1,500–16,000 Hz, that could also be switched to sawtooth waveforms, and a white noise generator. Audio processing of the output signals could employ reverb, echo, and a method for shifting the frequencies to different ranges. The vocoder was an especially effective device for applying tonal qualities of the human voice to any input signal. It consisted of 20 stacked band-pass filter channels, each tuned to a different frequency range with a bandwidth of 6,000 Hz. The vocoder could be likened to a smart, analog equalizer that measured the fundamental frequency of the incoming signal and then reproduced as nearly equivalent signals on the output for each channel.

Riedl was also interested in adding some level of control over the programming of tones, not unlike what he had learned about the punched paper recorder of the RCA synthesizer. For this purpose, the German engineers employed four telex-like punched paper tape recorders to store and play back binary commands controlling the pitch (up to 7 octaves using a 12-tone scale), volume (set in 32-step increments of 1.5 dB each), timbre (applying band-pass filters), and duration (for reproducing whole, quarter, eighth, and sixteenth notes). The method of coding the paper tape was more user-friendly than the RCA punched paper reader and allowed the composer to play a note on a piano-style keyboard before recording it as a hole on the paper tape. The volume and timbre of each note was determined using rotary dials. In 1960, the system was outfitted with a supplemental input device in the form of the *Bildabtaster* (image sensor)—an optical reader capable of converting graphic images into tones and volume settings—a gadget that inspired the creation of electronic music from freehand drawings and paintings.

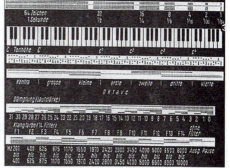

Figure 6.14
Four paper tape input devices were used in the Siemens studio to control the pitch, volume, duration, and filtering characteristics of electronic sounds.
(Siemens)

Figure 6.15   The Siemens Studio für Elektronische Musik, 1960. (Siemens)

The organization of the Siemens Studio für Elektronische Musik was completed by 1959, and included tape editing stations and a master mixing console. Between 1960 and 1966, the studio opened its doors to many outside composers and produce widely diverse output. Riedl worked continuously in the studio during this period and produced no fewer than 44 works, many for motion pictures and industrial films.

The studio achieved the status of a state-of-the-art studio in Europe much like the Columbia–Princeton Electronic Music Center had in the United States. It became the stopping-off point for many prominent visitors, including Pierre Boulez, Herbert Brün, Ernst Krenek, Karlheinz Stockhausen, Bruno Maderna, Henri Pousseur, Mauricio Kagel, Werner Meyer-Eppler, Abraham Moles, and many others, although only a few of these people—including Kagel, Pousseur, Brün, and Krenek—completed important electronic works there. The studio was closed in 1967 but its main control room and equipment have been preserved as part of a museum exhibit at the Siemens Museum in Munich.

Although not designed from the ground up as an integrated synthesizer like the Olson–Belar RCA synthesizer, the Siemens Studio für Elektronische Musik offered many of the same advantages for the composer, including a method for controlling its tone-generating facilities, modification and modulation of the sounds in real time, and the manipulation of recorded material into finished works.

Early Voltage-Controlled Components

Developments at both the Columbia–Princeton Electronic Music Center and the Siemens Studio für Elektronische Musik represented a bridge from the purely electro-mechanical synthesizer to voltage-controlled instruments that permitted improved programmability for the composer. **Voltage control** is a method of applying metered amounts of current to an electronic component to govern how it operates. The application of control voltages can be likened to manually turning the volume knob on a stereo system: the further up or down the dial is turned governs the amount of current fed to the amplification circuitry that drives the loudspeakers.

Analog electronic music components such as oscillators, amplifiers, and filters can all be controlled by control voltages. The **voltage-controlled oscillator (VCO)** is a simple example. The more voltage is applied to the input of the oscillator—e.g. through a manually rotated dial, patch cord, or preset switch—the more rapidly the oscillator will vibrate and the higher the frequency of its pitch.

Designing voltage-controlled electronic music components was less practical until the affordability of transistorized, solid-state electronic music components in the 1960s. Prior to the availability of low-powered solid-state circuit boards, the use of voltage control relied on significantly higher current levels, hardwired circuits, and vacuum tubes that had a short lifetime. Even so, voltage control was used as the basis for the design of some experimental components found in electronic music studios of the 1940s and 1950s. Homer Dudley's vocoder (1939), designed to analyze and reproduce the sound of the human voice, generated control voltages to shape the envelope and amplification of the input signal it was analyzing.[22] Harald Bode, a German engineer who developed many electronic instruments and components found in the first European studios, developed a voltage-controlled amplifier in 1959 as part of a broader modular sound modification system.[23] Composer Vladimir Ussachevsky of the Columbia–Princeton Electronic Music Center and Peter Mauzey, the lead technician of the studio, also experimented with voltage-controlled devices. Mauzey was one of Moog's instructors when he studied engineering at Columbia University in the 1950s. In 1965, Ussachevsky gave Moog specifications for the construction of a voltage-controlled envelope generator. Moog recalled the significance of the idea:

> I built two voltage-controlled amplifiers, two envelope generators, and two envelope followers. Ussachevsky wrote the specifications for these modules. He wanted the envelope generators to have four parts: Attack, Decay, Sustain, and Release. He was the first one to specify the ADSR envelope. Now it is standard on electronic synthesizers and keyboards.[24]

EARLY SYNTHESIZERS AND EXPERIMENTERS

1 *The Expression of Zaar* (alt. title *Wire Recorder Piece*, 1944) by Halim El-Dabh
   Middle East Radio, Cairo; composed using a magnetic wire recorder

2 *Dripsody* (1955) by Hugh Le Caine
   Using Le Caine's Special Purpose Tape Recorder

3 *Folge von 4 Studien* (1959–62) by Josef Anton Riedl
   Siemens Studio für Elektronische Musik

4 *Electronic Study No. 1* (1960) by Mario Davidovsky
   Columbia–Princeton Electronic Music Center

5 *Leiyla and the Poet* (1961) by Halim El-Dabh
   Columbia–Princeton Electronic Music Center

6 *Antithese* (1962) by Mauricio Kagel
   Siemens Studio für Elektronische Musik

7 *Ensembles for Synthesizer* (1961–63) by Milton Babbitt
   Using RCA Mark II Electronic Music Synthesizer

8 *Space Mystery* (1963) by Raymond Scott
   Using Scott's Electronium

9 *I of IV* (1966) by Pauline Oliveros
   Produced at the University of Toronto Electronic Music Studio using Hugh Le Caine's tape loop system

10 *Time's Encomium* (1968–69) by Charles Wuorinen
    Using RCA Mark II Electronic Music Synthesizer

LISTEN

The subject of voltage control and analog synthesis is more completely explored in Chapter 7.

Raymond Scott

Raymond Scott was a commercial musician and inventor of electronic musical instruments whose work largely went unnoticed because he worked privately rather than as part of an institution.[25] Yet anyone who grew up in the 1950s or 1960s heard his electronic music at one time or another. Scott was the composer and electronic architect of a myriad of jingles, special effects, mood pieces, and other commercial applications of electronic music for radio, television, and industrial films. His specialty was the snappy tune, space-age sounds, and joyful electronic abstractions—all for hire. His work was used for a diverse portfolio of organizations and products ranging from Nescafé coffee to spark plugs, Bufferin pain reliever, General Motors, IBM, Hostess Twinkies, and Baltimore Gas and Electric, to name a few.

Prior to his endeavors as a designer of "plastic sounds" and "audio logos" for commercial purposes, Scott was most visible as a bandleader. Many of his catchy melodies— *Powerhouse, Twilight in Turkey, Dinner Music for a Pack of Hungry Cannibals*—were adapted for use in cartoons by legendary Warner Brothers music director Carl Stalling (1888–1974) during the 1940s and 1950s.

The other side of this man was little known to the public. Scott was at heart a self-taught electronics wizard and spent many of his early years soldering, tinkering, and inventing musically oriented contraptions. By the late 1940s, he had accumulated enough wealth from his work as a bandleader and composer to purchase a large home in North Hills, Long Island. In it were eight rooms devoted to his electronic experiments. He had a professionally outfitted machine shop for making electronic equipment and a spacious recording studio with a disc lathe, reel-to-reel tape recorders, and a wide assortment of wall-mounted instruments, mixers, and controls that grew more complex from year to year as he continued to invent new audio processing devices and musical instruments.[26]

Scott occasionally reached out to other engineers to obtain gear. Robert Moog recalled a visit he and his father made to Scott's home around 1955. Scott was interested in using one of the younger Moog's Theremin circuits. Robert Moog later remarked:

> I can't remember the first time I saw that much stuff. But you don't
> go from having nothing one day to having 30 feet of equipment the
> next. Scott probably was fooling with that kind of stuff for years and years.[27]

During the 1950s and 1960s, Scott and Eric Siday—another early customer of Robert Moog's—were the two most sought-after composers of music for radio and television commercials. Scott formed Manhattan Research Inc. as an outlet for his commercial electronic music production. By about 1960, he was offering a grab bag of gadgets for various musical applications, including four models of electronic doorbells, an electronic music box, and three models of an instrument he called the Electronium. By the mid-1960s, Scott's printed advertising billed Manhattan Research Inc. as "Designers and Manufacturers of Electronic Music and Musique Concrète Devices and Systems."[28]

Figure 6.16 Raymond Scott in his home studio, 1959.
(Raymond Scott Archives, Manhattan Research Inc.)

His most unique inventions included a variety of keyboard instruments, multitrack recording machines, and automatic composing instruments.

Multitrack Tape Recorder (1953)

Scott invented two of the earliest multitrack magnetic tape recorders. His patented machines could record seven and fourteen tracks on a single reel of tape using multiple tape heads. Les Paul (1915–2009) had previously used the technique of recording sound-on-sound in the early 1940s, but that method only involved recording from one monophonic tape recorder to another while playing along in real time. Scott's multitrack machines recorded seven or fourteen parallel audio tracks on the same reel of tape. Paul made a prototype of an eight-track machine in 1954,[29] and in 1955 Hugh Le Caine (1914–77) invented a machine that mixed six separate but synchronized tapes down to one track.

Clavivox (1959)

This was a three-octave keyboard instrument resembling a small electronic organ. It used the beat frequency principles of the *Ondes Martenot* and Theremin but had the

Figure 6.17   Raymond Scott's Clavivox.
(Thom Holmes)

unique ability to slide notes from key to key at adjustable rates of portamento. The Clavivox also had left-hand controls for vibrato, hard attack, and soft attack, and a mute button that allowed the player to abruptly silence a note while it was on the rise.[30] The instrument was one of the few products that Scott marketed commercially, although relatively few were made.

Electronium (1959–72)

Scott once remarked that "the Electronium is not played, it is guided."[31] Scott's remarkable "instantaneous composition/performance machine" evolved many times over the years and grew in sophistication as he continually cannibalized components from his other equipment. The Electronium was a semi-automated composing synthesizer without a keyboard. Controlled by a series of switches on the face of the instrument, the composer could preset melodies, tempos, and timbres or recall previously prescribed settings. After making initial settings for the music, the Electronium was set into motion and made additional parameter changes on its own, automating the creation of tunes according to the basic rules initiated by the composer. Polyrhythms and multiple parts for the music were performed and recorded in real time without the aid of multitrack tape recording.[32] The Electronium also used "processes based on controlled randomness to generate rhythms, melodies, and timbres."[33] In an operator's manual for one version of the Electronium, the inventor described the composing process as follows:

> A composer "asks" the Electronium to "suggest" an idea, theme, or motive. To repeat it, but in a higher key, he pushes the appropriate button. Whatever the composer needs: faster, slower, a new rhythm design, a hold, a pause, a second theme, variation, an extension, elongation, diminution, counterpoint, a change of phrasing, an ornament, ad infinitum. It is capable of a seemingly inexhaustible palette of musical sounds and colors, rhythms, and harmonies. Whatever the composer requests, the Electronium accepts and acts out his directions. The Electronium adds to the composer's thoughts, and a duet relationship is set up.[34]

Scott designed the Electronium to produce in hours what would have normally taken days or weeks for a composer to write out as scored music. He envisioned the device as a cost-saving innovation for the production of television and motion picture music.

Scott also developed a sophisticated, electro-mechanical switching **sequencer** to control his racks of electronic music devices.[35] This predecessor of the voltage-controlled sequencers developed by Moog could produce rhythmically uniform sequences "in which 200 elements can be combined in infinite permutations of pitch, tempo, meter, timbre, or special mood."[36] Some of the components of the sequencer found their way into the design of the Electronium.

The Electronium took Scott ten years to perfect. When he offered it for sale in 1970, Motown Music Inc. immediately expressed interest in buying one. Motown hired Scott to be their technology consultant for several years. His one and only commercially produced Electronium was delivered to Motown in the early 1970s and now resides in the Hollywood-based studio of Devo member Mark Mothersbaugh, who hopes one day to restore it to operating condition.

Scott was secretive about his musical invention and feared that others would steal his trade secrets. Aside from filing for patents, Scott did little to reveal the technology of his inventions to others. He was not interested in explaining his technology to other engineers but was more than willing to give lively demonstrations at advertising and media conventions. Even those who supplied Scott with components had no idea what they would be used for. "He never bought our stuff with the idea that he would plug it in and use it," recalled Robert Moog. "He was developing his own instrumentation. During the early days of us making synthesizers, Scott wanted us to make little things that he would then incorporate into instruments he was working on."[37] As a result, Raymond Scott had minimal influence on the evolution of music technology.

Hugh Le Caine

Canadian Hugh Le Caine was a physicist who, after helping develop early radar systems during World War II, turned his attention to designing electronic music devices. Among his achievements, Le Caine invented an early voltage-controlled synthesizer nearly 20 years before similar technology became widely available through the work of Robert Moog and Donald Buchla.

Whereas Raymond Scott was reluctant to share his musical inventions with other engineers, Le Caine was a product of academia and made his work known as a matter of course. He frequently contributed to the engineering literature and by 1954 was employed full-time by Canada's National Research Center to work on his electronic music inventions. This was a privileged position seldom afforded to an engineer of music technology in any country. For 20 years, this gifted and affable inventor devised innovative audio processing and synthesizing gear and nearly "single-handedly equipped electronic music studios at the University of Toronto (opened in 1959) and at McGill University in Montreal (opened in 1964)."[38] Le Caine is acknowledged as a major influence by both electronic music composers and engineers. Robert Moog, who invented the first commercially successful voltage-controlled synthesizer in the mid-1960s, called Le Caine a "profound influence" on his work.[39] His inventions ranged from multitrack tape recording methods to electronic keyboard instruments and analog sequencers.

Even though Le Caine's inventions were never mass-marketed like those of Moog and others, his influence was nonetheless significant because his ideas and equipment were used every day by a host of composers and technicians who frequented the electronic music studios at the University of Toronto and McGill University. Even though he completed over a dozen tape pieces, Le Caine never considered himself a serious composer. This, despite the fact that he composed one of the most famous examples of *musique concrète*—the two-minute *Dripsody* (mono 1955, stereo 1957). His "étude for variable-speed tape recorder" consisted of tape manipulations of a single sound: a drop of water falling into a bucket. He transformed the sound of the drip into a series of pitched notes by adjusting its playback speed and re-recording it. For many years, *Dripsody* was undoubtedly the most often played tape composition in any college music course.[40] In 1966, Pauline Oliveros had been working with tape delay techniques in the San Francisco area, where she lived. The equipment at the San Francisco Tape Music Center consisted largely of a cleverly patched-together amalgam of tape recorders, oscillators, and filter banks. That summer, she went to Toronto to study circuit-making with Le Caine for two months, and while working there she suddenly found that she had access to some of the most innovative and sophisticated electronic sound processing and recording equipment available anywhere. "The techniques that I had invented for myself were very well supported by the studio setup at the University of Toronto," explained Oliveros. "He [Le Caine] was a very generous man and wished to share his knowledge. I worked with some of his devices there—like the 20-channel loop machine. But most of my work was done with my own system."[41] Not surprisingly, Oliveros responded with a deluge of output; some ten completed tape compositions and six ultrasonic tape studies in just a few short weeks.[42] Among these was one of her best-known electronic works, the 21-minute *I of IV* (1966), featuring tape delay and 12-tone generators connected to an organ keyboard. The keyboard and oscillators were already set up that way in the Toronto studio and were evidently one of the versions of Le Caine's various "oscillator bank" permutations, this one having been installed in 1961. Oliveros did what came naturally to her: she pushed "the edges as far as possible."[43]

Electronic Sackbut (1945–73)

Le Caine began working on the Electronic Sackbut synthesizer in 1945 and continued to upgrade the instrument in keeping with parallel advances in electronics for almost 30 years. A model called the Sackbut Synthesizer, completed in 1971, was launched commercially but met with little success in a market saturated with more visible synthesizers marketed by Moog, ARP, EMS, and Buchla. Tragically, Le Caine died in 1977 at the age of 63 from injuries suffered in a motorcycle accident before having an opportunity to fully realize the potential of the Sackbut in a market that had finally caught up with his innovative ideas.

The Electronic Sackbut used voltage control techniques to trigger and modify sounds. The Sackbut had a familiar-looking keyboard for the control of pitch in addition to several specially devised touch-sensitive controls for other sound parameters. The keys of the manual were spring-mounted and pressure-sensitive so that the volume of the sound would increase with the force being applied to them. A gliding transition between adjacent keys was achieved by pressing a key sideways toward the next higher or lower key. With a little practice, this effect could be accentuated to take on a portamento glide by releasing the first key and then quickly pressing a series of additional keys up or down the scale.

The type of waveform and timbre was modified using a touch-sensitive pad for the left hand that had individual controllers for each finger. Because the hand could remain in a stationary position, the dexterity and practice needed to effectively play the controls was greatly minimized. All selections could be made with the fingers and thumb. The thumb had two pads for controlling the balance of overtones in a note: one controlled the dominating frequencies, or "main formant," of the waveform, and the other controlled the "auxiliary formant." The index finger rested on a movable circular pad that could be pressed in any direction to continuously change the waveform and timbre of the sound. This deceptively simple controller provided the player with extraordinarily fluid manipulation of the waveform. The oscillator provided sawtooth and pulse waveshapes. The pad was marked so that the musician could equate locations on the pad to various approximations of tonal quality, such as the reedy timbre of an oboe, the brassy sound of a trumpet, or the more purely abstract "foundation tones" of the oscillator. The remaining three fingers of the hand each had a pressure pad that could be pressed to modify the strict "periodicity" or regularity of the wave-form, resulting in surprising and sometimes unpredictable changes to the tone.

Le Caine's success and popularity with musicians was the result of his interest in developing instruments with intuitive and easy-to-learn controls. The Electronic Sackbut, although mono-phonic, was conceived with enough synthesizing flexibility to serve as "the starting point of all musical thinking."[44]

Figure 6.18   Electronic Sackbut prototype, invented by Hugh Le Caine in 1948. This was the first voltage-controlled analog synthesizer. (© Hugh Le Caine Archive, National Research Council Canada)

Touch-Sensitive Organ (1952–57)

Another early Le Caine project was the creation of the first **pressure–sensitive keyboard** for an electronic organ. Although regarded as a standard feature on even the least expensive electronic keyboard instruments today, his invention of a keyboard whose output volume would vary in proportion to how hard the keys were pressed was a couple of decades ahead of its time. A prototype was made of this organ and the rights to the patent were acquired by the Baldwin Organ Company in 1955, but a commercial model was never mass-produced.[45] Le Caine himself sometimes used the Touch-Sensitive Organ as an audio source for his own tape compositions, as in his piece *Ninety-Nine Generators* (1957).

Special Purpose Tape Recorder (1955–67)

Otherwise known as the "Multi-Track," this was Le Caine's early version of a tape recorder capable of recording and mixing multiple individual tracks. Monophonic recording was still the industry standard when he first produced a six-track version of the machine. Unlike later multitrack recorders—and Raymond Scott's invention from two years earlier—the Multi-Track did not record its sound using multiple tape heads and a single reel of tape. Instead, Le Caine's device synchronized the playback and recording of six individual tape reels. The sound from all six was mixed down into a single track. It was possible to control the variable speed of each of the six tapes independently of one another, making the recorder ideally suited for tape composition of electronic music. The speed of each tape was controlled by a touch-sensitive, 36-key keyboard, providing preset speed changes in small, incremental steps. In practice, the keyboard-controlled feature of the tape recorder was an excellent tool for the composer, providing a measurable degree of control over speed transposition that would not have been easily achieved through conventional variable control or clutch-driven tape recorders. Le Caine demonstrated the utility of this device to the composer when he created his own work *Dripsody* (1955), the sound material for which was based largely on the sound of dripping water transposed to different speeds. The Special Purpose Tape Recorder was a key component of the University of Toronto Electronic Music Studio when it opened in 1959.[46] Le Caine refined the device over the years, eventually making a more compact, solid-state version in 1967.

Oscillator Banks (1959–61) and the Spectrogram (1959)

Le Caine built several versions of a device for controlling and experimenting with multiple audio oscillators. Each had a touch-sensitive keyboard for triggering the individual oscillators, each of which could be tuned and switched to play sine, pulse, and sawtooth waves. He built versions of the oscillator bank with 12, 16, 24, and 108 oscillators. In addition to the touch-sensitive keyboard controller, the oscillator bank could be programmed using an optical reader called the Spectrogram. Le Caine invented the Spectrogram to enable the graphical input of program instructions—a uniquely artistic method of sound programming even to this day. Images were fed into the Spectrogram using a roll of paper and scanned using an array of 100 photocells. Le Caine's interest in the optical input of graphic information to be used for composing purposes paralleled similar interest at both the Columbia–Princeton Electronic Music Center and the Siemens Studio für Elektronische Musik in Munich.

Serial Sound Generator (1966–70)

This forerunner of analog sequencers used hardwired switches to program a series of tones and related effects. Essentially, it was an analog computer dedicated to the programming of musical sequences. It gave the composer control over the pitch, duration, timbre, and repetition of sounds, and used a voltage-controlled oscillator as its sound source.

Sonde (1968)

The Sonde was another Le Caine instrument dedicated to controlling a large number of sine wave generators. In this case, it had 200 signals available, controlled by a panel of slide controls, one for each tone. Transistorized circuits greatly reduced the space needed to house all of this gear; the Sonde stood four feet high and two feet wide, giving it a much smaller footprint than Le Caine's earlier oscillator banks.

Polyphone Synthesizer (1970)

At the height of the monophonic Moog craze, Le Caine sat down to design what would become one of the most powerful and least-known analog synthesizers of all time.

The voltage-controlled instrument was built for the McGill University Electronic Music Studio and was fully polyphonic—a feature that other makers of voltage-controlled synthesizers would not introduce for several more years. Like the Minimoog that also appeared in 1970, the instrument was compact with many sound-shaping modules built in. Unlike any other synthesizers available at the time, however, the Polyphone had touch-sensitive keys and individual pitch and waveform controls for each key. Le Caine was able to include these capabilities by giving each of the 37 keys its own dedicated oscillator.

SUMMARY

- The conceptual and technical building blocks that would figure significantly in the development of the commercially available analog synthesizer took shape during the 1940s and 1950s with the increasingly sophisticated approach to synthesis developed by institutional electronic music studios.

- The Olson–Belar electronic music composing machine introduced binary programmability, through the use of punched paper tape, as a control element in the creation of electronic music.

- The RCA Mark II Electronic Music Synthesizer was provided for use to the Columbia–Princeton Electronic Music Center in 1959. Although its programmable composing feature was only used by a select few composers, the machine included a robust set of sound modification features, including multitrack tape recording, pitch, timbre, and envelope control, and an advanced filtering system for altering the quality and pitch of source audio signals.

- The modular design of the RCA Mark II Electronic Music Synthesizer and associated technology were precursors of solid-state analog synthesizers of the 1960s.

- The Columbia–Princeton Electronic Music Center was the first notable university-based electronic music studio in North America, and provided access to equipment for composers and students.

- The Siemens Studio für Elektronische Musik in Munich, which developed parallel to the Electronic Music Center at Columbia University, was another well-equipped facility with programmable control over wave generators and a wide variety of audio processing features. Although not designed from the ground up as an integrated synthesizer like the Olson–Belar RCA synthesizer, the equipment at the Siemens Studio für Elektronische Musik offered many of the same advantages and modularity in the process of creating music.

- Developments at both the Columbia–Princeton Electronic Music Center and the Siemens Studio für Elektronische Musik represented a bridge from the purely electro-mechanical synthesizer to voltage-controlled instruments that permitted improved programmability for the composer.

- Raymond Scott was a commercial musician and inventor of electronic musical instruments whose work was largely devoted to the making of music for films and television commercials. His inventions included a modular composing synthesizer, a multitrack tape recorder, and a programmable analog sequencer.

- Hugh Le Caine developed the first voltage-controlled synthesizer, the Electronic Sackbut, and designed the key audio components found in the electronic music studios of the University of Toronto and McGill University. His other achievements included the invention of the first touch-sensitive keyboard for an electronic organ, multitrack tape recording devices, an analog sequencer, and banks featuring controllable multiple oscillators.

KEY PEOPLE IN CHAPTER SIX

KEY TERMS IN CHAPTER SIX

MILESTONES

Early Synthesizers and Experimenters

Technical and scientific	Year	Instruments
– Homer Dudley of Bell Labs invented a means for controlling audio processing equipment voltage control.	1939	– The Dudley vocoder included voltage-controlled envelope and amplifier through components.
– Hugh Le Caine developed the first voltage-controlled synthesizer prototype.	1945	– Hugh Le Caine introduced his prototype synthesizer, the Electronic Sackbut.
– Transistor invented at Bell Labs.	1947	
– Olson and Belar invented the electronic music composing machine.	1950	
– Hugh Le Caine invented the touch-sensitive keyboard.	1952	– Hugh Le Caine introduced the Touch-Sensitive Organ.
– Raymond Scott invented the Multitrack Tape Recorder.	1953	
– Electronic music experiments began at Siemens corporation in Munich, Germany.	1955	– RCA Mark I Electronic Music Synthesizer demonstrated in Princeton. – Hugh Le Caine introduced the Special Purpose Tape Recorder.
– Columbia–Princeton Electronic Music Center founded.	1958	– RCA Mark II Electronic Music Synthesizer installed at the Columbia–Princeton Electronic Music Center; a multitrack tape recorder and punched paper reader enabled composers to compose multivoice electronic works that could be played in real time.
– Siemens Studio für Elektronische Musik opened its doors to outside composers. – Harald Bode developed a voltage-controlled amplifier. – Hugh Le Caine invented the first of many series of oscillator bank controllers.	1959	– The Siemens studio included four paper tape readers for controlling sound composition, a vocoder for filtering and shaping source signals, and multitrack mixing. – Raymond Scott introduced the Clavivox electronic keyboard and Electronium composition and performance synthesizer.
– Composer Vladimir Ussachevsky gave Robert Moog a specification for a voltage-controlled envelope generator.	1965	– The Ussachevsky/Moog voltage-controlled envelop generator was built for the Columbia–Princeton Electronic Music Center and also became the basis for envelope generation on Moog and other analog synthesizers.

Technical and scientific	Year	Music and instruments
	1966	– Hugh Le Caine introduced the Serial Sound Generator, an analog sequencer.
	1970	– Hugh Le Caine introduced the Polyphone Synthesizer.

CHAPTER 7

Principles of Analog Synthesis and Voltage Control

Brutal, caustic, volcanic. Evocative, flirting, caressing. Crisp, powerful, biting. Entrancing, embracing, exhilarating! Extend the stuff your music is made of with the Minimoog . . . The IN-strument of the Pros.
—Original Moog Minimoog brochure, 1971

Vladimir Ussachevsky and engineer Peter Mauzey in the Buchla studio of the Columbia–Princeton Electronic Music Center, *c.* 1970. (Columbia University Computer Music Center)

Electronic music is an art that marries technology and human imagination. This chapter provides a definitional background to the science behind audio phenomena and its application to the synthesis of musical sound. Understanding such fundamentals was essential to the early composers of electronic music whose equipment often had its origins in the audio engineering lab. Over time, even as the design of the instruments has become less technical and more comprehensible to the average person, the lexicon of electronic music terms and principles remains the same. Knowing the basics of waveforms, filters, cutoff frequencies, modulation, and other technical concepts is key to a thorough understanding of the making of electronic music and appreciation of the results.

In keeping with the generally chronological organization of the historical portion of this book, this chapter provides a grounding in the principles underlying the making of electronic music from the standpoint of analog synthesis and the application of these precepts to voltage-controlled synthesizers. As such, this material provides background in anticipation of discussions of both voltage-controlled analog synthesizers in Chapter 8 and their application in computer and digital synthesis as discussed in Chapters 10, 11, and 12.

UNDERSTANDING MUSICAL SOUND

The science of musical acoustics developed during the latter half of the nineteenth century in tandem with general discoveries in the field of electricity. The scientist Hermann von Helmholtz was a principal player in these discoveries and demonstrated that musical sound could be analyzed according to a few basic physical principles. Using combinations of tuning forks to illustrate his point, he showed that the quality (or timbre) of a tone was reliant on the intensity, order, and number of harmonics (overtones and partials) present in a note. Helmholtz showed that the vibrations found in a single musical tone consisted of a **fundamental** or base tone accompanied by related **harmonics** above the frequency of the fundamental. The harmonics of a tone are responsible for creating timbre or tone color. Timbre is what distinguishes the sound of a violin from the sound of a piano, even though both instruments might be playing the same note. Every instrument exhibits its own unique mixture of harmonics called its **harmonic spectrum**. Figure 7.1 visualizes the natural harmonic series of a tone.

When building sounds using electronic music techniques, the composer is working with the naturally occurring harmonic spectrum of predefined waveforms. Figures 7.2 and 7.3 depict a common method of illustrating the harmonic spectrum of waveforms, in this case a square and triangle wave. Figure 7.3 relates the harmonic spectrum inherent with each basic type of waveform to the musical scale.

The Helmholtz theory suggested that sound could be analyzed by its component parts and led directly to the engineering of electronic means for synthesizing sound, first in the form of Cahill's Telharmonium. An understanding of the wave structure of sound led to a robust reassessment of tonal systems used by composers. A technical understanding of consonance and dissonance stemmed from this scientific work. Helmholtz's theories also inspired a new, rational approach to analyzing sounds of all types, including noises. The Futurists categorized different types of sound for the purpose of using them in composition. Ferruccio Busoni saw in the scientific understanding of musical sound the possibility of inventing new instruments for extending the range of the 12-tone system. Busoni referred to Cahill's Telharmonium in this regard when he wrote in 1907:

Keyboard instruments, in particular, have so thoroughly schooled our ears that we are no longer capable of hearing anything else—incapable of hearing except through this impure medium, yet Nature created an *infinite gradation—infinite!* . . . He [Cahill] has constructed a comprehensive apparatus which makes it possible to transform an electric current into a fixed and mathematically exact number of vibrations. As pitch depends on the number of vibrations, and the apparatus may be "set" on any number desired, the infinite gradation of the octave may be accomplished by merely moving a lever corresponding to the pointer of a quadrant.[1]

All of these people had set the scene many years before the arrival of composer John Cage. Cage brought an artistic clarity to the nature of creating music. He did this by professing to remove his emotions from the process of composing and objectively examining the materials of music. Cage sought ways to let sounds be themselves, allowing the listener to provide whatever emotional or intellectual context he or she needed to assess the result. In this regard, Cage directly echoed the sentiments of Busoni, who once declared that "Music was born free; and to win freedom is its destiny."[2] Cage's approach was not unlike that of a scientist studying a natural phenomenon. He observed, measured, and experimented to carry out musical hypotheses in the form of compositions.

The natural harmonic series

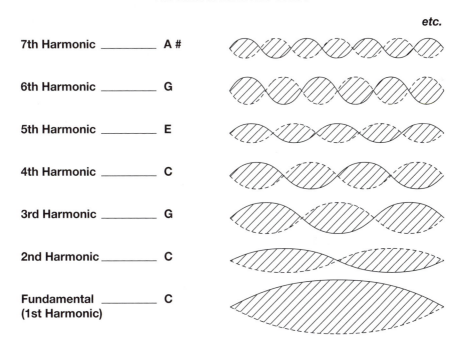

Figure 7.1 The harmonic content of a note comprises the dominant frequency known as the first harmonic, or fundamental. The first harmonic is the lowest frequency in the harmonic series of two or more frequencies that make up the content of a note. This diagram portrays the harmonic series for a note played by a string instrument. Electronic musical instruments can build notes using the addition and subtraction of harmonics to and from the fundamental tone. (After Friedman, 1986)

Harmonic spectrum of a square wave

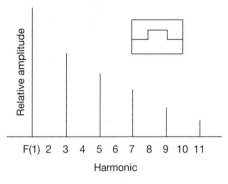

Harmonic spectrum of a sawtooth wave

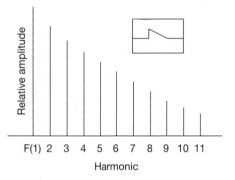

Figure 7.2   Harmonic spectra of square and sawtooth waveforms. (After Friedman, 1986)

Like Helmholtz, Cage was fascinated by the constituent parts that make up sound. In 1937, he gave a talk to an arts society in Seattle in which he suggested that music should be defined by its four basic components: the timbre ("overtone structure"), frequency, amplitude, and duration of sounds.[3] By 1957 he had added a fifth component to the list: the "morphology," or envelope, of the sound, otherwise known as its attack and decay characteristics, or "how the sound begins, goes on, and dies away."[4]

When Cage first proposed these ideas he also related them directly to the potential of using electronic musical devices to broaden our sound spectrum and create a new kind of music. The special nature of "electrical instruments" was that they provided total control over the principal components of sound. In perhaps his most prophetic statement, Cage said in 1937, "I believe that the use of noise to make music will continue and increase until we reach a music produced through the aid of electrical instruments which will make available for musical purposes any and all sounds that can be heard."[5]

Cage was by no means working in aesthetic isolation. He had the benefit of knowing and learning from several key figures in contemporary music, including Edgard Varèse, Henry Cowell, and Arnold Schoenberg. But in analyzing sound according to the five basic parameters—timbre, frequency, duration, amplitude, and envelope—Cage defined the

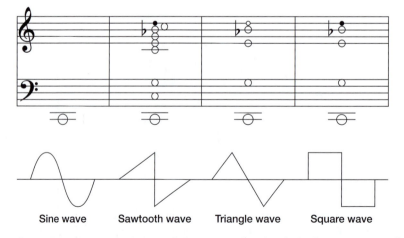

Sine wave   Sawtooth wave   Triangle wave   Square wave

Figure 7.3   Harmonic spectra of sine, sawtooth, triangle, and square waves, shown using musical notation. (After Strange, 1983)

common denominators by which all sound can be described. What set Cage apart was that he used these essentially scientific principles to rewrite the definition of music. Because all sounds are composed of the same primary components and because music is sound, then it must follow that all sounds can be defined as being musical.

The Components of Sound

Sound is produced by air pressure waves that cause the eardrum to vibrate. These vibrations are converted by auditory nerves into impulses that the brain recognizes as sounds. If a wave vibrates in a regular pattern, it is perceived as a pitched sound, such as those used in music. If the wave does not vibrate in a regular pattern, it is perceived as unpitched sound or noise.

Understanding the five components of sound is helpful for the appreciation of any music. They are especially pertinent to electronic music because the composer and musician are often working with direct control over these aspects of what you hear:

- **Frequency: the pitch of a sound**. Specifically, it is the number of vibrations per second that, when in the audible range, are detected as a certain pitch. In measuring frequency, a single vibration is called a **cycle** and the number of cycles can be expressed by a unit of measure known as the **hertz (Hz)**. In electronic music, this pitch becomes audible as an expression of the alternating electrical current that is used to vibrate the cone of a loudspeaker at a certain rate per second.
- **Amplitude: the loudness or volume of a sound and its constituent harmonics**. The simplest definition of amplitude is that it comprises the loudness of a sound and is conveyed through a loudspeaker by the distance that the speaker cone moves back and forth from its neutral position. Amplitude has multiple applications in the creation of electronic music. In addition to the overall volume of a given signal, one can selectively alter the amplitude of individual harmonics using controlled voltages, changing the timbre of a tone. In addition, amplitude may have its own shape or pattern that affects the envelope of a sound (see below).
- **Timbre: the nature or quality of a sound**. Sometimes known as tone color, timbre is what distinguishes the sounds of different musical instruments playing the same note. All sound waves are complex and contain more than just one simple frequency or fundamental tone. These additional wave structures are sometimes called *partials*, *overtones*, *harmonics*, and *transients*. If one harmonic, or fundamental, predominates, then the sound can be related to a note on the musical scale. A more complex set of harmonics—for example a sound in which the amplitudes of all harmonics have been made equal—makes it difficult to associate a tone with a specific note.
- **Duration: the length of time that a sound is audible**. Acoustic instruments have a limited ability to sustain sounds. The piano is designed with a pedal for the purpose of sustaining notes. Electronic instruments have the innate ability to sustain a sound indefinitely, making duration a key element in composition. The overall duration of a note can be further broken down into its envelope characteristics (see below).

- **Envelope: the attack, sustain, and decay characteristics of a sound**. The envelope of a sound is essentially the shape of the amplitude characteristics of a sound as it occurs over time—the way it begins, sustains, and ends. **Attack** refers to the beginning of a sound and how long it takes to reach its maximum loudness. **Sustain** is the length of time that a sound lasts at a fixed amplitude. **Decay** is the time it takes for the signal to go from its peak amplitude to its sustain amplitude. **Release** comprises the time it takes for a note to end and return to zero amplitude, for example after the finger is lifted from the key.

Fourier Analysis and Waveform Mathematics

The French mathematician and physicist Jean Baptiste Fourier (1768–1830) developed a theory of wave physics during the early nineteenth century that allowed for the scientific analysis of musical sound. In relation to the frequency relationships of periodic waveforms, the theory states that *any periodic vibration (waveform), however complex, is comprised or can be created by combining a series of simple vibrations whose frequencies are harmonically related.*

Fourier theory has two direct applications in electronic music. First, a sound wave is made of component parts and, by analyzing its characteristics (e.g. frequency, amplitude), one can measure and control such components to modify the sound. This is called **Fourier analysis**. Second, waveforms can be created with predictable and controllable results by combining simpler waves (e.g. sine waves) into more complex waves. This is a method of synthesis based on Fourier principles and is called *Fourier* or *additive synthesis*. In the case of harmonic sounds, the sidebands or harmonics all consist of integer multiples of the lowest or fundamental frequency. Non-harmonic musical sounds—such as that of a gong or bell—can be created by combining waveforms that are not integer multiples of one another. Figure 7.4 shows the results of combining several simple waveforms.

The frequency range of the 12-tone scale may contain higher and lower octaves. An **octave** is created by doubling or dividing in half the frequency of the first harmonic (fundamental) of a tone. Figure 7.5 provides a guide to the frequencies of fundamental tones in a standard set of octaves.

Making Music

It is evident from earlier chapters that there has been an evolution in the field of electronic music from the use of simpler, non-parametric instruments such as the Theremin, electronic organ, or even the tape recorder to instrumentation that provides the composer with increasingly programmatic control over the elemental components of musical sound. Allen Strange (1943–2008), in his classic text about the techniques of analog synthesis, pointed out that electronic musicians faced the same challenges as those learning conventional instruments: musical events involve practice in the making of a sound as well as the control or performance of the sound.[6] Table 7.1 provides a reminder of the many complexities of musical sound that must be managed in an electronic music environment and at the same time indicates how they are interrelated. For example, loudness is affected by both the filtering of the audio spectrum and amplitude.

Controlling all of the parameters available for generating and performing music on analog synthesizers was made practical by the introduction of the technique of voltage control.

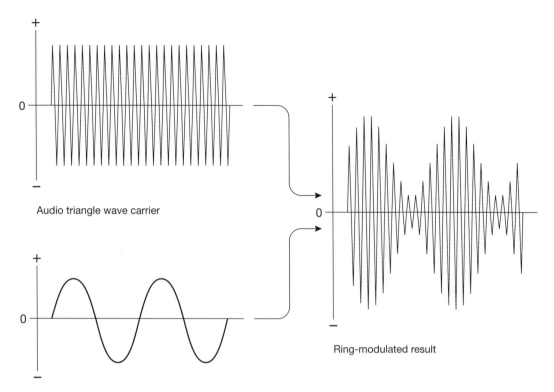

Figure 7.4   Ring modulation serves as a good illustration of the effects on waveshape when two different waveforms are combined. In this case, a triangle wave is modulated by a sub–audio sine wave, resulting in a waveform that combines and subtracts elements of both source signals. (After Naumann, 1985)

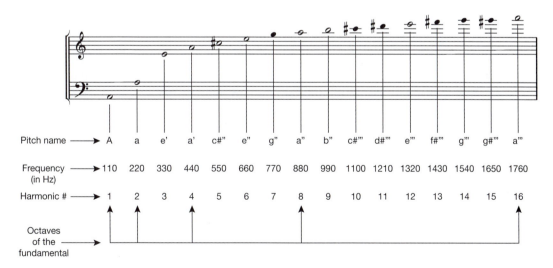

Figure 7.5   Frequencies expressed in Hz and related to the musical scale. (After Naumann, 1985)

Table 7.1   **Electronic music parameters[7]**

Frequency	*Audio spectrum*	*Amplitude*	*Structure*
Discrete pitch	Timbre	Loudness	Rhythm
Sliding pitches (portamento and glissando)	Loudness	Rhythm	Duration
Vibrato	Vibrato	Tremolo	Repetition
Timbre	Tremolo		Sequence
Associated techniques			
Frequency modulation	Band-pass filtering	Amplitude modulation	Looping
	Ring modulation	Delay	Sequencing
	Reverberation		Envelope generation
	Pulse width modulation		

ELECTRONIC SOUND GENERATION

Waveforms can be generated by an electronic circuit called an **oscillator**, which produces periodic vibrations in the form of an electric current. The resulting current precisely mirrors the shape of the waveform in a natural acoustic environment and is only audible once it reaches a loudspeaker. Oscillators can produce sounds in the full range of human hearing—from about 20 Hz to 20,000 Hz. They may also produce subsonic and ultrasonic waves, which cannot be heard but which, when combined with other waves, produce an audible result in keeping with Fourier principles of waveform behavior. Oscillators are the basic building blocks of sound in a synthesizer.

Oscillators have been made using many different techniques throughout the history of electronic music. In the late nineteenth century, Thaddeus Cahill invented the tone wheel—an electro-mechanical device that required the rotation of precisely milled notched metal cogs against a metal brush to produce pitch-making circuits. Vacuum tubes were used as oscillators in many early electronic musical instruments until the advent of the transistor in the 1950s. Solid-state oscillator circuits were found in voltage-controlled analog synthesizers from the 1960s to the mid-1980s, when digital synthesis using integrated circuits and software was adopted.

Waveforms

Common terminology is used in describing the characteristics of waveforms. Figure 7.6 provides a graphical representation of these aspects of a waveform.

The midpoint of a wave's propagation is called the **equilibrium point** and is denoted as point 0 on a waveform diagram. A **period** is the length of time required for a wave to complete one cycle from the equilibrium point to its apex, back through the equilibrium point to its base point and back again to the equilibrium point. The distance from the apex to the base of a waveform is called the **displacement**, another designation for

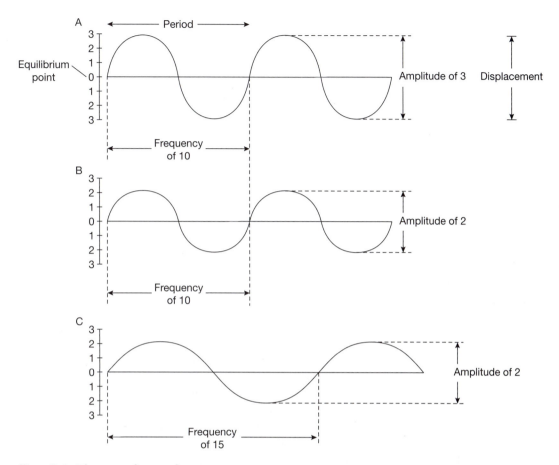

Figure 7.6   Elements of a waveform. (After Strange, 1983)

wave amplitude. The **duty cycle** of a wave is a ratio denoting the proportion of a single cycle that occurs above the equilibrium point versus time below the equilibrium point.

Waveforms can also be said to occupy a space in time, also known as the **phase**. Waveforms are said to be *in phase* if they are identical and occupy the same space and time in the conducting medium. If two identical waves are displaced slightly in the same conducting medium, one beginning before the other, they are said to be *out of phase*. This phenomenon produces audibly perceptible results and has been used as a recording technique by variably phasing two identical recorded tracks of any sound source, producing a gradually shifting spatial displacement of the sound (see Figure 7.7).

There are four basic waveforms used in electronic music composition. All of them may exist in any frequency range:

- **Sine wave**. This is the simplest type of waveform. It contains no harmonics. The sine wave undulates evenly. Although some liken the sound of a sine wave to that of a flute, even the flute has more body and depth than a pure sine tone, since it contains harmonics. The audible sine wave is a thin, precise tone, similar to a whistle. Multiple sine waves are often used as the building blocks of more complex tones.

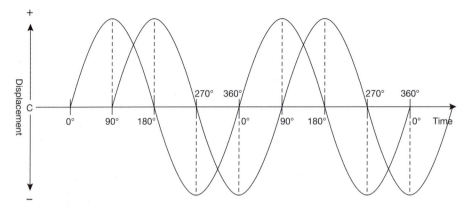

Figure 7.7   Phase relationships of two sine waves. (After Naumann, 1985)

- **Sawtooth wave**. The sawtooth or ramp wave contains all even and odd harmonics associated with a fundamental tone, making it a rich source for modeling other sounds. The amplitude of each overtone decreases exponentially as a ratio of the harmonic's frequency to that of the fundamental, providing a ramp shape to the wave. The sound of the sawtooth is rich and buzzy and is often used to reproduce the sound of reeds or bowed string instruments.
- **Triangle wave**. A triangle wave contains only the fundamental frequency and all of its odd-numbered harmonics. The amplitudes of the harmonics fall off in odd-integer ratios. The sound of the triangle wave has more body and depth than a sine wave, somewhat like a muted horn.
- **Pulse wave**. The pulse or *rectangular* wave has only the odd harmonics of the fundamental, like the triangle wave, but differs significantly in the amplitude relationships of these harmonics. Unlike sine, sawtooth, and triangle waves, which make a transition from the apex to the base of the wave cycle, the pulse wave instantaneously jumps from the apex to the base. Duty cycles of pulse waves can vary, with 1:3 being typical (1:3 indicates that the cycle spends one third above 0 and two thirds below 0 per cycle). The harmonic content of the pulse wave is determined by the duty cycle. A **square wave** is a type of pulse wave whose duty cycle is one half of the total cycle of the waveform, or 1:2, evenly divided between the upper and lower reaches of the wave, hence its square shape. The harmonic content of a pulse wave can be changed dramatically merely by altering its duty cycle. Pulse waves have a clear, resonant sound.

Each of these basic waveforms has a reliable structure that exhibits strict amplitude relationships between the harmonics and their fundamental. They can also be combined to create richer, more textured sounds or used to modulate the amplitude or frequency of another sound—techniques that will be explored below.

One more basic waveform needs to be mentioned. It is called **white noise**, and it does not exhibit the structural symmetry of sine, triangle, sawtooth, or pulse waves. In the simplest sense, white noise is to those four basic waveforms what the color gray is to the primary colors: it is a combination of all of them, with no particular element dominating the mix. White noise results when all the frequency and amplitude characteristics of a sound occur at random within the audio spectrum or contain energy at all

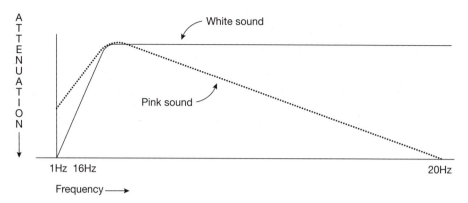

Figure 7.8   Graphic representation of white and pink noise frequency spectra. (After Strange, 1983)

frequencies within the audio spectrum. It is a continuous dense hiss. It can be filtered, modulated, and otherwise refined to sound like such things as the wind or the ocean, and is a rich source of background sound and texture for the composer of electronic music. Even The Beatles found an effective use for modulated white noise in their use of Moog-created undulating, wind-like noise at the end of "I Want You (She's So Heavy)" (1969). Composer Allen Strange defined white noise more precisely as containing all audible frequencies between 18 Hz and 22,000 Hz. A distilled form of white noise is called **pink noise**, which Strange defined as containing all frequencies between 18 Hz and 10,000 Hz (see Figure 7.8). At the other end of the audio spectrum, noise restricted to the frequency ranges between 10,000 Hz and 22,000 Hz would be **blue noise**.[8]

Electroacoustic Input

Natural sounds recorded using microphones and pickups are another common source of audio materials for electronic music composition. Recordings made using turntables and magnetic tape were key to the early practitioners of *musique concrète*. Since the early 1950s, the general practice has been to liberally combine sounds captured acoustically with electronically generated sounds on an as-needed basis to compose electronic music.

The term **electroacoustic music** is widely used to denote music that integrates sounds from the natural world with audio processing as well as synthesized sounds. The term "electroacoustic music" became more widely used during the 1970s and 1980s, a critical period of technology transition as the use of analog equipment began the switch to digital audio processing. The adoption of the term signaled a realization on the part of practitioners that it was important to leave behind previous definitions of electronic music, such as *musique concrète*, that carried dogmatic links to long since past formative stages in the history of the medium. By the late 1970s, the importance of electronic music techniques to all genres of music had become apparent, extending its reach well beyond the work of experimental music composers housed in institutional audio laboratories. But a definition of the field will vary depending on the expected outcomes. Contemporary practitioners are schooled in synthesis techniques (analog and digital), signal processing and sound manipulation, analysis and re-synthesis, spatialization, recording, and real-time or interactive software programming for live performance.

Dartmouth University, New Hampshire, has a graduate program in "electroacoustic music" that broadly "explores the interrelationships among music, technology, cognitive and computer science, acoustics, and related disciplines," an approach representing perhaps the most flexible definition of all, which not only considers the music but also the relationship of the human being to the listening experience, the cultural impact of such music, and the technology used to create it. For the purposes of this book, electroacoustic music is broadly defined as *music created using electronic and acoustic sound sources.*

Microphones and pickups are two common methods of capturing sound for use in electronic music. These devices fall into the broader category of *electroacoustic transducers,* as they are instruments designed to change vibrations in the air into an electric current so that it can be detected by an electronic device. The loudspeaker is also a transducer, only its function is to transform vibrations stored as electric current back into sound waves in the air. Two kinds of microphones or pickups have been commonly used in the production of electronic music:

- **Microphones**. Microphones respond to waves of varying air pressure. They can be built using two basic principles—the **dynamic** or electromagnetic microphone and the **condenser** or capacitor/electrostatic microphone.

  The dynamic microphone uses a diaphragm affixed to a coil within a magnetic field. Minute fluctuations of the diaphragm in response to sound vibrations create corresponding fluctuations in the magnetic field that can then be converted into a weak electric current. In the condenser microphone, the diaphragm is paired with a parallel metal plate to form a capacitor—an electrical device that can store energy between two such associated plates. When vibrations cause the diaphragm to fluctuate, changes in the static charges of the two plates are translated into a corresponding electric current.

  Dynamic microphones do not usually have the same frequency range response as a condenser microphone, although they may be ideal for certain ranges such as that of the singing voice. Most recording studios use condenser microphones to capture the full range of human hearing, frequencies from less than 100 Hz to about 20,000 Hz.

- **Contact microphones**. The **contact microphone**, or **pickup**, is not designed to detect vibrations in the air but rather to transduce vibrations from a solid surface with which it is in close proximity or in direct contact. Contact microphones are extremely limited in their frequency response, responding only to a narrow band of vibrations of no more than a few thousand hertz, usually at the lower end of the scale. Even so, contact microphones are a familiar staple of electroacoustic music because of their ability to amplify quiet, otherwise undetectable sounds. They can be inexpensively constructed using a few dollars' worth of parts from Radio Shack.

  Other kinds of pickups that can be used to detect sound waves include magnetic pickups such as those found on electric guitars, and the phonograph cartridge. In the late 1950s, John Cage and David Tudor discovered that they could get some startling results by using a phono-cartridge as a kind of contact microphone. The phono-cartridge is designed to transduce the vibrations present in the groove of a vinyl audio recording. It does this by way of a needle or stylus that converts the vibrations into an electric current that is amplified. Cage and Tudor made their new sounds by detaching the cartridge from its tone arm and using objects such as toothpicks, Slinkys, and straight-pins in place of the usual needle.

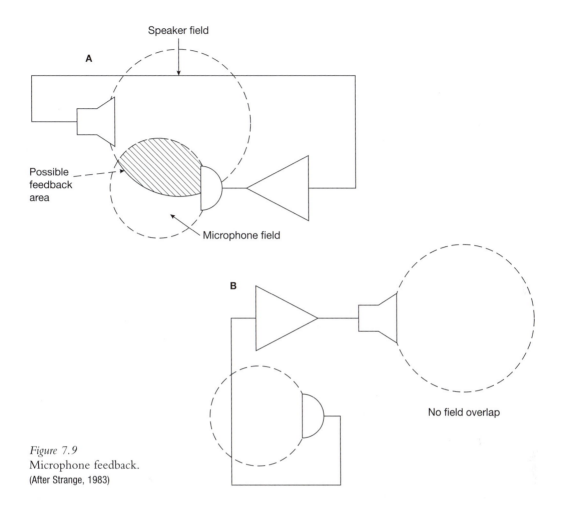

Figure 7.9
Microphone feedback.
(After Strange, 1983)

Audio Feedback

Composer Robert Ashley called **feedback** "the only sound that is intrinsic to electronic music."[9] Not only is it a natural effect that is available whenever a microphone or audio pickup is used, but it also introduces the use of sustained sounds, which are one of electronic music's inherent attributes. Feedback as a sound source is both abundantly available and difficult to control.

Acoustic Feedback

Acoustic feedback occurs when a signal is amplified and re-amplified within a closed system involving a microphone and a loudspeaker. In a situation such as a microphone placed too close to a loudspeaker, the audio signal created by the microphone is fed back into itself when it is projected by the loudspeaker (see Figure 7.9). The effect depends on the proximity of the microphone and loudspeaker, the amplitude of the output of the loudspeaker, the sensitivity of the microphone, and the reflective acoustic properties of the space.

The piercing, howling sound associated with uncontrolled feedback is normally undesirable, but some composers—and rock musicians—have used the principles behind feedback as the underlying source material for their music.

Robert Ashley's *The Wolfman* (1964) manipulates feedback intentionally through a clever performing technique requiring little equipment other than a microphone, amplifier, tape recorder, and speaker system. The level of amplification is set very high at the point of feedback for the given audio space. The performer delivers a set of vocal patterns while keeping the mouth in very close proximity to the microphone. Ashley described the effect:

> In *The Wolfman* the feedback is tuned for whatever place you're performing in. Then into that feedback are put different kinds of modulating materials on tape. That modulated feedback product is passing through the sole microphone in the space, the singer's microphone. That means that by just putting your mouth up against the microphone, and by doing very simple vocalisms, you can affect that whole feedback system in a very slow, modulation filtering sense. That's the principle of the piece. The feedback is a loop and the tape sound is being broadcast into that loop. The bottleneck in that loop is the microphone so that by treating the resonant cavity right in front of the microphone you actually create a model of the room in the size of the vocal cavity. It's a very simple principle. The room just keeps moving around and changing shape because of the way you shape your mouth. The act of doing it in the presence of that sound—the feedback—is so overpowering to the listener that no one ever understands how the sound is made.[10]

Steve Reich (b. 1936) arrived at his work called *Pendulum Music* (1968) by manipulating the acoustic properties of a swinging sound wave field. In this work, one or more loudspeakers were placed on their backs, aimed at the ceiling. Microphones were the source of the input signal. The amplitude was turned up to the point where feedback would occur if the microphones were brought within proximity of a loudspeaker. The microphones, suspended from the ceiling on long cables like pendulums, were then swung so that they would pass just over the loudspeakers. As a microphone crossed the space above a loudspeaker it would create a whooping feedback sound. As the swing of the microphones eventually decayed, they came to rest directly over the loudspeakers, causing uninterrupted feedback until the amplifier was shut off.

In *Pendulum Music*, what began as a straightforward compositional process ended with the cacophony of an opposing process: uncontrolled electronic feedback. Reich, whose highly determinist compositions stand in stark contrast to Cage's work, was amused by the combination of process and chaos that *Pendulum Music* represented:

> Over a period of ten minutes, which was a little too long for my taste, and as the pendulums come to rest, you entered a pulsing drone. Once it hit the drone, I would pull the plug on the machine and the whole thing ended. It's the ultimate process piece. It's me making my peace with Cage. It's audible sculpture. If it's done right, it's kind of funny.[11]

Feedback Circuits (Electronic Feedback)

Another form of feedback for generating audio signals is the use of **feedback circuits**. This type of feedback is not acoustical in the sense that it does not have its origins in the air of the listening space. Instead, circuit feedback is the result of signals generated within an electronic instrument whose design enables the recirculation of a signal within a closed circuit—taking the output back into the input— prior to its amplification in the listening space. Circuit feedback can take many forms in the hands of a tinkering composer.

David Tudor was one of the pioneers of circuit feedback and live electronic music. His important works *Untitled* (1972), *Toneburst* (1975), and *Pulsers* (1976) are based on the ability to feed the output of some of his devices back into their own inputs. The resulting signal paths could be manipulated by adjusting gain levels and filters.

Composer David Lee Myers (b. 1949) has been creating electronic music using only feedback circuits for over 20 years. Myers feeds electronic circuits back onto themselves to create interference noise that he can then mix, filter, and shape using audio processors:

Figure 7.10   Composer David Lee Myers uses feedback circuits to create music. (Thom Holmes)

> The idea is that an effects device is fed some of its own output—much like a squealing speaker which accidentally feeds the microphone supplying its input —and electrons begin to flow as they wish. The trick is to shape this flow, select the feedback paths which create an aesthetically pleasing, or whatever direction and shape. What is required is several devices whose business it is to bend sound into various shapes, and a routing scheme which allows them to speak to each other and to themselves.[12]

Using a variety of specialized "feedback workstations" that Myers has constructed over the years, the feedback system begins with a complex web of circuits that, once set in motion, spontaneously interfere with one another and generate output that can be amplified as sound. During a performance, Myers monitors and adjusts the process using a variety of audio components, including delays, ring modulation, an envelope generator, reverberation, an equalizer/filter, and a mixing panel. The result does not rely on the characteristics of the acoustic space but rather the way in which a multiple of circuit signals interfere with each other.

Japanese composer Toshimaru Nakamura (b. 1962) and the Netherlands' Marko Ciciliani (b. 1970) are two more practitioners who have recently devoted much work to feedback circuits and live performance. Both perform using the so-called "no-input mixer," an audio mixer wired such that its output is connected to its own input: no external signals are introduced. It thus becomes an instrument capable of being played via manipulation of its tone and volume controls, and the range of sounds that can be produced is extraordinary.

VOLTAGE CONTROL FUNDAMENTALS

As introduced in the previous chapter, **voltage control** is a method of applying metered amounts of current to an electronic component to govern how it operates. Using control voltages to manage an instrument became practical during the 1960s with the availability of solid-state circuitry and the ability to direct a small amount of current to the modular components of a synthesizer. Voltage-controlled technology was responsible for the commercial boom of electronic musical instruments during the 1960s and 1970s, leading to the adoption of control principles that continue to be applied, without the need for the control voltages themselves, in the algorithms used to drive digital synthesizers and software synthesizers.

A *control* voltage is discrete from the voltage used to generate an audio *signal*. Whereas the signal is the sound itself—a voltage in the audible spectrum—the control voltage affects the structure or flow of the sound and may itself be inaudible except in how it affects the audible signal. In the first modular synthesizers, patch cords were used to connect the output of one component to the input of another. Because of this, some components such as oscillators could be used as either signal sources or control sources, whichever suited the needs of the composer. Later performance instruments eliminated the patch cords and provided preset connections for governing signal and control voltages.

Voltage-Controlled Components

A significant advantage of voltage-controlled components was that special circuits could be designed to simultaneously manipulate a multitude of settings that might otherwise have been impractical to manage by hand. For example, it would be impossible to control by hand—manually turning individual dials and sliding levers—the frequencies of several oscillators, their changing amplitudes, envelopes, and filtering all at one time. Several basic types of voltage-controlled modules have been designed to automate this process.

The following voltage-controlled components are commonly used in analog synthesis. These were available as individual components (e.g. envelope generator) or packaged into a modular synthesizer with pots for connecting and combining individual components. Performing with these modules is accomplished through the use of various manual and programmable controllers (see pp. 221–5).

- **Voltage-controlled oscillator (VCO)**. A circuit for generating a periodic waveform, usually a sine, sawtooth, triangle, or pulse/square wave. Some oscillators had settings for more than one type of waveform. The VCO was the basic sound-generating source of the analog synthesizer. Typical voltage-controlled inputs would allow manipulation of oscillator frequency and waveshape.
- **Voltage-controlled filter (VCF)**. A circuit using control voltages to set the parameters filtering the audio spectrum of the sound source. A simple VCF employing a low-pass filter (allowing only lower frequencies to pass through) might only have simple settings for the cutoff frequency and resonance, with a voltage-controlled input for changing cutoff frequency. Other types of filters, such as high-pass, band-pass, and band-reject, provide other means of controlling specific ranges of the audio spectrum (see "Frequency Filtering," pp. 226–7).

- **Voltage-controlled amplifier (VCA)**. A voltage-controlled amplifier allows the musician to control the volume of a signal over a variable scale of amplitude. Amplitude is a fundamental element of sound production and rarely occurs on a scale that jumps from 0 (off) to peak (on) without some steps in between. These steps may be slow, as in a gradual swell of volume, to rapid and periodic as in vibrato. The VCA provides settings for making such gradual changes in volume possible.
- **Envelope generator (ENV)**. The voltage-controlled envelope generator is a special purpose amplitude controller dedicated to shaping the four stages of a sounds evolution: attack, decay, sustain, and release. It is most commonly associated with the characteristics of notes played using a keyboard trigger. The voltages generated by an ENV correspond to each of the multiple stages of a note's envelope.
- **Low-frequency oscillator (LFO)**. This oscillator circuit is restricted to subsonic frequencies and is an important source of modulation for other voltage-controlled modules. It is not used as an audible signal but as a control signal for other components. If fed to the input of a VCO, the LFO can control minute or radical fluctuations in the frequency of the oscillator's signal. If fed to the input of a VCA, the LFO creates periodic changes in the volume of the signal. An LFO signal fed to a VCF will modulate the filter by changing its cutoff frequency in a fluctuating pattern. If fed to a voltage-controlled pulse wave oscillator, an LFO can modulate its duty cycle and provide a pattern of changing harmonics in its output.

Sources of Control Voltage

The voltage-controlled modules described above could be managed by the composer through several means. One of the most flexible, and sometimes confusing, aspects of voltage-controlled systems is that voltage signals can be used for many different functions, often concurrently. For example, a voltage-controlled oscillator could be adjusted manually using a rotary dial to change its pitch or it could be triggered by a voltage source outside of the oscillator itself, such as a keyboard or sequencer. The same can be said for other voltage-controlled modules for generating or modifying the sound.

Sources of voltage control fall into two categories: *manually operated (kinesthetic) controls* or *programmable controllers*.

Manual Controls

Manually operated (kinesthetic) controls are those that are adjusted or played by hand in real time.

Keyboards

The organ-style keyboard was the most common voltage controller found on analog synthesizers and had obvious advantages for playing music. Every key was a voltage generator and could be used to trigger a specific note by sending a signal to the voltage-controlled oscillator. The earliest analog synthesizers were **monophonic**, capable of outputting only one voltage at a time, conventionally the lowest key to be depressed at any given moment. **Polyphonic** keyboards were capable of playing more than one note at a time but were often limited to no more than ten voices—one per finger—in the earliest models. The octave range of a keyboard could be scaled up or down in frequency range and keyboards on the most advanced analog synthesizers could also be split so that different parts of the keyboard were assigned to different instrumental voices. Some manufacturers provided keyboards that could modify the scale—frequency steps between notes—making composition possible with microtonal and other alternatives to the 12-tone scale. Because a synthesizer keyboard was essentially no more than a source of voltage output, it could also be used for managing modules other than pitch generators, providing timing triggers of preset parameters to VCAs, VCFs, and other components, permitting many actions to occur simultaneously.

The first commercially available synthesizer keyboards were not **touch-sensitive**, but by the 1970s this had become a common feature. There were two aspects of touch sensitivity important to voltage-controlled keyboards. A **velocity-sensitive keyboard** generated a voltage for a note that was proportional to the speed with which the keys were depressed. A **force-sensitive keyboard** produced a control voltage proportional to the amount of pressure put on a key. Both types of keyboard sensitivity could be included in the same keyboard.

Most keyboards also had expression controls such as wheels or levers for providing pitchbend or modulation:

- **Pitchbender wheel**. The pitchbender wheel allowed the performer to slide a note up or down, gliding the frequency smoothly between pitches. The control did this by sending a higher voltage to the VCO to raise the pitch or sending a lower voltage to lower the pitch. The range of the pitchbender could be adjusted either through preset switches or a sliding control. In the most flexible systems, pitches could be bent from a range as small as two adjacent keys to several octaves.
- **Modulation wheel**. The modulation wheel adjusted the amount of voltage from an LFO used to modify a VCO, VCA, or VCF. The audible result on the waveform depended on which voltage-controlled module was being modulated. If the VCA was modulated, tremolo was produced. If the VCO was modulated, vibrato was the result. If the output of the modulation wheel was sent to the VCF, a filter sweep was the result.

In addition to keyboards, several other unique methods of kinesthetic controls were developed as voltage sources for synthesizers. The Moog **ribbon controller** was a monophonic device for the linear control of voltage and essentially served the same function as the keyboard but without the keys. It was used by sliding a finger up and down a slender metallic ribbon to cause changes in pitch. Wavering the fingertip along the surface could create vibrato. This was a popular control technique that was modified and adapted by several manufacturers.

Joysticks

Joysticks were adapted for use on some performance synthesizers and combined both pitchbend and modulation voltage sources. Moving the joystick from front to back controlled one voltage source while moving it from right to left adjusted the second. Having one control for two manually adjusted parameters made the control of these voltage sources much easier for the performing musician. Theoretically, the joystick could be used to send voltages to any two voltage-controlled modules. Typically, the joystick was connected to an oscillator source to control pitchbend when it was moved in one direction (e.g. left to right) and was connected to a VCA to control amplitude when moved in the other direction (e.g. front to back). An infinite number of positions were available between the absolute front-to-back and right-to-left planes, providing many subtle combinations of the two control sources.

Other Kinesthetic Inputs

Buchla pioneered several early alternatives to organ-style keyboards including the Kinesthetic Input Port, which used flat, membrane contacts arrayed in the configuration of an organ-style keyboard. Unlike conventional keyboards, the Kinesthetic Input Port was equipped with outputs for connecting the membrane "keys" directly to other voltage-controlled inputs, allowing the port to act as both a performance interface and a simple, programmable aid for triggering other functions on the synthesizer. A simplified version of the membrane keyboard was used on the portable Buchla Electronic Music Box (1973), a self-contained synthesizer suitable for live performance.

Programmable Controllers

Another aspect of playing a synthesizer is the ability to program sounds, patterns, and modulations so that they can be performed automatically or possibly stored for retrieval and playback later. This element is widely accepted today in the design of computer-based instruments and music software. Prior to the application of computers to music, the programming of synthesizers was not as easily done, yet many innovative solutions were devised for applying voltage control to automate important aspects of creating electronic music.

Sequencers

The RCA Mark II Electronic Music Synthesizer and its coded paper input device was an early attempt to provide control over pitch, amplitude, timbre, and the organization of musical tones. Raymond Scott reportedly accomplished something similar in his home studio, as did the engineers of the Siemens Studio für Elektronische Musik in Munich around the same time. In all of these cases, the instruments were hardwired to the sound-generating and modifying circuits, greatly limiting their adaptability to all but certain preset values determined by the circuit builder. Nonetheless, all three attempts underscored the value of programmability to electronic music—one of its inherent traits. What RCA, Scott, and Siemens had done was demonstrate the potential usefulness of a control module or **sequencer**.

Buchla and Moog independently developed voltage-controlled sequencers for their synthesizers. The sequencer provided a means for structuring a sequence of voltage control signals that were then fed as control signals to other voltage-controlled modules. A number of schema were provided, from straightforward voltage pulses to controllers that also provided time settings for varying the duration of a given increment in a sequence. Most sequencers could be set to trigger control voltages in 8, 12, or 16 increments and there were often three such arrays available at a time (Figure 7.11 shows a 16-track set-up). Despite a limitation of 8, 12, or 16 steps, patches could be used to effectively string out all three rows into single long sequence comprising three times as many steps.

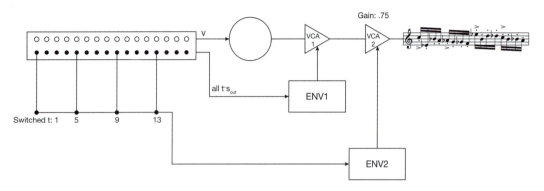

Figure 7.11   Setup for a 16-track voltage-controlled sequencer using a signal source, envelope generators (ENVs), and voltage-controlled amplifiers (VCAs) to produce a sequence of accented notes (t = trigger). (After Strange, 1983)

ANALOG SYNTHESIS AND SOUND MODIFICATION

1   *Cartridge Music* (1960) by John Cage
    A work for amplified small sounds that used phono cartridges as contact microphones

2   *The Wolfman* (1964) by Robert Ashley
    Acoustic feedback was used as the primary source of audio material for this work

3   *Safari: Eine kleine Klangfarbenmelodie* (1964) by Hugh Le Caine
    Used extensive additive synthesis and texturing by means of the Sonde, an instrument equipped with 200 closely tuned sine tones

4   *It's Going to Rain* (1965) by Steve Reich
    Tape piece experiment with tape loops and phasing of vocal passages

5   *Pendulum Music* (1968) by Steve Reich
    Used acoustic feedback

6   *Cambrian Sea* (1968) by Peter Klausmeyer
    Extensive use of modulated white noise and a Moog voltage-controlled envelope/amplitude generator

7   *Ambience* (1968) by Richard Allan Robinson
    Transformed electroacoustic sounds using voltage-controlled ring modulation, filters, and additive synthesis

8   "I Want You (She's So Heavy)" (1969) by The Beatles
    John Lennon added a modulated sequence of Moog-generated white noise to the last part of the song, providing a sound like that of relentlessly blowing wind

9   *Toneburst* (1975) by David Tudor
    Used feedback circuits

10 *Repeat* (1999) by Toshimaru Nakamura
    Used feedback circuits via the composer's "no-input mixing board"

Sequencers were a versatile source of output voltage and could be combined in banks so that the output of one could start and stop another. Sequencer outputs could be fed to any other voltage-controlled component for generating, modifying, mixing, and distributing sound.

Sequencers were typically triggered by a **timing pulse** output by a manual controller, such as a keyboard. This enabled a performer to trigger a sequence of control signals by only touching a single key. Pressing a key could trigger any variety of control sequences, from automatically playing an arpeggio, triggering a rhythm pattern in another module, changing the envelope of the sound, or activating a filter sweep. Any module that was voltage-controlled could be triggered by a sequencer.

Timing pulse generators were LFOs dedicated to generating pulses for controlling tempo or other repetitive processes commonly used in music. As a control signal, the timing pulse consisted only of a binary On/Off signal.

Sequencers were programmed either manually using a panel of rotary dials or by playing a sequence of voltages on the keyboard. When using the keyboard, a sequence could be recorded in *real time* as it was played or one note at a time using *step programming*. In either case, the sequencer acted somewhat like a player piano roll, keeping a record of the key depressions but not recording the sound of the notes themselves. This allowed a sequenced pattern to be used with any patch, regardless of the instrumental voices chosen. The tempo and key could each be changed without affecting the other.

Sequencers were forgiving when it came to recording key strokes. If the keyed notes were not precisely in correct time, a feature called **quantizing** was used to align each note to the nearest beat in a preset tempo, locking all key strokes into a perfect tempo. **Looping** was another feature that allowed a sequence to repeat as long as desired, providing a steady rhythmic backdrop for a piece of music. It was also possible to link multiple sequencers so that one could trigger the others, providing a cascading series of programmed sequences with nearly limitless possibilities. In addition to providing the fixed sequential output of a signal sequence, some sequencers could also be set to output a given sequence in *random* order.

SIGNAL PROCESSING

If audio signals may be considered the raw material of electronic music, signal processing represents the ways in which these signals can be dynamically modified and shaped. Signal processing is primarily aimed at modifying the frequency, amplitude, and timbre of sound. This is done through the use of a variety of circuits to modify the electrical voltage of a sound, or its digital equivalent in computer-based instruments.

The electrical signals generated by an audio circuit are not strong enough to drive a loudspeaker on their own and require amplification. **Gain** is the amount of voltage or power that an amplifier provides to increase the strength of a signal. The audible effect of increasing gain is a corresponding increase in volume from a loudspeaker. Within the circuits, however, gain is a factor in modifying other aspects of a waveform because it affects the amplitude of the signal to be modified.

Frequency Filtering

A **filter** is a specialized amplifier that controls the amount of gain to prescribed frequency ranges of a sound. Making such adjustments changes the balance of harmonics found in the source sound signal. Adjusting the perceptibility of harmonics is key to modifying the identity or timbre of a sound, making filters one of the most important sound modification components available to the composer.

Stereo systems are often equipped with a rudimentary filter called an **equalizer** for adjusting the amount of bass, midrange, and treble frequencies that will be heard in a piece of recorded music. Filters associated with electronic music can generally be adjusted to finer settings than those on a conventional stereo system. Some kinds of filters are designed for passing only certain ranges of frequencies and provide precise settings that can be easily repeated whenever needed. A **cutoff frequency** is the point at which a filter begins to omit a prescribed frequency range. Theoretically, a filter should attenuate or cut off a range of frequencies at the prescribed point, but this is not the case. Passing of the frequencies occurs as a **roll-off slope** that is generally equivalent to about 3 dB attenuation per octave. The precise roll-off specifications for a filter depends on its circuit design and will vary from manufacturer to manufacturer.

Some typical types of filters include the following (see also Figure 7.12):

• **Band-pass filter**. Allows only those sounds *between* specified high- and low-frequency cutoff points to be heard. It removes the high and low frequencies from a signal at the same time.
• **Band-reject filter**. Allows only those sounds *above* or *below* specified high- and low-frequency cutoff points to be heard. It removes the midrange frequencies from a signal.

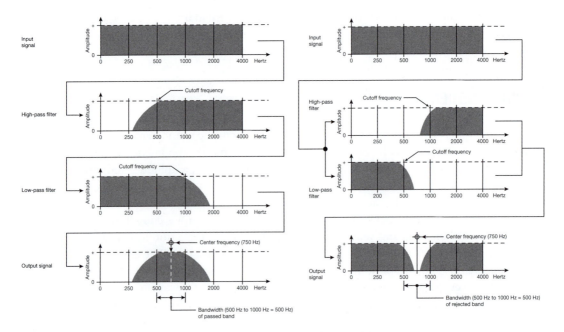

Figure 7.12   Band-pass filter (left) and band-reject filter (right). (After Naumann, 1985)

- **Low-pass filter**. Allows only frequencies *below* a specified cutoff point to be passed. It removes the high frequencies from a signal.
- **High-pass filter**. Allows only frequencies *above* a specified cutoff point to be passed. It removes the low frequencies from a signal.

While the degree of attenuation of a filter was sometimes a permanent fixture of its circuit design, most low-pass and band-pass filters also had a variable *regeneration* or *resonance* control sometimes referred to as the **Q factor**. This control changed the perceptible sharpness of the filtered sound. The Q factor was determined by dividing the center frequency of the filtered band by the bandwidth. For example, if the center frequency of a filtered band was 150 Hz and the bandwidth was 75 Hz, the Q factor was 2 (150 Hz/75 Hz = 2). Increasing the Q factor narrowed the width of the passed band, increasing the Q factor and further accentuating the remaining sidebands, giving the sound a hollow, harmonic chiming quality. Another technique was to keep the Q factor constant while varying the center frequency, resulting in a change to the bandwidth of the passed band while it maintained the same Q factor relationship with the center frequency.

Filters may be part of a synthesizer console, a software component for processing sounds, or a standalone device used like an effects box between an instrument and the mixing board or loudspeaker system.

Envelope Shaping

The envelope of a sound is the way the sound begins, continues, and then ends. It is the pattern of loudness of a sound. For example, a note played on the piano will begin sharply (attack) and will also end abruptly (release), but the middle part of the note can be extended by pressing the pedal (delay and sustain). Electronic musical instruments offer unique control over the envelope characteristics of a sound. This technique can be used to change the attack characteristics of all discretely generated sounds. Envelopes may be adjusted manually or programmed using an envelope generator.

Most envelope generators have four settings for different stages of a sound:

- **Attack**. The start of a sound as defined by the time it takes for the signal to go from zero amplitude to peak amplitude.
- **Decay**. The second stage of a sound as defined by the time it takes for the signal to go from its peak amplitude to its sustain amplitude.
- **Sustain**. Once a sound has passed through the attack and decay stages, it may be sustained at a fixed amplitude for as long as the note is held.
- **Release**. The end of a note's envelope, which drops off rapidly to zero amplitude. The term "release" is equivalent to releasing the key on a synthesizer.

These four stages of envelope generation are collectively known as the **ADSR** (attack, decay, sustain, release) characteristics (see Figures 7.13 and 7.14). Settings for the attack, decay, and release properties of a signal govern the duration of a sound regardless of how long a key is depressed. The sustain setting denotes a peak amplitude for as long as a signal is held.

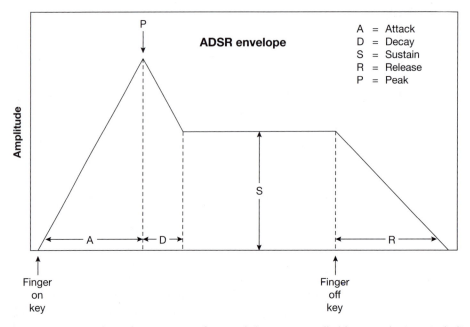

Figure 7.13   Envelope characteristics of a sound that are controlled by a synthesizer, including attack, decay, sustain, and release (ADSR). (After Friedman, 1986)

Other possible ADSR envelopes

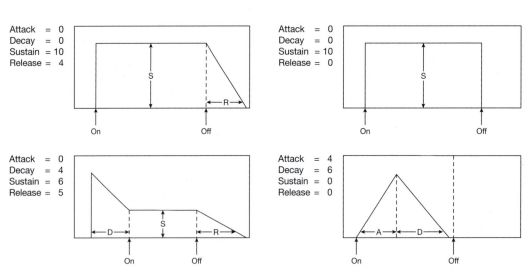

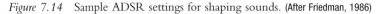

Figure 7.14   Sample ADSR settings for shaping sounds. (After Friedman, 1986)

Envelopes can be changed for any given sound signal. The attack, sustain, and decay characteristics are individually adjustable, providing the composer with infinite possibilities for altering a given sound source. In the voltage-controlled synthesizer, the envelope generator can be triggered by control voltages from other components, such as a low-frequency oscillator.

Echo, Reverberation, Looping, and Delay

The techniques of echo, reverberation, looping, and delay originated with tape composition and are described in that context in Chapter 5. When described using signal processing terminology, the definitions of these techniques can be applied apart from the tape recorder to both analog and digital signal processing.

Echo and *reverberation* comprise different degrees of the same phenomenon—the effect of reflected sound on the perceived depth or character of an audio signal. Reverberation comprises the sum total of all such reflections as expressed by a prolongation of the sound, where individual reflections are not discretely perceivable. The length of the reverberation is determined by the distance of the listener from the sound source, and the type of surrounding reflective surfaces. The length of reverberation is measured from the start of the sound to the point when it decays to 60 dB below its original amplitude. Echo is a form of reverberation in which the individual sound reflections, rather than being compressed into a short lapse of time, are spaced by 50 milliseconds or more, at which point they can be perceived individually.[13] Artificial reverberation and echo can be produced using a tape recorder or circuits designed to provide adjustable settings for room size and reflectivity.

The term *delay* is borrowed from the tape composition practice of stringing a length of recording tape through two tape recorders, recording a sound on the first machine, playing it back on the second, and then simultaneously feeding the signal back into the first machine where it is recorded again. The signal that is repeatedly re-recorded eventually diminishes with each generation of re-recording. Tape delay has been replaced with analog and digital delay circuits that reproduce the same effect with controllable parameters for the pace, duration, and rate of disintegration, if any, of the delay signal.

Looping a sound is similar to the use of a delay system except that the original signal is not re-recorded with each pass. Rather, a loop repeats without any loss of fidelity for as long as it is played. The concept of looping originated with locked grooves in turntable discs and was translated to the tape medium by splicing a short length of tape end to end so that it would play repeatedly.

Signal Modulation

The term **modulation** is used in music to denote a change from one key, or tonal center, to another—a technique that is commonly heard in the performance of popular music. In electronic music the term is borrowed from the field of telecommunications and refers to the use of one electronic signal to modify another, such as the output of an LFO changing an oscillator's frequency. Changes in pitch, amplitude, and timbre can all be controlled using modulation.

Amplitude Modulation

Amplitude modulation (AM) is the use of a control voltage to alter (modulate) the loudness of another signal. The sound that is being modulated is called the *carrier* signal. When a sub-audio signal is used to modulate a given sound wave, the result is a slow, undulating effect called tremolo, in which the volume of the sound becomes alternately louder and softer but without changing the pitch. The loudness rises and falls around a central amplitude.

All types of waveforms can be used as control signals. Using a sine wave to modulate the carrier will cause the loudness to rise and fall very smoothly. A triangle wave will effect a gradual rise in loudness that sharply turns down and gradually falls, only to switch directions again very sharply. The use of a pulse wave as an amplitude-modulating signal eliminates the various gradients between loud and soft, and causes the carrier to switch instantly between the two extremes.

When the control signal is a waveform in the audible range, the changes in loudness become much more difficult to perceive because of their rapidity, and the resultant effect is a change in the harmonic structure of the carrier through the creation of audible sideband frequencies. Sidebands are the partials or harmonics that make up part of a total sound but do not dominate it. They change the tone color or timbre of the carrier. Sidebands are mathematically related to the carrier: the upper sidebands are equal to the sum of the carrier and control frequencies, while the lower sidebands are equal to the difference between them. When sidebands become audible, the carrier signal still remains the dominant signal.

Frequency Modulation

Frequency modulation (FM) is the use of a control voltage to alter the frequency (pitch) of the sound. A sub-audio control voltage (less than 20 Hz) will produce a vibrato effect, which is an undulation of pitch around the carrier tone. As in amplitude modulation, when the control voltage is in the audible frequency range, the resultant signal contains sidebands of the carrier wave and the very rapid undulation of pitch is perceived as a change in timbre. The complexity and harmonics of FM sidebands are much more intricate and rich than those produced by AM. Unlike AM, FM sidebands may actually dominate the carrier tone. The degree of undulation of the pitch will vary in proportion to the amount of attenuation of the carrier as well as the type of waveform being used. Figure 7.15 visually shows the effect of using different waveshapes on FM modulation.

Ring Modulation

Ring modulation is a form of amplitude modulation in which special circuitry suppresses the carrier signal and reproduces only the sidebands. Two additional frequencies are created in place of the original carrier signal. One is equal to the sum of the two input frequencies, and the other is equal to the difference between them. If the input signal has many harmonics, such as a guitar or the human voice, the resulting output signal is complex and rich—a kind of ghost of the original sound. The analog ring modulator made by the Moog Music Co. has a second input signal in the form of an oscillator. This can be adjusted to narrow or widen the distance between the two frequencies generated by the effect.

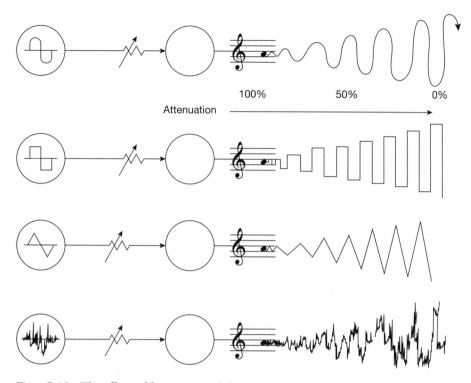

Figure 7.15   The effects of frequency modulation (FM) using different waveforms on a given signal source and attenuation increasing from 0 percent to 100 percent. (After Strange, 1983)

Pulse Width Modulation

Pulse width modulation (PWM) provides another technique for modulating the timbre of a frequency. This form of modulation takes advantage of the fact that the harmonics of a waveform will change according to the duty cycle of a pulse wave. The duty cycle—and pulse width—can be modulated by a low-frequency oscillator to provide subtle, although detectable modifications of the harmonic spectra associated with a pulse wave.

ANALOG SOUND SYNTHESIS

Synthesis is the ability to use the fundamental building blocks of sound to construct new sounds. Most electronic music composers prior to the 1960s had no purpose-made synthesizers at their disposal. Armed only with the basic building blocks comprising waveform oscillators, filters, tape recorders, and various other sound processing devices, they learned how to combine and modify existing sounds to make new ones from the simplest component parts. Through the development of solid-state miniaturization, early analog synthesizers provided many of the same audio processing components as an entire studio but in the guise of a few, integrated modular desktop components. But the actual synthesis of sounds relied on the same trial and error process that had been in use since the early 1950s.

The term "synthesis" connotes a desire to create unique electronic instrumental voices. Such voices may be designed by the composer to imitate the timbre and response of conventional instruments such as those found in the classical orchestra. But the possibility of modeling equally compelling new sounds is equally plausible. Prior to the advent of digital sampling and synthesis (see Chapter 11) the techniques for crafting electronic instrumentation using analog techniques were challenging, required much patience on the part of the composer, and were sometimes difficult to reproduce due to the precision needed to devise—and repeat—the parametric settings needed to produce the desired sound.

The simplest form of sound synthesis is the combination of two or more sine waves into a more complex waveform. This process is called **additive synthesis** and can be used to create diverse sounds by building up layers of many individual sounds. Additive synthesis is based on the observation from Fourier theory that a periodic sound is composed of a fundamental frequency, which is dominant, and partials that have a mathematically harmonious relationship to the carrier. In the electronic music studio, the individual frequencies and their amplitude relationships can be manipulated in such a way as to duplicate or modify the sound synthetically. Synthesizers allow for the construction of complex sounds from simpler individual components and offer the ability to manipulate their frequency and amplitude interrelationships. Additive synthesis was the method used by many of the earliest electronic music composers. Stockhausen's first experiments with sine wave generators began as exercises in additive synthesis.

Subtractive synthesis is another technique used since the early years of electronic music. Just as waveforms can be constructed by the addition of one sound to another, they can also be altered through the systematic elimination of certain parts of the sound, such as overtones or the fundamental frequency. Subtractive synthesis begins with a complex waveform and subjects it to filtering using any one of the techniques described earlier in this chapter. French composer Eliane Radigue (b. 1932) is a classic analog synthesist who has used subtractive synthesis as the focus of her works. She has been working with an ARP 2500 analog synthesizer since the early 1970s and makes use of the instrument's manual controls for mixing waveforms into gradually changing sound textures. Radigue first learned electronic music composition in Paris from Pierre Schaffer and Pierre Henry, but her affinity for music consisting of slowly unraveling processes is distinct from classic *musique concrète* in which tape manipulation and editing are such important elements.

Early performance synthesizers, such as the Moog Minimoog, incorporated some of the first logical steps away from the use of patch cords and manually controlled parameters to preset controls for instrumental voices based on additive and subtractive synthesis techniques. The Minimoog had no patch cords and although it did not include specific preset voices it greatly simplified the modification of sounds by providing only rudimentary controls over envelopes, amplitude, and other modulation. For example, an Emphasis dial with ten settings could be used in conjunction with a Cutoff Frequency (filter) dial to produce a sharp resonance in the filter. Eliminating the patch cords with preset circuits for controlling waveshaping parameters greatly freed the performing musician to concentrate on playing. This was an innovative improvement, but playing the Minimoog was still not as simple as flipping a switch to get the desired sound. By way of an example, note the following instructions taken from the Minimoog operating manual for adjusting the attack characteristics of a sound:

The ATTACK TIME control determines the duration of the initial rise in volume to a peak. Turn off the Noise Source and turn on Oscillator 1. Move control back and forth while repeatedly pressing down a key. Notice the different qualities which a note takes on as a sharp attack becomes a slow crescendo.[14]

The Minimoog was soon followed by more advanced analog synthesizers by Moog and other companies that incorporated an increasing number of presets made to approximate the distinctive voices of many instruments, such as violins, horns, and pianos, among others. By the end of the 1970s, the availability of increasingly affordable computer circuits began to improve the programmability and sequencing features of analog synthesizers, eventually leading to fully digital instruments using a new wave of diverse synthesizing techniques (see Chapter 11).

COMPONENTS OF THE VOLTAGE-CONTROLLED SYNTHESIZER

All analog, voltage-controlled synthesizers, whether modular or integrated by design, were comprised of several common building blocks. Although the specific way in which each manufacturer engineered these components varied, the expected results could be managed through the application of basic principles of voltage-controlled sound processing. The most common sound modules included the following:

- **Two or more oscillators for generating raw sound material**. The waveforms normally offered included sine, sawtooth, square, and sometimes triangle. Those waveforms could be combined to create variations on the default waveshapes through modulation.
- **Preset sounds, or instrumental "voices."** Modular synthesizers from the 1960s only came with basic waveform generators from which a composer would construct desired instrumental sounds. By the mid-1970s, the use of preset waveform generators and memory chips introduced the availability of preset voices requiring no additional programming.
- **White noise generator**. Variations on white noise generators—usually applying preset filters to produce specific bands of the noise spectrum—were offered by many manufacturers.
- **Voltage-controlled amplifier (VCA)**. Adjusted the loudness of a signal in proportion to a control voltage input.
- **Voltage-controlled filter (VCF)**. Provided a cutoff frequency that was adjustable in proportion to a control voltage input. Most VCFs also included voltage-controlled resonance, which accentuated frequencies near the cutoff and provided a hollow, ringing quality to the sound. VCFs were often designed for specific filtering functions and included band-pass, band-reject, high-pass, low-pass filters intended to pass only certain ranges of the sound spectrum.
- **Envelope generator (ENV)**. Controllers for modifying the way a sound starts, continues, and ends. Whereas an envelope generator is used to shape the loudness curve of a sound, an envelope *follower* is used to detect and respond to the loudness curve of an incoming signal.

KEY TO DIAGRAMMING NOMENCLATURE

Schematics of audio processing modules included in this and other chapters adopt the following visual nomenclature for diagramming components and the flow of a signal source.

The *signal path*, indicated in a left-to-right direction using an arrow, follows the path of a voltage signal through the necessary stages of sound processing required to complete the function of a given module (see Figure 7.16).

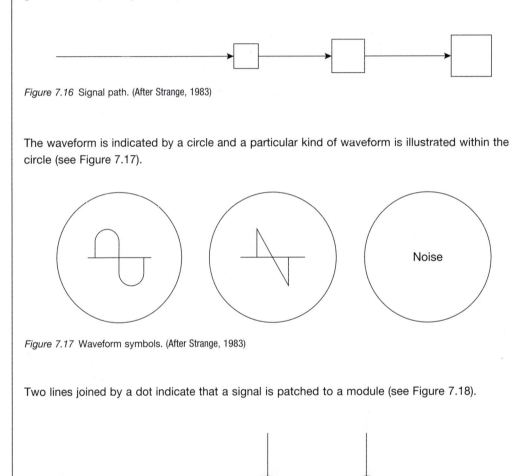

Figure 7.16 Signal path. (After Strange, 1983)

The waveform is indicated by a circle and a particular kind of waveform is illustrated within the circle (see Figure 7.17).

Figure 7.17 Waveform symbols. (After Strange, 1983)

Two lines joined by a dot indicate that a signal is patched to a module (see Figure 7.18).

Figure 7.18 Patch symbol. (After Strange, 1983)

The attenuation—adjustment—of a signal prior to its linkage to a module is indicated by the symbol in Figure 7.19.

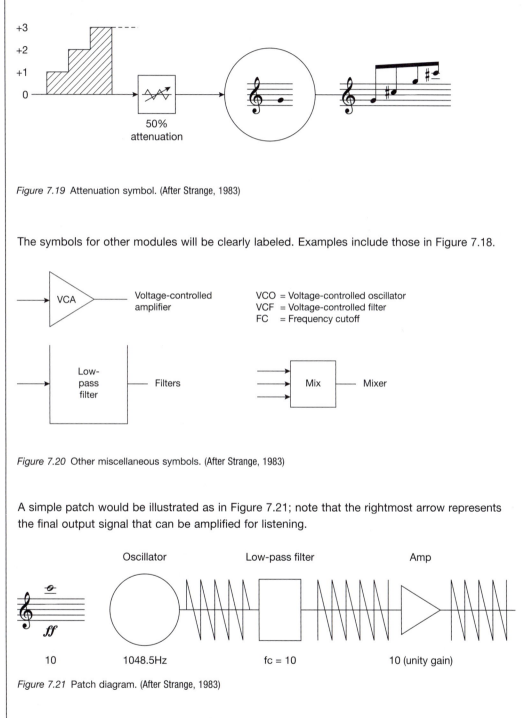

Figure 7.19 Attenuation symbol. (After Strange, 1983)

The symbols for other modules will be clearly labeled. Examples include those in Figure 7.18.

Figure 7.20 Other miscellaneous symbols. (After Strange, 1983)

A simple patch would be illustrated as in Figure 7.21; note that the rightmost arrow represents the final output signal that can be amplified for listening.

Figure 7.21 Patch diagram. (After Strange, 1983)

- **Sequencer**. One of the most diverse sources of voltage control, and could be used to generate patterns of tones or programmed changes in amplification, filter, mixing, modulation, and sound distribution.
- **MIDI**. MIDI IN/OUT/THRU for controlling one or more keyboards or interfacing a synthesizer with a computer in real time (see Chapter 8, pp. 259–64).

Synthesizer Configurations

See Figures 7.22 and 7.23.

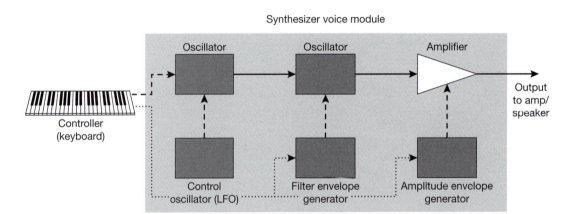

Figure 7.22   Schematic for a basic analog synthesizer. (After Crombie, 1982)

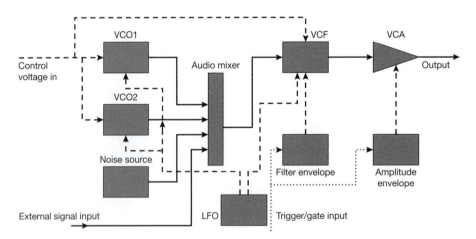

Figure 7.23   Schematic for a basic synthesizer voice module. (After Crombie, 1982)

SUMMARY

- Helmholtz showed that the vibrations found in a single musical tone consisted of a fundamental or base tone accompanied by related harmonics above the pitch of the fundamental.

- If a wave vibrates in a regular pattern, it is perceived as a pitched sound, such as those used in music. If the wave does not vibrate in a regular pattern, it is perceived as unpitched sound or noise.

- Components of sound include frequency, amplitude, timbre, duration, and envelope.

- Fourier theory states that any periodic vibration (waveform), however complex, is comprised of, or can be created by combining, a series of simple vibrations whose frequencies are harmonically related and that change in amplitude independently over time.

- Voltage control is a method of applying metered amounts of current to an electronic component to govern how it operates. It was a technique used to control the modules of analog synthesizers.

- A control voltage is discrete from the voltage used to generate an audio signal.

- Common voltage-controlled components of the analog electronic music studio included the voltage-controlled oscillator (VCO), voltage-controlled filter (VCF), voltage-controlled amplifier (VCA), envelope generator (ENV), and low-frequency oscillator (LFO).

- Waveforms can be generated by an electronic circuit called an oscillator, which produces periodic vibrations in the form of an electric current.

- Common waveforms used in music synthesis include sine, sawtooth, triangle, and pulse waves.

- White noise results when all the frequency and amplitude characteristics of a sound occur at random within the audio spectrum. White noise contains equally distributed energy at all frequencies within the audio spectrum.

- Electroacoustic music is broadly defined as music created using electronic and acoustic sound sources.

- Microphones and pickups are two common electroacoustic transducers and are designed to change vibrations in the air or on a solid surface to electric current.

- Acoustic feedback occurs when a sound amplified via a microphone or pickup is re-amplified again and again via the same microphone or pickup. A feedback circuit enables the internal generation of signals by connecting output back to input, prior to their amplification in the listening space.

- Forms of analog signal processing include frequency filtering, envelope shaping, echo, reverberation, loops, delay, and signal modulation such as amplitude modulation (AM), frequency modulation (FM), ring modulation, and pulse width modulation (PWM).

- Analog sound synthesis is commonly done using additive synthesis by combining waveforms, or subtractive synthesis by using filters to eliminate frequency ranges from a given sound.

KEY PEOPLE IN CHAPTER SEVEN

KEY TERMS IN CHAPTER SEVEN

CHAPTER 8

The Voltage-Controlled Synthesizer

There was never a notion that a synthesizer would be used by itself for anything.
—Robert Moog

Robert Moog and his Minimoog and Modular Synthesizers. (Bob Moog, 1971)

Hugh Le Caine invented the voltage-controlled synthesizer in 1945 but never achieved commercial success with his invention. That accomplishment fell to American engineer Robert Moog, whose finely crafted solid-state synthesizer modules, introduced during the mid-1960s, were the first to be sold with any success. Moog's instruments were classics in a field that soon became crowded with aggressive and often better-financed competitors. Over 40 years later, the classic synthesizers bearing the Moog name and his robust circuitry still represent the gold standard of the analog electronic music industry.

This chapter explores the history of the first commercially produced analog, voltage-controlled synthesizers and their inherent design features.

HISTORY OF THE VOLTAGE-CONTROLLED SYNTHESIZER

Moog was not the first person to build a synthesizer, but he has become the most recognized. The idea of the synthesizer is as old as Thaddeus Cahill's Telharmonium, when he first used the term in 1896 to describe that power-hungry dynamo. Cahill's idea was virtually the same as Moog's: to use a combination of tone-generating and modulating devices to build sounds from their component parts. The *Moog synthesizer*, produced in both **modular** and **performance** designs, was the most commonly used instrument in electronic music studios during the late 1960s and 1970s.

The secret of Moog's success was that he listened to musicians and solved the three most pressing challenges plaguing the use of synthesizers at that time: size, stability, and control. Transistorized and solid-state components solved the first two problems by reducing the size of the sound-generating components and producing stable oscillators. Providing controls over the myriad possible sounds that could be made with the synthesizer was a bigger challenge. Moog worked painstakingly to solve the problem of synthesizer control with the help of his many composer and musician friends.

Prior to the voltage-controlled synthesizer, the performance instruments and signal processing equipment found in electronic music studios were controlled through the manual adjustment of dials that directly affected the AC output of the device. This method was unreliable and required many trial and error adjustments because each separate component of a system, from the multiple oscillators to filters and other special devices, required precise manual adjustments to duplicate any given effect. Moog became the first synthesizer designer to popularize the technique of **voltage control** in analog electronic musical instruments. Donald Buchla in the United States and Paul Ketoff in Italy had been developing commercial synthesizers using the same principle at about the same time, but their equipment never reached the level of public acceptance of Moog's products and only a handful were sold.

In a voltage-controlled device, a small amount of current is applied to the control input of a given component to modify the output signal. This voltage signal can be preset, precise, and quick, and activated by such easy-to-use voltage control components as the synthesizer keyboard, thus making the analog synthesizer much easier to manage. What the keyboard was actually doing was sending a voltage signal of a particular amount to the sound-generating oscillator of the synthesizer and telling it to produce a note of a certain pitch. Moog's synthesizer was designed as a modular device with self-contained but connectable components to generate, modify, modulate, and output sounds. Moog succeeded in creating a product that could be manufactured with consistently high quality. A complete discussion of voltage control fundamentals is explored in the previous chapter.

The Moog Synthesizer

Robert Moog was an engineer with a bachelor's degree in physics from Queens College, New York (1957), a second degree in electrical engineering from Columbia University, and a Ph.D. in engineering physics from Cornell University (1965). Moog studied engineering at Columbia University during the late 1950s during the same period that the Columbia–Princeton Electronic Music Center was founded, yet he never set foot in the studio while he was there. This was despite the fact that Moog took a laboratory course led by Peter Mauzey, the lead engineer of the center. Moog's entrée into the world of electronic music came from a different direction. Before developing a complete synthesizer, Moog had been manufacturing a transistorized Theremin kit and experimenting with custom-made voltage-controlled modules for others. The synthesizer grew out of a meeting that Moog had with Hofstra University professor Herbert Deutsch (b. 1932), an electronic music composer. Moog recognized that his Theremin kits facilitated his connection with Deutsch. He recalled:

> Many people had those Theremins, including Herb Deutsch, a music instructor at Hofstra University on Long Island. He was also an experimental music composer. It was in the winter of 1963 that I was at a music teachers' conference—the New York State School Music Association—in the Catskills. I was demonstrating the Theremin. I didn't even have my own booth. I was at a friend of mine's booth. Herb Deutsch came along and he started a conversation off by saying that he had one of my Theremin kits and that he used it for sight-singing and ear-training exercises in the classroom, which was interesting. Then at one point he said, "Do you know anything about electronic music?" At that point I really didn't. I had never heard any. I only had the vaguest idea of what people like Ussachevsky were doing. Even though my undergraduate work was at Columbia, I never met Ussachevsky while I was there or heard any of his music. He said he was looking for equipment to compose electronic music.[1]

Deutsch invited Moog to attend a concert of his music in New York City in January 1964, just a few days after the New Year. The performance was at the studio of sculptor Jason Ceely, who was known for making sculptures out of automobile bumpers. Deutsch had composed a piece for magnetic tape using the sounds of a percussionist playing traditional instruments as well as Ceely's sculptures. Moog recalled, "He had composed this using the crudest possible equipment. The tape recorders were one or two Sony home tape recorders that one could buy for a couple of hundred dollars. I was completely hooked. I was very excited by it."[2] Moog knew from that moment that he wanted to get involved with electronic music.

Moog and Deutsch arranged to get together to brainstorm some electronic instrument ideas. In the summer of 1964, Deutsch brought his whole family up for a vacation in the Finger Lakes region of New York state, near where Moog lived in Trumansburg. Moog continued the story:

> The vacation consisted of his family hanging out at the local state park while Herb and I worked together. That was about two or three weeks, a relatively

Figure 8.1 Herb Deutsch and a prototype model of the Moog Modular Synthesizer. (Bob Moog, 1964)

short time. But I built stuff and he tried it out and at the end of that period he had a couple of tapes of interesting stuff and the two of us together had the basic ideas for a modular analog synthesizer. What I'm sure I came up with for Herb at that time were two voltage-controlled oscillators and one voltage-controlled amplifier. As for controls, I'm not sure. Maybe we used doorbells. I don't think we even had a keyboard at that time. He was perfectly content to set this thing up to make a sound, record that sound, and then splice it into his tape music. That's how everyone else was making tape music at that time.[3]

The result was a piece of music for demonstration purposes, Deutsch's *Jazz Images, A Worksong and Blues* (1964), but no real system to play it on. Moog continued his work, and by the end of the summer he had his first complete prototype ready. He wrote a paper entitled *Voltage-Controlled Electronic Music Modules* and was invited to present it at a convention of the Audio Engineering Society (AES) that fall. Even at such an early stage of development, Moog realized that the successful implementation of voltage-controlled modules would not only benefit the composer of tape music but could provide instruments that were responsive enough to be used for "live (real-time) performance."[4] His approach was to design a voltage-controlled instrument whose components—oscillators, filters, and amplifiers—produced results that were "directly proportional to the total charging current." To produce mathematically correct musical intervals such as those used with a keyboard, Moog added circuitry to establish an exponential relationship between an applied control voltage and the output of a voltage-controlled oscillator (VCO). In addition to using a control voltage to set the pitch of an oscillator, the VCO had two additional inputs for control voltages and he discussed the production of vibrato or the creation of a pattern of changing frequencies using such

The Evolution of the Moog Modular Synthesizer

Figure 8.2 Moog Modular Synthesizer, 1965. The earliest commercially available model. (Roger Luther, Moog Archives)

Figure 8.3 Moog Modular Synthesizer, 1967. (Roger Luther, Moog Archives)

Figure 8.4 Moog Modular Synthesizer, 1968. (Roger Luther, Moog Archives)

control voltages output from additional oscillators. The same paper discussed voltage-controlled circuits for a band-pass filter and amplifier and detailed the use of an organ-style monophonic keyboard and a "resistance ribbon" transducer to trigger voltages for notes or other modules. In closing the paper, Moog argued that designers of electronic musical instruments should to be mindful of the needs of musicians and that it was "worthwhile to investigate, in an objective and systematic way, what transducer configurations will most effectively translate the musician's intent into sound."[5]

Figure 8.5 Eric Siday, composer of music for radio and television commercials, was one of the first customers of Robert Moog. He is shown here in his private studio, *c.* 1967. (Roger Luther, Moog Archives)

The prototype that Moog eventually provided for Deutsch consisted of a module with two VCOs and two voltage-controlled amplifiers (VCAs) triggered by two keyboards.

After Moog took his "little box of stuff" to the AES in October 1964, the secret was out of the bag. He accepted his first orders at that convention and word began to spread among academics and musicians alike. Early adopters of Moog equipment were individual composers who wanted to have the synthesizer for their personal use. Moog's first makeshift modular system was purchased by Eric Siday, a New York composer of music for radio and television commercials and a competitor of Raymond Scott. After meeting at the AES conference, Siday and associates visited Moog in Trumansburg to work out the specifications for his system. "This is the first time when a system the size of a synthesizer was actually talked about between me and a central customer," recalled Moog.[6] Moog had to devise a cabinet to house the modules, a keyboard controller, and a satisfying configuration that would be useful to a professional musician. Moog also had to settle on a fair price for his labors and equipment. It was Moog's first inkling that a genuine business was taking shape. Siday's synthesizer was delivered about six months later in the spring of 1965.

Another composer who approached Moog about building some voltage-controlled components was Vladimir Ussachevsky, co-founder and director of the Columbia–Princeton Electronic Music Center in 1965. Having been an engineer as well as a composer, Ussachevsky was able to provide Moog with a technical specification for the devices he wanted to have constructed. Moog recalled:

> I still remember the letter, asking us to build what amounted to two voltage-controlled amplifiers, two envelope generators, and two envelope followers. He gave the specifications for all of these things. The specifications for the envelope generator called for a four-part envelope. Attack, initial decay, sustain, and release. That way of specifying an envelope is absolutely standard in today's electronic music. That came from Ussachevsky's specification. Ussachevsky wasn't interested in a keyboard. He had this rack with the six modules and for a long time that's how the Columbia–Princeton Electronic Music Center did their envelope shaping. In some of the pictures taken in the late 1960s you can see that piece of equipment right in the middle above the mixing console.[7]

The key component of Ussachevsky's specification was the four-part envelope generator or ADSR, the implementation of which, in Moog's hands, became the standardized approach for shaping the envelope of a sound.

Ussachevsky's needs were those of an academic studio and he eschewed the necessity for an organ-style keyboard controller in favor of patch cords and dials. But Moog remained committed to designing instruments for musicians other than those confined to the tape studio. By 1966, he was offering two additional controllers: an organ-style keyboard and a ribbon controller. The synthesizer was monophonic, which meant that only one note at a time could be triggered. On the keyboard, precedent was given to the lowest key depressed at any one time. As soon as one key was released, another could be played. One benefit of a monophonic system was that it gave Moog an opportunity to perfect his portamento feature. Portamento allowed the instrument to slide smoothly from one note to another as determined by the voltage values of two successively depressed keys. Moog added a Portamento switch to his keyboard to toggle the feature On or Off and a rotary dial to control the speed (volts changed per millisecond) of the gliding pitch change between notes. The ribbon controller consisted of a Teflon-coated thin metal band that was played by touching the finger up and down its length. A sliding note effect, not unlike that of the Theremin, could be created by running the finger up and down the ribbon. Expressive vibrato was created with the ribbon controller by merely rubbing the finger back and forth to effect a slight wavering of the tone.

In the spring of 1966, Moog sold his first production model of the synthesizer to Alwin Nikolais, director of the Alwin Nikolais Dance Theater, who composed many of his own scores on tape. By 1967, with customer interest slowly growing, Moog officially christened his product the "Moog Modular Synthesizer."

The basic studio model of the Moog Modular Synthesizer was assembled from a variety of independent components that could all be interconnected, all packaged in handsome walnut-framed cabinets that gave the instrument a superbly professional appearance. The wood cabinetry was a strategic choice on Moog's part because he did not want the design to be too bold or modern for fear of intimidating traditional composers and musicians. As a modular system, the customer ordered whatever components they wanted and Moog's technicians would assemble them for them. It was conceivable that every model could have been different from the one ordered before it because Moog's company was intent on keeping the system design as flexible and modular as the varied needs of its customers. Another early Moog customer was composer Joel Chadabe (b. 1938) at the State University of New York at Albany. In 1965, Chadabe received a small grant to create an electronic music studio. He bought a small synthesizer, but, as he explained:

> We didn't have enough money for a power supply so the first year we ran it on a car battery. It wasn't really strong enough to make a lot of interesting electronic sounds, but I could make collages and automate the collages in different ways. In fact, I asked Bob to make a kind of keyboard-mixer for me. It was actually a series of gates. It had about eight keys. As I pressed each key the sound could pass through a gate that was controlled by that particular key.[8]

Two years later, in 1967, Chadabe received a larger grant and devised a much more ambitious plan for his university studio:

Then, I remember, one night about two in the morning, I got an idea. It was for a completely programmable studio. Now, at that time—it was about 1967—to have something "programmable" could barely have meant a computer . . . I thought if we bought a computer to control this analog synthesizer it would probably take us a couple of years to develop software and learn about it and get it up and running. I wanted to be making music faster. So, I thought of an analog programmable studio and was lucky enough, in fact, to raise the money at the State University . . . So, I got a grant for about $18,000 and ordered a synthesizer from the R. A. Moog Company. We went back and forth a little bit about the design of it and the specific design of the sequencers. This was doubtless the single largest installation of the Moog sequencers in the world. The whole studio was controlled by a digital clock. It was delivered in 1969. I worked with it pretty intensively for the better part of a year to figure out the best way of using it. In the course of that, I started to work with different kinds of automated procedures. From an analog studio point of view, this was a serious deviation from the norm. Normally people were playing it as a musical instrument with a keyboard. It was about that time that Wendy Carlos came out with *Switched-On Bach*, for example, where she was playing it like an organ or harpsichord. This was a different matter altogether. It was a question of setting up automatic procedures and then guiding them.[9]

Customizations aside, the basic components that could be ordered as part of the Moog Modular Synthesizer included:

- **A five-octave, monophonic keyboard for triggering voltage control signals**. This could be set to operate like a chromatic keyboard using the 12-tone scale or adjusted for alternate pitch scales and microtonal systems. Only one pitch could be played at a time, represented by the highest voltage (highest key) being depressed on the keyboard at any given time.
- **Wide-range voltage-controlled oscillators (VCOs)**. These had a frequency range of 0.01 to 40,000 Hz. The range of human hearing is only about 20 to 20,000 Hz. The Moog provided frequencies above (ultrasonic) and below (sub-audio) this range that could be used as control voltages to modulate audible tones. The original Moog contained two VCOs as sound sources. Larger studio models such as the Moog 55 had up to seven VCOs. Each VCO was switch-selectable for sine, sawtooth, triangular, and rectangular (square/pulse) waves.
- **A voltage-controlled amplifier (VCA)**. The VCA can be used to amplify any voltage. It was most often used in conjunction with an envelope generator to change the loudness of a waveform during an attack-sustain-decay sequence.
- **A voltage-controlled filter (VCF)**. The voltage-controlled filter was one of the most cleverly engineered components of the system. Its design was so unique that several other synthesizer manufacturers copied it until Moog's company forced them to cease and desist. The ARP 2600 used this filter, as did synthesizers made by Crumar. Moog calls the filter "the only patent I ever got that is worth anything."[10]
- **An envelope generator**. This classic ADSR controlled the attack, decay, sustain, and release characteristics of the output signal.

- **A ribbon controller**. This was available as an optional triggering device. It consisted of a Teflon ribbon with a wire on its underside, suspended slightly above a contact strip. Pressing the ribbon against the contact strip at any point along its length would close a circuit and produce a corresponding voltage. This voltage was used to drive oscillators. A dial was used to adjust the frequency range of the ribbon controller.
- **Patch cords, used to make connections between the different modules**. All of this was done using RCA phone jacks on the front panel of the instrument, resulting in a dizzying tangle of cables required to set up patches for the creation of a desired sound or modulation pattern.
- **Sequencer**. The Moog sequencer provided a source of timed, stepped control voltages that could be programmed to create repeating note patterns or control sequences without using the keyboard. Sequencer-managed music became synonymous with the steady, trancelike rhythms that characterized the works of such artists as Tangerine Dream, Kraftwerk, Isao Tomita, and Klaus Schulze (b. 1947).

Popular accessories included spring reverberation, a ring modulator, pink and white noise generators, a vocoder, and frequency shifters.

During the period from 1966 to 1968, Moog pounded the pavement to get the word out about his new instrument. As an engineer, he frequented professional conferences and gave demonstrations of his equipment. He only had three salespeople, stationed in New York, Los Angeles, and London. The Moog Synthesizer had begun to appear on commercial records, but trying to pinpoint which album was released first is not easy. Less puzzling is knowing who played the instrument on these first recordings. Musician Paul Beaver (1925–75) was Moog's West Coast sales representative. Being one of the only people who knew how to set up and perform on the Moog meant that he was often recruited to sit in on recording sessions for other people.

Because of Beaver, the very first commercial recording featuring the Moog Synthesizer may have been *Zodiac Cosmic Sounds* by Mort Garson (Elektra EK 4009, mono, EKS 74009, stereo, 1967). It came about in a most serendipitous way. Moog recalled:

Figure 8.6 Zodiac Cosmic Sounds LP. (Elektra EKS-74009, 1967)

We went out to California to the Audio Engineering Society convention in April 1967. It was at the Hollywood Roosevelt Hotel. It was the first time we had ever been out to the West Coast. At that time, believe it or not, the Audio Engineering Society in Los Angeles was a very small show. Hollywood was sort of a backwater of New York. How things have changed. This was the very first synthesizer we had shipped west of the Rockies. We had arranged for a representative to sell these things on our behalf out there. He invited all of the session musicians that he knew to come down to see this thing. That began a whole wave of interest out on the West Coast. One night during that show, we took the modular synthesizer to the recording studio where they were working on *Zodiac Cosmic Sounds*. Our representative, Paul Beaver, produced the sounds, turning the knobs and hitting the keys. If you can get a hold of that album the very first sound on it is ooooaaaahhh—a big slow glissando.[11]

Figure 8.7   Paul Beaver and Bernard Krause from the album cover of *In a Wild Sanctuary* (1968). These two composers were largely responsible for the early use of the Moog Modular Synthesizer on a variety of early synthesizer jazz and rock albums. (Ergo, *In a Wild Sanctuary* album cover, Warner Brothers 1850, 1970)

Many strange instruments found within a 50-mile radius of Los Angeles were used in the same recording session. With the release of *Zodiac Cosmic Sounds*, and its 12 individually packaged sequels, the Moog entered the pantheon of exotic instruments being plundered to make popular recordings in the late 1960s. Mort Garson (1924–2008), the creator of *Zodiac Cosmic Sounds*, was a well-established musician, composer, and arranger, having worked with such popular music artists as Doris Day, Mel Tormé, and Glenn Campbell. Following *Zodiac Cosmic Sounds*, Garson acquired his own Moog and produced a peculiar series of record albums exploiting the sounds of the synthesizer. Among these now highly collectable records were *Electronic Hair Pieces* (1971, music from the hippie-generation Broadway musical *Hair*), *Z: Music for Sensuous Lovers* (1971, a collage of Moog sonics bubbling over the apparent sounds of a couple making love), *Black Mass Lucifer* (1971, Garson's dark electronic rock opera), and *Plantasia* (1976, music to help plants grow).

Beaver was also recruited later in 1967 for some other studio recording sessions. The first was by percussionist Hal Blaine for his spacey *Psychedelic Percussion* (1967), on which Beaver played the Moog and the "Beaver Electronics System." He also contributed Moog and Clavinet to an album by vibraphonist Emil Richards called *Stones* (1967).

In 1967, few people, including the musicians who hired Beaver, understood how to produce sounds on the Moog. The resulting records used the synthesizer primarily for seasoning the music played primarily by more familiar instruments. Nobody had yet to create a clearly identifiable sound that could be associated with the Moog and that was one reason why the inventor himself was unsure of its potential, even then. Moog would later say that, "There was never a notion that a synthesizer would be used by itself for anything."[12]

A little more than a year later, that opinion required serious revision when Columbia Records released *Switched-On Bach* (1968) by Wendy Carlos, the smash success needed to propel the Moog synthesizer into the public's consciousness.

LISTEN

EARLY MOOG RECORDINGS (BEFORE 1970)

1   *Zodiac Cosmic Sounds* (Elektra, 1967) by Mort Garson
    Paul Beaver provided Moog sounds

2   *Psychedelic Percussion* (Dunhill, 1967) by Hal Blaine
    Paul Beaver provided Moog and other electronic treatments for this jazzy
    percussion album by drummer Blaine

3   *Stones* (Uni, 1967) by Emil Richards New Sound Element
    Paul Beaver played Moog and Clavinet on this album by jazz–pap mallet player
    Richards, who also contributed some synthesizer sounds

4   *The Notorious Byrd Brothers* (Columbia, 1968) by The Byrds
    Producer Gary Usher was acknowledged for having included the Moog in this
    rock album; tracks including Moog sounds: *Space Odyssey*, *Goin Back* (played by
    Paul Beaver), *Natural Harmony*, and unreleased track *Moog Raga*

5   *Pisces, Aquarius, Capricorn, and Jones Ltd.* (Colgems, 1967) by the Monkees
    Moog effects provided by Micky Dolenz of the Monkees and Paul Beaver

6   *Kaleidoscopic Vibrations* (Vanguard, 1967) by Perry-Kingsley
    The first Moog album by this duo known for their electro-pop songs

7   *Switched-On Bach* (Columbia, 1968) by Wendy Carlos
    The most celebrated Moog album of all time and still a classic

8   *Moog Rock* (Calendar, 1968) by Les Baxter
    Les Baxter was the first crossover band leader from the easy-listening genre to adopt
    the Moog; Paul Beaver played the Moog on this disc

9   *Moogie Woogie* (Chess, 1969) by The Zeet Band
    Electronic boogie and blues by an ensemble including Paul Beaver, Erwin Helfer,
    Mark Naftalin, "Fastfingers" Finkelstein, and Norman Dayron

10 *The Blue Marble* (Together, 1969) by Sagittarius
    This was a studio group headed by Gary Usher, producer of The Byrds, who used
    the Moog extensively on this rock album

Wendy Carlos and *Switched-On Bach*

Wendy Carlos first met Robert Moog at the AES conference in New York in 1964.
Ussachevsky, her music instructor at Columbia University, had suggested that she visit
the conference because she was "one of his more technically curious graduate students."[13]
This is where she first saw Moog's early voltage-controlled modules and the two struck
up a conversation. Carlos was already a veteran of the Columbia–Princeton Electronic
Music Center that Ussachevsky directed, but her musical interests were not in the kinds
of experimental sounds that represented most of the output of the studio. She later
recalled, "I thought what ought to be done was obvious: to use the new technology
for creating new music that expanded from the best and most appealing earlier models.
Why wasn't it being used for anything but the academy approved 'ugly' music?"[14]

Carlos had flirted with tape and instrumental pieces much in the manner of Otto
Luening, but ultimately could not resist also exploring the electronic realization of

traditional musical forms. Having worked at the Columbia–Princeton studio, she became practiced in the usual methods of constructing music track by track, using oscillators, filters, amplifiers, envelope shapers, mixers, tape recorders, and tape splicing. Like most other composers working at the center, Carlos was not a fan of the RCA Mark II Electronic Music Synthesizer and did not use it. As she explained:

> I found it to be an indirect, clumsy way for creating music. That was long before performance controllers could be tied to music generating computers. You had to hand-punch long player-piano-like note lists, timbre lists, envelope lists, a conducting list, and then all of those consciously calculated commands were mechanically scanned. The rigid, un-felt, simulated performance results just drove me up the wall. It seemed even back then that such an approach was sadly wrong-headed.[15]

While an undergraduate at Brown University, Carlos pursued a crossover major that integrated music and physics. Her interest in astronomy has never waned, and for many years she has traveled the world photographing total eclipses of the sun.[16] Carlos sensed in Robert Moog an attentive inventor whose synthesizer had the potential of greatly simplifying the entire process of creating electronic music. Moog remembers that "every time we visited her there was not one but a whole handful of ideas."[17] Carlos left academia in 1966 and struck out on her own, hoping that a person with her taste for technology and musical innovation could find success in the emerging field of electronic music. She became one of Moog's first customers and, by early 1966, they were assembling a custom system for her. To help finance the project, Carlos offered her services to assist Moog in promoting his company. "I was able to 'barter' my time and skills in writing, recording, composing, and mastering a professional Moog demo LP," explained Carlos, "toward the purchase of additional synth components."[18]

Figure 8.8
The studio used by Wendy Carlos to produce *Switched-On Bach* in 1968. The Moog Modular Synthesizer was custom-made to Carlos's specifications. Patch cords in abundance, the photo shows two custom-made touch-sensitive keyboards as well as her retractable mixing board positioned below them. Tape recorders were to the left of the instrument, including an eight-track Ampex machine that she assembled from an assortment of used parts and homebuilt components.

Figure 8.9 Switched-On Bach LP. (Columbia Records MS 7194, 1968)

Moog personally delivered the first components that Carlos ordered, driving to New York City in his station wagon and helping the composer haul the gear up to her walk-up apartment. Many of these early Moog Modular components were built or modified according to Carlos's specifications. She was technically skilled with electronics and often designed circuits and built equipment as needed. She constructed her own one-inch eight-track tape recorder, an unusual piece of hardware at the time considering that even The Beatles were still using four-track machines in 1967.

The name Wendy Carlos is forever linked with the Moog synthesizer. This despite the fact that she gave up the Moog and analog synthesis more than 25 years ago while preparing the soundtrack for the movie *Tron* (1982), moving on as a pioneer in the field of digital synthesis. Her album *Switched-On Bach*, released in late 1968, became the top-selling classical music album at that time. Her warm and sparkling electronic interpretations of Bach's keyboard music single-handedly created the kind of buzz about electronic music that launched an industry of instrument makers and recording artists. *Switched-On Bach* was created after Carlos's departure from Columbia University and was in some ways her reaction against academic music making, especially avant-garde music that so dominated the electronic music scene at the time. "I tried to avoid gratuitous obsession with only dissonance," Carlos explained. "I tried to make music that was not ugly."[19]

For many months, Carlos had been working steadfastly with Moog's equipment to lay down her interpretations of Bach's keyboard music. The process was complicated by the fact that the Moog was a monophonic instrument. Playing two or more notes at the same time to construct even the simplest chords required multitracking, synchronization, and impeccable timing. The original Moog keyboard was not touch-sensitive, which would have made her performance of Bach that much more difficult to assemble. A little-known fact is that Carlos commissioned Moog to build two touch-sensitive keyboards for her. Each key rocked mechanically on a small vane and used optical sensors to detect the velocity and depth of a key being depressed.[20] According to Carlos, the keyboards were impossible to play rapidly. "I had to clatter away slower than [at] actual speed. You could never play faster than moderato. Sixteenth notes at a good clip? Forget it!"[21]

Carlos explained her approach to transcribing Bach's keyboard music:

> The Moog wasn't all that elaborate. There were three to six oscillators, and you adjusted them to track the octaves. You would pick a waveshape from the four available: sine, triangle, pulse wave, and sawtooth. There was a white noise source, and a filter to reduce the high end of the wave to make it sound more mellow, to add resonance, or take out the bottom. Then there were envelopers that came from Ussachevsky's ideas: attack time, decay, sustain, and release. Set the thing to ramp-up at some rate: slow for an organ or fast for a plucked string. Make it decay immediately for a harpsichord, or sustain for a piano. Have the final release-time based on the need; short and dry, or longer for the vibrating body of a cello or drum. Easy.[22]

In addition to her custom-built Moog, Carlos used a stereo Ampex 440B tape recorder, a homemade eight-track tape recorder,[23] a homemade varispeed box, a homemade voltage-controlled oscillator, and a homemade mixing panel.

The Moog was sensitive to temperature fluctuations and frequently went out of tune during Carlos's *Switched-On Bach* sessions. This made the multitracking process of recording anything tedious. "You would adjust the tuning, play a phrase, then check the tuning again. If OK, continue. Otherwise, go back and do it again."[24] Chords were created by recording one part per track and synchronizing them, "which was particularly challenging." For contrapuntal melodies, a slight error was allowable in the Sel-Synching (multitrack recording synchronization) of individual lines.

Columbia Records didn't expect much from *Switched-On Bach*. It was good timing in that it fit with Columbia's "Bach to Rock" sales campaign at the time. At the time of its release, the record was one of three new Columbia albums being promoted. Another was *In C* by Terry Riley, which was part of the Columbia Masterworks, Music of Our Time series produced, interestingly enough, by electronic music composer David Behrman. A third new album was expected to be the biggest commercial success of the three—a rock album called *Rock and Other Four Letter Words*, by two rock journalists, J. Marks and Shipen Lebzelter. The latter album featured a collage of free jazz and psychedelic music intermixed with snippets of interviews with rock notables, including Brian Wilson, Jefferson Airplane, Tim Buckley, Ginger Baker, and a host of others.

The New York press party for the three albums was held at Columbia's famous 30th Street studio in New York. Carlos dropped in to make a brief appearance, "grabbed a press kit and snuck back out."[25] Robert Moog was asked to demonstrate his synthesizer:

> I remember there was a nice big bowl of joints on top of the mixing console, and Terry Riley was there in his white Jesus suit, up on a pedestal, playing live on a Farfisa organ against a backdrop of tape delays. *Rock and Other Four Letter Words* went on to sell a few thousand records. *In C* sold a few tens of thousands. *Switched-On Bach* sold over a million and just keeps going on and on.[26]

In 1969, *Switched-On Bach* sold so many copies that it began to climb the industry sales charts for popular as well as classical music. It received a gold record in August 1969 from the Recording Industry Association of America (RIAA) for having sold more than 500,000 copies. In time it became the first classical music album to ever sell more than a million copies, giving it RIAA certification as a platinum record. *Switched-On Bach* also received three Grammies in 1969, for Best Classical Performance, Instrumental Soloist; Best Engineered Classical Recording; and Classical Album of the Year. Wendy Carlos was recognized as the first virtuoso player of the Moog synthesizer. Her record had unusual appeal because it was palatable to non-classicists and classicists alike. "We tried to do something with the medium that was musical and likable," says Carlos.[27]

One reason for the success of the Carlos recording was that the genius of her musical performance vastly offset the ambivalence of the public toward electronic music. Pianist Glenn Gould described Carlos's interpretation of Bach's *Brandenburg Concerto No. 4* as "the finest performance of any of the Brandenburgs—live, canned, or intuited—I've ever heard."[28] Because of the album's popularity, "synthesizer" became a household word and the once-impenetrable mystique that shrouded the world of electronic music was vaporized. The interest generated by this one record was responsible for the burgeoning use of synthesizers in all music genres, from rock and jazz to classical and the avant-garde. Synthesizers were in demand and every hip musician and commercial recording studio wanted one. Carlos herself produced four additional albums of predominantly Moog music before converting her own studio to digital instruments, including *The Well-Tempered Synthesizer* (Columbia 1969), *Switched-On Bach II* (Columbia 1974), *By Request* (Columbia 1975), and *Switched-On Brandenburgs Volumes 1 & 2* (Columbia 1979).

The success of *Switched-On Bach* belied the difficulties encountered by Carlos in crafting the finished product. The Moog Modular Synthesizer was not an easy instrument to learn. Using it required some fundamental knowledge of wave physics and the way in which voltage-controlled components behaved. Notating electronic music was impractical and unfamiliar to most composers who instead were faced with a bewildering matrix of patch cord connections, control panel settings, and rigorous procedures to produce a set of sounds. Composers were sometimes given patch panel diagrams, not unlike pages from a coloring book, upon which they could draw the various connections for any given setup of patch cords and dial settings. Using these drawings, a performer could reconstruct, sound by sound, the various settings and steps needed to recreate whatever effects were required (see Figure 8.10). The Moog Modular Synthesizer was not designed for live, real-time performance. It was conceived as a tool for the electronic music studio. In working with it, most composers simply recorded the sounds of every experimental patch on tape and later processed, modified, and assembled the finished work as a composite of pre-recorded sounds.

Standardized operating instructions for patch cord setups were not generally available for the Moog because each installation of the synthesizer was configured to the unique needs of the customer. Composers worked by trial and error to explore the potential of the synthesizer. The first electronic music composer's bible was the textbook *Electronic Music: Systems, Techniques, and Controls* by Allen Strange. This softcover manual was the first successful attempt to structure information about the newly evolving field of electronic musical instruments with "pedagogical sensibility."[29] Strange was a practiced composer, musician, and electronic musician. Thirty years later, the first and second editions of his book were still highly valued as exquisitely detailed documents of the analog past.

While the Moog Modular Synthesizer was best suited for studio use, there was increasing demand for a portable version that could be easily taken on the road. In 1969, Moog's company set another precedent by introducing the *Minimoog*—a simple, compact monophonic synthesizer designed for live performance situations. With sales of about 12,000 units, this model became the most popular and widely used synthesizer of all time. Most of the patching between modules was preset ("hardwired") and controlled by rocker switches and dials. The keyboard featured two unique performance controls that were widely imitated: the "pitch wheel" for bending notes, and the "mod wheel" for adjusting the degree of modulation of the output signal. The original Minimoog was in production until the late 1980s.

Robert Moog's original company went through several periods of transition. It was acquired twice by larger companies. Moog himself left Moog Music in 1977 to pursue his engineering interests independently, working as a much sought-after consultant for many years. In 1978, Moog founded a new instrument-manufacturing company called

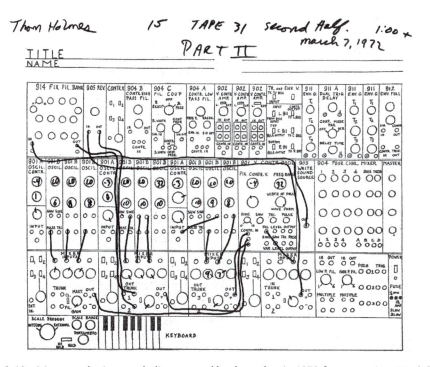

Figure 8.10   Moog synthesizer patch diagram used by the author in 1972 for composing. Worksheets like this were essential for documenting one's patch setup and settings on the instrument.
(Thom Holmes)

Big Briar Inc. in North Carolina to continue manufacturing voltage-controlled synthesizer components and instruments. As a consulting engineer, Moog headed new production research at Kurzweil Music Systems from 1984 through 1989. He began manufacturing a new line of solid-state Theremins during the 1990s as well as high-quality analog sound processing modules under the brand name of Moogerfoogers. Moog regained the rights to the Moog Music and Minimoog trademarks in 2002, changed the name of Big Briar back to Moog Music and resurrected the Minimoog with a new model called the Voyager. Unfortunately, Moog died in August 2005 from brain cancer. His company lives on to continue the work of this pioneer who was the most influential engineer in and advocate of electronic music for 50 years.

Moog's success encouraged many manufacturers to enter the market for commercial synthesizers. Collectively, these companies revolutionized the design of synthesizing equipment by employing the latest in integrated circuitry to produce entirely self-contained electronic music machines. As the instruments became more affordable, they began to migrate from institutional electronic music studios into the homes of composers and musicians.

The Buchla Synthesizer

In 1965, Morton Subotnick and Ramón Sender of the San Francisco Tape Music Center (SFTMC) contracted engineer Donald Buchla to design a synthesizer for their studio.

At that time, the SFTMC had no more than half a dozen oscillators, filters, and tape recorders at its disposal.

Like Robert Moog and Hugh Le Caine, Buchla was convinced that voltage control was the most practical approach for producing a synthesizer that could be managed effectively by a composer. Unlike Moog, Buchla was a musician and had a strong, natural affinity for the needs of the composer. Moog's original synthesizer was designed strictly as a studio tool. "There was never a notion that a synthesizer would be used by itself for anything."[30] In contrast, Buchla, Subotnick, and Sender envisioned an instrument that could be used in live performance.

In 1964, at about the same time that Moog was also working on voltage-controlled synthesizer design, Buchla created the basic parts for what would become the 100 series Modular Electronic Music System. He used this work as a foundation for the instrument that he built for Subotnick and Sender at the SFTMC, which was then sold in 1966 as a commercial product.

Buchla emphasized two aspects of synthesizer design to accommodate the needs of composers. First, he offered great flexibility in the modification of tone color. Next, he provided a way to "program" a series of repeatable sounds using a pattern of repeating control voltages. This was the first sequencer available on a commercial synthesizer. Moog admired Buchla's work, recently stating that Buchla designed a system not only for "making new sounds but [for] making textures out of these sounds by specifying when these sounds could change and how regular those changes would be."[31] The implications for composers were enormous because Buchla's synthesizer provided real-time controls over shaping the timbre of sounds that would normally have been done using multiple stages of sound processing in a conventional electronic music studio.

Buchla began delivering prototype components of the synthesizer modules to the SFTMC "one by one as they were developed."[32] William Maginnis was one of the first people to compose a piece of music on the system. Called *Flight*, it was realized on the first night that the initial components arrived in 1965.

The solid-state *Buchla 100* was outfitted similarly to the Moog in its use of voltage-controlled oscillators, amplifiers, and filters. Instead of a keyboard, the Buchla employed various arrays of touch-sensitive plates. These capacitance-sensitive plates could each trigger sounds that had been manually programmed using patch cords on the control panel, or they could be set to emulate an actual keyboard tuned to the chromatic scale. The SFTMC instrument had two sets of touch-sensitive plates. Subotnick explained how they were used:

> One had 12 keys and you could tune it straight across the board. You could get a chromatic scale if you chose to. It had three control voltages per position. The other one had ten keys and one output per key. We often used this one to control the amplitudes of concrète tapes during playback. You could literally play ten loops with your fingers.[33]

The most innovative features of the Buchla 100 were its sequencer options. The Buchla sequencers functioned in a manner similar to those of the Moog Modular System (see above) but offered some configuration options that were unique to the Buchla design. Three Sequential Voltage Source generators were provided. Two accommodated up to eight programmed voltages in sequence and the third provided a sequence up to 16 voltages. Up to three outputs were available per sequencer and the controls consisted of rotary dials, one for each of the available voltage steps, arrayed horizontally in three rows. Adjusting any of the dials would set the voltage for an output pulse that could then be patched into another module as a control voltage. Having more than one sequencer provided many combinations of control sequences for the composer. Morton Subotnick described a typical configuration in which he would run multiple sequencers simultaneously to control pitch, amplitude, and the stereo projection of the sound in space. A separate pulse generator module was also available for controlling the sequencers, allowing the composer to modify the voltage values controlling the rhythm of each individual sequencer. "You could literally program a very complex rhythm over a long period of time, for example, by running five stages against 13."[34]

Figure 8.11   Vladimir Ussachevsky in 1970 with the Buchla synthesizer acquired by the Columbia–Princeton Electronic Music Center. (Columbia University Computer Music Center)

The *Buchla 200* (1970) expanded on the already formidable sequencing features of the Buchla 100 with the addition of two new control voltage sources. Whereas typical sequencers were restricted to the output of rigidly stepped voltages, the Multiple Arbitrary Function Generator allowed the composer to enter interval time values governing the rate of pulses, from 0.001 to 120 seconds for up to 16 individual control voltages in a sequence. Even more specialized was the whimsically named Source of Uncertainty module, which could generate any combination of two continuously varying random voltages, two pulse-actuated random voltages, and white noise with three spectral distributions.

Subotnick became the foremost virtuoso of Buchla's synthesizer. Although the instrument was suited for real-time performance and improvisation, Subotnick's early synthesized works were more highly composed. His pioneering work with the Buchla 100 resulted in a series of landmark realizations that were released by Nonesuch Records: *Silver Apples of the Moon* (1967) and *The Wild Bull* (1968) were the first works of electronic music commissioned solely for release as long-playing record albums. In addition to the SFTMC, Buchla's synthesizers were popular with other studios, including the Columbia–Princeton Electronic Music Center.

Buchla's instruments never experienced the runaway popularity that Moog enjoyed. Yet, by retaining control over his products and only manufacturing them in limited numbers, Buchla was able to remain independent and relatively unaffected by the synthesizer marketing wars that came and went along with many companies and products during the 1970s and 1980s. Philadelphia composer Charles Cohen (b. 1945) is an original owner of a *Buchla Music Easel*, only about 25 of which were manufactured in 1972. He still uses it for live performance, remarking:

> The instantaneous and very light touch of the keyboard is part of what I like. The ability to smoothly and/or rapidly move around amongst and between all the basic electronic sound textures is the other big plus. While I no doubt could replicate the sounds with modern instruments, its playability and stability in the free-flowing, wide-ranging, and fast-moving genre of live performance group improvisation is very satisfying.[35]

Figure 8.12   Charles Cohen in 2001 performing with one of the rarest of all Buchla synthesizers, the Buchla Music Easel—a portable analog synthesizer used in live performance. (Thom Holmes)

The Buchla synthesizer went through several stages of development over the years, successfully bridging the gap from analog to digital synthesis. In 1970, Buchla introduced the 200 series Electronic Music Box, which became one of the centerpieces of the studios of the Mills Center for Contemporary Music. During the mid-1970s, Buchla built several analog/digital hybrid instruments and a model with a keyboard (the Touché, 1978). By the mid-1980s, MIDI was so prevalent that Buchla shifted his attention from designing synthesizers to making unique MIDI-compatible controllers for musicians other than keyboardists. Then, in 1987, he introduced the model 700 with MIDI controls.

During the mid-1980s, Buchla turned his attention to the development of other new electronic instruments, the Thunder and Lightning—light-controlled wands for triggering MIDI signals using any MIDI-compatible synthesizer. Buchla upgraded these in 1996 with the improved Lightning II. In 1999–2000, Buchla introduced the Marimba Lumina, a mallet-style MIDI controller with an onboard synthesizer. The mallets were programmable and triggered tones and control signals when they were "played" on a flat, touch-sensitive matrix of tiles configured like a marimba. In 2005, Buchla revived the series 200 family of analog synthesizers with the model 200e. Buchla also collaborated with Moog Music in 2004 to develop the PianoBar, a device for capturing sound from a conventional piano and transforming it into MIDI signals that could be further processed.

Figure 8.13   The EMS Synthi 100, the British-made alternative to the Moog Modular Synthesizer. (EMS, 1971)

Other Commercial Synthesizers

Following the success of the Moog and Buchla systems in the late 1960s, many new manufacturers entered the market with variations on the modular voltage-controlled synthesizer. Japanese manufacturers in particular designed innovative and less costly technology. Among the instrument makers to join the synthesizer wars were ARP, Oberheim, Korg, Yamaha, Roland, EMS, and Crumar, some of which continue to make electronic music products to this day. Over the years, analog technology evolved into hybrid analog/digital technology, then into microcomputers with sound cards, and finally into purely digital performance instruments. One predominant trend at the time of writing is the "virtual analog" instrument: software or digital keyboards using sound-generating algorithms and controls that emulate the manual control and tone color of classic analog instruments.

OTHER EARLY SYNTHESIZER RECORDINGS (PRE-MIDI, NOT MOOG)

1 *Alien Bog* (1967) by Pauline Oliveros
   Used prototype Buchla 100 at Mills College

2 *Silver Apples of the Moon* (LP, 1967) by Morton Subotnick
   Used Buchla 100

3 *Concert Piece for Synket and Symphony Orchestra* (Turnabout, 1968) by John Eaton
   Used the Synket, an Italian-made modular synthesizer of which only six may have been made

4 *Entropical Paradise* (Seraphim, 1970) by Douglas Leedy
   Six "sonic environments" using the Buchla Modular Electronic Music System and Moog Modular Synthesizer

5 *Space Experience* (LP, 1972) by John Keating
   Used EMS Synthi VCS3

6 *The Eden Electronic Ensemble Plays Joplin* (LP, 1974) by the Eden Electronic Ensemble
   Used EMS Synthi AKS and Minimoog

7 *Beyond the Sun* (LP, 1976) by Patrick Gleeson
   Used Eu Polyphonic Synthesizer

8 *Oxygene* (1977) by Jean Michel Jarre
   Used ARP Odyssey, EMS Synthi AKS and Synthi VCS3, RMI Harmonic Synthesizer

9 *Kosmos* (LP, 1978) by Isao Tomita
   Used Roland System 700, Roland Strings RS-202, Roland Revo 30, in addition to Moog Modular III, Moog System 55, and Polymoog

10 *The Ethereal Time Shadow* (1981–82) by Terry Riley
    Used two Prophet V synthesizers, tuned to just intonation and employing sequencing

LISTEN

MIDI

The development of the analog synthesizer was reaching its summit by the late 1970s, at about the same time as the emergence of the first personal computers. The field of electronic music was clearly on a path to digital synthesis, a topic fully explored in Part III, but there was a transitional period from about 1975 to 1985 during which analog instruments became increasingly computerized and the ability to link synthesizers to personal computers underwent a transformative stage of development. No industry standard existed for linking synthesizers and computers until 1984 and the introduction of the **Musical Instrument Digital Interface (MIDI)**. In its earliest incarnation, MIDI was a digital technology attached to analog instrumentation, signifying a transition in the development of electronic musical instruments from analog systems to digital systems and software.

Although MIDI is essentially a digital technology, it is included in this concluding discussion of analog synthesis because it represents a bridge between those two fundamental paradigms of electronic instrumentation.

The Early History of MIDI

By the early 1980s, the makers of commercial synthesizers and PCs were feeling pressure from consumers to provide universal connectivity of their gear. When a manufacturer chose to connect a computer with a synthesizer, it did so using expensive and quickly outdated proprietary methods that were unique to its own products.

The MIDI interface and communications protocol was introduced in 1984 after many months of behind-the-scenes cooperation and squabbling by several leading electronic instrument manufacturers, including Roland, Oberheim, Sequential Circuits, Yamaha, Korg, and Kawai. Note the absence of Moog Music and Buchla from this list, both of whom were, by that time, considered minor players in a market then dominated by relatively low-cost performance synthesizers competing for visibility in the world of popular music production. The original specification for MIDI was the result of a collaboration between competitors in the then explosive market for commercial synthesizers. Roland, Yamaha, Korg, Kawai, and Sequential Circuits all contributed to version 1.0 of the spec, which was completed in August 1983.[36]

The MIDI interface was designed with two basic applications in mind:

- **Connecting and controlling synthesizers**. MIDI can connect standalone electronic musical instruments and permit one instrument to control the sounds being made on several others. This can be done without a separate computer. The instruments may or may not have keyboards, although in a typical multi-instrumental setup there is at least one keyboard that triggers all of the activity. Standalone MIDI controllers are also available independently of the instruments themselves, providing a variety of control methods ranging from the conventional keyboard to any number of kinesthetically controlled devices that might be useful in the creation of music.
- **Linking computers to synthesizers**. MIDI can connect standalone electronic musical instruments to a PC. In this configuration, the computer is used to trigger sounds and patterns on the connected instruments. MIDI is also used to manage and control software-based synthesizers that do not exist as standalone performance synthesizers or outside of the laptop computer.

The coded MIDI control signal communicates several parameters about musical notes that are device-independent, meaning that the codes can be interpreted by any device—synthesizer or computer—that is compatible with the MIDI communications protocol. MIDI succeeded in providing genuine compatibility among different instruments and the computer and led to explosive growth in the making of software and hardware for the music industry.

MIDI Basics

MIDI communicates the values of notes played on the keyboard, including the pitch, amplitude, and duration. This should not be confused with recording the sounds played by the keyboard since MIDI is only a data stream representing a sequence of note values and associated parameters. The timbre, or quality of the sound, is the provenance of the synthesizer that receives the MIDI signal. The same sequence of note values can be played on different instruments using different voices.

The MIDI standard includes specifications for a *communications messaging* protocol for connecting musical instruments and associated devices and an *interface* standard for making the physical connection between these devices.

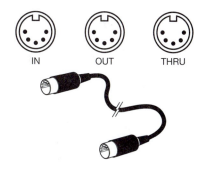

Figure 8.14   MIDI ports and cable.

The physical interface between MIDI instruments and between MIDI instruments and computers uses a cable with a standard 5-pin DIN connector. There are three ports on an electronic musical instrument that can use such MIDI cables: MIDI OUT, for sending data from the instrument; MIDI IN for accepting data into the instrument; and MIDI THRU for daisy-chaining multiple instruments in series (see Figure 8.14). When a computer is added to the configuration as a controller, MIDI THRU is effectively replaced by the use of software for mixing and managing incoming and outgoing MIDI channel signals. The instrument or controller that manages the signals is thought of as the **master unit** and satellite instruments are known as **slave units** (see Figures 8.15, 8.16, and 8.17).

MIDI messages are sent in one direction through a MIDI cable but the ability to multiplex signals allows up to 16 channels of data, each capable of controlling an instrument. Channel 1 is the default channel for MIDI devices but the master unit—whether an electronic musical instrument or computer—can be used to set the additional channels for other instruments in a daisy chain. There are some limitations on the number of instruments that can be daisy-chained depending on the instruments themselves. Instruments with more than one sound-generating module—e.g. percussion plus a separate instrumental voice—may require two or more channels to accommodate controls signals for each of the modules. Another practical limitation is the lag involved when multiple instruments are daisy-chained: as MIDI control signals are passed from one to the next, a very noticeable delay is accrued.

MIDI communications protocol, also known as performance codes, are divided into two broad categories: **channel messages**, which direct a MIDI command to any one of the 16 available channels; and **system messages**, which comprise commands broadcast to all devices on all channels.

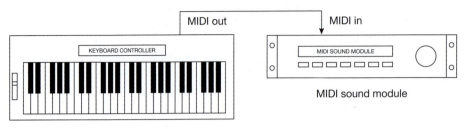

Figure 8.15 Schematic of a simple MIDI connection between two synthesizers.

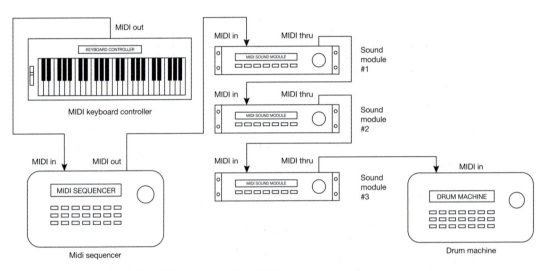

Figure 8.16 Schematic of a MIDI network of multiple instruments.

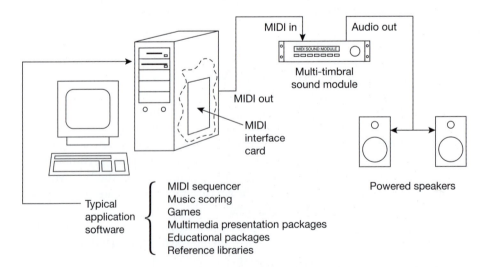

Figure 8.17 Schematic of a computer–controlled MIDI network.

MIDI Channel Messages

Channel messages are MIDI commands delivered on a single channel. There are channel messages for voice commands that designate performance aspects for a particular MIDI device set up to respond to one or more channels, such as which notes to play and expressive features.

MIDI messages consist of binary data organized into ten-bit units or words. The first and last bits comprise the START and STOP bits and do not convey MIDI data. The eight bits (one byte) in between are codes for a given MIDI control element, although frequently only seven bits are employed, as in the Note On example in Figure 8.18, where note and velocity values are seven-bit values, giving a binary range of 0–127. MIDI commands require from one to three bytes to convey all of the aspects needed to complete a command. For example, the Note On command requires three bytes as shown in Figure 8.18. Each ten-bit sequence is sent one after another in a data stream, each one requiring 320 microseconds. MIDI is thus a *serial* protocol: only one command is sent at a time, and although this happens so rapidly that a chord might sound as if all the notes were played simultaneously, in fact they are played sequentially.

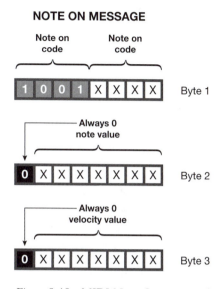

Figure 8.18   MIDI Note On command sequence. (After Scarff, 2007)

MIDI channel messages (see Table 8.1) are available for the following controls and parameters:

- **Note On**. This command begins to play a designated note. The MIDI tuning range is broad—five octaves below middle C to five octaves above the G above middle C. Notes can be designated in whole tones or semitones. Part of a Note On message is a byte representing *velocity*, which corresponds to how fast a key on a keyboard was depressed, and is thus a measure of the force with which the note was played. A remote MIDI device "down the chain" can be set to respond with greater or lesser sensitivity to velocity values.
- **Note Off**. In the world of MIDI commands, stopping a note is a command that is separate from starting a note (Note On). The Note Off command is sent when a note ends, as when the finger is lifted from the key. It is also possible to turn off a note by issuing a Note On command with a velocity value of zero.
- **Polyphonic Key Pressure**. This command, also known as Aftertouch or Poly Pressure, can be sent to instruments that can apply pressure changes to a note while it is being played. Separate data bytes are provided to designate the key and the pressure level to be applied. Channel Aftertouch, which applies the same key pressure information to all keys, is handled by a separate command—Channel Key Pressure.
- **Channel Key Pressure**. This command applies a measure of Aftertouch equally to all keys. It differs from Polyphonic Key Pressure, which can apply individualized pressures to different notes in a polyphonic sequence. Bytes are sent to identify the keys and the pressure level for all keys.

- **Pitch Wheel Change**. This command is generated by a pitchbend wheel, responding to changes in the wheel and applying them to a single channel. Two data bytes are required to represent a 14-bit pitchbend value, which is heard as a smooth, gliding change with indistinguishable steps, an important feature when modifying the pitch over several octaves.
- **Control Change**. This widely adoptable command is responsible for changing the performance of a variety of expressive sound properties such as vibrato, envelope shape, amplitude, portamento, foot controllers, and many more. The command consists of three bytes: the first byte is a status byte activating a control change and it is followed by two data bytes—the first being for controller number, which identifies a parameter such as panning, overall volume of a device, an effect, or another aspect of a sound, and the second byte being a value (occupying seven bits, or 0–127) for that parameter. The availability of controllable aspects of a sound is dependent on the design of the electronic instrument being controlled, so the Control Change message has been designed with many possible settings to accommodate many manufacturers and applications. There are 127 controller numbers in all, many of which remained undefined for future use and expansion. Table 8.2 lists currently assigned controller numbers.
- **Program Change**. This command message is sent to an instrument on a specified channel to recall another patch or program. The message includes channel data and information identifying the instrumental voice (e.g. violin, trumpet). There was little standardization of instrumental codes during the early days of synthesizer development, requiring the composer to know the vendor-specific codes for each instrument being controlled. The introduction of the **General MIDI** specification in 1991, a standard developed jointly by the MIDI Manufacturers Association (MMA) and the Japan MIDI Standards Committee (JMSC), defined specific instrumental codes that have since been adopted by most manufacturers for the most commonly used synthesizer voices.

Table 8.1 **MIDI channel messages**

Command	Meaning	Number of parameters	Parameter 1	Parameter 2
0 × **80**	Note Off	2	key	velocity
0 × **90**	Note On	2	key	velocity
0 × **A0**	Polyphonic Key Pressure (Aftertouch)	2	key	touch
0 × **B0**	Continuous Controller	2	controller #	controller value
0 × **C0**	Patch Change	2	instrument #	
0 × **D0**	Channel Key Pressure	1	pressure	
0 × **E0**	Pitch Wheel Change	2	lsb (7 bits)	msb (7 bits)
0 × **F0**	Control Change	–	–	–

Notes

msb = most significant bit, the leftmost bit position in the lead MIDI byte that determines whether the binary integer is a data byte or command byte.

lsb = less significant bit, or value bit in a binary integer.

Table 8.2   **Control Change module assignments**

No.	Function/module assignment	No.	Function/module assignment
0	Bank Select	68	Legato Footswitch
1	Modulation Wheel or Lever	69	Hold 2
2	Breath Controller	70	Sound Controller 1 (default: Sound Variation)
3	Undefined	71	Sound Controller 2 (default: Timbre/Harmonic Intensity)
4	Foot Controller		
5	Portamento Time	72	Sound Controller 3 (default: Release Time)
6	Data Entry MSB	73	Sound Controller 4 (default: Attack Time)
7	Channel Volume (formerly Main Volume)	74	Sound Controller 5 (default: Brightness)
8	Balance	75	Sound Controller 6 (default: Decay Time—see MMA RP-021)
9	Undefined		
10	Pan	76	Sound Controller 7 (default: Vibrato Rate—see MMA RP-021)
11	Expression Controller		
12	Effect Control 1	77	Sound Controller 8 (default: Vibrato Depth—see MMA RP-021)
13	Effect Control 2		
14	Undefined	78	Sound Controller 9 (default: Vibrato Delay—see MMA RP-021)
15	Undefined		
16	General Purpose Controller 1	79	Sound Controller 10 (default undefined—see MMA RP-021)
17	General Purpose Controller 2		
18	General Purpose Controller 3	80	General Purpose Controller 5
19	General Purpose Controller 4	81	General Purpose Controller 6
20–31	Undefined	82	General Purpose Controller 7
32	LSB for Control 0 (Bank Select)	83	General Purpose Controller 8
33	LSB for Control 1 (Modulation Wheel or Lever)	84	Portamento Control
34	LSB for Control 2 (Breath Controller)	85–90	Undefined
35	LSB for Control 3 (Undefined)	91	Effects 1 Depth (default: Reverb Send Level—see MMA RP-023) (formerly External Effects Depth)
36	LSB for Control 4 (Foot Controller)		
37	LSB for Control 5 (Portamento Time)		
38	LSB for Control 6 (Data Entry)	92	Effects 2 Depth (formerly Tremolo Depth)
39	LSB for Control 7 (Channel Volume, formerly Main Volume)	93	Effects 3 Depth (default: Chorus Send Level—see MMA RP-023) (formerly Chorus Depth)
40	LSB for Control 8 (Balance)		
41	LSB for Control 9 (Undefined)	94	Effects 4 Depth (formerly Celeste [Detune] Depth)
42	LSB for Control 10 (Pan)	95	Effects 5 Depth (formerly Phaser Depth)
43	LSB for Control 11 (Expression Controller)	96	Data Increment (Data Entry +1) (see MMA RP-018)
44	LSB for Control 12 (Effect control 1)	97	Data Decrement (Data Entry −1) (see MMA RP-018)
45	LSB for Control 13 (Effect control 2)	98	Non-Registered Parameter Number (NRPN)—LSB
46	LSB for Control 14 (Undefined)	99	Non-Registered Parameter Number (NRPN)—MSB
47	LSB for Control 15 (Undefined)	100	Registered Parameter Number (RPN)—LSB*
48	LSB for Control 16 (General Purpose Controller 1)	101	Registered Parameter Number (RPN)—MSB*
49	LSB for Control 17 (General Purpose Controller 2)	102–119	Undefined
50	LSB for Control 18 (General Purpose Controller 3)	120	All Sound Off
51	LSB for Control 19 (General Purpose Controller 4)	121	Reset All Controllers
52	LSB for Control 20 (Undefined)	122	Local Control On/Off
53–63	Undefined LSB for Control 21–31	123	All Notes Off
64	Damper Pedal On/Off (Sustain)	124	Omni Mode Off (+ all notes off)
65	Portamento On/Off	125	Omni Mode On (+ all notes off)
66	Sustenuto On/Off	126	Poly Mode On/Off (+ all notes off)
67	Soft Pedal On/Off	127	Poly Mode On (+ mono off + all notes off)

Notes

MSB = most significant byte, the leftmost bit position in the lead MIDI byte that determines whether the binary integer is a data byte or command byte. LSB = less significant byte, or value bit in a binary integer.

Source: MIDI Manufacturer's Association (www.midi.org/about-midi/table3.shtml, accessed July 14, 2007).

MIDI System Messages

MIDI system messages are not channel-specific and affect all MIDI devices that have been networked. Used to control timing events, sequences of data, and special effects, system messages fall into three categories: common, system exclusive, and real time:

- **System common messages**. These messages can be interpreted by all systems in the network and include several functions:

  - *MTC Quarter Frame Message*: MIDI time code information used to synchronize MIDI systems and other equipment, such as audio or video players.
  - *Song Select Message*: Used to recall a song that was stored on another MIDI device such as a sequencer or drum machine.
  - *Tune Request Message*: Used primarily with analog synthesizers to automatically retune their internal oscillators. Many analog synthesizers would go notoriously out of tune while being used or when subjected to varying temperature and humidity conditions. Retuning is not generally an issue with digital synthesizers.
  - *EOX Message*: Denotes the end of a system exclusive message (see below).

- **System exclusive messages**. These messages provide each manufacturer with the ability to provide a set of commands dedicated to the particular functions of its own MIDI devices. Examples include special patches for instrumental voices, which can be "dumped" as bundles of bytes for storage on a computer or other device, and later transmitted back to the instrument.

- **System real-time messages**. These messages are used to synchronize all MIDI clock-controlled devices on a MIDI network, a particularly useful tool when connecting a number of sequencers, drum machines, and synthesizers that need to work in unison. Using commands such as Timing Clock, Start, Continue, and Stop, the musician can set a tempo to which all devices will be synchronized and can control playback of the sequence. One common MIDI problem is that notes sometimes get stuck and continue to play indefinitely until some action is taken. This may occur, for example, if a MIDI cable is accidentally disconnected. The Active Sensing command is used to eliminate this problem and then triggers the System Reset command for reinitializing the sequence.

Adaptability of MIDI

As with any industry standard, the creation of the MIDI protocol was not completed without some compromises. The primary limitation of MIDI is that it was conceived with the production of keyboard music in mind. This was rightfully viewed as providing the most widespread commercial application of the standard, but it potentially left in the lurch many composers who had ideas unrelated to keyboard music. Over the years, however, MIDI has proved to be eminently adaptable by engineers and composers alike, so that today its limitations are often overcome in many creative ways.

Not long after the introduction of MIDI, the same protocols used to generate control signals between keyboard synthesizers were being adopted for a wide variety of other musical applications. Wind instruments, drum machines, and effects boxes all became MIDI-compatible. Moog, Buchla, and other makers of voltage-controlled synthesizers invented their own interfaces to translate information from voltage controls into MIDI data and back again, thus adapting vintage analog synthesizers to interface with a new generation of technology. Engineer and musician David Rokeby in Toronto created a way to translate images from a video camera into MIDI signals. His Very Nervous System was first used in 1991 to interpret and translate the images of a dancer into musical accompaniment. Much of Donald Buchla's most recent development has revolved around innovative new MIDI controllers. Buchla updated his touch-pad technology, a feature of his early voltage-controlled synthesizers, with a MIDI-compatible version called Thunder (1990). The Buchla Lightning (1991) was an optically induced MIDI controller that used infrared beams to transmit control data from handheld wands to any MIDI-compatible synthesizer equipped with a receiver. The speed and position of the wands could be set to trigger a variety of MIDI parameters, including pitch, but also the panning of sound and volume level. In 2000, a Lightning II model was introduced, with the added feature of a 32-voice synthesizer, making it a complete, ready-to-play instrument. Another Buchla instrument, the Marimba Lumina, allowed the sounds, program switches, and editing controls of a normal synthesizer to be managed using a marimba-like surface with controller membrane pads instead of wooden keys. The strips were played by four different programmable mallets. One used the Marimba Lumina in place of a keyboard to control MIDI-compatible synthesizers. Buchla also co-developed the PianoBar with Moog Music, a device that converts the movement of a piano's keys into MIDI compatible signals.

Dutch composer Michel Waisvisz (1949–2008) was director of the Studio for Electro-Instrumental Music (STEIM) in Amsterdam, and specialized in the creation of **gestural controllers** for live electronic music performance. He was on the crest of the MIDI wave in 1984. One of his earliest electro-mechanical controllers was called The Hands, first used in 1984. It consisted of a pair of metal devices strapped to his hands. Each contained touch-sensitive keys that could be played by the fingertips as well as sensors that responded to the tilt and changing distance between the two "hands." They sent control signals to sound modules to generate sound in real time. Modified and repro-grammed many times over the years, The Hands generate MIDI signals via a small computer worn by the performer.[37]

Figure 8.19   Michel Waisvisz demonstrating his electro-mechanical MIDI-controllers, *The Hands*. (STEIM, 2008)

American composer Robert Ashley also embraced the use of MIDI almost immediately, realizing that to some extent MIDI freed him from having to enlist an orchestra of musicians to simply test certain kinds of compositions that he was considering. One result of Ashley's early MIDI work was *Superior Seven* (1986). He explained it this way:

> When *Superior Seven* was composed, the MIDI system was a barely workable technology, and I must say that because I did not own a computer then and because I was not much interested in "computer music," the idea of a composition that is so appropriate to MIDI could not have occurred to me. But *Superior Seven* is very appropriate to realization in MIDI, and MIDI— not an orchestra of acoustical instruments—is the technology of this recording.[38]

The piano part of *Superior Seven* played cues (MIDI control signals) for other instruments. The other instruments were intended to play the same notes in the same register in precise synchronization with the piano cues: "Thus, the cue lines serve the same function as a sequence of note-instructions from the computer, and the cue lines 'conduct' the entrances of all the other instruments in the orchestra."[39] If he had used a live orchestra to perform the work, Ashley likened the role of the conductor to that of "the mixer at a recording console." The use of MIDI provided an ideal solution for a work that was, in some part, intended to be mechanized or programmed during its performance.

Despite some the conceptual limitations of the MIDI standard, it has proven to be invaluable to the growth of electronic music in the way that instruments are designed and because of the benefits to the composer and performer of music using such instruments. When it was introduced in 1984, MIDI represented the first important stage in a standardized transition from analog to digital music systems, leading directly to the current generation of software synthesizers, controllers, and instruments, all of which continue to take advantage of the MIDI specification.

SUMMARY

- The secret of Robert Moog's successful synthesizer design was that he listened to musicians and overcame three important technical challenges: size, stability, and control.

- In a voltage-controlled device, a small amount of current is applied to the control input of a given component to modify the output signal. This voltage signal can be preset, precise, and quick, and activated by such easy-to-use voltage-controlled components as the synthesizer keyboard, thus making the analog synthesizer much easier to manage.

- Moog presented a paper at the 1964 AES conference detailing his design for a modular, voltage-controlled electronic music synthesizer and began taking orders.

- Moog developed an influential design for voltage-controlled ADSR envelope generation based on a specification created by composer Vladimir Ussachevsky.

- The first voltage-controlled synthesizers were monophonic and modular.

- *Switched-On Bach* (1968) by Wendy Carlos was a popular recording using the Moog synthesizer and helped popularize electronic music and spawned a new industry of industry makers.

- Buchla created his first voltage-controlled synthesizer modules for the San Francisco Tape Music Center in 1965. Buchla's synthesizer became a commercial product in 1966.

- Buchla created innovative sequencing designs that helped automate analog synthesizer functions.

- *Silver Apples of the Moon* (1967) by Subotnick was the first work of electronic music commissioned solely for release as a long-playing record.

- Following the success of the Moog and Buchla systems in the late 1960s, many new manufacturers entered the market with variations on the modular voltage-controlled synthesizer.

- No industry standard existed for linking synthesizers and computers until 1984 and the introduction of the Musical Instrument Digital Interface (MIDI).

- The MIDI communications interface was designed to link and control multiple synthesizers and to connect synthesizers to personal computers.

KEY PEOPLE IN CHAPTER EIGHT

KEY TERMS IN CHAPTER EIGHT

MILESTONES

The Voltage-Controlled Synthesizer

Technical and scientific	Year	Artists and music
– Hugh Le Caine invented the first voltage-controlled synthesizer.	1945	
– Buchla developed early voltage-controlled modules. Moog developed voltage-controlled modules. – Moog published paper *Voltage-Controlled Electronic Music Modules* and began taking orders at the annual AES conference.	1964	– Herb Deutsch, working with Moog, composed *Jazz Images* with Moog components. – Among early customers that Moog met at the AES conference were Wendy Carlos and Eric Siday.
– Buchla completed modular synthesizer for the San Francisco Tape Music Center. – Moog began to build custom modular synthesizers for early customers. – Ussachevsky provided design for voltage-controlled envelope generation that Moog built.	1965	– *Flight* by William Maginnis was one of the first works composed with Buchla synthesizer modules. – Moog built a custom modular synthesizer for Eric Siday.
– Moog built first commercial model of his modular synthesizer for the Alwin Nikolais Dance Theater.	1966	– Wendy Carlos ordered some voltage-controlled modules from Moog.
– The Buchla 100 was introduced. – Moog developed touch-sensitive keyboard for Wendy Carlos.	1967	– The sound of the Moog was used on several commercial recordings, often played by Paul Beaver. – *Silver Apples of the Moon* by Morton Subotnick was released.
	1968	– *Switched-On Bach* by Wendy Carlos was released.
– Minimoog was introduced.	1969	
– Buchla 200 was introduced.	1970	
– Buchla Music Easel was introduced.	1971	
– MIDI standard was approved.	1984	

PART III

Digital Synthesis and Computer Music

CHAPTER 9

Early Computer Music (1953–85)

There are no theoretical limitations to the performance of the computer as a source of musical sounds, in contrast to the performance of ordinary instruments.[1]
—Max Mathews

Max Mathews (right) and L. Rosler (left) at Bell Labs, with *Graphic 1* workstation, *c.* 1967. (Lucent/Bell Labs)

The programming of music was not the "killer app" for which computers were invented. But audio technology figured prominently in the early uses of computers, particularly in the quest to improve the automation of one of the keystones of American industrial success—the telephone and communications infrastructure. More than ten years before IBM rose to prominence in the 1950s to become the world's leading manufacturer of general-purpose computers, the founders of Hewlett-Packard produced their first product, the 200A Audio Oscillator. This rugged piece of testing equipment found its way into Walt Disney Studios where eight of them were used to produce sound effects for the movie *Fantasia* (1940).[2] Bell Laboratories, the research and development division of American Telephone and Telegraph (AT&T), was manufacturing calculators by the early 1940s and performing calculations remotely by Teletype connection, an early example of remote access computing using analog technology. In 1943, at the bidding of the United States Army, Bell Labs and resident engineer George Stibitz developed an analog relay-based calculator for weapons testing. The device was programmable by paper tape, providing the design for later control systems using hardwired, analog connections, not the least of which were early music synthesizers made by RCA and Siemens.

The first general-purpose computers were monolithic, powered by vacuum tubes, and used analog relays and switches to make digital calculations. The engineers who designed those machines had three fundamental killer apps in mind: crunching numbers, automating communications, and controlling complex processes. Just *which* numbers, communications, and processes were up to the programmer and every exercise in application development was a major research project. Early computers were engineered primarily to solve mathematical and logic problems. Then in 1948, due largely to the work of pioneering information scientist Claude E. Shannon (1916–2001), the fledgling field of computer science was broadened to encompass any form of information that the user wanted to encode and transmit. In his landmark paper entitled *A Mathematical Theory of Communication*, Shannon leveled the playing field for the processing of any kind of information that could be represented digitally. "Any stochastic process," wrote Shannon, "which produces a discrete sequence of symbols chosen from a finite set may be considered a discrete source." He then cited three all-encompassing examples of such signals:

1 Natural written languages such as English, German, Chinese.
2 Continuous information sources that have been rendered discrete by some quantizing process. For example, the quantized speech from a PCM transmitter, or a quantized television signal.
3 Mathematical cases where we merely define abstractly a stochastic process which generates a sequence of symbols.[3]

This important paper by Shannon extended computer science beyond the detection and calculation of discrete signals into realms of noise assessment, probability theory, and the way in which a statistical structure could be applied to virtually any kind of information. The effect was one of greatly broadening the concept of computing into realms that might have practical applications in the real world of information assessment and communication.

Shannon happened to be working at Bell Labs at the time when he developed this theory of information science. It was the *Bell System Technical Journal* that published his work. Shannon's work did not escape the notice of his colleagues, some of whom viewed the mathematical regularity of musical form as ideally suited for exploration using computers. The digitization and control of sound became an important mission of Bell Labs, leading to the development of the first computer music systems.

This chapter traces the early history of computer music and the foundations of digitally produced electronic music.

FOUNDATIONS OF COMPUTER MUSIC

The development of computer technology historically paralleled the development of the modern electronic music studio and synthesizer, leading to a cross-fertilization of the two fields that greatly benefited electronic music. The ultimate objective of computer music was always the development of a **musical programming language** and a method for the direct synthesis of digital signals into audible sound. However grand, these goals were not entirely feasible during the early days of computers from the standpoint of economics and the availability of processing power that was up to the task. The result was an extensive period of basic research lasting 30 years that provided a template for the modern development of computer-based music.

In 1957, the same year that Edgard Varèse was working on *Poème électronique* and Luening and Ussachevsky were experimenting with the RCA Mark I Electronic Music Synthesizer in Princeton, New Jersey, Bell Labs engineer Max Mathews succeeded in programming a computer to synthesize a few notes of music. The result was a short monophonic piece lasting a mere 17 seconds, but it was the first program written to generate sound directly from a computer. The programming language that Mathews created was called *MUSIC I* and it was limited to one voice, one waveform (triangular wave), and had no expressive controls over the dynamics of the sound. All it could do was program a sequence of pitches at prescribed intervals of a given loudness for a given length of time.

MUSIC I was followed by several improved versions, with Mathews leading their development through the 1960s. *MUSIC II* (1958) added four voices and the concept of the wavetable synthesizer, in which all digital parameters for sounds are called from predefined tables, providing a kind of shorthand for the composer, greatly simplifying the process of calling into action the great amount of data required to define and shape a sound. With *MUSIC III* (1960), Mathews added several other concepts to the program to simplify its operation:

- **Control function tables**. Provided simple signal processing routines.
- **Unit generators**. Small, modular programs for generating sound could be combined and driven using text commands to build instruments that could be stored. These programs could define parameters such as control rates and audio rates for sound generators.
- **Orchestras**. A set of user-definable instructions for combining instruments into a set to be used for a composition.
- **Scores**. A set of user-definable parameters for structuring or organizing the musical content of a piece and calling instruments from the orchestra into play.

LISTENING GUIDE 9.1

Title: *Numerology*

Artist: Max Mathews   **Year**: 1960   **Duration**: 2:43

Genre: Computer music

Electronic Instrumentation: IBM 7090 mainframe computer, *MUSIC III* programming language.

Background: While working at Bell Labs in telecommunications research, Max Mathews became one of the earliest engineers to use a general-purpose computer to program music and digitally synthesize musical sound. His programming language *MUSIC III* allowed composers to design their own virtual instruments, a breakthrough during those pioneering days of computer music. *Numerology* was composed to demonstrate the various parameters, or building blocks, available to the composer using this programming language: vibrato (frequency modulation), attack and decay characteristics, glissando, tremolo (amplitude modulation), and the creation of new waveshapes. The short piece has eight sections.

	Listen For: The introduction of various forms of dynamic effects including vibrato, tremolo, glissando, envelope characteristics, and amplitude changes; programmed melodies in one and two voices; the frequency range of the melodies.
0:00–0:10	The piece begins with a steady sine-like tone that increases in loudness (crescendo) and expresses increasing levels of vibrato. At about 0:08 seconds, a second, lower-pitched voice fades in and forms an audible bridge to the second section of the work.
0:11–0:30	Following a short, five-note beat, a duet begins between a percussive instrument sound in the upper range (the loudest voice) and a sliding, melodic bass accompaniment at a lower volume level. The attack and decay characteristics of the louder, percussive voice are slowly modified so that the voice changes from a sharp piano-like sound to a softer string-like sonority. This sequence is repeated once.
0:31–0:42	The bass voice from the previous section is shifted to a higher-pitch range and becomes the dominant voice. A chorusing, or multiplying, effect is created by momentarily dividing each note of the melody into three fractional tones and then recombining them at the next note of the melody. This happens so quickly that it is difficult to detect, but the effect is that of a momentary cascade of microtones between each fundamental tone of the melody.
0:43–0:59	In this duet section, a melody is played three times, first in the upper range, then in the bass range, and once again in the treble range. The accompanying bass or treble parts in each section consist of slowly wavering tones using a variety of vibrato effects. Note how the rhythm varies slightly during the middle interation when the melody is played in the bass voice. The third iteration is marked by a sharper attack of the notes and a slight portamento effect of sliding between notes.
1:00–1:24	In this section, a bass part is played twice, first with unadulterated notes and then with distorted tones. This effect was accomplished by modifying the waveform used to define the instrumental voice of the melody.
1:25–1:49	A melody with glissando accompaniment is used to demonstrate vibrato effects applied to a waveform.
1:50–2:00	Here the composer experiments with rhythm, playing a canon in which two melodies are separated by one beat. Notice the ability of the program to reproduce a sharp, rapid, melodic rhythm, a characteristic emulated in the late 1960s using analog synthesis.
2:01–2:31	For the finale, Mathews pushes several parameters to the extreme. Note how the tempo of the melody gradually increases until it becomes a blur, the accompanying voices consist of rapid harmonic sweeps up to five octaves in range, and the time sequence for executing each section becomes increasingly compressed. The resulting sounds have an organic presence, similar to taped sounds that are sped up on a reel-to-reel tape recorder.

Compare and Contrast

Two-Part Invention in F Major (1968) by Wendy Carlos

Etunytude (1983) by Barton McLean

Home Zone (2007) by Digitalism

After Mathews completed *MUSIC IV*, the development of computer music languages began to extend to his colleagues outside of Bell Labs. Hubert Howe and Godfrey Winham developed *Music IVB* at Princeton University. This was quickly updated to *Music IVBF*, programmed entirely in the higher-level language *FORTRAN*. *FORTRAN* was a general-purpose computing language that could be run on any conventional computer of the time, a development that opened the doors to the development and modifications of the *MUSIC N* series by other composers and programmers.[4]

At about the same time as Howe and Winham were working on *Music IVB*, Barry Vercoe at MIT developed *Music 360*, written in *assembly language* for IBM 360 mainframe computers. Vercoe also created a more portable version, *Music 11*, written for the new DEC PDP-11 minicomputer, a general-purpose system that was somewhat smaller and less expensive than the IBM 360. Although mostly written in *C* language, *Music 11* still contained some legacy code in assembly language, making it more platform specific.

At Princeton, Paul Lansky created a port of *Music IVBF* that incorporated a random soundfile access feature allowing users to combine soundfiles after they had been synthesized. This language was written entirely in *FORTRAN* and was called *mix*. In 1969, Max Mathews released his own *MUSIC V* written in *FORTRAN*.

After releasing *MUSIC V*, Mathews moved on to develop *GROOVE* in 1970, or *Generated Real-time Output Operations on Voltage-controlled Equipment*, a computer system with a display screen interface to simplify the management of digital music synthesis in real time. As Mathews explained:

> The computer performer should not attempt to define the entire sound in real time. Instead the computer should retain a score and the performer should influence the way in which the score is played . . . the mode of conducting consists of turning knobs and pressing keys rather than waving a stick, but this is a minor detail.[5]

To further simplify the process of composing electronically generated music, Mathews and L. Rosler, also of Bell Labs, developed *Graphic 1* (1968), an interactive computer system that could translate images drawn with a light-pen on a display terminal into synthesized sound. "The *Graphic 1* allows a person to insert pictures and graphs directly into a computer memory by the very act of drawing these objects," wrote Mathews. "Moreover, the power of the computer is available to modify, erase, duplicate, and remember the drawings." With the development of *Graphic 1*, Mathews was responsible for introducing the concept of interactive, real-time composition on a computer screen with cut-and-paste capabilities, years before personal computers would make this functionality commonplace.

MUSIC N, *GROOVE*, and *Graphic 1* were just a few of the accomplishments that earned Mathews his much-deserved reputation as the father of computer music.

With the exception of Bell Labs, experiments with computer music during the 1950s and 1960s were largely backdoor operations at research institutions and corporations with large-scale computers and spare processing time to offer musicians. Mainframe computers were expensive devices, isolated in clean-rooms where they could be maintained and safeguarded. Programming them required an acute knowledge of computer languages, mathematics, and, in the case of music, acoustics as well. Most facilities could not synthesize sounds directly from computers so many early musical applications for computers encompassed the composition of music for conventional instruments. This activity proved to be a fruitful line of exploration that provided composers with a powerful tool to more fully realize their visions of complex, mathematically rendered compositions.

The composition of mathematically derived music was of particular interest to post-war contemporary music composers. Although working without computers, the early composers of the Cologne studio during the early 1950s were preoccupied with using serialist techniques to generate electronic music, exemplified by Stockhausen in his compositions *Studie I* and *Studie II*.

Lejaren Hiller, working at the University of Illinois, first explored the use of the computer as an aid to composing instrumental music during the mid-1950s. Already equipped with degrees in chemistry and music, Hiller was also a student of information theory. Being familiar with the work of Shannon and Norbert Weiner, Hiller made connections between the flow and communication of data and musical structures. "A person becomes more disturbed when the number of possibilities increase;" wrote Hiller, "disorder increases and you build tension, and then resolutions come when one arrives at more organized, more static situations. This is what causes the ebb and flow of drama in a piece."[6] Hiller's thinking about information fluxes became an integral part of his algorithms for composing music on the computer. Working with Robert A. Baker, Hiller wrote the program *MUSICOMP* for the IBM 7094 computer. Not a program for the synthesis of sounds, *MUSICOMP* organized compositional functions into computer subroutines to automate parts of the composing process. *MUSICOMP* was important for its reliance on a rules-based approach to constructing a piece of music from predefined variables—a preview of things to come many decades before the availability of MIDI and personal computers made rules-based software tools widely available for composing, editing, and performing.

Hiller invited German composer Herbert Brün (1918–2000) to join him as a research associate at the University of Illinois in 1963. Although familiar with psychoacoustic research prior to joining the faculty at Illinois, Brün had not yet used a computer to compose music and found it challenging to keep pace with the brilliant Hiller, eventually learning to program in *FORTRAN* and composing music for instruments and taped sounds, including *Infraudibles* (1968). His stated desire was to counter the popular belief that music composed using a computer could not retain the personality of the individual.[7]

Romanian-born Greek composer Iannis Xenakis had conceived of a music based on probability theory and associated mathematical processes during the mid-1950s and devised formulae for composing works, many of which involved the generation of large masses of sounds that were difficult if not impossible to compose manually. His first **stochastic** compositions were calculated manually. One remarkable example was the orchestral work *Metastasis* (1964), built around a swarm of independently sliding instrumental glissandi. The piece required an orchestra of 61 musicians, each playing a different part in the form of a sliding note. The sound mass, dominated by the aura of string instruments, began in unison and gradually broadened into different pitch ranges, eventually disintegrating as players one by one completed their assigned glissandi parts of different durations. The score was partly graphic and Xenakis integrated 12-tone techniques as well as a Fibonacci series in devising the parts for the work (see Figure 9.1).

It wasn't until about 1961 that Xenakis gained access to a computer at the Paris facilities of IBM, giving him an opportunity to automate the kinds of complex processes he had conceived of in earlier works.[8] His use of the computer was largely for the purpose

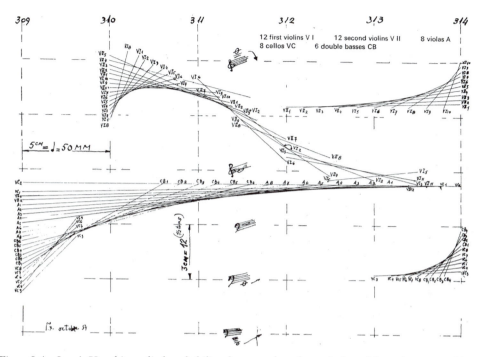

Figure 9.1   Iannis Xenakis applied probability theory and mathematical models to the composition of his music. The graphic score for *Metastasis* (1964) visually defined the nature of the sound to be performed and has corollaries in the composition of electronic and computer music. (Éditions Salabert)

of conducting calculations, based on mathematical functions he would program, using the output to create a score for an instrumental or electronic work. Working with an IBM 7090 computer, Xenakis composed many mathematically based works during the early 1960s, including his ST series instrumental ensembles of many sizes.

The journey of German composer Gottfried Michael Koenig (b. 1926) exemplified the path taken by many composers during the pioneering days of computer music. From 1954 to 1964, Koenig worked in the electronic music studios of West German Radio in Cologne. As a composer, he was steeped in serial techniques and assisted such composers as Stockhausen and Ligeti in the realization of their works in the studio. Koenig was a student of musical theory and contributed frequently to the German journal of contemporary music, *die Reihe*. He became interested in computer programming in the early 1960s with the goal of translating processes associated with serial music into a system to help him compose music. He completed his first program, *Project 1* (*PR1*) in 1964, about the same time he moved to the Netherlands, where he worked at the Institute of Sonology at the University of Utrecht. *PR1* extended the reach of serial music beyond the tone row, adding choices for varying degrees of randomness and permutations of instrumental sounds. "It was thus necessary," explained Koenig, "to limit the procedure to a compositional model containing important elements of the serial method, and to test that model under various conditions with different musical goals in mind."[9] A composition was created in *PR1* section by section, each of which could be assigned one of seven "processes," ranging from totally non-rhythmic and random ("irregular") to the highly repetitive ("regular"). Musical parameters could be set for instrument:

duration, pitch, octave register, and dynamics of all tones. The result was output onto paper in the form of a numeric table that was used to developed a written score for instrumentalists. *PR1* was an exceptional exercise in organizing musical values and choices using a computer. Koenig continued to improve the program and finished a version called *Project 2* (*PR2*) in 1966, providing more flexibility in the organization of a composition beyond "sections" and giving the composer additional parameters that could be regulated, such as harmonic series based on predefined chords, tone rows, or user-defined interval tables and the ability to score parts for multiple ensembles playing with different parameters as subgroups of the whole orchestra. Koenig's work on the programs continued to evolve and took a step toward direct synthesis of output when the Institute of Sonology acquired a new computer in 1971. After several years of experiments, a programming bridge and appropriate digital-to-analog converters gave a synthesized voice to Koenig's programs, resulting in a system called the *SSP Sound Synthesis Program*. During his explorations, Koenig had become well versed in music composition and computer programming and taught both. Other composers faced with similar opportunities became fellow members of a rarified fellowship of musical savants who translated their digitally fashioned musical conceptions for an ever-growing new generation of composers.

By 1970, the cost effectiveness of using computers to synthesize electronic music had improved significantly over the early years of direct synthesis at Bell Labs.

While a graduate student in music at Stanford University, John Chowning (b. 1934) visited Max Mathews at Bell Labs in 1964 for a demonstration of *MUSIC IV*. This led to Chowning's efforts to get the program up and running on a computer at Stanford and his first experiments in computer music. Working with his programming partner, David Poole, the two of them ported *MUSIC IV* to the Digital Equipment Corp. (DEC) PDP-1 platform and then by 1966 to the newest generation of DEC computers, the PDP-6. In the course of converting the code from the IBM platform for which *MUSIC IV* was written to the DEC, Chowning and Poole were among the first people to make Mathew's music programming language available outside of Bell Labs.

After having successfully ported *MUSIC IV* to the Stanford computer, Chowning turned his attention to improving the quality of sounds that could be directly synthesized from the computer. He visited Jean-Claude Risset at Bell Labs in 1968 and learned about his attempts to synthesize the sounds of brass instruments through the analysis of trumpet sounds.[10] In using a computer and finite waveform measurements to analyze the sound of a trumpet, Risset discovered the telltale fingerprint of the sound that made it so rich and difficult to synthesize. There was a correlation between the growth of the amplitude of the sound and its corresponding frequency spectra. The intensity of the signal during its first few milliseconds was concentrated around the fundamental frequency but then rapidly radiated to other harmonics at progressively louder volumes. The waveform analysis allowed Risset to then synthesize the sounds using the complicated process of additive synthesis and more than a dozen finely tuned oscillators. Chowning had a realization: "I could do something similar with simple FM," he explained, "just by using the intensity envelope as a modulation index."[11]

Chowning experimented with FM synthesis in 1971 to see if he could apply what he learned from Risset. Using only two oscillators, and fiddling with the relationship between increased amplitude and frequency bandwidth, Chowning suddenly found himself producing brass-like tones that were strikingly similar to those created by Risset's complicated computer-based simulations:

That was the moment when I realized that the technique was really of some consequence, because with just two oscillators I was able to produce tones that had a richness and quality about them that was attractive to the ear—sounds which by other means were quite complicated to create.[12]

As a reality check, Chowning played his brass tones for his friends at Bell Labs. They immediately told him to patent it.[13] This technology was shopped around and acquired by Yamaha in 1975 to become the basis for the DX-7 digital synthesizer, introduced in 1983, probably the top-selling synthesizer of all time.

The success of Chowning's FM synthesis method was due in part to its extensibility. Chowning not only tested his synthesis method using two oscillators—one carrier and one modulator—but devised branching schemes where one modulator could affect several carriers or several modulators could drive a single carrier. Chowning's composition *Turenas* (1972) was an avid demonstration of these techniques. The three-part, ten-minute piece used FM synthesis to generate a wide spectrum of natural-sounding percussion sounds. Using the *Music 10* programming language, the composer created spatially directed paths for the sounds to travel in relation to four channels and loudspeakers (see Figure 9.2). The effect rendered a remarkably living atmosphere in which organically

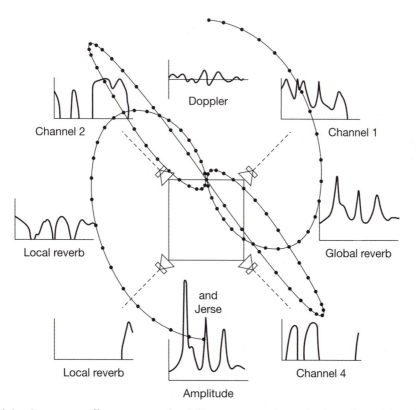

Figure 9.2 Computers offer composers the ability to manage the projection of sound as well as its generation. This diagram created by John Chowning illustrates the sound paths used in his work *Turenas* (1972), written using the *Music 10* programming language used at Stanford University. (After Dodge and Jerse, 1985)

LISTENING GUIDE 9.2

Title: *Stria*

Artist: John Chowning   **Year**: 1977   **Duration**: 5:14

Genre: Computer music using FM synthesis

Electronic Instrumentation: DEC PDP-10 computer, *Music 10* and *SAIL* software.

Background: This rigorously composed work was the result of early experiments in FM synthesis by John Chowning. Using high-level computer programming to organize and synthesize the sounds, Chowning sought to develop a work based on the naturally occurring inharmonic ratios between carrier signals and modulators. He used the Golden Mean (1.618) as the basic unit of his calculations, wherein a carrier/modulator ratio would equal 1 to some power of 1.618, the resulting characteristics of the music all being derived in this way. Writing computer code to compose using this organizational principle, the result is an inharmonic piece for 26 sine wave instruments, each programmed to play varying notes with a variety of possible envelopes. The overall shape or micro-structure of the composition is also reflected in each individual tone of the program. The work has several sections, each characterized by events determined by ratios of the Golden Mean.

	Listen For: Frequency and timbral ranges and the variety of sound envelopes. The attack, sustain, decay, frequency, amplitude, and reverberation of each tone were computer controlled. Notice how the piece changes gradually over time, experimenting with the psychoacoustic effects of sliding tones within a dense tone cloud.
0:10–1:00	The piece begins with a frequency of 1,618 Hz (equal to the Golden Mean), soon joined by a series of low, sustained, bell-like tones that accumulate and overlap. Notice between 0:35 and 1:00 how multiple tones stabilize a sustained chord-like tone and then break apart as additional frequencies begin to dominate the mix. The overall effect is one of gradual, large-scale harmonic shifts that dissolve from one to the next, without a true tonal center.
1:01–1:50	Between 1:05 and 1:50 the tonal center of the piece shifts to the upper registers and one hears several high-pitched tones clustered close together. Note the vibrato effect as waves of similar frequencies vibrate in and out of phase with one another.
1:51–4:00	The piece gradually shifts to lower and lower pitches over the course of two minutes, creating vibrato and slightly disorienting effects as individual tones waver up and down within the mass.
4:01–5:14	Reverberation, sliding notes (glissandi), and the spatial distribution of the tones within the stereo field add to the complexity of the final portion of the work.

Compare and Contrast

Computer Piece No. 1 (1968) by Vladimir Ussachevsky

Cavis Muris (1986) by Laurie Spiegel

resonating beats, clicks, and thumps reminiscent of naturally occurring sounds traveled around the listener like insects flying in the night. *Turenas* was decidedly unlike most computer music being composed at that time and factored importantly into bridging the gap between the computer lab and the music hall.

Chowning's algorithms were in good hands at Yamaha. With the composer's input, Yamaha engineers devised a method of dynamically modifying the spectra of a digital oscillator by scaling the pitch—called *key scaling*—to avoid the introduction of distortion that normally occurred in analog systems during frequency modulation. The recognizable bright tonalities of the DX-7 were also due in part to an overachieving sampling rate of 57 kHz in the instrument's digital-to-analog converter.[14]

The licensing of Chowning's patent to Yamaha and others was a generous source of income for Stanford, earning the university as much as $20 million between 1975 and 1995.[15] Some of this funding found its way back to the Stanford Center for Computer Research in Music and Acoustics. Chowning and colleagues James Moorer, Loren Rush, John Grey, and instrument designer Peter Samson channeled more than $100,000 into a Stanford project to create a digital synthesizer of their own, driven by a DEC PDP-10 minicomputer and running a ported version of *MUSIC V*. The Systems Concepts Digital Synthesizer, affectionately known as the Samson Box after its creator, was delivered to the university in 1977. Julius O. Smith was one university composer who used the Samson Box, lovingly describing it as a "green refrigerator."[16] The synthesizer was designed with *MUSIC V* in mind and included hardware equivalents of many of the predefined *unit* instrument generators associated with the program. It featured 256 waveform generators and was capable of numerous kinds of synthesis including FM, waveshaping, additive, subtractive, and non-linear. It was used at the lab for 12 years, eventually being superseded by faster, smarter programmable tools that required much less maintenance, a fate that also led to the demise of large-scale general-purpose mainframe computers as processing technology became less expensive and the market for PCs created a new paradigm in the application of computers.

In the early 1980s, Lansky and Vercoe engaged in a friendly competition to see who could create the faster and more elegant music programming language. Princeton acquired two DEC micro-Vax computers running *UNIX* and Lanksy rewrote *mix* entirely in *C*, eventually renaming it *cmix*. Barry Vercoe created *Csound* based on his earlier program *Music 11*. Being written entirely in *C* language, *mix* and *Csound* were easily portable to other machines and extensible by the user. As for the friendly competition, each programmer succeeded in developing a highly adaptable music programming environment. *Cmix*—later renamed *RTcmix* for *real-time cmix*—was generally considered to be faster, but *Csound* became the more popular program and currently has over 1,200 unit generators. Both are available for free and are still used at most computer music centers in the United States.

Although the early history of computer music was dominated by developments in the United States, research began to shift to Europe and other countries as computer centers became more prevalent across the globe. Of most significance was the founding in Paris in 1969 of IRCAM (Institut de Recherche et Coordination Acoustique/Musique), a government-supported laboratory for the exploration of computer applications in the arts. Established by President Georges Pompidou, the institute appointed composer Pierre Boulez as director and to lead its efforts in musical research. Boulez hired Jean-Claude Risset to direct its computer operations. Construction of IRCAM was

completed in 1974 and it remains to this day a vital center of computer music development connected to the Centre Pompidou in Paris. This international center for the exploration of computer music and media has since hosted many projects and developed software tools for the use of composers. Chowning perfected some of his FM synthesis techniques while visiting the center as a guest. A student of Barry Vercoe's at MIT by the name of Miller Puckette spearheaded the *4X* development team and eventually created *Max*, one of the most widely used computer music environments for personal computers. A number of other important IRCAM milestones are recounted below in "A Concise History of Computer Music" (see p. 287).

Figure 9.3   IRCAM today. (Thom Holmes)

EARLY COMPUTER MUSIC

LISTEN

1 *The Illiac Suite for String Quartet* (1957) by Lejaren Hiller and Leonard Isaacson
   Computer-assisted composition at the University of Illinois

2 *Five Stochastic Studies* (1961) by James Tenney
   Used direct synthesis at Bell Labs

3 *Metastasis* (1964) by Iannis Xenakis
   Computer-assisted composition

4 *HPSCHD* (1967–69) by John Cage and Lejaren Hiller
   Computer-assisted composing and sound control

5 *Turenas* (1972) by John Chowning
   Used FM synthesis at Stanford University

6 *Love in the Asylum* (1981) by Michael McNabb
   Realized at Stanford University using the Systems Concepts Digital Synthesizer and mainframe computer

7 *Tron* (1982) by Wendy Carlos
   Used the Crumar GDS digital synthesizer

8 *Two Melodramas for Synclavier* (1983) by Jon Appleton
   Used the Synclavier II digital music synthesizer

9 *Zoolook* (1984) by Jean-Michel Jarre
   Used the Fairlight CMI

10 *Metropolitan Suite* (1987) by Larry Fast
    Used the E-mu Emulator, Yamaha DX-7, and other instruments

In the early 1990s, IRCAM developed a new software package called *PatchWork*, more specifically designed for the intended purpose of music composition. In France, a new school of thought regarding music composition evolved around the developers of *PatchWork*. Working with a technique they called "spectral music," composers including Gérard Grisey (1946–98) and Claude Vivier (1948–83) from Toronto and Tristan Murail (b. 1947) from France began to apply techniques of *spectral analysis* to the composition of electronic and non-electronic instrumental music. They were interested in creating new harmonies based on the mathematical principles of frequency modulation, amplitude modulation, and ring modulation.

The technique of ring modulation can be used to illustrate how a spectral composer might work. When two sounds are subjected to ring modulation, neither of the source frequencies is heard, just two new frequencies based on the sum and difference of the original signals. By using a computer to analyze the spectra or overtone series of a sound that changes over time, a composer could use that data to mathematically calculate which frequencies would be produced if that sound were subjected to ring modulation. These calculations could lead to new harmonies based entirely on the actual overtone structure of a specific instrument or sound if modulated in the same way. These new frequential calculations—the preferred term of these composers is *frequential* not *spectral* music—could then be transcribed into a musical composition that could be played by a chamber ensemble or orchestra. Spectral analysis often results in music based on microtonal scales, revealing new harmonies that often require new skills and instruments. Instrumental ensembles playing this music have been augmented with live electronics and electronic processing to help the players attain the new timbres created by such frequential harmonies. *Instrumental additive synthesis* is the name given to the process of orchestration or assignment of different frequency components to the players, a term with obvious connections to the concept of additive synthesis in electronic music.[17]

PatchWork was developed at IRCAM by Mikael Laursen, Jacques Duthen, and Camilo Rueda. This composition environment has been in continual development since the 1990s and was rebranded *Open Music* in 1998. In essence, the software succeeded in automating some of the tedious calculations that composers such as Stockhausen, Grisey, and Murail had been making by hand. It allowed the creation of music at any frequency, including microtones, and was no longer tied to the 12-tone equal-tempered system. Equipped with this software, frequential composers we able to extend their control over sound beyond the harmonies, applying computer analysis to many other parameters of the music such as density, duration, and harmonic paths of modulation.

Much of the research in the early part of this century has been devoted to creating a real-time *Fast Fourier Transform (FFT)* for music—an algorithm that contains the spectral frequencies, relative amplitudes, and phase data needed to re-create and process the spectra of a sound over time. FFT functionality is available to *Open Music* through the use of external sound processing tools. A composer can use an FFT to study a spectral phenomenon and apply its characteristics to various parameters of a musical composition. The process known as *data mapping* involves some method of data mining and the visualization or auralization of that data, then mapping it to the inputs of a system used to create musical output electronically.

Popular among composers, *Open Music* is often used alongside other IRCAM programs such as *AudioSculpt* or American Michael Klingbeil's *SPEAR* program. *AudioSculpt* or *SPEAR* allow the user to analyze the frequential components of a sound and then import the data into *Open Music* where it can be manipulated and transformed. Together these programs enable the composer to edit the spectra of a sound, morph between the spectra of two sounds, combine them, subtract them—almost anything you can think of. A major work of this genre composed at IRCAM using spectral software was Tristan Murail's *Désintégrations*, first performed in 1983. The work was divided into 11 sections, each exploring a different range of spectra, rhythms, and unique harmonic timbres based on spectral analysis.

IRCAM continues to be a major player in the development of computer music languages and tools. In addition to *Open Music* and *AudioSculpt*, newer programs include *Modalys* for physical modeling, *Chant* for formant analysis, *Spatialisateur* for the spatialization of sound signals in real time intended for musical creation, postproduction, and live performances, and *Orchidée* for orchestration.

The ability to analyze and manipulate the spectral content of music is a resource for composers of electronic and acoustic music. Being able to visualize and understand the components of sound can lead to nonstandard ideas that simply would not be possible if one were composing music in the conventional way, thinking of it merely as a process of moving from one tone to another. Spectral analysis led composer Jonathan Harvey (b. 1939) to make new connections between the timbres of an orchestra and those of human speech. In 2008, he premiered the work *Speakings* for large orchestra and electronics in which his analysis of speech timbres was used as a toolkit for prescribing ways to make an orchestra "speak."

THE ROLE OF COMPUTERS IN MUSIC

Traditionally, the term "computer music" referred to the ways in which large, general-purpose mainframe computers were applied to the making of music. These same roles translate to the use of today's personal computers, usually in the form of modular software programs designed to accomplish the following tasks.

Computer Composition and Scoring

In this role, the computer aids the composer in producing a printed score to be played using traditional musical instruments. When Lejaren Hiller and Leonard Isaacson first attempted to make a computer create a musical score at the University of Illinois in 1955, the computer was allowed to create sequences of notes that were then selected and organized by the composers and transcribed onto sheet music for a string quartet. Their intention was to aid the composer in the process of composition, harnessing the computational and organizational power of the computer.

Computer Synthesis of Sounds

The direct synthesis of sounds is based on numeric algorithms created for this purpose and digital tone-generating circuits (see Chapter 11). The tones may be triggered directly by playing a MIDI-compatible instrument or be generated by a software-based synthesizer. A digital-to-analog converter (DAC) is used to convert digital binary codes into analogous electrical waves that can drive a loudspeaker system.

Figure 9.4 John Cage and Lejaren Hiller preparing the computer-generated music for the piece *HPSCHD* at the University of Illinois, 1969.

The quality and robustness of digital synthesis depends on the power of the computer being used. Many software programs have been written to control and produce sounds on general-purpose desktop and laptop computers, but they are limited by their processing speed—real-time modeling of digitally produced sound waves is a processor-intensive operation—and the power of their onboard sound chips. Sound cards and chips designed specifically for digital signal processing (DSP) are required for more advanced and responsive real-time sound generation. Today's computers have the versatility and power to control most interactive, multimedia performances and installations. One or more computers may be used for these purposes.

Computer Control Over External Synthesizers

Standalone electronic musical instruments may be controlled using MIDI or proprietary computer-interface software. Software on a computer is used to designate the pitch, timbre, amplitude, duration, and envelope of sounds being played on instruments connected to the computer. The computer may act merely as an elaborate sequencer to aid a performing musician, or it may control multiple aspects of the production of a piece of music that are really beyond the control of any single individual in real time. Widely used software including *Max/MSP/Jitter* and *SuperCollider* provides graphical user interfaces in which composers can construct instruments and orchestras of electronically generated sounds as well as manage their organization, playback, and spatial deployment in real time.

Computer Sampling of Audio Input

The term **sampling** can refer to the sampling rate of sounds that are directly synthesized by a computer or the digital reproduction of externally generated sounds, both of which are explored more fully in Chapter 10. In an analog-to-digital conversion, input from a microphone, tape recorder, or other analog audio input is converted into binary code, which can then be processed and reorganized at will on a computer. This is the basis for the sound sampling that is such a familiar element of popular music. Conceptually,

---

SPECTRAL MUSIC

LISTEN

1   *Mantra* (1970) by Karlheinz Stockhausen
    Two pianos were processed through ring modulators to produce new frequential material. An early precursor to *spectral* or *frequentially* composed music. Stockhausen's *Stimmung* (1972) can also be seen as an early precursor to frequentially based music

2   *Partiels* (1975) by Gérard Grisey
    An exploration of the natural harmonic scale for 18 musicians based on the study of sonograms of a trombone

3   *Modulations* (1976–77) by Gérard Grisey for Orchestra
    Another key work in the spectral canon that explores the timbral differences between harmonic and non-harmonic (noise) textures

4   *Mortuous Plango, Vivos Voco* (1980) by Jonathan Harvey
    FFT analysis and re-synthesis of timbres derived from samples of his son, who was a chorister at Winchester cathedral, and the largest of the cathedral bells. Created at IRCAM

5   *Gondwana* (1980) by Tristan Murail
    An exploration of inharmonic spectra. Data were also mapped to the interpolation of amplitude envelopes and duration curves

6   *Lonely Child* (1980) by Claude Vivier
    An early *frequential* work for soprano and orchestra based on a single tone and its sum and difference pitches

7   *Désintégrations* (1982) by Tristan Murail
    Using spectral analysis to create both harmony and timbre

8   *NoaNoa* (1991) by Kaija Saariaho
    For flute an interactive electronics created at IRCAM

9   *Engine* (1996) by Magnus Lindberg
    This work employs a complex computer-generated counterpoint

10 *Speakings* (2008) by Jonathan Harvey
    Composition for large orchestra and electronics based on speech analysis to make the orchestra "speak"; employed the IRCAM software *Orchidée* to suggest possible orchestration ideas

sound sampling provides a digitized means for creating *musique concrète*, much as the French were doing in the 1940s. Bell Labs were experimenting with the computer digitization of analog sounds as early as 1958.[18]

External Control of the Computer

These same computer music languages—*Max/MSP/Jitter*, *SuperCollider*, *RTCmix*, *Csound*, *ChucK*, and *Processing*—can communicate with controllers via computer cables and through wireless networks and *Bluetooth*. This can allow external controllers to be used for gestural maneuvers over various parameters of a performance. A small cottage industry has developed to build and write programs for a wide variety of controllers and sensors, from motion detection to accelerometers. The data from these devices (the physical world) are then mapped to compositional or performance parameters in real time.

It is clear throughout this history how the creation of computer hardware and software developed hand in hand. From large mainframe computers at Bell Labs to the laptop, software has sought to use the full resources of its host computer.

Unfortunately for composers, until the popularity of Windows- and Mac OS-based personal computers, some of the most music-friendly computers were short-lived in the marketplace. The *NeXT* computer (1988–90), developed by the late Steve Jobs during his temporary departure from Apple in the late 1980s, was the first desktop computer available for serious music-related computations and programming. When NeXT went out of business, computer musicians turned to the Silicon Graphics *Indy* computers (1993–97). Although expensive at $5,000 a workstation, the Indy was within the budgets of many major universities and available in computer music centers. When SGI went out of business, computer musicians turned to the Apple *Macintosh*. These desktop and laptop computers were fast enough to run the real-time audio and video processing software needed for music computing. Another important milestone came in 1994 when *Max/MSP/Jitter* was ported to Windows, greatly increasing the potential pool of users at a relatively inexpensive entry point.

A CONCISE HISTORY OF COMPUTER MUSIC

The early history of computer music is detailed below in two parts: first, the formative experiments in computer composition, programming, and synthesis; and, second, the rise of the dedicated, digital synthesizer prior to the transition in the late 1980s to software-based synthesis.

Formative Experiments in Computer Music

1955–57:   At the University of Illinois, using the ILLIAC computer, Lejaren Hiller and Leonard Isaacson developed a computer program to generate sequences of data that could be applied as pitches and parameters of a musical score. The two men selected portions of this output and assembled it into the first significant piece of music composed with the aid of a computer, the *Illiac Suite for String Quartet* (1957). The ILLIAC was the first large-scale computer built and operated by a university in the United States.

1956:   Two computer engineers at the Burroughs Corporation, Martin L. Klein and Douglas Bolitho, programmed a Datatron computer to compose popular songs automatically. Affectionately nicknamed "Push-Button Bertha," the unit reportedly composed some 4,000 pop tunes after being fed the characteristics of 100 that were then popular.

1961–62:   In Paris, Iannis Xenakis wrote some probabilistic computer programs to aid in the composition of music. Rather than having the computer itself compose a piece, Xenakis fed the computer previously calculated information and employed it to work out complex parameters of scores for various sizes of instrumental groups. Works he composed using this approach and the IBM 7090 computer included the "ST" series (e.g. *ST/10–1,080262 for Ten Instruments,* 1962), *Atrées (Law of Necessity, ST/10–3,060962,* 1962), *Morsima-Amorsima (ST/4–1,030762,* 1962), and *ST/48–1,240162 for 48 Instruments* (1962).

1957:   At Bell Labs, researcher Max Mathews successfully demonstrated the computer generation of sound for the first time using a digital-to-analog converter (DAC) and the first musical programming language, *MUSIC I.* For Mathews, this was the beginning of a long association with computer music.

1959–66:   Mathews and his Bell Lab associates experimented widely with computer-synthesized music. Their compositions ranged from sonic demonstrations (e.g. *Pitch Variations* by Newman Guttman, *Sea Sounds* by John Pierce) to abstract musical soundscapes (e.g. *Noise Study* by James Tenney) to simple renditions of familiar tunes and more complex pieces using classical music forms (e.g. *Five Stochastic Studies* and *Ergodos* by Tenney). The Bell Labs team developed a series of programs for automating the digital processing and organization of such works. These programs began with *MUSIC I* in 1957 and were updated regularly by Mathews for more than ten years. *MUSIC IV* (1962) was used widely during the 1960s. Many of these early experiments were released on a recording called *Music from Mathematics* (IBM, 1962), providing composers and listeners outside of Bell Labs an opportunity to hear the sounds of early computer music.

1965:   At Bell Labs, French physicist and composer Jean-Claude Risset conducted analysis and synthesis experiments using programs by Max Mathews and Joan Miller. This experiment in analog-to-digital conversion was particularly significant because previous programs had been unsuccessful in faithfully reproducing the sound of a brass instrument.[19] Risset continued this work for several years and developed an extensive catalog of programmed instrumental sounds.

1968:   Mathews and L. Rosler at Bell Labs developed a graphical interface called *Graphic 1* for composing music. A light-pen was used to draw parameters of pitch, amplitude, duration, and glissando onto the grid of a cathode ray tube representing the passing of musical notes in time. The output was permanently stored and could be played back using computer synthesis. This was the first successful composer-friendly experiment using software to draw, copy, erase, and edit musical values on a computer.

1967–69:   At the University of Illinois, John Cage and Lejaren Hiller collaborated on an extensive multimedia piece called *HPSCHD.* The work was scored for 7 harpsichords and 51 computer-generated sound tapes. It was prepared by Cage and Hiller using a computer to assemble sound patterns based on calculations derived from *I Ching* chance operations. A commercially available recording of the work (Nonesuch, 1969) included an individually randomized computer printout that could be used by the listener to control the output parameters of a stereo system to "perform" the work at home.

1969–74:   Max Mathews, F. R. Moore, and Jean-Claude Risset at Bell Labs released the *MUSIC V* program, written in *FORTRAN* and adaptable to any general-purpose computer. In response to a call for a computer music program that could be used in performance situations, the group developed a program called *GROOVE*, which permitted a computer to be used as a voltage-controlled signal generator for an analog synthesizer.

1975–82:   Mini- and microcomputers began to be used as control devices for analog synthesizers. Developments in microprocessor technology introduced the use of sound-synthesizing "chips" in consumer musical instruments and professional synthesizers. The first all-digital synthesizers for the commercial market were introduced. Computer music programs became available for use with personal computers made by such companies as Apple, Commodore, and Atari (see Chapter 10).

1976:   The *4A Digital Sound Processor* was completed at IRCAM by a team headed by Giuseppe Di Giugno. Additional versions of this software synthesizer were released between 1976 and 1981 as the *4B*, *4C*, and collectively as the *4X* series.

1979:   An IRCAM team headed by Xavier Rodet completed the first release of a computer program called *Chant*, which created synthesized sounds based on computer models of the singing voice.

1979:   Bell Labs introduced the first integrated, single-chip digital signal processor (DSP), the multimedia processing heart of audio synthesizers, cell phones, and other digital systems that process sound.

1981:   The first computer work composed by Pierre Boulez at IRCAM, *Répons*, was premiered during the Donaueschingen festival. It was created using the *4X* software synthesizer developed at the institute. The work was performed by 24 musicians, with the sounds of the soloists each being modulated by the synthesizer and distributed to a network of loudspeakers in the concert hall.

1981–83:   Personal computers from IBM and Apple Computer began to dominate the market for home computing. Rudimentary and inexpensive music software packages began to appear for the creation of computer music.

1984:   IRCAM released *Iana* software for the psychoacoustic analysis of sounds. It was developed by a team led by Gérard Assayag.

1985:   IRCAM released its first musical software for personal computers. It was developed by a team led by David Wessel. In addition, a library of computer functions for computer-assisted composition was completed by Claudy Malherbe, Gérard Assayag, and Jean-Baptiste Barrière.

Early Digital Synthesizers

1974–75:   The first commercially available portable digital synthesizer was created at Dartmouth University, New Hampshire, and developed by the composer Jon Appleton and the engineers Sydney Alonso and Cameron Jones.

Figure 9.5   Jon Appleton and the Synclavier II, 1982. (Jonathan Sa'adah, *Four Fantasies for Synclavier* album cover, Folkways FTS 37461)

Called the *Synclavier*, the instrument used FM synthesis, was performance-oriented, and included a means to store tracks of sound that could be used interactively with real-time keyboard performance. The Synclavier set the early standard for computer-based synthesizers. New England Digital Corp. was established to manufacture and sell the product. The average cost of a Synclavier ranged from $200,000 to $300,000.

In the United States, Joel Chadabe purchased the first commercially available Synclavier but without its keyboard controller. Instead, he asked Robert Moog to develop Theremin-like gestural controllers for the synthesizer. "I used them not to make sounds as the Theremin makes sounds but rather to control the computer. He [Moog] designed frequency voltage converters in the base of the Theremins that I plugged into the synthesizer."[20]

1978–84:   The Fairlight *CMI* (*Computer Music Instrument*) digital synthesizer was developed in Australia and introduced in 1979. The Fairlight CMI was designed by Peter Vogel and Kim Ryrie and used a dual microprocessor architecture engineered by Tony Furse. Providing a full complement of sound-design features, it was equipped with its own dedicated computer, dual eight-inch disk drives, a six-octave touch-sensitive keyboard, and software for the creation and manipulation of sounds. Its most innovative feature was an analog-to-digital converter for processing incoming audio signals from analog sources. The Fairlight CMI was the first commercially available digital sampling instrument. It featured a sequencer, 400 preset sounds, and the ability to create new tonal scales tuned in increments as small as one-hundredth of a semitone. An external audio signal could be used as a controlling signal, much like earlier voltage-controlled synthesizers. A light-pen and CRT display provided a means for drawing and editing waveshapes. As a recording device, live tracks could be merged with recorded passages for overdubbing. In the studio, the system could control the synchronization of up to 56 parts on an eight-track tape recorder. The cost of the average Fairlight was $25,000 to $30,000.

1980:   Another digital synthesizer called the *General Development System* (*GDS*) was introduced by Crumar. Based on Bell Labs designs, it was designed for additive synthesis and had two eight-inch floppy disk drives, a Z-80 microprocessor, computer terminal, and keyboard controller. It sold for $27,500. It was the first stage of a product line to introduce the lower-priced Synergy (see below) in 1982.

1980:   Casio introduced the first portable digital electronic musical instrument, the Casio *VL-Tone*. Selling for about $70, this small monophonic instrument with its two and a half-octave mini-keyboard included presets for rhythms and instrument voices and permitted the player to store a sequence of up to 100 notes in memory. It was programmed by entering an eight-digit number to select a waveform (e.g. piano, guitar, fantasy) and envelope. Three waveforms could be modulated by a low-frequency oscillator. It was the first low-priced digital synthesizer.

1981:   E-mu Systems introduced the *Emulator*, a dedicated digital sampling keyboard. Its sample time was only two seconds, but at about $10,000 the Emulator was the first professional-quality sampling keyboard priced lower than the $35,000 Fairlight CMI. It had eight-voice polyphony, a sequencer, real-time looping, and used 5.25-inch floppy disks to load its programs.

1982:   Crumar introduced the *Synergy*, a relatively low-cost digital synthesizer with a retail price of about $6,000, a significant price drop at the time. Wendy Carlos became an avid user of the Synergy, after working with its expensive precursor, the GDS.

Figure 9.6   E-mu Emulator II, 1985, linked to an early Apple Macintosh. (E-mu Systems)

Her score for the motion picture *Tron* combined original orchestral music with analog Moog sounds and GDS digital synthesis as part of the same instrumental ensemble.

1983:   Casio introduced the *PT-20*, a 31-key monophonic instrument with two and a half octaves. It included seven preset voices, including piano, organ, violin, and flute, and 17 background rhythms. Preset algorithms for chords were played by buttons with designations for chords such as major, minor, and seventh. Using a feature called an "automatic judging chord generator," the keyboard could be played with one finger and the PT-20 could automatically select and play an accompanying chord. The keyboard could also store up to 508 notes for playback. This device was introduced at a retail price under $100. The PT-20 was a breakthrough not only in terms of price but in the way that Casio engineers used the computer as an interpretive tool and accompanist for the user.

1983:   The *Synclavier II* was introduced by New England Digital. It featured the same general capabilities as the Fairlight CMI but was designed more as a musical instrument than as a computer. The control panel featured dozens of buttons that were logically arranged by functions such as volume, envelope, recorder control, vibrato, and timbre bank. The instrument featured 16 digital oscillator voices and 16–track recording. A digital sampling feature could digitize analog sounds using a higher frequency range than the Fairlight instrument. Its digital memory recorder could store a sequence of 2,000 notes, and could be expanded to record 15,000 notes. The Synclavier II became the premier product in the market for proprietary digital synthesizers. It cost from $28,000 for a basic configuration up to about $55,000 for a fully equipped system.

1983:   Kurzweil Music Systems introduced the *K250*, a performance keyboard instrument using proprietary wavetable algorithms to emulate the sounds of acoustic instruments. Stored in ROM, the digital instruments faithfully reproduced piano, strings, choirs, drums, and other acoustic instruments with great clarity. The well-equipped instrument was designed with the help of musician Stevie Wonder, with a design that leaned more to the needs of a musician than a computer programmer. It featured an 88-note velocity-sensitive, wooden keyboard, 341 standard presets from 96 ROM-based instruments, user-controlled sampling with rates up to 50 kHz, and full sample editing. It was remarkably multitasking with up to 31 samples per setup, up to 87-way keyboard splits, and a 12,000-note multitrack sequencer with event editing, MIDI, and tape sync. The keyboard could also be linked to an Apple

Figure 9.7   One feature of the Fairlight CMI digital synthesizer was a light pen and monitor for drawing sounds to be created by the instrument. (Fairlight, 1980)

Macintosh computer interface for managing samples and setups. The K250 became the benchmark for digital sampling keyboards using preset instrumental algorithms.

1983:   Syntauri Corporation introduced its *alphaSyntauri* system, designed to enable a desktop computer to create music. This system used a 48K Apple II computer as its brain, one or two 5.25-inch floppy disk drives for storage, and a video monitor. The digital audio oscillators were contained on a plug-in sound card developed by Mountain Computer. Syntauri provided software, a four- or five-octave piano-type keyboard, interface hardware, and instructions to start creating digital music with its system. Laurie Spiegel, who had previously been working at Bell Labs, was a member of the team that developed the alphaSyntauri music system. Although not as powerful as the Fairlight CMI or Synclavier II, the alphaSyntauri marked the beginning of a trend toward less expensive electronic music systems built around personal computers. The most elaborate model, including a five-octave keyboard and 100 preset sounds, cost around $2,000, not including the computer, which cost another $1,500 to $2,000 at the time.

1984:   *MIDI* was introduced as a standard interface language for synthesizers and personal computers.

1984:   Roland introduced yet another method of using an Apple II computer to make music. The Roland *Compu Music CMU-800R* system was an external add-on to the computer and provided six digital tone generators and seven rhythm voices. The unit was plugged into the Apple II through an interface circuit board and was played or programmed through the computer keyboard. External controls were also provided for the envelope generator and volume of the melody, chord, and rhythm components of the sound. The $500 product was as short-lived as the Apple II after the introduction of the Macintosh, but anticipated by many years the trend toward the use of external slave synthesizers with personal computers.

1985:   Mark of the Unicorn, a software developer, introduced *Performer* (later *Digital Performer*), one of the first MIDI sequencing programs for the Macintosh computer.

1988:   Korg introduced the *M1 Music Workstation*, a dedicated computer-based synthesizer with onboard display, sequencer, drum machine, digitally sampled sounds, and digital effects. About 250,000 units were sold, a breakthrough for a computer-based music system.

1988:   IRCAM released its first version of *Max*, a graphical programming language for music applications, created by Miller Puckette. It was developed to support real-time interaction between the performer and computer and provided a rich array of virtual patches and controllers for the management of audio processing. The first client for a *Max* patch was Philippe Manoury, for his composition *Pluton*.

1989:   IRCAM began developing the *Max* hardware board for the *Max* computer and Ariel systems. *Max* was ported to the *Max* to drive the events, with the signal processing part of the patcher (FTS, faster than sound) running the hardware on the IRCAM Signal Processing Workstation.

1990:   A musician-friendly version of *Max* was introduced by Opcode, with its design improved by David Zicarelli. This microcomputer program for the Macintosh became an instant success and continues to be the most widely used software controller for real-time music synthesis today. Other popular programming languages—many available for free and using open-source code—include *Csound* (by Barry Vercoe, 1985), *RTCmix* (by Brad Garton, John Gibson, Dave Topper, Doug Scott, Mara Helmuth, 1995), *SuperCollider* (by James McCartney, 2002), *ChucK* (by Perry Cook and Ge Wang, 2003), and *MetaSynth* (by Eric Wenger, 2000), which features granular synthesis.

1990:   Symbolic Sound introduced a two-processor microcomputer-based electronic music system. The software controller was called *Kyma*, and worked with a proprietary set of sound processors called *Capybara*. Like *Max/MSP*, but with its own dedicated audio processing hardware, it is well suited to the real-time processing of audio signals during live performance.

1996:   Miller Puckette released *Pure Data* (*Pd*), a rewrite of *Max* as an open-source, software-only platform, with both logic and audio (DSP) capabilities.

1997:   David Zicarelli founded *cycling74* and released *MSP* (named after Miller Puckette), a set of audio extensions for Opcode's *Max* that used the PowerPC chip for real-time signal processing on the Macintosh platform with no additional hardware. The *MSP* engine and object API were initially based on the *Pd* system released the previous year by Puckette.

1999:   IRCAM, with development led by François Déchelle, completed *jMax*, a new real-time version of its performance software for personal computers.

SUMMARY

- The new field of information science inspired composers to explore the use of computers to compose and synthesize music, beginning in the 1950s.

- The development of computer technology historically paralleled the development of the modern electronic music studio and synthesizer, leading to a cross-fertilization of the two fields that greatly benefited electronic music.

- The development of computer music requires a musical programming language and a method for the direct synthesis of digital signals into audible sound.

- The first music programming language was developed by Max Mathews at Bell Labs in 1957.

- Lejaren Hiller and Iannis Xenakis explored the use of computers for musical composition during the late 1950s and 1960s.

- The direct synthesis of music by computers became feasible during the 1970s and resulted in the creation of large-scale digital synthesizers at Bell Labs, Stanford University, the Institute of Sonology in The Netherlands, IRCAM, and other computer centers.

- John Chowning's work in FM synthesis led to an economical way to harness computing power to create a wide palette of easily shaped sounds that could be accomplished with a minimum of processing power.

- The four roles of computers in music include composition and scoring, computer synthesis, computer control over audio processing functions and performance, and computer sampling of audio input.

- Computer music research at IRCAM from the 1990s to the present day has provided new software tools for composers interested in creating *frequential music* based on the spectral analysis of tones, timbres, and other elements of sound.

KEY PEOPLE IN CHAPTER NINE

KEY TERMS IN CHAPTER NINE

MILESTONES

Early Computer Music

Technical and scientific	Year	Artists and music
– Claude E. Shannon published *A Mathematical Theory of Communication*.	1948	
– Max Mathews of Bell Labs produced the first example of direct synthesis with a computer using the *MUSIC I* programming language. – Lejaren Hiller and Robert Baker of the University of Illinois produced *MUSICOMP*, a music composition programming language.	1957	– Hiller and Leonard Isaacson composed the *Illiac Suite for String Quartet* using the ILLIAC computer and *MUSICOMP*.
	1962	– Max Matthews realized *Bicycle Built for Two* using *MUSIC N* software at Bell Labs. – James Tenney composed *Five Stochastic Studies* using *MUSIC N* software at Bell Labs.
– Gottfried Michael Koenig of the Institute of Sonology in the Netherlands produced *Project 1*, a musical programming language for musical scoring.	1964	
– Max Mathews and L. Rosler of Bell Labs developed *Graphic 1*, an interactive music composing system controlled by video input on a CRT.	1967	– Gottfried Michael Koenig composed *Funktion Grün* and *Terminus II* at the Institute of Sonology in the Netherlands using *Project 1* composing software.
– IRCAM was founded in Paris under the direction of Pierre Boulez.	1969	
– Max Mathews of Bell Labs produced *GROOVE*, a musical programming language for real-time performance.	1970	
– Gottfried Michael Koenig of the Institute of Sonology in the Netherlands directed the development of the *SSP Sound Synthesis Program*, a direct synthesis computer.	1971	– Emanuel Ghent composed *Phosphons* using the *GROOVE* system at Bell Labs.
	1972	– John Chowning composed *Turenas* using his FM synthesis techniques and the *Music 10* programming language.
– John Chowning at Stanford University published *The Synthesis of Complex Audio Spectra by Means of Frequency Modulation*	1973	
– The Samson Box was delivered to Stanford University.	1977	– John Chowning, working at IRCAM, composed *Stria* for magnetic tape.
– Yamaha manufactured the DX-7 digital synthesizer	1983	– Janis Mattox composed *Shaman* using the "Samson Box" at the Center for Computer Research in Music and Acoustics at Stanford University.

CHAPTER 10

The Microprocessor Revolution (1975–2011)

Making the transition was very interesting. I was resistant initially. I had taken a summer course in computers when they were like mainframes and PDP-11 computers and I found them very counter-intuitive and, of course, not portable . . . Then, when I was dragging my heels, Paul DeMarinis said, 'Don't think of it as a computer. Think of it as a big, expensive logic chip.' It was like a mantra. That got me going.
—Nicolas Collins

Matt Rogalsky and performance equipment. (Künstlerhaus)

By 1990, the use of analog synthesizers in the tradition of Moog, Buchla, ARP, Roland, and others was entirely superseded by the availability of inexpensive, computer-based, digital synthesizing techniques. Computer processors are used in every kind of music equipment imaginable. They are at the core of digital synthesizers, effects boxes, mixers, multitrack recorders, and other basic devices used by the working musician. Most commercial recordings are now recorded, mixed, and mastered using digital means.

The personal computer has become an essential component of the electronic musician's equipment arsenal, fulfilling the traditional functions of the computer in music for composition and scoring, synthesis and sound processing, control over external synthesizers and other performance equipment, and the sampling of audio and video input, and real-time video manipulation.

This chapter traces the transition of computer music from large, mainframe systems to microprocessors and personal computers, a shift in the paradigm of computer technology that made electronic music systems affordable and widely accessible. Related improvements in chip technology and sound processing also led to the development of the first digital synthesizers, the origins of which were explored in Chapter 10.

FROM TRANSISTORS TO MICROPROCESSORS

As the 1970s began, the technology paradigm of the computer was making a dramatic changeover to increasingly miniaturized components. Transistors, originally used individually in analog devices, became part of the integrated circuit by the early 1960s. The *integrated circuit* (IC) is a miniaturized electronic circuit manufactured on a thin substrate of semiconductor material. In addition to transistors, an IC may contain blocks associated with RAM, logic functions, and the input and output of signals. The IC, also known as the silicon chip or microchip, can be adapted to many functions and provides the brains and circuitry for any digital electronic device, from computers, to cell phones, MP3 players, and televisions. The first ICs were manufactured by Texas Instruments during the early 1960s. Following advances in miniaturization, such chips became widely used as logic function devices in portable calculators.

A *microprocessor* is a programmable integrated circuit. It contains all of the basic functions of a central processing unit (CPU) on a single chip. Prior to the development of the microprocessor, computers operated using transistorized components and switching systems, making them relatively large and expensive. The introduction of the micro-processor greatly reduced the size and manufacturing cost of computers. There are usually one or more microprocessors in a computer, each with potentially thousands or hundreds-of-thousands of embedded transistors. The dramatic reduction in the cost of processing power brought on by the microprocessor led to the introduction of the *microcomputer* by the end of the 1970s. At the same time, there was a shift in the development of computer music from large-scale computer environments to the desktop of the composer.

Before there were microprocessors dedicated to audio signal processing, there were ICs with sound-specific applications in toys, appliances, and telephones. The first "oscillator on a chip" that was both inexpensive and widely available was the Signetics NE/SE566, designed for use in touch-tone telephones. It was the first audio chip that composer Nicolas Collins (b. 1954) acquired. The year was 1972 and he was in his last year of high school and about to embark on undergraduate study with Alvin Lucier at Wesleyan University, Connecticut. Collins taught himself to assemble a little gadget that could make satisfying boops and beeps with the SE566: "It cost $5, which seemed like a lot of money at the time. But, you know, the synthesizer was $5,000."[1] This was several years before the widespread availability of home computers, when chip technology was first being built into appliances, calculators, toys, and other household items.

It turned out that Collins' discovery had also been made by several other soldering composers. A few years later he was able to look "under the hood" of one of David Behrman's early homemade synthesizers. This was not a computer, nor even a synthesizer in the traditional sense, because it had none of the usual paraphernalia found on commercial instruments, such as voltage-controlled filters, envelope generators, and modulation wheels. All Behrman wanted was a lot of oscillators. He soldered them together along with logic circuits and pitch sensors to create an early logic-based interactive sound synthesizer. It was used in his work for synthesized music with sliding pitches. Tones were triggered by several musicians and sustained by the synthesizer, dying out after a few seconds. As a tone died out, it modulated or deflected the pitches of other tones that were being played and this caused sliding pitches to occur during the attack and decay parts of a tone. The soldering composer had crossed the first line into the digital age. The chips provided him with a sonic wall of wavering, digital bliss. Behrman had become the "Phil Spector of Downtown,"[2] the father figure of a new wave of electronic music tinkering.

Collins calls the Signetics chip the "cultural linchpin for an entire generation" of composer-hackers. A lot of tinkerers learned basic IC breadboard design with the SE566. Even more significant was that, before too long, the Signetics chip was already obsolete, only to be replaced by the next generation. Each successive IC was more versatile yet less expensive. The economics of technology were for once working in favor of the electronic musician. Composers Collins and Ron Kuivila (b. 1955) had just started taking classes at Wesleyan:

> We were like the idiot twin children of Alvin Lucier. We were desperately trying to learn electronics. I don't think either of us had any real intuition for it. We just forced ourselves to do it. What else could you do? You were a student, you had time and no money, so you were trying stuff.
>
> But here's what happened. Technology got cheaper and more sophisticated and there was a generation of composers who taught themselves this stuff. There was Ron, myself, John Bischoff, Tim Perkis, Paul DeMarinis. Those are the names that come to mind offhand. And we're all about the same age. It is 2001 now. We're all essentially between 45 and 55 years old.[3]

Behrman found himself immersed in a new generation of electronics once again, hitting the books, trying to keep up with the changes. "I remember riding on the Cunningham bus in the early 1970s with manuals about logic gates," explained Behrman. "There was a period several years before the computer entered the picture where I remember we could do switching networks."[4]

As a new generation of composers was discovering the work of Mumma, Tudor, and Behrman, they began to ask for help in learning how to build their own instruments. A watershed event for a select group of these young composers was the "New Music in New Hampshire" workshop in Chocorua, New Hampshire in the summer of 1973. For a little more than two weeks, more than a dozen students participated, alternately, in classes on composing music and building instruments.

David Behrman and Gordon Mumma both taught courses in building homemade instruments. The classes preceded the final workshop, which was simply called "Rainforest" and was taught by David Tudor. His workshop in "sound transformation without modulation" gave birth to the remarkable installation version of his most famous work, *Rainforest IV* (1973), but also brought together a core of young composers— including John Driscoll, Ralph Jones, Bill Viola, and Martin Kalve—who continued to be Tudor's collaborators in performance for several years. Tudor aptly named the group Composers Inside Electronics because, instead of using electronics as given instruments, they were working with the circuitry, trying to alter it, influence it, discover what it can do.[5]

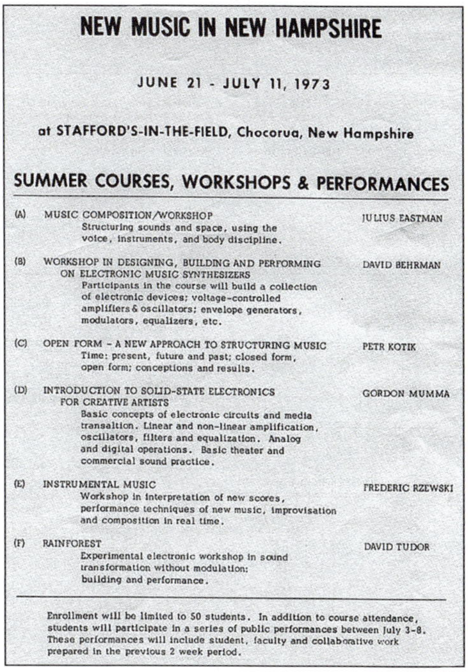

The purpose of the workshop was for the

NEW MUSIC IN NEW HAMPSHIRE

JUNE 21 - JULY 11, 1973

at STAFFORD'S-IN-THE-FIELD, Chocorua, New Hampshire

SUMMER COURSES, WORKSHOPS & PERFORMANCES

(A)	MUSIC COMPOSITION/WORKSHOP Structuring sounds and space, using the voice, instruments, and body discipline.	JULIUS EASTMAN
(B)	WORKSHOP IN DESIGNING, BUILDING AND PERFORMING ON ELECTRONIC MUSIC SYNTHESIZERS Participants in the course will build a collection of electronic devices: voltage-controlled amplifiers & oscillators; envelope generators, modulators, equalizers, etc.	DAVID BEHRMAN
(C)	OPEN FORM - A NEW APPROACH TO STRUCTURING MUSIC Time: present, future and past; closed form, open form; conceptions and results.	PETR KOTIK
(D)	INTRODUCTION TO SOLID-STATE ELECTRONICS FOR CREATIVE ARTISTS Basic concepts of electronic circuits and media translation. Linear and non-linear amplification, oscillators, filters and equalization. Analog and digital operations. Basic theater and commercial sound practice.	GORDON MUMMA
(E)	INSTRUMENTAL MUSIC Workshop in interpretation of new scores, performance techniques of new music, improvisation and composition in real time.	FREDERIC RZEWSKI
(F)	RAINFOREST Experimental electronic workshop in sound transformation without modulation: building and performance.	DAVID TUDOR

Enrollment will be limited to 50 students. In addition to course attendance, students will participate in a series of public performances between July 3-8. These performances will include student, faculty and collaborative work prepared in the previous 2 week period.

Figure 10.1 Promotional flyer for the Chocorua summer workshop. (Gordon Mumma)

students to compose and perform live electronic music using only instruments of their own design. Tudor wanted them to learn what it was like to begin with nothing and build something that suited their needs. *Rainforest IV* was an interactive installation of suspended objects that were wired so that sound could be run through them as if they were loudspeakers. The result was reverberant electroacoustic music generated by the vibrating objects, without further electronic modification. It had previously been performed only in a more concert-like version, as Mumma explained:

> This was the first "large-scale" *Rainforest* production. The previous were performances that David Tudor and I did with the Merce Cunningham Dance Company, from the premiere of *Rainforest* [in late 1968] up to the Chocorua project [July 1973]. The MCDC performances were, in character, a special kind of "chamber music," in comparison with the large-scale twelve (or so) performers at Chocorua.[6]

Gordon Mumma and David Behrman next went to California. Mumma had been invited to the University of California at Santa Cruz (in 1973) to establish an electronic music studio there. Behrman joined Robert Ashley at Mills College in northern California in 1975. The Bay Area became the West Coast's experimental station for soldering composers. Rooted in Silicon Valley and drawing nourishment from the proximity of the first microcomputer manufacturers, the Mills program attracted many young soldering composers, including Paul DeMarinis, Ron Kuivila, Laetitia deCompiegne, and John Bischoff.

The KIM-1

David Behrman was begrudgingly becoming aware of the advantages offered by microcomputers:

> I remember saying to myself, "No, I'm not going to go down this path into computer software" . . . There were lots of people there who were interested in this new microcomputer thing that was just coming out. Students started coming in with the very first kits.[7]

Up until then, the synthesizers Behrman had been building were hardwired to do only one thing, such as play a defined set of oscillators: "It seemed that this new device called the microcomputer could simulate one of these switching networks for a while and then change, whenever you wanted, to some other one."

The breakthrough in microcomputers came with the arrival of the KIM-1 (1975), a predecessor of the Apple computer that used the same chip set. One individual from the Bay Area scene was largely responsible for moving the gadget composers from soldering chips to programming the KIM-1. Jim Horton (1944–98), by all accounts the leading underground computer evangelist in Berkeley, preached the miracles of the KIM-1 at regular meetings at the Mediterranean Café near UC Berkeley. Collins explained:

> he was the first person to get a single-board computer—a KIM-1—for use for music. This caught on. These computers were made for controlling machines and for learning how a microprocessor worked. They looked like autoharps. They had a little keypad in the corner, a little seven-segment display.[8]

The KIM-1 was a primitive, industrial-strength microcomputer for process control applications. It could be programmed with coded instructions—machine-language software—but these were entered by pressing keys on a hexadecimal pad. It had no keyboard or computer monitor like microcomputers do today. One entered a sequence of codes and hit the run button. The composer was operating very close to the level of the machinery itself. Behrman, Paul DeMarinis (b. 1948), and other composers found that the KIM-1 was ideal for controlling their primitive, chip-based synthesizers.

Figure 10.2
A homemade interface between a KIM-1-era microcomputer and the homemade synthesizers of David Behrman. (Thom Holmes, from Behrman's collection)

They built in cable ports, not unlike printer connections, to connect homemade synthesizers to the KIM-1.

Horton's work, dedication, and know-how led to the development of live performances of microcomputer music in the Bay Area during the early 1970s. One group founded by Horton was the League of Automatic Music Composers, which also included John Bischoff (b. 1949), Tim Perkis, and Rich Gold. Members of the group have continued to work over the years on the creation of computer music using networked machines, inexpensive technology, and low-level programming languages. One extension of the League of Automatic Music Composers was The Hub, a group of six individual computer composer-performers connected into an interactive network. The Hub took shape around 1989 and included members Mark Trayle (b. 1955), Phil Stone, Scot Gresham-Lancaster (b. 1954), John Bischoff, Chris Brown, and Tim Perkis. Their music is a "kind of enhanced improvisation, wherein players and computers share the responsibility for the music's evolution, with no one able to determine the exact outcome, but everyone having influence in setting the direction."[9]

EARLY MUSIC FROM MICROPROCESSORS

1   *Figure in a Clearing* (1977) by David Behrman
    A KIM-1 computer controlled harmonic changes for 33 electronic generators and accompanying cello

2   *Rondo from Sonata in B flat for Clarinet and Piano* (by Wanhal), realized in 1979 by Dorothy Siegel
    Created using an Altair S-100 microcomputer

3   *Artificial Intelligence* (1980) by Larry Fast
    Music generated by a microcomputer self-composing program

4   *A Harmonic Algorithm* (1981) by Laurie Spiegel
    Created on an Apple II computer with Mountain Hardware oscillator boards

5   *Little Spiders* (1982) by Nicolas Collins
    For two microcomputers equipped with gestural sensing programs, which generated sounds based on analysis of keystrokes

6   *Than Particle* (1985) by Gordon Mumma
    For computer percussion and a percussionist

7   *And the Butterflies Begin to Sing* (1988) by Morton Subotnick
    For string quartet, bass, MIDI keyboard, and microcomputer

8   *Dovetail* (1989) by John Bischoff, Mark Trayle, Tim Perkis
    Three microcomputer programs interact and respond to each other in real time

9   *Wax Lips* (1992) by Tim Perkis
    Performed by The Hub, an electronic music ensemble networked by a microcomputer

10 *Electric Changgo Permutations* (1993) by Jin Hi Kim
    Early *Max* implementation

LISTEN

Table 10.1 Evolution of computer technology

Computer generation	Era	Processing speed (instructions per second)	Data storage capacity (cost per MB)	Progression of computer music applications
1st generation (vacuum tube)	1939–54	5,000	$40,000	• Composition and scoring
2nd generation (transistor)	1954–59	10,000	$10,000	• Analog to digital conversion of audio sources • Audio spectrum analysis • Simple audio signal generation
3rd generation (integrated circuit)	1959–71	10,000 to 1 million	$10,000 to $5,000	• Additive and subtractive synthesis audio synthesis
4th generation (microprocessor)	1971	1 million	$2,000	• Wavetable synthesis
	1975	5 million	$800	• FM synthesis • Granular synthesis
	1980	7 million	$300	• Digital audio sampling
	1985	8.5 million	$150	• Digital audio signal processing • Digital audio recording
	1990	50 million	$10	• Digital audio workstations
	1995	540 million	$1	
	2000	3,560 million	$0.015	
	2007	6,400 million	$0.000000015	

Source: Based in part on data from www.littletechshoppe.com/ns1625/winchest.html.

By the early 1980s, the affordability of integrated circuits and microprocessors was directing development toward the production of sophisticated, multifunction sound chips and digital signal processing components for electronic music. This began with relatively simple audio chips built into the first widely used microcomputers such as the Apple II Plus (1977) and IBM PC (1981), the purpose of which was primarily to provide alert sounds while using the computer. There was no facility built into these early personal computers for porting audio signals in or out. Any music created on these early microcomputers was limited to simple tone generation, a throwback to the earliest days of direct synthesis at Bell Labs in the 1950s.

Laurie Spiegel

Laurie Spiegel (b. 1945) is a composer and musician at heart—a skilled player of the lute and banjo—who also nurtures a fascination with computer music dating back to the early 1970s. Spiegel took a job as a software engineer at Bell Labs and in six productive years, from 1973 to 1979, worked alongside pioneer Max Mathews, Emmanuel Ghent, and other talented engineers to explore the outer reaches of computer music. It was a heady time for computer music and one that was often viewed with skepticism by those outside the Lab. "Whereas back then we were most commonly accused of attempting to completely dehumanize the arts," explained Spiegel, "at this point there has become such widespread acceptance of these machines in the arts that there is now a good bit of interest in how this came to be." While at Bell Labs, Spiegel wrote programs to operate *GROOVE*, Mathews' minicomputer-based real-time synthesis project. Among Spiegel's compositions with *GROOVE* were *Appalachian Grove* (1974) and *The Expanding Universe* (1975). *GROOVE* was rooted in the technology of the late 1960s, however, and by 1979 its performance and capabilities were being rapidly eclipsed by new technology. About this time, Spiegel made a decision to leave Bell Labs to work as a consultant on new microcomputer-based products as computer engineer and composer. Spiegel dove headfirst into exploring the music applications of microcomputers:

> There were wonderful electronics parts shops all over this neighborhood [Tribeca, New York City] until gentrification replaced them with expensive restaurants. Especially important was one place on West Broadway just below Chambers that sold little kits they made up with things like buzzers and frequency divider circuits, with a breadboard and all the parts and instructions. I suspect a few of us composers used some of the same kits. I didn't do nearly as much of this as several of my friends, but I kludged up a little synth back in the late 1970s inside a seven-inch tape box that I played live into a microphone like any other acoustic instrument, including through a digital signal processor.[10]

Figure 10.3   Laurie Spiegel, 1981. (Carlo Carnevali, courtesy of Laurie Spiegel)

Among Spiegel's consulting projects from 1981 to 1985 were the alphaSyntauri music system for the low-cost Apple II computer and the design of a high-end analog musical instrument, the Canadian-made computer-controlled McLeyvier, that never came to market. After the McLeyvier project fell apart in 1985, Spiegel oscillated back in the direction of small, inexpensive desktop computers and created her best-known music program, the astonishingly modest but capable *Music Mouse* for the then new Apple Macintosh 512k computer and later Amiga and Atari computers. *Music Mouse* was an enabler of music-making rather than a programming environment. It provided a choice of several possible music scales (e.g. "chromatic," "octatonic," "middle eastern"), tempos, transposition, and other controls that were all played using a "polyphonic" cursor that was moved with the mouse on a visual grid representing a two-dimensional pitch range. The simple *Music Mouse* was an elegant example of what Spiegel called an "intelligent instrument" that could manage some of the basic structural rules of harmonic music-making for the user.

Following the availability of the Apple II and IBM PC home computers, the next stage in the development of computer music was the use of specially designed sound chips for use in home entertainment systems such as Atari and Sega video game consoles. One common sound chip was the Texas Instruments SN76489 Four-Channel Programmable Sound Generator. It included three programmable square wave generators, a white noise oscillator, and amplitude modulation of the signal. Chips like these were used to create the tunes that were played while a video game was operating. Each of the major game manufacturers, including Atari, Nintendo, and Commodore, released chips specialized for use with their game consoles. After acquiring the license for John Chowning's FM synthesis patent in 1975, Yamaha released a series of chips of varied sophistication that could also be used in home computers and game consoles. The limiting factor for all sound chips was the computer hardware itself; the only way to output the sound signal was through the tinny speaker built into the personal computer.

The availability of MIDI in 1984 incentivized microcomputer makers to develop more robust methods of producing computer music. The most adaptable solution was to provide an *expansion card* dedicated to sound synthesis and other audio processing tasks that could be plugged directly into a peripheral slot in a computer's microprocessor motherboard. Some of the best-known sound cards are the *Sound Blaster* family produced since 1988 by the firm Creative Technology in Singapore.

The original *Sound Blaster* quickly became a de facto standard for common music applications. This sound card included a sound chip for synthesizing sound, a MIDI port, and a digital-to-analog converter for porting the signal out to an analog stereo system through built-in stereo output jacks. The popularity of the *Sound Blaster* led to the development of a variety of sound cards from many manufacturers, some of them also involved in the making of synthesizers, such as Roland and Ensoniq.

By 2000, as the processing power of the microcomputer improved, manufacturers of personal computers were able to replace the need for an add-on sound card for most consumers by making music with built-in chips and codecs for processing sound from the motherboard. While these sound audio processing components provide most of the features of sound cards, they are generally limited in processing power and reduce the performance and response time of the computer when engaging in MIDI control and other computationally demanding DSP functions. The need for peak performance instruments and improved synthesis, especially in real-time situations, led to an ancillary industry devoted to providing high-end sound-generating hardware. These devices come in a variety of hardware configurations, from plug-in boards, to slave synthesizers (boxes without a keyboard), to rack-mounted components connected by Firewire or USB cables rather than being housed inside the computer.

As the power of the microcomputer has improved over the years there has been a shift of functionality from hardware and dedicated chip sets to the use of software to provide many of the synthesizing and control functions needed to make computer music. The rise of software synthesizers and ancillary programs is explored below.

MUSIC SOFTWARE FOR MICROCOMPUTERS

With the invention of the microprocessor, the next frontier for computer music lay in the development of new music programming languages. By 1978, microcomputers had advanced to the point where they could accept commands written in coded software languages, such as *Forth* and *Turtle Logo*, using some form of alphanumeric display and a keyboard for input. Composers were then faced with learning about software. It was yet another distraction in a series of distractions that conspired to steal away their composing time, and was a growing source of frustration for many. Nicolas Collins was about ready to give up:

> Making the transition was very interesting. I was resistant initially. I had taken
> a summer course in computers when they were like mainframes and PDP-11
> computers and I found them very counterintuitive and, of course, not portable.

I was completely committed to live performance and therefore portability was
the essential factor. Then, when I was dragging my heels, Paul DeMarinis was
thinking about buying a KIM, and he said, "Don't think of it as a computer.
Think of it as a big, expensive logic chip." In other words, just think of it as a
big chip. It was like a mantra. That got me going.[11]

Moving from soldering circuits to composing with software required a mental
adjustment for the composers as well. Composing with circuits in the tradition of Tudor
and Mumma was a real-time, action–reaction medium. You turned it on, flipped a switch,
and it just happened in parallel with whatever else was going on: another circuit, a circuit
affecting another circuit, a musician playing along, a voltage-controlled device modifying
the output of the circuit, and so forth. It was also transient activity that could not be
repeated, because analog systems were more like organisms growing old. Eventually
they burned out, fried to a crisp, changing slightly all along the way until total failure.
The Barrons had used this characteristic of analog electronics to their advantage when
they were composing with tube-based oscillators and circuits in the 1950s. Working
with analog instruments was more like playing an instrument in real time: a performance
existed as a function of human awareness and memory, passing in time, never to be
repeated.

What made microcomputer music different was the concept of computer memory
as an adjunct to human memory. Software allowed one to save a control sequence.
Actions could be stored and repeated as originally conceived, and repeatedly performed
by the computer as often as one liked. The circuits themselves were transitory rather
than hardwired. One's actions were reversible, unlike soldering, where you could
permanently melt your best work away with one false move of the heating element.
Conceptually, the composer could think differently about the organization, variation,
and playback of music because there were endless permutations possible through the
modification of software controls. Software was also, because of the nature of coding,
a linear process consisting of a sequence of instructions to the computer. This departed
from the solid-state idea of soldering, in which all things could happen at the same time
as long as the switches were flipped on. Whereas it was easy with soldered circuits to
run activities at the same time, the linear sequencing of software control was by its very
nature stretched out in time.

Soldered systems were vertical in conception: stacked and parallel. Software systems
were horizontal in nature: sequential and time-based. When working with computers,
composers had to adapt their thinking process for creating music. "So you had to stop
thinking about parallelism," explained Collins, "and start thinking in sequential terms.
It changed the way people worked."[12]

As microcomputers became more powerful and standardized during the 1980s, the
emphasis on music for computers shifted mostly to the use of software. Soldering was
rendered unnecessary for everyone except those few dedicated tinkerers who understood
the richness of circuit sounds and the direct manipulation of electronics without the
interloping influence of software. Mumma embraced it all: "I've never left the analog
world, because there are processes unique to it that are not transferable to the digital
world. I use them both."[13]

Software has in many ways equalized the opportunities for electronic music
composers. The graphical user interface, developed by Xerox and made popular first by

the Apple Macintosh and Microsoft Windows, provided a less daunting working environ-ment for the musician and composer who stopped short of learning a programming language. Some of the first successful music applications for the microcomputer were simply MIDI sequencers such as *Digital Performer* (1984) that stored and provided for the editing of notes played on a keyboard or other instrument.

Types of Computer Music Software

The potential uses of electronic music have expanded exponentially through the availa-bility of programs for making music with a personal computer. Computers have become the hub around which other music production functions now orbit. Whether in the music labs of academia, inside the commercial music studio, on stage with a performing musician, or in the private home studio, software for creating, editing, and controlling electronic music is pervasive. This section provides a tour of some of the most frequently encountered music software applications and prominent products.

Software Instruments

A software instrument is a *virtual synthesizer* than can be performed in real time. An organ- or piano-style keyboard is the most common type of MIDI controller used with a software synthesizer ("softsynth"), but they may also be manipulated using virtual dials and patches implemented on screen or through alternative MIDI controllers such as touch pads (e.g. the *Trigger Finger* by M-Audio, *Monome* by Brian Crabtree and Kelli Cain, *Manta* by Snyderphonics), guitar interfaces, and wind instruments (e.g. the Yamaha *WX5* and Akai *EWI4000S*).

A software synthesizer is operated using a computer's on-board sound processor or expansion sound card. The quality of the audio signal from a softsynth depends on its **sampling rate**—a numerical representation of a waveform that is converted to an analog voltage signal for reproduction by a loudspeaker. The sampling rate equates to the number of samples per second of a continuous waveform signal. Sampling and reproducing a sound requires an enormous amount of computer processing power. CD audio quality is standardized at a sampling rate of 44.1 kHz. Because of the Nyquist sampling theorem (see Chapter 11, p. 332) studios usually double or triple that resolution to 88,200 or 176,400 Hz while producing the original recording sessions, giving them the highest-quality signal possible to withstand post-production digital signal processing—special effects, speed changes—without any noticeable degradation in quality. The size of the byte used to sample audio is another factor affecting its quality. Common sampling resolutions include 8-, 12-, and 16-bit levels, with 16-bit being the quality necessary to produce audio CD-quality reproduction. For the purpose of overcompensating, some software synthesizers can run at bit rates of 24, 32, and 64 bits. Each incremental increase in quality has a proportional increase in the amount of processing time and disk storage required to retain and edit the sound.

The processing power required to delivery high-quality synthesis has only recently become commonplace on personal computers. Many programs can now run at higher than CD quality sampling rates, often in the range of 48, 96, or 192 kHz. These numbers equate to 48,000, 96,000, and 192,000 samples *per second* of a given waveform, a task that could not have been handled even by the best-equipped mainframe computer during the first two decades of computer music synthesis. The choice of sampling rate and bit rate will be determined by the capability of the software first, but also by the degree of quality required for a given piece of music, the processing power of the computer, and the amount of disk storage available to retain the music files. A 16-bit, 44.1 kHz signal is adequate for most home recording applications, unless the music is going to be processed later for commercial distribution. Sampling rates below 44.1 kHz will lose some of the highest frequencies in a signal. A bit rate lower than 16 bits will also have more jagged, or noisy, waveforms.

Software synthesizers are available as *standalone* programs or as *plug-ins* for a host application. The format for plug-ins is proprietary for different manufacturers and many software synthesizers can accommodate several host applications. Such host applications usually consist of umbrella-like programs with an integrated package of applications. The most common host program environments include *Virtual Studio Technology* (*VST*) by Steinberg, *DirectX* by Microsoft (Windows only), *MAS* by Mark of the Unicorn, and *Real Time Audio Suite* (*RTAS*) by Digidesign. Such host applications are not software synthesizers themselves but consist of a music workstation environment for editing, mixing, processing, mastering, and controlling the entire multitrack music production process. The ability to add and control a synthesizer as part of such a suite allows the user to have all of their music applications under the control of one interface.

Plug-ins are also available for standalone software synthesizers, either from the original manufacturer of the software or independent developers. Being able to update a software synthesizer with additional algorithms for new instrumental voices is one of the advantages of using a softsynth over a conventional hardware performance instrument.

Software synthesizers can be grouped into several varieties.

Virtual Analog

One class of software synthesizers is designed to mimic the circuitry of analog synthesizers, providing the warm, fuzzy tones and fat sound qualities often associated with classic instruments. These **virtual analog** instruments are usually provided with a wealth of preset instrumental voices and controls for manually adjusting the filter, envelope, amplitude, modulation, and effects applied to a voice. Native Instruments *Absynth* is an example of one of the most robust virtual analog softsynths. It includes an on-screen keyboard controller or output to an external MIDI controller and offers multiple synthesis techniques, including subtractive, frequency modulation, amplitude modulation, granular, and direct sampling of analog audio data. Like most virtual analog softsynths, *Absynth* offers several interface views for controlling different aspects of the workstation, two of which are shown in Figures 10.4 and 10.5. Other work spaces within this program include windows for editing the envelopes and waveshape of a sound. Other noteworthy virtual analog synthesizers include Muon *Electron*, Antares *Kantos*, and VirSyn *Tera*.

Another approach to virtual analog software synthesizers is the modeling of classic brand-name instruments and providing a computer-based emulation, complete with a graphical user interface that represents every last detail of the original hardware. This has been a popular area of development in recent years and several options are available now if one wants to have a classic Minimoog, ARP Odyssey, Roland Juno, or almost any other once-popular instrument to run on their laptop computer. The French company Arturia has done much to revive such classic machines. One of Arturia's most interesting emulations is that of the *Moog Modular V*, a classic studio synthesizer from

Figure 10.4 (LEFT) Native Instruments *Absynth* software synthesizer performance screen. (Thom Holmes)

Figure 10.5 (ABOVE) Native Instruments *Absynth* software synthesizer—screen for selecting instruments. (Thom Holmes)

Figure 10.6 (LEFT) The Arturia virtual *Moog Modular* software synthesizer simulates the interface of the original Moog Modular Synthesizer, complete with adjustable patch cords. (Thom Holmes)

about 1970 (see Figure 10.6). The original instrument was programmed using patch cords and rotary dials, all of which have been faithfully reproduced in the interface for the software version. Translating such classic analog instruments to the computer also provided advantages over the original instruments, including the availability of preset voices—the original Moog Modular had none—as well as MIDI and vastly extended sequencer capabilities.

Audio Development Environments

Whereas the virtual analog instruments described above are ready to use out of the box, providing a wealth of preset voice and functions for the performing synthesist, there is another class of flexible audio processing tools requiring a higher level of familiarity with computer programming. An **audio development environment** brings many possible functions under the control of an object-oriented graphical programming environment. The most widely used of these are often free, having been originally developed by research institutions such as IRCAM.

Audio development environments have roots in the musical programming languages first developed at Bell Labs. The IRCAM program *Max* (now combined with *MSP* and *Jitter*) was, in fact, named after Max Mathews, the father of computer music, and *MSP* after Miller S. Puckette, one of the original programmers of *Max*. An *object-oriented programming language* is one in which many sets of modular, predefined functions and instructions can be stored for easy assembly within a graphical user interface. In an environment such as *Max/MSP*, one adds and connects objects on screen that represent instructions for a musically related action or sequence of actions. Each individual object can be modified by the user and many routines already exist in the form of shared libraries. In Figure 10.7, a simple *Max/MSP* patch, read top to bottom, is used to generate a short sequence of notes.

Audio development environments allow for the use of plug-in synthesizers and other DSP modules. Many of these programs are optimized to maximize processing time and are ideally suited for real-time processing and performance. They can be used for functions as simple as MIDI control, but their true power lies in mastering the graphical programming language and use of objects. Composers who dabble in programming their own audio processing routines often use *Max/MSP* to control the performance of such

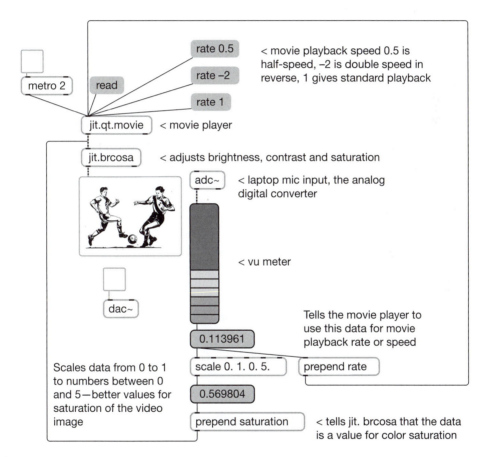

Key: In this patch, the volume of the microphone (audio input) is used to control both the color saturation and the rate of playback of a video image. The microphone comes in through the *adc~* (analog-to-digital converter). The volume is a number between 0 and 1. The *jit.brcosa* object adjusts the saturation: 0 is no color, 1 gives a normal color level and anything above that increases the saturation. The 0 to 1 value from the mic is scaled or *mapped* to 0 to 5 since those are better values for saturation. The volume of the microphone also controls the speed of video playback. This value is tapped off the vu (volume units) meter before it gets scaled. A value of 0 means stop playback, a value of 1 is standard playback with 0.5 being half-speed and 2.0 being double speed.

Figure 10.7   *Max/MSP* simple patch using audio input to control a video image. (Terry Pender)

routines. Being essentially designed for multitasking, *Max/MSP* can trigger audio processing routines at the same time that it manages other aspects of a performance, such as the spatial distribution of sound to loudspeakers, the triggering of MIDI devices, and the multitrack recording of the outcome. The time needed to master an audio development environment such as *Max/MSP* can be daunting, just as learning any programming language. With the increased power of modern laptops, new avenues of exploration have opened up for creative artists. Using programs such as *Max/MSP/Jitter* it is now possible to have real-time control of video, use *openGL* to create 3D animations, employ FFTs to shape and convolve the spectrum of audio signals in real time, and use *convolution reverbs* that are digitally modeled spaces into which you can place your sound or performance. Despite its steep learning curve, *Max/MSP* is widely used by a wide variety of artists, including Autechre, Aphex Twin, David Behrman, Ikue Mori, Matt Rogalsky, Pamela Z, Merzbow, and many more.

Max/MSP is currently available through Cycling '74. Other notable audio development environments include IRCAM's *Open Music* (a favorite of frequential composers), *Csound* and *RTCmix*, *SuperCollider*, *Pd*, and *ChucK*. All of these programs are available for free download with the exception of IRCAM's *Open Music*, and several commercially available programs that are somewhat easier to use, such as Native Instruments *Reaktor* and *Dynamo*, and Applied Acoustic Systems *Tassman*.

By 2006, the state of the art had advanced to the point where Dan Trueman and Perry Cook were able to form PLOrk—The Princeton Laptop Orchestra—the first real-time laptop orchestra.

Software Samplers

Some software applications are designed specifically to record, edit, modify, and optimize audio samples from analog sources. Until recently, most software samplers could only modify previously sampled sounds, the job of capturing the audio having been dedicated to an ancillary hardware device or sampling instrument. Recent improvements in the processing speed of microcomputers have made it possible to capture sound using a software sampler and a line input such as a microphone or stereo cable. The latest generation of software samplers also begin to bridge the gap between sampler and synthesizer, providing means for using samplers to model new instrumental voices. Typical software sampler features include loop editing, time stretching, pitch shifting, sample editing, libraries of preset sample sounds, and special effects processing for reverberation, echo, phasing, and other classic treatments. Some of the manufacturers producing software samplers include E-mu Systems, Native Instruments, TASCAM, Digidesign, Mark of the Unicorn, and Steinberg, among others.

Percussion Synthesizers

Rhythm is such a key component of music that the ability to program and generate percussion sounds has become a dedicated specialty within the world of electronic music. Some of the original applications of digital sampling technology were drum machines produced during the 1980s, some before the advent of MIDI. One of the first direct-synthesis applications on the original Apple Macintosh computer was *MacDrums* (1988), a simple rhythm generator that provided an easy-to-use grid of rows and columns for assigning a sequence of beats to a number of predefined percussion voices. *Percussion synthesizers* remain a special application within software synthesis and are available either

Figure 10.8   Percussion synthesis is one area where many musicians still prefer the tactile interaction provided by using a hardware controller to program drum tracks, such as the Akai MPC5000 controller. (Akai Professional LP)

as standalone programs or plug-ins for use with other host applications. Some programs use digital samples to generate sounds, while others provide percussion sounds using direct synthesis. Distinguishing features of percussion synthesizers include the number of simultaneous voices that can be played, the breadth of available preset sounds, the programming of rhythm patterns, use of polyrhythms, assignment of accents, and other typically rhythmic functions. *Groove Agent 3* by Steinberg includes drum riffs sampled from the live drum styles of celebrity drummers through the use of pre-recorded audio loops.

Percussion synthesis is one area, however, where many musicians still prefer the tactile interaction provided by using a **hardware controller** to program drum tracks. Stand-alone hardware controllers such as the Akai MPC5000, the Korg padKONTROL, and the Alesis ControlPad all have small drum pads played by hand.

The success of software synthesizers has spawned a vibrant cottage industry that provides the latest drum sounds and sample sets of any imaginable sound. Sound designers create sample sets that range from the Vienna Symphonic Library to world music percussion instruments and the latest dance music sounds.

Digital Audio Workstations

The first commercially available hard disk audio recording system was introduced in 1984 by the British firm AMS NEVE Ltd. Designed for professional music and broadcasting studios, the AMS *AudioFile* system combined microprocessor control with hard disk storage and pioneered such digital editing functions as non-linear access to recording sound and non-destructive editing. In 1991, an American-based company named Digidesign introduced *Pro Tools*, an audio editing workstation for the home user that quickly emerged, and evolved, into a de facto industry standard for many composers. The first version of *Pro Tools* only supported four tracks and 16-bit audio, but by 1994 the program had been upgraded to support 24-bit audio and up to 48 tracks. The market for digital audio workstations is currently divided into segments supporting various needs, from the home composer interested in making simple mixes of music to fully featured systems providing high-quality sound that is ready for mastering for commercial distribution.

The fundamental purpose of a **digital audio workstation** is to record, edit, and synchronize multiple tracks of music input. The ability to edit and modify sounds, rearrange parts, add effects, import video to score a picture, and perform various kinds of digital signal processing is now an inherent feature of these programs. Leading professional-grade products include Digidesign *Pro Tools*, Apple Computer *Logic*, Mark of The Unicorn *Digital Performer*, Cakewalk *Sonar*, Steinberg *Cubase*, Ableton *Live*, Propellerhead *Reason* and *Record*, and Cockos *Reaper*. Each of these companies also provides entry-level versions for the composer on a budget.

Most of these programs have also evolved to include some form of music notation capability, allowing one to capture sound played on a MIDI device or develop a score note by note on screen for output as sheet music. More sophisticated, fully featured notational software programs including Make Music *Finale*, Avid/Sibelius *Sibelius*, and the free *LilyPond* are all capable of interfacing directly with the user's digital audio workstation software for use in scoring to picture, exporting both parts and scores for print or as MIDI files that can be imported to the workstation's samplers and synthesizers. Other features that make digital audio workstations increasingly versatile include the addition of synthesizer plug-in programs, digital signal processing of recorded sound, equalization and filtering, and the application of sound effects.

All of the major digital audio workstations are, in one sense, the more expensive and upscale cousins of no-frills audio development environments such as *Max/MSP* and *SuperCollider* (see Figures 10.10 and 10.11). Some digital audio workstations perform quickly enough to be used in live performance with minimum **latency**—the lag in response time experienced when the CPU is performing signal processing and other tasks at the same time.

Physical Modeling

The **physical modeling** of sound is another useful software function for the electronic music composer. Physical modeling refers to the synthesis of sound waves and harmonics that closely resemble those of an acoustic sound source, such as a musical instrument. This technique differs from digital sampling, which converts an analog sound into a digital imprint, because it relies on a scalable set of mathematical formulas, equations, and algorithms that consider the way in which a sound can be modeled based on the changing physical dimensions and materials that comprise the acoustic instrument. Physical models may also consider variables such as the response time of the instrument based on the energy applied by the player.

Physical models intended for music synthesis fall into two categories: lumped and distributed. *Lumped models* simulate mechanical and physiological elements related to a musical instrument—a singer's vocal cords, the hammer mechanism of a piano, contortions of a brass player's lips, and other tangible and mechanical aspects of playing a musical instrument. *Distributed models* concern themselves with the wave propagation properties of physical materials. Distributed models result in digital waveguides, the mathematically defined vibrations of idealized strings, acoustic tubes, and anything else that propagates waves.[14]

Physical modeling functions are available in several software applications, including Cycling '74 *Max*, Modartt *Pianoteq*, Arturia *BRASS*, Apple *Logic Studio*, Native Instruments *Reaktor*, and Keolab *Spicy Guitar*.

Figure 10.9 AudioSculpt from IRCAM is a popular spectral analysis program. (IRCAM)

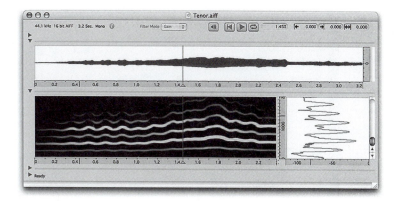

A BRIEF HISTORY OF SOLDERING AND COMPOSING

There is a tradition of non-commercial instrument-making in the field of electronic music. Beginning in the post-World War II years, in the era of vacuum tubes and continuing to the present, there have always been independently operating individuals who took it upon themselves to make their own equipment. These were the persistent soldering composers, the circuit builders who imagined sounds and then found ways to create them. Not content with—and unable to afford—the kinds of synthesizing equipment that only rock stars could buy, they worked with the trickle-down technology of the computer industry, the cheapest chips, and mass-produced kits and circuits. These instrument builders came from the Radio Shack school of electronic music begun by David Tudor and promulgated in successive generations primarily by Gordon Mumma, David Behrman, Pauline Oliveros, Joel Chadabe, Paul DeMarinis, Laurie Spiegel, John Bischoff, Tim Perkis, Nicolas Collins, Ron Kuivila, and Matt Rogalsky, among others. This is a brief history of their work—the computer music tinkerers.

Consider what it would be like for an auto mechanic if the technology of automotive engines changed drastically—fundamentally—every five years. The mechanic either learns the new technology and survives, or falls behind and becomes unemployed. The challenge facing this imaginary auto mechanic is not unlike the actual dilemma faced by electronic musicians over the past 40 or 50 years. These were times of unprecedented paradigm shifts in the field of electronics. Electronic musicians were obligated to muddle through several stages of re-education just to keep pace with the changing working environment of their livelihood. The most rapid changes occurred in the 1970s with the coming of affordable integrated circuits and microcomputers.

The name of Gordon Mumma is frequently intoned with great reverence in any discussion about the origin of tinkering-and-soldering composers. The late David Tudor, once the elder statesman of the movement and about ten years Mumma's senior, admitted that it was Mumma who first made him aware of the possibilities of making his own musical circuits:

> He had been around radio men, broadcast engineers, and electronics buffs for years, so his suggestions were always to the point, although he never offered any solutions. He didn't say "do this," or "do that." He just told me about

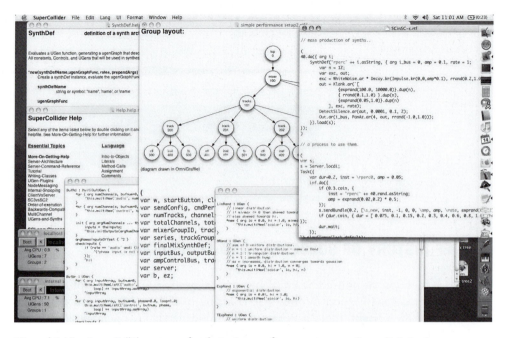

Figure 10.10   SuperCollider screens for designing performance setups. (James McCartney)

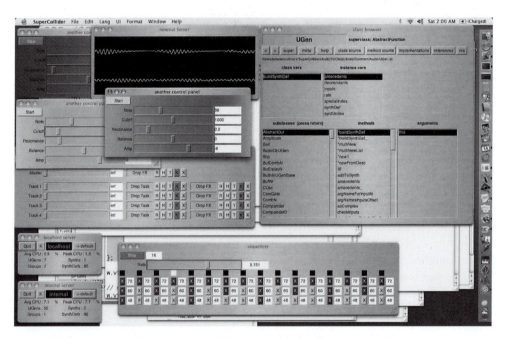

Figure 10.11   SuperCollider screens and windows for defining functions and instruments. (James McCartney)

PHYSICAL MODELING AND INTERACTIVE MUSIC

1 *Speech Songs* (1980) by Charles Dodge
   Early work based on speech synthesis

2 *Idle Chatter* series (1980s) by Paul Lansky
   Speech analysis synthesis (*LPC—linear predictive coding*) and *granular synthesis*

3 *Silicon Valley Breakdown* (1982) by David Jaffe
   Symphony of *physically modeled* plucked string instruments (Strong, Karplus, Jaffe, Smith) created at the Center for Computer Research in Music and Acoustics, Stanford University

4 *Rough Raga Riffs* (1991) by Brad Garton
   Physically modeled (Charlie Sullivan's version of the Karplus-Strong algorithm) and *style-modeled* using *LISP* on a NeXT computer

5 *Still Time* (1994) Paul Lanksy
   Uses Perry Cook's *physical waveguide* model of a slide flute on a NeXT computer

KEY INTERACTIVE/PERFORMANCE ART WORKS

6 *The Hands* (1984–86) by Michel Waisvisz
   Live performance using interactive, gestural hand controllers

7 *Jupiter* (1985–86) Phillipe Manourey
   A work for interactive flute and scored using a *Max* patch programmed by Miller Puckette

8 *Voyager* (1986–88) by George Lewis
   Using software that allows instruments to listen and respond to performers. This work asks the question, "What is an instrument—what is a player?"

9 *Trois études en duo pour piano acoustique interactif* (2008) by Jean-Claude Risset
   The playing of a "live" pianist is transformed and reflected in real time on the same instrument, a Yamaha Disklavier

10 *Fashionably Late For The Relationship* (2008) by R. Luke DuBois
   A feature-length video work that digitally compresses all 72 hours of a continuous street performance by Lián Amaris. The film is an edit of a multi-channel HD shoot of a three-day outdoor performance, accelerated at 60 speed, in which a woman prepares for a night out on the town in slow motion. Created with *Max/MSP/Jitter*

LISTEN

> something that somebody had told him or he said, "maybe you should look at
> the cables," suggestions really of practical help.[15]

A few years later, Mumma tutored David Behrman in the making of audio
components by writing step-by-step do-it-yourself instructions in the form of electronics
experiments:

> I started soldering around 1965. Gordon wrote me. He was in Ann Arbor with the
> ONCE group. We became friends and he started writing me letters. I have a
> collection of letters from him that describe these projects, starting with a preamp
> and a ring modulator, voltage-controlled amplifiers, and envelope followers and
> things like that. You couldn't buy synthesizers yet.[16]

One factor that enabled them to make their own equipment was the tumbling
cost of electronic parts. Mumma began by re-purposing war-surplus parts in the 1950s.
By the mid-1960s, the transistor had become inexpensive and widely available. Transistors
were, in essence, shortcuts for creating circuits. They were more compact than the equivalent
amount of hardwired parts required to perform the same functions. They could also be
powered by batteries, which improved the portability of electronic music components.

A community of electronic music tinkerers began to grow during the mid-1960s.
Oliveros, Mumma, Tudor, and Behrman were trading circuit diagrams. Whenever a
composer friend went to a technical conference where people like Robert Moog and
Hugh Le Caine were speaking, they would quickly circulate any papers being handed
out for the purpose of distributing new and inventive ways of making their own
instruments. The era of the voltage-controlled synthesizer was also upon them, making
available high-quality modular components with which to experiment.

The technology was not inexpensive enough yet for these composers to build
their own synthesizers. So, taking a cue from Mumma's work, they focused on creating
black boxes for modulating and processing acoustic or electronic sounds in real time:
ring modulators, filters, delay circuits, phase shifters, and the like. These were all basic
tools found in the analog composer's bag of tricks.

By the mid-1960s, Mumma had advanced to making performance circuits that could
actively respond to signals during a live performance. His *cybersonic* components, the earliest
of which dated back to 1958, were an example of these. He explained the idea:

> The word "cybersonics" derives from the Greek *kybernan*, meaning to steer or
> guide. The work "sonics," from the Latin *sonus*, pertains to sound. Cybernetics,
> the science of control and communication, is concerned with interactions
> between automatic control and living organisms. The cybersonic sound controls
> are derived from the sound materials themselves and applied directly to their
> own musical modification and articulation.[17]

Mumma's cybersonic circuits self-adjusted to the acoustic properties of sounds in a
given performance space, generating electronic responses in the form of modulated
feedback and control signals that could also trigger other sound-generating circuits. During
this adjustment, some circuits would become imbalanced and "attempt to rebalance
themselves," which was a desirable performance variable for Mumma's experimental

works. For example, in *Medium Size Mograph* (1963) the cybersonic process involved mostly changing the articulation of piano sounds using an envelope follower—that is, readjusting the natural acoustical envelope of the piano's attack and decay so as to have the attack characteristic occur shortly after the piano sound had already begun. "Near the end of the performance an accompaniment was added: a recording of further cybersonic processing of the piano sounds."[18]

Mumma's devotion to the design of interactive, adaptable electronic circuits responsive to both the performing space and the players added a significant new aesthetic consideration to electronic music. For Mumma, who was also a serious student of jazz, his circuits provided something that had been lacking in the development of most electronic music—an element of interaction and improvisation during performance. Mumma's live performance work with the Merce Cunningham Dance Company, John Cage, and the ONCE festivals in Ann Arbor influenced a new generation of composer tinkerers who were practitioners of live, improvised electronic music, including AMM, MEV, David Behrman, Paul DeMarinis, and many others.

Circuits did not always work as expected, which was a constant source of discovery for these composers. Their trial and error approach to making circuits sometimes paid unexpected dividends. The sound character of Behrman's *Runthrough* was largely due to imperfections in an off-the-shelf electronics kit that he used to build one of the key circuits:

> That was a collection of analog homemade circuits that had some components from Lafayette Radio kits that were supposed to make sounds. And sometimes they didn't work properly. I remember one of the components of *Runthrough* was a Lafayette kit for tremolo. It was supposed to make the sound get louder and softer. But somehow because of some feedback or impedance thing it made it go up and down in pitch, which is sort of an accident and the basis for that *Runthrough* sound.[19]

The invention of their own circuits for making music implied a radical shift in the way that music itself was being conceived. The technical pioneers at Bell Labs "thought that they understood music when in fact they only had a very fuzzy understanding of music."[20] Composers who could afford to use commercially manufactured synthesizers were working with cookie-cutter sounds, rhythms, and preset controls. The tinkerers, on the other hand, were in many ways reinventing music itself. Composer Nicolas Collins was well aware of the rules that were being broken:

> You were not tiptoeing slowly away from tonality through chromaticism to serialism. It wasn't like a one-step thing. It was like suddenly wiping the slate clean and starting over again. What if we violate the first rule and then set off? . . . What if we went back and stepped on that bug in the year 2 billion BC. How would life be different? Let's interfere with the past. I think that there was an ethos at that time about starting over.[21]

The shift in technological paradigms during the 1970s and early 1980s drove some composers of electronic music back to the use of packaged synthesizers or out of the genre entirely. There is a noticeable gap in available recordings of computer music during this period, punctuated only occasionally by the experimental works of pioneers of microprocessor music. This situation changed dramatically by the late 1990s when continually dropping prices of personal computers and software made computer music available to a wide audience of potential users in all fields of music.

The most popular open-source electronics prototyping platform is called *Arduino*. Originally created by Massimo Banzi and David Cuartielles in Ivra, Italy, in 2005, they have shipped well over 100,000 Arduino micro-controllers, which can be easily connected to a myriad of sensors that transmit their physical data to programs such as *Max/MSP/Jitter*, *Processing* (Ben Fry and Casey Reas, 2001) or Adobe *Flash* running on a laptop. Arduino was designed especially for artists interested in creating interactive objects or environments. Different types of sensors are hooked up to the Arduino board, including anything from a three-axis accelerometer to a fingerprint scanner.

The growth of the soldering composer paradigm has been helped by the availability of micro-controllers by Arduino and has also benefitted from organizations like Douglas Repetto's *Dorkbot* and *ArtBot* meetings and competitions. Dorkbots were started by Repetto at the Columbia University Computer Music Center in 2001 as monthly gatherings where people get together to share ideas and celebrate people "doing strange things with electricity." There are now close to a hundred groups meeting monthly worldwide under the Dorkbot umbrella from Las Vegas to Mumbai. In addition to Dorkbots, Repetto also launched ArtBots: The Robot Talent Show.

In addition to the resurgence in what is now more commonly referred to as "circuit bending," there has been substantial growth in "handmade" hardware controllers that a performer plays like an "instrument," such as Snyderphonics *Manta*, Brian Crabtree and Kelli Cain's *Monome*, Don Buchla's *Lightning Rods*, *The Eigenharp* and the Haken *Continuum*. The success of these boutique-type controllers has fostered knockoffs from the major manufacturers (Korg *Kaos Pad*) hoping to appeal to digital artists striving to retain that elusive sense of "feel" or "groove" in an all-digital project.

Everything that's old is new again in the production of electronic music with a resurgence of analog hardware, especially drum machines, and software synthesizers that strive to emulate the classic sounds of analog synthesis. There has even been a rebirth for hardware analog synthesizers such as Don Buchla's redesigned patchbay synthesizer, the *Buchla 200*e series with several new modules, the Moog *Slim Phatty*, and the Arturia *Origin Keyboard*.

SUMMARY

- The availability of the microprocessor in 1971 ushered in a paradigm shift from large, mainframe computer music systems to the personal computer.

- One of the first "oscillators on a chip" used by musicians was the inexpensive and widely available Signetics NE/SE566, designed for use in touch-tone telephones.

- A breakthrough in microcomputers came with the arrival of the KIM-1, a predecessor of the Apple computer that used the same chip set. Composers began to adopt the KIM-1 for musical applications during the early 1970s.

- By the early 1980s, the affordability of integrated circuits and microprocessors was directing development toward the production of sophisticated, multifunction sound chips and digital signal processing components for electronic music.

- The availability of MIDI in 1984 incentivized microcomputer makers to develop more robust methods of producing computer music. One result of this activity was the sound card, or expansion card, which could be added to a personal computer to expand its synthesizing capabilities and provide analog audio output of the sound signal.

- Software instruments and digital audio workstation programs provide software tools for the electronic music composer on a microcomputer.

- There is a tradition of instrument-making in the field of electronic music involving composers who construct electronic musical instruments from inexpensive components for the purpose of realizing works for media or live performance.

MILESTONES

The Microprocessor Revolution (1975–91)

Technical and scientific	Year	Artists and music products
– The first microprocessors became available.	1971	
– Audio sound chips became available.	1972	
	1973	– "New Music in New Hampshire" workshop in Chocorua, NH.
– KIM-1 microcomputer introduced.	1975	
– Apple II Plus computer introduced.	1977	
– IBM Personal Computer introduced.	1981	
– Texas Instruments SN76489 Four-Channel Programmable Sound Generator chip introduced.	1983	
– MIDI introduced. – Apple Macintosh computer introduced.	1984	– Mark of the Unicorn released *Professional Composer*, a music notation program for Macintosh.
	1985	– Mark of the Unicorn released *Performer*, a MIDI sequencing program for Macintosh.
– *Sound Blaster* PC sound card introduced.	1988	– *MacDrums* drum synthesizer introduced.
	1989	– The *Max* audio development environment was introduced by IRCAM.
	1991	– Digidesign introduced *Pro Tools* digital audio workstation software.

CHAPTER 11

The Principles of Computer Music

It is a popular assumption that the computer can create any sound. While this may be theoretically possible, the difficulty lies in specifying the sound with sufficient accuracy without getting bogged down in minute details.[1]
—John Strawn

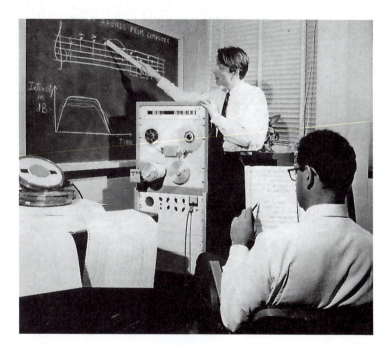

Jean-Claude Risset describing computer analysis of instrumental sound spectra at Bell Labs, 1968. (Lucent/Bell Labs)

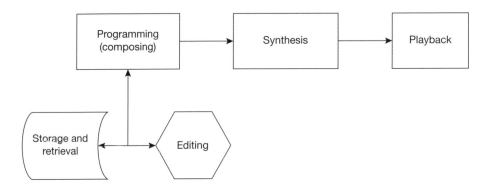

Figure 11.1   Five basic stages of computer music production.

As explored in the previous chapters, the foundations of computer music were laid down even before the term "digital" was applied to computers. Experiments at RCA, Siemens, and the University of Illinois were especially important in the exploration of machine-assisted composing and sound synthesis techniques. In each case, composition using binary codes aided the musician in creating a piece of music in machine-readable form. Although the audio output from such systems was generated using analog synthesis techniques, such early experiments with computers established a broader working approach to music development encompassing several sub-disciplines: the *programming* of musical parameters using a central processor, the *storage and retrieval* of said parameters, audio *synthesis* of the parameters, *editing*, and the *playback or synthesis* of completed works represented by such parameters (see Figure 11.1). In early computer music environments, playback or recording of the synthesized result may frequently have involved additional editing using the analog tape medium. By the late 1970s, however, the availability of microprocessors, more affordable computer memory and storage, and the development of music-related software led to the continuing improvement and affordability of digital music tools for all aspects of the process, from composing to synthesis and the management of live real-time performance.

This chapter leaps ahead from the history of the medium to the present, providing background on the basic processes and terminology associated with digital music synthesis and audio processing. Digital audio processing builds on the principles of analog sound synthesis described in Chapter 7. The reader should continue to turn back to that chapter and other earlier chapters for descriptions of the basic lexicon of editing and sound processing techniques that remain constant in the world of digitally produced electronic music. Digital synthesis and audio processing represents a paradigm shift from analog synthesis—and voltage-controlled synthesis in particular—to the use of the computer and associated software to provide similar and expanded music production capabilities.

DIGITAL AUDIO PROCESSING

An analog system uses continuous means to represent changing values. Small fluctuations in an analog system are meaningful and can be measured. The measurement is also made through a medium that operates in tandem with the thing being measured. An old-fashioned mechanical bathroom scale is an example of an analog device: it displays a person's weight as a reading using the medium of a beam scale and the movement of a needle on a gauge to provide a reading. The degree of movement of the needle is dependent on the amount of weight on the scale and this movement is said to be analogous to the weight.

In electrical devices, such as an analog synthesizer, some property of electrical voltage (e.g. frequency, amplitude) served as the medium to convey a signal. The signal, in turn, represented sound of a given quality, control voltage, or some other property of sound manipulation. The turning of a dial, the transmission of a voltage pulse using a sequencer, and other analog processes were the driving force behind such technology. The output of an analog electronic music system was a voltage that represented the shape and characteristics of its corresponding air pressure waveform.

Whereas an analog system operates on the basis of continuous values, digital systems operate on the basis of discrete values. Quantities are expressed as numbers. A digital bathroom scale translates one's weight into a specific number value that is then displayed on a digital display. This differs from the analog bathroom scale, which uses a continuously traveling meter to represent one's weight.

In a digital music system, quantities representing the frequency, amplitude, timbre, duration, and envelope of a sound are also expressed as discrete numbers. Numbers are input and calculated to produce the desired results, such as increases in volume, or changes in timbre. Instructions for making these changes might be made through software on a computer or directly from physical controls (e.g. dials and switches) on an electronic musical instrument.

Sound in the real world is formed by a continuous acoustic waveform. A digital system converts this analog waveform into numeric, binary data that can be stored, processed, and then reproduced again as an analogous air pressure waveform.

A *binary* number is a number for which each individual digit may have two values: 0 or 1, or On and Off. Computers are designed to interpret and manipulate ordinary decimal numbers that are stored as binary numbers using only 1s and 0s. A binary notation system is ideal for use with computers because digital electronic circuits exist in only one of two states: On or Off. A binary number is composed of any sequence of binary digits, or *bits*, each digit of which is represented by 0 or 1. A pattern of bits comprises the content of a command or instruction. By example, two bits can assume four different configurations—00, 01, 10, 11—providing a compact method of conveying distinct values in binary code. Each bit, reading from the right, represents a greater power of two, thus counting from zero to three is accomplished by the four two-bit numbers in the previous sentence. The *byte* is a universally accepted convention for creating binary code and consists of eight bits, making up to 256 distinct values possible with each byte. Computer instructions, such as those described for MIDI in Chapter 8, may comprise one or more bytes depending on the specification of the assigned programming language. Instructions may also vary in byte length depending on the purpose. This system using eight-bit bytes (two values per bit) is also called the *hexadecimal* system and was introduced in 1956 by the computer maker IBM.

Computers are operated by providing a list of procedures (algorithms) that can be organized as a sequence of instructions using binary code. A *programming language* is used to communicate such instructions to a given computer. Many different programming languages have been devised over the years for the creation of music-related applications, many of which were mentioned in the previous chapter about the early history of computer music. The first general purpose music languages developed for a computer were *MUSIC I* through *MUSIC V* (1957–68) by Max Mathews, who worked at Bell Laboratories.

Digital Sound Resources and Synthesis

Sound can be generated from a computer either by synthesizing original tones from scratch or by converting analog audio signals into a digital signal that can be further manipulated. In either case, a computer represents sound as discrete numeric values. The ability to represent analog musical information in this way provides the composer and musician with many options for managing, playing, editing, and performing music.

Several techniques have been developed over the years to create sounds using computers and digital synthesizers. These include *direct digital synthesis*, *complete sampling*, *note sampling*, and *wavetable synthesis*.

Direct Digital Synthesis

Direct digital synthesis creates a sound from numeric values generated through the use of a computer music programming language. The process of building a sound from scratch is not unlike that employed by early electronic music composers who used entirely analog techniques, except that the use of a computer can greatly simplify the mathematical aspects of defining, modifying, storing, and playing sounds.

The digital oscillator is the sound-generating circuit or program of a computer-based music system. A digital oscillator represents a waveform as a series of numbers. Its output is converted to a smooth, analog waveform that can played through a loudspeaker. Programmatic controls, or algorithms, determine the characteristics of a waveform produced by a digital oscillator. The type of waveform (e.g. sine, sawtooth, triangle, pulse), its frequency, and amplitude are all numerically controlled aspects of a digital oscillator. Because a digital oscillator is simply a table of numbers, it can be easily manipulated mathematically to produce complex sounds: for instance, frequency modulation effects may be obtained by continuously varying the rate at which the table is read. The accurate reproduction of complex real-world instrumental sounds, such as those of the violin or piano, are usually accomplished with special techniques that rely on wavetable synthesis. Makers of digital synthesizers usually employ their own proprietary wavetables for instrumental sounds.

Csound is an example of a programming language used to synthesize sound directly through a computer. It was originally developed by Barry Vercoe at MIT and continues to be upgraded as an open-source programming language. The program is controlled by simple text command statements that enable it to render sound through a digital audio device such as a sound card or other digital synthesizer. Modules within *Csound* include:

- **Orchestra file**. A text file in which the composer describes, using special abbreviations, the "instruments" they wish to use.
- **Score file**. A second text file in which the composer defines what sound events are going to be played, using which instruments, and how they will be organized in time.

The score file contains *note lists* for activating an instrument, tabular *function tables* for creating waveshapes, envelopes, and other sound-related properties, and other commands used to direct the non-sound-generating aspects of a work such as its organization and tempo.

The *Csound* function table (f-table) is used for the direct synthesis of sounds. For example, the following command statement generates a sine wave with a 16-point sample resolution per wave cycle:[2]

$$f\ 101\ 0\ 16\ 10\ 1$$

Csound can also represent function tables visually. Figure 11.2 illustrates the above coded statement, showing 16 points of the sine wave and related numeric values.

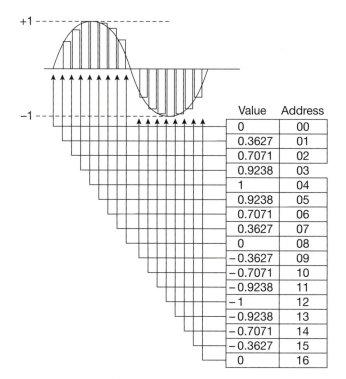

Value	Address
0	00
0.3627	01
0.7071	02
0.9238	03
1	04
0.9238	05
0.7071	06
0.3627	07
0	08
−0.3627	09
−0.7071	10
−0.9238	11
−1	12
−0.9238	13
−0.7071	14
−0.3627	15
0	16

Figure 11.2   A 16-point sine wave function definition in *Csound*. (After Boulanger, 2007)

Programming languages such as *Csound, RTCmix, SuperCollider, Pd (Pure Data), ChucK,* and *Max/MSP/Jitter* can usually be supplemented with function tables and algorithms for generating sounds that have been previously developed, but the composer is able to invent new sounds as well by directly inputting numeric values for the desired sounds.

Complete Sampling

A **sample** is a numerical representation of an analog sound that can be converted back to a voltage for the purpose of driving a loudspeaker. Samples can be used in various ways, the most straightforward being the *complete sample*. In this form, a sample is the

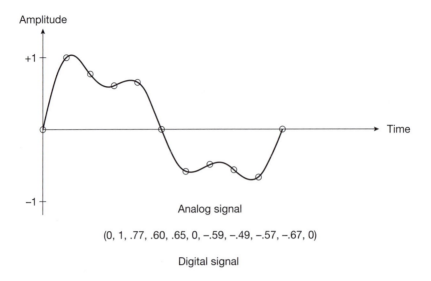

Figure 11.3   Digital sampling of analog sounds. (After Mathews, 1969)

equivalent of an analog tape recording of a sound from the real world. Sound for the complete sample is typically captured using a microphone or a line input from an electronic source, such as a turntable, CD player, or other device with analog sound output. An **analog-to-digital converter (ADC)** is used to convert analog sound to digital form by *sampling* the analog signal many times per second and storing those instantaneous values as a table in memory or in a file. On the playback end of the process, a **digital-to-analog converter (DAC)** is used to reverse the process, reading the digital values sequentially, and smoothing them out into a continuous analog signal again, which can be made audible through a loudspeaker system. Figure 11.3 visually depicts the sampling process.

A complete sample can be of any length that computer memory and storage capacity will allow. The sound is captured as a complete unit or passage of the original, such as a person speaking a phrase or the recording of a bird's song. Once sampled, audio processing software can be used to edit, manipulate, and otherwise modify the sample for the purposes of composing music. This practice is the digital equivalent of tape composition.

The **sampling rate** is a setting that determines how many times per second an analog sound source will be sampled. A single sample is a number corresponding to a measurement of the voltage level of the analog signal at one moment in time. The higher the sampling rate (the closer together the measurements of the analog signal), the better the digital representation of the analog sound's waveform. Figures 11.4 and 11.5 visually depict the sampling process.

The size of the binary number used to represent each digital sample is another factor affecting its quality. The larger the number, the greater the range of values that can represent gradations of amplitude of the analog signal. Early sampling instruments employed 8 or 12-bit values. Audio CDs, introduced in the 1980s, employ a 16-bit standard. Common sampling resolutions today include 24- and 48-bit levels. The choice of resolution depends on whatever quality is acceptable for a given sound and the amount

(a)

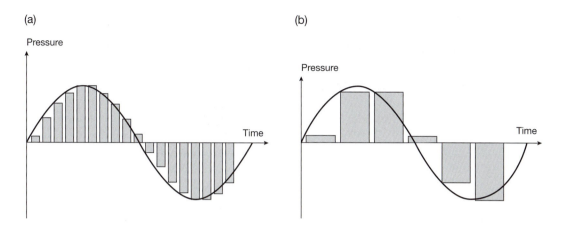

(b)

Figure 11.4 Digital sampling rates. (After Mathews, 1969)

of storage available to store it. An 8-bit sample provides 256 gradations of amplitude, a 12-bit sample provides 4,096 gradations, and a 16-bit sample provides a resolution of 65,536 gradations of amplitude, now considered an acceptable but not ideal resolution for high-end audio work. The higher the sampling rate and the greater the number of bits used to represent an analog signal, the more detail can be achieved when manipulating the sampled sound: for instance, audibly smoother reverberation effects and fade-outs. Sometimes, however, low sampling rates and bit depths are still deliberately used by electronic musicians to provide "gritty" sound qualities.

The sampling rate, bit depth, and duration of a sample determine how much storage space it will require. Note that the analog sound content itself has no bearing on the size of the digitized file—silence requires just as much space to sample as the sound of a full orchestra. Audio CDs have a resolution of 16-bits and a sampling rate of 44.1 kHz (44,100 samples per second), which requires about 183 K of storage per second, or 11 MB per minute of sampled stereo analog sound. This factor is reduced dramatically if the resolution is set for 8-bits and the sampling rate to 22 kHz, requiring more than

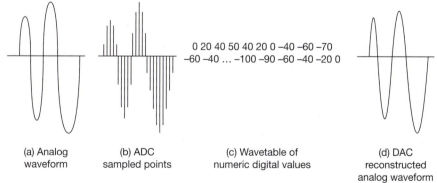

0 20 40 50 40 20 0 −40 −60 −70
−60 −40 ... −100 −90 −60 −40 −20 0

(a) Analog
waveform

(b) ADC
sampled points

(c) Wavetable of
numeric digital values

(d) DAC
reconstructed
analog waveform
from sampled
points

Figure 11.5 Steps in the sampling of sounds. (After Williams, 1999)

four times less storage at about 2.5 MB. Much consumer and professional audio software now offers higher bit depths of 24 or 48 bits, and sampling rates of 96 kHz or even greater, producing correspondingly large sound files. Some types of audio, such as the spoken word, do not always require the highest-quality settings, so composers can experiment with the level of quality that best suits their purposes.

Many of the techniques associated with tape editing and analog sound processing are shared by software programs designed for editing and processing digital samples. As in any computer editing environment, one has the ability to cut and paste content, which is the equivalent of using a razor blade and splicing tape to make broad additions, deletions, and reorganizations of sounds. However, digital editing has obvious advantages over the magnetic tape equivalent, not the least of which is that it allows one to isolate such edits by track and to undo unwanted changes. Digital editing provides many other functions as well and offers processing tools for modifying even small parts of a work without affecting the whole: typically, edits are now made in software only, without modifying the original samples stored on hard disk or other storage medium. A catalog of common audio editing and processing terms is offered in Tables 11.1 and 11.2. Software used to edit sound may offer a variety of ways to view, test, and construct audio signals. A basic editing screen for a two-track composition is seen in Figure 11.6.

Table 11.1 **Common digital audio editing functions**

Feature	Function
Cut, copy, paste	Removes, copies, and inserts audio; may be possible by individual tracks
Crop	Removes all but the selected audio
Silence	Replaces any selected portion of an audio track with silence
Insert	Inserts another audio signal (apart from the audio being edited) at a selected insertion point; controls are usually provided for specifying the type, duration, frequency, or other dynamics of the audio to be inserted; types of audio often include silence, noise, simple tone (sine, sawtooth, triangle, pulse), or a frequency-modulated sine wave
Loop	Repeats an entire audio file or only loops a selected part; for a performance sample player, *sustain loop* allows a loop to occur only while a key is depressed; *release loop* allows a loop to continue after a key is released
Edit splice	For a performance sample player, allows two samples to be joined end to end to form a loop; a *butt* control provides an immediate jump from one sample to the other; *crossfade* provides a gradual transition from one sample to the other
Start/end point	Deletes unwanted sound or silence at the start or end of a sampled sound
Mix/merge	Mixes audio stored in the computer's memory clipboard (from a cut or copy function) with another passage of sound; the amplitude of the incoming audio can be adjusted
Swap channels	Switches the contents of designated channels
Fourier spectrum analysis	Provides a frequency spectrum analysis of the selected audio, graphing the average levels of various frequency bands

Table 11.2   **Common digital audio processing functions**

Feature	Process
Normalize	Sets the amplitude of the loudest part of the sound to a target level (e.g. specific dB level or a percentage of its current state) and then scales the rest of the audio file accordingly; can be done by individual track or by all tracks
Amplitude/ volume	Increases or decreases the volume of selected audio to a target level (e.g. specific dB level or a percentage of its current state)
Resample	Changes the sampling rate and bit depth for a given sample
Adjust pitch/ speed	Like changing the speed of a tape deck, adjusting the sampling rate will change the pitch and duration of a sound; programs facilitate pitch/speed changes by making it possible to adjust any one of three factors: sampling rate, pitch (as a percentage of original sample), and duration
Reverse	Plays the audio file backwards
Envelope	Designs a custom envelope for a selected sound or sample; this is often done using an amplitude scale and the ability to set adjustable points throughout the span of the selected audio signal
Fade in/ fade out	Applies a preset or adjustable envelope to fade in a sound from silence or fade out a sound to silence
Compressor	Reduces the differences in volume between the loudest and quietest parts of an audio file; used to compensate for portions of the file that are too loud; performed dynamically after setting thresholds for attack and release times (in microseconds) and compression ratio
Expander	Increases the differences in volume between the loudest and quietest parts of an audio file; used to compensate for portions of the file that are too quiet; performed dynamically after setting thresholds for attack and release times (in microseconds) and compression ratio
Noise gate	An extreme "expander" that silences any audio that falls beneath a threshold volume; can be used to create silence between sounds such as drum beats or spoken dialog
Add noise	Adds white noise or other available preset noise types
Filter	Filters specific frequency bands within the spectrum of an audio file; *graphic EQ* provides preset options for filtering (e.g. 3-band, 10-band, custom); *high-pass* permits frequencies above a specified level to pass; *low-pass* permits frequencies below a specified level to pass
Chorus	Adds one or more slightly delayed versions of a sound to its original signal to create depth and the impression of multiple voices; this is done by providing variable-length delay on top of the original audio signal; a low-frequency oscillator (LFO) (e.g. sine or triangle wave) controls the amount of delay and the degree of variance from the pitch of the original; the shape of the delay sweep over the original audio signal is a function of the waveshape (e.g. smooth sine wave or angular triangle wave)
Delay/echo	Adds a specified degree of echo/delay to a signal; adjusts the proportion of the original audio versus echo that can be heard; with *feedback*, the signal gradually fades as it repeats; without feedback, the signal repeats at 100 percent of its original gain, like a tape loop
Reverberation	Adds natural reverberation to an audio signal; presets are often provided for hypothetical spaces, such as a room, a hall, or a stadium
Flanger/ phaser	Adds a phasing effect in which the original audio signal is mixed with an exact copy that slowly goes in and out of phase with the original; like Chorus, settings can be adjusted for an LFO that controls the sweep and the amplitude levels of the signals being phased

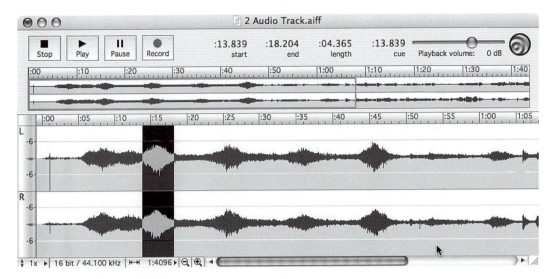

Figure 11.6   Typical sound editing software provides a means to play, edit, and record sounds using a visualization of the sound as a guide. (Sound Studio)

Spectral Editors

There is now a new breed of **spectral editors** such as Michael Klingbeil's *SPEAR* (available for free) and *AudioSculpt* from IRCAM (see Chapter 10). These software editors give the user the ability to analyze, edit and transform the spectrum of a sound, alter the timbre by adjusting the relative strength of various partials above the fundamental frequency, change the length of a sound file without altering its pitch, or alter the pitch without altering the length of the sound.

Note Sampling

In addition to making a complete sample—the digital equivalent to making an analog tape recording of a sound from the real world—a smaller sample can also be made and then scaled to operate at different control points on a keyboard. Known as **note sampling**, this approach to digital sound generation has roots in the early computer music work of Max Mathews and Jean-Claude Risset at Bell Labs during the mid-1960s. Even with the ability to directly synthesize tones on a computer using additive synthesis techniques, the properties of psychoacoustic timbres associated with real instruments made the direct computing of interesting sounds difficult. "The synthetic sounds produced in the late fifties and the early sixties lacked variety, richness and identity," remarked Risset. "One could not get exciting new sounds by varying parameters haphazardly."[3] Without the benefit of sampling technology, their approach was to use a computer to first analyze the recorded tonal parameters of acoustic instruments and then mathematically reconstruct those tones in the form of algorithms to synthesize similar sounds. Mathews and Risset input musical sounds into a mainframe computer using an experimental analog-to-digital converter designed at Bell Labs. The results often compared favorably with the sounds of acoustic instruments, although some classes of sounds such as those of brass instruments presented unique challenges.[4] Risset discovered that the signatory elements of an instrument were found in its overtone structure and envelope characteristics, a finding that led to his systematic analysis of a variety of instrumental sounds and the programming of their numeric values. By 1969, Risset had compiled a substantial catalog of digital instrument parameters that served as the foundation for the next generation of digital synthesis development.

The work of Mathews and Risset captured all of the characteristics of a single note or tone played by an instrument: the frequency spectrum, amplitude, and envelope of the sound. This basic technique was later applied to the first commercially available digital samplers such as the Fairlight CMI (1979) and E-mu Emulator (1981).

Note sampling digitally captures the parameters of a single tone played on an instrument. Once loaded into a computer or digital musical instrument, the sample can be transposed up and down the scale as it is played on the keyboard. The most accurate method of reproducing such sampled tones on a keyboard is to provide a sample for every individual note, thus avoiding distortion that naturally occurs when transposing a single note sample across one or more octaves. This technique, called **multisampling**, can be applied to every note on the keyboard or for narrow pitch ranges when software can be used to manage an accurate transposition of tones up and down a small section of the scale. Multiple samples are the most effective way to accurately reproduce an instrument's timbres for each note.

Wavetable Synthesis

There are three major kinds of wavetable synthesis techniques: additive, subtractive, and modulation. Digital electronic music systems and software can take advantage of traditional additive and subtractive approaches to synthesis, the fundamentals of which are discussed in earlier chapters on analog processes. As a quick review, *additive synthesis* comprises the combining of elementary waveforms to create a more complex waveform. *Subtractive synthesis* does quite the opposite, beginning with a spectrally rich audio signal and using filters to omit unwanted portions. In the case of additive and subtractive synthesis, processes for generating envelopes, modulating sounds, and other signal processing functions can be sequenced, programmed, and automated, often employing linear, time-based functions.

The frequency of a digital waveform can be specified directly in hertz or through the use of a **wavetable**. A wavetable is a mathematical method for defining *one cycle* of a specified waveform. The numeric values of the waveform may be derived from an analog sample or through direct digital synthesis, as described above in relation to *Csound*. The wavetable contains a sequence of numbers that define the shape of a waveform throughout each part of its cycle. Unlike a longer sample of a musical instrument, which captures the envelope and amplitude characteristics of a tone, a wavetable only deals with harmonic spectral data—the frequency and overtones of a single wave cycle. A waveform lookup table extrapolates values needed to modify a waveform when its characteristics are changed. Wavetables are stored in memory and are often selectable either by controls on the operating panel of a digital synthesizer or as a command in the algorithms used in software synthesis. Ancillary algorithms and tables are used to modify the amplitude, envelope, and other characteristics of a tone generated using wavetable synthesis.

While the term "sample" is commonly used to refer to any digitally recorded sound, it more specifically refers to each instananeous value that is an element of the digital representation of a sound: a wavetable cycle is comprised of many such single samples, each representing microseconds of the total cycle.

A mathematical model called the **Nyquist sampling theorem** provides guidance for the creation of the most accurate samples. According to this theorem, a sound may be adequately recorded digitally only if it is sampled at a frequency at least twice that of the highest desired frequency present in that sound. The upper limit of human hearing is around 20 kHz: the Nyquist sampling theorem is the reason why the sampling rate used in commercial CD recordings is slightly more than twice that at 44.1 kHz. To use a sampling rate less than twice the highest frequency results in distortion in the resulting digital recording: frequency "aliasing" or "foldover" results, which are audible as unpleasant lower-frequency components in the digital representation.

A wavetable stores waveforms as numerical values representing only a single cycle of a periodic wave. To play a tone, the computer accesses the wavetable in a rapidly repeating cycle to reproduce a continuous sound. The concept of sampling rate is also important to wavetable synthesis even if the numeric values are generated by direct synthesis. A wavetable with a low sampling rate will only reproduce the rough shape of a sound. A more robust sampling rate will fill in gaps and produce a more faithful reproduction of the wave.

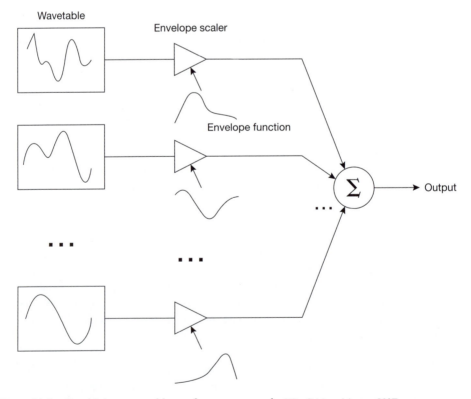

Figure 11.7 Combining wavetables to form new sounds. (After Bristow-Johnson, 2007)

More than one wavetable can be mixed to change characteristics of the sound over time. Figure 11.7 is an example of a process using envelope generators to manage the mixing of wavetables—a process called *sequential crossfading* or *windowing*, which is used as a method of generating evolving timbres.

The classic application of wavetable synthesis, developed by Mathews and associates at Bell Labs, was based on a time domain process and direct synthesis in which predefined waveform cycles were stored in memory and repeated to create periodic waveforms. Wavetable synthesis can also be approached from the frequency domain, using a harmonic spectrum based on direct input of numeric values or spectral analysis of sampled tones. Spectral wavetable synthesis provides **interpolation** among timbres, a task made easier because phase can be readily normalized using this kind of synthesis.[5]

Wavetables have proved to be a valuable shorthand method of storing pre-programmed sounds and have been used widely to create preset instrumental voices for digital music synthesizers. Without the use of wavetable synthesis, the complex nature of changing wave parameters in real time as well as mixing and crossfading from one instrumental voice to another is cumbersome to manage, even for a talented programmer.

Frequency Modulation Technique

Frequency modulation (FM) grew from the analog spectrum analysis efforts at Bell Labs and Stanford University. The early work of Mathews and Risset at Bell Labs was characterized as *synthesis from analysis*, in which the frequency spectra of acoustic sounds were analysed, and then experimentally re-synthesized with the computer, using the data obtained. This proved to be very successful. Following on from the work of Risset and Mathews, John Chowning developed FM synthesis as a means of emulating the qualities of acoustic instruments, using a method he described as *analysis by synthesis*, since it involved first experimentally synthesizing tones and then comparing them with acoustic instruments (see Figure 11.8).[6]

Chowning's research at Stanford University was greatly influenced by Mathews and Risset and their analysis of the frequency spectra of synthesized and natural sounds. Chowning devised a unique application of the tried-and-true process of frequency modulation. In traditional FM applications, a subsonic low-frequency oscillator (the *modulator*) was used to change the pitch of an oscillator in an audible frequency range (the *carrier*). A typical result was a slightly rising and falling periodic pitch variation (*vibrato*) in the carrier. Using a computer to simplify the management of complex frequency modulation, Chowning found that, when the modulating frequency entered the audio

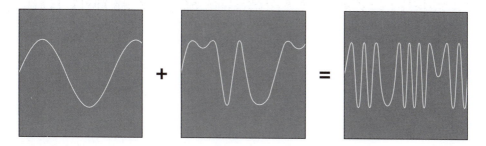

Figure 11.8   Classic FM synthesis combines two simple sine waves to generate a third that is more complex. (After Aikin, 2003)

range (upwards of about 20 Hz), the rising and falling of the pitch of the carrier was no longer heard as vibrato, but rather as a complex change in its spectrum (see Figure 11.9). Chowning was able to patent his findings, which provided an elegant and efficient technique for modifying the timbre or spectral qualities of digitally synthesized sounds. This technique is called *non-linear* because a wide spectrum of overtones is produced from the modification of relatively few inputs and parameters. Frequency modulation (FM) produces a rich, and precisely definable, assortment of sidebands around the carrier frequency. The depth of pitch variation in the carrier signal is "proportional to the amplitude of the modulating wave."[7] The harmonic content of a signal produced using FM synthesis is determined by the ratio of the carrier and modulating frequencies and the depth of modulation.[8] In practice, this means that the timbre of one oscillator could be controlled by the another, and that both could be managed using envelope generators to dynamically modify the timbre and shape of a note. As the modulating wave gets louder, the overtones become more complex.

Chowning's FM technique required fairly simply algorithms that could be processed by early solid-state digital synthesizers and analog–digital hybrids. Yamaha acquired rights to Chowning's algorithms and produced the Yamaha DX (1983) family of FM synthesizers, arguably the best-selling synthesizers of the last 50 years. The technique was equally good at approximating the sounds of acoustic instruments as well as generating a uniquely electronic sound palette.

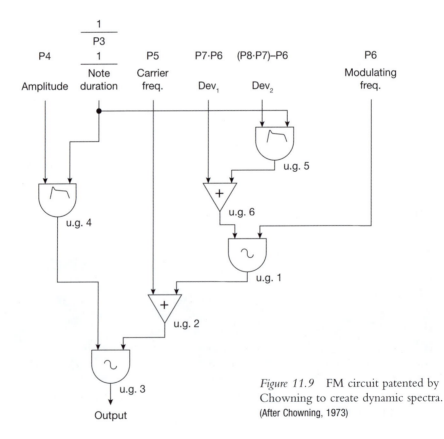

Figure 11.9 FM circuit patented by Chowning to create dynamic spectra. (After Chowning, 1973)

The use of the computer to synthesize waveforms digitally has led to many algorithmic approaches to sound analysis and generation, each using numeric tables to replicate given audio parameters. The following sections describe some of the most prominent of these.

Waveshaping Synthesis

Also known as *distortion* or *non-linear synthesis*, **wave-shaping synthesis** is similar to FM synthesis in that complex changes are made to an audio signal by warping it according to another signal, or mathematical function. Waveshaping is a method of developing dynamically evolving sound spectra for complex timbres. It distorts an audio signal in order to modify its waveform. Foundational waveshaping work was done by Risset who used it to replicate the timbres of complex acoustic sounds such as that of a trumpet. Waveshaping requires a *non-linear* processor. Rather than passing a waveform through its circuitry intact—as with a *linear* processor such as an amplifier—a non-linear processor modifies the waveform in direct proportion to the amplitude of the input circuit (see Figure 11.10). When a waveform is modified in this way, its frequency spectrum is altered, giving the output signal a different timbre from that which was fed into the processor.[9]

A lookup table provides algorithms for the non-linear processing function. In the non-linear processor, the *transfer function* is a calculation that determines output values based on input values. Figure 11.11 illustrates the change in harmonic content of a waveform during waveshaping synthesis.

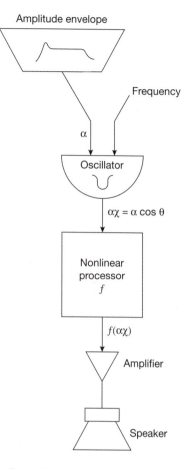

Figure 11.10   Basic waveshaping software instrument. (After Roads, 1979)

Like FM synthesis, waveshaping is more efficient in changing the timbre of a sound than additive synthesis and lends itself to the use of computational tables, or indexes, to store algorithmic values. Because it uses polynomial expressions in its transfer function, waveshaping provides the ability to limit the output spectrum to a specified bandwidth, a feature not inherent in FM synthesis, which is more prone to *aliasing*—distortion artifacts of the FM signal sampling technique.

Granular Synthesis

Granular synthesis introduced a different paradigm for conceptualizing sound signals. Based on the pioneering work in 1947 by Hungarian physicist Dennis Gabor (1900–79), granular synthesis breaks the audio signal down into small overlapping *grains* typically lasting no more than 50 microseconds. This concept was in stark contrast to traditional wave theory supported by the Fourier analysis of frequency cycles. Gabor stated that "sound has a time pattern as well as a frequency pattern,"[10] and set about to develop a mathematical principle for representing sound as being composed of minute grains, each with its own waveform, envelope, duration, density, and position in space. The

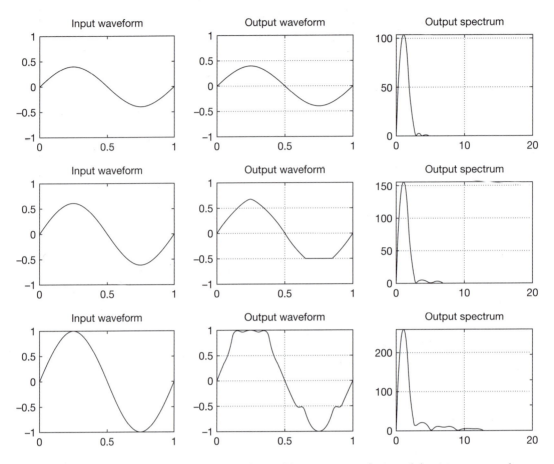

Figure 11.11   Transfer function: The shape of the output waveform, and thus its spectrum, changes with the amplitude of the input signal, becoming richer as the amplitude increases. (After Smythe, 2007)

complexities of working with individual grains becomes quickly evident if one considers the challenge of controlling all of the parameters for each of the grains for even a minute.[11] Iannis Xenakis was probably the first composer to develop compositional strategies for using grains of sound. Curtis Roads of the University of California was one of the first computer music composers to successfully translate Gabor's theories into a practical programming environment. Roads realized that one of the first challenges of granular synthesis was to find a practical way to control all of the possible parameters of grains. In 1975, using a mainframe computer, he developed a program for "compositional control" that provided "a higher level unit of organization for the grains."[12] The raw material is conceptually viewed as a cloud consisting of hundreds of thousands of grains. Because so many parameters need to be set, Roads created an interface that only required the composer to define a beginning set of parameters, after which the program would systematically generate the traits for each individual grain. The higher-level organization of the material consisted of *events*, each of which was comprised of data for the beginning time and duration of a sound as well as the initial setting and rate of change for a waveform, center frequency, bandwidth, grain density, and amplitude, all of which led to a unique dispersal pattern of grains during an event. One resulting piece was *prototype* (1975), a graphical representation of which is shown in Figure 11.12.

Improvements to the processing speed of computers have made granular synthesis a more practical technique explored by contemporary composers. In the mid-1980s, Canadian composer Barry Truax developed the first real-time system for granular synthesis at his PODX studio at Simon Fraser University, British Columbia, and numerous electroacoustic works were composed with this system by him and many other visiting composers. Granular synthesis is now commonly available as a feature of numerous plug-ins for commercial music software.

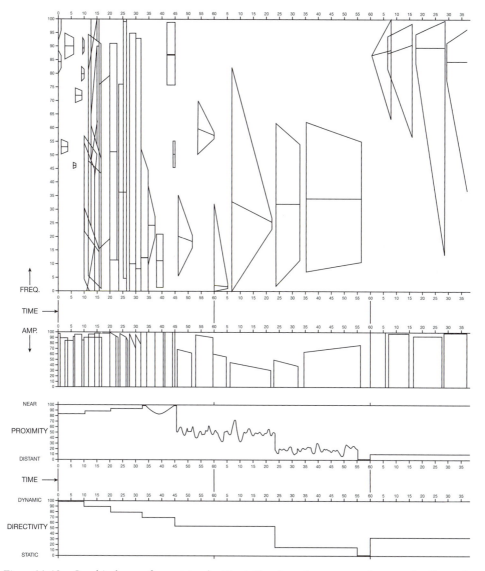

Figure 11.12   Graphical score for *prototype* by Curtis Roads, an important early example of granular synthesis using large computers. (Roads, 1978)

In practice, granular synthesis often begins with a sound sample and divides it up into small grains of sound. By controlling parameters such as grain size, the frequency of individual grains, their density, the way that grains might overlap, and degrees of randomness introduced into the process, one can generate interesting, amorphous effects and transformations of familiar sounds. A sound may be modified in pitch without changing its duration, and changed in duration without affecting its pitch. It is possible to move "through" a sample extremely slowly, and even "freeze" a sound in the middle—a method of exploring the harmonic content of a sound that was previously impossible.

EARLY COMPUTER SYNTHESIS

1 *Numerology* (1960) by Max Mathews
   Direct computer synthesis using an IBM 7090 mainframe computer and the *MUSIC III* programming language

2 *Analog #1: Noise Study* (1961) by James Tenney
   Used direct synthesis and filtering of noise bands at Bell Labs' facilities

3 *Computer Cantata* (1963) by Lejaren Hiller
   Direct computer synthesis using an IBM 7094 mainframe computer and the *MUSICOMP* programming language

4 *Mutations I* (1969) by Jean-Claude Risset
   Used frequency modulation

5 *The Earth's Magnetic Field* (1970) by Charles Dodge
   Used an IBM mainframe computer and the *MUSIC 4BF* programming language to convert geophysical data regarding the Earth's magnetic field into music

6 *Appalachian Grove I* (1974) by Laurie Spiegel
   Used the *GROOVE* program at Bell Labs

7 *prototype* (1975) by Curtis Roads
   Used granular synthesis

8 *Stria* (1977) by John Chowning
   Used the composer's patented FM synthesis algorithms

9 *Chreode* (1983) by Jean-Baptiste Barriere
   Granular synthesis using the *Chant* program at IRCAM. Computer-controlled organization of material—a grammar of musical processes prepared with IRCAM's *Formes* software.

10 *Riverrun* (1986) by Barry Truax
   Composed using only granulated sampled sound, using Truax's real-time PODX system

NOISE REDUCTION

The presence of unwanted noise or hiss in analog recordings was a vexing problem for manufacturers of tape recorders and other analog components. The biggest noise-contributing culprit was the magnetic tape process itself. There was a direct correspondence between the size of the magnetic oxide particles that could be slurried onto the emulsion of the recording tape and the degree of resulting *tape hiss*. The amount of noise was also affected by tape speed and interference caused by the buildup of a residual magnetic charge on the head, a natural by-product of the tape recording process. Other components in an analog system also contributed degrees of noise, from loose or inferior cable connections to improper grounding. This problem led to the development of several techniques for reducing noise in an analog audio recording. These developments are important to the understanding of digital audio because of the base of knowledge gained in developing noise reduction circuits and their implications for digital audio and compression techniques used today.

One of the first **noise reduction** systems dates from 1953 and was aimed at reducing the surface noise heard when playing vinyl discs on a turntable. Developed by prolific British engineer D. T. N. Williamson, this noise reduction system analyzed waveforms as they were played and blocked those that exceeded a preset click frequency. So elegantly simple and effective was this method for dealing with the surface noise of records that the Williamson concept of a dynamic noise filter became the basis for several more well-known breakthroughs in noise reduction using solid-state components.

The most prominent of these analog noise reduction systems was first produced by Raymond M. Dolby in 1966. The goal of the *Dolby noise reduction system* was to increase the signal-to-noise ratio of a recording by *compressing* the signal during recording and *expanding* it again during playback. During the recording process, parts of the signal also receive *pre-emphasis*—a boost in its gain level that helps to overcome low-level tape hiss. When the tape is played back through the appropriate Dolby decoding circuitry, the signal is de-emphasized, and restored to its original balance of frequencies.

Dolby A was developed for professional recording studio applications, and reduced noise across the entire frequency range by analyzing the input signal in four bands. Dolby B, a less expensive option, was developed for consumer applications and became the most widely available system, commonly found on home cassette tape players beginning in the 1970s.

Tape hiss and other sources of analog noise are not problems with digital systems, but digital processing itself can lead to the introduction of noise. The process of sampling and **quantizing** sound can introduce erroneous bits that can cause distortion. This is because algorithms use a preset mathematical model to analyze and store a waveform and any such sampling scheme is prone to error. If the same sampling formula is used repeatedly on the same waveform, the process of re-sampling can repeat, emphasize, or multiply any errors found in the original. The process of *dithering* was developed to avoid this problem by using an algorithm that rounds up and down in a partly random pattern. As a result, any errors introduced by the sampling and quantizing process remain isolated rather than magnified, keeping such digital noise below a perceptible threshold.

In an interesting flashback to the problem that Williamson tackled in filtering out clicks and surface noise from phonograph records, the National Sound Archive in London, working with Cambridge Electronic Design, developed a digital noise reduction process in 1990 with 78 rpm records in mind. Called *Computer Enhanced Digital Audio Restoration* (*CEDAR*), the program employs digital signal processing tools to restore old analog recordings through a staged process of special application routines. Each algorithm is dedicated to a task such as removing clicks (scratches), crackles (high-density, small-amplitude disturbances), buzz (closely spaced regular clicks caused by electrical faults), hiss (magnetic tape noise), and thumps (vibratory disturbances such as the unintentionally recorded sound of the piano being closed). The same type of processing is now widely available in simplified consumer-oriented versions, such as the plug-in *SoundSoap*.

AUDIO COMPRESSION

With digital audio processing comes another advantage for which iPod users the world over can be thankful to computers: audio data compression. Without the availability of such compression schemes, which can reduce the size of audio files dramatically, an eight-GB iPod Nano might only hold 182 four-minute songs instead of 2,000. This type of compression is widely used to reduce the time and bandwidth required to download or play sound files over the Internet. To compress files, a **codec** (compression/decompression algorithm) typically uses psychoacoustic principles to analyse and convert certain parts of the original audio signal into more compact code. The file is then decompressed upon playback, restoring the signal to a listenable approximation of the original.

MP3 is an abbreviation for MPEG Audio Layer 3, the audio component of a digital media compression protocol that is widely used for reducing the size of digital media files with minimum loss of quality. Development of the audio compression form format began in Germany in 1987 under the direction of Dieter Seitzer at the University of Erlangen in Nuremberg. Key patents for the technology are held by the Fraunhofer Institut Integrierte Schaltungen. As an industry-wide standard, MP3 was the first such audio file format of significant importance to be adopted by the Industry Standards Organization (ISO).[13]

The *MPEG Layer 3* codec, introduced in 1997 and now known as MP3, reduced an audio signal by as much as 90 percent. That allowed the digital storage of high fidelity-quality sound files in one tenth of the space required by uncompressed audio files. MP3 is now a widely used audio compression scheme. The user can set the bit rate (kilobits per second) for an MP3 file, which specifies how many bits per second will be used to

Table 11.3 **MP3 file bit rates and audio quality**

Bit rate (kbit/s)	Quality equivalency	Comparative duration
32	AM radio; acceptable for voice	4 hours
64–96	FM radio; excellent for voice and acceptable for music	2 to 1.5 hours
128–160	Near CD; the most commonly used MP3 format for music	1 hour to 37.5 minutes
192–320	Approaching CD and lossless quality	45 to 18.75 minutes

represent the recorded signal. The higher the bit rate, the better the quality. Table 11.3 compares the quality of the audio provided by sample bit rate settings for an MP3 file.

One approach used in developing algorithms for MP3-type codecs is **perceptual audio coding**, which applies principles from the field of psychoacoustics in the development of data compression schemes. Perceptual audio coding exploits the normal limits of human hearing by permanently removing theoretically inaudible components of audio signals. Such psychoacoustic principles are based on research that has identified such aspects of audio perception as acoustic masking, the hearing thresholds, and the time-frequency analysis capabilities of the human ear.[14] The parts of a signal that are "thrown away" after being identified as perceptually inaudible (or less significant, at any rate) are not restored when the compressed signal is later played back, thus this type of compression is referred to as *lossy*. Sound files compressed at too low a bit rate suffer from audible artifacts, sometimes heard as a background "warbling," making these files unappealing for even casual listening. Much work is being done in this field with the expectation that increasingly radical compression can be accomplished while maintaining better-quality sound.

The growth of the Internet has led to the widespread development of competing lossy audio compression schemes. In addition to MP3, the most prevalent commercial codecs include *RealAudio*, various *QuickTime* codecs, **Advanced Audio Coding (AAC)**, and *Windows Media Audio*. A number of non-commercial codecs have also been developed under General Public License, including *Ogg Vorbis*. Some of these schemes can also compress video signals. In 1998, the MPEG4 codec was introduced as a method of audio and video compression, introducing an easy method to distribute music videos and movies over the Internet. AAC rose to prominence in 2001 as one of the most widely used compression schemes when Apple Computer adopted a secure version of it as the file format for its popular iTunes Music Store and iPod portable music player.

Lossy audio compression and decompression inevitably compromise the fidelity of the original signal. Currently, no industry standards govern the quality of compressed audio signals, and results can vary from codec to codec. *Lossless* data compression algorithms have also been developed that retain the full spectral fidelity of the original audio. Commercially developed lossless audio compression algorithms include *Windows Media Audio 9*, and the *Apple Lossless Audio Codec* (*ALAC*). Non-commercial, freely distributed lossless codecs include *FLAC* and *Shorten*, which are widely used within the community of traders and collectors of live "bootleg" concert recordings.

None of these lossless techniques provide a compression ratio as impressive as MP3 and AAC, most reducing audio file size only by about 35 to 45 percent, making them less practical for portable music players.[15]

MP3 and other lossy codecs are primarily used for making consumer copies of audio files for distribution. Lossy formats are not adequate for composing and mastering archival copies of electronic music. Electronic works are generally composed and distributed using an uncompressed format such as WAV or AIFF, each of which is typically available as a storage option with most software synthesizers and multitracking programs. A certain irony has been noted that, while digital technologies were once touted as a way of achieving higher-quality audio recording and reproduction—offering the possibility of eliminating tape hiss and other distortions in recorded sound—the widespread everyday use of lossy audio files and playback technologies almost always involves a reproduction of sound that many listeners perceive as being inferior to analog technologies such as LP recordings and cassette tapes.

DIGITAL RIGHTS MANAGEMENT (DRM)

The ease with which digital music can be copied, downloaded, and distributed has led to concern over the protection of copyrighted works. Digital Rights Management (DRM) is an umbrella term for various hardware and software initiatives undertaken voluntarily by music product manufacturers to safeguard the sales and use of copyrighted content such as recorded music. The Open Mobile Alliance is an industry organization charged with developing standards for DRM that are operable across different mobile product platforms, such as cell phones, PDAs, and portable MP3 players. One prominent application of DRM is the adoption of Protected AAC by Apple Computer to secure the protection of digital music downloads from its popular iTunes Music Store. Apple's proprietary Fairplay file protection scheme is praiseworthy for managing the way in which music downloads can be distributed, but the incompatibility of this scheme with music players manufactured by other companies has led to a growing industry struggle over DRMs. The market is moving toward the liberalization of DRM schemes in favor of allowing purchasers to freely copy their own files and creating widespread compatibility between the schemes of competing music distributors. Steve Jobs, the former CEO of Apple, acknowledged threats from the European Union to block the availability of the Apple iTunes Music Store in EU nations and wrote an open letter to the industry recommending the abolishment of all DRM schemes in favor of the worldwide distribution of music files in an open, licensable format:

> Why would the big four music companies agree to let Apple and others distribute their music without using DRM systems to protect it? The simplest answer is because DRMs haven't worked, and may never work, to halt music piracy. Though the big four music companies require that all their music sold online be protected with DRMs, these same music companies continue to sell billions of CDs a year which contain completely unprotected music.[16]

The motivation behind Jobs' bold suggestion was quite plain. If Apple were to comply with the EU's demand to share its proprietary Fairplay DRM scheme with other manufacturers, the technology would surely be leaked, and workaround programs would be developed by independent developers "which will disable the DRM protection so that formerly protected songs can be played on unauthorized players."[17] As a result, Apple would no longer be able to guarantee protection of the music that it licenses from music companies.

Other opponents of DRM come from outside the music business. Noted pioneering computer programmer John Walker views DRM as another intrusive step in the gradual control and censorship of the Internet by government. "DRM will implement several categories of right to use content," wrote Walker, "some of which have no direct analogues in traditional publishing."[18] Like the battle fought decades earlier over the consumer's right to make personal copies of television programs and movies onto videotape, DRM calls into question traditional practices in the purchase and ownership of media. What separates DRM from previous arguments over the private use of copyrighted materials is the use of technology to manage the process, effectively restricting the consumer's use of purchased goods without consent. Richard Stallman, a software developer and founder of the non-profit Free Software Foundation, is an ardent defender of an individual's right to own and operate their own computer without outside interference. Stallman launched a campaign called Defective by Design in 2006 to fight the development of DRM-enabled products. "Using Digital *Restrictions* Management (DRM) to lock down citizens is unethical," wrote Stallman. "It strips us of our rights to control the devices and computers we own, and takes away the traditional uses we have made of music and video."[19]

In the United States, the Digital Millennium Copyright Act (DMCA) of 1996 established the legal basis for DRM by making it illegal to circumvent electronic measures implemented to protect access to a copyrighted property, even in the absence of any infringement of the copyright itself. In 2001, the EU passed a similar provision as part of the European Copyright Directive, criminalizing the reverse engineering of access controls such as DRM. These legal policies encouraged the deployment of DRM measures that have become increasingly restrictive and difficult to circumvent. In the music industry, the enormous success of Apple's iPod and iTunes Music Store, de facto monopolies in the market, have stimulated consumers and competing manufacturers alike to campaign for less restrictive DRM measures or their elimination entirely. Operating on the fringes of legality, technically minded consumers, offended by efforts of the entertainment industry to limit the use and distribution of media files, have inevitably taken it upon themselves to develop and make available means of defeating each attempt: with a little Internet research one may easily find programs that remove many types of DRM restrictions.

SUMMARY

- A working approach to music development on computers encompasses the *programming* of musical parameters using a central processor, the *storage and retrieval* of said parameters, audio *synthesis* of the parameters, *editing*, and the *playback or synthesis* of completed works represented by such parameters.

- In a digital music system, quantities representing the frequency, amplitude, timbre, duration, and envelope of a sound are expressed as numbers. Computers are designed to interpret and manipulate ordinary decimal numbers that are stored as binary numbers using only 1s and 0s.

- Computers are operated by providing a list of procedures (algorithms) that can be organized as a sequence of instructions using binary code.

- Sound can be generated from a computer by either synthesizing original tones from scratch or by converting analog audio signals into a digital signal that can be further manipulated.

- Techniques for generating sounds using a computer include direct digital synthesis, complete sampling, note sampling, and wavetable synthesis.

- Three major kinds of wavetable synthesis techniques are *additive*, *subtractive*, and *modulation* synthesis.

- The Nyquist sampling theorem states that a time-sampled waveform can only be adequately represented if the sampling frequency is at least twice that of the highest desired frequency being sampled.

- Although noise reduction systems as once implemented with analog music production systems are not required for digital music production, the DSP function of *dithering* is used to avoid noise introduced during the sampling process.

- Data compression algorithms that retain the full spectral fidelity of the original audio file are termed *lossless* and contrast with so-called *lossy* data compression algorithms that cannot reconstruct the compressed signal to its original specifications.

KEY PEOPLE IN CHAPTER ELEVEN

John Chowning 333	Curtis Roads 336
Raymond M. Dolby 339	Dieter Seitzer 340
Dennis Gabor 335	Richard Stallman 342
Steve Jobs 342	Barry Truax 337
Max Mathews 324	John Walker 342
Jean-Claude Risset 330	D. T. N. Williamson 339

KEY TERMS IN CHAPTER ELEVEN

Advanced Audio Coding (AAC) 341	interpolation 333
aliasing 335	lossless 341
analog-to-digital converter (ADC) 326	lossy 341
binary 323	MPEG Layer 3 (MP3) 340
bit 323	multisampling 331
byte 323	noise reduction 339
codec 340	note sampling 330
complete sample 325	Nyquist sampling theorem 332
digital-to-analog converter (DAC) 326	perceptual audio coding 341
Digital Millenium Copyright Act 343	programming language 323
Digital Rights Management (DRM) 342	quantizing 339
dithering 339	sample 325
Dolby noise reduction system 339	sampler 331
European Copyright Directive 343	sampling rate 326
frequency modulation (FM) 333	spectral editor 330
granular synthesis 335	waveshaping synthesis 335
hexadecimal 323	wavetable 331

MILESTONES

Computer Music Synthesis

Technical and scientific	Year	Music and instruments
– Engineer Harry Nyquist published *Certain Topics in Telegraph Transmission Theory*, laying the groundwork for Nyquist sampling theory.	1928	
– Physicist Dennis Gabor published *Acoustical Quanta and the Theory of Hearing*, introducing the principles of granular synthesis.	1947	
– D. T. N. Williamson invented the first practical noise reduction system for filtering out surface noise from turntable recordings.	1953	
– IBM introduced hexadecimal coding using eight-bit bytes.	1956	
– Max Mathews completed *MUSIC I*, a general-purpose music programming language.	1957	– Mathews completed the first work of direct synthesis using *MUSIC I*, a 17-second composition using an IBM 704 computer.
– Work at Bell Labs continued with Mathews developing *MUSIC II–V* and Jean-Claude Risset conducting analysis of synthesized waveforms.	1960–68	
– Raymond M. Dolby invented the Dolby noise reduction system for analog recording and playback.	1966	
– Risset released *An Introductory Catalog of Computer Synthesized Sounds*.	1969	– Risset composed *Mutations* for magnetic tape ay Bell Labs.
– John Chowning published *Digital Sound Synthesis, Acoustics, And Perception: A Rich Intersection*, laying the groundwork for FM spectral synthesis.	1973	
	1975	– Curtis Roads created a granular synthesis programming language based on Gabor's theories. He composed the work *prototype* using the technique.
	1979	– Fairlight *CMI* digital sampling keyboard introduced.
	1981	– E-mu *Emulator* digital sampling keyboard introduced.

Technical and scientific	Year	Music and instruments
	1983	– Yamaha *DX-7* introduced, using Chowning's FM synthesis algorithms.
– Barry Vercoe introduced the *Csound* music programming language.	1985	
– United States Congress approved the Digital Millennium Copyright Act.	1996	
– MP3 audio compression format developed by Dieter Seitzer in Germany.	1997	
– Apple computer introduced AAC, its audio compression scheme incorporating digital data management. – The European Union approved the European Copyright Directive.	2001	

PART IV

The Music

CHAPTER 12

Classical and Experimental Music

Rarely in the history of music has the musician found himself in a more radical position, faced with as unaccustomed a task as the creation of the very sound itself.[1]
—Pierre Boulez

Edgard Varèse. (Edgard Varèse Collection, Paul Sacher Foundation, Basel)

Earlier chapters were focused primarily on the chronology of inventions, instruments, and other technological innovations that made electronic music possible. This part explores the musical outcomes of the technology and key innovators in various musical genres who made it possible.

Electronic music had its roots in post–World War II classical music, one branch of which ventured into experimental new forms with and without the help of electronics. These pioneers shaped the early direction of electronic music and greatly influenced the dispersion of new music ideas into other musical idioms. The electronic music work of classical and experimental music composers is a fitting place to begin the discussion and is the subject of this chapter.

PERSPECTIVES ON ELECTRONIC MUSIC

"Despite the fact that electronic music is the outcome of decades of technical development, it is only in most recent times that it has reached a stage at which it may be considered as part of the legitimate musical sphere."[2] These were the thoughts of Herbert Eimert, one of the founding scholars of electronic music. He wrote this in 1955, just four years after establishing the electronic music studio of West German Radio (WDR). By "legitimate musical sphere," Eimert meant that he intended purely electronic tones to become the new raw material for realizing serialist works in the mold of Anton Webern. The German studio was in fact launched into prominence on the reputation of several serialist-inspired pieces consisting of purely electronic signals. In stark contrast were the pioneering tape works of *musique concrète* created at the GRM studio in Paris under the guidance of Pierre Schaffer. The French composed freely, modifying and re-contextualizing naturally occurring sounds into montages that defied any stylistic precedent. The aesthetic clash between the French and Germans was short-lived due to the refusal of electronic music to be contained by any single school of thought or dogmatic approach to organizing such sounds.

Even though Eimert may have been unable, or unwilling, to accept a style of electronic music other than one embracing his devotion to serialism, there was perhaps an even more significant undercurrent in his pronouncement. It seemed clear that, because electronic music was reliant on technology, the music itself was going to become a testing ground for new aesthetic ideas about the art of musical sound. Just as an electronic sound can be sustained as long as the electricity is turned on, the medium effectively stretches to its limits the conception and manipulation of the five basic elements of all musical sound: pitch, amplitude, envelope, duration, and timbre.

In the same 1955 issue of the journal *die Reihe* that featured Eimert's thoughts, Pierre Boulez offered a cautionary tale of composers gone astray in the electronic music studio, their once-fixed audio limitations having become unlimited, leading to the "negative cliché" of special effects gone mad.[3] The underlying message? The taste that governs the writing of traditional music can well serve the composer of electronic music.

By its nature as a music using a new medium, the composing and performing of electronic music will naturally lead to new sounds, techniques, and styles of music.

In 1969, looking back at the decade of the Sixties, no less a musical figurehead than composer Igor Stravinsky commented that the most telling index of musical progress in the 1960s:

[was] not in the work of any composer . . . but in the status of electronic music . . . the young musician takes his degree in computer technology now, and settles down to his Moog or his mini-synthesizer as routinely as in my day he would have taken it in counterpoint and harmony and gone to work at the piano.[4]

With that remark, Stravinsky reinforced the legitimacy of electronic music and its continued evolution within all musical circles. By 1970, after 20 years of experimentation, the field of electronic music established a niche for itself founded on three cultural perspectives:

- Technology naturally leads to *experimentation* and eventual acceptance of new sounds, styles, and techniques for making music.
- The *acceptance* of electronic music will succeed by comparing it to other forms of music, even if that comparison is unnecessary to accept electronic music as a musical form of its own.
- Composing and listening to electronic music require *new skills*.

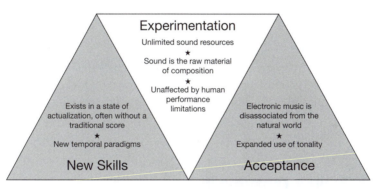

Figure 12.1 Perspectives and traits of electronic music.

Figure 12.1 associates the above perspectives with the seven fundamental traits of electronic music described in Chapter 5.

The golden age of synthesizers (1968–78) did indeed offer composers improved control over the shaping of pitch, amplitude, duration, and timbre. But the synthesizer itself was a changeable beast, was too expensive for most people to own, was found mostly in institutions, and rapidly became obsolete. Despite the fact that many synthesizer composers went "astray," producing "negative clichés" in nearly unimaginable quantities, there was also the continued evolution of an aesthetic of music that electronics made possible.

While synthesizers came and went, the effect of electronic music permeated all musical culture. In this way the work of even the most experimental composers influenced practitioners of rock, pop, jazz, and other musical genres. Writing about music in 1973, British musicologist Jack Bornoff discovered that understanding what was happening in music also meant understanding the technology that affected it:

> Even more than a kind of music, there is a kind of *sound* of music which we might call typical of the space age. It is the amplification to the *nth* degree of any music—whether produced by traditional or electronic instruments—which is invariably used in performances of pop music . . . Not the least interesting aspect of this fashion in pop music is the fact that it would not have happened if "serious" music had not earlier, with composers such as Stockhausen, integrated electronics in their work.[5]

In the 1970s and 1980s, while musicologists pondered how the steady influx of electronic sound generation was changing the course of music, tinkering composers such as David Tudor, Pauline Oliveros, Maryanne Amacher (b. 1943), Eliane Radigue, Gordon Mumma, and David Behrman were hacking together new instruments from early digital components. "I remember riding on the [Merce] Cunningham bus in the early 1970s with manuals about logic circuits," recalls Behrman as he hit the books yet again to learn about a new generation of electronics.[6] These pioneers created instruments to propagate a new aesthetic of music—experiments that required new skills, required experimentation, and eventually led to varying degrees of acceptance of electronic music techniques in most world cultures. These composers in turn taught a new generation of tinkerers, including Nicolas Collins, Ron Kuivila, Paul DeMarinis, and many others.

What is the aesthetic that electronic music enables? On one hand, it is a music of *continuity* and *non-continuity*. Boulez characterized this aesthetic as "the concept of continuity which faces the composer in all directions."[7] Looking back at the extensive work of David Tudor, composer Forrest Warthman wrote that Tudor's approach was to "shape sound in all its dimensions, without limitation."[8] So it seems that we have developed a continuously expanding universe of sounds in which pitch, envelope amplitude, duration, and timbre comprise the elemental particles that explode from the center of the musical universe.

THE DEBATE OVER TERMINOLOGY

In the preface of this book, I provided my rationale for using the term *electronic and experimental music* to describe the subject of this book. The evolution of electronic music technology has always been shadowed by a debate over what to call the music. This debate essentially has no purpose other than to narrowly describe specific approaches to making the music, or a stylistic tendency for which there is an existing body of works. But many find this debate to be an interesting lightning rod for opinions and discussion over the nature and aesthetics of electronic music. I am providing this background of that discussion for readers who would like to engage in this debate.

When viewed from the standpoint of history, it is possible to view each term within the context of its own time and place, but oftentimes they do not translate to the present day in a meaningful way. Take Pierre Schaeffer's term *musique concrète*. For Schaeffer, this was a work conceived with the recording medium in mind that was composed directly on that medium and was played through the medium as a finished work. In *musique concrète*, therefore, one worked directly with the modification of sound material, often obscuring beyond recognition the identity of the original source. You could literally describe music made using computer software and recorded on a thumb drive in much the same way, so why don't we? Schaeffer was so fixated on the transformative aspect of *musique concrète* that he apparently expelled one of his own understudies, Luc Ferrari, from the Paris studios in 1964 for having allowed many of the natural sounds in his material to remain recognizable.[9] Schaeffer had a difficult personality and by 1958 had alienated so many of the staff at the Paris studio that Pierre Henry left, taking all of his friends and assistants with him.[10] Schaeffer's stubborn insistence on a rigid doctrine for *musique concrète* ultimately led to the disuse of the term by most other studios.

In Germany, of course, the composers in the Cologne studio insisted on the term *elektronische Musik* to describe what they were doing. For the briefest of moments in 1951 there may have actually existed a technological distinction between these two schools of thought: *musique concrète* embracing the manipulation of recorded natural sounds and *elektronische Musik* comprising only electronically generated tones. However, composers working in these rival studios were much less interested in the debate than in the fantastic sounds they were making, and soon realized that, once a sound was recorded, no matter what the original source, a sound was simply a sound like any other on tape. Once composers had essentially broken all the rules of their institutional mentors, the fizzle was spent for both the French and German terms.

The earliest electronic music of all was named for the communication wires over which it was distributed. The output of the Musical Telegraph was sometimes known as "telegraphic" music and the output of the Telharmonium was referred to as "telephonic" music.[11] During the 1950s, Varèse sidestepped the entire debate of the French and Germans and referred to his own electronic music as "organized sound." Cage adopted similar terminology, but considered "sound" to consist of noise as well. By 1960, the general term "electronic music" had been widely adopted in America to describe any and all music produced using recorded sound, tape machines, and sound generators, whether for movies, television, stage, dance, or in the halls of academic music studios. In Great Britain during this same time, the term "radiophonic" was used to describe the programmatic electronic music produced by the BBC.

During the 1970s the use of general-purpose music synthesizers simplified the production of electronic music and the debate over terminology gradually became decoupled from the technical means used for producing the music. The terms *electronic* and *electroacoustic* music became widely used and referred more to a style of music than to the instruments used to create it. A hiccup in terminology occurred once more with the introduction of digital instruments and the use of personal computers to create music. This advance in technology was significant because it gradually took the tape medium out of the picture and led to the development of software and digital circuitry for creating virtually any style of music electronically. Until about 1985, the term *computer music* was used to describe new instruments and experiments in the creation of electronic music. After that, most music has been produced with the aid of a computer and we return to the naming of various genres or styles of music.

Following is a quick assessment of many of the most familiar terms that have been used to describe electronic music. Some are based in the history of technology, others in an attempt to describe a style or aesthetic of the music.

- **Telegraphic and telephonic**: Dating from the late nineteenth and early twentieth centuries, these terms refer to the electrical means for distributing early experiments in electronic music using telegraph wires and telephone lines.

- **Organized sound**: Varèse's general term for his musical compositions, whether they were electronic or instrumental. This is generally understood to be the creation of music intended for a concert hall or other audience situation, such as the Philips Pavilion at the Brussels World's Fair.
- *Musique concrète*: Schaeffer's term for a work conceived with the recording medium in mind that was composed directly on that medium and was played through the medium as a finished work. This term is often synonymous with early tape music.
- *Elektronische Musik*: Beyer and Meyer-Eppler's term for music comprised entirely of electronically generated sounds. This term is also synonymous with early tape music.
- **Acousmatic**: Schaeffer's later term for tape music —*acousmatique*.[12] It is generally considered synonymous with *musique concrète*, and was preferred by composers who wanted to avoid being associated with earlier debates over terminology.[13] The term is widely used in academia to refer to contemporary works of *musique concrète* using digital media and whose source material consists primarily of pre-recorded sounds. The term *electroacoustic* (see below) is often used synonymously with *acousmatic*.
- **Electroacoustic**: This is music for which the primary content consists of electronically modified acoustic sounds.[14] Electroacoustic techniques vary widely from working with the manipulation of previously recorded sounds to the treatment and modification of instrumental sounds in real time. The term is often used synonymously with electronic music, although to many it refers to art music incorporating electronic effects.
- **Radiophonic**: British term referring to electronic sound effects and music for radio and television programming. The composition techniques closely parallel those of *musique concrète*. The *BBC Radiophonic Workshop* was a sound laboratory and studio created by the BBC in 1958 for the production of electronic music.
- **Sound art**: Electronic music not necessarily intended for the concert hall and that might be used as an audio installation in a gallery or other environmental context.
- **Computer music**: Music created solely with the aid of computers, either in the composition, audio production, or both. Prior to the availability of standalone, computer-based electronic music synthesizers in the early 1980s, *computer music* was considered an experimental form of producing music electronically. Like the term *musique concrète*, computer music is no longer in general use unless it is describing the historical development of music using computers.
- **Electronica**: A contemporary term that covers a wide range of electronic music styles. Generally referring to popular music relying heavily on electronic sonorities, beats, and sound manipulations, it may be intended for dancing or for private listening. *Electronica* may stand alone as a purely electronic form of music, or its elements may be combined with those of rock and pop bands and vocalists.
- **Electronic music**: A broad term encompassing any form of music that incorporates largely electronic elements, whether originating as acoustic source material or purely electronic tones.

From the standpoint of history, this book explores the connections between the evolution of technology and the making of electronic music, each stage of which seems to be associated with a change in terminology. That is why, as a general principle for organizing the discussion across many decades, I have chosen the term *electronic music* as the most widely applicable and least controversial for those who wish to discuss the field.

VARÈSE AND THE LISTENER'S EXPERIMENT

When *musique concrète* came into its own around 1950, Varèse was already 65 years old. The explosion in electronic music was vaunted by a new generation of experimental composers who held him in high regard. Varèse had been seeking access to practicable electronic musical instruments for many years, so upon the establishment of electronic music studios during the early 1950s he quickly went about getting up to speed on the new technology. What he found was not entirely encouraging because working with magnetic tape was a far cry from conceiving music for a soloist playing an electronic musical instrument such as the Theremin. While living in Greenwich Village in New York City in 1953, Varèse received an anonymous gift in the form of an Ampex 400 tape recorder. This began his personal exploration of magnetic tape music and he dragged the machine with him on this travels to record sounds and learn how to edit tape.[15] His first project was more of an exercise in tape editing techniques as he labored over constructing a three-minute soundtrack for part of the biographical film *Around and About Jean Miró*. Varèse completed his short section of the soundtrack, known as *Good Friday Procession in Verges*, and next proceeded to plan his first major work to include electronic music, *Déserts* (1954).

Varèse left the confines of his inadequately equipped home studio in New York to compose *Déserts* in Paris at the studios of GRM. The work consisted of seven parts—four instrumental and three for magnetic tape. The parts were closely dovetailed, nearly overlapped, so as to disguise the transition from orchestra to tape, but at no time did the orchestra play at the same time as the tape (see Figure 12.2). Varèse scored the instrumental parts as was his normal practice and left places where the electronic tape would be played. The instrumental parts of the work underscore his use of rhythm, tone color, and radical dynamic changes, techniques that he perfected long before the advent of tape composition. The tape part explored many of the same elements, but with concrete and electronic sounds. Varèse composed it in this way as if to demonstrate that all music—instrumental or electronic—shared many of the same resources. The piece was performed live several times using stereo loudspeakers to project the sound. A young Stockhausen proudly operated the volume controls for one of the early performances.

Déserts was premiered in Paris in 1955 under the baton of Hermann Scherchen (1891–1966), a respected conductor of new music responsible for previous world premieres of works by Schoenberg, Webern, and Berg. It was not well received by an audience that was most interested in hearing another work on the program, Tchaikovsky's *Pathétique Symphony*. A reviewer writing in *The Score* revealed:

> A riot almost as furious and bloody as that provoked by the first performance of *Le Sacre* ensued [Stravinsky's *Rite of Spring* which premiered in the same theater 42 years earlier], and the work was often unaudible through the barrage of stamping, clapping, and catcalls that arose after a few minutes. Even for those listening to the radio broadcast, the music was often completely submerged in the general mêlée.[16]

It was a painful experience for Varèse to have his first work in nearly 20 years hounded so demonstrably by a mob of concertgoers and it reportedly drove him to tears. Yet he spent the rest of the night following the concert at the RTF studios remixing the tapes

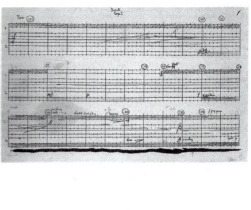

Figure 12.2   The handwritten score for *Déserts*, prepared by Varèse's assistant Chou Wen-chung, consisted of two parts. The orchestral score (left) is shown here with an attached list of instruments written by Varèse. The continuity score for the first magnetic tape interpolation (right) included instructions for synchronizing and setting the volume level of the tape recorder with the live orchestra. (Edgard Varèse Collection, Paul Sacher Foundation, Basel)

to improve their fidelity.[17] Several other performances of *Déserts* followed in Europe and were much better received. By the time Varèse returned to America with the work, audiences had been primed for the new experience of witnessing tape music played with an orchestra. One review in particular by Louis Chapin of the *Christian Science Monitor* touched on both the promise and pitfalls of the work:

> Where instruments can be percussive, electronics can approach the concussive. "Noise," we think, as we are assaulted by Mr. Varèse's tape-recorded sounds, either abrasive, explosive, or knifing through the pile with high-frequency squeals. But before we dot the "i" in noise, we can do well to listen to what is ingenious and selective in what we hear, to enjoy modulations of massive rhythm and space . . . One wonders, though, whether the two media here—instruments and tape—might work together more, might not develop more continuity instead of merely taking turns at the audience.[18]

The criticism offered by Chapin regarding the organization of *Déserts* was widely regarded as the major flaw of the work. Why include a tape and orchestra if there is no facility for these elements to play against one another? Moving ahead, Varèse would finally realize his dream of creating a work only for recorded sound in the making of *Poème électronique*.

As disastrous as it was, the Paris premiere of *Déserts* provided an important link for Varèse to the creation of his next and final work of electronic music. The Swiss architect Charles-Edouard Jeanneret (1887–1965), better known to the world as Le Corbusier, was in attendance in Paris when the crowds roared at the electronic music of Varèse.[19] Soon thereafter, the architect was contracted to build a pavilion for the Philips Radio Corporation for the 1958 Brussels World's Fair. Philips was a leading record company and responsible for publishing the earliest works of *musique concrète* produced by Schaeffer and company in Paris. At Le Corbusier's urging, Philips contracted Varèse to provide tape music to be used in the pavilion. Along with Iannis Xenakis, Le Corbusier's architect assistant at the time, Varèse and Le Corbusier conceived a union of architecture and electronic music that has seldom been matched.

The Philips Pavilion was designed for the express purpose of presenting Varèse's tape piece. It was built in the shape of a circus tent with three peaks, a shape that was also likened to that of a sheep's stomach. Inside were 400 loudspeakers to broadcast the sound in sweeping arcs throughout the pavilion. The music was accompanied by visual projections selected by Le Corbusier.

Varèse was a familiar face in New York and visited Ussachevsky and Luening at the Columbia Tape Music Center just prior to beginning work on *Poème électronique*. Although he would actually compose the piece in the well-equipped studios of Philips, Eindhoven, the sponsoring client of the pavilion, Varèse wanted to brush up on tape composition techniques and was assisted by composer Chou Wen-chung (b. 1923) in learning more about composing with oscillators, microphones, and tape recorders at Columbia. Varèse was then off to Eindhoven where he composed the work under the watchful eye of Philips technicians.

The directors of Philips did not understand the music of Varèse and for several weeks tried to remove him from the project. Le Corbusier had gone off to India to supervise another project, leaving Xenakis to fill in for him. Xenakis reported to Le Corbusier in

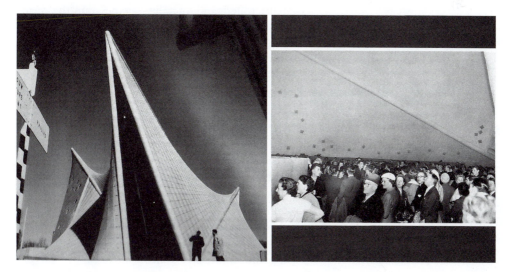

Figure 12.3   Exterior and interior of the Philips Pavilion at the Brussels World's Fair, 1958. Inside the pavilion, hundreds of small loudspeakers were mounted on the walls to create a moving path of sound. (Philips International BV, Eindhoven)

writing that the Philips executives were being openly hostile to Varèse. Le Corbusier's reply was as bold an endorsement as Varèse could have hoped for: "The *Poème élec-tronique* cannot be carried out except by Varèse's strange music. There cannot for a moment be a question of giving up Varèse. If that should happen, I will withdraw from the project entirely." The Philips people bothered Varèse no more.[20]

A lesser-known side note to the Philips Pavilion story is that Xenakis, too, contributed a piece of electronic music to the project. His *Concret PH* (1958) was played after every two performances of *Poème électronique*. The short work, only 2′ 45″ in length, was composed by modifying the amplified sounds of burning embers. Xenakis spliced the sounds into one-second lengths, modified their speeds, filtered them to give the crackling sounds a metallic effect, then layered the result into a thick, continuous rain of drifting sound-specks in space. Like *Poème électronique*, *Concret PH* had been composed with the design of the pavilion in mind and was an equally compelling work, if not as melodramatic as Varèse's piece.

Poème électronique and *Concret PH* were composed knowing that they would be projected spatially using a matrix of loudspeakers and three channels of tape inside the Philips Pavilion. The works were played using a 3-track, 35 mm perforated magnetic tape system, the output of which was fed to 325 wall-mounted speakers and 25 sub-woofers around the floor. The projection of the sound and images was controlled by 15-track control tape that automatically switched the audio amplifiers and image projectors. The amplifiers were connected to groups of five speakers and they were switched on and off in a sequence across the space so that the three tracks of sound appeared to be moving in two or three directions at the same time around the audience.

Varèse called *Poème électronique* a work of "organized sound." It was created using electroacoustic sounds, electronically generated tones, tape effects, and magnetic tape editing techniques. The work was one of the first completed at the Center for Electronic Music of the Philips Research Laboratories in Eindhoven. The eight-minute work combined passages of familiar sounds with stark electronic effects and treatments. Church bells tolled and metallic scrapes cut the space in shreds. Organ-like tones droned quietly as ominous electronic sounds built a threatening crescendo. A voice moaned, thunderous crashes interrupted, and dark sonorities lurked in the background. All of this was contrasted by the brilliant use of pauses and silence, ever increasing the tension of the work. The lights were dimmed for each performance and the music was accompanied by a light show of projected colors. *Poème électronique* was experienced by 500 people at a time who stood inside the pavilion during the summer of 1958. No prior piece of electronic music had been so thoroughly integrated into a performance space nor implemented on such a grand, immersive scale.

Figure 12.4   The architect Le Corbusier with Edgard Varèse, 1958. (Edgard Varèse Collection, Paul Sacher Foundation, Basel)

Poème électronique was received more warmly than *Desérts* and represented a watershed event in the history of electronic music. The work

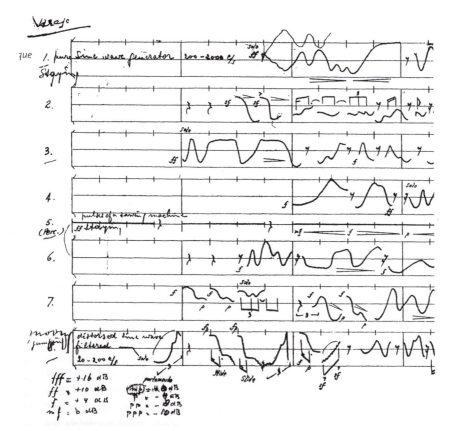

Figure 12.5   Early sketch of score for *Poème électronique* by Varèse. (Philips International BV, Eindhoven)

introduced an intriguing musical experiment to the general public and demonstrated that multimedia applications were an effective venue for electronic music. *Poème électronique* was premiered in America at the Village Gate, a club in Greenwich Village—Varèse's stomping ground in New York City, where he lived for 40 years. In the view of the *Musical America* critic who witnessed the American premiere, *Poème électronique* deserved a spot alongside Cage's *Williams Mix* as a milestone in the young history of electronic music. The critic noted:

> The focus of the concert . . . was on Edgard Varèse. Samuel Baron conducted his *Octandre*, which is now 34 years old. In this piece Varèse demonstrates his peculiarly architectural sense of space, combined with extremely idiomatic writing for the eight instruments. Varèse then spoke, saying among other things that an artist was never ahead of his time, but most people were behind it . . . Then came the major event—the United States premiere of Varèse's *Poème électronique*. There were loudspeakers all over the large hall, and fragments of sirens, drums, choirs, solo voices, and many electronically derived sounds poured from them, in new and almost frightening counterpoint. Alone with John Cage's *Williams Mix*, this is one of the most impressive electronic compositions to date. And wild as the sounds seem to us now, it is hard to doubt a future for

LISTENING GUIDE 12.1

Title: *Poème électronique*

Artist: Edgard Varèse   **Year**: 1958   **Duration**: 8:02

Genre: Tape composition

Electronic Instrumentation: Recorded acoustic sounds, audio generators, reverberation, tape editing.

Background: Perhaps the best known of all works of classic electronic music, Varèse's *Poème électronique* was designed for the interior space of the Philips Pavilion at the 1958 World's Fair in Brussels. It was composed at the electronic music studios of Philips in Eindhoven. Its use of recorded and processed natural sounds as well as electronically generated tones marked a period in which academic electronic music was becoming more widely influential in popular media. It also signified a departure from the earlier distinctions in the making of tape music among French and German practitioners, inviting the use of any and all sounds to produce a potent and highly personal musical expression.

	Listen For: The combination and sequencing of natural sounds, electronically generated sounds, and sounds of each type modified by tape manipulation. Also note the drama and emotional impact intended by this music. Imagine standing in a dark space with other audience members hearing this music for the first time.
0:00–1:10	The piece opens with the ominous tolling of a bell, grasping the attention of the listener and leading them innocently into unfamiliar sonic territory. A few percussion instruments are heard at 0:16 following by stinging electronic tones that waver broadly up and down the pitch range. The texture of the work is sparse at this stage and filled with moments of rest. At 0:45, one hears percussion instruments played in reverse. During this section, the music comprises many contrasting sounds, one after another—loud and soft, rough and smooth, high and low. The sequences of continuous oscillator tones were produced by manually adjusting dials (e.g., 0:21–0:25; 1:00–1:10).
1:11–1:45	The texture thickens at this point, using three tracks of noisy percussion instruments. A short tape loop of a jangling instrument is clearly heard at 1:20, repeating four times. This is followed by a momentary clash combining electronic tones and smashing percussion sounds, after which occurs another relatively quiet section of manually adjusted electronic tones.
1:46–2:30	This section applies tape echo to several percussive and electronic sounds.
2:31–5:45	The bell tolls again at 2:34, marking the start of a passage of purely electronic tones, sustained, chord-like, and more musical than earlier electronic passages. At 3:25, the piece returns to a section of processed acoustic sounds. Voices are clearly heard for the first time, first a solo female voice singing and then several vocalizations that are processed and filtered. The vocals are joined by caustic, explosive sounds, additional shadow vocals, and the sound of someone walking on gravel (beginning at 4:44) moves back and forth between the right and left channels. The voices become increasingly abstracted and unearthly.
5:46–8:08	The piece returns to an extended section of electronic tones and percussion instruments. Varèse creates slowly building crescendos of electronic tones, punctuated by sharp percussion sounds. A distorted tape loop of an orchestral percussion section is heard at about 6:01 and repeats several times at different volume levels. A snare drum is heard at 6:14. A jet plane cuts across the sound at 6:34 followed by noisy market sounds and the distorted voice of an opera singer. From 7:12 to 7:28, several sharply cut sounds of an orchestra and organ are played repeatedly as a short loop, spaced by contrasting passages of quieter sounds. The jet plane sound returns, combined with an alarming onslaught of loud, distorted, electronic tones. The piece ends abruptly when the final collage of noise and tones rises to a peak before being sharply cut.

Compare and Contrast

Gesang der Jünglinge (1956) by Karlheinz Stockhausen
Diamorphoses (1959) by Iannis Xenakis
Apocalypse (1961) by Tod Dockstader

such means of composition. In a world of jet planes, man-made moons, atomic submarines, and hydrogen bombs, who is to say this music does not have a place?[21]

Varèse is famous for having said, "My experimenting is done before I make the music. Afterwards, it is the listener who must experiment."[22] With *Poème électronique*, Varèse succeeded in bringing many a new listener into the experiment of electronic music.

There is a New York footnote to the Varèse story that reconnects him to the Columbia–Princeton Electronic Music Center as well as to the father of computer music working at Bell Labs. Varèse had become acquainted with Max Mathews and Newman Guttman of Bell Labs in 1959 and the two Bell researchers offered to assist the composer in creating tape mix for *Desérts*. While visiting Bell Labs and demonstrating their experiments in computer music, Mathews conjured up the digitally sampled sound of a buzz saw that Varèse decided would make a good addition to his piece. Bell Labs did not have the necessary tape studio facilities to work with pre-recorded sound material, so Varèse contacted his friend Vladimir Ussachevsky, director of the Columbia studio, requesting some time there. Ussachevsky was delighted and replied to Varèse in February 1960, writing:

> It has long been agreed that our facilities are open for your use, it would be our pleasure to make the arrangements for a regular use of the studio by you. It is my impression that your scientist friends from the Bell Laboratory would be interested in assisting you and we could arrange a time in the evening when they are more likely to be able to come.[23]

Beginning in April of 1960, Varèse, Mathews, and Guttman made regular evening visits to the Columbia studio, usually on Friday and Saturday nights. Columbia composer and technician Bülent Arel also joined the team and contributed to the creation of the definitive version of *Desérts* that is dated 1960–61. Arel's graphical editing notes for *Desérts* would suggest that he was largely responsible for managing the actual editing of the final tapes under the watchful eye of the composer.

Varèse became a regular fixture at Columbia during this time, working several months at a time in the studio and serving as a guest lecturer from time to time. Having such great access to Varèse led Ussachevsky to propose a concert in his honor. An evening of Varèse's music was presented at Town Hall in New York on May 1, 1961 and included performances of six works, including his two electronic works, *Poème électronique* and *Desérts*. The event involved many of the students and staff of the Columbia Center.

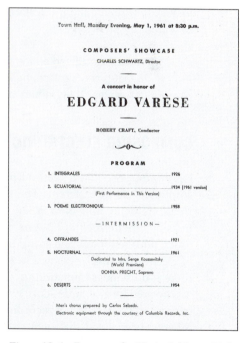

Figure 12.6 Program for Varèse's Town Hall Concert, New York, 1961. (Columbia University Computer Music Center)

Varèse's energy level and enthusiasm for electronic music remained high during his closing years despite the fact that his health was beginning to deteriorate. During the spring of 1962, Varèse continued to work in the studio on works, learning first-hand "how to operate every knob and switch, and to manipulate the tape recorders himself."[24] In 1963, realizing that it was a strain for Varèse to visit the Columbia studio as regularly as before, Ussachevsky solicited funds from the dean of faculties and provosts of Columbia University to pay for the creation of a small studio in the composer's apartment, "so that he could experiment to his heart's content, and have him come to Columbia whenever he is ready for those more complex manipulations of his materials."[25]

Varèse died on November 6, 1965. Within two days of his death, Ussachevsky was actively recruiting financial support to produce yet another concert of Varèse's music, this time a tribute that included performances of his music as well as a documentary film about Varèse, the three-minute segment of the short film about Miró for which Varèse provided his first electronic music composition, a recorded speech by Varèse, and tributes from his colleagues. Alice Shields was recruited to assist Ussachevsky in re-mastering a two-channel stereo mix of the three-channel version of *Poème électronique* that had been used for the Philips Pavilion in 1958. Shields listened to each of the three tapes and graphically sketched audio cues and timings onto ruled paper to aid her in synchronizing the separate parts. The concert was held on December 15, 1965 in the McMillan Academic Theater of Columbia University. The loss of Varèse was especially difficult for the Columbia staff, of whom no fewer than seven composers had been closely associated with Varèse either through friendship, productions of his music, knowing him as a colleague through his teaching, or working directly with him in the studio. Composer Chou Wen-chung, a member of the Columbia faculty, became the executor of Varèse's literary and musical estate. Fellow composer Otto Luening closed his tribute to Varèse by saying:

> Varèse speculated on the future, lived fully in the present, remembered the past. In that grand tradition, he believed it to be his duty to work with and for his colleagues. They, in turn, admired him and loved him.[26]

COMPOSING ELECTRONIC MUSIC

Every composer has a method for developing a piece of music and electronic music composers are no different. The first post-World War II electronic music composers in Paris, Cologne, and New York benefited from a variety of compositional styles that preceded them, such as 12-tone music (serialism), the use of alternate scales and micro-tones, non-harmomic and atonal music, and non-traditional time signatures. The medium of electronic music presented its own unique problems for the composer and to this day there is no standard notation used for this medium. Most electronic works do not exist in a notated form at all. A score would be of no value to most electronic music composers because the outcome is a recording rather than a transcript of notes to be performed by others. Having said that, it is also true that much thought has been given to ways in which to organize the process of composing electronic music.

One might broadly group methods of composing electronic music into several categories:

• **Sound crafting**—This method is the most intuitive and least specific approach to planning a piece of electronic music. The composer works directly with the sound material and the most general concept of a structural plan. A graphical representation of the sound, as created by Varèse for *Poème électronique* (see Figure 12.5), might be employed to help the composer organize the work and make macro-level changes to its composition. Sound crafting or *sound montage* is the most widely used approach to composing electronic music and had its origins in the first works completed by Pierre Schaeffer in the late 1940s.

• **Graphic score**—This kind of score is a detailed visual representation of the form and substance of a work in a degree of specificity that could be faithfully reproduced by others. In a graphic score, symbols other than those used in traditional musical notation are used to specify the music. Prior to the availability of computer software to visualize electronic compositions, many composers of electronic music invented their own systems for graphically documenting their scores. Figures 12.7, 12.10, and 12.11 are examples of graphic scores. Stockhausen's detailed graphical specifications for *Studie I* and *Studie II* left no stone unturned, providing all of the required parameters needed to create the work using any sine wave generator. An idea related to the graphic score is the **listening score** (see Figure 12.15), a visual aid to the listener for studying the structure and form of a piece of music.

• **Technical score**—A score for a work can be specified by the technical parameters of the required sounds. This technique will theoretically provide a score that can be

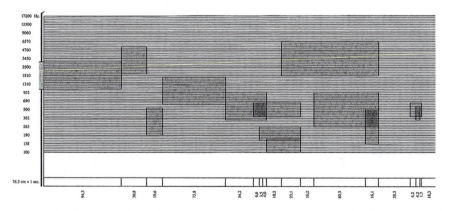

Figure 12.7   Graphic score: close view of the score for *Studie II* (1954) by Stockhausen visually depicting specifications for the amplitude, duration, and frequency of sine waves used in the piece. (Stockhausen Verlag)

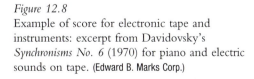

Figure 12.8
Example of score for electronic tape and instruments: excerpt from Davidovsky's *Synchronisms No. 6* (1970) for piano and electric sounds on tape. (Edward B. Marks Corp.)

reproduced by others. Pierre Henry's graphical score for *Antiphonie* (1952) provided specific measurements for the duration and envelope of given sounds, although the sound sources themselves could vary.

• **Electronics with other instruments**—Electronic sounds, either pre-recorded or performed live, can be combined with music played by classical instrumentalists. This was an early approach developed by Luening and Ussachevsky at Columbia University and continues to be developed. In such a work, a score is generally provided for the instrumentalist that specifies some concurrent activity generated electronically. An example that combined magnetic tape with instrumentalists was *Synchronisms No. 6 for Piano and Electric Sounds* (1970) by Mario Davidovsky, in which instructions are provided on the musical score for starting and stopping a pre-recorded tape (see Figure 12.8). Another example, specifying pitches and timings for electronically generated sounds on tape, can be seen in Figure 12.9, an excerpt from an innovative score by Roger Reynolds. The work *Superior Seven* (1988) by Robert Ashley, for solo flute and MIDI orchestra (1988), provides written music for a flute player and pianist, and audible cues that trigger the engagement of MIDI instrumental functions controlled by a participating electronic musician.

• **Instructional composition**—Some electronic works are realized by following written instructions that are not specific to any particular sound source, but provide a detailed framework for completing the work. Cage's *Williams Mix* provided detailed instructions for the editing and assembly of pieces of magnetic tape (see Figure 3.3).

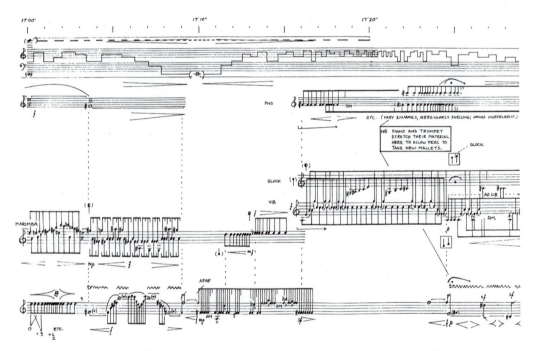

Figure 12.9 Example score for electronic tape and other instruments: excerpt from . . . *the serpent snapping eye* (1978) for trumpet, percussion, piano, and computer synthesized tape by Roger Reynolds (b.1934). (C.F. Peters Music Corp.)

Any realization of that work would utilize the same envelope characteristics and durations specified by Cage, even though the sources of sounds could vary from realization to realization. At the other end of the instructional spectrum are works for which only the most general of instructions are provided. Annea Lockwood's *From the River Archive* (1973) instructs the performer as follows:

> Find a brook or fast flowing river in as isolated a place as you can reach. Placing the microphone(s) near the surface at a spot where the water is creating a richly textured sound, make a tape recording at least a half-hour long. Note the name of the river, the place and date.

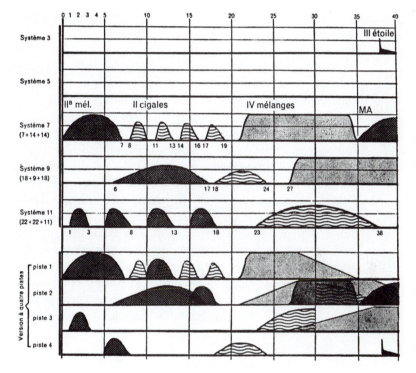

Figure 12.10 Example technical score with graphical elements: *Eclipses musique électronique pour quatre colonnes sonores* (1964), for four-track tape, by Swiss composer Werner Kaegi (b. 1926).

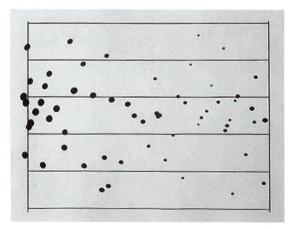

Figure 12.11 Example graphical score: *Transicion I* (1959) by Mauricio Kagel.

> Play the tape back on a cassette recorder, in some public place, for one person at a time (using headphones). Turn the listener's head very gently from side to side, tilted toward one shoulder, then toward the other as he or she is listening. Suggest that the listener closes his or her eyes to listen. Tell each other personal experiences with rivers/brooks/etc; dreams involving them; memories.[27]

There was an effort during the early history of electronic music to find a workable approach to notating such works. At the GRM studios in Paris, Pierre Schaeffer led investigations into the spectral analysis of music for the purpose of understanding the nature of sound objects (see Figure 12.12). This analysis was key to understanding the physical properties of sound and ways in which parameters such as pitch, amplitude, timbre, envelope, and duration could be manipulated using the resources of the electronic music studio.

Although Schaeffer was well grounded in classical music composition, he struggled to find a way of translating a music composed of sound objects into written music using conventional techniques. His colleague Pierre Henry was a more practiced composer and immediately grasped some useful techniques for visualizing his electronic works as scores. One early experiment was Henry's *Antiphonie* (1952), for which he scored several components of the sound without specifying particular notes or rhythms.

Antiphonie represented a break from the purely montage formula behind much of the earliest *musique concrète*. Henry used the *Phonogène* for this short work, a special tape player designed by Pierre Schaeffer that allowed the speed of a tape to be shifted instantaneously to any one of 12 preset speeds under the control of a keyboard. The three-minute composition was specified using a visual grid of 12 sections. Graphic symbols were used to specify the parameters for two opposing instrumental voices, noting general pitch range, the envelope of a sound, duration of each sound, the occurrence of silence, and the manner in which the sounds were mixed. This systematic, quasi-serial approach to composing electronic music was also being explored in Cologne by Stockhausen and his colleagues. Stockhausen himself would elevate the application of serial techniques in

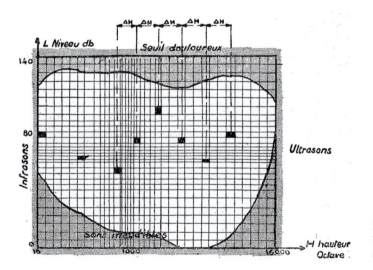

Figure 12.12
Sound spectra analysis
by Pierre Schaeffer.
(Schaeffer, 1952)

electronic music to a fine art prior to branching out into a less formulaic, albeit controlled approach to his works.

The application of chance operations is frequently employed to realize electronic music, especially with the addition of computers to the composing process. Software such as *Max/MSP* provides a ready means to apply randomizing routines to any aspect of a performance, from the operation of software instruments to the channeling of MIDI signals to the spatial distribution of the resulting music. Yet, even with the aid of computers, true randomness is really a definition provided by whomever is writing the routine. Cage remarked to the author that there was no such thing as true randomness, just somebody's definition of true randomness.[28] Christian Wolff, who worked closely with Cage for many years, was well aware that individual composers applied the concept of chance to suit their own motivations:

> What was so shocking intellectually to everybody was this notion of randomness, that you gave up control. And yet it was clear that control operates at many different levels or angles, and that there was just as much control in John's work as there might be in Stockhausen's or Boulez's. It was just a question of where you applied it and how you focused it.[29]

So with electronic music came just about every method of composing imaginable: graphical scores on paper or transparent sheets of plastic; computer-generated algorithms; written instructions; oral commands; audible performance cues; and so on. In a field of music where no standardized method exists for notating works, traditionalists still debate the value of electronic music as music at all. Pauline Oliveros has wrestled with this perception for most of her career:

> My way of composing is seen either as a substantial contribution to the field or it is dismissed as not real music because it is not written in the conventional way and cannot be judged conventionally. It is dismissed because of a lack of written notes, or because participants are asked to invent pitches and rhythms according to recipes or to respond to metaphors. Musicians accustomed to reading notes and rhythms often are shocked by the bareness of the notation compared to familiar conventional scores which direct their attention to specific pitches and rhythms which to them seem predictable and repeatable. What I value is the more unpredictable and unknowable possibilities that can be activated by not specifying pitches and rhythms. I prefer organic rhythms rather than exclusively metrical rhythms. I prefer full spectrum sound rather than a limited scalar system. I sometimes use meter and scales within this fuller context of sound oriented composition.[30]

Artikulation—The Story of a Composition

György Ligeti (1923–2006) was born in Transylvania, Romania, to Jewish parents. During World War II, he survived a forced labor camp but lost his brother and father to the Holocaust. Living in Hungary after the war, he completed his studies and became an instructor in music theory. But once again his life was disrupted when the Soviet Union violently struck down the Hungarian revolution for independence in 1956 and became an occupying force. Ligeti and many other artists fled the country. He went to Austria and eventually became an Austrian citizen. This displaced composer found sympathetic artists in Cologne, where he began composing avant garde instrumental compositions. In 1957, an encounter with Karlheinz Stockhausen and Gottfried Michael Koenig of the electronic music studio of West German Radio would change his approach to writing music forever. Ligeti became immersed in the physical analysis of sound and its application in shaping the sound of musical works. Although Ligeti only completed three short works of electronic music before returning to instrumental composition—*Glissandi* (1957), *Pièce électronique* (unfinished, 1958), and *Artikulation* (1958)—it seems clear that he could not have conceived some of his later works had he not learned the techniques of composing with slowly modulating textures and timbres that came with producing tape music. Each of his best-known instrumental works, *Atmosphères* (1961) for orchestra and *Lux Aeterna* (1966) for sixteen voices, was a highly textural piece that one can imagine being produced electronically. In fact, when heard today, the sweeping, microtonal harmonies of these works have more in common with modern spectral composing than any conventions in use in the 1960s.

Ligeti's best-known electronic work is *Artikulation*. He composed this piece for tape in early 1958 under the tutorship of engineer and composer Koenig and British composer Cornelius Cardew (1936–81), who was Stockhausen's assistant at the time. In composing *Artikulation*, Ligeti took a path that diverged from Stockhausen's serial approach in which every minute detail was managed by an overall schema. Ligeti combined chance operations in the selection of specific sound passages while maintaining a general plan for the overall structure of the work.[31]

Ligeti planned the work and collected recorded sounds during January and February of 1958 and assembled the tape piece during February and March. It was premiered on the radio in Cologne on March 25 of the same year. The work was an extension of Ligeti's interest in phonetics at the time, specifically the spectral properties of noise in vocal sounds and the nature of phonemes in spoken words and phrases. *Artikulation* was conceived as a work that would be composed of artificial speech: electronic sounds imitating the spectral properties and dynamic characteristics of the spoken word. Taking this approach he hoped to establish "conditions of aggregation," beginning with individual categories of sounds and gradually combining and recombining them in mixtures, or articulations, of artificial phonemes, words, and sentences. He described his plan of attack in this way:

> First I chose types with various group-characteristics and various types of internal organization, as: grainy, friable, fibrous, slimy, sticky and compact materials. An investigation of the relative permeability of these characters indicated which could be mixed and which resisted mixture.[32]

Ligeti electronically created a collection of artificial phonemes in the studio and then categorized them into 42 types of basic materials. Some of the sounds were longer than others. Because he did not want any category of sound to dominate the piece, he devised a formula to determine how much of a given sound could be used so as not to favor those that were longer. His notes for the piece included tables spelling out the durations and number of instances for each of the 42 categories of sound materials. These tables provided values for cutting up the magnetic tape recordings into small pieces

JOHN CAGE ON COMPOSING MUSIC

Figure 12.13   John Cage performing *Improvisation I—Child of Tree or Branches* (1975). It consisted of playing on cacti and other plant materials amplified using contact microphones. "My reason for improvising on them," explained Cage, "is because the instruments are so unknown that as you explore, say the spines of a cactus, you're not really dealing with your memory or your taste. You're exploring." (John Cage Trust)

1985, I asked John Cage the following question: How do you make music? His reply:

> I have found a variety of ways of making music (and I continue to look for others) in which sounds are free of a theory as to their relationships. I do not hear music before making it, my purpose being to hear as beautiful something I have not before heard. Most of the ways I have found involve the asking of questions rather than the making of choices, and *I Ching* chance operations pinpoint among all the possible answers the natural ones to be used. These questions generally have to do with the writing of music which is later to be practiced and finally performed and heard. Though they sometimes take advantage of technological means (recording means, the activation of electronic sound systems, the programming of computer output of actual sounds), or just acoustic means, instruments over which I have no control (a music of contingency). I hear ambient sound as music. Therefore I have no need to make music, though I continue, as cheerfully as I can, to do so.[33]

INNOVATION

matching the prescribed lengths. Ligeti then placed snippets of sounds with similar sonic characteristics into separate bins. The process of assembling the work proceeded in five successive stages during which he blindly selected bits of tape from the bins, edited them together into longer pieces of tape, and divided them up again by cutting them in half. The shortest snippets, which he called "sounds," were spliced together to become longer segments called "texts," which, after being divided in half, became "words," and so forth. Figure 12.14 illustrates Ligeti's staged process for composing *Artikulation*. At each step of the process, some of the sounds would be further modified through studio techniques such as filtering and reverberation. The completed piece was intended to be heard using four channels, two in front of the listener and two in the rear.

Ligeti's notes and tables for producing *Artikulation* resemble the elements of a technical score, but they are not complete enough for any other person to reproduce the work

Figure 12.14 Ligeti's staged process for composing the tape piece *Artikulation*.

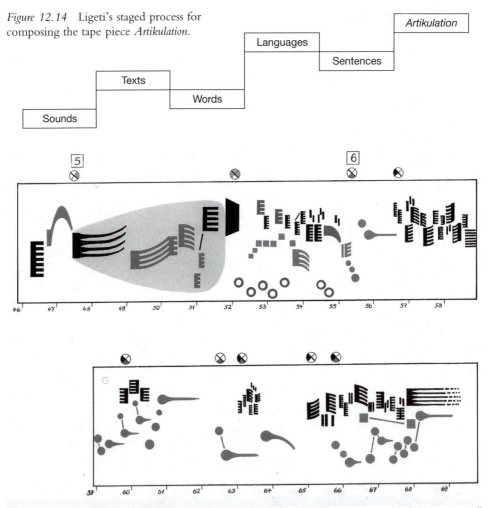

Figure 12.15 Rainer Wehinger's "score for listening" for Ligeti's tape piece, *Artikulation*, a small section of which is shown here, provides the listener with a visual roadmap of the piece. This aural score contains a key to various symbols used in the graphic to depict pitch ranges and other dynamics of the tape sound. (Schott, 1970)

from scratch. Interestingly, in 1970, music educator Rainer Wehinger of the Academy of Music in Stuttgart created a "score for listening" (*hörpartitur*) for *Artikulation*, a section of which is shown in Figure 12.15. Wehinger's aural score attempted to provide the listener with a visual roadmap of the piece, and used graphic symbols to represent a variety of sound parameters, from pitch range and filtered noise to subharmonic waves and pulses. The aural score included a time scale along the bottom so that one could follow along while listening to the recording. The artistic value in visualizing this work of electronic music is plain to see, but it becomes even more vivid when one follows along to any of several available YouTube videos that track the score while listening to the work.

STOCKHAUSEN: VIBRATIONS OF HIS UNIVERSE

Stockhausen's tape works during the 1960s were few in number but highly influential. *Telemusik* (1966), which he composed in the studio of Radio Nippon Hōsō Kyōkai (NHK) in Tokyo, can legitimately be called the first recording of global or world music in the modern sense—a work that weaves influences from various cultures into one musical entity. Like *Gesang der Jünglinge*, it consisted of a seamless contour of electronic and acoustic sounds. The acoustic sounds in this case were drawn from recordings of the indigenous music of Japan, Bali, China, Spain, North Africa, Hungary, and the Amazon. Stockhausen called it his first step in composing a "music of the whole world, of all countries and all races."[34]

Telemusik was also important because it was designed to join composed elements of electronic music with elements that could be performed in a live setting. The work had a performable score that could be realized using electronic sound generators, filters, and mixing controls in tandem with pre-recorded material.

Stockhausen's most influential piece of electronic music was *Hymnen* (1966–67). It remains the finest example of formal tape composition of the 1960s. The word *Hymnen* means "anthems." The piece was 113 minutes long and occupied four album sides when it was originally released on record. Each side, or "region," used a number of national anthems as source material. Most of the anthems were taken from commercial recordings that Stockhausen then modified and processed as part of his overall sound design. At least one anthem, the Russian, was beautifully realized in a stripped-down form using purely electronic means. The work had

Figure 12.16   Stockhausen in the Cologne studio during the composition of *Hymnen*, 1966. (Stockhausen Verlag)

LISTENING GUIDE 12.2

Title: *Hymnen: Region III* (opening)

Artist: Karlheinz Stockhausen   **Year**: 1966–67   **Duration**: 2:28

Genre: Tape composition

Electronic Instrumentation: Tape composition.

Background: This is an excerpt from an extended work of electronic music called *Hymnen*, an elaborate combination of electronic music and concrete sounds incorporating the recordings of worldwide national anthems as well as other sounds. The length of the piece is variable, although the original recorded version lasted 113 minutes. The composer often performed the work live, combining taped sounds with those of live acoustic musicians and amplified sounds, and employing a system for manually adjusting the distribution of the sound throughout the performance space using a four-speaker system. The work is divided into four "regions" or parts. This excerpt is from the beginning of *Region III* (dedicated to John Cage). It continues the realization of the Russian anthem in purely electronic tones. This piece, with its nearly indefinable form and spacey effects was a pinnacle of tape composition techniques originating in the NWDR electronic music studios in Cologne. It was also an influential work in the early development of "space music."

	Listen For: Hints of the Russian national anthem, the combination of natural and electronic tonalities, special tape effects including echo, and the use of the Springer device for suspending taped sounds.
0:00–0:45	The piece opens with a sequence of nine booming electronic chords accompanied by a cloud of chirping sounds. The chords are part of the electronic realization of the Russian anthem continued from the previous section of the piece. The blocks of chords appear to have been sustained artificially by the use of a device called the Springer, used to loop and suspend tape sounds in real time. Several snippets of other anthems are heard beginning at 0:14, all of which are radically processed through variable speed adjustments, reverberation, filtering, and intermixing with electronic tones.
0:46–2:28	The cloud of chirping sounds multiplies in density and is joined by crowd voices and an electronic drone. The electronic tones and crowd sounds gradually rise in pitch, breaking up to become part of the fabric of a broader palette of electronic tones. At about 1:55, the crowd sounds gradually lower in pitch, become muted by a low-pass filter, and appear to be part of a repeating tape loop. The crowd sounds eventually resemble those of a flock of squawking sea gulls, accented by a loop of short electronic bird-like sounds.

Compare and Contrast

Tête et queue du dragon (1959) by Luc Ferrari

Ludwig von Bayern (1978) by Klause Schulze

Low of Vibration (1994) by Tetsu Inoue

the unpredictable atmosphere of a collage, but moved in precise, well-planned stages that unfolded musically through changing sounds and textures. It was replete with broadcast sounds, miscellaneous noises, shortwave radio interference, crowd sounds, and Stockhausen's breathing—which inspired the eerie breathing sequence in the movie *2001: A Space Odyssey* (1968) when HAL the computer was being shut down. Stockhausen used the *Springer* device to suspend sounds in time, allowing him to freeze a moment of music and further transform it in real time as it floated, seemingly weightless and detached from the way that sounds are expected to behave. This technique was a central textural motif of the work.

Stockhausen underscored his personal indebtedness to the composers Pierre Boulez, Henri Pousseur, John Cage, and Luciano Berio by dedicating each of the four regions to one of them. *Hymnen* was presented many times using a quadraphonic sound setup, and Stockhausen also composed a concert version that included parts for six soloists. *Hymnen* is an authentically original masterwork of electronic music—a piece that continues to inspire new composers. It has an undeniable humanity that launched an entire generation of imitators in what might be called electronic space music.

Aus den sieben Tagen (*From the Seven Days*, 1968) is a cycle of works representing, perhaps, the least obsessive side of Stockhausen's personality. Drawn up as a series of 12 compositions, each for different instrumentation, the score for each merely consists of a simple, interpretive text instruction. The performers of *Es* (*It*) were asked to play:

> only when one has achieved the state of non-thinking, and to stop whenever one begins to think . . . As soon as a player thinks of something (e.g. that he is playing; what he is playing; what someone else is playing or has played; how he should react; that a car is driving past outside etc.) he should stop, and only start again when he is just listening, and at one with what is heard.[35]

The instructions were even more abstract for *Aufwärts* (*Upwards*):

> – Play a vibration in the rhythm of your smallest particles.
> – Play a vibration in the rhythm of the universe.
> – Play all the rhythms that you can distinguish today between the rhythms of your smallest particles and the rhythm of the universe, one after another and each one for so long, until the air carries it on.[36]

Stockhausen clearly owed a debt of gratitude to John Cage, La Monte Young, Yoko Ono, and Fluxus composers for having paved the way for music consisting of highly subjective instructional inspiration. Legendary avant-garde jazz composer Sun Ra was himself a little unsure of what to make of *Aus den sieben Tagen* for on his personal copy of the recordings he scribbled the note: "This is totally insane."[37] There is an unintentionally amusing footnote on the liner sleeve of the original recording bearing the above instructions for *Aufwärts*: "It should be mentioned here, that the musicians had previously interpreted several other texts in which rhythms of the limbs, cells, molecules, atoms, or rhythms of the body, heart, breathing, thinking, intuition etc. occur."[38] This note was added to explain that by the time the performers had recorded *Aufwärts*, they had already gone through several earlier pieces in the cycle under Stockhausen's coaching to fine-tune their meditative skills. Stockhausen was not at all comfortable with spontaneity, but this was not readily apparent to anyone who merely listens to the seemingly formless sonic beauty of these recordings.

In 1971, the author was composing music scored for small ensembles of electronic musicians, each of whom was required to wear headphones connected to one of the other players. They were instructed to play in response to what they were hearing, but they could not hear the sounds of their own playing because of the headphones. Upon sharing this piece with Cage and naively suggesting that it was an attempt to produce a form of improvisation like Stockhausen's *Aus den sieben Tagen*, Cage remarked, "I think it is different from Stockhausen. He lets people play freely, but before the audience hears it he controls it from a master panel."[39]

Stockhausen's output of magnetic tape compositions diminished during the 1960s as he became increasingly interested in working with electronic music in a live setting. In 1964, he began to tour extensively with a group of players and set out to compose works involving the electronic modification and accompaniment of music being played by instrumentalists. He called this music "intuitive," a term that suggests free improvisation, but it was not. His intuitive music was scored, albeit minimally or graphically in many cases, providing great freedom for the individual performers within the boundary lines established by the composer. This set of works consisted largely of the amplification and modulation of the sounds of acoustic instruments with electronic effects. *Mixtur* (1964) and *Mikrophonie I* (1964) were the first of these.

Mixtur was scored for an ensemble consisting of woodwinds, brass, cymbals, and tam tams, plus four ring modulators and four sine wave generators. Microphones picked up the sounds of the instruments and fed them into the ring modulators. Four musicians played sine wave oscillators to modulate the ring modulators, changing the texture and width of the sidebands being triggered by the processed sounds of the instruments. The smallest, inaudible sounds of the cymbals and tam-tams were amplified using contact microphones and modified in the same manner. All of this was played and mixed according to Stockhausen's instructions, and he controlled the final blend that was amplified and projected by loudspeakers. It was music of timbres and textures and amplified small sounds—a blast of continuously changing, seemingly formless playing. Stockhausen also composed a version of *Mixtur* for a smaller ensemble and, taking a page out of Cage's book, gave the conductor the freedom to vary the number of players in any way.

Stockhausen's passion for live performance led to many pieces following the same general approach: instruments played live and modified by electronics in real time. What differed from work to work were the instrumental timbres he chose, the changes to filtering, volume, duration, spatial projection, and other dynamics that he controlled as the "mixer," and the nature of his instructions to the musicians. *Mikrophonie I* fully exploited the amplification of the small sounds of the tam-tam. *Mikrophonie II* (1965) used 12 singers, 4 ring modulators, a Hammond organ, and tape. *Solo* (1965–66) was for any solo melody instrument and tape, wherein the musician's playing was amplified and mixed with the sounds of a pre-recorded tape. The frequently performed *Prozession* (1967) was written for his five touring players, including Fred Alings and Rolf Gehlhaar (tam-tam), Johannes Fritsch (viola), Harald Bojé (Electronium), and Aloys Kontarsky (piano). In this work, the musicians' previous experience with earlier Stockhausen works forms the basis for their parts. Stockhausen explained, "The musical events are not individually notated, but are variants of parts of my earlier compositions played from memory by the performers."[40] The tam-tam players and the "microphonist" used

Mikrophonie I as their reference point; the viola player referred to *Gesang der Jünglinge*, *Kontakte*, and *Momente*; the Electronium player referred to *Telemusik* and *Solo*; and the pianist referred to *Klavierstücke I–XI* (1952–56) and *Kontakte*. All the time, Stockhausen manned the "monitoring desk," where he mixed and controlled the spatial projection of the sound through loudspeakers. He also frequently recycled tape music from previous compositions as material to be mixed with the live performances.

Even the most astute listener of Stockhausen's live electronic works will have trouble understanding what was "composed" and what was not in this music. Yet underlying all of this so-called spontaneity is the mind of Stockhausen. In *Kurzweillen* (1968), six players reacted spontaneously to the sounds being broadcast over six shortwave radios. The composer himself asked the performers to react "on the spur of the moment," yet he defined the processes and rules by which they reacted:

> What I have composed is the process of transforming: how they react to what they hear on the radio; how they imitate it and then modulate or transpose it in time—longer or shorter, with greater or lesser rhythmic articulation—and in space—higher or lower, louder or softer; when and how and how often they are to play together or alternately in duos, trios or quartets; how they call out to

Figure 12.17 Stockhausen at the control console during the live electronic music performances of his troupe at the Osaka World's Fair, 1970. (Stockhausen Verlag)

each other, issue invitations, so that together they can observe a single event passing amongst them for a stretch of time, letting it shrink and grow, bundling it up and spreading it out, darkening it and brightening it, condensing it and losing it in embellishments.[41]

One crowning technical achievement of Stockhausen's concertizing days were the performances given at the 1970 World's Fair in Osaka Japan. He was asked to collaborate with an architect in designing a performance space for his electronic music. Like Varèse before him, Stockhausen was able to design an auditorium from scratch conceived only for the purpose of listening to electronic music. It was the perfect opportunity to fully explore his interest in the spatial deployment of sounds. The resulting hall was a huge globe that could seat 600 people on a metal platform in the middle, which consisted of a grid so that sound could travel through it. Loudspeakers were organized in circles to surround the audience by sound, and there were seven circles of speakers from the bottom of the globe to its top—three below the audience and four above. The music consisted of various Stockhausen works played on tape, sung, or performed by live musicians perched in six balconies around and above the audience. All of the sound was piped into a mixer ("soundmill") controlled by Stockhausen or one of his assistants. The mixer had two pods for directing the sound to any vertical or horizontal configuration of speakers. The sound could be manually rotated at speeds up to five revolutions per second in any direction.

Stockhausen described how he could control the sound:

> I could decide to make a voice go in an upward spiral movement for two or three minutes, either clockwise or anti-clockwise, while at the same time another player's sound moved in a circle using the other soundmill, and a third crossed in a straight line, using just two potentiometers.[42]

This was one of Stockhausen's most elaborate experiments in spatial composition. The troupe of 20 musicians from five countries worked for six and a half hours every day for 183 days. Over a million visitors experienced the spectacle in Osaka during the World's Fair.

During the past 30 years, Stockhausen largely turned his attention back to instrumental and orchestral works, and also opera. The criteria he developed for composing electronic music continued to serve him well, and he often found ways to integrate electronic elements into his work. One reason for his success and longevity in the field was that he was always meticulous about documenting and scoring his works. It is not unusual, even to this day, to find independent groups staging recitals of such works as *Prozession* or the various versions of *Mikrophonie* because the composer's instructions were clear and the equipment needed to realize them in a live setting was readily available and not proprietary only to Stockhausen.

Stockhausen's electronic music was greatly enhanced by the addition of the EMS Synthi 100 analog synthesizer to the Cologne studio in the early 1970s, giving him greater control over musical scales, the recorded sequencing of notes, and the manipulation of all dynamic parameters of the sound in real time. The first piece on which he used the Synthi 100 to full effect was *Sirius* (1975–77) for electronic music, trumpet, soprano, bass clarinet, and bass. Stockhausen's comments about the electronic music for *Sirius* show us that he has come to view electronic music as a means for experiencing a unification with natural forces in the universe:

> By listening to this music . . . one perceives how the newly discovered means and structural possibilities of electronic music can awaken in us a completely new consciousness for revelations, transformations and fusions of forms, which would never have been possible with the old musical means, and become increasingly similar to art of the metamorphosis in nature.[43]

EXPERIMENTAL ELECTRONIC MUSIC

1 *Antiphonie* (1953) by Pierre Henry
   Early serial tape composition

2 *Poème électronique* (1958) by Edgard Varèse
   Classic tape composition using montage

3 *Concret PH* (1958) by Iannis Xenakis
   Modified and amplified small sounds

4 *Sound Patterns* (1961) by Pauline Oliveros
   For voices and electronic modification on tape

5 *White Cockatoo* (1966) by İlhan Mimaroğlu
   Tape composition using abstract sounds applied to sonata form

6 *Telemusik* (1966) by Karlheinz Stockhausen
   Tape composition using world music recordings; also had a component for live performance

7 *Hymnen* (1966–67) by Karlheinz Stockhausen
   Classic tape composition

8 *Bird Cage* (1972) by John Cage
   Tape composition using chance operations

9 *Points* (1973–74) by Ruth Anderson
   Synthesis using sine tones

10 *Resonate (noise)* (2006) by Matt Rogalsky
   Computer music

LISTEN

WENDY CARLOS: IN A MORE CLASSICAL TRADITION

After ten intensive years of analog synthesizer experience coaxing sounds out of the Moog, Wendy Carlos and her producer, Rachel Elkind, did some serious homework before considering digital synthesis. They visited Bell Labs in the mid-1970s. They tried the Fairlight CMI, which Carlos described as being "sample-playback-oriented, quite limited at the time. It was only playing back a single sample at a time. You couldn't filter it. You couldn't merge samples. You couldn't put them together in a key-map.

It was very limited."[44] At Dartmouth, they played with the early Synclavier. Carlos thought it was too expensive and "architecturally kind of thin." She explained:

> What was thin wasn't the sound. The distinction here is that you could sample with it and get very rich timbres if they were rich samples. Architecturally, it just had four layers that could either be an oscillator pair or a sample. That's not enough. It did not have much meat on the bones for advanced synthesis, additive and complex.[45]

An engineer was hired to build a digital synthesizer to her specifications, but that experiment became too expensive to continue: "It was an amusing, deep device, but we didn't have the money or the staff to develop it further, or market it. It's foolish for a composer to try to do that on his or her own."[46]

Of all the digital synthesizers being developed at the time, she took a liking to the one made by Digital Keyboards Inc. Their first model was the General Development System (GDS), then came the less-expensive Synergy. In evaluating musical technology, Carlos's standards are high:

> The GDS/Synergy was a machine I got very deeply involved with in 1981, my first significant involvement with a digital machine. It is still superior in certain areas to the machines that have come out since . . . No one else has bothered to do some of the things the Synergy could do. Yes, others have done it quieter, with greater fidelity, better high frequencies, and less hiss. But they have not developed the real difficult tasks, like full additive synthesis with complex modulation.[47]

Figure 12.18
Wendy Carlos with her two Synergy digital synthesizers, October 1986. Her left hand is operating the instrument's fader knob, which she used to shape the notes being played by the right hand. (Vernon L. Smith, © 2001 Serendip LLC—All Rights Reserved)

Some of the "other" brands that also took up residence in her studio included the Yamaha DX models and later SY77, the Kurzweil K2000/2500/2600 digital keyboards, and the Korg Z1 for modeling several acoustic sounds. Carlos is apt to use any and all of these instruments in her current work, along with *Digital Performer* MIDI software from Mark of the Unicorn, to orchestrate the many instrumental and electronic timbres of her music.

Carlos wants to get inside the sound when she composes. Much like Stockhausen, she composes the sound itself, often transforming it into a rich *"**Klangfarbenmelodie**"*— a melody of changing timbres. Because of this, she is more interested in the precision controls of a synthesizer than the bells and whistles:

> You can't have a synthesizer that purports to be a great musical instrument if basically all it has are a few canned sounds. You try to find an instrument that is fairly open-ended—like the old first synthesizers from the days of the RCA and eventually the Moog and the Buchla synthesizers—that they have enough things that you can control with enough degree of precision so you can begin to shape even a small palette according to your own taste and the desires of what you need for a particular context.
>
> You are looking for a device that is of high quality—like a Steinway is an excellent-sounding piano and the Stradivarius is an excellent-sounding violin— but you need more than that. You also need it to be responsive to a human being's performance touch, to an orchestrator or instrument designer's needs on variations of timbre and have enough subtleties that the things that are weak about the instrument can be overridden by dint of willpower when you sit down to come up with a sound that might not be the easiest kind of sound for this device to make. There should be enough supersets of things you can get at that can allow one to come pretty close to the sound that's in your head, that you are going to look for. That's how I approach things. I usually have some pretty good ideas in my head of what I'm looking for and try to have enough versatility under the hood to let me get at it.
>
> Finally, you need a good interface. You need something which is a little less tedious to get at all of those parameters than some of the early-'80s devices. There were some instruments that made it really very painful to get at a few basic properties. Manufacturers made it too difficult to bother with. I think that if you put too many hurdles in the way it ceases to be of much use.[48]

Carlos's major works over the years cover a lot of musical territory. What unifies them all is a remarkable sense of wonder, and joy. Even *Tales of Heaven and Hell*—with its dark sound palette and sense of foreboding—manages to emote a kind of unearthly mystery for its disembodied souls. She uses less-common tonal scales and often microtonal scales of her own invention. Timbre and tone color are constructed with the same care as a melody or counterpoint. It is music that springs from the intuition of a gifted composer.

The *Switched-On* series established Carlos as a master at synthesizing classical works as electronic music, a path down which many imitators followed. After creating two albums of Bach interpretations, she was recruited by Stanley Kubrick to do much of the same for the soundtrack of *A Clockwork Orange*. The challenge facing Carlos in that case was monumental—creating convincing orchestrations of Beethoven's *Ninth Symphony* and other symphonic music. It was far different from transcribing small-ensemble or keyboard music and required a seriously altered palette of new sounds. This project immersed Carlos for the first time in one of her continuing musical passions: the modeling and synthesis of acoustic orchestral instruments. Adding to the multilayered arrangements for *A Clockwork Orange* were the sounds of a synthesized choir created by Carlos using a vocoder and many vocal performances by Elkind that added a haunting humanity to the music.

The soundtrack to *A Clockwork Orange* also gave Carlos a chance to leave the idiom of classical interpretation and compose some new music of her own. Most notable were two works that were only sparingly used in the movie: *Timesteps* and *Country Lane*. These works established Carlos as a composer with a new voice in electronic music. This was music of rhythm, harmony, melody, and a rich timbral palette: an exposé of movement and emotion.

Carlos's work immediately following *A Clockwork Orange* was yet another dramatic departure from Bach and Beethoven. *Sonic Seasonings* (1972), originally released as a double album, was instrumental in starting the movement in "new age" music that persists today: soothing harmonies, electronic meditations, and blends of music with the sounds of nature. It was Carlos's version of *musique concrète* but without the melodrama. She and Elkind combined electronic simulations of natural sounds created on the Moog with actual recordings of outdoor environments and quietly strung it together with musical themes that dissolved in and out of the sonic whole.

Several years after *Sonic Seasonings*, in 1980, Carlos embarked on a mission to upgrade her equipment so that she could more easily endeavor to create the music she was imagining. The digital technology provided by the Crumar GDS and Synergy instruments gave her the tools she needed to perfect synthesized replicas of orchestral sounds, putting the entire orchestra and many extrapolations at her fingertips. This required many months of methodical work with the programming of these digital synthesizers, but the results were stunningly robust and have been of use to her for many years.

Digital Moonscapes (1984) was completed using what Carlos dubbed the "LSI Philharmonic"—programs using large-scale integration circuits to churn out realistic-sounding orchestral instruments. This was the first digitally synthesized orchestra of any significance that a single composer could command.

When faced by critics who only view her achievement as that of replacing the human musician with a digital one, she scoffed by focusing rightfully on the promise of the resulting music:

> But why do all this? Do we now have the "orchestra in a box"? Not really, considering the time and effort required to produce an orchestral recording in this manner. Rather, we should consider the reality of replication as only a measure of the quality of the synthesis, not as the ultimate goal. The goal ought to be providing the base on which to build new sounds with orchestral qualities that have not been heard before but are equally satisfying to the ear . . . look for the next steps using the experimental hybrid and imaginary sounds which have grown out of this work.[49]

Carlos's successive works have delivered on her promise of creating new and unimagined sounds that can be managed and played within the context of an orchestra.

Beauty in the Beast (1986) and *Tales of Heaven and Hell* (1998) are two of the most fully realized works of electronic music ever to apply the techniques of the traditional symphonic composer.

Even though Carlos has been the consummate electronic tinkerer throughout her career, she has now reached a point where she is more interested in composing than finding yet another new big technology to embrace:

> I don't think that any of the technologies have done anything but to tap the surface of a very rich vein that still lies, for the most part, buried. It will be explored in time, but not in my lifetime. That's fine. You would expect this to go on for decades, probably even a few centuries. The dream of the general-purpose, do-anything synthesizer has never arrived.[50]

The music of Wendy Carlos is experimental in its redrafting of scales and digital abstraction of acoustic sounds, yet familiar at its core of human sentiment and intellect. Synthesist Larry Fast, a collaborator of Carlos's, encapsulated her achievement: "By the time *Switched-On Bach* came out in 1968, Wendy Carlos proved to me that one person could use electronics to express a personal sonic vision."[51]

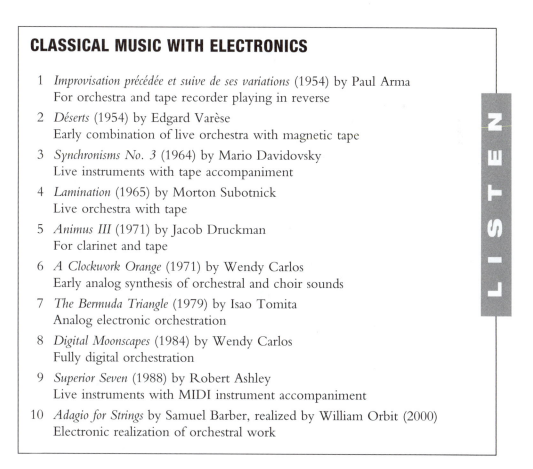

CLASSICAL MUSIC WITH ELECTRONICS

1 *Improvisation précédée et suive de ses variations* (1954) by Paul Arma
For orchestra and tape recorder playing in reverse

2 *Déserts* (1954) by Edgard Varèse
Early combination of live orchestra with magnetic tape

3 *Synchronisms No. 3* (1964) by Mario Davidovsky
Live instruments with tape accompaniment

4 *Lamination* (1965) by Morton Subotnick
Live orchestra with tape

5 *Animus III* (1971) by Jacob Druckman
For clarinet and tape

6 *A Clockwork Orange* (1971) by Wendy Carlos
Early analog synthesis of orchestral and choir sounds

7 *The Bermuda Triangle* (1979) by Isao Tomita
Analog electronic orchestration

8 *Digital Moonscapes* (1984) by Wendy Carlos
Fully digital orchestration

9 *Superior Seven* (1988) by Robert Ashley
Live instruments with MIDI instrument accompaniment

10 *Adagio for Strings* by Samuel Barber, realized by William Orbit (2000)
Electronic realization of orchestral work

LISTEN

The ability to put it all in perspective is a defining force behind Carlos's career:

> Music is something you are very lucky to be able to do. You are lucky to have this time in history when the field is morphing into something new and maybe a few of the little tidbits that you've been able to scratch out of the clay and the mud will have lasting effect . . . You can laugh at those who call you a nerd or laugh at those who say you're obsessive because that's how it's done. There's no way to get around that without doing a poor or clichéd job of it. You have to know what you're doing. Feeling and thinking.[52]

Although composing remains her focus, Carlos continues to work on the development of innovative electronic musical instruments. The latest is a supercharged digital pipe organ with four manuals, a touch-sensitive pedalboard, and a bevy of sound-shaping controls. The instrument uses high resolution digital samples of actual pipe organs and is MIDI controlled. The pedalboard includes note pedals as well as special control and expression pedals. "The paradigm of pipe organ turns out to be pretty good with synth timbres and even with orchestral instruments, too, explained Carlos. "But it *is* hard to learn how to play: you really have to have your wits about you at all times!"[53] A full report on the development of this custom instrument can be found at the composer's personal web site (www.wendycarlos.com).

THE ART OF DRONES AND MINIMALISM

Terry Riley and La Monte Young (b. 1935) were classmates at the University of California at Berkeley in 1959. They knew of Cage's work, were immersed in the world of classical music, the German school of serialism, and *musique concrète*, and were highly aware of the tape music experiments taking place at the Columbia–Princeton Electronic Music Center. Even though they were both rooted in the new music scene of northern California, both Riley and Young split from the core community of composers at Berkeley and the San Francisco Tape Music Center to pursue their own individual musical missions. Electronic music played a role in the development of their approaches to composition, but the two are most widely recognized as being key influences on a style of music called *minimalism*, which has had its own powerful impact on new music.

In 1959, Young attended a summer music course in Darmstadt, Germany, where he studied with Karlheinz Stockhausen. While in Germany he also happened to experience the piano recitals of David Tudor and performances by John Cage, both of which greatly affected his musical direction. Tudor later featured one of Young's compositions— *X for Henry Flynt*—at one of his Darmstadt performances. Terry Riley was impressed by him, later saying, "La Monte was definitely the focal point of the class. He was so radical. I had never come across anyone like that in my life before."[54]

Classmates of Young and Riley included Pauline Oliveros, Paul Epstein, Loren Rush, David Del Tredici, and Doug Lee. While Young and Riley were attending UC Berkeley, they were also working as co–musical directors for Ann Halprin's (b. 1920) Dancer's Workshop. There was a healthy rivalry growing between this group of composers. Riley remembers, "Everybody in that class was trying to out-do each other in being far-out and seeing what could be the most new and mind-blowing thing that somebody could do in music."[55]

La Monte Young: Musical Reductionist

Prior to Darmstadt, La Monte Young had already begun to explore the possibilities of lengthening the duration of the notes in his music. His *Trio for Strings* (1958) was a serial piece requiring about an hour to perform because it was constructed of lengthy sustained tones and long silences. It has been called the work that established Young as the "father of minimalism."[56]

After experiencing Cage for the first time in Darmstadt, Young boldly began to add chance elements to his work and to strip it of complexity altogether. There was also a touch of Zen, possibly inspired by Cage as well, in his newly developed reductionist point of view. One of his first works following Germany was *Vision* (1959), which Young calls his "assimilation of Darmstadt."[57] It prescribed a time frame of 13 minutes during which 11 precise sounds were made, the timing and spacing of which were governed by chance operations.[58] Inspired by Cage, Young was clearly conscious of the differences in his work that would set him apart from the elder statesman of experimental music. Cage's work from the early 1960s was imbued with a complexity mediated by chance operations. Cage's definition of modernism was that it consisted of "collage and juxtaposition."[59] This was evidenced by works exhibiting an extraordinarily busy mingling of audiovisual events. It was as if Cage were dropping an asteroid in a reflecting pool: ripples became tidal waves that saturated one's perceptions. In contrast, Young only slowly submerged himself in a still lake, minimizing the ripples that could break the surface. His work was about concentrating on a single thing very intensely, be it a sound, a process, an action, a thought, an environment, or some other possible element of a performance.

In 1960, Young moved to New York and worked from a loft in Greenwich Village. He began to explore radical interactions with audiences. He established contact with George Maciunas and contributed some works to the Fluxus movement in the early 1960s, a forum for exploring the radical aspects of social interaction with the audience. Some of his works from the early 1960s were reduced to simple textual instructions, another innovation that followed Cage but also led to similar practices by Oliveros, Stockhausen, Yoko Ono, and others. *Composition #5 1960* (1960) consisted of a series of instructions, such as:

> Turn a butterfly (or any number of butterflies) loose in the performance area.
> When the composition is over, be sure to allow the butterfly to fly away outside.
> The composition may be any length but if an unlimited amount of time is available,
> the doors and windows may be opened before the butterfly is turned loose and
> the composition may be considered finished when the butterfly flies away.[60]

Young met Marian Zazeela in 1962 and the two have worked together ever since. While her expertise has been the creating of light environments for Young's performances, she is also one of the musicians who contributes to his work. From 1962 to 1965, Young's interest in extended sounds and drones led to the formation of a performance group that was eventually called the Theater of Eternal Music. Members included Young and

Zazeela (vocal drones), Tony Conrad (violin), John Cale (viola), and Angus MacLise (percussion). (Cale and MacLise would go on to be founding members of the Velvet Underground.) Sine wave oscillators were used to create sustained electronic pitches, as was a small aquarium pump that vibrated with an audible hum. One of the extended works that they did was *The Tortoise, His Dreams and Journeys* (1964). Pitches to be performed were determined ahead of time by Young and consisted only of intervals that were multiples of seven, three, two, and one. The group would improvise around this predefined sound palette, mostly holding and allowing the tones to permutate for as long as they could. It was played loudly so that the tones would intersect, producing new sidebands and beat frequencies. A performance could last four or five hours.

Young first encountered Indian musician Pandit Pran Nath (1918–96) in 1970. Learning about the art of the raga reinforced the kind of improvisation he had been practicing in the 1960s, but also suggested some subtle changes that became a part of his compositional thinking. Rather than begin a piece with a strong musical statement, as he was apt to do when playing the saxophone, he learned to let a work unfold slowly from the very first note, resulting in a more suspended, organically evolving sound. Around this time, he and Zazeela created the concept of the Dream House for expanded musical experiences. The Dream House was at once a physical location, a sound and light environment, and a performance that lasted over an extended period of time. The couple did performances in various places. Some were a week long, others two weeks. One performance in Germany was for 90 days, where the performers played the piece every day for a week and then the electronic tones were left to continue sounding for the remaining days.[61] It was performed using voices and electronic drones.

Terry Riley: The Pulse of a New Sound

Riley wrote *String Quartet* (1960), which was influenced in part by Young's *Trio for Strings* with its long sustained tones, but also by the fog horns that he could hear from his home in San Francisco. He then became involved in tape composition for a time with Morton Subotnick at the San Francisco Tape Music Center. Riley was probably the first composer to experiment with extended tape delay and the accumulating effect of running a single loop of tape through several tape machines, recording and re-recording signals in real time during the course of a performance. Riley came to his music of repeating figures and pulse rhythms largely by way of the tape recorder:

> My interest then was to have some good tape recorders and work with tape loops and tape-loop feedback. The electronics were opening up new ideas in music for me. But I had no money to obtain a tape recorder. So I always used my skills as a pianist playing in bars to try to finance that part of my career.[62]

There was another aspect of Young's music that resonated with Riley. He recognized it as Young's tendency to repeat lines of notes many times and to strip the structure of a piece down to its bare essentials. By doing this, Young greatly reduced the motion and tension of a piece of music, so that it did not appear to move. It evolved slowly, through whatever process had been defined ahead of time.

In C, Riley's seminal work from this period, could not have existed without the influence of La Monte Young.[63] Riley knew that the key to *In C* was its static nature, its motionlessness even in the midst of a complex production involving many instruments and musicians. Like the complex and machine-made player piano music of Conlon Nancarrow (1912–97), *In C* was a conceptual precursor to the idea of programming and sequencing in electronic music. Not surprisingly, Riley went from the acoustic environment of *In C* to create electronic works for organ and other keyboards, including *A Rainbow in Curved Air* (1969) and the lovely *Shri Camel* (1980), which used a Yamaha synthesizer tuned for just intonation. He also became immersed in Indian music and has succeeded for many years in creating music with a tendency toward the transcendental listening experience.

PROCESS MUSIC

At the heart of many works of electronic music is a process. Sometimes the process itself becomes the piece of music.

A few minutes after a piece of **process music** begins, the perceptive listener is usually thinking, "Oh, I get it." The composer has made her or his intentions obvious as the work unfolds. The piece is a kind of game that evolves by its own natural rules.

Much of the minimalist instrumental music of Steve Reich and Philip Glass is clearly process music: rules are established by the composers for the instrumentalists to follow unwaveringly. The controls available for electronic musical instruments, old and new, encourage a composer to think in terms of a process, whether that process is a hardwired patch of cables, a virtual patch inside a computer, or the turning of dials to various increments that shape the development of a piece of music.

Reich authored a personal manifesto about his process approach to composition in 1968, famously stating, "I do not mean the process of composition, but rather pieces of music that are, literally, processes."[64] He continued by explaining that he was interested in processes that could be clearly perceived, and that revealed themselves gradually, and then praised the use of "electro-mechanical means," although not to the exclusion of human players. He wanted to reveal all in the listening, leaving no hidden intentions or prejudices, to some extent excluding his personal taste from the music other than by choosing the manner and instrumentation by which it would be realized.

The tape recorder has inspired process music from the early days of its use. It can be used as a means for recording and composing electronic music, or, in the case of process music, the tape machine itself becomes an integral cog in the process. An early process piece that also served as an installation was *Music for the Stadler Gallery* (1964) by Earle Brown, in which four recordings of the same instrumental piece were continuously replayed on four separate tape recorders, with the four tracks becoming increasingly out of phase with one another. The total duration of this piece was 30 days. An even earlier experiment using tape as the crux of the process was *Improvisation précédée et suive de ses variations* (1954) by Paul Arma, in which a tape recording of an orchestra was played in reverse at the same time as the same orchestra was performing the work live.[65]

Tape composition using tape loops is an example of process music. When Oliveros set up one tape loop running through two tape recorders for *I of IV* (1966), she was taking advantage of the phenomenon of tape delays that was made possible by using two tape recorders. This was the defining concept or process behind the piece. Another was that the realization had to be possible in real time—a requirement of much process music. Oliveros was committed to performance pieces that could be engineered in front of an audience. The sounds were recorded on the first tape recorder, and were then played back on the second tape machine after an eight-second delay. Once played, the sound was fed directly back to the record channels of the first tape recorder. With the addition of reverberation, the result was a barrage of slowly unfolding undulations that changed dynamically as sounds continued to be repeated. Oliveros played an active role during a performance of *I of IV* by continuously triggering new sounds to add to the evolving mix. Every sound that entered the loop was slowly transformed as other sounds were continuously layered on top.

Brian Eno also worked with tape delay much in the manner defined by Oliveros. However, he expressed a somewhat indifferent attitude toward the outcome. He described the realization of *Discreet Music* (1975):

> Since I have always preferred making plans to executing them, I have gravitated toward situations and systems that, once set into operation, could create music with little or no intervention on my part. That is to say, I tend toward the roles of planner and programmer, and then become an audience to the results.[66]

Eno's composition existed of a diagram of the devices used to generate the music. His approach was identical to that of Oliveros except that the sound material was specifically melodic and he did not modify or interact with the sound once the process was set in motion. The result in *Discreet Music* is the gradual transformation of a recognizable musical phrase that starts the process. Along with collaborator Robert Fripp, Eno continued to produce several works and performances using this process technique, but with the increasing involvement of the performer as a real-time wild card for throwing sonic monkey wrenches into the steadily turning wheels of tape-delayed sound.

Steve Reich has composed some of the purest forms of process music. His early tape compositions dating from 1965 and 1966 used tape loops to explore the process of phasing—identical segments of recorded sound were played synchronously using more than one tape recorder and then were allowed to drift out of phase as the speed of one of the players was increased or decreased. As the sounds went in and out of "phase" with one another, they created new combinations of timbres, beats, and harmonics. When the sound material had a natural cadence, the process of phasing often created continuously shifting changes to the rhythm as the sound drifted in and out of phase. Adding additional tracks and loops of the same source sound increased the possibilities for phasing relationships.

Reich's first tape works using this phasing process were based on recordings of the human voice. He discovered the phasing process by accident while playing tape loops of a Pentecostal street preacher he had recorded in San Francisco. The resulting work, *It's Gonna Rain* (1965), began with the simplest demonstration of phasing as two loops began in unison, moved completely out of phase with one another, and then gradually came back together in unison. The same process began again with two longer loops to which Reich added another two and then eventually eight to create a multilayered series of phasing sequences happening in parallel. *Come Out* (1966) was shorter and used a brief tape loop of a young man describing the aftermath of a beating he was given at a police station in New York City. In this case a short phrase of the young man's voice was first played using two loops going gradually out of phase. The natural rhythm and

LISTENING GUIDE 12.3

Title: *Come Out* (excerpt)

Artist: Steve Reich   **Year**: 1966   **Duration**: 3:00

Genre: Tape composition using a phasing process

Electronic Instrumentation: Recorded voice, tape loops, filters, tape editing.

Background: Steve Reich, one of the founders of the contemporary classical musical style known as minimalism, attributes his interest in process forms of music to his early experiments with tape music. *Come Out* is built around a single snippet of recorded tape during which a teen states the words, "I had to like, open the bruise up and let some of the bruise blood come out to show them." Reich picks up the phrase "come out to show them" and builds his piece around the rhythms and tonalities of the young man's voice. He played two loops of this phrase going gradually out of phase, creating new rhythms and accentuating the melodic features of the spoken words. The two tracks were further embellished by an additional eight tracks to accentuate various tones and timbres of the original material.

	Listen For: The rhythms and changes created by the tape loops as they go out of phase. Additional tape effects added to embellish the result.
0:00–1:00	The full text of the young man's statement is played three times in a row, then the phrase "come out to show them" is begun using two loops of the phrase starting at exactly the same time on two different tape recorders. The two tape loops begin to go out of phase almost immediately, creating the drifting effect of the sound from right to left at about 0:22.
1:01–3:00	By this point, the two loops are only slightly out of phase, causing a spatial reverberation effect, but not affecting the rhythm of the music. By about 1:40, the strong accents of the words "Come out" begin to distinguish themselves as individual beats across the two tracks. By 2:26, this delay begins to sound like echo. By about 2:45, the echo effect is replaced by a natural compound rhythm that accents the replaying of each loop. The evolution of the piece continues in this fashion for another ten minutes as Reich introduces additional tracks one by one to increase the rhythmic complexity of the phasing process. Eventually, the meaning of the words is lost in the timbres and tonalities of the sounds as Reich uses tape delay to accumulate the dominant elements in the loops and allows them to degenerate in clarity and eventually fade out.

Compare and Contrast
Beautiful Soop (1967) by Pauline Oliveros
She Was a Visitor (1967) by Robert Ashley
I Am Sitting in a Room (1969) by Alvin Lucier

melody of the voice led to a kind of two-voice canon. Reich enriched the canon or "round" effect by then using four and finally eight tracks, the last consisting of a beautifully undulating pulse that sounds more like the reverberating sound of a ticking clock in a tunnel than the human voice.

Reich's use of the human voice as source material was a departure from the norm in electronic music of that time. He recalled why he made that choice in his first electronic music experiments:

> I was interested in real sounds, what was called musique concrète in those days, but I wasn't really interested in the pieces that had been done. I thought that they were boring, partly because the composers had tried to mask the real sounds. I was interested in using understandable sounds, so that the documentary aspect would be a part of the piece.[67]

Reich felt that by not altering the dynamics of the voice—its pitch and tone color—it retained its naturally emotive power. His phasing treatment then magnified the expression of the voice through rhythm and repetition.

After realizing *Come Out*, Reich moved on to compose music for live instrumentalists. His love of the phasing process was so strong that some of his first instrumental works from this period, such as *Piano Phase* (1967), recreated the effect with live musicians. He gradually applied a process approach to an entire canon of works, which placed him on the map as a leading proponent of minimalist music. *Four Organs* (1970), for four electric organs and maracas, was a tour de force of process composition. The piece was based on the augmentation of a single chord of music that was played, note by note, in a slowly unfolding sequence by four organists. Reich described the work in this way:

> *Four Organs* is an example of music that is a "gradual process." By that I do not mean the process of composition, but rather pieces of music that are, literally, processes. The distinctive thing about musical processes is that they determine all the note-to-note (sound-to-sound) details and the overall form simultaneously. (Think of a round or an infinite canon.) I am interested in perceptible processes. I want to be able to hear the process happening throughout the sounding music. To facilitate closely detailed listening, a musical process should happen extremely gradually.[68]

Four Organs is a 24-minute piece of music consisting of a single chord. The work had structure only because of the process through which the chord was disassembled and recombined.

A conceptual cousin to Reich's *Four Organs* music is *Points* (1973–74) by Ruth Anderson, which used only sine waves as the raw threads of the piece. Individual tones of different frequencies entered at intervals of five seconds, building up a multilayered fabric of sound that gradually began to thin again as the earlier threads of sound were pulled out. The process repeated several times but with different choices of pitches making up the threads.

Computer music is a particularly fertile field of possibilities for applying processes. This fact has been recognized by anyone working with any size or vintage of computer.

Figure in a Clearing (1977) by David Behrman used one of his homemade synthesizers based on the KIM-1 microcomputer. The process used in that work consisted of rules being carried out by the computer in real time during the performance. A live cellist responded to chord changes played by the computer, which employed 16 triangle wave oscillators. The computer could also choose those chord changes from any one of several preset tunings. The tempo of the chords was determined by an algorithm modeling the velocity of a satellite in a falling elliptical orbit around a planet. While the computer ran on its own using rules for making chord and tuning changes, the live cellist improvised using six pitches specified by the composer.

Alvin Lucier is the godfather of process music. He is widely known for works that begin with a process or idea that is then carried out according to written guidelines. The process in most of Lucier's works is often a physics lesson of some sort. In *Vespers* (1968), performers walked through a darkened space using handheld echo-location devices to find their way. In a version of *Clocker* (1978) that he produced with Nicolas Collins, Lucier wired himself to a galvanic skin response monitor that could measure the differences in skin resistance caused by mood changes. The electrical signal of the device was amplified and used as a control voltage to modify the speed of a ticking clock. The ticking was amplified and sent through a delay system, creating layers of ticking that Lucier could manipulate, much in the manner of Reich's phasing idea, but in real time rather than on tape: "I wanted to make a work in which a performer could speed up and slow down time, stopping it, if possible, simply by thinking."[69] *Clocker* was the literal implementation of this desire.

Lucier's list of process works is extensive, each one unique. *I Am Sitting in a Room* (1970) explored the process of sound filtering by the natural acoustics of a room by repeated playback and re-recording of successive generations of Lucier's voice reciting a short paragraph. *Music for Piano with One or More Snare Drums* (1990) picked up the sympathetically vibrating sounds of snare drums as "a pianist plays a series of notated pitches in chronological order, repeating them freely in overlapping patterns."[70] In *Music on a Long Thin Wire* (1980), a single piano wire was made to vibrate through the action of a horseshoe magnet and the current from an oscillator. As it vibrated, it began to sound. The acoustics of the room determined how the oscillator would have to be adjusted to get it to work.

The passing of time can also be the basis for a process piece. Cage was known for a series of "number" pieces, the titles of which all specified the precise length of the works down to the second. Two of these included *31' 57.9864" for a Pianist* (1954), and *27' 10.554" for a Percussionist* (1956). A stopwatch was required to perform these.

Composer Laurie Spiegel has worked with mainframe and microcomputers to compose music. Her approach often integrates a predefined logical process running in real time on a computer with actions that she can take during the generation of the sound:

> What computers excel at is the manipulation of patterns of information. Music consists of patterns of sound. One of the computer's greatest strengths is the opportunity it presents to integrate direct interaction with an instrument and its sound with the ability to compose musical experiences much more complex and well designed than can be done live in one take.[71]

Old Wave (1980) was composed using a Bell Labs computer that controlled analog synthesis equipment through a program called *GROOVE*. With the computer, Spiegel applied weighted mathematical probabilities to develop the pitches and rhythms of melodic lines. The weightings could be made to change "continuously or at given time, so that certain notes would dominate under certain conditions."[72]

In another Spiegel work, *Pentachrome* (1980), an algorithm is used to continuously accelerate the music, but Spiegel performed the rate and scale of the acceleration by adjusting knobs and dials in real time. This combination of real-time, almost improvisatory action on the part of a performer who is otherwise following a process is not an uncommon approach to process music when it is performed live. Spiegel always kept something of the human touch in her music:

> What I could control with the knobs was the apparent rate of acceleration (the amount of time it took to double the tempo), and the overall tempo at which this happened (the extremes of slow and fast that were cycled between). This was only one of the processes going on in the piece. Stereo placement (voicing) was automated, too, except for the percussion voice, which just doubled the melodic line. I did the timbral changes completely by hand.[73]

One of Spiegel's early microcomputer works was *A Harmonic Algorithm* (1980), composed with an Apple II computer. This piece is comprised of a program that "goes on composing music as long as the program is allowed to run,"[74] making it the ultimate self-fulfilling prophecy of process composition.

The Sheer Frost Orchestra (1999) by Marina Rosenfeld (b. 1968) is a performance work combining elements of process (time and structure controls) with improvisation. The work called for 17 women to play electric guitars or computers. The guitars were placed on the floor in front of each performer. Rosenfeld taught the players six techniques for playing the guitar with a nail polish bottle (hence the "Sheer Frost" brand name of the title). The score specified various combinations of players using these techniques over the course of 110 30-second segments played without pause for the duration of the 55-minute work. A large digital clock was mounted in the space so that the performers could keep time. Rosenfeld also combined elements of process control and improvisation in her solo work for turntable, *theforestthegardenthesea* (1999), part of a larger work called *Fragment Opera*. The sound material for this work consisted of sounds composed and recorded by Rosenfeld onto acetate discs. A live performance involved playing and processing a sequence of the disc sounds, all of which were modified in real time using turntable techniques and audio processors. She explained her approach:

> These are compositions that are superimposable, or modular. With each suite of records I am assuming that the beginning of the performance will somehow start with an unmanipulated superimposition of the "fragments" and as the performance evolves, transformations start to take place with new juxtapositions and so on . . . It's improvisation but there is usually a structure that is notated at some point. My scores have to do with a sequence of events, but they are not exact instructions to go from point A to point F with B-C-D-E regimented in between. I don't make scores for myself when I perform solo but as soon as I am in an ensemble situation there is usually some kind of score which might look more like a grid, a sequence of events, or something like that.[75]

An approach to process that is not as frequently used is that of gradually changing dynamics in a sound field, perhaps coupled with a steady increase of a given isolated dynamic, such as volume. Iannis Xenakis's *Bohor* (1962) was a tape piece using the amplified sounds of Asian jewelry and a Laotian mouth organ. He composed it during a period in which he was exploring the gradual transformation of sounds within a cloud of seemingly unchanging density. "You start with a sound made up of many particles, then see how you can make it change imperceptibly, growing, changing, and developing, until an entirely new sound results." Xenakis said he likened this process to the "onset of madness, when a person suddenly realizes that an environment that had seemed familiar to him has now become altered in a profound, threatening sense."[76] The piece has also been likened to the experience of listening to the clanging of a large bell—from inside the bell.[77]

The clangorous tones of *Bohor* begin quietly and then steadily build to an extremely loud conclusion that ends so abruptly that it must have been cut off with a pair of scissors. The 22-minute work is largely about the process of increasing volume, and is so extreme in its execution that even Pierre Schaeffer, to whom it was dedicated, could do little but make fun of it. Referring back to Xenakis's *Concret PH*, the pleasant piece composed of the sounds of burning embers and played in the Philips Pavilion at the 1958 Brussels World's Fair along with Varèse's *Poème électronique*, Schaeffer said:

> No longer were we dealing with the crackling of small embers [*Concret PH*], but with a huge firecracker, an offensive accumulation of whacks of a scalpel in your ears at the highest level on the potentiometer.[78]

A crowd that witnessed a live performance of *Bohor* in Paris in 1968 was strongly divided about the work. According to one observer, "By the end of the piece, some were affected by the high sound level to the point of screaming; others were standing and cheering."[79]

MINIMALIST AND PROCESS MUSIC WITH ELECTRONICS

1 *The Tortoise, His Dreams and Journeys* (1964) by La Monte Young
   Early minimalist work employing electronic drones

2 *Music for the Stadler Gallery* (1964) by Earle Brown
   Process work for four tape recorders

3 *It's Gonna Rain* (1965) by Steve Reich
   Process piece using tape loops and phasing

4 *A Rainbow in Curved Air* (1969) by Terry Riley
   Minimalist work for electronic organ

5 *Four Organs* (1970) by Steve Reich
   Process piece for four electronic organs

6 *Discreet Music* (1975) by Brian Eno
   Process piece for synthesizers

7 *Figure in a Clearing* (1977) by David Behrman
   Process piece using the KIM-1 microcomputer

8 *A Harmonic Algorithm* (1980) by Laurie Spiegel
   Self-composing program running on an Apple II computer

9 *Music for Piano with One or More Snare Drums* (1990) by Alvin Lucier
   Process piece for amplified piano and snare drum

10 *The Sheer Frost Orchestra* (1999) by Marina Rosenfeld
   Process piece for a timed improvisational live performance

LISTEN

THE SAN FRANCISCO TAPE MUSIC CENTER

The San Francisco Tape Music Center (SFTMC) is important not only because of the composers who worked there but also because its early history reflects the dilemmas faced by many American composers of electronic music in the early 1960s. There was no funding or institutional support for their efforts, making it necessary to pool their equipment, locate performance spaces, and raise funds for publicity on their own. The SFTMC was also unique among private American electronic music studios in that its success led directly to a sizable grant to become a part of Mills College. What had begun as a makeshift operation run by a handful of dedicated composers became one of the greatest success stories of any university-based electronic music studio in the world. After 40 years, it is still in operation as a vital part of the program of the Center for Contemporary Music at Mills College.

The artistic climate in San Francisco in 1961 was ringing with new ideas. A number of young composers, including Ramón Sender, Pauline Oliveros, and Morton Subotnick, had been experimenting with tape composition. Oliveros completed her first work in 1961. Called *Time Perspectives*, it was a piece of *musique concrète* using natural sounds that she had recorded with her Sears and Roebuck Silvertone home tape recorder. Without any other equipment at her disposal, she used the natural acoustics of her bathroom and some cardboard tubes to filter and enhance the raw sounds.[80]

Ramón Sender was a student at the San Francisco Conservatory of Music when he met Oliveros. He had received a little financial support from the conservatory to start an electronic music studio and he and Oliveros teamed up to organize the project, calling it Sonics. "The first program we gave," recalls Oliveros, "included first tape works by Ramón Sender, Terry Riley, Phil Winsor, and me."[81]

Figure 12.19
Composers of the San Francisco Tape Music Center, 1963. Left to right: Tony Martin, Bill Maginnis, Ramón Sender, Morton Subotnick, and Pauline Oliveros.
(John Bischoff, Mills College Center for Contemporary Music)

Later in 1961, Sender and Morton Subotnick decided to pool their tape recording and audio equipment and founded the San Francisco Tape Music Center. Oliveros soon joined them. The center was first located in a condemned building. Enough interest was stirred by their first few months of work that Sender and Subotnick worked out a plan to move into new quarters as part of a larger cooperative involving radio station KPFA, Ann Halprin's Dancer's Workshop (for which Subotnick was musical director), and Canyon Cinema. Their new address on Divisadero Street was spacious and well organized for their purposes. The Tape Center occupied the upstairs office and shared a large room for performances with Canyon Cinema. The dance workshop occupied another hall, and the radio station set up a remote studio in an adjoining office so that it could broadcast concerts. The cooperative held monthly performances to pay the rent. Terry Riley's *In C* (1965) was premiered in that space.[82] Tony Martin (b. 1936) joined the group as their visual artist in charge of light projections for the performances, and William Maginnis signed on as both engineer and composer from 1964 to 1967.

Maginnis defined the center as a "nonprofit cultural and educational corporation, the aim of which was to present concerts and offer a place to learn about work within the tape music medium." The center itself had little more equipment than six audio oscillators and some tape recorders.[83] This forced the composers to develop some novel approaches to making electronic music, including Oliveros's elaborate tape delay setups. The composers were also very interested in creating music that could be presented live, which led them to the use of light projections to accompany tape pieces. The collective was highly successful and influential. It undertook regional and national tours during the mid-1960s.

As noted earlier, engineer Donald Buchla worked with Morton Subotnick and Ramón Sender in 1965 to design an instrument for the SFTMC. The first Buchla synthesizer was installed in the SFTMC at the end of 1965, and Subotnick continued to collaborate with Buchla on the further development of electronic music synthesizers. The availability of this device rapidly changed the nature of the music that could be produced at the Center. No longer dependent upon using recorded natural sounds, audio oscillators, and tape manipulation to compose their music, the sound palette of works produced by Subotnick, Sender, and Oliveros began to shift toward new and increasingly complex sonorities.

The Rockefeller Foundation was interested in the SFTMC and granted it $15,000 in operating funds. In 1966, the center worked with the foundation to secure an even longer-term commitment. An agreement was struck whereby the foundation would grant the center $400,000 for four years under the stipulation that it would agree to move to Mills College. Oliveros explained, "The foundation did not consider the Tape Center capable of administering the funds, so the move was deemed necessary in order to utilize the Mills College administration and to insure continuity when the grant period was over."[84] At Mills, the center was first known as the Mills Tape Music Center, and later as the Center for Contemporary Music (CCM). The new electronic music studio was going to be built from scratch, although some basic equipment—including a Bode frequency shifter, a Fairchild compressor, and a Buchla 100 synthesizer—pre-dated its construction.[85]

For the center, 1966 and 1967 were years of transition. Not only was it moving to a new location, but it was having difficulty finding someone to be its director. Subotnick, who had been teaching at Mills, was the natural choice. He had to decline, however, because he was taking a position at New York University. Another choice would have been Sender, but he was also unavailable. Oliveros was next in line and accepted the position, only to leave the following year after being offered the position of lecturer at the University of California in San Diego. Before leaving, one of her accomplishments while director of the center was to convince the Mills administration that the studios should have a public-access policy.[86]

Changes in leadership at the Mills Tape Music Center delayed plans to complete the new electronic music studio. It wasn't until 1969, when composer Robert Ashley was appointed director at Mills, that work started in earnest on the new facilities. This was three years after the initial grant. Although prior to Ashley's arrival much work had been initiated by Tony Gnazzo and Lowell Cross to configure existing equipment into a working studio, Ashley was faced with bringing in new gear to realize the ultimate plan of creating a professionally equipped environment. He recalled the state of affairs when he was recruited for the job:

> Part of that grant that Mills got had been designed to build an electronic music facility. It had never really become anything because each person who was supposed to run it left . . . So, they invited me to come there because apparently I was known for being able to do this stuff. I took a wonderful guy, a friend of mine, Nick Bertoni, as the engineer. We started from scratch and built a really nice studio.
>
> There was a recording studio, a work studio where students could build their own synthesizers and learn electronics, and then there was a Moog synthesizer studio and a Buchla synthesizer studio, and there were a couple of smaller studios where people could do mixing and those kinds of things. They were all attached to the main studio. We had a four-track in one studio and an eight-track in another studio. We had a very nice mixing board that I designed and Nick Bertoni built. We made something that I was very proud of.[87]

Ashley also managed to keep alive Oliveros's recommendation for a public-access facility:

> After we got the studio built—which took a couple of years—we were able to offer anybody in the Bay Area, any band in the Bay Area, access to that studio with an engineer at very low cost. I think the recording studio was like $10 an hour . . . I think we invented the public-access studio . . . There were rock bands and rap bands and everything. People coming in to learn the Moog equipment and that kind of thing. There is nothing like it in the world and hasn't been since.[88]

Composer John Bischoff, currently an instructor and studio coordinator at the CCM, believes that in 1972 anyone in the neighborhood could rent the Buchla studio for a mere $2.50 an hour or the Moog studio for $5.00 an hour. Composers Maggi Payne (b. 1945), who has been at Mills since 1970, and Robert Sheff (aka Blue Gene Tyranny, b. 1945) "alternated weeks as recording technicians for the community users." Payne is currently an associate professor and co-director of the CCM. About the hourly rates, she added, "If people wanted instruction, I taught Moog and Buchla for an additional $5.00 and hour."[89]

Figure 12.20
David Tudor performing with a Buchla 100 synthesizer during a live concert of electronic music at Mills College, January 1968. (John Bischoff, Mills College Center for Contemporary Music)

If there was a distinction between Oliveros's original concept of a "public-access" studio and Ashley's, it might have been that Ashley opened the doors to people who were not necessarily associated with the composing community or staff of the college.[90] Ashley was director of the CCM until 1981. He created a master's degree program in "Electronic Music and Recorded Media," and also received Ford Foundation funding to grant 16 composers a month's residency in the studio to work with the latest multitrack recording equipment that they had installed. "No composer at that time in 1970 had any experience with a multitrack studio," explained Ashley. "Only The Beatles and the Rolling Stones had multitrack studios. So, we had Alvin [Lucier] and David [Behrman], and Christian Wolff and David Tudor and people like that."[91] The grant program lasted two years.[92]

In the generally underfunded and unsupported world of electronic music development, what Subotnick, Oliveros, Ashley, and others accomplished between 1961 and 1970 was simply remarkable. But it also made sense to Mills. Ashley again:

> When I proposed this idea to the Rockefeller Foundation and we got the money to do the public access studio, I think Mills was very proud because the campus itself had become very isolated from the city of Oakland. It improved our relationship with the community a lot. I have to say that the people who were responsible for helping me—like Margaret Lyon, who was the head of the music department, who I think is really a total genius—and the dean of faculty, Mary Wood Bennett, equally a genius, they saw the social potential of this in a positive way. They were very supportive. That allowed me to do things that I couldn't have gotten away with in any other institution. Mills was so independent itself that if they decided that something was a good idea they would do it.[93]

Maggi Payne remarked that the studio facilities have since expanded to about double the size of the facilities in the 1970s, "although it's still not enough."[94] This is surely a healthy sign for the state of new music at Mills College, and new music culture in general.

SUMMARY

- The aesthetic clash over approaches to electronic music between the French and Germans during the 1950s was short-lived due to the refusal of artists to be contained by any single school of thought or dogmatic approach to organizing such sounds.

- Because electronic music was reliant on technology, the music itself was going to become a testing ground for new aesthetic ideas about the art of musical sound.

- Three cultural perspectives on electronic music assume that technology naturally leads to *experimentation*, the *acceptance* of electronic music will succeed by comparing it to other forms of music, and composing and listening to electronic music requires *new skills*.

- *Poème électronique* was perhaps the first work of electronic music to be so thoroughly integrated into a performance space and implemented on such a grand, immersive scale.

- Techniques for composing electronic music include *sound crafting/montage*, the use of a *technical score*, the combining of *electronics with other instruments*, and *instructional composition* that follows a set of directions written in text.

- Among his many contributions to electronic music, Stockhausen pioneered the orchestration of live electronic musicians accompanied by recorded passages.

- Wendy Carlos pioneered the synthesizing of orchestral sounds using both analog synthesis and digital algorithms of her own design.

- Elements of minimalism include a tendency to repeat lines of notes many times, greatly reducing the motion and tension of a piece of music so that it does not appear to change or progress.

- Process music involves rules established by a composer that govern the way that a piece unfolds, sometimes with a minimum of human intervention. A piece of process music lasts as long as it takes to complete the predefined process.

- The Center for Contemporary Music (CCM) at Mills College was founded in 1966 and grew out of the efforts of the original San Francisco Tape Music Center. The Mills CCM remains one of the foremost institutions providing instruction in electronic music in the United States.

KEY PEOPLE IN CHAPTER TWELVE

KEY TERMS IN CHAPTER TWELVE

MILESTONES

Classical and Experimental Music

Musical work	Year	Significance
– *Antiphonie* by Pierre Henry.	1952	– Tape work that utilized serial composition techniques.
– *Williams Mix* by John Cage.	1952	– Tape work that utilized instructional composition technique to assemble the final tape edit; also influenced by chance decision-making operations.
– *Déserts* by Edgard Varèse.	1954	– One of the first works to combine a live orchestra with a tape of electronic music.
– *Poème électronique* by Edgard Varèse.	1958	– One of the first widely known and publicly accessible works of electronic music.
– *Trio for Strings* by La Monte Young.	1958	– One of the earliest recognized works of minimalism.
– *In C* by Terry Riley.	1964	– Extended instrumental minimalist work for an ensemble of any instruments.
– *Music for the Stadler Gallery* by Earle Brown.	1964	– Early process piece for four tape recorders that played for 30 days.
– *The Tortoise, His Dreams and Journeys* by La Monte Young.	1965	– Extended minimalist work using electronics.
– *It's Gonna Rain* by Steve Reich.	1965	– Early tape loop process piece exploring the phenomenon of phasing.
– *Telemusik* by Karlheinz Stockhausen.	1966	– Example of electronic work with a performable score.
– *Four Organs* by Steve Reich.	1970	– Process piece for four electronic organs.
– *I Am Sitting in a Room* by Alvin Lucier.	1970	– Process piece that explored the audio degradation of repeatedly re-recorded tape sounds.
– *Discreet Music* by Brian Eno.	1975	– Process piece for synthesizer and tape delay.
– *Digital Moonscapes* by Wendy Carlos.	1984	– Early example of digital orchestration.

CHAPTER 13

Jazz, Live Electronic Music, and Ambient Music

Musical intuition is as essential to a jazz musician as to the electronic composer in such exploratory musical ventures. Improvisation is the common denominator.[1]
—Gil Mellé

Sun Ra performing "Space is the Place," with June Tyson, 1971. Note the Minimoog upper right. (Francis Davis)

The mid-1960s were a time of enormous experimentation with the staging of live performances. Elements of theater, dance, film, and music were often combined to create new and unexpected performance situations. John Cage was, as usual, right in the thick of the revolution. His works involving electronic music during this period—*Variations I–VI* (1958–66) for any number of players and instruments; *Rozart Mix* (1965) for 12 tape recorders, performers, and 88 tape loops; *Assemblage* (1968); and *HPSCHD* (1967–69) for harpsichords and computer-generated sound tapes—were always produced and performed in collaboration with other musicians. Cage, along with the dancer and choreographer Merce Cunningham and their numerous collaborators, pushed the concept of performance art to its most experimental and thought-provoking outer reaches.

While the work of Cage and Cunningham was regularly showcased in national media, they were not alone during the 1950s and 1960s in pioneering the possibilities of performing electronic music in a live setting. Electronic music was also making inroads into the world of jazz, America's "classical music," with its long tradition of musicianship, improvisation and live performance. This chapter explores the historic evolution of electronic music in jazz and the roots of electronic music in live performance across the arts.

JAZZ AND ELECTRONIC MUSIC

The intersection of jazz and electronic music was intermittent at best until the explosion of fusion jazz in the 1970s. This is not surprising considering that each of these genres approached music from different branches of the musical family tree. Modern jazz of the 1960s was a vibrant art based on a long-established tradition and affinity for live performance, expert musicianship, and improvisation. Electronic music of the 1960s had only recently developed and was largely viewed as an experimental stem of classical music. Furthermore, electronic music of that time could hardly be called spontaneous. No matter what the stylistic outcome—from the mathematically calculated art music of academia to the television themes of the BBC Radiophonic Workshop—all electronic music of the time had to be painstakingly assembled on magnetic tape using a razor blade and splicing block and involved little in the way of traditional musicianship. Except for the work of a few extreme experimenters such as Cage, Tudor, Mumma, and Ashley, the concept of live performance in early electronic music meant little more than playing a tape over loudspeakers.

During the 1960s, only a handful of unrelated, future-minded musicians could imagine a union of electronic music with jazz. But even for them, the melding of jazz with this new technology must have seemed virtually, if not practically, unattainable because of the technical obstacles to overcome. Yet, for several years before the

Figure 13.1 Jazz musician Gil Mellé invented electronic instruments such as the Electar, a tone generator made in 1966, to be played by musicians in his jazz ensemble. (*JazzTimes*)

introduction of the first commercial keyboard synthesizers, there were a few pioneers in both jazz and experimental music who believed that a union of electronic music with the expressive energy of jazz had great potential.

Early Experiments in Electronic Jazz

Miles Davis once said that the way to judge a jazz artist was not by technique but by his or her ideas. There were probably many jazz artists of the 1960s who had ideas for combining jazz and electronic music, but only a select few had the resources available to make it happen. Even by the early 1960s, most individual artists could not afford the elaborate and expensive equipment needed to make, modify, record, and edit electronic sounds. There were no off-the-shelf solutions for creating electronic music until the availability of affordable voltage-controlled synthesizers by the early 1970s. Accordingly, early experimenters in *electronic jazz* mostly followed individual rather than institutional paths of discovery, taking advantage of whatever resources were available. Each had a personal approach that somehow managed to circumvent the technical barriers of the time while still finding a uniquely jazz-like approach to using electronic music. This is a brief chronicle of their achievements.

A catalyst for the use of electronic music in jazz was an openly experimental attitude that embraced the world of jazz around 1960. Electronic music was considered highly experimental at the time and existed at the intersection of many kinds of music, especially classical, music for movies and television, popular song, and modern dance. Jazz was also undergoing a period of exploration with the emergence of styles including *modal jazz* and *free jazz* and the integration of classical music elements in a genre called *third stream jazz*. This atmosphere motivated jazz musicians using various styles and approaches to seek new sounds and means of expression. A few turned to experimenting with electronic music.

Early creators of electronic jazz invented several different approaches to making this new kind of music. Their experiments may be grouped into two broad categories:

* Jazz incorporating prerecorded electronic music on tape (1960–72).
* Jazz using electronic instruments and/or the sound modification of jazz instruments in performance (early years 1965–75).

This small but remarkable body of experimental works was a response to the times, born of a passion to bring new ideas into jazz and facilitated by the latest changes in technology that made electronic music possible. Historically, these early experiments might be viewed as testing the waters by introducing a new sound vocabulary to jazz that would later mature with the introduction of easier-to-use instruments and digital audio processing.

Jazz with Pre-Recorded Tape Music

From the standpoint of technology, jazz musicians working with electronic music around 1960 had little choice other than to compose their experimental sounds on magnetic tape. This led to two general practices: works incorporating jazz elements that were intended only as recorded works of *musique concrète*; and works that were performed by a live jazz ensemble accompanied by a magnetic tape part. In both cases, the inherent limitations of tape music—one was working with raw sound material that had to be meticulously edited as opposed to a musical instrument that could be played as part of an ensemble—tested the resourcefulness of the musician to embellish jazz with new sounds.

Given that the early years of electronic music were dominated by the rivalry between French *musique concrète* and German *elektronische Musik*, it is interesting to note that early jazz experiments with tape leaned heavily toward the French approach. Why was this? *Musique concrète* can be characterized as having a more likable naturalness than the unemotional synthesis of *elektronische Musik*. The explosive range of *musique concrète* was grounded in the real world and leveraged audio trickery to mask, modify, and pulverize the familiar into something new and surprising. The emotional range of *musique concrète* varied from the serene to the terrifying and even jocular at times. It hit the gut of the listener, and in this way shared an affinity with the emotional impact of jazz. *Elektronische Musik*, on the other hand, when practiced using the purest of tones, was a more objectified style, less emotional and, to many, less stimulating. The equipment used to create *elektronische Musik*—including tone generators, filters, and modulation circuitry—also depended on a method of composition that might be viewed as more detached than working with tape effects to manipulate recordings of natural sounds. The creation of *musique concrète*, on the other hand, more closely paralleled an approach to music that was already familiar to the jazz musician, that of shaping the expressive content of raw sound material.

In electronic jazz works intended only as tape pieces, composers familiar with the techniques of Schaeffer's Paris studio freely added the sounds of jazz instruments to the melting pot of jet engines, automobile crashes, and kitchen pans that comprised the audio palette of *musique concrète*. These works were less jazz-like in conception but clearly inspired by elements of jazz. Unlike jazz, there was nothing improvisatory about the creation of a tape work. A hint of jazz can be heard in one of *musique concrète's* earliest milestones. *Symphonie pour un homme seul* (1949–50) by Pierre Henry and Pierre Schaeffer, composed entirely of sound material from pre-recorded phonograph records, included the sound of a jazz ensemble, highly distorted, in one short section of the work called *Apostrophe*. Croatian composer Ivo Malec (b. 1925) composed the tape piece *Dahovi* (1962) in Paris, a work whose structure is more like that of the verse-solo format of a jazz composition than a typical *concrète* exercise in starkly contrasting sounds. *Dixi* (1967) was composed in the Experimental Music Studio of Polish Radio by Eugeniusz Rudnick (b. 1933) to explore the gradual mixing of extended sonorities, a lengthy sequence of which appears to begin with the mellow, electronically modified tones of a trumpet. François Bayle's *Solitioude* (1969) is a more emphatic blend of traffic noise, orchestral strings, and distorted jazz horns, drums, and electric guitar that effectively blended the rock-heavy rhythms of amplified jazz with electronic collage. Jazz trombonist and bass player Günter Christmann (b. 1942) and drummer Detlef Schönenberg (b. 1944) were members of the German experimental free jazz movement of the early 1970s, and composed some *concrète* works for tape, including *Gruppenimprovisation* (1971). Another artist who deserves mention is American Frank Zappa (1940–93), a rock and jazz guitarist who delighted in spoofing pop and rock music. A devoted admirer of Edgard Varèse, Zappa's early work including the album *Lumpy Gravy* (1967), a daring admixture of pop rock, polyrhythmic jazz, and *musique concrète*, delivered enthusiastically for the value of its shock effect.

The next stage of development for electronic jazz was the combination of tape music with clearly jazz-like instrumental compositions. A model for doing this already existed in avant-garde classical music. Many of the earliest institutional and academic works of electronic music of the 1950s combined live performers and pre-recorded electronic sounds. This example served as a template for musicians interested in accomplishing the same in jazz.

An early experiment combining jazz with tape music was *Jazz et Jazz* (1960) by French jazz critic and composer André Hodeir (1921–2011). *Jazz et Jazz* was a short, three-minute work composed for jazz ensemble in a swing style. Hodeir realized the work in three stages. During the first, Hodeir separately recorded a big band playing several composed passages and a rhythm section (bass and drums) playing along with a chord progression from the ensemble work. In the second stage, Hodeir transformed the recording of the big band passages using tape-editing techniques such as speed changes, tape reversal, filtering, and transposition (playing the tape upside down). He next added a rhythm section track, unchanged, to the electronically modified big band track. For the third stage, a piano player improvised "as indicated by the composer" along with the "composite tape background," creating the final realization.[2] The *musique concrète* treatment of the band included horns and drums in reverse, piano slowed down and sped up, chirping microphone taps, and a variety of comical percussive effects. The result was a carefully orchestrated crowd pleasure that could be performed live with a solo pianist exchanging passages with his or her mutated electronic doppelganger.

Avant-garde composer Luciano Berio, a veteran of the RAI electronic music laboratory in Milan, composed a large ensemble work with tape and jazz elements called *Laborintus 2* (1963–65). The work was created in California while Berio was teaching at Mills College, but was commissioned by both French and Italian radio to commemorate the 700th anniversary of Dante's birth. The piece was written for narrator, voices, tape, and jazz drummer. Berio was already known for his experimental music that emphasized verbal expression and a fusing of modern music with past influences. *Laborintus 2* is a 35-minute work that brought the influence of jazz into Berio's collection of quotable musical influences. Sometimes called a "no story opera," the work was largely without a fixed rhythm except for the short but potent jazz-like sequence that occupied about seven minutes in the middle of the work. During this passage, a drummer and bass player kept time at a frantic pace, leading to the introduction of a contrasting, arrhythmic sequence of electronic tape sounds. The electronic music was joined by a chorus of voices, horns, and woodwinds that exchanged phrases and noises until the beat disintegrated. Although Berio's use of jazz in this work was more decorative than central to the premise of the piece, it was nonetheless a notoriously original work that caught the ears of many jazz musicians at the time.

Beginning around 1963, a number of individual jazz artists began to combine their jazz music with taped electronic music in new ways, some of which could be performed live. Sun Ra had been experimenting with free jazz since the late 1950s and by the early 1960s had augmented his sound with a variety of electronic keyboards, including the electric piano, electric celeste, Hammond organ, and the Clavioline, a specialized organ with vacuum tube oscillators and frequency modifiers designed primarily for novelty effects (it was used for the signature space sounds of the hit song "Telstar" by the Tornados and on The Beatles' "Baby, You're a Rich Man"). In 1963, Sun Ra recorded an album called *Cosmic Tones for Mental Therapy* (not released until 1967) on which he used abundant reverb, echo, and amplified small sounds to embellish this set of compositions for large jazz ensemble. The track "Clusters of Galaxies" forgoes traditional jazz form and became Sun Ra's version of *musique concrète*, a soundscape of suspended sounds, tinkling piano strings, and the sonorous drone of an amplified gong or cymbal. This was not strictly a tape composition and could probably have been performed in real time, but was clearly an imitation of tape music that Sun Ra had heard coming from any number of institutional electronic music studios. Sun Ra's early experiments in electronic jazz encouraged many other artists to develop a fascination with new sounds. Sun Ra continued to experiment with electronic music in a jazz context. After befriending Robert Moog, the inventor provided a prototype Minimoog for Sun Ra to use in 1970, a year before the commercial model was released. Sun Ra was one of the first jazz keyboardists to record using a Minimoog, heard on the album *My Brother the Wind, Vol. II* (1970).

Another early jazz connection to tape music was Terry Riley, whose experiment with tape delay in Paris in 1963 found him collaborating with noted trumpeter Chet Baker. The result was a stage production called *The Gift* for which Riley provided the music. Riley first recorded a jazz quartet featuring Baker, both as a unit and then individually, each musician playing solo parts in both sessions. The taped material was used to create a tape delay sequence over which the live performers also improvised another set of solos. The result was a set of looped phrases, blending and overlapping with a variable delay pattern, creating rhythm loops juxtaposed with the tempo of the recorded jazz tracks.[3] This was a sign of sounds to come many years later when jazz artists embraced the use of digital delay as a performance and compositional tool.

These early experiments were followed by a host of other efforts by jazz musicians to connect with tape music. Sculptor Walter De Maria (b. 1935), known for his works of environmental art, is also a jazz-rock drummer. While establishing his career in art during the early 1960s, De Maria also dabbled in music and created two astonishingly fresh works on which he drummed to field recordings of environmental sounds. *Cricket Music* (1964) comprised 24 minutes of drumming set to the sounds of crickets and *Ocean Music* (1968) did much the same with the sounds of crashing waves. In each case, De Maria carefully adjusted the level of the field recordings and drumming so that, at times, the environmental sounds were the dominant elements to which he created complementary rhythms. De Maria's approach combined ambient and instrumental sounds in a ritualistic way, drawing parallels to early minimalism.

Other musicians found ways to connect the open-ended format of free jazz with tape music. Keyboardist Bob James (b. 1939) and his trio recorded the album *Explosions* in 1964 for the experimental music label ESP. The selections combined tape music composed by avant-garde composers Gordon Mumma and Robert Ashley, then working in Ann Arbor, with free jazz improvisations by the jazz trio. The electronic music comprised previously recorded materials that Mumma and Ashley provided for that purpose, but they were not involved in the jazz portion of the production, which James produced. The result was quirky, often noisy, and remains one of the most daring contrasts in musical styles to have been recorded in the name of jazz. French *musique concrète* composer Bernard Parmegiani (b. 1927) used a similar approach in creating *JazzEx* (1966) for electronic tape and jazz quartet, which premiered at the *Festival international d'art contemporain de Royan*, a French arts and music festival.

LISTENING GUIDE 13.1

Title: *JazzEx* (excerpt)

Artist: Bernard Parmegiani   **Year**: 1966   **Duration**: 3:00

Genre: Electronic jazz

Electronic Instrumentation: Tape composition with jazz quartet.

Background: Composed by Bernard Parmegiani, an early innovator from the French school of *musique concrète* in Paris, the work combines free jazz with electronic music on tape. This early experiment in combining jazz and electronic music was accomplished before the commercial availability of music synthesizers. Parmegiani composed the tape music with a jazz quartet in mind, assembling an arrhythmic sequence of colorful tones and noises to which he felt jazz musicians could freely improvise.

	Listen For: the contrasting sounds of electronic music and jazz musicians and the interaction between the two. Note the way in which the jazz players complement the electronic sounds with their own unconventional techniques.
0:00–1:00	The piece begins with the frantic sounds of the sax and trumpet, accompanied by a quietly scraping drone. This is followed by a passage of trumpet and electronic tones that blend so well that they are almost indistinguishable. The drummer and bass player join the fray.
1:01–2:00	There is a bass solo accompanied by a 2.5-second tape loop comprised of a wavering drone. The loop creates a slow rhythm to which the bass player responds.
2:01–3:00	At 2:04, the bass solo and electronic drone are interrupted by an eruption of the sax and a short, rapid sequence of cascading electronic tones that blend with the percussion. A sustained tone on the saxophone anticipates the entrance of a low-pitched electronic tone at about 2:11. The drone continues, unwavering, over which the sax player solos. At about 2:50, the electronic tone increases in volume and begins to waver with vibrato. At the same time, a thread of filtered white noise begins to increase in volume. This excerpt ends with a flourish by the quartet playing all at once, during which a sympathetic burst of white noise accompanies the drummer's cymbals, and a touch of echo is added as the white noise diminishes.

Compare and Contrast
Explosions (1964) by the Bob James Trio
Auto Jazz: Tragic Destiny of Lorenzo Bandini (1968) by Barney Wilen
Oba (1969) by Don Cherry and Jon Appleton

Barney Wilen (1937–96) was a noted French free jazz alto saxophonist and composer. He was also a fan of Grand Prix auto racing and in 1967 attended a race in Monaco equipped with three portable reel-to-reel tape recorders to capture the sound of the entire event for a film. Tragically, near the end of the race, Italian driver Lorenzo Bandini was killed when his axle snapped and the car flipped over in a fiery crash. Saddened but inspired by the tragedy, Wilen used the audio tapes of the race as the basis for a tribute piece he called *Auto Jazz: Tragic Destiny of Lorenzo Bandini* (1968). The work was divided into five parts corresponding to stages of the race and featured his free jazz combo playing to the accompaniment of actual race sounds. Wilen was careful to let the sounds be themselves, the music being constantly jarred and buoyed by the roaring of passing race cars, crowd sounds, PA announcers, and pit crews. The work was performed live in New York along with a film of the race.

Several other quirky but classic jazz and tape works are worth mentioning. They were created at what was effectively the end of the era of using electronic music on tape in a jazz format. In 1969, veteran record label executive, jazz producer, and composer Bob Thiele (1922–96) put together a collective of jazz musicians to collaborate on a contemporary jazz album called *Head Start*. The work included two LPs and touched on many musical styles, from jazz interpretations of Beatle tunes to a history of traditional jazz styles and a tribute to John Coltrane (who had recently died), concluding with an extended work of electronic music taking up all 17 minutes of the final LP side. For the tape piece, called "A Few Thoughts for the Day," Thiele worked with electronic music composer Jon Appleton of Dartmouth College to combine phrases of music composed for a big band with spoken passages from news headlines, a narrator, and tape music. Intended to "make you think about the social conditions, the horrors of the world," Thiele described the piece as comprising ". . . new orchestral music and the latest in electronic sounds, together with the voices and sounds of the destruction of the world."[4] Perhaps not surprisingly for that era, a short version of the work was released as a single to encourage radio airplay.

Composer George Russell (1923–2009) was noted for his work with third-stream jazz that combined jazz with elements of classical music. In 1969, working with producer Bob Thiele, he produced the eclectic *Electronic Sonata for Souls Loved by Nature*. Russell was another socially conscious composer and conceived his jazz sonata to feature "a pan-stylistic electronic tape; a tape composed of fragments of many different styles of music, avant-garde, jazz, ragas, blues, rock, serial music etc., treated electronically." He then used this tape as a backdrop for the instrumental portion of the work played by a large jazz ensemble, the hope being to reveal connecting tissue between cultures but also to humanize technology, using it to enrich the collective soul of humankind.[5] The electronic tape was produced at the studios of Swedish Radio, and the work was premiered in a live performance in Norway.

Another noteworthy work of electronic jazz was the created by İlhan Mimaroğlu (b. 1926), an electronic music composer associated with the early years of the Columbia–Princeton Electronic Music Center and later a producer of jazz recordings. In 1971, he combined these two interests and composed *Sing Me a Song of Songmy*, a work combining spoken word, poetry, avant-garde jazz, and electronic music on tape. The recording featured jazz trumpeter Freddie Hubbard. Thematically, the work was heavy on social commentary, dealing with topics as loosely connected as the war in Vietnam, the administration of President Richard Nixon, the notorious Hollywood murder of Sharon Tate, and the continuing civil rights struggle of African Americans. This uniquely compelling recorded work was overshadowed at the time by other activities in modern jazz, not the least of which was the new fusion of electronic instruments and efforts to combine jazz and rock by the likes of Miles Davis, Herbie Hancock, Weather Report, and the Mahavishnu Orchestra.

Figure 13.2   The album *Sing Me a Song of Songmy* (1971) by İlhan Mimaroğlu, featuring Freddie Hubbard, was one of the last great jazz works including tape music prior to the synthesizer age in jazz. (Atlantic SD 1576)

Jazz Using Electronic Instruments in Performance

The arrival of the analog music synthesizer in the late 1960s and early 1970s made it possible to add electronic instrumentation to a performing jazz ensemble. Underlying this trend was the availability of synthesizers with preset sound circuits that could be played using a keyboard, much like a piano or organ. The first instruments were relatively unsophisticated and could only play one note at a time like the Minimoog (1971) or two notes at a time like the original ARP Odyssey (1972). But the new sounds and expressive controls—modulation and pitch wheels—made these instruments a welcome addition to the cadre of traditional jazz instruments. By the mid-1970s, as synthesizers became more sophisticated, polyphonic, and programmable, their role expanded beyond that of the soloist. The ability to program patterns of sounds that could be played back automatically allowed the musician to generate a pattern of accompaniment to which they could solo or improvise. Synthesizers used in this way gave jazz added textures and complexity. By the end of the 1970s, pianists were no longer just pianists—they were keyboardists. The typical fusion jazz concert featured a keyboard player surrounded by a half dozen or more synthesizers, pianos, and organs, each required to produce a different effect. The coming of digital synthesis in the 1980s made it possible to shrink all of these various instrumental voices into the circuitry of just a few instruments, making life much easier for the traveling musician.

Keyboardist Herbie Hancock (b. 1940) was one of the most innovative early adopters of music synthesizers in jazz. After having played electric piano with Miles Davis in the late 1960s, he formed his own group and dove headlong into the exploration of the synthesizer. Four albums during this period—*Fat Albert Rotunda* (1969), *Mwandishi* (1970), *Crossings* (1972), and *Sextant* (1972)—reveal a rapid evolution of his music from the tight electric jazz style of the Davis quintet to a more spacious style of jazz-funk fusion that relied heavily on synthesis. *Crossings* and *Sextant* rank with Davis's recordings as some of the most experimental and imaginative works in electronic performance jazz. Hancock's lineup for these records introduced the idea of a synthesizer player as a sideman, whose role was not only that of soloist, but creator of sonic backdrops and effects to accompany instrumental solos and rhythm parts.

Figure 13.3   The Music Improvisation Company (1968–71), from the United Kingdom, was an early jazz performance group featuring live electronics. Members included Hugh Davies (electronic music), Evan Parker (soprano saxophone), Derek Bailey (electric guitar), Jamie Muir (drums), and Christine Jeffrey (voice). (Werner Bethsold from ECM 1005)

Figure 13.4
Herbie Hancock and a
bevy of electronic
keyboards (1978),
including (clockwise from
left) an Oberheim
Polyphonic, Yamaha
Polyphonic, ARP 2600,
Sequential Circuits
Prophet, ARP String
Ensemble, Hohner D6
Clavinet, Micromoog,
Minimoog, and ARP
Odyssey (no. 2) and
Polymoog. (Kaz Tsuruta from
Columbia 34907)

In addition to synthesizers, there existed several less standard approaches to augmenting a jazz ensemble with electronic instrumentation. These included the modification of acoustic instrument sounds and the use of non-keyboard electronic instruments.

Eddie Harris (1936–96) was an American tenor saxophone player in the hard bop style. After a period of mainstream success in the mid-1960s, Harris began to experiment with novel ways to modify the sounds of the saxophone. In this vein, he is best known as the pioneering user of the Varitone, a device for electrically amplifying and changing the sound of the saxophone. The device, produced by saxophone maker Selmer, included a small microphone located on the neck of the saxophone and a set of controls mounted on the side of the instrument. The saxophone was then attached to an amplifier. Using the device, the player could harmonize with him- or herself by producing a secondary tone, change the tone of the instrument, and use special effects such as tremolo and echo. Harris was one of the first sax players to embrace the Varitone and showcased it on his 1967 album, *The Electrifying Eddie Harris*. In the late 1960s, Harris invented a breath-controlled synthesizer that could be played like a saxophone, enabling a player to produce five-part harmony.

JAZZ WITH ELECTRONIC MUSIC ON TAPE

1 *Jazz et Jazz* (1960) by André Hodeir
   Music for big band transformed using tape-editing techniques and effects

2 *Laborintus 2* (1963–65) by Luciano Berio
   Avant-garde performance piece for narrator, voices, tape, and jazz drummer; featured a jazz-style section set against electronic music on tape

3 "Clusters of Galaxies" (1963) by Sun Ra
   Real-time jazz performance patterned after *musique concrète* form; a soundscape of extended sonorities and amplified small sounds, from the album *Cosmic Tones for Mental Therapy*

4 *Music for the Gift, Part 3* (1963) by Terry Riley and Chet Baker
   An early experiment using interactive tape delay created by Terry Riley and featuring a quartet led by Chet Baker

5 *Cricket Music* (1964) by Walter De Maria
   Artist and drummer De Maria played drums to a field recording mix of cricket sounds

6 *Explosions* (1964) by the Bob James Trio
   Free jazz improvisations set to electronic tape music provided by Gordon Mumma and Robert Ashley

7 *JazzEx* (1966) by Bernard Parmegiani
   French free jazz combined with a tape of electronic music in the style of *musique concrète*

8 *Auto Jazz: Tragic Destiny of Lorenzo Bandini* (1968) by Barney Wilen
   French free jazz played over a field recording of a 1967 Grand Prix automobile race

9 *A Few Thoughts for the Day* (1969) by the Bob Thiele Emergency
   Tape piece combining big band jazz, spoken word, and a collage of electronic sounds. Produced with composer Jon Appleton and included on the LP *Head Start*

10 *Sing Me a Song of Songmy* (1971) by İlhan Mimaroğlu, featuring Freddie Hubbard
   One of the last great works combining jazz and tape music

Gil Mellé (1931–2004) was an American baritone saxophonist, visual artist, composer, and record producer. A tinkerer who was fascinated by electronic technology, he thought that a marriage of jazz and electronic instruments would make for a new and interesting hybrid musical sound. Noting that previous attempts at creating "electronic jazz" (his term) relied on composing sounds on tape, he was determined to invent a set of instruments that could be played live.[6] In 1966, during a lull in his jazz recording career, and while working primarily with Army-surplus electrical components, Mellé handmade several electronic instruments for use in a jazz combo. He formed a group called the *Jazz Electronauts*, consisting of a conventional jazz quartet. Mellé provided each player with a specially made electronic instrument to be used in addition to their conventional instruments. These instruments included the *Electar* (a tone generator and arpeggiator), the *Envelope* (for shaping the attack of a cello or string bass sound), the *Doomsday Machine* (a noise generator and filter), the *Tome VI* (a soprano saxophone outfitted with oscillator circuitry to produce five different types of voices), the *Direktor* (a multiple oscillator controller), and various consoles and devices, including the *Percussotron*, an early drum machine. With these instruments, the Electronauts created a breezy blend of cool jazz and modal jazz with electronic sounds interwoven naturally into the mix. Mellé released the album *Tome IV* in 1967 on the Verve jazz label. The group made several live appearances including the Monterey Jazz Festival in 1968. Mellé only made one other jazz album using his electronic instruments—the obscure *Waterbirds* in 1970—but he continued to use electronic instruments in soundtrack and television work, most notably the music for the science fiction film *Andromeda Strain* in 1971.

Another approach to electronic jazz worth noting from the late 1960s was the work of several live performance groups specializing in free jazz. In some cases, they incorporated the use of portable modular synthesizers, such as the EMS Synthi made in Great Britain, but also electronic effects often found in rock groups. Among these ensembles were MEV (United States and Italy), AMM, Iskra 1903, Hugh Davies and Derek Bailey (The Music Improvisation Company, United Kingdom), Gruppo Di Improvisazione Nuova (Italy), New Phonic Art (France), and Wired (Germany).

LIVE ELECTRONIC MUSIC

Cage and Cunningham began working together in the early 1940s when the two first established their radical approach to developing musical accompaniment for modern dance. Until about 1950, when pianist David Tudor joined the company to work with Cage, all of the musical accompaniment for the troupe had been produced acoustically, often with percussion and prepared piano. With the coming of the tape recorder in the early 1950s, Cage and Tudor shifted their attention from acoustic to electroacoustic music for Cunningham's choreography. Their first efforts were dance performances set to pre-recorded loudspeaker music: *Symphonie pour un homme seule* by Schaeffer and Henry in 1952, and Christian Wolff's *For Magnetic Tape* in 1953.[7] It was not long, however, until Cage realized the chief liability of relying on pre-recorded tape music:

> I was at a concert of electronic music in Cologne and I noticed that even though it was the most recent electronic music, the audience was all falling asleep. No matter how interesting the music was, the audience couldn't stay

awake. That was because the music was coming out of loudspeakers.
Then, in 1958—the Town Hall program of mine—we were rehearsing the
Williams Mix, which is not an uninteresting piece, and the piano tuner came
in to tune the piano. Everyone's attention went away from the *Williams Mix*
to the piano tuner because he was live.[8]

The artistic backlash to loudspeaker music began with Cage and Tudor. The necessity of creating interesting electronic music for Cunningham "stimulated us very much, and it led to the use of microphones for purposes other than to amplify."[9] Some of their earliest experiments were merely to move the sound around in the performance space. This led directly to works such as *Cartridge Music* (1960), in which phono cartridges were plugged with different styli and scraped against objects to magnify their sounds. This seminal work resulted in electronic music conceived primarily for live performance—a critical stage in the evolution of avant-garde music.

Cage's growing interest in chance music paralleled his first electronic works for the Cunningham Dance Company. The abstract and untested potential of electronic music was a natural complement to Cunningham's equally original choreographic vision. While the two had sometimes composed the music first and then the dance, or the other way around, they came to the realization that the two were co-equal partners, unified by the element of time: "The relationship between the dance and music is one of co-existence, that is, being related simply because they exist at the same time."[10]

The company soon became Cage's laboratory for experimenting with live electronic music, a tradition that he oversaw with help primarily from David Tudor, Alvin Lucier, David Behrman, and Gordon Mumma for 30 years.[11] This was the mountain spring from which all live electronic performance music eventually flowed.

The reason that Cage got involved with dance in the first place was another motivating factor leading to the development of live electronic music. As a composer working in the 1940s, he found it increasingly difficult to find large ensembles of musicians willing to learn and play his music: "I soon learned that if you were writing music that orchestras just weren't interested in—or string quartets, I made several attempts, I didn't give up immediately—that you could get things done very easily by modern dance groups."[12] After establishing a base of operations with the Cunningham Dance Company, and having brought David Tudor on board as his chief musical collaborator, the two began to take their live electroacoustic performances on the road in the early 1960s. These performances throughout the United States and Europe defied all conventional wisdom in the field of classical music. Rather than sitting around writing instrumental music and waiting for someone to perform it, these classically trained composer-musicians took control of their careers by packing up their own gear and doing it all themselves. Theirs was the antithesis of the Cologne loudspeaker roadshow: no theory, no proselytizing, just performers making live electronic music.

In 1958, Cage composed the first in a series of *Variations* for any number and combination of instruments. The works were improvisatory in the sense that performers were allowed to make "immediate but disciplined decisions, and within specific structural boundaries," a mode of composing used at the time by composers including Cage, Earle Brown, and Christian Wolff.[13] Wolff himself noted that the *Variations* were most significant for the following reasons:

> [they] really pushed the notion of what constituted a piece of music, because
> nothing was said about anything except you had to make yourself something out
> of these lines and dots and things that were on plastic sheets. And that seemed
> to be about as far away from a musical identity as possible. But what always
> struck me as so mysterious was that what people did with those things almost
> all the time would come out sounding like John's work . . . There's this
> mysterious thing that in those days people would try some of John's chance
> techniques, but their music wouldn't come out sounding like John's.[14]

Variations V (1965) was certainly the most ambitious of these pieces. The "score" was written after the first performance, and, as Cage later said, it merely consisted of "remarks that would enable one to perform *Variations V*," a fine example of an *instructional score*.[15] The piece sprang from the idea of electrically triggering sounds through the physical movement of people. Preparation for the first performance at the Lincoln Center in New York (July 23, 1965) became something of a Manhattan Project for new music technology. The performance featured the Cunningham dancers on stage and an assemblage of musicians and electronic gear on a raised platform at the rear of the stage. Experimental film by Stan Vanderbeek and video images by Nam June Paik were also featured.[16]

Some of the sounds were triggered by movements of the dancers on stage; others were controlled and mixed by the musicians. Audio sources included continuously operating tape machines (at least six) playing sounds composed by Cage, Tudor, and Mumma; shortwave receivers (at least six); audio oscillators; electronically generated sounds triggered by proximity-sensing antennae (similar in principal to the Theremin); light beams aimed at photocells that could be interrupted to generate sounds; contact microphones attached to objects on stage (e.g. chairs and a table) that could be used by the dancers; and other homebrewed electronic sound generators that were manually adjusted as needed. Cage recruited several engineers to fabricate the equipment he needed to produce the music. Max Mathews from Bell Labs built a 96-port input mixer into which all of the sound sources were fed. Robert Moog, so familiar with Theremin technology, was retained to make the proximity-sensing antennae that were triggered when a dancer came near them. The light beams were in the base of the antennae and aimed at photocells to close a sound-generating circuit; when a dancer broke one of the beams by stepping into it, whatever sound being fed by that circuit was interrupted.

As one might imagine, the performances resulting from this assemblage of interactive gear were remarkably chaotic. Moog was somewhat puzzled by the whole plan, but knew that he was taking part in a legendary event:

> John Cage retained us to build some equipment for the first production of
> *Variations V*. It was done but it didn't work all that well. There were six
> Theremin-like antennae that the Merce Cunningham dancers would dance
> around and they would turn on different sounds. That was our part of *Variations
> V*. We had the antennae tuned so that if a dancer came within four feet of one it
> would set something off. They were scattered around the stage. There was so
> much stuff . . . I can't remember all that there was, but there was just a lot going
> on. It was an experience for me. All these wires at the edge of the dance area,
> where all of the technicians like me were set up, there were so many cables and

what-not that it was like walking on a forest floor. You couldn't determine
whether something was working or not. I think John Cage knew. But I don't
think anybody else knew. It was serious business, though.[17]

Composer Ron Kuivila became acquainted with the history of this event while
working with David Tudor, acknowledging that Moog was not alone in being puzzled
by the piece's technological complexity. The proximity-sensing antennae apparently did
not work as they had hoped during the Lincoln Center premiere. One had to get very
close to them to get a response. The idea had been for the dancers to trigger them by
moving about more freely on the stage.[18] But the show did indeed go on the road with
more success. According to Mumma, "we always used the proximity antennae and the
photo cell emitters, though we cut back on the number (about one half) of them because
of the logistic challenges in touring performances."[19] Mumma also made some
modifications to the equipment so that it worked better.

Another performance that must go down in history as one of the most complex
multimedia events ever staged occurred in 1969 at the University of Illinois. John Cage
and Lejaren Hiller teamed up to present a joint composition called *HPSCHD*. Using a
computer-derived extrapolation of the *I Ching* developed for Cage, the two assembled
51 sound tapes generated by computer and combined them in a live setting with the
activities of seven harpsichordists. The work was presented in a sports arena, with the
electronic sounds amplified by 51 individual speakers mounted along the ceiling. Seven
additional speakers were also used to amplify the harpsichords. In addition, 52 slide
projectors provided streams of unrelated imagery, which was projected onto a large
hanging screen measuring 100 feet by 160 feet as well as a semicircular screen that ran
340 feet around the inside rim of the ceiling. For five hours, hundreds of people sat in

Figure 13.5
John Cage, David
Tudor, and Gordon
Mumma with the
Merce Cunningham
Dance Company
performing *Variations
V* at the Lincoln
Center, New York,
1965. "There were
so many cables and
what-not that it
was like walking
on a forest floor,"
said Robert Moog,
who acted as an
audio engineer for
the performance.
(John Cage Trust)

the bleachers and milled around on the main floor of the arena immersed in this sensory bath. It was big and absorbing and live. The commercial recording of *HPSCHD* released by Nonesuch Records (H–71224) in 1969 included a computer printout (individualized for each copy of the record) with a randomly generated set of instructions for controlling the volume, treble, and bass knobs on one's stereo while listening to the music. Each printout was individually numbered. Mine happens to be "Output Sheet No. 374."

Cage's Influence

John Cage was without question one of the most important and influential composers of the twentieth century. His work had a ripple effect that permeated not only the fields of classical music, but also jazz, rock, dance, and other performance art. The fact that he often used electronics in his work was only secondarily important. The true impact of his music was in changing people's expectations about what was musical and what was not. In 1937, he said, "Wherever we are, what we hear is mostly noise. When we ignore it, it disturbs us. When we listen to it, we find it fascinating."[20]

His dissatisfaction with tape composition was amplified by his thoughts about musical indeterminacy delivered in a lecture entitled "Composition as Process":

> An experimental action is one, the outcome of which is not foreseen. Being unforeseen, this action is not concerned with its excuse. Like the land, like the air, it needs none. A performance of a composition which is indeterminate of its performance is necessarily unique. It cannot be repeated. When performed for a second time, the outcome is other than it was. Nothing therefore is accomplished by such a performance, since that performance cannot be grasped as an object in time. A recording of such a work has no more value than a postcard; it provides a knowledge of something that happened, whereas the action was a non-knowledge of something that had not yet happened.[21]

In a conversation with the author, Cage characterized his experience with chance music in this way:

> I think the thing that underlies my works since the use of chance operations— whether it's determinate or indeterminate—is the absence of intention. I've used the chance operations as a discipline to free the music precisely from my taste, memory, and any intentions that I might have. It's a discipline equivalent, I think, to that of sitting cross-legged, but the cross-leggedness would carry one, so to speak, in toward the world of dreams, the subconscious and so forth, whereas this discipline of chance operations carries one out to the world of relativity.[22]

Improvisation

There is a close affinity between the pioneers of live electronic music and jazz musicians. They often worked together, played to the same audiences, and crossed over as musicians from one idiom to the other. They also share the sociological experience, at least following the 1960s, of being cut off from most arts funding because of increasing corporate and institutional pressures to support more mainstream tastes in music.

Improvisation in electronic music is a 45-year tradition going back to the late 1950s, when the possibilities of live performance in this idiom were first being explored. Cage and Tudor were working with the Merce Cunningham Dance Company about the same time that Mumma and Ashley were performing live improvised electronic music in Ann Arbor, Michigan. Its practice has benefited from the evolution of smaller and more compact electronic instruments and computers. The widespread growth of digital sampling, keyboards, turntables, and other real-time audio processing technology has formed entirely new subcultures of music based on live electronic performance, including hip-hop, techno, and electronica, all of which are sustained by the social settings of raves, clubs, and other performance events.

Improvisation defies clear definition. Even though most musicians have difficulty explaining what it is, many can tell you the basic way that they approach it. Unlike jazz, which often deals with improvisatory rules in a kind of gamelike exchange of modes and melodies, electronic music often lacks the qualities of rhythm, harmony, and melody that many jazz musicians rely on. Instead, electronic music improvisation is largely based on the spontaneous modification of non-pitched aspects of sound: the shape of the envelope, timbre, rhythm, layers or filtering, effects (echo, delay, ring modulation, etc.), amplitude, and duration. A seasoned improviser learns how to listen to many layers of sound activity as part of a performance.

As members of composer Paul Epstein's improvisation ensemble in the mid-1970s, we spent much of our time tuning our senses to the performance space and other musicians with whom we would be working. Most of the work we did was without any instruments at all. We used body movement and vocal sounds as our main musical resource. There were two essential talents necessary to improvise successfully in an environment where any sound was fair game: *listening* and *patience*. You listened so as to comprehend the dynamics of the sound relationships being explored by other performers, and carefully chose a moment to make a contribution after having been subsumed by the experience.

The improvisatory process just described had the following attributes:

1 listening;
2 reacting;
3 augmenting (adding a sound to any fragment of what others were doing);
4 creating new sounds, or fragments to explore.

Those steps in and of themselves might constitute a composition or plan of action for an improvisation using any sound source.

Live, improvised electronic music can be heard in multiple venues in New York City, London, Tokyo, Rome, Berlin, and most other large cities any night of the week. In New York, a number of musicians and composers are in great demand for what they contribute to the improvisational situation. Familiar names include Elliot Sharp, Ikue Mori, John Zorn, Thurston Moore, Christian Marclay, Zeena Parkins, and Charles Cohen. What do these people bring to a performance that their collaborators so admire? Aside from being good listeners, Parkins thinks that it has something to do with the personality of the sound offered by each performer:

> People might be drawn to the personalized sound palette that we have. When you hear the electric harp, it is pretty unlikely that you are going to think of

anything else besides what it is. I think the same is true for when you hear Ikue on drum machines. Her sound is pretty unmistakably her sound. We have developed this very distinctive language. For those that have imagination to think of situations where that language might be well suited it's a really great thing to have such personalized sounds to work with.[23]

Pauline Oliveros has focused on the art of improvisation for many years. Instrumentation is much less important to her than the art of *practiced listening*:

The central concern in all my prose or oral instructions is to provide attentional strategies for the participants. Attentional strategies are nothing more than ways of listening and responding in consideration of oneself, others and the environment. The result of using these strategies is listening. If performers are listening then the audience is also likely to listen.[24]

The instructions for one of her works are worth considering within the context of any improvisatory situation:

My instructions are intended to start an *attentional* process within a participant and among a group which can deepen gradually with repeated experience. Here is an example of a piece for voices or instruments: *Three Strategic Options*. Listen together. When you are ready to begin choose an option. Return to listening before choosing another option. Options are to be freely chosen throughout the duration of the piece. The piece ends when all return to listening together. 1) Sound before another performer 2) Sound after another performer 3) Sound with another performer. If performing as a soloist substitute sound from the environment for another performer.

In order to perform *Three Strategic Options* all players have to listen to one another. Attention shifts with each option. Sounding before another could have a competitive edge. One has to listen for a silence which is the opportunity. Sounding after another implies patience. One has to listen for the end of a sound. Sounding with another takes intuition—direct knowing of when to start and to end. A definitive performance is not expected as each performance can vary considerably even though the integrity of the guidelines will not be disturbed and the piece could be recognizable each time it is performed by the same group. Style would change according to the performers, instrumentation and environment.[25]

Being aware of these dynamics, even as an audience member, can greatly embellish the experience of listening to live electronic music.

THE ONCE FESTIVALS: A COALITION OF ELECTRONIC MUSIC PIONEERS

In Ann Arbor, Michigan, in the late 1950s, Robert Ashley and Gordon Mumma successfully staged weekly performances of live electronic music and avant-garde theater in the Space Theater of Milton Cohen. The success of the Space Theater and a burgeoning community of performing artists in Ann Arbor provided the momentum to take their efforts to the next level. Beginning in 1961, composers Ashley, Mumma, Roger Reynolds (b. 1934), George Cacioppo (1927–84), Bruce Wise, and Donald Scavarda (b. 1928) joined forces with the local Dramatic Arts Center of Wilfrid Kaplan to produce the first ONCE festival of contemporary music. They were joined by artists in other disciplines, including architects Harold Borkin and Joseph Wehrer, filmmaker George Manupelli, and painter-sculptors Mary Ashley and Milton Cohen.[26]

Prior to the ONCE festivals, the only periodic showcase for new music had been in Darmstadt, Germany, and by the early 1960s those had become more of an aesthetic battleground than a showcase. Darmstadt was also institutional in its backing and those who managed it exercised judgmental control over the selection—and censorship— of works to be featured. The ONCE festival, on the other hand, grew out of the devotion of its artist-performers and was sustained both by the efforts of Kaplan as the initial patron and by the tremendous public support that the series gained. Gordon Mumma explained:

> The ONCE festival happened because a community of artists took matters into their own hands. They extended their responsibilities beyond the limits of producing their art into the organization and promotion of their art before the public. In this process they simultaneously took advantage of the means of commerce, private and public patronage, and pedagogy. But for the most part they did this outside of the established avenues of artistic commerce, pedagogy and patronage.[27]

Even though the ONCE festivals took place in Ann Arbor, they existed without any support from the University of Michigan. Being outside of the normal avenues of commerce for the arts, it was difficult finding financial and other support for the festivals. Despite the fact that some of the participants were employed by the university, Mumma noted:

> virtually all efforts at enlisting support from this institution precipitated resistance and animosity to the project. Applications and contacts with numerous foundations, continuously for more than six years, produced no responses beyond a growing file of polite, through sometimes enthusiastic, fine-bond, raised-letterhead replies.[28]

Ashley recalled that one of their principal benefactors withdrew his support in 1965 because the festivals were getting too far-out: "He and his wife were amateur musicians who had friends in the University of Michigan music department, which I think it is fair to say was ferociously jealous of our success. I think his departure was under their influence."[29]

Contrary to its name, the festival did occur more than once and continued to grow year by year, filling successively larger auditoriums. There were six ONCE festivals in all between 1961 and 1965 (two occurred in 1965, the final one being called ONCE AGAIN).

From the start, Ashley, Mumma, and Reynolds made an effort to attract European composers and conductors to the festival. They also opened their arms to influential jazz musicians who were exploring the outer reaches of that idiom. The concerts were an immediate international success, and a potent antidote to the musical dogma associated with Darmstadt.

The first ONCE festival took place in a 200-seat Unitarian church in Ann Arbor and consisted of four concerts. The subsequent festivals comprised four to eight performances spread out over a week or two, usually in February and March. According to Ashley, only one performance during the entire eight years had less than standing room-only attendance. Apart from the festivals themselves, there were also year-round concerts and performances given by individual members of the collective, which came to be known as the ONCE group. The fame of the concerts eventually inspired similar events around the country, particularly on college campuses.

The programs of the ONCE festivals featured the hottest new music performers and musicians. Live and taped electronic music was at the heart of many performances. In all, 29 concerts of new music were offered during the six ONCE festivals, including 67 premiere performances out of a total of 215 works by 88 contemporary composers.[30]

The fourth festival was preceded by a publicity controversy that enraged the critics almost as much as the music itself did. Mumma recalled:

> Mary Ashley designed an accordion-folded, purple and white flyer that featured on one side the enormously detailed programs. On the other side was a photograph of the composers Ashley, Cacioppo, Scavarda, and myself, looking like the Mafia in drag, standing behind a voluptuous nude reclining on the lunch counter of a well-known local eatery called "Red's Rite Spot."
>
> The appearance of this flyer created a small hysteria, and the Dramatic Arts Center called an emergency meeting. Suggestions that the flyer be withdrawn were overcome: the ultimate problem was obtaining further funds for reprinting it to meet the demand for souvenir copies. The extent of this flyer's success was indicated to me dramatically in New York City the following April. At the seminar following one of Max Polikoff's "Music in our Time" concerts, on which Ashley and I had just performed, the first question from the audience concerned the availability of autographed copies of the purple ONCE flyer.[31]

A list of the programs themselves shows that the history of the ONCE festivals evolved from that of mostly musical performances in a normal proscenium setting to more open-ended stagings including dancers, multimedia, and lighting effects. By the time Alvin Lucier took part in 1965, the musicians were beginning to mingle with the audience in the performance space for some pieces, as was the case with the first performances of Lucier's *Vespers* for an ensemble using small echo-location (pulse wave oscillators) devices called Sondols (sonar dolphin):

> I first did the piece called *Vespers* in Ann Arbor at the ONCE festival[32] in the ballroom at the graduate center. I wasn't anxious about it. I didn't know how it was going to play out. I needed to see the space and the performers. I had all these ideas. It was just a question about who was going to play the Sondols

and what they would do. So, I designed the performance that afternoon for the space: "You go there"; "Somebody start here"; "Don't do this—do this." And so you make the piece. In all honesty to the music, you couldn't really plan it in advance because that was not the way it was. I don't know if I blindfolded them or not on this occasion. I actually made up some of the performance during the performance, if you can imagine. I had leather shoes on and the floor was made of wood. The lights went down and I walked around the space and you could hear echoes from my feet. Now most people wouldn't pay attention to that because it was just walking. I opened the drapes on the windows to get a more reverberant space. I was preparing the space, actually. I was giving the audience clues as to what might be going on. Everybody knows if you open the drapes there's more reverberation. Then I had stacked some chairs up. I deployed some of those as obstacles. I think there were even potted plants that I put as obstacles. It was kind of like someone preparing for a dinner party. I went around and rearranged some of the furniture.

I had four players. They were in four parts of the room. I instructed them to try, by means of hearing the echoes that came back to them, to move as if they were blind. And that they should only play when it made sense to. To hear the echoes. That they shouldn't just play the instruments as instruments, they shouldn't decide to speed up or slow down for musical effect. That kills the performance immediately. It had to be based on survival and task. That was my score. This built the task into the performance. It was in the dark.[33] [Gordon Mumma added that the performers were also blindfolded for this performance.[34]]

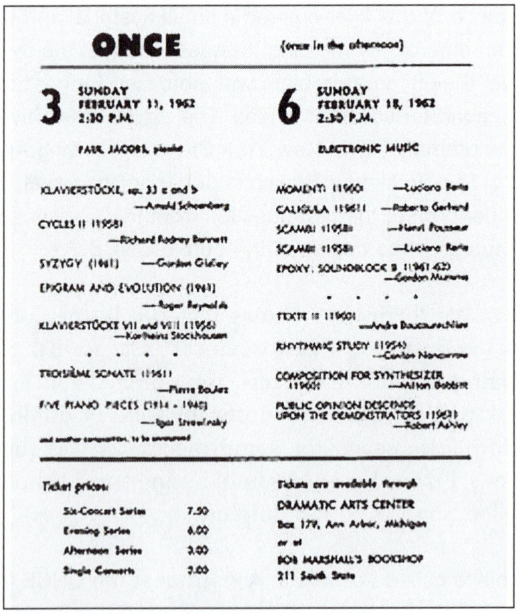

Figure 13.6   ONCE festival poster showing scheduled performances of electronic music by Berio, Mumma, Pousseur, Babbitt, and Ashley. (Gordon Mumma)

In spite of the perennial ribbing of media music critics—many of whom enjoyed beginning reviews, as Robert Ashley recalls, with a line such as "Once is enough"—the ONCE festivals served as a major influence on the contemporary-music scene. Their successful run had a galvanizing effect on the experimental music community, bringing together American composers from both coasts and ensuring that the spirit of radical experimentation of Cage and Tudor would continue into the next generation. While it would be contrary to its spirit to suggest that all of this experimental activity formed a cohesive school, it did indeed propel several movements in new American music. Many of these artists from New York, San Francisco, and Ann Arbor shared similar challenges and a common purpose: to create something new and original in contemporary music that was a reaction against what had come before and what was being lauded by the European avant-garde. As Gordon Mumma reflects, "The origins of the jazz traditions occurred in the same way—collaborative and interactive. While the Darmstadt model established fences on musical creativity, jazz traditions and the ONCE festival example let things grow, without putting limits on creative innovation."[35]

The live performance work of the SFTMC continued to evolve during this time as well, including instrumental and electronic performances using tape and live electronic music, theater and dance pieces, and visual projections. The ONCE and SFTMC groups developed an ongoing correspondence and shared many ideas related to their common

---

LIVE ELECTRONIC MUSIC

1 *Cartridge Music* (1960) by John Cage
   Amplified small sounds

2 *Greys* (1963) by Gordon Mumma
   Music from the ONCE festival

3 *Music for Solo Performer* (1964–65) by Alvin Lucier
   Music for amplified brainwaves

4 *Variations V* (1965) by John Cage
   Live multimedia performance

5 *In the Realm of Nothing Whatever* (1966) by AMM
   Live improvised music with electronics

6 *Hornpipe* (1967) by Gordon Mumma
   Modified horn sounds

7 *Runthrough* (1967–68) by David Behrman
   Homemade synthesizers and photocell mixers

8 *Spacecraft* (1970) by Musica Elettronica Viva (MEV)
   Analog synthesizers and amplified instruments

9 *Automatic Writing* (1974–79) by Robert Ashley
   Electronics and voice

10 *Contraband* (2006) by Ikue Mori and Zeena Parkins
   Improvisation for laptop electronics and instruments

LISTEN

experiences. Oliveros was invited to perform at the ONCE festival in 1965. In 1966 she returned to Ann Arbor with a new work written for the ONCE group called *C(s) for Once*. It was scored for trumpets, flutes, voices, organ, and three tape recorders, with one tape threaded through all three to modify the sounds of the live performers. This work led to some interesting collaborations in later years between veterans of both groups, including Oliveros's production of *Valentine* (1968), which was commissioned by the Sonic Arts Union of Ashley, Mumma, Behrman, and Lucier.

LEADING INDICATORS FOR THE FUTURE: THE SONIC ARTS UNION

By 1966, Robert Ashley, Gordon Mumma, David Behrman, and Alvin Lucier had become well acquainted because of their mutual collaborations and performances with John Cage, David Tudor, the Cunningham Dance Company (after 1966), and the instrumental performances of the ONCE festivals. With the festivals coming to an end, the four of them decided to join forces as a touring group, the Sonic Arts Group, later known as the Sonic Arts Union (1966–76).

The inspiration for doing this was clearly the success that Cage and Tudor had experienced by taking their music on the road. Lucier explained:

> David Tudor really freed a lot of us . . . That was a great stimulation—that you could design your own equipment, that you could find it at Radio Shack. You could configure it in certain ways and you could make your own work. That was very important.[36]

What the world received as a part of this union were four very individual voices ready to break another set of sound barriers.

Each of the members of the Sonic Arts Union is still active in music today. In speaking to them individually about their work, it is clear that the Sonic Arts Union was an especially bright period in each of their remarkable histories. Behrman thinks that the unifying element behind their individual work was an interest in doing pieces "in which established techniques were thrown away and the nature of sound was dealt with from scratch."[37]

Forming the group was largely a matter of practicality. Some of the members had been receiving invitations to perform in Europe and elsewhere, but the expense of producing a concert on one's own would have made it economically impractical to accept such offers. By teaming up, they could pool their equipment and eliminate other costs by serving as both technicians and musicians. Because there was often little or no payment for such performances, the union served as a hedge against unnecessary expenses.

The Sonic Arts Union toured North America and Europe into the early 1970s. Even though they pooled their equipment, they didn't often collaborate on compositions except by helping each other out during performances. Each composer would bring a piece to a concert and the others would act as musicians by manning the equipment. "A Sonic Arts Union concert was about 1,000 miles of wire and all these little boxes that plugged into each other," recalls Ashley.[38]

The Sonic Arts Union was happening during a period of transition for each of its members. Behrman was nearing the end of a successful period of producing for Columbia Records, during which he added the names of Cage, Oliveros, Babbitt, Lucier, Reich, Riley, Pousseur, and other avant-garde composers to the repertoire of artists represented on the Columbia Masterworks label of classical music recordings. Even as he worked with the Sonic Arts Union, he was busy touring with the Cunningham Dance Company and assisting John Cage on several projects. By the end of the union's run, he had become co-director of the Center for Contemporary Music at Mills College with Ashley.

At the time of the formation of the Sonic Arts Union, Lucier had been teaching at Brandeis University in Massachusetts (1962–69), where he conducted the Brandeis University Chamber Chorus, devoting much of its time to new music. His own work was commissioned by the Cunningham Dance Company in 1970. During his stint with the Sonic Arts Union, he took a teaching post at Wesleyan University, Connecticut (1970), where he continues to work today.

Ashley and Mumma had concluded the ONCE festivals in 1966 in Ann Arbor and were moving on to wider vistas. Mumma became increasingly active as a musician for the Cunningham Dance Company, working closely in the design and performance of electronic music with David Tudor. In 1970 he collaborated with Tudor on the design of the audio system for the Pepsi pavilion at the World's Fair in Osaka, Japan. Mumma calls his association with the Sonic Arts Union "one of the two most nourishing artistic situations I've ever been in," the other being the Cunningham Dance Company.[39]

Ashley took an entirely unexpected turn. One morning in April 1968, he decided to stop composing. He made this decision as if it were going to last forever. His reasons were many, including the economic pressures of trying to produce concerts while eking out a living with day jobs. With little money available for composers, he began to believe that "there was no reality" to his dreams.[40] He had also been deeply discouraged by one of the last performances of the touring ONCE group, an event during which the audience physically assaulted the musicians:

> The performance we did at Brandeis was a beautiful piece called *Night Train*. It involved, among a lot of other things, giving the audience something when they came in. The idea of the piece was that we were aliens and trying to make friends with the Earth people. So, everybody who came in along with their ticket got something edible, like an apple or an onion or a fish or a loaf of bread or something like that. Somehow in the middle of the performance the audience kind of lost it and started attacking us. Of course, the way humans would attack aliens. They literally attacked us. They were throwing things. The main problem that I had was that they were throwing things at the performers on stage and a lot of the things were dangerous to throw. Besides the hard pieces of vegetable, like an onion, we were passing out lights. Harold Borkin had a group of ten or so students there who were soldering one end of a flashlight bulb to one end of a battery and then soldering a wire to the other end of the battery. When the audience started throwing those I knew we were in deep trouble. We got through the performance but it was very ugly. I didn't like it at all. It was 1967 or '68. That's the only time we ever performed the piece. It was very discouraging and I stopped composing soon after that. I had had enough. And I didn't compose music for another five years or something like that. It was really extremely discouraging.[41]

Ashley didn't want his music to only "end up in his filing cabinet." He stopped composing, but was determined to stay involved in music and find a way to further the cause. The Sonic Arts Union gave him the chance to continue performing with like-minded individuals. He also took the job of director of the Center for Contemporary Music at Mills College in 1969 and revitalized one of the most influential music programs in the country during a time when several of its founding members—most notably Subotnick and Oliveros—had left for other opportunities.

Ashley, of course, returned to composing after about five years, the discouragement of audience attacks behind him and several fulfilling years with the Sonic Arts Union and Mills College under his belt. Ultimately, it was Mimi Johnson who challenged him by saying, "Well, if you are a famous composer you've got to compose music."[42] Which is what he did by inventing the field of contemporary opera for television with *Music with Roots in the Aether* (1975).

One can only describe the music of the Sonic Arts Union by understanding the interests and tendencies of its four composers. If Cage represented the first wave of live electronic music production—the use of magnetic tape and the amplification of small sounds—then Ashley, Behrman, Lucier, and Mumma surely represented four important extensions of that early electronic music. There is no greater testament to the gravity of their work than to realize that the four paths explored by these innovators were the leading indicators of musical practices that are still with us today.

Gordon Mumma

Gordon Mumma extended Cage's use of tape and amplification of small sounds to the real-time, adaptive electronic processing of sounds using acoustic and electronic sources. Most of this work has been done with circuits that he builds himself. He and Tudor were responsible for creating the performing culture of a table full of black boxes and wires, of interconnected components that can be mixed and modulated at will. Mumma says:

Figure 13.7   Gordon Mumma performing *Hornpipe*, 1967. (Gordon Mumma)

> In spite of my fairly solid education in the "Euro-American traditions," I found no conflicts or contradictions in my developing work with electronic music, though most of my teachers, and a good number my "traditional" peers, thought I was "off the track" or downright crazy.[43]

Hornpipe (1967) by Gordon Mumma is a solo work in which Mumma played the waldhorn and French horn, at first unmodified, working from four predetermined types of sound materials: sustained tones; natural reed horn; articulated reed horn; and staccato reed horn. On his belt was a "cybersonic console"—a black box containing adaptive resonant circuitry of his own design. Mumma noted, "The cybersonic console monitors the resonances of the horn in the performance space and adjusts its electronic circuits to complement these resonances."[44] This can be likened to controlled feedback, but the feedback was first run through additional circuitry where it was further modulated and articulated prior to being made audible through loudspeakers.

Because of its dependence on the resonant behavior of the performance space, each rendering of *Hornpipe* is different. It is improvisatory in that the musician must concentrate on what is happening and react to the electronic sounds being triggered by his own playing. The first part of the piece allows the player and cybersonic console to "train the space," so to speak, learning how sounds made with the horn will be electronically modified. Mumma then provides guidelines for what should follow this learning stage: horn playing with electronic sounds; long unmodified sequences of unmodified cybersonic replies; and electronic sounds "articulated directly by horn sounds."[45]

Robert Ashley

Robert Ashley has explored narrative music—storytelling music—for new media, including television and live performance with multimedia elements. In his words:

> I thought and still think that television is an ideal place for music. Especially for opera. It hasn't happened in my lifetime except in my work. But I think it will eventually happen. I think that it is inevitable that there will be operas for television . . . The television medium allows for a new kind of opera because it eliminates all of that machinery of the opera stage that slows an opera down. You can write an opera that goes as fast as any sitcom.[46]

Automatic Writing (1974–79) was much talked about when it was released on record by Lovely Music Ltd. in 1979. Ashley wrote it over a five-year period after having just come back from his self-imposed exile from composing in the early 1970s. He performed it many times in various formative stages with the Sonic Arts Union before finally committing it to disc.

Automatic Writing was frequently lauded as an early work of ambient music because of its quiet, tinkling sound. It consisted of 46 minutes of music that was so quiet that you would miss most of it if you left your volume control at its normal setting. The underlying keyboard music that makes up a layer of the work's texture was so muted that it sounded like it was coming from another room. *Automatic Writing* was compared to minimalism because it was sparse and repetitive and had some of those other characteristics that are often thought to be minimalist. It was also called "text-sound" composition because it included spoken dialog. While all of those descriptions were superficially accurate, most attempts to assign *Automatic Writing* to a genre were unhelpful. They failed to notice that Ashley was pointing to a place up the road ahead. The piece was Ashley's first extended attempt to find a new form of musical storytelling using the English language. It was opera in the Robert Ashley way.

The basic musical material of *Automatic Writing* was the spoken voice, closely miked, uttering what Ashley characterized as "involuntary speech": random, seemingly rational comments that might not make sense at all, depending on the context in which they were heard. He was searching for the essence of character and narrative, of human

Figure 13.8   Robert Ashley in his studio, 2001. (Thom Holmes)

emotion translated through language and sound into performance. This essence, this emotion, was not always communicated by words. The shape and quality of the voices, the level of amplification, and the musical accompaniment were all potent musical resources in *Automatic Writing*. Ashley was very aware of what he was up to.

Not long after the release of the first recording, he told me:

> In *Automatic Writing* I had become interested in the idea of characters in an operatic or dramatic sense. Of characters actually being manifested through a particular sound. I was fumbling around looking for ways I could work in an operatic sense that would be practical. I didn't want to start writing things that wouldn't be performed for 25 years without forming a group. So, I went toward the idea of sounds having a kind of magical function. Of being able to actually conjure characters. It's sort of complicated for me to think about it because I don't entirely understand it. It seemed to me that in a sort of psychophysical sense sounds can actually make you see things, can give you images that are quite specific.[47]

The piece evolved slowly over a number of years. All along, Ashley was aiming for four characters, four personalities to weave a sense of story and interaction. Two of these ended up being vocal, two instrumental. He first used some tape materials for the character part that was later replaced by the organ. Then he added the second speaker in the guise of Mimi Johnson, who acted like a "shadow talker." They staged it using live electronics and some reactive computer circuitry by Paul DeMarinis so that they could interact electronically in real time. The idea to add the French-language reading came to him when he went to Paris for the premiere of *Music with Roots in the Aether*:

> I felt this weird desire, which was totally unwarranted, to put a French translation along with the monologue. You can hardly understand the English, so to put a French translation—I don't know what made me do it. But I did it, and as soon as I heard that sound of the French translation I realized that I had three of the four characters.[48]

That became the part read by Johnson in the final version.

After several years of development, Ashley was ready to produce a definitive recording of *Automatic Writing*. He set up the recording studio at Mills College one summer while everyone was on vacation so he could work totally alone. He recorded his own vocal part by himself, adjusting the recording level for the microphone just at the point of feedback: "The microphone was probably not more than an inch from my mouth. It was about as close as it could be. That was the core of the piece, that sound of the close miking."[49] He added the subtle and eerie modulations of the voice to complete the track for the first character, rendering most of the words he read incomprehensible. The other three characters were added later to complete the recording, with the help of Mimi Johnson and Paul DeMarinis. This brought the life cycle of *Automatic Writing* to a natural conclusion:

> I had the monologue itself with the electronics. I had the synthesizer accompaniment to that, the inversion of that. I had the sound of the French language. Then, I realized that I just needed a fourth character and finally I found it in that *Polymoog* part. So, those four characters had been performed in various different manifestations for a couple of years before I did the record. Then when I did the record the piece was over and I never wanted to perform it after that. I had finished it—I had found the four characters.[50]

Alvin Lucier

Alvin Lucier has advocated music designed around simple acoustic processes, exploring the real-time processing of sounds in resonant environments. Lucier noted:

> So often, when I'm in school and teaching, I try to get students just to think clearly about something . . . The first papers they write are very confusing. They hear this, their opinions are confusing. Then I say that I'm not interested in your opinions. I say that you've got to have perceptions, not opinions. Everyone's got opinions. But perceptions. What are you hearing? So that is why my work is simple.[51]

Music for Solo Performer (1964–65) by Alvin Lucier was the first piece of music composed for amplified brainwaves—and certainly not the last. Lucier got the idea from research being done by physicist Edmond Dewan at the Air Force Research Labs in Cambridge, Massachusetts. With the aid of an electroencephalograph (EEG), Dewan's subjects were able to control the amplitude of their brains' alpha rhythms and transmit them to a teleprinter in the form of Morse code. In his adaptation of this idea, Lucier skipped the Morse code and worked directly with amplified brainwaves as a musical resource.

Music for Solo Performer was first performed on May 5, 1965, at Brandeis University in Massachusetts. "The brainwave piece is as much about resonance as it is about brainwaves. In fact, it isn't very much about brainwaves," admits Lucier.[52] It was really about using the room as an acoustic filter, one of his earliest experiments in this area that has occupied his projects for many years.

At the time of this work, the phenomenon of high-fidelity stereo was making a big splash. Bose and KLH had just introduced high-quality suspension loudspeakers for the home. Loudspeakers were a critical element in the success of any work of electronic music. Lucier recalled, "When you think about the violin makers in Italy in the early eighteenth century—Amati

Figure 13.9   Alvin Lucier, 2001.
(Thom Holmes)

and Stradivari—all the composers made pieces for those violins. We were making pieces for loudspeakers."[53] His idea was not only to generate sounds by amplifying the brainwaves but to place the vibrating surfaces of the loudspeakers in contact with percussion instruments that would, in turn, make sounds of their own. Snare drums, gongs, and other small objects were used. They were placed underneath, on top of, or against the loudspeakers:

> For the snare drums, I put little loudspeakers right on the skins of the snare drums. For the gongs, I put the gongs mostly touching the edge of the speakers, either near or almost touching. I'm trying to make the connection between sympathetic vibration, which is a physical thing, and the next idea is the room as a speaker.[54]

The intensity of the brainwaves would increase as one attained an alpha state. The different percussion instruments responded to differing levels of intensity in the brainwaves. The vibrating, rattling, chiming, and buzzing sounds changed with the flow of the performer's mental state. A performance of *Music for Solo Performer* was a captivating experience. When performing it himself, Lucier generally sat at the center of the stage, alone in a chair, with electrodes attached to his head by a headband. Loudspeakers flanked him on either side, arranged within proximity of a multitude of percussion instruments. Except for his facial expressions, and the opening and closing of his eyes, there was no visible correspondence between the performer and the sounds being heard on the loudspeakers. Alpha waves became strongest when he closed his eyes and stopped when he opened them. The humming persisted as long as he could concentrate on forming alpha waves.

A radical experiment such as this cannot be without at least one amusing mishap, and *Music for Solo Performer* is no exception. David Tudor was preparing for a performance of the piece at the University of California at Davis in 1967. Lucier was not involved, and when it came time to set up the proper equipment, they realized that they needed a special amplifier—a differential amplifier. It so happened that the veterinary school on campus had such a thing and was more than willing to help. Composer Larry Austin was also taking part and retrieved one of his own loudspeakers and a stereo amplifier to complete the complement of equipment for the test. At the lab, there was a doctor who knew how to place the sensors for the detection of brainwaves, but he had only done it with chickens. He placed the electrodes on David Tudor's forehead. Tudor noted: "And it was fine, but . . . in Alvin's original version, you controlled the sound by closing your eyes. If you opened your eyes, then the sound would stop."[55] In the case of the chicken doctor, just the opposite was true: if you closed your eyes, the sound would stop. This was amusing, but unacceptable, so they repositioned the electrodes to the back of Tudor's head to see what would happen. Suddenly, they had signals of a much greater amplitude. They were so strong, in fact, that before too long the loudspeaker went up in a puff of smoke and caught fire. It was smoking from David Tudor's brainwaves, a backhanded compliment if there ever was one. Larry Austin had sacrificed one of his prized loudspeakers for science, but a successful performance was nonetheless given using other equipment.

David Behrman

David Behrman is one of the earliest adapters of semiconductors and then micro-computers and software in the creation of interactive, responsive computer music systems. Behrman says:

> When I think back, I don't know, there hasn't been any generation of artists who have lived through an experience like this. Going from tubes to transistors to chips to microcomputers to very, very, powerful, tiny computers. It's never happened before. God knows what the future holds.[56]

Long before the word "computer" became associated with any music by David Behrman, he was creating works that provided interactivity between the performers and the electronics. Behrman described *Runthrough* (1967–68) as a piece that required no special performance skills other than the ability to turn knobs and aim flashlights, making this early work of interactive live electronic music as playable by non-musicians as by musicians. It was one of Behrman's earliest experiments in electronic interactivity, pre-dating his landmark work with computer circuits by nearly ten years.

The piece required two to four players and was often performed by the Sonic Arts Union. Sound was generated and modified using homemade synthesizers that were manually controlled by dials and switches. One or two of the people would play those. Behrman described this equipment:

> The homemade synthesizers, built into small aluminum boxes and powered by batteries, consisted of various devices that were not too difficult or expensive to build at that time—sine, triangle, and ramp wave generators, voltage-controlled amplifiers, frequency and ring modulators.[57]

Figure 13.10
David Behrman, 2007.
(Thom Holmes)

Homemade "photocell mixers" were used to direct the sound to four or eight loud-speakers that were normally set up surrounding the audience. The light-sensitive mixers consisted of a flat panel with several rows of photocells. Aiming a flashlight at a photocell would pipe the sound of the synthesizers to one of the speakers. The two players assigned to the photocell mixer each used two flashlights. The mixer required a darkened hall, which added yet another dramatic touch to what must have seemed like a work of magic to some members of the audience.

Sounds would result from any combination of dials being turned, switches being flipped, and photocells being activated. Players generally felt their way along on this sonic beachfront, learning to work together to produce astonishing effects. The more practiced players, including the Sonic Arts Union members themselves, could propel the work along, "riding a sound" they liked in a kind of wavy unison.

Runthrough had no score. It consisted only of circuit diagrams. But that did not deter a couple of recent attempts to realize *Runthrough* with digital technology. Composer Mark Trayle, who is currently chair of the composition program at the California Institute of the Arts, was able to recreate the piece using digital audio software. His students worked on it and played it for Behrman while he was there for a residency. This encouraged Behrman to revive some of his other earlier interactive pieces:

> I just did a revival of homemade synthesizer music with sliding pitches running in *Max/MSP* on a *PowerBook*. It sounds sort of the same. It's very easy to do. I mean it's not exactly the same. Then, of course, it can do a million other things that you couldn't do in those days.[58]

LIVE ELECTRONIC MUSIC PERFORMANCE

The history of live electronic music is rich. The recordings of two groups that are rooted in the 1960s are worth seeking out. MEV (Musica Elettronica Viva) was formed in 1966 by American composers Alan Bryant, Alvin Curran, Jon Phetteplace, and Frederic Rzewski. The members of the group varied, so at times it also included Richard Teitelbaum, Ivan Vandor, Edith Schloss, Carol Plantamura, Steven Lacy, and others. They toured heavily during the late 1960s, giving more than 100 concerts in 30 cities in Europe. In addition to their own works, they performed pieces by other composers including Cage, Behrman, Lucier, Cardew, Gelmetti, and Kosugi.

The music of MEV was free-form and radical in the most liberal tradition of Cage and Tudor. Instrumentation varied widely, from the simple amplification of room noise and outside sounds to the inclusion of electronic instruments such as the Moog synthesizer and traditional jazz and rock instruments.

London-based AMM was another touring group of electronic and jazz musicians formed in 1966. Composers Cornelius Cardew and

Figure 13.11   MEV (Musica Elettronica Viva). (Album photo, Mainstream MS 5002, 1968)

Christopher Hobbs were the only members of the group with formal education in classical music. The other members included jazz musicians Lou Gare, Edwin Prévost, and Keith Rowe.

Cardew, who was also a member of the musical wing of the Fluxus art movement in England, was the lecturer of the group:

> Written compositions are fired off into the future; even if never performed, the writing remains as a point of reference. Improvisation is in the present, its effect may live on in the souls of the participants, both active and passive (i.e., audience), but in its concrete form it is gone forever from the moment that it occurs, nor did it have any previous existence before the moment that it occurred, so neither is there any historical reference available . . .
>
> You choose the sound you hear. But listening for effects is only first steps in AMM listening. After a while you stop skimming, start tracking, and go where it takes you.[59]

Ikue Mori (b. 1953) is something of an underground legend in New York. She arrived in the United States in 1977 with a musician friend who was immediately approached to join bands by such punk luminaries as Lydia Lunch and James Chance. Mori, not yet a practiced musician, met guitarist Arto Lindsay who was looking for a drummer. She tried drumming and they started jamming. The threesome of Ikue Mori, Arto Lindsay, and Tim Wright became the recombinant punk band DNA.

DNA also proved to be Mori's first practice with improvisation. She recalled:

> In the beginning, when we were making pieces out of noise, we were doing a lot of improvisation. We probably made a song list of ten songs. We kept playing the same set for five years. I don't think it was musically developed, but it went beyond. DNA had become something beyond music.[60]

After DNA, John Zorn introduced Mori to other improvisers in town. "Before that," she admits, "I really didn't know how to improvise. I was just playing a beat."

It was about that time that someone gave Mori a drum machine. It wasn't long after that, faced with the impracticality of hauling a set of drums up to her tiny new sixth-floor apartment, that she gave up conventional drumming entirely in favor of the drum machine. She has been composing and improvising, most recently with a PowerBook (equipped with *Max/ MSP* software) and two small drum machines. It all fits into a backpack. She is without doubt the most requested *laptop* performer in town. She lays down a backdrop of arrhythmic clangs and clacks to which other performers love to improvise. She has a sound, an electronic signature, that is all her own. Her music consists of mutations of signals generated by drum machines and other sources. Some occur in real time during a performance, while others are stored on her PowerBook for

Figure 13.12   AMM (Keith Rowe, Cornelius Cardew, Lou Gare, Eddie Prévost). (Album photo, Mainstream MS 5002, 1968)

recall and modification using *Max*. Noise and pitches commingle freely, at her command. They are sometimes rhythmic and structured, but often more amorphous, bounding in an omnidirectional manner about the performing space. She works like a painter, adding colors, depth, and textures to the lines being drawn by other artists.

A performance sometimes becomes an orchestration of people and instincts rather than music. For each production of her *The Sheer Frost Orchestra*, Marina Rosenfeld recruits a new group of 17 female musicians and performers. The lifeblood of the piece results from the unpredictable interaction of the performers, who are teamed up in various changing combinations as specified by her score. Rosenfeld explains:

> Some of the interests I have as a music composer have crossed over into how I'm dealing with people. I realized that some of the ideas I have about composing music are just as relevant to composing the participation of people in my music. I'm especially interested in the differences between people and their idiosyncrasies as human beings. This is a feature of *The Sheer Frost Orchestra*, where I am often inviting women to participate based on some ambiance or feeling I get of their personality, as opposed to knowing what kind of musician they are, or might become. Each *Orchestra* performance has been close to an explosion of strong personalities.[61]

Improvisation is part of the experimental spirit that makes up the soul of electronic music. As Alvin Lucier so aptly put it, improvisation challengers players and listeners alike to "go in by yourself and perceive it."[62]

Figure 13.13   PLOrk (The Princeton Laptop Orchestra)—the first real-time laptop orchestra—in performance at The Kitchen in New York in 2009. (PLOrk, Lorene Lavora)

AMBIENT MUSIC

Ambient and environmental music has roots in the 1950s and 1960s, particularly in the work of Cage and Tudor, who drew attention to ambient sounds through the inclusion of silent patches in their works, *4′ 33″* (1952) for a pianist—Cage's so-called silent sonata —being the earliest unequivocal plea to embrace ambient sound as part of music. Cage had an affinity for ambient sounds that he voiced throughout his career. In a piece written in 1950, he spoke about the experiential context within which his plundering of silence would take place:

> This psychological turning leads to the world of nature, where, gradually or suddenly, one sees that humanity and nature, not separate, are in this world together; that nothing was lost when everything was given away. In fact, everything is gained. In musical terms, any sounds may occur in any combination and in any continuity.[63]

The first version of *4′ 33″* was composed in 1952 using chance-determined timings for a work in three parts. First performed by David Tudor, the movements lasted 33″, 2′ 40″, and 1′ 20″, with Tudor using a stopwatch to measure the duration. Tudor's interpretation of the work included closing the lid of the keyboard cover during each movement and opening it up between movements, all the time with the score and stopwatch placed in front of him on the piano. All of this was done with as little theatricality as possible. Cage later discarded the three movements and recast the piece for any instrument or combination of instruments and duration. The point of the piece, as Cage was fond of explaining, was that true silence does not exist and that one could realize this by only opening one's ears.

Experimental music that made use of ambient sounds came into its own during the 1960s. Cage and Tudor amplified remote sounds from rooms and piped them into an auditorium (*Variations IV*, 1964). Alvin Lucier has an extensive body of work exploring the natural acoustics of a given performing space. Max Neuhaus, widely credited with inventing the sound "installation," provided continuously playing music within the context of public spaces. David Behrman composed what could be called the first musical composition of electronic sounds with environmental sounds in 1968 for the Robert Watts (1923–88) film *Cascade*. It was a tape work consisting of environmental sounds with electronics murmuring underneath and had much of the atmosphere and flavor associated with works by others that were given the label **ambient music**. He called it a collage piece at the time and remembered that its composition was done independently of the motion picture: "I had seen the film before making the music, but didn't coordinate any of the sounds with any specific action in the film."[64] The film made the rounds of art house theaters at the time but was not highly visible and therefore does not seem to qualify as a major influence on other composers. Thankfully, the music is now available on CD in the form of a piece called *Sounds for a Film by Robert Watts* (Italy, Alga Marghen, Plana B 5NmN.020, 1998).

Considered individually, one might not normally draw comparisons between the work of Wendy Carlos, Annea Lockwood (b. 1939), and Brian Eno. Each was responsible, however, for experimenting in ambient sound composition in ways that would be much imitated in the future.

Wendy Carlos composed the remarkable *Sonic Seasonings* in 1972, combining synthesized sounds with environmental sounds. Nobody knew quite what to make of it at the time, since it fit none of the convenient names being given to record bins in the store. It consisted of two LPs' worth of quiet, subtle sounds, carefully composed to gently bob the imagination. They were mood pieces, intended to invoke the essence of the four seasons. Carlos's own words explain the concept best:

> *Sonic Seasonings* has the form of a musical suite, made of four contrasting movements. Each is loosely based on images of the four basic seasons on our planet: Spring, Summer, Fall, and Winter . . .
>
> There is no real plot in any of the movements. Instead they suggest a cyclic point of view that moves onto a few other musical locations, and eventually returns to a similar setting from whence it began.[65]

By the early 1970s, composer Annea Lockwood had created a niche for herself in new music as the composer who burned and drowned pianos and made electroacoustic music with shards of glass. She had worked widely with choreographers and visual artists and was very much in tune with the environmental aspects of the performance space. It was about this time that she turned her attention to the creation of pieces and installations using recorded sounds from the natural world. She had been making remote recordings of natural phenomena such as river sounds since the late 1960s, and many of these elements figured prominently in her tape composition *World Rhythms* (1975). *World Rhythms* was a musical travelog of nature sounds that was pieced together as carefully as a dovetail joint to mesh the rhythms of one segment with those of the next.

Lockwood's approach to using taped sounds differed significantly from *musique concrète*. Like Steve Reich, whose looped works used unadulterated sound sources to generate tension and rhythm, she was interested in using sounds as themselves so that their intrinsic qualities could be heard. Unlike Reich, Lockwood avoided using tape manipulation or loops so that the sounds could unfold on their own. Her process was that of selecting and carefully organizing natural sounds. She explained:

> I've never done much manipulation of the sound sources I'm working with. What I have been doing all of this time is selecting what I want to record very carefully, listening to it very closely, and figuring out angles, situations, and times of day in which to record to get maximum presence. I'm really interested in acoustic commonalities amongst various disparate sounds and tracing them. That's been one of my focal points for my electroacoustic works rather than treating these sound sources as intrinsically raw material and then working them over and transforming them. I regard them all as self-sufficient, certainly as intricately complex and complete audio phenomena in and of themselves. I'm looking at the relationships amongst them.
>
> In terms of assembling the sound materials for a piece . . . very often what will lead me to select sound X to follow what I am currently doing rather than sound Y is something very specific in their respective rhythms or something to do with the frequency band. Similarity which can show that I can make a transition, a smooth sort of interface transition between the two sounds. I'm interested in making those sorts of transitions where you really don't realize that you've slipped over into another sound until a second or so.[66]

World Rhythms wasn't only conceived as a recorded work, however, and had an important beginning as a live performance piece:

> World Rhythms was composed in 1974–75 and was a ten-channel live
> improvised mix, together with a performer on a very large tam-tam. The ten
> speakers formed a circle around the audience, placed at various heights
> (the speakers!). The gong player and person mixing both sat in the center.
> The gong part is designed to create an actual biorhythm, not an analog for the
> heartbeat or anything like that. The player strikes the gong then turns inward,
> tracking her/his body's responses to that action (not to the mix or even to the
> sound of the gong per se). When all responses seem to have ebbed away,
> sh/e sounds the gong again. So it is a rhythm of action and response which
> is being added to the general mix, but which is created independently of
> the mix.[67]

Following *World Rhythms*, Lockwood's fascination with river sounds led to the creation of *The River Archive*—a library of natural river sounds that continues to grow to this day. "I've not counted how many rivers the Archive now has, contributed by friends and acquaintances, as well as my own collecting."[68] The idea was triggered by a passage she once read in a book about a Peruvian culture that believed that the sound of a river had healing powers:

> They were taking people who were off-balance in various ways, out of balance,
> to rivers for entire days at a time because they felt that that environment
> rebalanced mental processes. That really stuck in my head. I was living near
> London and not long after that living in Manhattan and was drawn to river
> sounds in any case from childhood memories but also because of their textural
> complexity. They are really complicated masses of interlocking rhythms. That
> interested me greatly. I came up with the idea of collecting river recordings and
> making installations from them for city people who were deprived of rivers.[69]

The archive includes the watery pinnacle of Lockwood's installation work, *A Sound Map of the Hudson River* (1980)—a two-hour continuously playing/looping tape comprised of sounds recorded at 26 sites, from the source to the mouth of the Hudson River.

These works by Carlos and Lockwood laid the foundation for environmental and ambient music by deftly blending electronics and the recorded manipulation of natural sounds. The next step—a decidedly musical one—was taken by Brian Eno with the release of *Music for Airports* in 1978. His was not music *from* the environment but music *for* the environment. *Music for Airports* consisted of short pieces of electronic background music, splashes of sound for the blank audio canvas of imaginary airports. Eno borrowed the term "ambient" to describe the work:

> An ambience is defined as an atmosphere or a surrounding influence: a tint.
> My intention is to produce original pieces ostensibly (but not exclusively) for
> particular times and situations with a view to building up a small but versatile
> catalogue of environmental music suited to a wide variety of moods and

> atmospheres . . . Ambient Music must be able to accommodate many levels of
> listening attention without enforcing one in particular: it must be as ignorable as
> it is interesting.[70]

This was a new way of listening as much as it was a new way of composing with sound. It assumed that there was a quieter side of the human psyche to which music could appeal. The ambient work of Eno and Harold Budd, his first collaborator in this style, invoked a resilient strength that many found soothing. Some called it meditative music, and this led to the idea of healing music and the phenomenon of "new age" music. Although ambient is widely accepted today as an alternative style of music, pioneers such as Eno did not find record companies to be receptive to the idea back in the 1970s:

> Ambient music was a completely obscure and oblique idea. I remember taking
> that into record companies, and them saying, "Nobody wants to listen to music
> that doesn't have a beat, doesn't have a melody, doesn't have a singer, doesn't
> have words." All they could see were all the things it didn't have. Well, it turns
> out they were wrong: people's tastes have very much drifted in that direction,
> and people are very able to handle long pieces of music with or without
> structures and key chord changes.[71]

Harold Budd is a pioneer of ambient music by virtue of his association with Eno. However, "ambient" is not a term he ever uses to describe the work, and he strongly disagrees with people who find something "meditative" or "healing" about this music. He remarked that the trouble with most "new age" and "meditative" music was that "it had absolutely no evil in it."[72] His music comes from a darker corner of the human psyche:

> I find that it comes from a rather unpeaceful sort of place. I think an element of
> danger and a kind of unsettled quality. Unresolved issues. I don't find it
> meditative at all, just the opposite. If that were meditation, I for one would give it
> up immediately.[73]

About the time that Eno composed *Music for Airports*, he heard a cassette of a work by Budd that had been performed at Wesleyan University. *Madrigals of the Rose Angel* (1972) was written for female chorus, harp, percussion, and keyboard. Budd had conceived a piano part that was so radically quiet that he couldn't get anyone to play it adequately. "There didn't seem to be any way to notate it," he explained:

> I could say, "play softly," or "play at the very edge like you're just about to
> ruin the whole piece." So I decided that in my role as composer I really had to
> switch over to be the performer as well because I was the only one that really
> understood what should be done. By default, I became a keyboard player not
> out of any great desire to express myself but out of the desire to protect my
> idea.[74]

The piece was performed in the mid-1970s at Wesleyan and, unbeknownst to Budd, a cassette began circulating around the music world. Gavin Bryars and Michael Nyman had a copy of the tape and gave it to Brian Eno. Eno was soon on the phone to Budd asking him if he wanted to turn the work into a commercial recording project.

Madrigals of the Rose Angel became part of a collection of pieces that were called *The Pavilion of Dreams* (1978), consisting of four chamber works composed between 1972 and 1975. Following that, Eno recruited Budd to collaborate with him on "something that no one had ever done before."[75] This became the recording *Ambient 2: The Plateaux of Mirror* (1980), a seminal work of musically inclined ambient music. It was followed by a second piano-based collaboration between the two called *The Pearl* (1984). These two studio works established a quiet, moody style of music of translucent beauty. Budd's elemental musical themes were the ideal foil for Eno's whispery electronic treatments.

The haunting afterimages of sound and beautifully engineered works that comprise *The Plateaux of Mirror* and *The Pearl* were all improvised. Budd would work things out on the keyboard and Eno added his treatments, delays, and mutational processes to the music in real time:

> As you can tell, I am not a professional piano player. My fingerings are all incorrect. I have no athletic skill at the keyboard. I have no formal training at the keyboard. It's all very much what I can come up with at the point of actually doing it. The music is improvised, by and large, or at least extemporaneous. Which is different from something that you can do with a large ensemble of pieces. Neither one of us knew how it was going to turn out. So, we just started. You have to start somewhere so we started inside the studio, inside a pop music studio, with all the Lexicons and the electronic loops and all that stuff that is taken for granted. We didn't know. We didn't have a clue. The quality of the sound is very much due to Brian's skill, period. It wasn't added afterward. It was real time.[76]

Budd and Eno seemed to have discovered a rarity in new music these days: a blank canvas. They invented a new palette of sounds and directed the softest of electronic brush strokes to create a dazzling body of highly evocative sound paintings.

The more "musically composed" work of Carlos, Eno, Budd, Jon Hassell, Jon Gibson, and Michael Snow led directly to what is called ambient music today: subtle rhythms and electronic drones. Tetsu Inoue, one of the 1990s' generation of electronic composers, made his mark with a hybrid form of ambient music that deftly blended world rhythms, documentary sounds, and twittering electronics into a less edgy form of *house* music. There is also a persistent strand of quieter, harmonious ambient music that is placed under the heading of "new age" music.

It is difficult to draw a line showing where ambient music ends and "other" music begins. The definition of ambient music has evolved to include elements of jazz, classical, and electronic music closely associated with house or *electronica*. Once considered a music of quiet, background sounds, the current definition of "ambient" embraces a diverse sonic range of music. If there is a unifying element in all ambient music it appears to be a continuity of energy that enables a suspension of tension. Like minimalism, contemporary ambient music often relies on a persistent rhythm and slowly evolving wash of sound textures. **Ambient dub** is a style that borrows liberally from the layering techniques of Jamaican sound artists and fuses them with elements of world music, subterranean bass lines such as those used by Bill Laswell, and evolving harmonic sounds of electronica. Ambient dub has a sustaining quality to it that immerses the listener in a wash of non-invasive undulations. Other tributaries of the ambient stream include dark or **industrial ambient**, consisting of modified mechanical noises, drones, and auditory science experiments (e.g. Susumu Yokota, Hafler Trio, Merzbow, and Nocturnal Emissions).

Another subgenre of ambient that has a large following is **space music**, so named because of the often spacey or dreamy nature of the music. Largely a by-product of the analog synthesizer sequencer, the early makers of space music included Tangerine Dream, Klaus Schulze, Vangelis, Isao Tomita, and Jean-Michel Jarre. These creators of space music were early adopters of modular synthesizers and technically savvy musicians. Space music has been characterized by long, meditative electronic works built on slowly evolving chord changes and an unrelenting rhythmic pulse. Noted acts in this field are often associated with spectacular concert events using multimedia resources to package the space music experience, an idea borrowed from planetarium presentations.

The roots of space music are varied and include jazz experimenters such as Sun Ra and the electronic works of Karlheinz Stockhausen. The genre continues to have a loyal following and its works are often classified with other genres such as "new age" and electronica. At least three public broadcasting programs in the United States have served listeners of this genre for many years: *Hearts of Space* (originally *Music from the Hearts of Space*, Berkeley, 1973), *Stars End* (Philadelphia, 1976), *Musical Starstreams* (San Francisco, 1981), and *Echoes*, produced by John Diliberto and Kimberly Haas (Chester Springs,

---

AMBIENT AND SPACE MUSIC

1 *Sounds for a Film by Robert Watts* (1968) by David Behrman
Electronic and environmental sounds

2 *Sonic Seasonings* (1972) by Wendy Carlos
Electronic and environmental sounds

3 *Ricochet* (1974) by Tangerine Dream
Analog space music

4 *World Rhythms* (1975) by Annea Lockwood
Nature sounds mixed and edited

5 *Spiral* (1976) by Vangelis
Analog space music

6 *Music for Airports* (1978) by Brian Eno
Synthesizer music

7 *X* (1978) by Klaus Schulze
Analog space music

8 *Ambient 2: The Plateaux of Mirror* (1980) by Brian Eno and Harold Budd
Synthesizer music

9 *World Receiver* (1996) by Tetsu Inoue
World music and digital synthesis

10 *Lightning Teleportation* (2001) by Bill Laswell
Ambient dub jazz

Pennsylvania, 1989). *Stars End*, which was originated by Diliberto while he was working at a Philadelphia college radio station, was billed as a "journey to the outer limits of your aural universe"[77]—a fitting description for the space music genre. These popular programs are often broadcast during the graveyard shift when space music might double as a potent inducement for sleep. Contemporary space music artists include Steve Roach, Robert Rich, James Bernard, Rudy Adrian, and a host of veterans including Schulze, Tangerine Dream, Conrad Schnitzler, and many others.

Klaus Schulze is a pioneering German synthesist whose trance-like instrumental music made him one of the key innovators in the "space music" genre. As a drummer, Schulze was an early member of Tangerine Dream and Ash Ra Tempel, but became a solo artist in 1971. Working with classic analog synthesizers, Schulze crafted lengthy electronic instrumentals and developed a following devoted to his spectacular multimedia performances. Classic recordings from his most prolific period include *Moondawn* (1976), *X* (1978), and *Dig It* (1980), which marked his transition to digital instrumentation. His current work continues to blend many influences such as jazz, opera, and trance music. His interest in electronic music technology came down to always using "the best available instruments for my special kind of music. I think, here I'm not much different from a violin player, or from a piano player," explained the composer, continuing:

> I just cannot imagine that Glenn Gould would be too happy with a Casio VL-Tone. I'm a musician, not a technician. I rarely think much about *technology*—I just use it. Have I told you that I *never* read the operating manuals? Not in 1975 and not today.[78]

SUMMARY

- Jazz musicians began to experiment with the use of electronic music around 1960. Initial experiments combined the playing of jazz musicians with tapes made in the fashion of *musique concrète*. By the mid- to late 1960s, jazz musicians began to include the use of electronic instruments and sound modifying devices in live performances.

- Early electronic jazz works incorporating tape pieces included *Jazz et Jazz* by André Hodeir, *Music for the Gift* (1963) by Terry Riley and Chet Baker, *Cricket Music* (1964) by Walter De Maria, *Explosions* (1964) by the Bob James Trio, and *JazzEx* (1966) by Bernard Parmegiani.

- *Sing Me a Song of Songmy* (1971) by İlhan Mimaroğlu and Freddie Hubbard marked the end of the era of jazz and tape music.

- Gil Mellé was one of the first jazz artists to introduce specially made electronic music instruments that could be played within the context of a live jazz performance. He recorded *Tome IV* in 1967.

- Cage and Tudor produced their first live electronic music for dance performance in the late 1950s.

- *Variations* by Cage was a series of multimedia performances, or happenings, that were staged during the mid- to late 1960s, combining dance, projected visuals, and live electronic music.

- Improvisation in electronic music is a 45-year tradition going back to the late 1950s, when the possibilities of live performance in this idiom were first being explored.

- The ONCE festivals were a series of new music and performance festivals held in Ann Arbor from 1961 to 1965. Live electronic music works were frequently performed during the festivals.

- The Sonic Arts Union (1966–76), comprised of Robert Ashley, Gordon Mumma, David Behrman, and Alvin Lucier, was a performance group that largely focused on works of live electronic music.

- Two European-based live electronic music groups of the late 1960s were Musica Elettronica Viva (MEV, Rome) and AMM (London).

- Ambient and environmental music has roots in the 1950s and 1960s, particularly with Cage's work, *4′ 33″* (1952) for a pianist—the so-called silent sonata.

- Early recorded works of ambient music often combined environmental sounds with electronic music.

- Once considered a music of quiet, background sounds, the current definition of "ambient" embraces a diverse sonic range of music, such as ambient dub, industrial ambient, and space music.

MILESTONES

Live Electronic Music and Ambient Music

Musical work	Year	Significance
– *Cartridge Music* by John Cage.	1960	– Work for amplified small sounds and an early departure from taped music in favor of live performance.
– *Variations V* by John Cage.	1965	– Elaborate live electronic music work for multimedia and dance.
– *Vespers* by Alvin Lucier.	1965	– Live interactive electronic work shaped by the acoustic properties of the performance space.
– *In the Realm of Nothing Whatever* by AMM.	1966	– Live improvised electronic music ensemble (England).
– *Sounds for a Film by Robert Watts* by David Behrman.	1968	– Early ambient work using environmental sounds.
– *Spacecraft* by MEV.	1970	– Live improvised electronic music ensemble (Italy).
– *Sonic Seasonings* by Wendy Carlos.	1972	– Ambient work using synthesized and environmental sounds.
– *Music for Airports* by Brian Eno.	1978	– Defining work of synthesized ambient music.
– *X* by Klaus Schulze.	1978	– Fully realized works of space music employing analog synthesizer orchestration.

CHAPTER 14

Rock, Space Age Pop, and Turntablism

They would often bring in bits of tape and say, "Listen to this!" as they tried to outdo one another in a de facto weird sound contest.
—Geoff Emerick, Abbey Road studio engineer during
The Beatles' *Revolver* recording sessions

Beatles Paul McCartney and George Harrison are given guidance in using the Moog Modular Synthesizer by Mike Vickers, who was employed to program the Moog during the *Abbey Road* recording sessions.
(© 2009 Apple Corps Ltd)

Electronic music and rock music were separated at birth but destined to meet again after reaching adolescence. Rising from the same transistorized technology that made tape recorders possible were the keyboards, effects boxes, and other gadgets that embellished the sound of rock and roll. By the late 1960s, as the professional recording of rock music adapted to multitrack tape recorders and the availability of synthesizers and other electronic instruments, rock and jazz fusion artists became the standard bearers for the dissemination of electronic music to the masses. This chapter examines important artists who contributed to the popularization of electronic music in commercial music and examines the subgenre of turntablism.

ROCK AND ELECTRONIC MUSIC

There is the notion of the *hook* in rock and roll music: a memorable snippet of a song that grabs the attention and demands to be heard over and over. The hook is the *l'objet sonore* of rock—a molecule of sound with unique timbral and psychoacoustic properties that make it easy for the listener to commit to memory: a special sound with its own personality that could stand alone outside of the context of a song. Furthermore, the hook is the product of the uniquely crafted sound of a rock group—an instrumental blend of guitars, amplifiers, effects pedals, and other elements that combine to give a group its sonic identity. Rock music is very much about crafting and shaping sounds, so it was only natural that many of the early adopters of electronic music techniques would be in the recording studios producing hit records. Any rock group worth remembering has a distinctive sound and the best musicians, producers, and engineers are in the business of perfecting that sound.

The Beatles

Discussing the entire history of rock and roll is beyond the scope of this book. Fortunately, one need look no further than The Beatles for examples of classic electronic music techniques and analog synthesis in rock music. Much has been written about the importance of the recording studio to The Beatles who, at the peak of their popularity in 1966, stopped touring and spent the remaining four years of their partnership solely as recording artists. With the aid of the extraordinarily gifted producer George Martin and a cadre of talented and inquisitive recording engineers, many of the sounds of electronic music began to slip into the music of The Beatles.

The Beatles became fascinated with tape loops during the recording sessions for the album *Revolver* (1966). One of the first loops the group used was set up by engineer Geoff Emerick for the hypnotic rhythm of the song "Tomorrow Never Knows" (1966). Paul McCartney was so taken with the effect that he went home and recorded a batch of additional tape loops using his guitar, the ringing sound of wine glasses, and other noises. He came back to the studio and handed Emerick a little plastic bag full of tape snippets that the engineer dutifully threaded onto a tape deck for the band to audition.[1] This led to a session devoted to the live mixing of tape loops during which all five tape decks of the Abbey Road studio were employed. Many of the loops were long and required technicians to stand nearby spooling them in the air with uplifted pencils. In the control room, Emerick conducted the live mix, controlling the sound balance while others adjusted the panning and levels. Emerick likened the result to a human-enabled synthesizer. Some of the sounds were mixed into "Tomorrow Never Knows," including the seagull-like noise that was made with a distorted guitar.[2] Another effect used on the song was the continuously varying speed of some of the background tracks, the result of The Beatles having access to a varispeed tape recorder.

The use of tape reversal in a Beatles' song first occurs in the single release "Rain," also produced in 1966 just a week after "Tomorrow Never Knows." There are two conflicting stories about how this happened. One is that John Lennon took his vocal track home and accidentally threaded it upside down on his reel-to-reel tape recorder, causing the sound to be played back in reverse. The other is that George Martin intentionally mounted the tape backwards on a tape deck in the studio to demonstrate the effect to Lennon, who had stepped out of the studio for a minute. When Lennon returned and played the tape, he was "amazed." One way or the other, "Rain" "was backwards forever after that."[3] Experiments with tape loops continued to be used on various Beatle albums, from the whirling calliope effects of "Being For the Benefit of Mr. Kite" (1967) to the atmospheric nature sounds that form an aural bridge between "Here Comes the Sun" and "Sun King" on the album *Abbey Road* (1969).

Carnival of Light

Paul McCartney recently shed a little more light on another famed Beatle excursion into tape music. In December of 1966, McCartney was asked by to contribute a recording for an event known as the *Million Volt Light and Sound Rave* to be held at the Roundhouse in London. There were two scheduled events, one on January 28, 1967 and another on February 4, 1967. Posters for both events advertised "music composed by Paul McCartney" and the tape work was played several times at each of the two events. In addition to a number of rock groups, the concerts also featured a collective of BBC Radiophonic Workshop composers, including Delia Derbyshire and Brian Hodgson and their electronic music group Unit Delta Plus.

In a recent interview with BBC Radio 4, McCartney expressed hope that the piece —13′ 48″ long—could finally be officially released to the public if Ringo Starr and the estates of Harrison and Lennon could agree. Back in 1967, the free-form improvisation was considered too "adventurous" for release.[4] George Harrison and producer George Martin, in particular, were not fond of this particular sonic experiment.

Although the piece hasn't been heard publicly since 1967, the existence of the tape has long been known. McCartney tried to include it on *The Beatles Anthology* in the late 1990s but was again thwarted by one of his band mates. "It was up for consideration on *The Anthology* and George vetoed it," explained McCartney in a 2002 interview. "He didn't like it."[5]

What's not to like? The piece was the result of a brief recording session that McCartney organized while The Beatles had a free half hour of studio time after recording vocal overdubs for "Penny Lane." The date was January 5, 1967. The work was McCartney's idea but he enlisted all of The Beatles for the in-studio realization. "There's no lyrics, it's avant-garde music," said McCartney. "You would class it as . . . well you wouldn't class it actually, but it would come in the Stockhausen/John Cage bracket . . . John Cage would be the nearest. It's very free-form. Yeah man, it's the coolest piece of music since sliced bread!"[6]

Lewisohn acknowledged the recording of the work, then simply called *Untitled*, in *The Beatles Recording Sessions*. The track is also known as *Carnival of Light*, which was an alternative name for the Million Volt Light and Sound Rave at which it was premiered. The piece comprised four tracks mixed in real time. McCartney gave the other members of The Beatles instructions for the performance:

> I said "all I want you to do is just wander around all the stuff, bang it, shout, play it, it doesn't need to make any sense. Hit a drum then wander on to the piano, hit a few notes, just wander around." So that's what we did and then put a bit of an echo on it. It's very free.[7]

Lewisohn listened to the track while writing his book. He described *Carnival of Light* as follows:

> Track one of the tape was full of distorted, hypnotic drum and organ sounds; track two had a distorted lead guitar; track three had the sounds of a church organ, various effects (the gargling of water was one) and voices; track four featured various indescribable sound effects with heaps of tape echo and manic tambourine.
> 　　But of all the frightening sounds it was the voices on track three which really set the scene, John and Paul screaming dementedly and bawling aloud random phrases like "Are you all right?" and "Barcelona!"[8]

McCartney still hopes to release the piece, now more than 45 years old. "I like it because it's The Beatles free, going off piste," offers McCartney. "The time has come for it to get its moment."[9]

"Revolution 9"

Carnival of Light was influenced by McCartney's interest in the experimental and electronic music of John Cage and Karlheinz Stockhausen. The same can be said for John Lennon and Yoko Ono about "Revolution 9" from *The Beatles*—better known as "The White Album." "Revolution 9" was a montage of tape loops mixed with recorded sounds from the BBC archives and live studio improvisations. The piece was constructed in a manner similar to the way that "Tomorrow Never Knows" was produced two years earlier. Dating from the June 1968 recording sessions for *The Beatles*, the 8′ 13″-long work was produced by Lennon with help from Harrison and Ono, both of whom contributed occasional recitations and, in the case of Ono, high-pitched singing.[10] All of the resources and technicians were once again recruited to keep the tape loops flying and to manage the mixing in the control room. Although the final stereo version consists of several overdubs, each original track comprised a live-studio mix of whatever sounds were being looped at the time. Martin had the job of mixing the elements of "Revolution 9" into a whole. As Martin explained:

> I was painting a picture in sound, and if you sat in front of the speakers you just lost yourself in stereo. All sorts of things are happening in there: you can see people running all over the place and fires burning, it was real imagery in sound. It was funny in places too, but I suppose it went on a bit long."[11]

A Beatle Touch of Moog

The Beatles are not normally associated with synthesizer music but were actually one of the first groups to effectively integrate the sounds of the Moog into their music. This came about through the efforts of Paul Beaver and Bernie Krause, a musical duo who also acted as sales representatives for Robert Moog and his synthesizer. Krause had already sold Moog instruments to George Martin and Mick Jagger and, in the fall of 1968, was contacted by George Harrison for a demonstration. Harrison hired Krause to play the synthesizer on a Jackie Lomax record being produced in Hollywood. After the session, Harrison reportedly asked Krause to hang out for a bit and give him a demonstration. Krause gladly obliged and played a few patches he had been working on with Paul Beaver for a record they were producing called *Gandharva*. Harrison recorded the demonstration and headed back to England. He eventually purchased a Moog through Krause in early 1969 and asked him to come to London to set it up and teach him how to play it. As the story goes, Krause arrived at Harrison's home, where the synthesizer was set up in the Beatle guitarist's living room. Before starting the lesson, Harrison wanted to play Krause a bit of dabbling on the Moog that he had already recorded. "Apple will release it in the next few months."[12] To the amazement of Krause, the sounds on the tape were none other than the demonstration sounds that he himself had played for Harrison during the Jackie Lomax demonstration months earlier. Krause confronted Harrison on the spot, but to no avail. In spite of Krause's complaints, the album *Electronic Sound* was released in May 1969. Unwilling to spend the money required to sue a Beatle, Krause demanded that his name be removed from the album jacket. Rather than replace the original album cover, Apple smudged over his name with silver metallic ink. *Electronic Sound* was by no measure successful and sounded like nothing more than what it truly was: a demonstration of Moog sound effects and patches.

In the summer of 1969, while The Beatles were recording their final album, *Abbey Road*, Harrison had his synthesizer transported to the EMI studios for all of the group members to access. The Moog was used subtly on the album and appears on nearly every track. Producer George Martin felt that the Moog was a challenge to use but sparked the imagination of The Beatles. "When you had been used to playing real instruments," explained Martin, "this was an innovation, and we put it to good use."[13]

McCartney was playing with loops again and assembled a collection of Moog and other sounds for use on the album. Beatles' archivist Mark Lewisohn writes:

> Paul took a plastic bag containing a dozen loose strands of mono tape into *Abbey Road*, where—together with the production staff—he spent the afternoon in the studio three control room transferring the best of these onto professional four-track tape. The effects—sounding like bells, birds, bubbles and crickets chirping—allowed for a perfect crossfade in the medley from *Sun King* into *You Never Give Me Your Money*.[14]

Musician Mike Vickers (from the group Manfred Mann) was hired to tame the Moog and provide patches for The Beatles. The instrument was installed in a booth of its own and wired into all of the available control rooms, and all of group members utilized it in one way or another. The Moog solo played on "Maxwell's Silver Hammer" was performed by McCartney using a ribbon controller.[15] Perhaps the most extreme Moog effect employed on the album was the three-minute span of modulated white noise added by Lennon to the conclusion of "I Want You (She's So Heavy)." In 1969, Lennon mused about using the Moog on this track, saying:

> It's pretty heavy at the ending, you know, because we used the Moog synthesizers on it and the range of sound is from minus to way over . . . well, you can't hear it; that instrument can do all sounds and we did it on the end, if you're a dog you can hear a lot more."[16]

While the Moog found its way onto *Abbey Road*, it was merely just one more tool in the group's bag of aural trickery. Martin recalled:

> We played the synthesizer on something like *Because* or *Maxwell's Silver Hammer* just as a different extra sound, but we were using other original sounds that weren't synthetic . . . and our own innovations of using different speeds and weird sounds for harmoniums and mouth organs and that sort of thing . . .You have to remember that for most of the Beatles' time, we had the Mellotron, which was a kind of synthesizer, but not an electronic one. It was simple tape passing over heads and things. We didn't get computers in those days; we didn't get anything that we have today.[17]

The Beatles did for rock what Varèse, Cage, and Stockhausen had done for classical music—they opened up the world of music to any and all possible sounds.

Rock artists became heavily invested in synthesizer equipment during the 1970s and there was much competition among manufacturers in a burgeoning market for modular and performance synthesizers. The development of polyphonic synthesizers, touch-sensitive keyboards, preset patches for sounds, sequencing, controller options, MIDI control, and digital sampling were significant innovations that appeared during the 15 years spanning 1970 to 1985. By the end of the 1980s, most instruments had switched over to digital technology because of the falling cost of computer-based components, the result being a stabilization of basic performance and control features and increasing emphasis on new sound algorithms, digital signal processing, and the use of software to manage instruments, audio recording, editing, and performance.

Yoko Ono is a Japanese-born artist, musician, and activist who is well known for having been married to Beatle John Lennon. During the early 1960s in New York, prior to meeting Lennon, Ono was a prominent member of Fluxus and her performance art was influenced by composer friends John Cage and La Monte Young. John Lennon once described Ono as "the world's most famous unknown artist: everybody knows her name, but nobody knows what she does."[18] As a recording artist, she used electronic music techniques as one of her tools on such albums as *Yoko Ono Plastic Ono Band* (1970) and *Fly* (1971), a double album blending her Fluxus-style text-based pieces with the resources of the rock music recording studio. "I was always into expanding the horizon of musical soundscape by using the existing technology in new ways," she explained. "When I was in the studio, I was like a kid in a toy shop. I got totally excited by the fact that one could step into a realm of previously unexplored sound maps by experimenting with the use of technology."[19] One of Ono's early pre-Beatles musical performances occurred in 1961 at Carnegie Recital Hall. Said Ono:

> In those days, tape recorders were used to record things and listen. In that particular concert, I used tape recorders as instruments on stage and off. It was the beginning of the Plastic Ono Band. There's a photo of the band—which did not have any humans in it . . . just technological machines.[20]

Other Early Electronic Rock Practitioners

The Beatles were hardly alone in experimenting with electronic music in rock. Before the Moog synthesizer, several types of electronic organs had found a home in the sound of such classic songs as "Runaway" (1961) by Del Shannon, featuring a modified Clavioline called the Musitron; "Telstar" (1962) by the Tornados, using the Clavioline; "House of the Rising Sun" (1964) by the Animals, featuring a Vox Continental organ; "96 Tears" (1966) by Question Mark and the Mysterians, using the Farfisa Combo Compact organ; "Light My Fire" (1967) by the Doors, featuring the Gibson G101 organ; and "A Whiter Shade of Pale" (1967) by Procol Harum, featuring a Hammond Organ.

The *Mellotron* was another favorite special effects keyboard with rock bands. Invented by American Harry Chamberlain in 1947, this electro-mechanical instrument was actually a tape sampler with a separate playback head for each key on its organ-like keyboard. The instrument did not become popular until Chamberlain licensed the British firm Streetly Electronics, near Birmingham, to build a version in the UK, which they called the Mellotron. The BBC was one of Streetly's first customers, purchasing two Mellotrons around 1963, but only using them for cuing up special effects. Mellotrons intended as musical instruments were typically pre-loaded with the sounds of orchestral instruments, including strings. This lent an eerie, unearthly sound to the music of many rock bands, including The Beatles ("Strawberry Fields Forever," 1967), the Rolling Stones ("2000 Light Years from Home," 1967), and many other bands, most notably the Moody Blues whose Mellotron specialist, Mike Pinder (b. 1941), also happened to be a local sales and service representative for Streetly Electronics. Pinder's experience came in handy on those occasions when the instrument literally broke open and spilled its tapes on the floor while the band was setting up for performances. About 2,500 Mellotrons were built between 1963 and 1986 and they were most widely used during the progressive rock era of the 1970s.

Aside from The Beatles, the original Pink Floyd probably made the most vivid use of *musique concrète* techniques in composing much of its early music. The original lineup of the group in 1966 was essentially a rock band and included Syd Barrett (1946–2006) on guitar and vocals, Roger Waters (b. 1943) on bass guitar and vocals, Richard Wright (1943–2008) on Farfisa and Hammond organs, piano, and vocals, and Nick Mason (b. 1944) on drums. David Gilmour (b. 1946), playing guitar and vocals, joined the group during the making of its second album and replaced Barrett, who suffered from a mental breakdown. Pink Floyd's first two albums—*The Piper at the Gates of Dawn* (1967) and *A Saucerful of Secrets* (1968)—were branded as psychedelic music at the time due to the group's penchant for long, dreamy instrumentals and often puzzling lyrical content. Like Sun Ra in jazz, early Pink Floyd succeeded in exploiting the electronic sonorities of rock as a sonic experiment with a form and presentation reminiscent of *musique concrète*, only done with guitar, organ, vocals, and a generous amount of reverb. The track "A Saucerful of Secrets" (1968) from the album of the same name, was a multi-part sonic excursion lasting about 12 minutes. Among the electronic music techniques used on the track were the amplified small sounds of a cymbal, crossfading organ sounds, tape loops of percussion sounds, distorted guitar, Farfisa organ, Mellotron, and reverberating vocals. This piece still seems contemporary by modern standards and not so different from present-day space music and the sound of such groups as Sigur Rós.

Figure 14.1 Instruments for a 1969 Pink Floyd concert include a tape recorder to accompany the band's live rendition of "A Saucerful of Secrets." Pictured are roadies for the band. (Hipgnosis from Capitol STBB-388)

Figure 14.2 Keith Emerson, *c.* 1971, in an early performance with Emerson, Lake & Palmer. Emerson was one of only a few rock musicians to travel with a fully equipped Moog Modular Synthesizer.

(Eddy Van Mossevelde)

The American duo Silver Apples was yet another bold experiment in blending electronic music with rock. The group emerged from the New York rock scene of 1967 and comprised Danny Taylor on drums and Simeon Coxe III, who sang and played an assemblage of audio oscillators and filters that he called *The Simeon*. Stripped of the familiar sound of rock guitar, Silver Apples created a pulsing, trance-like music that took advantage of the beat-making attributes of oscillators. Without a synthesizer or keyboard, Simeon manually adjusted the rotary dials on his battlement of oscillators, filters, and mixers to the prescribed settings for each song, improvising with drummer Taylor during instrumental breaks by turning knobs and adjusting levels. Their setup appeared as if they had removed a rack of engineering equipment from a radio lab and set it upon a stage.

Once the Moog synthesizer became available by about 1968, various studios bought them and invited their rock stars to tinker away. Early rock Moog recordings ran the gamut and include such albums as the Monkees, *Pisces, Aquarius, Capricorn & Jones Ltd.* (1967); the Byrds, *The Notorious Byrd Brothers* (1968), and Emerson, Lake & Palmer (ELP), "Lucky Man" (1970). Keith Emerson, of ELP, was one of the first true stars of synthesizer rock, able to blow any electric guitarist off the stage with a single swipe of the ribbon controller on his massive Moog Modular Synthesizer, which he took on tour.

The coming of the synthesizer age spawned many rock groups whose primary sound was that of the electronic keyboard. Gary Numan (b. 1958) is a British composer and rock musician who came to prominence in the late 1970s and 1980s with his unique synthesizer-heavy sound and themes of alienation. His early albums such as *Replicas* (1979) and *The Pleasure Principle* (1979) eschewed guitars entirely in favor of keyboards that were often processed using guitar effects and accompanied by synthetic percussion. His trademark song "Cars" (1979) has been remixed and revived numerous times over the years. Numan is active today as a composer and performer of new electronic music and, although the technology has undergone vast change since the 1980s, his approach to composing is not that different:

> I feel that I am technology led and so it affects the way I compose music completely. Once the basic melody is written, a process which has changed little over the years, I then adapt the way I produce and develop the songs to suit the new technologies as they come along.[21]

Contemporary Electronic Rock

Modern electronic rock is a genre of rock music that goes by many names, including electro-pop, synth-rock, trip-hop, and downtempo. What qualifies all of these styles as

Figure 14.3 Simeon of Silver Apples,
pictured in 1968, who sang and played an
assemblage of audio oscillators and filters
accompanied by drummer Danny Taylor.
(Barry Bryant)

ROCK AND ELECTRONIC MUSIC

1 "Tomorrow Never Knows" (1966) by The Beatles
   Tape loops and Lennon's voice fed through the rotating Leslie speaker of a
   Hammond organ

2 *Ceremony* (1970) by Spooky Tooth and Pierre Henry
   Featured tape composition by the French master as part of a rock opera

3 *Emerson, Lake, & Palmer* (1971) by Emerson, Lake, & Palmer
   Featured the Moog played by Keith Emerson and one of the first rock hits in
   which a Moog was the featured solo instrument ("Lucky Man")

4 *Fragile* (1971) by Yes
   Featured the Moog and other electronic keyboards played by Rick Wakeman

5 *Goodbye Yellow Brick Road* (1973) by Elton John
   Featured the ARP 2600 played by Dave Henschel

6 *Low* (1977) by David Bowie
   Produced by Brian Eno

7 *Touch and Gone* (1977) by Gary Wright
   Used Polymoog, Clavinet, Oberheim, and Fender–Rhodes electronic keyboards

8 *The Pleasure Principle* (1979) by Gary Numan
   Early synth-rock success using electronic keyboards without guitar

9 *(Who's Afraid Of?) The Art of Noise* (1984) by The Art of Noise
   Art rock devised by Anne Dudley and Trevor Horn using the sampling capabilities
   of the Fairlight CMI

10 *Slave to the Rhythm* (1985) by Grace Jones
    Featured the Synclavier played and programmed by Trevor Horn

LISTEN

Table 14.1   **Contemporary electronic rock artists**

Artist	Founded	Country	Members	Key albums
Air	1995	France	Nicolas Godin and Jean-Benoît Dunckel	1998: *Moon Safari* 2001: *10 000 Hz Legend* 2007: *Pocket Symphony*
Digitalism	2004	Germany	Jens Moelle and İsmail Tüfekçi	2007: *Idealism*
DJ Shadow	1989	United States	Joshua Paul Davis	1996: *Endtroducing . . .* 2002: *The Private Press* 2006: *The Outsider*
Four Tet	1998	United Kingdom	Kieran Hebden	2001: *Pause* 2003: *Rounds* 2008: *Ringer* 2010: *There Is Love in You*
Ladytron	1999	United Kingdom	Reuben Wu, Daniel Hunt, Helen Marnie and Mira Aroyo	2001: *604* 2002: *Light & Magic* 2005: *Witching Hour* 2008: *Velocifero*
M83	2001	France	Anthony Gonzalez and guest musicians	2001: *M83* 2005: *Before the Dawn Heals Us* 2008: *Saturdays = Youth*
Matmos	1995	United States	M. C. (Martin) Schmidt and Drew Daniel	1998: *Matmos* 2001: *A Chance to Cut Is a Chance to Cure* 2006: *The Rose Has Teeth in the Mouth of a Beast* 2008: *Balloon*
Outputmessage	2001	United States	Bernard Farley	2003: *Idol Tryouts 1* 2006: *Idol Tryouts 2* 2004: *Oneiros* 2009: *Autonomous*
Rinôçérôse	1997	France	Jean-Philippe Freu and Patrice Carrié	1999: *Installation Sonore* 2006: *Rinôçérôse* 2009: *Futurinô*
Susumu Yokota	1992	Japan	Susumu Yokota	1998: *Magic Thread* 2002: *Sound of Sky* 2006: *Wonder Waltz* 2007: *Skintone Collection* 2009: *Mother*
Trentemøller	1997	Denmark	Anders Trentemøller	2006: *The Last Resort* 2007: *The Trentemøller Chronicles*
Zero 7	1999	United Kingdom	Henry Binns and Sam Hardaker	2001: *Simple Things* 2004: *When It Falls* 2009: *Yeah Ghost*

electronic rock is use of predominantly electrified instrumentation, often with vocals, to produce a song-driven music that leans heavily on the use of electronic and computer-generated editing and effects. Electronic rock absorbs techniques from many other genres of electronic music, including ambient, electronica, trance, glitch, DJ beat juggling, and looping. What separates this style from other electronic music is an attempt by the artists to craft music that is harmonically appealing to a wide audience, complete with memorable hooks and choruses. The use of computers to manage the production of music is a key element behind the rise of electronic rock. In many cases, an electronic rock "band" may only consist of one or two individuals who command a bevy of electronic instruments through the use of laptops and multi-track recording. Key practitioners of electronic rock include the artists listed in Table 14.1.

THE THEREMIN REVIVAL

Several years before his famed synthesizer would materialize as a commercial product, Robert Moog began a small business building transistorized Theremins. An electronics hobbyist since his youth, Moog had learned how to build Theremins while still in high school. In 1962 he was a married graduate student at Cornell University looking to earn a little extra money, so he rekindled his old hobby and began to build Theremins to order, mostly for educational use. Moog recalled:

> The height of my Theremin building was in college. We had a three-room apartment on the top floor of a house. For $10 a month, the landlord let me have the furnace room to build Theremins in. So, all through graduate school I had a 10' × 11' furnace room as my shop. I built quite a few Theremins there.[22]

"Quite a few" translated to about 1,000 Theremin kits sold during the height of Moog's little business. Moog's love for the Theremin and the mysterious Russian inventor whom he had never met set him squarely on the path to the invention of his groundbreaking Moog synthesizer several years later.

After having served as the musical staple of many horror and science fiction movie soundtracks, the 1960s witnessed the emergence of the Theremin in other forms of popular music, especially rock music and jazz. An instrument sounding peculiarly like a Theremin surfaced as the signature sound of the 1966 hit song *Good Vibrations* by The Beach Boys. Although the instrument heard on that record was not actually a Theremin, The Beach Boys' story has a tangible connection to Robert Moog.

Paul Tanner (b. 1917) was a top-notch trombonist in Hollywood working in movies and television. He was in great demand as a session man. About 1958, Tanner sat in as a musician on the re-recording sessions for the *Spellbound* soundtrack, which was being updated to produce a stereophonic version of the music. It was during these sessions that he first observed Dr. Samuel Hoffman coaxing his mesmerizing electronic sounds from the Theremin. Tanner could relate the space-controlled nature of Theremin performance to the inexact science of moving the slide on a trombone. This motivated him to go into competition with Hoffman as another provider of spooky musical effects.

Tanner turned to a local actor, Robert Whitsell, for help in making a Theremin. Whitsell had made a few of the instruments as a teenager. But as the two of them discussed the project further, it was clear that Tanner wanted an instrument that could be controlled more easily than the traditional space-controlled Theremin used by Hoffman. Although they originally had a Theremin in mind, what Whitsell built was something else entirely. The "instrument" was no more than two off-the-shelf components from Heathkit: an oscillator and an amplifier. Whitsell designed a clever way to house the components that both disguised them from the observant eye and made the oscillator easy to play for a musician. The oscillator was hidden inside a wooden box. On top of the box was a strip of paper with a 15-inch image of a keyboard. A sliding handle could be moved along the length of the paper keyboard. The handle itself was attached though a pulley-and-cable mechanism to the rotary dial of the oscillator hidden inside the box. Moving the sliding handle turned the dial in one direction or another, changing the pitch. Volume was controlled simply by turning the volume control of the amplifier component.[23] This design offered Tanner the control he needed to accurately play a sequence of prescribed notes.

Tanner had apparently offered his services as a "Theremin" player prior even to having an electronic musical instrument in hand. Whitsell's "instrument with no name" was finished in the early morning hours of the day of their first gig: a recording session in 1958 for an album that would be called *Music for Heavenly Bodies* (1958), with an orchestra conducted by André Montero and arrangements by Warren Baker. Both Tanner and Whitsell took part, with Tanner doing the playing.[24] Whitsell was on hand in case the instrument broke.

The nameless instrument was apparently christened the "electro-Theremin" by the producer of the recording or by Cy Schneider, the author of the liner notes.[25] Schneider's words were chosen carefully to distinguish the instrument from its Russian-born relative:

> Its eerie sound is not unlike Dr. Samuel Hoffman's famous Theremin, but it is easily distinguishable to those who have heard both. Tanner's instrument is mechanically controlled, while Hoffman's is played by moving the hands in front of it without touching the instrument. It operates on a slide, and those who know about electronics will guess immediately that the sound is being created by a variable oscillator. The audio range of the electro-Theremin covers the complete sound spectrum, from 0 to over 20,000 cycles per second. Its highs and lows can only be measured on an oscilloscope. Its sounds are pure sine waves without any harmonics, making it an ideal instrument with which to test your audio equipment.[26]

Tanner and his electro-Theremin were an instant hit with Hollywood music producers. After making some adjustments to the design—specifically to improve the manual articulation of the notes—Whitsell stepped out of the picture and Tanner was off and running with the novel new instrument. He went on to do sound effects for several Warner Brothers' movies as well as television shows for ABC, CBS, and NBC.[27] The electro-Theremin can be heard in films such as *The Giant Gila Monster* (1959) and *Strait Jacket* (1964). The instrument was often used for sound effects for the TV shows *I Love Lucy* and *My Favorite Martian*. In the latter, the electro-Theremin was heard every time Uncle Martin's antennae popped up. Tanner also played on the theme music for the shows *Dark Shadows* and *Lost in Space*.[28]

Tanner's most famous electro-Theremin gig came when Brian Wilson (b. 1942) of The Beach Boys asked him to join their 1966 recording sessions. These were the sessions leading up to the album *Pet Sounds* and the single "Good Vibrations." The first piece on which Tanner played was "I Just Wasn't Made for These Times." It was followed a few days later by the first of many sessions for the landmark "Good Vibrations."

When it came time to take the show on the road, The Beach Boys asked Tanner to come along, but he declined. He was a busy musician and instructor in California and could not take time out to join them. The group had by this time heard of Robert Moog and his Theremins. They called him and asked if he would construct a portable instrument that could be used in concerts. It is a popular

Figure 14.4   Paul Tanner and the electro-Theremin, 1958. (David Miller)

misconception that what Moog built for them was a Theremin. What he actually provided was a transistorized audio oscillator housed in a slim walnut box about two feet long and six inches wide that was played by sliding the finger along a ribbon controller: "a thin metal band, covered with Teflon-impregnated cloth."[29] It was handheld, had a volume control, and was powered by being plugged into the wall. It could be marked at the places where the finger had to stop to play the notes of a song. Interestingly, for his current concertizing, Brian Wilson brought back the electro-Theremin in the form of a replica built by Tom Polk, which is played by multi-instrumentalist Probyn Gregory of Brian Wilson's band.

In the world of jazz, American composer Eric Ross (b. 1929) has composed more than 15 works for the Theremin since 1982, including one for 14 instruments. Jazz trumpeter and thereminist Youseff Yancy, born in Belgium, has been playing the Theremin since the late 1960s and often teams up with Ross.

There is also a footnote to the story of the inventor of the Theremin himself. After having disappeared back to the Soviet Union for more than 50 years, Leon Theremin returned to the West in 1989. An award-winning documentary about his life was produced by Steven Martin (*Theremin: An Electronic Odyssey*, 1993) and several concerts were given in honor of the 93-year-old inventor.

SPACE AGE ELECTRONIC POP MUSIC

Avant-garde experiments in electronic music naturally spawned many commercial applications of the same techniques. Raymond Scott is most notable because he was a knowledgeable tinkerer and inventor in the field. But several other composers and musicians became better known than Scott by composing electronic pop music for the masses.

The term *exotica* describes a genre of easy-listening music that incorporates exotic instrumentation from around the world to play popular songs and mood music. It was popular in the 1950s and 1960s and there were frequent efforts within the genre to incorporate electronic instruments into the arrangements. One of the earliest exotica records to feature the Theremin was produced by composer Harry Revel (1905–58) in 1948 and released on two 78 rpm records: *Music Out of the Moon* and *Music for Peace of Mind*. Revel is best known as a composer of Broadway musicals. This departure in easy-listening music featured the Theremin playing of Dr. Samuel Hoffmann, the podiatrist from Hollywood, and arrangements by Les Baxter. Baxter, Esquivel, and many other easy-listening arrangers continued to bring electronic instrumentation to exotica through the 1950s and 1960s. Prior to the availability of the Moog synthesizer, the most commonly used electronic instruments in easy-listening music were the Theremin and various electronic organs such as the Ondioline and Novachord.

When the age of stereo was first upon us, producer Enoch Light (1907–78) and his Command label were there to fill our walnut-veneered record cabinets with exciting new sounds. He employed an eclectic stable of studio musicians who could adapt their stylings to whatever trend popular music was embracing. One of his more venerable performers was keyboardist Dick Hyman (b. 1927). This most versatile of musicians could be relied upon to take a turn at whatever keyboard instrument or musical style was popular at the time. His list of album credits is nearly countless, and he played everything from jazz piano to funky organ and "happening" harpsichord. He was one of the first artists to release a Moog album following the overnight success of Wendy Carlos's *Switched-On Bach* in late 1968: *The Electric Eclectics of Dick Hyman* and *The Age of Electronicus*, both released in 1969. His songs had fun titles such as "Topless Dancers of Corfu Hyman," "The Moog and Me," and "Tap Dance in the Memory Banks," belying how truly tedious it was for a skilled keyboard player to piece together music layer by layer using the monophonic Moog. Hyman recently recalled his days with the Moog in this way:

> I got started on the Moog at the urging of the Command people, Enoch Light and Bobby Byrne, and learned what the basics were from Walter Sear. I eased out of the field when it became more specialized and I felt I had reached the limits of my interest. Still, I used the *Minimoog* as an occasional double on various recording sessions. I last tried Walter Sear's equipment as an overdub for a sequence in Woody Allen's *Everyone Says I Love You* around 1998, but we rejected the effect.[30]

Two of the earliest composers to create purely electronic pop music were Tom Dissevelt and Dick Raaijmakers from the Netherlands. Working in various studios, including the Philips Eindhoven Research Laboratories and the University of Utrecht, they crafted short, syncopated melodies with instrumental voices synthesized from the most basic of tools: oscillators, filters, and tape recorders. Both composers had one foot in the camp of avant-garde composition and one in pop music. Perhaps it was to protect his standing as a serious composer that Raaijmakers used the pseudonym of Kid Baltan when he released his pop tunes on several recordings issued by Philips in the early 1960s. "Song of the Second Moon" (1957), a pleasant little song lasting only 2′ 49″, was composed the same year and in the same studio as Varèse's *Poème électronique*. Philips also altered the titles of Dissevelt's and Baltan's works when they packaged them for North America, giving them such kitschy titles as "Moon Maid" (formerly "Drifting"), "The Visitor from Inner Space" (formerly "Vibration"), "Sonik Re-entry" (formerly

SPACE AGE POP MUSIC

1 *Music Out of the Moon* (1948) by Harry Revel
   Featured the Theremin playing of Dr. Samuel Hoffmann

2 *Song of the Second Moon* (1957) by Tom Dissevelt and Dick Raaijmakers
   Tape music from the Netherlands

3 *Music From Outer Space* (1962) by Frank Comstock
   Featured the electro-Theremin playing of Paul Tanner

4 *The In Sounds from Way Out* (1966) by Jean-Jacques Perrey and Gershon Kingsley
   Tape music featuring the Ondioline

5 *Amazing Electronic Pop Sounds* (1968) Jean-Jacques Perrey
   First Moog album by Perrey

6 *The Electric Eclectics of Dick Hyman* (1969) by Dick Hyman
   Moog recording

7 *Exotic Moog* (1970) by Martin Denny
   Moog-heavy album by familiar easy-listening bandleader

8 *Moog!* (1970) by Claude Denjean
   Moog renditions of hit songs

9 *Space Experience* (1972) by John Keating
   Songs with an outer space theme, played on the EMS Synthi

10 *Hot Butter* (1973) by Stan Free
   Moog pop tunes

LISTEN

"Whirling"), and "Twilight Ozone" (formerly "Intersection"). The following endorsement graced the American release:

> Never before has electronic music been so melodic, so fully arranged, and such pleasant listening. Tom Dissevelt and Kid Baltan have created groovy vibrations and singing sounds to delight the ears of all who hear.[31]

Jean-Jacques Perrey (b. 1929) and Gershon Kingsley (b. 1925) teamed up for two whimsical albums of electronic pop music. They purchased their first Moog synthesizer in 1966, the same year that they released their first album, entitled *The In Sounds from Way Out* (1966), but this record did not feature the Moog. It was composed using tape loops and classic tape composition techniques, Frenchman Perrey having learned about loops and editing from Pierre Schaeffer. He also played the Ondioline, a compact French electronic keyboard instrument invented by Georges Jenny and dating from 1941. The composers became fast friends with Robert Moog and received personal assistance from the inventor in learning the new instrument.[32] Perrey's first album featuring the Moog was *Amazing Electronic Pop Sounds of Jean-Jacques Perrey* (1968). After their collaboration of several years, both went on to work separately in the field of popular electronic music stylings, and continue to do so today. Perrey released several other pop albums. Kingsley

LISTENING GUIDE 14.1

Title: Song of the Second Moon

Artist: Dick Raaijmakers   **Year**: 1957   **Duration**: 3:08

Genre: Tape composition

Electronic Instrumentation: *Ondes Martenot*, audio oscillators (sawtooth, sine, pulse), tape recorders, pulse-generator with reverberation circuits, noise-generator, octave and half-octave filters, and whistling.

Background: Dick Raaijmakers was employed at the Philips Research Laboratory as an assistant in the acoustics department when, in 1957, he was asked by the director of the studio, Roelof Vermeulen, to compose a piece of popular music using electronic music techniques. The result was *Song of the Second Moon*, one of the first works of electro-pop music. This strikingly original, fun piece was composed using techniques of the classic electronic music studio—recorded audio tones, modified, filtered, reversed, and edited by hand using a razor blade and splicing tape. He used an electronic instrument called the *Ondes Martenot* to play most of the melodic material and an experimental spring reverb unit that was developed at the lab. The work was completed at about the same time that the Soviet Union launched its first Sputnik satellite, which explains the title because, as Raaijmakers recalled, "the second moon was now a fact." *Song of the Second Moon* exists in two versions, the original being longer than the second version. This listening guide is written for the original version.

	Listen For: Tape sounds versus melodies played on the *Ondes Martenot*; artificial reverberation; pulse tones, filtered noise tones, tape loops, multi-tracking; variable speed tape manipulation.
0:00–1:11	The piece begins with a sequence of pulse tones forming a basic rhythm. The tones are modified by a reverberation circuit and repeated by means of a tape loop. At about 0:19 seconds, a second loop repeats a short bass line played by a sawtooth generator and a third adds a short, repeating high-pitched glissandi tone to accentuate the rhythmic pulse. At the same time, the pulsing rhythm that opened the piece is replaced by a less distinct, crackly rhythm of filtered noise in the background. At the 0:24 mark, three separate tracks can be heard.
	At 0:25, a melody track is added to the three underlying rhythm tracks. The melody is played on the *Ondes Martenot*, a monophonic electronic music instrument using the same principle as the Theremin, only with a keyboard for triggering the notes. A generous amount of tape echo is applied to the melody. At about 1:12, this section comes to a conclusion with a burst of short, cascading, tones constructed of short tape sections that were spliced together and modified using octave and half-octave filters to generate the falling pitches.
1:12–2:11	As the cascading sounds conclude, the rhythmic tape loop of pulse tones used in the beginning of the work is repeated, although at a slightly faster tempo. This rhythm remains throughout the section and is supplemented by a loop of less organized noise pulses, giving this section a denser, more complex quality than the first section. Both of these tracks are joined by a third track of rapidly pulsing high-pitched tones. At about 1:15, the bass loop from the first part is added, but is played at a faster tempo than before, giving it a higher pitch. The volume of the bass track is lower than in the first section, adding to the density of the texture. At 1:24, the melody returns but this time it is whistled by Raaijmakers. The melody is heavily treated with reverberation circuits to add resonance and tape echo. Even though many of the same sound materials found in the first section are used to construct this section, notice how the composer modifies them by using frequency filters, varying the speed, and combining them in different ways to produce a different overall sound texture.
2:12–3:08	This section begins sharply with a dense, rhythmic passage reminiscent of honky tonk piano. The main melody is played on the *Ondes Martenot*. The backing track consists of a variety of taped sounds played using loops to form a rhythm of pulsing beats and chords. The sound of a piano can be detected, as well as a sawtooth bass, some whistling, and high-pitched glissandi notes.

At about 2:55, the individual tracks begin to drop out, leaving only the whistling loop. The piece ends with quickly pulsing glissandi that drops in pitch from high to low, followed by a single booming bass tone produced by an audio oscillator processed using a reverberation circuit.

Compare and Contrast
Chimera: Dance 1 (1966) by Alwin Nikolais
Circuit Breaker (1969) by Walter Sear
Brakes On (1999) by Air
It's Not Up To You (2001) by Björk

Figure 14.5 Dick Raaijmakers in the Philips Research Laboratories, *c.* 1959. Note the adjustable "T" rail attachment on the back of the tape recorder tracking tape loops up in the air and back down into the machine. (Philips International BV, Eindhoven)

organized a Moog Quartet for a Carnegie Hall performance in 1970. Speaking about their interest in making electronic music fun and accessible to the public, Perrey remarked:

> Technology gives technical progress but forsakes other emotions. We have to rediscover the sensibility that makes the instruments speak to the heart and to the soul of the listeners. That's why I advise the new generation of electronic musicians to work hard and not to be ruled by the sound capacities of the machines.[33]

A veritable blizzard of Moog recordings from many artists stormed the market in the years immediately following *Switched-On Bach*, not the least of which were every variation imaginable of the "switched-on" theme: *Switched-On Rock* (1970) by the Moog Machine, *Switched-On Gershwin* (1970) by Leonid Hambro and Gershon Kingsley,

Switched-On Nashville (1970) by Gilbert Trythall, and *Switched-On Bacharach* (1969) by Christopher Scott. Most are collectors' items today, although at the time they were written off by most people as genuinely uninspired imitations designed to make a quick buck. But they didn't, and it wasn't long before those expensive synthesizers were collecting cobwebs in some of the busiest commercial recording studios in the business.

TURNTABLISM

Twentieth-century culture has had a love affair with the record player. The turntable has always been a technology of mass consumption. Those of us who were raised prior to the coming of the audio CD—I guess that means every human being on earth who is older than 20—has childhood memories accompanied by the remembered sounds of scratchy, skipping, vinyl records. For us, the sound of a record being played is charged with such memories. This artifact of "contemporary household culture," as Thurston Moore calls it, has had a long history in the performance of music as well.[34]

Paul Hindemith and Ernst Toch first transformed turntables into instruments in 1930, mixing tracks using a disc lathe to create short experiments with variable playback speed. In 1936, Varèse had experimented with turntables that could play in reverse and had variably adjustable speeds.[35] In Cage's apocryphal credo on experimental music written in 1937, he mentioned turntables as one of several electrical instruments that would help usher in a new era in the history of music.[36] Recordings of music on 78 rpm discs were widely available at the time and provided the only practical means for making sound recordings until the availability of the tape recorder by about 1950. Cage composed a piece for pre-recorded discs called *Imaginary Landscape No. 1* in 1939, for which test records were played simultaneously and their speeds variably adjusted according to Cage's instructions. In 1948, Pierre Schaeffer completed his first work of *musique concrète*—the *Études de bruits*—using turntable technology to collect, play back, and record the final version of the piece.

Turntablism is the use of the turntable as a musical instrument. A vital and broadening DJ performance culture has emerged during the past 30 years. Since about 1977, when Grand Wizard Theodore invented the "scratch" technique, turntablism has been at the center of several musical idioms, most notably hip-hop, techno, electronica, and other kinds of house or dance music. Each style has its own use of the turntable. What they have in common is an affinity for active sound mixing as a performance element and the application of electronic effects and synthesizer modules to broaden the sound spectrum of the turntable.

A repertoire of DJ skills has evolved. *Scratching* is the manual reversal of the spin of a record to run the needle backwards over the sound in a quick, rhythmic swipe. The manipulation of beats is another intrinsic characteristic of turntablism. A spinning record is itself a loop, especially when the needle is made to hug a groove rather than move ahead with the natural spiral of the track. *Beat juggling* uses either two identical turntable recordings or one disc and a digital sampler to repeat the same sounds as a *breakbeat*. Digital looping and delay are also common to beat manipulation. These techniques are for the turntablist what finger exercises are for the piano player.

Like any performance medium, turntablism has its radicals, its experimentalists, who push the form in unexpected directions. The omnipresence of turntable music in today's culture has been likened to an earlier generation that grew up emulating rock and roll artists. "The electric guitar is an instrument that's fifty years old," remarked turntablist Christian Marclay (b. 1955). "It's already become a nostalgic instrument for baby boomers. Today's new guitar is the turntable."[37] These experimental artists use the same equipment as their more popular DJ counterparts, but with a different musical object in mind. They are no different from composers who write experimental works for other instruments and remain vastly outnumbered by those who write conventionally for the widest commercial appeal. They view their instrument as a resource for new musical possibilities.

Marclay is a key figure in the revival of experimental turntablism. He began in 1979 when hip-hop turntablism was emerging. Nicolas Collins calls him the "in-between man" in the development of this style. Marclay approached the music from the perspective of an art school student. He sometimes shared the stage with hip-hop artists, but also organized installations and events that were more common to the gallery scene. After ten years or so devoted to turntable music, he returned to art again. Now he is back and in great demand as a music improviser. Collins thinks that maybe "he's been forgotten by a generation. A lot of DJs came up and started doing the same stuff. He came back in and people noticed him."[38]

Marclay's approach to his instrument is much like Cage's toward the piano. He does not use the trendiest turntable technology, preferring to lug around industrial-strength record players that look like they came from a garage sale at an elementary school. Some of these are not always in the best working order. He has also re-purposed the content of the music on old recordings through his real-time editing of old sounds into new forms—the ultimate recontextualization of reality in music. His palette is rich and he is as likely to break a record as preserve it for future use. He is not a collector of records; he is a living channel through which the recorded history of our culture is collected and expressed—a human audio filter.

Marclay also brought black boxes to turntablism. He would be equally at home setting up shop for a Merce Cunningham performance as for a club date in the East Village. He stacks his records, unsheathed, so that they will be scratched and damaged, adding to the noise elements that become an intriguing sub-theme of turntable music.

Figure 14.6 Turntablist Christian Marclay and equipment. (Thom Holmes)

Watching him perform is not unlike watching any other highly focused musician. He is intent on the next moment, anticipating changes, listening to haphazard collisions of sound that sometime coalesce, all under his watchful eye. He works with four to eight turntables, digital delay, distortion boxes, and other gizmos thrown together to produce a live mix. His recordings are often prepared using "abusive manipulation": rubbing two records together, cracking them, breaking them apart and gluing them back together, and allowing them to get extremely dirty.[39]

In a recent compilation of his early work, he explained his approach to performance this way:

> I worked on these pieces until I found the right combination of records, then integrated them into my set. Usually lasting between 20 and 30 minutes, the set was an uninterrupted flow of records mixed on multiple turntables—four, six, or sometimes up to eight turntables. It evolved continuously, as records got damaged beyond use and new ones were found. The records were annotated, numbered and stacked in original piles. These stacks of prepared records were my score. Later I preferred improvising with just a few markings on the records, which were ordered only by sound types. I do not remember specifically which records were used on most of these mixes; to my ears they were only sounds, very abstract and detached from their original sources. They lost their identity and became fragments to be mixed—a loop, a texture, a transition, a beat, an intro, a word.[40]

Marclay's most provocative avant-garde statement may have been his 1989 installation piece called *Footsteps*. For this work, he first pressed 3,500 copies of a vinyl disc featuring the sound of recorded footsteps. For six weeks during the summer of 1989, these discs were laid out on the floor of one of the Shedhalle Galleries in Zurich. Visitors to the gallery had to walk on top of the loosely piled recordings, marking the discs with scratches, cracks, dirt, and other physical elements of wear and tear. Each record suffered its own unique form of damage, producing the kind of "abusive manipulation" en masse that Marclay applied individually to his performance discs. After six weeks, 1,100 of the records were packaged and sold (100 as a signed edition). The recordings were art objects with an aura of impermanence. Marclay had done something like this on a smaller scale in 1985 with his legendary *Record without a Cover*. Thurston Moore notes, "Christian encouraged the owner to progressively destroy the edition. This destruction enabled the listener to create a personal stamp and therefore eradicate any question of value to the object."[41]

A turntablist who has been influenced by Marclay is DJ Olive, the Audio Janitor (Gregor Asch). Like Marclay, he has an art background and became involved in turntablism when he had to provide music for installations. He uses the standard-issue equipment for most DJs: two or three Technics SL-1200 turntables. Rather than working with recordings of recognizable or popular music, his tendency is to shape abstract sounds, electronic or electroacoustic in origin. Using digital delay and sampling, he jockeys sound fragments back and forth, progressively mutating them in conceptual ways that are close to the roots of tape composition. His work sometimes emulates Stockhausen's work with the *Springer* machine, suspending sounds in time, eradicating all tempo, and then gradually transforming them into something else. His use of recording techniques in real time adds a dimension of complexity to turntablism that is critical to the overall effect of his work. His turntable sources share the audio space with ghosts of themselves that persist sometimes long after the records have been switched.

While Marclay's "score" consists of a stack of records, DJ Olive has devised what he calls the "vinyl score" as a way to extend his work to other turntablists. A vinyl score is a collection of sounds that DJ Olive has created and committed to disc so that other DJs can use them. Each disc includes about 50 tracks. His instructions are simple. "The rules are that you have three turntables. You mix between ten and twenty minutes. Record it and send it to me."[42] This approach brings out the improvisatory nature of turntablism, which is purposefully encouraged by DJ Olive's less-than-rigorous rules of engagement:

> What you would paint and what I would paint with a disc would have to be completely different. What you would pull out of it and what I might pull out of it would be totally different. And you can't play the whole thing because you can only play for ten or twenty minutes. So you can just kind of find some stuff you like and make your interpretation this time like working just this one band. This is open-ended composition. It can never be played the same way twice and there is no correct way to play it. It kind of shows you what the DJ does and what the instrument is. I've done shows with five different DJs and you see one after the next play it and it sounds so radically different. You sense, OK, it's the DJ that's making a difference.[43]

A recording featuring largely improvised experimental electronic music by DJ Olive, Ikue Mori, and Kim Gordon was released by Sonic Youth Records (SYR). In performance, this trio complements each other in a manner that you might expect from a traditional rock guitar-bass-drum trio, only they do so with the often unpredictable nuance of electronic music. "My part is pretty open," explains electronic musician Ikue Mori, who plays improvised sounds on her laptop. "Olive has this beat. Kim's singing is kind of fixed. She has songs and lyrics to sing. When she sings, we imagine all kinds of sounds."[44] Gordon steps up front, guitar slung over her shoulder, and becomes the visual focus of the performance as a hail of often calamitous sounds emanates into the

Figure 14.7
DJ Olive, 2001.
(Thom Holmes)

space. It is the perfect demonstration that the turntable and laptop have arrived as the garage-band instruments of the new century.

Another artist riding the experimental edge of turntablism is DJ Spooky, That Subliminal Kid (Paul D. Miller, b. 1970). He is the most widely known of the abstract turntable artists. Also based in New York, he was one of the early performers on the protoplasmic *illbient* scene in the East Village in the 1990s. This was a music without dance rhythms, yet it was neither trance nor ambient in conception. It was too harsh, too urban for that. Illbient artists use the noise and energy of the city to weave their soundscapes. DJ Spooky's gigs are part performance and part installation, sometimes piping in room noise from other locations, an environment reminiscent of Cage and Tudor's work in 1964 on *Variations IV*. He mixes audio verité to form a kind of real-time *musique concrète*, weaving electronic tones into the mix, sampling, dubbing, and rearranging chunks of sound like pieces of time. It is a heavy brew of noise, voice, electronic distortion, sampling, and an occasional musical or rap riff.

DJ Spooky is also a prolific writer and immersed in questions of ontology and the semiotics of popular media and urban culture. His artistic references span the gamut of the avant-garde. He makes his sources known in the detailed notes that accompany each of his commercially available recordings, dropping the names of Cage, Stockhausen, Olly Wilson, Gertrude Stein, Pauline Oliveros, Iannis Xenakis, Philip Glass, Ben Neill, Vernon Reid, Bill Laswell, and a host of others. His language is imbued with the vocabulary of a graduate student in philosophy. He takes a classroom discussion of the social significance of music culture to his audience through his liner notes:

> Translating the untranslatable in a prismatic fashion through the union of form and content, the DJ refracts meaning from the dense locale of culture and places the rays of meaning, in a rhizomatic fashion, back in their original locale in the human mind.[45]

Figure 14.8 Marina Rosenfeld in performance, 2001. (Thom Holmes)

Despite this academically tuned prose, DJ Spooky has not lost touch with the social significance of the DJ culture and club scene. His thoughts on the place of electronic music in our culture are clearly expressed:

> Electronic music is, in a way, the folk music of the 21st century. Instead of, say, the '20s, where you had everyone who knew a blues riff playing a guitar, you now have everyone who knows certain beats and things like that putting them together and then circulating them—this scene is about mixing and mix tapes. Technology is making the creative process democratic.[46]

Marina Rosenfeld represents yet another discipline in turntable performance. Rosenfeld is a schooled composer, having studied composition at Cal Arts with Mel Powell. She acknowledges that Morton Feldman is one of her most beloved influences. She has worked with turntable composition and performance as one of several outlets for her work.

Figure 14.9
Prepared disc by
Marina Rosenfeld.
(Photo by Thom Holmes)

Rosenfeld's *Fragment Opera*, mentioned earlier in the discussion of process music, utilizes a set of acetate discs that she created herself. These form the sound palette for a live performance of the work that follows a structural sequence suggested by her instructions for the performer. Like Marclay, Rosenfeld diddles with the physical material of her recorded discs to create manipulative patterns and noises. She is attracted to the physicality of turntable performance and often prepares her discs by gluing nails to them:

> I like the fact that the turntable is mechanical. It's mechanical like the way a piano is mechanical. I was a pianist first, and still feel like my hands have to make the music on some level. My hands are where all the ideas are hiding, plus, from the point of view of a performance, where the idea is to expose the music and not conceal it, or conceal your means of production. It's a plus that you and the audience can see the whole thing in front of you and go anywhere without rewinding something or fast-forwarding something or pressing a button. It's a visual medium and visually exposed.
>
> In my first pieces with turntables, all of my records had nails or pins inserted in them. Like everyone else who ever got into this technique, I was into loops that you could see. I was making these pieces where the arm of the record player was going in and then it hit a nail and started to make a bouncing noise. So, you could see it's a loop—and hear the possibly obnoxious bumping noise it made each time the loop repeated. The benefit was that there was something so concrete about it. Not even descriptive. It was a loop. You could see it. You could hear it. I like to look at the instrument that way. I think eventually I'm going to get tired of the precomposition that goes into making the LPs first and spinning them later, and will do it from scratch on the spot.[47]

Another Marclay-inspired turntablist with a twist is Philip Jeck from England. He first saw Marclay perform while visiting the United States on a work assignment. It was about the same time that he was beginning to explore turntablism. The experience liberated his thinking about what he could do as a composer using previously recorded works. Jeck has been more interested in composing a wall of vinyl sounds, often repeating loops in long sequences. He places stickers on his records to keep the tone arm stuck

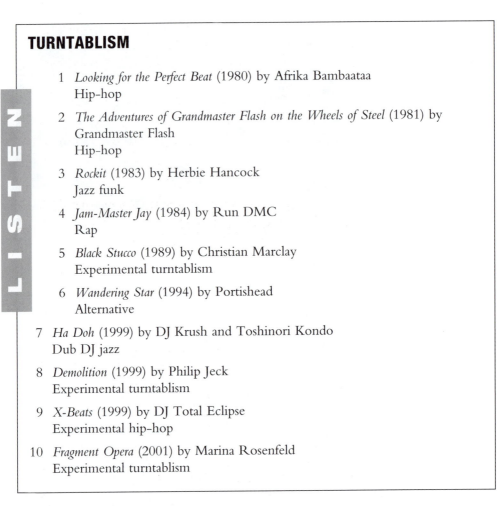

LISTEN

TURNTABLISM

1 *Looking for the Perfect Beat* (1980) by Afrika Bambaataa
   Hip-hop

2 *The Adventures of Grandmaster Flash on the Wheels of Steel* (1981) by
   Grandmaster Flash
   Hip-hop

3 *Rockit* (1983) by Herbie Hancock
   Jazz funk

4 *Jam-Master Jay* (1984) by Run DMC
   Rap

5 *Black Stucco* (1989) by Christian Marclay
   Experimental turntablism

6 *Wandering Star* (1994) by Portishead
   Alternative

7 *Ha Doh* (1999) by DJ Krush and Toshinori Kondo
   Dub DJ jazz

8 *Demolition* (1999) by Philip Jeck
   Experimental turntablism

9 *X-Beats* (1999) by DJ Total Eclipse
   Experimental hip-hop

10 *Fragment Opera* (2001) by Marina Rosenfeld
   Experimental turntablism

in a given groove. His works are long and extended excursions that owe as much to the continuously droning energy of La Monte Young and Terry Riley as to Marclay. He builds layers and loops of interweaving sounds and repeating patterns that change gradually over time. His *Vinyl Requiem* (1993) was the most ambitious piece of turntable industrialism yet conceived. It consisted of a performance for 180 Dansette record players and a visual show provided by 12 slide projectors and two movie projectors.

Following the examples of these composers, and many others who are working in this field, a new generation of turntablists has clearly reclaimed the record player as an instrument of the avant-garde.

SUMMARY

- Rock music embraced the tape editing and synthesizing techniques of electronic music beginning around the mid-1960s.

- The Beatles were influential in being among the first rock groups to use tape loops, tape reversal, variable-speed playback, the Moog synthesizer, and musical collage in their recordings, turning the recording studio into an important tool for creating their music.

- Other early practitioners of electronic music in rock included Pink Floyd, whose track "A Saucerful of Secrets" (1968) was, essentially, a rock version of *musique concrète*.

- Exotica was a popular genre of easy-listening music during the 1950s and 1960s that sometimes incorporated electronic musical instruments.

- Turntablism is the use of the turntable as a musical instrument.

- Modern turntablism has origins in hip-hop and rap music and is also practiced in the work of many experimental music composers.

Pioneering Works of Electronic Music

The many works of electronic music discussed in *Electronic and Experimental Music* are but a sampling of the many innovative and important achievements in this field of music. Although a comprehensive discography of electronic music is beyond the scope of these pages, the annotated recommendations below provide a supplementary list of key works of electronic music for those who wish to explore some of the "greatest hits" of the field. These recommended recordings add depth to the *Listen* playlists and *Listening Guides* already found throughout the book and keyed to the context of each chapter.

These recommended tracks include many classics of electronic music, some reaching back to the origins of the discipline. In selecting the music, I was looking for pieces that were well enough known even in their day to influence other people working in the field. Many of these works have been mentioned to me repeatedly as key influences by composers and musicians in the field. Some of these works are widely known to the public, while others are rarely heard outside of the canon of avant-garde and experimental music. The works are organized alphabetically by the last name of the composer.

Automatic Writing **(1974–79) by Robert Ashley**. This work has been variously described as minimalist, ambient, or spoken word. This early Ashley opera, consisting of text in the manner of involuntary speech, is one of the composer's many works exploring the storytelling powers of new media.

Ensembles for Synthesizer **(1961–63) by Milton Babbitt**. This appealing serial composition, produced using the RCA Electronic Music Synthesizer at the Columbia–Princeton Electronic Music Center, was also an early application of computer-like composition using binary input.

"Tomorrow Never Knows" (1966) by The Beatles. "Tomorrow Never Knows," from the album *Revolver*, was produced shortly after the Beatles abandoned live concerts and retreated to the recording studio. The song utilized classic tape manipulation techniques such as looping and variable speed changes and ushered in a new era in the use of electronic music in rock and pop music.

Runthrough **(1967–68) by David Behrman**. Behrman put homemade synthesizers and photosensitive mixers in the hands of musicians and non-musicians to produce this early, interactive work based on handmade analog hardware hacking. This work was a breakthrough for soldering composers and improvised electronic music.

On the Other Ocean **and** *Figure in a Clearing* **(1977) by David Behrman**. These were two early works of interactive microcomputer music. For *On the Other Ocean*, a KIM-1 computer would sense the order and timing of six pitches played by two performers, subsequently generating "harmony-changing messages to two homemade synthesizers." The computer reacted directly to pitches being played by the performers, and the performers, in turn, were "influenced in their improvising" by the computer's responses. This was among the first recorded works of micro-computer-based, interactive music.

Thema–Omaggio a Joyce (1958) by Luciano Berio. An early tape composition in which the sound of the voice was the primary source material, adapting text from James Joyce's *Ulysses*, spoken and sung by vocalist Cathy Berberian. Berio applied tape editing and mixing techniques to modify the sounds electronically, paying particular attention to the envelopes—attack, sustain, and decay characteristics—of the result. The work is an important example of early work composed at the RAI studio in Milan.

Williams Mix (1952) by John Cage. Representing the introduction of chance operations in the composition of electronic music, this work was also the antithesis of all other electronic music being done at the time in Germany, France, and the United States. *Williams Mix* established an outpost for the most experimental practices in electronic music.

Switched-On Bach (1968) by Wendy Carlos. This work single-handedly popularized the Moog synthesizer and spawned a new industry for commercial electronic musical instruments as well as countless musical imitations. *Switched-On Bach* proved that electronic music did not only dwell in the realm of the experimental.

Stria (1977) by John Chowning. This rigorously composed work was the result of early experiments in FM synthesis by John Chowning. Using high-level computer programming to organize and synthesize the sounds, Chowning sought to develop a work based on the naturally occurring inharmonic ratios between carrier signals and modulators. Writing computer code to compose using the organizational principle of the Golden Mean, the result is an inharmonic piece for 26 sine wave instruments, each programmed to play varying notes with a variety of possible envelopes.

Leiyla and the Poet (1959) by Halim El-Dabh. Many composers remember having heard this work on an early recording of electronic music from Columbia Records. It is remarkable because of its organic textures and raw energy and inspired many composers who decided to work in electronic music. It is one of the most familiar and popular works produced during the early years of the Columbia–Princeton Electronic Music Center.

Music for Airports (1978) by Brian Eno. This was the first widely known ambient work based on purely electronic tonalities. Eno coined the term "ambient" by putting it in his liner notes, although Eno was not the first to experiment with such soundscapes—David Berhman, Pauline Oliveros, and Teresa Rampazzi all having explored similar concepts earlier.

Dripsody (1955) by Hugh Le Caine. An early tour de force of basic tape composition techniques using only the sound of a drop of water falling into a bucket. This classic work demonstrated the use of Le Caine's multi-tracking tape machine, which synchronized the playback of six individual tape reels, mixing them down to a single monophonic track.

World Rhythms (1975) by Annea Lockwood. Simply the first widely heard work of environmental music using only natural sounds as sources. Although a mixture of recordings of various natural sounds, Lockwood's work did not employ tape manipulation, loops, or other effects to modify the sounds. She carefully organized and transitioned the sounds to create a slowly unfolding soundscape, allowing the audio material to stand on its own merits.

I Am Sitting in a Room (1970) by **Alvin Lucier**. This is a work whose reputation often precedes it, and many composers mention it as an influence even if they've only read about it. The piece explores the degenerative effects of recording and re-recording the same sound through the use of microphone and two tape recorders. The composition consists of a set of instructions for making these recordings and splicing them together in the order in which they were recorded.

Record Without a Cover (1985) by **Christian Marclay**. He revived the field of experimental turntablism during the early and mid-1980s. This work, the vinyl recording of which bears no protective sleeve, was intended to get increasingly scratched and damaged with each successive handling.

Hornpipe (1967) by **Gordon Mumma**. A performance piece for live Waldhorn—a valveless hunting horn—and French horn, with adaptive analog circuits that responded to the horns by making their own sounds. Mumma's work in this area, dating back to the 1950s, was the archetype for the real-time electronic processing of sounds during a performance.

I of IV (1966) by **Pauline Oliveros**. This piece is built around a performance process that was conducted in real time. Therefore, the technique for creating this work is essentially that of live electronic music. The piece is based on real-time tape manipulation and audio processing techniques using tape delay, echo, and reverberation with audio oscillators as sound sources.

Four Aspects (1960) by **Daphne Oram**. This piece demonstrated Oram's interest in creating works that were longer than the short snippets of music that she had composed for the BBC Radiophonic Workshop. It was composed using a strikingly harmonic tone field of slowly evolving sounds and was very unlike most of the commercial and academic electronic music being produced at the time.

Come Out (1966) by **Steve Reich**. Minimalist composer Steve Reich created *Come Out* to explore the process of gradually playing tape loops in and out of phase. The work is built around a single snippet of recorded voice. He played two loops of this snippet going gradually out of phase, creating new rhythms and accentuating the melodic features of the spoken words. This is a classic exercise in composing tape music using a predetermined mechanical process, the outcome of which varies depending on the sound source and the tape machines being used.

Symphonie pour un homme seul (*Symphony for a Man Alone*, 1949–50) by **Pierre Schaeffer and Pierre Henry**. This early work of *musique concrète* was composed using only pre-recorded sounds on disc. This piece represents the beginning of the modern era of electronic music and is significant because it established many of the audio manipulation concepts still in use today—sound reversal, transposition, speed variation, editing, and mixing.

X (1978) by **Klaus Schulze**. An influential work of space music, *X* was a double album comprising six extended-length instrumentals ranging from 11 to 30 minutes each. Schulze performed using Moog modular, EMS, and ARP synthesizers and some sections include drums and string orchestra.

The Expanding Universe (1975) by **Laurie Spiegel**. Composed by Spiegel using the *GROOVE* computer music studio at Bell Labs, near the end of the era of musical software applications for general-purpose mainframe computers.

***Gesang der Jünglinge (Song of the Youths, 1955–56)* by Karlheinz Stockhausen**. *Gesang der Jünglinge* was the work that leveled the wall between *musique concrète* and *elektronische Musik*. It was significant for several reasons, not the least of which was the composer's meticulous planning and scoring that stand today as a major aesthetic contribution to the art of electronic music thinking and composition.

***Hymnen (Anthems, 1966–67)* by Karlheinz Stockhausen**. This is the *Pet Sounds* of electronic music, possibly even more influential than Stockhausen's earlier *Gesang der Jünglinge*. This pensive work represents the pinnacle of classic tape composition technique. At about two hours long, it elevated the stature of electronic music from that of a novel program break to an experience of operatic proportions. It also influenced a younger generation of German musicians in the early 1970s, spawning the genre of space music.

***Silver Apples of the Moon* (1967) by Morton Subotnick**. The first electronic composition conceived and recorded specifically for release as a commercial recording. (Stockhausen can claim to have edited the four parts of *Hymnen* the previous year so that they would fit on four sides of two discs, but his work was conceived for live performance.) It uses the Buchla synthesizer and was the first widely recognized work by this important composer of electronic music.

***Rainforest IV* (1973) by David Tudor**. *Rainforest IV* (the installation version) is perhaps the most influential work of interactive, ambient, electronic music using handmade electronics. The work is like an organism that continues to grow and change with each manifestation. Gordon Mumma deserves mention as an important collaborator on this work.

***Sonic Contours* (1952) by Vladimir Ussachevsky**. This piece of tape composition was based solely on recorded piano sounds. It was composed using only tape speed changes, reverberation, and tape editing. It is an early example of tape composition using traditional instruments. It was played at the first recital of electronic music in the United States at the Composers Forum in New York City on May 9, 1952.

***Déserts* (1954) by Edgard Varèse**. The first work to combine a live orchestra and a magnetic tape part in live performance. Although the composer intentionally segregated the electronic sounds from the live orchestra—the tape part consisted of interludes between orchestral parts—both the tape and instrumental parts were composed to complement and contrast with one another, making the whole an extraordinary exploration of unique sonic textures.

***Poème électronique* (1958) by Edgard Varèse**. The culmination, if not the end, of the classic era of *musique concrète*, this is one of the best known and most widely heard pieces of tape music. Its design for the spatial projection of sound using hundreds of loudspeakers in the Philips Pavilion of the 1958 Brussels World's Fair underscores its significance as one of the first works of electronic music designed and composed for a specific acoustic space, and broad listening public.

***Bohor* (1962) by Iannis Xenakis**. The influence of this thundering mass of ever-loudening clangings is epochal. It marked the germination of noise and industrial music that flowered in the late 1960s and 1970s and still blooms periodically. The stochastic methods employed by Xenakis to compose his electronic works hint at the use of granular synthesis in conceiving music comprised of sound particles.

The Evolution of Analog Synthesizers

This appendix provides an evolutionary timeline tracing the major technological developments, manufacturers, and models of analog synthesizers. While most of the instruments contained in the accompanying diagrammatic history were developed between 1960 and 1982, some earlier synthesizers have also been included because of the importance of the foundational technologies that they represented.

The development of analog synthesizers reached its peak during the 1970s, when dozens of manufacturers the world over offered an ever-changing variety of new modular and performance electronic musical instruments. An estimated 375 manufacturers produced as many as 1,100 different analog synthesizer models by the time that digital instrumentation began to transform the market in the mid-1980s.[1] For every familiar and well-established manufacturer such as Moog, Korg, Roland, and Yamaha, there were dozens of less stellar performers with names ranging from the seriously technical, such as Evos Research and Process Electronics, to the musically evocative and whimsical, such as Sequential Circuits, Polyfusion, and Electronic Dream Plant.

This appendix comprises three annotated diagrams tracing the evolution of analog synthesis technology:

- Figure AI.1: Evolution of Electronic Organs (1897–1970)
- Figure AI.2: Evolution of Electronic Pianos (1926–72)
- Figure AI.3: Evolution of Analog Synthesizers (1945–82)

Grouping instruments by related technology in this way provides a means for tracing the historical development of synthesizers as well as acknowledging groundbreaking products. Instruments were chosen for the diagrams based on their significance to the overall continuum of electronic musical development. While some of these products met with respectable market success, such as the Moog Minimoog, some were largely unsuccessful but represented an important milestone in the development of musical instrument technology, such as the Le Caine Electronic Sackbut (1945)—the first voltage-controlled synthesizer.

Each diagram is annotated with additional information for each instrument, including the name of the inventor or manufacturer, the name of the instrument (in italics), the year that the instrument was patented, invented or commercially introduced, a brief note about the technology, and the country of origin.

EVOLUTION OF ELECTRONIC ORGANS (1897–1970)

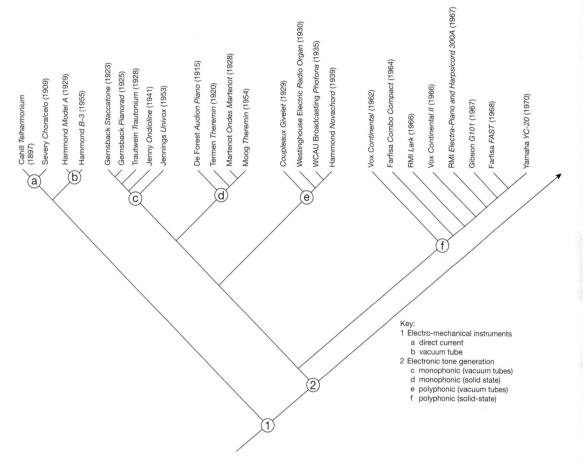

Figure AI.1 Evolution of electronic organs (1897–1970).

1 Electro-Mechanical Instruments

(a) Direct Current

- Cahill *Telharmonium* (1897); mammoth, polyphonic, direct-current instrument using axles and tone wheels, which was installed in New York to provide live music wired into hotels by telephone lines (United States).
- Severy *Choralcelo* (1909); used electromagnetically vibrating strings to create organ-like tones without hammers; the body of the instrument was an upright piano; the sound was amplified using non-electronic resonating chambers (United States).

(b) Vacuum Tube

- Hammond *Model A* (1929); a practical application of Cahill's tone wheel design using vacuum tubes to reduce the bulk of the instrument (United States).
- Hammond *B-3* (1955); popular organ using drawbars to vary timbre and a rotating speaker (Leslie) to create a unique swirling sound effect (United States).

2   Electronic Tone Generation

(c) Monophonic (Vacuum Tubes)

- Gernsback *Staccatone* (1923); polyphonic, using one sine wave tube oscillator per note; keys were simple on/off switches producing a sharp staccato note with little control over the attack of a sound (United States).
- Gernsback *Pianorad* (1925); an improved version of the Staccatone, also polyphonic, which produced pure sine wave tones with little overtones using tube oscillators (United States).
- Trautwein *Trautonium* (1928); monophonic instrument using sawtooth tube oscillators; it was played using a fingerboard, or pressure-sensitive band on which sliding notes could be produced; it had two or three fingerboards to enable the playing of more than one note at a time; the Trautonium was noted for its excellent control over the timbre of a sound using filters and the use of subtractive synthesis as a sound-shaping technique; it was used for sound effects and music in movies, including *The Birds* by Alfred Hitchcock (Germany).
- Jenny *Ondioline* (1941); four-octave monophonic melody instrument using tube oscillators; notes could be bent by wiggling the keys, producing vibrato; octave transposer switch generated four additional octaves (France).
- Jennings *Univox* (1953); monophonic keyboard that used frequency shifting to create its three-octave range (United States).
- De Forest *Audion Piano* (1915); the inventor of the vacuum tube created one of the earliest electronic organs using this new technology; beat frequency sound generation; a single triode vacuum tube per each of three octaves on a keyboard; sounds "resembling a violin, cello, woodwind, muted brass," could be produced by fine-tuning the vacuum tubes to adjust their timbral qualities; a fully polyphonic version was planned but never produced (United States).
- Termen *Theremin* (1920); beat frequency instrument invented by Russian Lev Termen ("Theremin") using gesture control in proximity to two antennae, one controlling amplitude, the other controlling pitch. Neither organ nor synthesizer, the unique Theremin produced a distinctly sonorous tone and provided a range of articulations (e.g. vibrato, tremolo) made possible by movements of the hand in space (Russia).
- Martenot *Ondes Martenot* (1928); French instrument that used the same beat frequency principle as the Theremin but had a keyboard template and a movable ring on a cable for varying the pitch in precise increments. Later models had keyboards and allowed for the production of vibrato by pressing a key from side to side (France).

(d) Monophonic (Solid-State)

- Moog *Theremin* (1954); Robert Moog began to sell kits for making a transistorized Theremin, the ancestor of all modern, solid-state Theremins (United States).

(e) Polyphonic (Vacuum Tubes)

- *Coupleaux–Givelet* (1929); combining tube oscillators and a paper tape reader similar to those used in reproducing pianos, the "programmer" could use the paper reader to specify the pitch, amplitude, tremolo, envelope, and timbre of the instrument; the paper tape reader was a precursor of binary programming as a means for controlling the playback of an electronic instrument (France).
- Westinghouse Electric *Radio Organ* (1930); used vacuum tube oscillators and played using a three-octave keyboard similar to that of a pipe organ (United States).
- WCAU Broadcasting *Photona* (1935); electronic organ design that combined the use of photoelectric sensors with vacuum tube oscillators (United States).
- Hammond *Novachord* (1939); one of the first polyphonic electronic instruments, used circuitry to derive all 72 notes of its keyboard from a mere 12 oscillators, in this case vacuum tube oscillators; it was designed with easy-to-operate controls for the envelope and timbre of its instrumental voices; like other instruments using vacuum tube instruments, frequencies tended to drift out of tune and tone color was often unreliably variable due to the heat of the tubes and complexity of the circuitry (United States).

(f) Polyphonic (Solid-State)

- Vox *Continental* (1962); early transistorized polyphonic organ; became popular with rock and roll groups including the Animals, the Dave Clark Five, and the Doors; the instrument had four drawbars including settings for sine and sawtooth sounds plus a combination (England).
- Farfisa *Combo Compact* (1964); inexpensive, portable combo organ heard frequently on rock and roll recordings of the 1960s, including the song *In-A-Gadda-Da-Vida* by Iron Butterfly (Italy).
- RMI *Lark* (1966); combo organ that was available with a three-octave or four-octave keyboard; used split frequency circuitry to derive its full range of notes from a lesser number of oscillators (United States).
- Vox *Continental II* (1966); a two-keyboard version of the Vox Continental (England).
- RMI *Electra-Piano and Harpsichord 300A* (1967); used one oscillator per note and a five-octave keyboard; five models of the Electra-Piano and Harpsichord were produced between 1967 and 1980, each with voice settings for a variety of piano and harpsichord tones as well as lute and organ (United States).
- Gibson *G101* (1967); five-octave keyboard with three split sections for different voices; known for its variety of preset voices and special effects, including fuzz bass, gliding notes, wow-wow, staccato, sustain, and reverb (United States).
- Farfisa *FAST* (1968); five-octave split keyboard available in five models featuring various voice combinations (Italy).
- Yamaha *YC-20* (1970); basic combo organ with five-octave split keyboard and vibrato (Japan).

EVOLUTION OF ELECTRONIC PIANOS (1926–72)

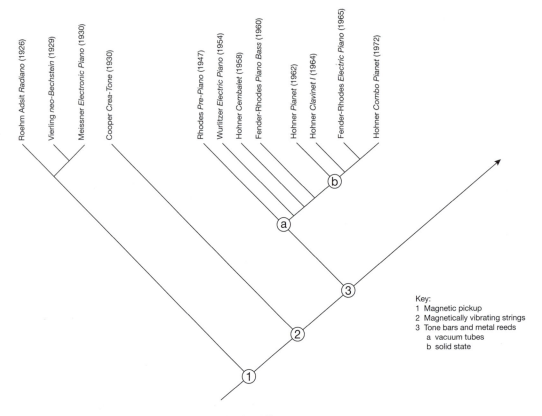

Figure AI.2   Evolution of electronic pianos (1926–72).

1   Magnetic Pickup

- Roehm–Adsit *Radiano* (1926); used contact pickups to electronically amplify an acoustic piano (United States).
- Vierling *Neo-Bechstein* (1929); a grand piano body lacking a sound board; strings were arranged in groups and amplified using electromagnetic pickups, much like an electric guitar (Germany).
- Miessner *Electronic Piano* (1930); also using magnetic pickups to amplify the vibrations of piano strings, this instrument had one pickup per 88 strings, giving it superior reproduction over earlier attempts to amplify an acoustic piano; treble and bass controls were provided to adjust tone color (United States).

2   Magnetically Vibrating Strings

- Cooper *Crea-Tone* (1930); electromagnets were used to excite the strings of a piano so that they vibrated audibly without electronic amplification; the instrument could sustain a tone for a long period and also provided a means to play staccato notes; lacking natural vibrato, the tones sounded electronically produced (United States).

3   Tone Bars and Metal Reeds

(a) Vacuum Tubes

- Rhodes *Pre-Piano* (1947); a small electric piano used in schools with a three-octave keyboard and built-in tube amplifier; used a piezo pickup to reproduce its toy piano-like sound (United States).
- Wurlitzer *Electric Piano* (1954); six-octave keyboard and built-in vacuum tube amplifier; used felt-cushioned hammers and metallic tines with electromagnetic pickup; included tremolo feature (United States).
- Hohner *Cembalet* (1958); five-octave keyboard; used rubber plectra to pluck metal reeds; likened to an electric harpsichord; one voice (Germany).
- Fender–Rhodes *Piano Bass* (1960); used the company's first-generation tine and tonebar mechanism to create sounds; a three-octave instrument covering the lower register of the scale; famously used by Ray Manzarek of the Doors (United States).

(b) Solid-State

- Hohner *Pianet* (1962); six-octave range with no expression controls; electromagnetic pickups and hammered metal reeds (Germany).
- Hohner *Clavinet I* (1964); used 60 plucked strings played by a keyboard, similar in principle to an electric guitar; some models had amplifiers and tone controls; made famous by Stevie Wonder (Germany).
- Fender–Rhodes *Electric Piano* (1965); popular tonebar design and transistorized circuitry; sustain pedal, six-octave range, and a bass control (United States).
- Hohner *Combo Pianet* (1972); compact version of Pianet for stage use; five-octave range (Germany).

EVOLUTION OF ANALOG SYNTHESIZERS (1945–82)

1   Early Programmable Modular Synthesizers

(a) Vacuum Tube

- RCA *Mark I Electronic Music Synthesizer* (1955); used tuning fork oscillators; one punched paper roll recorder/player for storing compositions; two-channel audio output; disc lathe for recording audio (United States).
- RCA *Mark II Electronic Music Synthesizer* (1958); expanded version of Mark I featuring two punched paper recorder/players, four-channel audio output, ten-chamber electronic resonators, ten-octave range, white noise generator, two banks of vacuum tube oscillators producing sawtooth and triangle waveforms to supplement the tuning fork oscillators, frequency shifter, and four-channel mixer with magnetic tape recorder (United States).

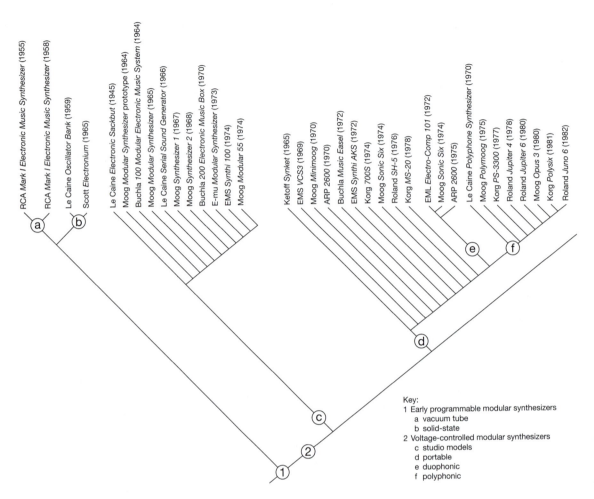

Figure AI.3   Evolution of analog synthesizers (1945–82).

(b) Solid-State

- Le Caine *Oscillator Bank* (1959); a bank of multiple oscillators controlled by a touch-sensitive keyboard; oscillators could be switched to produce sine, pulse, and sawtooth waves (Canada).
- Scott *Electronium* (1965); semi-automated composing synthesizer without a keyboard; the composer could preset melodies, tempos, and timbres or recall previously prescribed settings (United States).

2 Voltage-Controlled Modular Synthesizers

(c) Studio Models

- Le Caine *Electronic Sackbut* (1945); first voltage-controlled synthesizer prototype; vacuum tube circuitry and touch-sensitive keyboard; keys could be pressed to the side to create a gliding note up or down to the adjacent key; rotary, pressure-sensitive controls for timbre and the selection of waveforms (sine, pulse, sawtooth) (Canada).

- Moog *Modular Synthesizer* prototype (1964); began the era of solid-state circuitry synthesizers; included two voltage-controlled oscillators, two five-octave keyboard controllers, one envelope generator, filter, and white noise generator (United States).
- Buchla *100 Modular Electronic Music System* (1964); wooden cabinet with touch-sensitive plates used as controllers and room for up to 25 modular components such as oscillators, filters, mixer, envelope generator, ring modulator, and early sequencer (United States).
- Moog *Modular Synthesizer* (1965); expanded the prototype version with a larger cabinet to house modular components, a modified five-octave keyboard, oscillators, ribbon controller, and foot pedal controller (United States).
- Le Caine *Serial Sound Generator* (1966); an analog computer dedicated to the programming of musical sequences; provided control over the pitch, duration, timbre, and repetition of sounds, and used a voltage-controlled oscillator as its sound source; early analog sequencer (Canada).
- Moog *Synthesizer 1* (1967); module package including five-octave keyboard, not-quite portable folding cabinets, oscillators, ribbon controller, spring reverberation, low-pass filter, envelope generator, white noise generator, voltage-controlled amplifier, filter bank, and optional eight-step sequencer (United States).
- Moog *Synthesizer 2* (1968); module package including five-octave keyboard, wooden cabinet for housing modules, oscillators, ribbon controller, spring reverberation, low-pass filter, envelope generator, white noise generator, voltage-controlled amplifier, filter bank, eight-step sequencer, and mixer (United States).
- Buchla *200 Electronic Music Box* (1970); wooden cabinet with 17-note touch-sensitive membrane keyboard, also available with a four-octave touch-sensitive membrane keyboard with eight assignable sections, joystick controller, envelope followers, frequency detector, multiple arbitrary function generator, reverberation, oscillators, filters, mixer, envelope generator, ring modulator, stored program module, noise source, random voltage generator, sequencer, and the Source of Uncertainty random noise generator (United States).
- E-mu *Modular Synthesizer* (1973); medium to large modular system with unique ability to make patches with cords on the face of the machine or "firm" patches on the rear of the instrument for settings that were not often changed; five-octave keyboard; full range of filters, envelope generators, mixer, and eight-step sequencer (United States).
- EMS *Synthi 100* (1974); large, expandable synthesizer with 12 oscillator banks, two five-octave keyboards, dual 64 × 64 matrix patch panels, filters, envelope controllers, mixer, and 3-track sequencer; its sophisticated Euro-style cabinetry was at home in professional studios, including Stockhausen's WDR facilities (England).
- Moog *Modular 55* (1974); the top-of-the-line Moog modular package included a wooden cabinet for housing modules, five-octave keyboard, ribbon controller, spring reverberation, low-pass filter, high-pass filter, fixed filter bank, envelope generator, white noise generator, random signal generator, voltage-controlled amplifier, dual trigger delay, sample and hold, eight-step sequencer, and mixer (United States).

(d) Portable

- Ketoff *Synket* (1965); one of the earliest portable performance synthesizers; three, small two-octave keyboards, stacked vertically; three sound-generating modules, each triggered by one of the keyboards; frequency dividers, filters, and amplitude modulators; the keys could be wiggled from side to side to create vibrato; an influential instrument that sold very poorly but clearly suggested solutions for instrument makers who followed in the 1970s (Italy).
- EMS *VCS3* (1969); table-top unit with two voltage-controlled oscillators, low-frequency oscillator, velocity-sensitive three-octave keyboard, ring modulator, envelope shaper, spring reverb, joystick control, and stereo output; known in the United States as the Putney (England).
- Moog *Minimoog* (1970); three voltage-controlled oscillators, low-pass filter, two envelope generators, and 44-key monophonic keyboard with pitch wheel and modulation wheel (United States).
- ARP *2600* (1970); matrix-switch patching without patch cords; three voltage-controlled oscillators, low-pass filter, voltage-controlled amplifier, two envelope generators, ring modulation, sample and hold, white noise, spring reverb, and four-octave keyboard. Used widely in rock and jazz, including such artists as David Hentschel (for Elton John), Edgar Winter, Pete Townshend (The Who), Joe Zawinul (Weather Report), and Herbie Hancock (United States).
- Buchla *Music Easel* (1972); 2.5-octave touch plate keyboard, voltage-controlled oscillators, sequencer, preamplifier, envelope detector, octave shifter, portamento, and program cards for recording and restoring patch settings (United States).
- EMS *Synthi AKS* (1972); identical to the EMS VCS3 with the addition of a 2.5-octave touch plate controller, monophonic sequencer, and a fold-up case (England).
- Korg *700S* (1974); early Japanese-made synthesizer with three-octave keyboard, two oscillators, pitchbend, filter, envelope, portamento, simple delay, chorus, noise source, and vibrato (Japan).
- Moog *Sonic Six* (1974); synthesizer in a briefcase intended for schools; four-octave duophonic keyboard, two voltage-controlled oscillators, low-pass filter, and envelope generator (United States).
- Roland *SH-5* (1976); 3.5-octave keyboard, two voltage-controlled oscillators, two low-frequency oscillators, two filters, and two voltage-controlled envelope generators (Japan).
- Korg *MS-20* (1978); three-octave keyboard, preset voices or patches, two voltage-controlled oscillators, low-frequency oscillator, dual multimode filters (low-pass, high-pass, notch, band-reject), and envelope generator (Japan).

(e) Duophonic

- EML *Electro-Comp 101* (1972); 3.5-octave keyboard, four voltage-controlled oscillators, one low-pass filter, multimode filter (low-pass, high-pass, band-pass), envelope generator, ring modulator, amplitude modulator, sample and hold, and folding case for portability (United States).
- Moog *Sonic Six* (1974); duophonic portable synthesizer in a briefcase (United States).
- ARP *2600* (1975); later models of the ARP 2600 were duophonic synthesizers.

(f) Polyphonic

- Le Caine *Polyphone Synthesizer* (1970); touch-sensitive keyboard and three-octave range; fully polyphonic with individual oscillator, and pitch and waveform controls for each key (Canada).
- Moog *Polymoog* (1975); five-octave velocity-sensitive keyboard with up to three keyboard splits; fully polyphonic; preset voices, filters, eight preset and one user-modifiable memory settings, and envelope generator (United States).
- Korg *PS-3300* (1977); semi-modular synthesizer with full polyphonic four-octave keyboard (one of the first completely polyphonic voltage-controlled synthesizers), 48 voltage-controlled oscillators, three-band equalizer, filter, and envelope generator (Japan).
- Roland *Jupiter 4* (1978); four-voice polyphonic four-octave keyboard; ensemble mode for synching all four oscillators for a thick lead sound; filter, low-frequency oscillator, an early arpeggiator, ten preset voices, and eight memory settings (Japan).
- Roland *Jupiter 6* (1980); six-voice polyphonic five-octave keyboard, low-frequency oscillator, multimode filter (low-pass, high-pass, band-pass), envelope generator, arpeggiator, 32 preset voices, and early MIDI implementation; one of Roland's most popular synthesizers (Japan).
- Moog *Opus 3* (1980); polyphonic four-octave keyboard known for its string, brass, and organ sounds; two multimode voltage-controlled filters (low-pass, high-pass, band-pass), panning, and envelope generator (United States).
- Korg *Polysix* (1981); early low-cost programmable analog synthesizer; six-voice five-octave keyboard, 32 user-programmable presets, six voltage-controlled oscillators, low-pass filter, envelope generator, chorus, phaser, and ensemble (Japan).
- Roland *Juno 6* (1982); six-voice five-octave keyboard, low- and high-pass filters, envelope generator, optional sequencer, chorus, and digitally controlled analog oscillators (Japan).

The Evolution of Computer Music

This appendix provides an evolutionary timeline tracing the major technological developments, developers, and models of computer musical instruments and software. The diagrammatic history below spans the modern history of computer music through four technological generations of equipment from 1957 to 2011. In addition to including music made with general-purpose computers, the diagrams also include important milestones in the development of digital synthesizers (hardware and software) based solely on digital technology.

The first 20 years of computer music development were largely a clean-room phenomenon hosted by major computer centers at educational, scientific, and government-funded institutions. It was not until the early 1970s, and the availability of sound chips and microprocessors, that small, affordable microcomputers were applied to making music. By the year 2000, the availability of increasingly affordable memory and processing power led to a wholesale migration of computer music activity to the desktop or laptop platform, broadening its reach and appeal well beyond academia into all genres of music.

This appendix comprises three annotated diagrams tracing the evolution of digital music synthesis technology:

- Figure AII.1: Evolution of Computer Synthesis Software (1957–2011)
- Figure AII.2: Evolution of Digital Synthesizers (1975–2011)
- Figure AII.3: Evolution of Audio Sampling Instruments, Software, and Controllers (1917–2011)

Grouping instruments by related technology in this way provides a means for tracing the historical development of synthesizers as well as acknowledging groundbreaking products. Instruments and programs were chosen for the diagrams based on their significance to an overall continuum of computer music development. They range from the earliest attempts to synthesize sounds using second-generation mainframe computers to fully digital performance instruments and software programs for laptops. The category of Audio Sampling Instruments and Software has a history dating back to analog attempts to provide a means for playing back pre-recorded sounds. For this reason, it makes sense to include such analog devices as the Mellotron in this appendix rather than Appendix I, which traces the evolution of analog synthesizers, because, in principle, early tape-based sampling instruments were not synthesizers and could be viewed as conceptually more closely related to digital samplers.

Each diagram is annotated with additional information about each hardware, software, or computer-based instrument, including the name of the inventor or manufacturer, the name of the instrument (in italics), the year that the instrument was patented, invented, or commercially introduced, a brief note about the technology, and the country of origin.

EVOLUTION OF COMPUTER SYNTHESIS SOFTWARE (1957–2011)

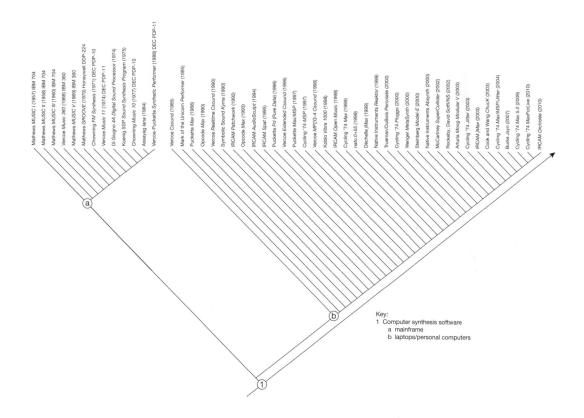

Figure AII.1   Evolution of computer synthesis software (1957–2011).

1   Computer Synthesis Software

(a) Mainframe

- Mathews *MUSIC I* (1957) IBM 704; the first computer synthesis programming language, written in assembly code; *MUSIC I* was developed at Bell Labs by Max Mathews and spawned several improved versions throughout the 1960s, eventually being converted to other programming languages and hardware platforms (United States).
- Mathews *MUSIC II* (1958) IBM 704; revision of *MUSIC I* (United States).
- Mathews *MUSIC III* (1960) IBM 7094; revision of *MUSIC II* and the first music synthesis program written for the third generation of increasingly transistorized IBM computers (United States).
- Vercoe *Music 360* (1968) IBM 360; a modified version of *MUSIC IV* created at MIT and written in *FORTRAN* and *IBM 360* assembly languages (United States).
- Mathews *MUSIC V* (1969) IBM 360; upgrade of earlier versions of *MUSIC* and the first to be completely written in the *FORTRAN*—a machine independent programming language—allowing transferability to other types of computers and the ability of programmers other than Mathews to continue the development of *MUSIC*. *Music 360* by Vercoe and *MUSIC V* by Mathews were widely circulated within the university community and used to compose several hundred works (United States).
- Mathews *GROOVE* (1970) Honeywell DDP-224; early real-time performance computer-based music synthesis system; input and control through computer keyboards, rotary dials, and a joystick; tone generation via twelve 8-bit and two 12-bit digital-to-analog converters; CRT workstation added to permit a composer to create and edit waveforms graphically (United States).
- Chowning *FM Synthesis* (1971) DEC PDP-10; innovative algorithms for digital FM synthesis based on earlier demonstrations by Risset at Bell Labs; algorithms modeled the correlation between the rate of intensity of the attack portion of a tone and the growth of the bandwidth of the signal; Yamaha acquired the patent to produce the DX-7 synthesizer (United States).
- Vercoe *Music 11* (1973) DEC PDP-11; one of the earliest music programming languages developed for a minicomputer and the forerunner of a trend toward machine-independent music programs; the forerunner of *Csound*; used real-time audio processing and synthesis; introduced *control-rate* signals for controlling the shape and motion of vibrato, filets, amplitude, and envelopes (United States).
- Di Giugno *4A Digital Sound Processor* (1974); digital synthesizer developed for IRCAM; design incorporated 256 voices in the form of fixed waveform oscillators and programmable connections for synthesizing circuits; models *4A, 4B, 4C, 4X* produced by 1976 (France).
- Koenig *SSP Sound Synthesis Program* (1975); music software language represented sound as a sequence of amplitudes in time; also utilized earlier routines, *Project 1* (1964) and *Project 2* (1966), which had been written previously to define and organize tones for serial composition (Netherlands).
- Chowning *Music 10* (1977) DEC PDP-10; used FM synthesis and included routines for directing the spatial distribution of sound across four channels (United States).

- Assayag *Iana* (1984); program for aiding in the psychoacoustic analysis of sounds; used to produce data that could be interpreted by other programs for synthesizing tasks (France).
- Vercoe Puckette *Synthetic Performer* (1988) DEC PDP-11 model 55 and Di Giugno *4X* sound processor; software for a minicomputer designed to track the tempo and follow pitches in real time being produced by a live performer, extract musical information from the sounds that it detected, and synthesize a digitally produced part in response the player (France).

(b) Laptops/Personal Computers

- Vercoe *Csound* (1985); early musical programming language written in C language code for minicomputers (United States).
- Mark of the Unicorn *Performer* (1985); early MIDI sequencing, recorder, and playback software for Macintosh computers (United States).
- Puckette *Max* (1988); developed at IRCAM; a graphical programming language for music applications; could be used in real-time performance; ancestor of current versions of *Max/MSP* and *jMax* (France).
- Vercoe *Realtime Csound* (1990); version of *Csound* that added interactive, real-time sensing and interaction with performers, similar in execution to Vercoe's earlier *Synthetic Performer* (United States).
- Opcode *Max* (1990); Opcode *Max* was released using source code licensed from IRCAM; at this point it was a MIDI-only program with no DSP functionality.
- Symbolic Sound *Kyma* (1990); first commercial release version of this proprietary sound design program with a graphical programming language and digital signal processing tools; prototype versions written in 1987 for the Macintosh 512 computer using *Smalltalk* programming language; currently still in production and used by professional sound designers for motion pictures and other media (United States).
- IRCAM *PatchWork* (1992); visual music software program for computer aided composition.
- Opcode *Max* (1993); Opcode *Max 3.0* was released allowing third-party externals, opening up the development of objects by other people.
- IRCAM *AudioSculpt* (1994); visual, spectral audio editor.
- Miller Puckette left IRCAM and went to UCSD (1995); IRCAM began development on *Max/FTS* for the *DEC/Alpha* (software only).
- IRCAM *Spat* (1995); software for concert hall acoustics and spatialization.
- Puckette *Pd* (*Pure Data*) (1996); Miller Puckette released a clean-room rewrite of *Max* as an open-source, software-only platform, with both logic and audio (DSP) capabilities.
- Vercoe *Extended Csound* (1996); alternative architecture for *Csound* utilizing multiprocessors; the central processor host of a microcomputer was used to manage all compiling of instruction code, disk access, the graphical user software interface, sound editing, and sequencing; a second processor in the form of a sound card was tasked with all digitial audio processing (United States).
- Puckette *Max/MSP* (1997); a revision of *Max* that provided extended real-time digital signal processing via the *MSP* module; allowed users to configure and create their own software synthesis and effects using processor modules (France).

- Cycling '74 *MSP* (1997); David Zicarelli founded Cycling '74 and released *MSP*, a set of audio extensions for Opcode's *Max* that used the PowerPC chip for real-time signal processing on the Macintosh computer with no additional hardware; the *MSP* engine and object API were initially based on the *Pd* system developed the previous year by Puckette.
- Vercoe *MPEG-4 Csound* (1998); extended version of *Csound* capable of compiling MPEG-4-compatible audio (United States).
- IRCAM *Open Music* (1998); software for computer-assisted composition.
- Koblo *Vibra 1000* (1998); MIDI-compatible monophonic software synthesizer; one switchable oscillator, filter, and envelope generator; designed for Macintosh (Denmark).
- Cycling '74 *Max* (1999); David Zicarelli and Cycling '74 acquired the *Max* software assets and began work on *Max 4*.
- *nato.0+55* (1999); NATO was released by "Netochka Nezvanova," an anonymous programming team, providing a real-time video framework for *Max 3.5*.
- Déchelle *jMax* (1999); browser-compatible version of *Max* written in *Java*; cross-platform musical programming language (France).
- Native Instruments *Reaktor* (1999); cross-platform software synthesizer and sampler; over 200 preset voice modules; polyphonic; sampler with range of 22 to 132 kHz; FM synthesis and granular synthesis; output to AIFF and WAV audio formats (Germany).
- *Percolate* (2000); Dan Trueman and R. Luke DuBois; an early *Max/MSP* port of synthesis and signal processing routines originally developed for other platforms, namely the *CCRMA Synthesis Toolkit*, *STK* (Perry Cook and Gary Scavone, 1995) and the *Makegen* routines from *RTcmix*. This early work led many other programmers to create their own open-source externals and helped to expand the *Max/MSP/Jitter* platform. This development continues at Columbia University under Brad Garton (b. 1957), who has created externals allowing code from the following software programs to be run inside *Max*: *rtcmix~* for *RTcmix*, *sc3~* for *SuperCollider 3*, *chuck~* for *ChucK*, *maxlispj* and *maxlisp* for different flavors of *CommonLisp*.
- Cycling '74 *Pluggo* (2000); allowed *Max/MSP* patchers to be turned into audio plug-ins for digital audio workstation software made by various companies.
- Wenger *MetaSynth* (2000); software sound design and audio processing environment with graphical editing system; envelope controllable digital sound processing; effects processor; modification of sound samples; sequencer; image filter converts drawable screen art into sound processing elements (France).
- Steinberg *Model-E* (2000); plug-in software synthesizer emulation of Moog Minimoog (Germany).
- Native Instruments *Absynth* (2000); semi-modular cross-platform entry-level software synthesizer; 86-note virtual keyboard; three oscillators; filters, envelopes, drawable waveforms, ring modulator, and delay (Germany).
- McCartney *SuperCollider* (2002); musical programming language for real-time audio synthesis; multiplatform; open-source code; considered somewhat easier to learn than *Max*; provides graphical user interface; large library of synthesis and audio processing functions (United States).
- Rokeby, David *SoftVNS* (2002); another real-time video object set for *Max*.

- Arturia *Moog Modular V* (2003); virtual version of the Moog Modular synthesizer; graphical user interface included moveable virtual patch cords (France).
- Cycling '74 *Jitter* (2003); a set of objects for video, 3D and matrix processing.
- IRCAM *jMax* (2003); IRCAM halted development of *jMax* and focused its real-time research on developing extensions for the commercial Cycling '74 version of *Max*.
- Cook and Wang *ChucK* (2003); Perry Cook and Ge Wang's free software for the analysis of concurrent programming.
- Cycling '74 *Max/MSP/Jitter* (2004); ported to the Windows platform.
- Burke *Jsyn* (2007); Phil Burke's audio API for Java; software to develop interactive computer music programs that could run as standalone programs or applets on a web page.
- Cycling '74 *Max 5.0* (2009); became a monolithic product (*MSP* and *Jitter* were included in all versions); the software featured a rewritten interface.
- Cycling '74 *MaxForLive* (2010); allowed for the embedding of *Max* patchers as "devices" within Ableton *Live*.
- IRCAM *Orchidée* (2010); computer-aided orchestration software designed for the orchestration of speech sound by an instrumental ensemble.

EVOLUTION OF DIGITAL SYNTHESIZERS (1975–2011)

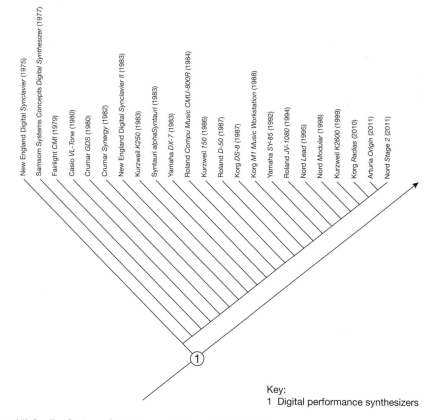

Figure AII.2   Evolution of digital synthesizers (1975–2011).

1 Digital Performance Synthesizers

- New England Digital *Synclavier I* (1975); early high-end turnkey fully digital performance instrument; polyphonic (64-note); 6-octave velocity- and touch-sensitive keyboard; 8-bit FM and additive synthesis; sampling component with 16-bit, 100 kHz samples up to 32 MB in size; on-board 16-track recorder; 32-track sequencer; push-button console and preset voices (United States).
- Samson Systems Concepts *Digital Synthesizer* (1977); the Samson Box, as it was known, was at the heart of the computer music department at Stanford for ten years; 256 waveform generators; amplitude and frequency modulation; delay; random-number generator; programmable wavetables; 4-channel output; highly programmable for many musical applications; not a commercial product (United States).
- Fairlight *CMI* (1979); high-end, 16-note polyphonic synthesizer; 6-octave, velocity-sensitive keyboard; dual keyboard option; Fast Fourier Transforming synthesis; waveform editing; graphical user interface for drawing waveforms on a monitor; rhythm sequencer; 80-track polyphonic sequencer; music composition language; 16-bit sampler with sample rates variable up to 100 kHz (Australia).
- Casio *VL-Tone* (1980); inexpensive and one of the first digital synthesizers, although largely a novelty item combining a calculator with a small 29-note keyboard, regarded as a toy; one oscillator; vibrato and tremolo; 5 preset voices; 10 preset rhythms; keyboard was switchable to 3 octave ranges (Japan).
- Crumar *GDS* (1980); highly programmable digital synthesizer; 32 oscillators; 16-bit digital sound; 5-octave velocity-sensitive keyboard; video monitor and control panel; sequencer; noted for the usefulness of its software for designing instrumental voices (United States).
- Crumar *Synergy* (1982); moderately priced preset version of the GDS system comprised of a single unit with 6-octave velocity-sensitive keyboard; not directly programmable; keyboard splittable into 4 sounds; joystick and pitchbend controls; 24 internal patches; additional patches could be used via an add-in cartridge; keyboard could be programmed for microtonal scales (United States).
- New England Digital *Synclavier II* (1983); expanded version of the Synclavier I with a video monitor for editing waveforms and the first 16-bit sample-to-disk option for making monophonic samples; 200-track sequencer; permitted the re-synthesis of sampled sounds (United States).
- Kurzweil *K250* (1983); ROM-based digital sampling keyboard that successfully emulated the sounds of the grand piano, orchestral instruments, choirs, and percussion; designed for live performance; 7-octave touch-sensitive keyboard; 12-note polyphonic; additional sounds could be sampled at 50,000 kHz; 12-track sequencer; could also be connected to a personal computer for sound modeling and the development of MIDI-based scores (United States).
- Syntauri *alphaSyntauri* (1983); low-end sound card, software, and 4- or 5-octave velocity-sensitive keyboard for the Apple II Plus personal computer; 15-note polyphony; 3,000-note disk recorder; vibrato, tremolo, and transposition; looping; sustain and portamento (United States).
- Yamaha *DX-7* (1983); moderately priced 16-note polyphonic synthesizer; 5-octave velocity-sensitive keyboard; 16-bit FM synthesis; 32-patch memory; MIDI-compatible (Japan).

- Roland *Compu Music CMU-800R* (1984); low-end polyphonic 4-note digital slave synthesizer (no keyboard); controlled by an Apple II computer; rudimentary voice and percussion sounds (Japan).
- Kurzweil *150* (1986); keyboardless slave digital synth; 240 oscillators; 256-stage programmable envelopes; up to 255 patches; MIDI-compatible (United States).
- Roland *D-50* (1987); 16-note polyphonic synth; 5-octave velocity-sensitive keyboard; 32 oscillators (Japan).
- Korg *DS-8* (1987); 8-note polyphonic; FM synthesis; 5-octave velocity-sensitive keyboard; 2 oscillators; joystick; 100 user-programmable patches; delay, flanger, and chorus module (Japan).
- Korg *M1 Music Workstation* (1988); 16-note poplyphonic synthesizer using sampled and wavetable waveforms; 5-octave velocity-sensitive keyboard; reverb, delay, overdrive, and rotating speaker effects; MIDI-compatible (Japan).
- Yamaha *SY-85* (1992); 32-note polyphonic using digitally sampled instruments; 5-octave velocity-sensitive keyboard (Japan).
- Roland *JV-1080* (1994); 64-note polyphonic slave synthesizer (no keyboard); 16-part multitimbral synthesis; 4 expansion slots for adding voices; MIDI-compatible (Japan).
- Nord *Lead* (1995); early virtual analog keyboard using waveform models of classic analog synthesizer sounds; led to line of virtual analog synthesizers that remains popular (Sweden).
- Nord *Modular* (1998); modeled the audio processing of classic analog modular synthesizers; maximum 32 voices; with or without keyboard; knobs and function keys used to program the voices and DSP functions (Sweden).
- Kurzweil *K2600* (1999); high-end digital performance synthesizer; 6-octave velocity-sensitive keyboard; 238 present memory patches plus 200 user-programmable patches; 32-track sequencer; 60 DSP functions (United States).
- Korg *Radias Rack Synthesizer* (2010); an old-style rack synth using digital routing instead of patch cords.
- Arturia *Origin* (2011); synthesizer/workstation providing the ability to mix and match virtual oscillators, filters, and other components from instruments such as the Minimoog, ARP 2600, Jupiter 8, and more.
- Korg *Kronos* (2011); a major workstation with nine different synth engines and 88-, 73-, or 61-note piano-action keyboards; additional performance controls include a joystick and full-color 8-inch touchscreen.
- Nord *Stage 2* (2011); includes patches from their piano, organ and synthesizer lines with fully weighted, 76-note and 88-note keyboards.

EVOLUTION OF AUDIO SAMPLING INSTRUMENTS, SOFTWARE, AND CONTROLLERS (1917–2011)

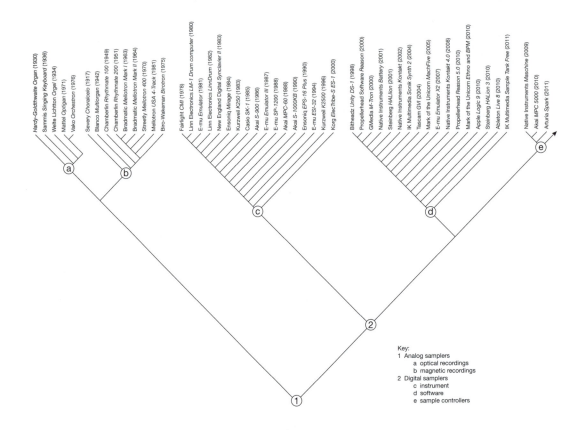

Figure AII.3 Evolution of audio sampling instruments, software, and controllers (1917–2011).

1 Analog Samplers

(a) Optical Recordings

- *Hardy–Goldthwaite Organ* (1930); used photoelectric recordings on disk converted from the recorded sounds of actual instruments; pitch range of 71 notes (United States).
- Sammis *Singing Keyboard* (1936); played samples of instrumental sounds recorded optically onto film strips (United States).
- *Welte Lichtton Orgel* (1934); played disk recordings of pipe organs (Germany).
- Mattel *Optigan* (1971); "OPTIcal orGAN," produced by toy maker Mattel; used optically recorded sounds of actual instruments stored on 12-inch discs; 3-octave keyboard; chord buttons; rhythm machine; spring reverb; 37 voice tracks per disc; built-in loudspeaker (United States).

- Vako *Orchestron* (1976); professional version of the Optigan; lacked the chord buttons of the Optigan in favor or providing more instrumental voice tracks per disk (57 voices) (United States).

(b) Magnetic Recordings

- Severy *Choralcelo* (1917); in the patent for the Choralcelo, the inventor suggested that magnetic disk recordings of the human voice could be added to the instrument and played through the use of the keyboard (United States).
- Blanco *Multiorgan* (1942); this instrument was conceived to use magnetically recorded wire loops but was not built (Cuba).
- Chamberlin *Rhythmate 100* (1949); used 14 tape loops of percussion sounds; an early drum machine; no keyboard (United States).
- Chamberlin *Rhythmate 200* (1951); expanded version of the Rhythmate 100 included two 3-octave keyboards side by side (one for melody, one for rhythm and fill accompaniment) and the recorded sounds of flutes, vibraphones, and violins in addition to drum sounds; used ¼-inch full track magnetic tape; the ancestor of the Mellotron (United States).
- Bradmatic *Mellotron Mark I* (1963); descendant of the Chamberlin Rhythmate 200; two 3-octave keyboards, side by side as in the Rhythmate 200; 3-track ⅜-inch magnetic tapes; vacuum tube amplifier (England).
- Bradmatic *Mellotron Mark II* (1964); upgrade of Mark I model; 18 of the rhythm and fill sounds from the left keyboard were replaced with individual lead sounds, providing more instrumental sounds; tube amplifier replaced with transistorized amplifier; volume, varispeed, and spring reverb controls; the first successful Mellotron and the one most commonly heard on classic recordings by The Beatles, the Moody Blues, and the Rolling Stones, among others (England).
- Streetly *Mellotron 400* (1970); simpler and more reliable instrument; one 3-octave keyboard; tapes were easily swapped out; wide variety of recorded sounds including full orchestra, jazz instruments, organ, honkytonk piano, Clavinet, Rhodes, vibes, marimba, Minimoog, VCS3, electric and acoustic guitars, mandolin, and small and large choirs (England).
- Mellotron USA *4-Track* (1981); 4-track instrument using ¼-inch tape; tone controls; 4 separate amplifiers and line output jacks for the 4 tracks (United States).
- Biro–Wakeman *Birotron* (1975); developed by David Biro and funded by Rick Wakeman (of Yes); used 8-track tapes; 3-octave keyboard; sounds included strings, choirs, brass, and flutes; only 17 to 35 units were made and sold (England).

2 Digital Samplers

(c) Instruments

- Fairlight *CMI* (1978); high-end, early digital sampling keyboard; 6-octave, velocity-sensitive keyboard; dual keyboard option; 16-bit sampler with sample rates variable up to 100 kHz (Australia).
- Linn Electronics *LM-1 Drum Computer* (1980); the ancestor of modern drum machines; used samples of acoustic drum sounds; twelve 28 kHz samples including snare, kick, three toms, hi-hats, tambourine, congas, claps, cowbell, and rimshot;

100 memory patches; no keyboard; 12-voice polyphonic; popularized the step-time creation of patterns; quantize function (United States).

- E-mu *Emulator* (1981); classic, moderately high-priced keyboard sampling instrument; 4-octave keyboard; 8-bit, 27 kHz sampler for sounds up to 2 seconds long; 8-note polyphonic; vibrato; floppy-disk initialized; MIDI and sequencer added to later models (United States).

- Linn Electronics *LinnDrum* (1982); upgraded LM-1 with crash and ride cymbal sounds added; 42 preset patterns; 56 user-programmable patterns; no keyboard; 28 to 35 kHz sample rate; 12-voice polyphonic; no MIDI (United States).

- New England Digital *Synclavier II* (1983); expanded version of the Synclavier I digital synthesizer; 16-bit, 100 kHz selectable sampling rate (maximum 32 MB of sample storage) ; the first 16-bit sample-to-disk option for making monophonic samples; 200-track sequencer; permitted the re-synthesis of sampled sounds (United States).

- Ensoniq *Mirage* (1984); low-priced digital sampling keyboard; diskette initialized; and 8-bit, 32 kHz sampling rate; 5-octave, 8-note polyphonic keyboard; sample time of 6.5 seconds; split keyboard; samples loaded by diskette; editing via keypad on console; 333-note sequencer; MIDI compatible (United States).

- Kurzweil *K250* (1983); high-end early keyboard sampler; 7-octave, 12-voice polyphonic keyboard; 16-bit samples of 1 to 4 MB; 12,000-note, 12-track sequencer; 96 preset voices; chorus, transpose (United States).

- Casio *SK-1* (1985); inexpensive, toy 4-octave digital sampling keyboard; 8-bit, 9.38 kHz sampler (maximum 1.4 seconds); 4-note polyphonic mini-keyboard (Japan).

- Akai *S-900* (1986); early rack-mounted professional sampler; 12-bit stereo sampling, 7.5 to 40 kHz variable sampling rates (maximum 63 seconds; storage of 32 samples to disk; 8-note polyphonic (Japan).

- E-mu *Emulator III* (1987); 16-note, polyphonic digital audio workstation; first sampler to provide CD-quality samples; 16-track sequencer; 5-octave keyboard; MIDI (United States).

- E-mu *SP-1200* (1988); 8-note polyphonic sampler and drum machine; had 8 touch-pads instead of a keyboard; 12-bit , up to 22 kHz sampler (maximum 42.5 seconds); popular with rap, DJ, and hip-hop artists (United States).

- Akai *MPC-60* (1988); 16-note polyphonic sampler; 12-bit, 40 kHz; stereo; drum machine; 16 touchpad controllers; 60,000-note capacity sequencer; MIDI; popular with rap, DJ, and hip-hop musicians (Japan).

- Akai *S-1000KB* (1990); 16-note polyphonic sampler; 5-octave keyboard; 16-bit, up to 44.1 kHz, sampler (maximum 47.4 seconds); MIDI (Japan).

- Ensoniq *EPS-16 Plus* (1990); up to 20-note polyphonic monophonic sampler; 16-bit, 11.2 to 44.6 kHz sampler (maximum 11.5 seconds); 5-octave keyboard; filters; MIDI (United States).

- E-mu *ESI-32* (1994); rack-mounted, 32-note polyphonic sampler; 16-bit, 22 to 44.1 kHz sampler (maximum 11 seconds); reverb, delay, chorus, and other effects; filters and MIDI (United States).

- Kurzweil *K2500* (1996); moderately high-end 48-note polyphonic (24-note stereo) sampler, keyboard workstation; 6-octave keyboard; 32-track sequencer; 238 preset patches; 200 user-programmable patches; 60 DSP functions; MIDI (United States).

- Korg *ElecTribe-S ES-1* (2000); low-end tabletop module with 12-note polyphony; 32 kHz sampler (maximum 95 seconds); storage for 100 monophonic or 50 stereo samples; 11 effects modules; 16 touchpad controllers; MIDI (Japan).

(d) Software

- Bitheadz *Unity DS-1* (1998); 64-note polyphonic sampler and instrument; 16-bit, 44.1 kHz sampler; DSP functions (United States).
- Propellerhead Software *Reason* (2000); up to 99-note polyphonic sampler and synthesizer; sample player; drum machine (Sweden).
- GMedia *M-Tron* (2000); fully polyphonic software plug-in and virtual Mellotron; 28 classic Mellotron tape banks including strings, choirs, flutes, brass, and some rhythms; 3-octave on-screen keyboard; 16-bit samples of actual Mellotron tapes (England).
- Native Instruments *Battery* (2001); 128-note polyphonic sample player and drum machine; 32-bit samples and a graphical matrix interface to program sequences; looping and reverse; extensive drum library (Germany).
- Steinberg *HALion* (2001); 256-note polyphonic sample player, recorder, and editor; 32-bit samples; 12 modulation sources; tuning, octave shift, glides, LFOs, and sample quality; filters; envelope editor; scrollable virtual keyboard (Germany).
- Native Instruments *Kontakt* (2002); 256-note polyphonic sample player, recorder, and editor; virtual 10-octave keyboard; extensive effects banks; library of sampled sounds; editing of source samples (Germany).
- IK Multimedia *Sonik Synth 2* (2004); 256-note polyphonic sample player and synthesizer; ability to combine samples with synthesizer voices to create combination voices; filters and envelopes; 80 effects (Italy).
- *Tascam GVI* (2004); professional, fully polyphonic sample player; 24-bit , 96 kHz sampler; multisampling of instrument sounds (Japan).
- Mark of the Unicorn *MachFive* (2005); fully polyphonic sample player, recorder, and editor; 24-bit, 192 kHz sampler; samples, loops, synthesis, and effects; 200 discrete audio outputs; graphical mixer; multipoint envelope editing; multisampled instrument samples (United States).
- E-mu *Emulator X2* (2007); fully polyphonic sample recorder, player, editor, and synthesizer; 24-bit, 192 kHz sampler; fully editable samples; synthesis features; filters, envelopes (United States).
- Native Instruments *Kontakt 4.0* (2008); still one of the most popular professional software samplers (Germany).
- Propellerhead *Reason 5.0* (2010); this digital audio workstation included the NN-19 Digital Sampler and the NN-XT Advanced Sampler (Sweden).
- Mark of the Unicorn *Ethno* and *BPM* (2010); *Digital Performer 7.0's* two high-performance drum samplers (United States).
- Apple *Logic 9* (2010); this digital audio workstation included the EXS-24 Sampler (United States).
- Steinberg *HALion 3* (2010); Steinberg's VST-sampler, originally released in 2001, *HALion* is known for its ability to load almost any sample set (Germany).
- Ableton *Live 8* (2010); music production software; Ableton's software sampler is called *Sampler* (Germany).
- IK Multimedia *SampleTank Free* (2011); a fully featured version of *SampleTank 2.5* available for free download (Italy).

(e) Sample Controllers

- Native Instruments *Maschine* (2009); hands-on hardware drum controller for Native Instruments' drum sample sets (Germany).
- Akai *MPC5000* (2010); the popular Akai *MPC* line continues to be updated regularly (Japan).
- Arturia *Spark* (2011); an analog-style drum machine with pads, dials, wheels and a library of Arturia drum samples (France).

Glossary

12-tone music *see* **twelve-tone music**

acousmatic   A style of electronic music generally considered synonymous with the term *musique concrète*; the term was coined by French composer Pierre Schaeffer as an alternative term for tape music—*acousmatique*; the term was originally preferred by composers who wanted to avoid being associated with earlier debates over terminology.

ADC *see* **analog-to-digital converter**

additive synthesis   The creation of complex waveforms through the combination of two or more individual waveforms; relies on the principle from Fourier theory that a periodic sound is composed of a fundamental frequency, which is dominant, and partials that have a mathematically harmonious relationship to the fundamental.

ADSR   Abbreviation for the envelope characteristics of a waveform: attack, decay, sustain, and release.

Advanced Audio Coding (AAC)   A commercial codec for compressing music files; used by Apple.

ambient dub   Musical style combining the layering techniques of Jamaican sound artists and fusing them with elements of world music, drum and bass, and electronica.

ambient music   Musical style consisting of electronic textures, often dominated by sustained harmonies rather than beats, played quietly with a continuity of energy that conveys a suspension of tension.

amplitude   The loudness or volume of a sound and its constituent harmonics; the strength of an audio waveform signal during synthesis, as represented graphically by wave height.

amplitude modulation (AM)   In analog synthesis, the use of a control voltage to alter (modulate) the loudness of another signal.

analog   The use of signals or information represented by a continuously variable physical property or quantity, such as a voltage or spatial configuration.

analog-to-digital converter (ADC)   In digital audio sampling, a device used to convert analog sound to digital form by sampling the analog signal many times per second and storing it as numeric values. The resulting values can be played using a digital-to-analog converter (DAC) that reverses the process, reading the digital values sequentially, smoothing them out into a continuous analog signal again, which is made audible through an amplifier and loudspeaker.

atonal music   Music composed using a method such as the 12-tone system, lacking a tonal center or familiar chord patterns, emphasizing the importance of individual notes.

attack   In relation to the envelope of a sound, the start of a sound as defined by the time that it takes for the signal to go from zero amplitude to peak amplitude.

audio development environment   Digital audio processing tools allowing the customization and programming of audio processing and control functions for making music; *Max/MSP* is an audio development environment.

band-pass filter   An audio filter that allows only those sounds between specified high- and low-frequency cutoff points to be heard. It removes the high and low frequencies from a signal at the same time.

band-reject filter   An audio filter that allows only those sounds above or below specified high- and low-frequency cutoff points to be heard. It removes the midrange frequencies from a signal.

blue noise   A subset of white noise containing all frequencies between 10,000 Hz and 22,000 Hz.

capstan   In relation to tape recorders, a tiny rotating, motor-driven spindle that pinches the tape against a rubber roller and pulls it from the supply reel to the take-up reel; changing the diameter of the capstan alters the transport speed.

chance operations   In musical composition, an approach developed by John Cage who also described many of his compositions as being *indeterminate* of their performance; a composition process dictated by chance operations in which the score is created using a system for making chance decisions about notes, duration, amplitude, timbre, and other possible dynamics.

channel message   In a MIDI performance setup, a signal that directs a MIDI command to any one of the 16 available channels.

codec   A compression/decompression algorithm.

computer music   A style of electronic music created with the aid of computers for composing, audio production, performance, or all of these.

condenser microphone   A type of microphone using a diaphragm paired to a parallel metal plate to form a capacitor—an electrical device that can store energy between two such associated plates; when vibrations cause the diaphragm to fluctuate, changes in the static charges of the two plates are translated into a corresponding electric that has a wave shape analogous to the incoming sound; also known as a capacitor/electrostatic microphone.

contact microphone   A type of microphone that operates by transducing vibrations from a solid surface rather than by converting sound vibrations detected in the air; the contact microphone, also called a pickup, is in close proximity to, or in direct contact with, the solid surface that is the source of the vibrations; a variation is the magnetic pickup that converts the vibrations into an electric signal, as with a guitar pickup or phono cartridge.

cutoff frequency   In audio filtering, the point at which a filter begins to omit a prescribed frequency range.

cycle   In waveform analysis, a single vibration of a frequency; a unit of waveform measurement from the equilibrium point to its apex, back through the equilibrium point to its base point and back again to the equilibrium point.

decay   In relation to the envelope of a sound, the second stage of a sound as defined by the time it takes for the signal to go from its peak amplitude to its sustain amplitude.

digital audio workstation   A combination of computer hardware and software used to record, edit, and synchronize multiple tracks of music input. Other software-based features may include audio editing and effects processing. Digidesign *Pro Tools* operating on a laptop is an example of a digital audio workstation.

digital-to-analog converter (DAC)   In digital audio sampling, a device used to convert digitally stored sounds that were captured using an analog-to-digital converter; the DAC reads the digital values sequentially, smoothing them out into a continuous analog signal again, which is made audible through an amplifier and loudspeaker.

displacement   In waveform analysis, the distance from the apex (highest amplitude) to the base (lowest amplitude) of a waveform.

dissonance   Exhibiting a lack of harmony among musical notes.

duration   The length of time that a sound is audible, a factor that can be controlled via the envelope generator of a synthesized sound.

duty cycle   In waveform analysis, the ratio denoting the proportion of a single cycle that occurs above the equilibrium point versus time below the equilibrium point.

dynamic microphone   A type of microphone using a diaphragm affixed to a coil within a magnetic field; minute fluctuations of the diaphragm respond to sound vibrations to create corresponding fluctuations in the magnetic field that are then converted to a weak electric current that has a wave shape analogous to the incoming sound; also known as an electromagnetic microphone.

echo   In regard to audio signal processing, a form of reverberation in which the individual sound reflections, rather than being compressed into a short lapse of time, are spaced by 50 milliseconds or more, at which point they can be perceived individually.

electroacoustic   A style of electronic music for which the primary content consists of electronically modified acoustic sounds; electroacoustic techniques vary widely from working with the manipulation of previously recorded sounds to the treatment and modification of instrumental sounds in real time; the term is often used synonymously with electronic music.

electro-mechanical   An electrically powered, analog mechanical device, e.g. an electronic organ or piano.

electronica   A contemporary style of electronic music that generally refers to popular music relying heavily on electronic sonorities, beats, and sound manipulations; electronica may stand alone as a purely electronic form of music, or its elements may be combined with those of rock and pop bands and vocalists.

electronic music   A broad term encompassing any form of music that incorporates largely electronic elements, whether originating as acoustic source material or purely electronic tones.

elektronische Musik   A historic style of electronic music developed in Germany that was comprised entirely of electronically generated sounds.

envelope   The attack, decay, sustain, and release characteristics of a waveform; the shape of a waveform as determined by its changing amplitude characteristics.

envelope generator (ENV)   In sound synthesis, a special-purpose amplitude controller dedicated to shaping the four stages of a sound's evolution: attack, decay, sustain, and release.

equalizer   An audio filter, generally with preset band settings, for adjusting the amount of bass, midrange, and treble frequencies that will be heard from a sound source, such as a recorded tape or live feed.

equilibrium point   In waveform analysis, the midpoint of a wave's propagation, denoted as point 0.

feedback   An electroacoustic phenomenon that occurs when an audio signal is amplified and re-amplified within a circuit consisting of a microphone or magnetic pickup and a loudspeaker; e.g., when a microphone is placed too close to a loudspeaker, the audio signal created by the microphone is fed back into the microphone when the sound is projected by the loudspeaker.

feedback circuit   A type of audio signal feedback that is based on regenerative electronic audio signals rather than acoustic feedback; a feedback circuit permits signals generated within an electronic instrument to recirculate within a closed circuit—taking the output back into the input—prior to its amplification in the listening space.

Fibonacci series   A numeric sequence in which each new value in a series is simply the sum of the two before it; a mathematical series often used in music composition.

filter   In sound synthesis, a specialized amplifier that controls the amount of gain to prescribed frequency ranges of a sound; making such adjustments changes the balance of harmonics found in the source sound signal.

force-sensitive keyboard   An attribute of an electronic keyboard controller that can respond to the length of time that a key is depressed, which affects how long a note is sustained; also known as pressure sensitivity.

Fourier analysis   Theory of waveform physics stating that any periodic vibration (waveform), however complex, is comprised of, or can be created by combining, a series of simple vibrations whose frequencies are harmonically related.

frequency   The pitch of a sound; specifically, the number of vibrations per second that, when in the audible range, are detected as a certain pitch; frequency is measured by the number of vibrations, or cycles, per second, and expressed as a measure of hertz (Hz).

frequency modulation (FM)   In analog synthesis, the use of a control voltage to alter the frequency (pitch) of an audio signal.

frequency shifter   An audio signal processor that takes a designated waveform frequency and through a process of frequency division and multiplication adds harmonics to produce a modified waveform, e.g. converting a sine tone into a sawtooth tone composed of all even and odd harmonics; also known as an octaver.

full-track   In relation to tape recorders, a monophonic recorder capable of recording only one track in one direction across the entire width of the magnetic tape.

fundamental   In waveform analysis, the base, or carrier portion, of a given tone.

Futurist music   Futurism was a European art movement, originating in Italy in 1912, that consisted of a small coalition of artists, poets, composers, and writers who were fascinated with the machine age and new technology; Futurist music was produced using acoustic noise-making machines, a foreshadowing of industrial noise music and electronic music incorporating acoustic sounds.

gain   The amount of voltage or power that an amplifier provides to increase the strength of an electrical signal; the audible effect is an increase in volume.

General MIDI *see* **MIDI (Musical Instrument Digital Interface)**

gestural controller   An electronic musical interface, generally employing MIDI, providing musical expression and artistic control through the use of devices other than a keyboard, e.g. through hand and arm movements, facial expressions, and other forms of body motion.

Gramophone   A nineteenth-century mechanical audio recording and playback device that inscribed a recording of sound onto a rotating disc by means of a metallic needle or other stylus; discs were made of metal, glass, shellac, or vinyl; the term Phonograph later replaced the term Gramophone in popular usage.

granular synthesis   Method of computer synthesis that uses small overlapping *grains* of sound, typically lasting no more than 50 microseconds each, to build a piece of music.

graphic score   An electronic music score providing a detailed visual representation of the form and substance of a work to a degree of specificity that could be faithfully reproduced by others; in a graphic score, symbols other than those used in traditional musical notation are often used to specify musical elements.

half-track stereo   In relation to tape recorders, the ability to record two tracks in one direction across the full width of magnetic recording tape, permitting two-channel stereo recording.

hardware controller   A device with tactile controls for triggering and manipulating the sounds generated by an electronic music instrument or computer; keyboard control pads are examples of hardware controllers.

hardwired   Term used to describe analog technology, typically consisting of permanent electronic circuits that are designed with a single purpose in mind.

harmonics   In waveform analysis, the lesser frequencies above the fundamental tone of a waveform; harmonics create the timbre of an instrumental voice.

harmonic spectrum   The mixture of harmonics associated with a given instrument, giving it a unique timbral voice distinguishable from other instruments.

hertz (Hz)   In waveform analysis, a measurement for cycles per second.

heterodyning   A phenomenon of electromagnetic waves that occurs when two ultrasonic signals of nearly equal frequency are mixed; the combination of the two results in a third signal that is equal to the difference between the first two frequencies; the resulting signal is also called the beat frequency; this phenomenon was the basic for generating tones in several early electronic music instruments, including the Audion Piano, Theremin, and *Ondes Martenot*.

high-pass filter   An audio filter that allows only frequencies above a specified cutoff point to be passed. It removes the low frequencies from a signal.

industrial ambient   Musical style consisting of modified mechanical noises, drones, and auditory science experiments.

instructional composition   An electronic work realized by following written instructions that are not specific to any particular sound source, and only provide a verbal framework for completing the work.

interpolation   An abrupt change in the elements of a piece of music, which can be facilitated and managed using wavetable synthesis.

joystick   A synthesizer controller combining the functions of the pitchbending and modulation wheels.

Klangfarbenmelodie   In musical composition, distributing a melody among several instruments.

latency   The lag in response time experienced when a computer is performing signal processing.

leader tape   In relation to tape recorders, the non-magnetic protective tape at the beginning or end of a reel; it can be used to insert silence into a tape composition.

listening score   A visual aid for studying the structure and form of a piece of electronic music, typically representing the flow and structure of a work using graphics.

lock groove   In turntablism, a closed, rather than continuous groove in a recorded disc that repeats the same audio track with each revolution of the disc.

looping   (1) The repeated playback of the same passage of recorded sound, as with a tape loop; a loop repeats without any loss of fidelity; (2) a feature used by a programmable sequencer to repeat a preset sequence of notes for as long as desired, a technique typically used in analog synthesis to form the underlying chord pattern or rhythm of a piece of music.

low-frequency oscillator (LFO)   In sound synthesis, an oscillator circuit restricted to subsonic frequencies and used for the modulation of other voltage-controlled modules; it is not used as an audible signal but as a control signal for other components.

low-pass filter   An audio filter that allows only frequencies below a specified cutoff point to be passed. It removes the high frequencies from a signal.

magnetic pickup *see* **pickup**

magnetic tape   Audio recording medium comprised of thin plastic tape coated with magnetic (iron oxide) powder.

master unit   In a MIDI performance setup, the instrument or controller that manages the signals and satellite instruments (slave units).

microtonal   Music composed using note intervals smaller than the conventional Western semitone; microtonal music can be facilitated by programmable electronic music instrumentation or software.

MIDI (Musical Instrument Digital Interface)   A standardized industry specification for a communication messaging protocol that connects musical instruments, computers and associated devices and an interface standard for making the physical connection between these devices; MIDI is used to communicate performance information to and from musical instruments.

modular synthesizer   A synthesizer intended for studio use rather than live performance, featuring a set of modular audio-generation and processing components that can be expanded to meet the needs of the musician.

modulation   The use of one electronic signal to modify another, such as the output of an LFO changing an oscillator's frequency; changes in pitch, amplitude, and timbre can all be controlled using modulation.

modulation wheel   An expressive control found on a synthesizer keyboard used to modify the pitch, amplitude, or frequency range of a waveform; commonly used to create a vibrato effect; originally associated with voltage-controlled synthesizers.

monophonic   Capable of producing only one note at a time; a term usually applied to first-generation analog synthesizers which, in practice, could output only one control voltage at a time, conventionally the lowest key to be depressed on the keyboard at any given moment.

multisampling Individually sampling every note of an acoustic instrument that will be reproduced, as digital samples, on a piano-style keyboard; the most accurate method of reproducing an instrument's individual note timbres.

multitracking In relation to the tape recorder, using more than one recording track or channel to combine multiple sounds across the same span of recorded time; tape recorders equipped with multiple track recording capability; synthesizer programming technique providing control and playback of more than one instrumental voice at the same time.

musical programming language A computer programming language dedicated to the control and synthesis of sound.

Musical Telegraph A category of nineteenth-century experiments in electrically produced musical sounds using the clicking sounds inherent in the sending of telegraph messages.

musique concrète A historic style of electronic music developed in France, describing a work conceived with a recording medium in mind that was composed directly on a given medium (e.g. disc or magnetic tape) and played through the medium as a finished work.

noise reduction In analog audio, circuitry used to reduce extraneous noise or hiss during recording or playback.

note sampling The use of a short digital sample, such as a single musical note played on an acoustic instrument, that can then be used to programmatically extrapolate additional notes, such as control points across a piano-style keyboard. *See also* **multisampling**.

Nyquist sampling theorem A mathematical model providing guidelines for the creation of the most accurate digital samples; the theorem states that a sound may be adequately recorded digitally only if it is sampled at a frequency at least twice that of the highest desired frequency present in that sound.

objet sonore, l' **(the sound object)** French term associated with *musique concrète*, indicating the characteristics of sound material that could be objectified and defined by the three dimensions of amplitude, frequency, and time, and which might fall outside of what was normally considered musical or harmonic (noise); a sound that exists apart from human perception.

octaver *see* **frequency shifter**

organized sound Varèse's general term for his musical compositions, whether they were electronic or instrumental; generally understood to be the creation of music intended for a concert hall or other public performance.

oscillator An electronic sound-generating circuit.

perceptual audio coding A data compression algorithm that permanently removes theoretically inaudible components of audio signals.

performance synthesizer A compact synthesizer designed with a keyboard and preset audio settings; intended for live performance situations.

period In waveform analysis, the length of time required for a wave to complete one cycle from the equilibrium point to its apex, back through the equilibrium point to its base point, and back again to the equilibrium point.

phase   In waveform analysis, the displacement relationship between two identical signals; the signals are said to be in phase if they occupy the same space and time in the conducting medium; if two identical waves are displaced slightly in the same conducting medium, e.g. one beginning before the other, they are said to be out of phase.

Phonograph   A nineteenth-century mechanical audio recording and playback device that inscribed a recording of sound onto a rotating cylinder, covered with tin foil or wax, by means of a metallic needle or other stylus; the term Phonograph was eventually used to refer to disc recording and playback machines, originally called Gramophones.

photoelectric   Sound generation by beaming a light through the slits of a rotating disc onto a photoelectric cell. The rotation speed of the disc and the distance between the equidistant slits produced a prescribed frequency, or signal. The photoelectric cell converted the light signal into an electrical impulse equivalent to a musical tone and triggered a vacuum tube oscillator to produce an audible note.

physical modeling   The computer synthesis of sound waves and harmonics that closely resemble those of an acoustic sound source, such as a musical instrument.

pickup   A type of contact microphone positioned in close proximity to, or in direct contact with, the solid surface that is the source of the vibrations; a magnetic field in the pickup converts the vibrations into an electric signal, as with a guitar pickup or phono cartridge.

pink noise   A subset of white noise containing all frequencies between 18 Hz and 10,000 Hz.

pitchbender wheel   An expressive control found on a synthesizer keyboard, the pitchbender wheel allows the performer to slide a note up or down, gliding the frequency smoothly between pitches; originally associated with voltage-controlled synthesizers.

polyphonic   Capable of playing two or more notes at a time; a term usually applied to the second generation of analog synthesizers, which could play two or more notes depressed on the keyboard at the same time.

portamento   An electronic keyboard effect producing a sliding transition from one note, or frequency, to another, across the span of notes being played from the lowest to highest, or in reverse; the effect is typically triggered by playing two notes on a keyboard, the first to define the starting point and the second to define the ending point; the rate, or speed, of portamento is usually assignable by the musician.

pressure-sensitive keyboard *see* **force-sensitive keyboard**

process music   A composition method in which the process of creating the music is an analog for the music itself; minimalist music often includes elements of process music.

pulse wave   A type of basic waveform containing only the odd harmonics of the fundamental frequency, but having a sharp duty cycle that instantly jumps from the apex to the base, creating a sharp sound; also called a rectangular wave. *See also* **square wave**.

pulse width modulation (PWM)   In audio signal processing, modulation of the duty cycle (pulse width) of a waveform by a low-frequency oscillator to create subtle modifications of the harmonic spectra associated with a pulse wave.

Q factor In audio filters, a variable regeneration or resonance control that changes the perceptible sharpness of the filtered sound; often found as a control associated with low-pass and band-pass filters.

quantizing A feature used by a programmable sequencer to correct and align manually played notes to the nearest beat in a preset tempo.

radiophonic British term referring to electronic sound effects and music for radio and television programming. The composition techniques closely parallel those of *musique concrète*. The BBC Radiophonic Workshop was a sound laboratory and studio created by the BBC in 1958 for the production of electronic music.

ramp wave *see* **sawtooth waveform**

realization The act of creating and assembling a completed work of electronic music; most often associated with works intended for recorded media.

reel-to-reel tape recorder An audio recording device using magnetic tape as its recording media, so named because the tape was transported using rotating reels to feed and take up the tape.

release In relation to the envelope of a sound, the time it takes for a sound to end and return to zero amplitude; often associated with the way that a musical note ends when the finger is lifted from the keyboard.

reverberation In regard to audio signal processing, the effect of reflected sound on the perceived depth or character of an audio signal; reverberation comprises the sum total of all such reflections as expressed by a prolongation of the sound, where individual reflections are not discretely perceivable. *See also* **echo**.

ribbon controller A synthesizer controller consisting of a touch-sensitive ribbon providing linear control over the pitch of a waveform; commonly used to produce sliding notes.

ring modulation In sound synthesis, a form of amplitude modulation in which the fundamental tone of a waveform is suppressed, leaving only the sidebands; in the processing of simple waveforms, two additional frequencies are created in place of the original carrier signal—one is equal to the sum of the two input frequencies, and the other is equal to the difference between them.

roll-off slope In audio filtering, the slight attenuation of a sound at the cutoff point, generally equivalent to about 3 dB attenuation per octave.

sample A digitally reproduced version of an analog sound.

sampling The digital conversion of an analog audio signal so that it can be stored and reproduced by a computer music system or synthesizer.

sampling rate In digital audio sampling, the setting that determines how many times per second an analog sound source will be digitally sampled; a higher sampling rate equates to higher fidelity.

sawtooth waveform A type of basic waveform containing all even and odd harmonics associated with a fundamental tone; also called a ramp wave.

sequencer A programmable control device for defining a preset sequence of notes to be played on a synthesizer; originally developed for voltage-controlled synthesizers, the sequencer provided a means for structuring a sequence of voltage control signals that were then fed as control signals to other voltage-controlled modules.

serialism Composition method with rules for prescribing a fixed series of musical elements such as pitch, timbre, rhythm, and amplitude. *See also* **twelve-tone music**.

sine wave   A type of basic waveform with no harmonics that undulates evenly; the least complex waveform.

slave unit   In a MIDI performance setup, a satellite instrument connected to a master unit or controller.

sound art   Electronic music not necessarily intended for the concert hall and that might be used as an audio installation in a gallery or other environmental context.

sound crafting   An electronic music composition technique in which the composer works directly with sound materials guided by a general structural plan but without a specific written score.

sound installation   A work of electronic music designed for a specific audio space, event, or activity, as opposed as to stage performance.

sound object *see **objet sonore, l'***

sound-on-film   An audio recording and playback system, originally devised for motion pictures, by which audio signals were converted to electrical waveforms and photographically recorded on the edge of motion picture film; the soundtrack was made audible again by means of a photoelectric cell.

space music   A genre of electronic music characterized by long, meditative electronic passages built on slowly evolving chord changes, a rhythmic pulse, and suspension of tension.

spectral editor   Audio processing software that permits the analyzing, editing, and transformation of the spectrum of a sound, the relative strength of various partials above the fundamental frequency, and other inherent characteristics of a waveform.

splicing   The physical act of editing magnetic tape using a razor blade.

splicing block   A tool used to guide the splicing of magnetic tape.

square wave   A type of basic waveform whose duty cycle is one half of the total cycle of the waveform, or 1:2, evenly divided between the upper and lower reaches of the wave; a form of pulse wave.

stochastic   Information having a random probability distribution or structure that can be analyzed statistically.

subtractive synthesis   Audio synthesis that employs the selective removal of sidebands or the fundamental frequency to change the timbral qualities of a sound.

sustain   In relation to the envelope of a sound, the length of time that a sound lasts at a fixed amplitude, between the decay and release constituents of a waveform.

synthesis   The use of the fundamental building blocks of sound to construct new sounds.

synthesizer   An electronic musical instrument containing several integrated components to create, modify, amplify, and play sounds; the basic components may include two or more audio signal generators (oscillators) for creating raw sound material, preset sounds or instrumental voices, a white noise generator, audio filters, methods for accommodating amplitude and frequency modulation, envelope generation, and organizing and sequencing sounds; controllers may include a physical controller, such as a keyboard, or may consist of audio-processing modules only that are controlled by computer software or another instrument connected by means of MIDI.

system message   In a MIDI performance setup, a command signal broadcast on all channels to all available MIDI devices.

tape delay   In regard to tape recording technology, the practice of stringing a length of recording tape through two tape recorders, recording a sound on the first machine, playing it back on the second, and then simultaneously feeding the signal back into the first machine where it is recorded again; the signal that is repeatedly re-recorded eventually diminishes with each generation of re-recording.

tape loop   A short length of magnetic tape, spliced end to end and threaded through a tape recorder, for recording and playback purposes; a sound played back using a tape loop will repeat continuously without any loss of signal quality.

tape recorder   An electro-mechanical device for the recording and playback of sound by means of electromagnetic signals; the signals were recorded onto a moving reel of paper or plastic tape coated with magnetic (iron oxide) powder.

tape reversal   In relation to tape recorders, playing a recorded sound in reverse, usually accomplished by exchanging the places of the feeder reel and the take-up reel.

tape speed manipulation   In relation to tape recorders, playing a recording at a speed other than that at which it was recorded, primarily to produce audio effects; likewise, a sound may also be recorded at a speed other than that at which playback is intended, providing a similar effect; in the classic tape studio, some tape recorders had fixed speed settings while others had variably adjustable speeds within a given range.

technical score   An electronic music score specifying the technical parameters and settings for producing a specific piece of music; a technical score provides the means for others to faithfully reproduce a given composition.

telegraphic and telephonic   Term associated with early electronic music dating from the late nineteenth and early twentieth centuries, referring to the electrical means for distributing early experiments in electronic music by means of telegraph wires and telephone lines.

text–sound composition   The electronic manipulation of live or recorded vocal sounds to create a musical work that transforms the reading or singing of a text.

timbre   The nature or quality of a sound that distinguishes it from other sounds; tone color; timbre is defined by the constituent elements of waveform structure: the fundamental tone plus partials, overtones, harmonics, and transients.

timing pulse   A control signal, typically triggered by a keyboard, used to activate a voltage-controlled sequencer on an analog synthesizer.

tone wheel   In electro-mechanical musical instruments, a notched metal disc that, when rotated on a pitch shaft, comes in contact with a metal brush and produces an electrical current equivalent to a given frequency; method of tone generation used in the Telharmonium and Hammond organ.

touch-sensitive keyboard   A type of keyboard controller that can respond to the amount of energy applied to the keys (velocity-sensitive), which alters the amplitude of the note, and/or the length of time that a key is depressed (force-sensitive), which affects how long a note is sustained; the term was originally applied to second-generation analog synthesizers.

tremolo   A periodic undulation in the amplitude of a tone.

triangle (triangular) wave   A type of basic waveform containing only the fundamental frequency and all of its odd-numbered harmonics.

turntablism   Music produced using turntables and recorded discs.

twelve-tone music   A compositional system devised by Arnold Schoenberg that was based on the relationship between individual notes of the 12-tone chromatic scale, as opposed to chords; the system could be applied to any set of adjacent 12 notes, called the tone row; each tone was given equal importance; and the 12 tones could be used in a melody in any order, provided that no tones were repeated before any others were used.

ultrasonic   Electromagnetic waves at a frequency above the range of human hearing.

vacuum tube   The first widely used miniaturized electronic component, capable of amplifying a weak electrical signal; invented in 1907, the vacuum tube was widely used in the production of radios, televisions, musical instruments, sound amplifications, and other applications until the early 1960s when transistors became widely available.

velocity-sensitive keyboard   An electronic keyboard controller that can respond to the amount of energy applied to the keys (velocity-sensitive), which alters the amplitude of the note.

vibrato   A periodic undulation in the pitch of a tone.

virtual analog   An electronic music instrument or software that uses digital technology to imitate and replicate analog synthesis techniques or vintage analog synthesis sounds.

vocoder (voice encoder)   An audio processing device for applying tonal qualities of the human voice to any input signal.

voltage control   A method of applying metered amounts of current to an electronic component to govern how it operates; an approach applied to the control of solid-state, analog electronic music synthesizers; a *control* voltage is discrete from the voltage used to generate an audio signal.

voltage-controlled amplifier (VCA)   A sound synthesis component that allows the musician to control the amplitude of a signal over a variable scale. *See also* **envelope generator (ENV)**.

voltage-controlled filter (VCF)   A circuit using control voltages to set the parameters for filtering the audio spectrum of an electronic sound source, e.g. a VCF employing a low-pass filter with settings for the cutoff frequency and resonance, using a voltage-controlled input for changing the cutoff frequency.

voltage-controlled oscillator (VCO)   The basic sound-generating component of the analog synthesizer; a circuit for generating a periodic waveform, usually a sine, sawtooth, triangle, or pulse/square wave.

waveshaping synthesis   Making complex changes to an audio signal by means of another signal, or mathematical function; also known as distortion or non-linear synthesis.

wavetable   A mathematical method for defining one cycle of a specified waveform.

white noise   A type of basic waveform containing all frequencies at once, when all frequency and amplitude characteristics occur at random within the audio spectrum; white noise can be filtered, modulated, and refined to produce a variety of electronic textures.

wire recording   Use of an electro-mechanical device to record and play back sound by means of electromagnetic signals. The signals were recorded onto a moving reel of metal wire coated with magnetic (iron oxide) powder.

Notes

Preface

1   Brian Hodgson, "Delia Derbyshire, Obituary," *The Guardian*, July 7, 2001.

1   Electronic Music Before 1945

1   Alan Clayson, *Edgard Varèse* (London: Sanctuary, 2002), 121.
2   Melvin Kranzberg, "Technology and History: 'Kranzberg's Laws,'" *Technology and Culture* 27 (1986), 544–60.
3   Robert Brown, *Science for All* (London: Casell, Petter, Galpin, 1880), 182.
4   G. P. Hachenburg, "Musical Telegraphy," *Electrical Review*, November 14, 1891, 172–3.
5   Reynold Weidenaar, *Magic Music from the Telharmonium* (Metuchen, NJ: Scarecrow Press, 1995), 182.
6   Ibid., 213.
7   Marion Melius, "Music by Electricity," *The World's Work*, June, 1906, 7660–3.
8   Thomas Commerford Martin, "The Telharmonium: Electricity's Alliance with Music," *Review of Reviews*, April 1906, 420–3.
9   Weidenaar, *Magic Music from the Telharmonium*, 253.
10   Ray Stannard Baker, "New Music for an Old World," *McClure's Magazine* XXVII(3) (July 1906, New York), 291–301.
11   "The Generating and Distributing of Music by Means of Alternators," *Electrical World* XLVII(10) (1906, New York), 519–21.
12   Feruccio Busoni, "Sketch of a New Esthetic of Music (1911)," in *Three Classics in the Aesthetic of Music* (New York: Dover, 1962).
13   Ibid.
14   Ibid.
15   Filippo Tommaso Marinetti, "The Futurist Manifesto," *Le Figaro* (Paris, February 20, 1909).
16   Ibid.
17   Luigi Russolo, *The Art of Noise*, trans. Barclay Brown (Stuyvesant, NY: Pendragon, 1986).
18   Ibid.
19   One of the factors leading to the disturbance was the fact that Marinetti and Russolo had a habit of overbooking their venues. Alessandro Rizzo, "Zang Tumb Tumb; Las Musica Futurista, Futurism." Available online: www.futurism.fsnet.co.uk.
20   Simon Crab, "120 Years of Electronic Music (update v3.0)." Available online: www.obsolete.com/120_years/machines/futurist/index.html (accessed April 15, 2007).
21   Bob Osborn, "Futurism and the Futurists." Available online: www.futurism.org.uk/futurism.htm (accessed April 15, 2007).
22   Crab, "120 Years of Electronic Music (update v3.0)."

23   Louise Varèse, *Varèse* (New York: W. W. Norton, 1972), 47.

24   Ibid., 123.

25   Peter S. Hansen, *An Introduction to Twentieth Century Music* (New York: Allyn & Bacon, 1969), 316.

26   Edgard Varèse, interview, *Christian Science Monitor*, July 8, 1922.

27   Edgard Varèse, *391*, no. 5 (1917).

28   William W. Austin, *Music in the 20th Century* (New York: W. W. Norton, 1966), 377.

29   Russolo, *The Art of Noise*.

30   Lee De Forest, *The Father of Radio* (Chicago, IL: Wilcox and Follett, 1950), 331–2.

31   RCA Theremin Service Notes, collection of the author (New York: Radio-Victor Corporation of America, 1929), 5.

32   John Cage, *Silence* (Middletown, CT: Wesleyan University Press, 1961), 4.

33   Lucie Bigelow Rosen, private notes (Archive of the Caramoor Estate, undated).

34   David Miller, personal communication with Thom Holmes, May 9, 2001.

35   Albert Glinsky, *Theremin: Ether Music and Espionage* (Urbana, IL: University of Illinois Press, 2000), 190.

36   Ibid., 190.

37   Ibid., 158.

38   Charlie Lester, personal recollection communicated to Thom Holmes, April 20, 2001.

39   Charlie Lester, "Samuel J. Hoffman." Available online: www.137.com/hoffman/ (accessed April 15, 2007).

40   Ibid. As noted in Samuel Hoffman's personal scrapbook and transcribed by Charlie Lester. Verification of titles, alternative titles, and dates contributed by Saul Fisher.

41   Jeanne Loriod, liner notes, *Music for Ondes Martenot* (Musical Heritage Society, MHS 821, *c*. 1970).

42   Crab, "120 Years of Electronic Music (update v3.0)."

43   Tom Darter and Greg Armbruster, *The Art of Electronic Music* (New York: Quill, 1984), 8–9.

44   Ibid., 9

45   Ibid., 16–17.

46   Ibid., 32.

47   Phil Cirocco, *The Novachord Restoration Project*. Cirocco extensively restored an original Novachord to working order. An account of his project can be found online at www.discretesynthesizers.com/nova/intro.htm (accessed August 2, 2011).

48   Oskar Sala, liner notes, *Subharmonische Mixturen* (Erdenklang, 70963, Germany), 27–8.

49   Doepfer Musikelektronik, "The Trautonium Project." Available online: www.doepfer.de/traut/traut_e.htm (accessed April 20, 2007).

50   Georg Misch, "The Trautonium, the Difference Engine," *Wired* (September 1997), 42–6.

51   Ibid., 45.

52   Austin, *Music in the 20th Century*, 379.

53   Fernand Ouellette, *Edgard Varèse* (London: Caldar and Boyars, 1973), 102–3.

54   Clayson, *Edgard Varèse*.

2   Early Electronic Music in Europe

1   John Cage, *Silence* (Middletown, CT: Wesleyan University Press, 1961).

2   Melvin Kranzberg, "Technology and History: 'Kranzberg's Laws,'" *Technology and Culture*, 27 (1986), 544–60.

3   John D. Cutnell and Kenneth W. Johnson, *Physics*, 4th edn (New York: Wiley, 1998), 466.

4   Mark Katz, *Capturing Sound* (Berkeley, CA: University of California Press, 2004), 100.

5   Ibid., 102.

6   Ibid.

7   Halim El-Dabh, personal correspondence with Thom Holmes through associate David Badagnani (Kent State University), August 6, 2006.

8   Ibid.

9   Ibid.

10 Abraham Moles, *Les Musiques expérimentales*, excerpts translated by the author (Paris: Éditions du Cercle d'Art Contemporain, 1960), 42.

11 Jacques Poullin, "L'apport des techniques d'enregistrement dans la fabrication de matières et de formes musicales nouvelles: Applications à la *musique concrète* (1955) (ARS Sonara, No. 9, 1999). Available online: www.ars-sonora.org/html/numeros/numero09/09.htm (accessed April 30, 2007).

12 Moles, *Les Musiques expérimentales*, 32.

13 Groupe de Recherches Musicales (GRM), "Words" (Institut National de l'Audiovisuel). Available online: www.ina.fr/grm/presentation/mots/en.html (accessed April 29, 2007).

14 Carlos Palombini, "*Musique concrète* Revisited," *Electronic Musicological Review* 4 (June 1999). Available online: www.rem.ufpr.br/REMv4/vol4/arti-palombini.htm (accessed April 29, 2007). The work was broadcast over French radio in eight one-hour segments.

15 John Dack, "Pierre Schaeffer and the Significance of Radiophonic Art," in *Contemporary Music Review* 2 (Harwood Academic Publishers, 1994). Available online: www.zainea.com/PierreSchaeffer1994.pdf (accessed April 29, 2007).

16 Pierre Schaeffer, *Machines à communiquer* (Paris: Editions du Seuil, 1970), 108–9.

17 Palombini, "*Musique concrète* Revisited."

18 Ibid.

19 Ibid.

20 Pierre Schaeffer, *A la recherche d'une musique concrète* (*The Search for a Concrete Music*) (Paris: Editions du Seuil, 1952).

21 Maurice Béjart, liner notes, *Variations for a Door and a Sigh* (Limelight, LS 86059, 1966).

22 Ibid.

23 Ios Smolders, "Pierre Henry Interview," *EST Magazine*. Available online: http://media.hyperreal.org/zines/est/intervs/henry.html (accessed April 29, 2007).

24 Ibid.

25 Tim Hodgkinson, "Interview with Pierre Schaeffer," *Recommended Records Quarterly* 2(1) (1987).

26 Jason Gross, "Interview with Konrad Boehmer," *OHM: The Early Gurus of Electronic Music* (Ellipsis Arts, 1999). Available online: www.furious.com/perfect.ohm/eimert.html (accessed April 29, 2007).

27 Hodgkinson, "Interview with Pierre Schaeffer."

28 David Ewen, *The Complete Book of 20th Century Music* (Englewood Cliffs, NJ: Prentice Hall, 1959), 348.

29 Joseph Machlis, *Introduction to Contemporary Music* (New York: Norton, 1961), 388.

30 H. H. Herbert Stuckenschmidt, "The Third Stage: Some Observations on the Aesthetics of Electronic Music," *die Reihe* 1 (1955), 11.

31 Moles, *Les Musiques expérimentales*, 34.

32 Pierre Schaeffer, as quoted by Herbert Russcol, *The Liberation of Sound* (Englewood Cliffs, NJ: Prentice Hall, 1972), 83.

33 Herbert Eimert, "What is Electronic Music?," *die Reihe* 1 (1955), 1.

34 Otto Luening, "An Unfinished History of Electronic Music," *Music Educator's Journal* 55(3) (November 1968), 46–7.

35 Teresa Rampazzi, liner notes, *Musica Endoscopica*, 2007.

36 Tom Rhea, "Beginning of the Modern Age," in Alan Douglas (ed.) *The Electronic Musical Instrument Manual* (Blue Ridge Summit, PA: TAB Books, 1976), 61.

37 Robert Beyer, "First Experiments" (1954). WDR web site by Marietta Morawska Buengeler: www.musikwiss.uni-halle.de/musicweb/elemusik/technik.htm.

38 Karl. H. Wörner, *Stockhausen: Life and Work* (Berkeley, CA: University of California Press, 1977), 122.

39 Gross, "Interview with Konrad Boehmer."

40 Konrad Boehmer, liner notes, *Cologne–WDR, Early Electronic Music* (Acousmatrix, 6 CD 9106, 1999).

41 Michael Manion, "From Tape Loops to MIDI: Karlheinz Stockhausen's Forty Years of Electronic Music," an interview. Available online: www.stockhausen.org/tape_loops.html (accessed May 24, 2007).

42 Ibid.

43   Ibid.

44   Ibid.

45   Ibid.

46   Ibid.

47   Karlheinz Stockhausen, liner notes for *Studie I and Studie II* (CD3, Stockhausen Verlag).

48   Karlheinz Stockhausen, ". . . how time passes . . .," *die Reihe* 3 (1959), trans. Cornelius Cardew, 10.

49   Robin Maconie (ed.), *Stockhausen on Music: Lectures and Interviews* (London: Marion Boyars, 2000), 95–111.

50   Wörner, *Stockhausen: Life and Work*, 41.

51   Ibid.

52   Karlheinz Stockhausen, *Gesang der Jünglinge* (score) (Stockhausen Verlag, 2001), 2. Available online: www.stockhausen.org/gesang_der_junglinge.pdf (accessed April 29, 2007).

53   Wörner, *Stockhausen: Life and Work*, 41.

54   Jon H. Appleton and Ronald C. Perera (eds), *The Development and Practice of Electronic Music* (Englewood Cliffs, NJ: Prentice Hall, 1975), 109.

55   Karlheinz Stockhausen, personal communication with Thom Holmes, April 10, 2000.

56   Jan W. Morthenson, "Aesthetic Dilemmas in Electronic Music," in Robin Julian Heifetz (ed.) *On the Wires of Our Nerves: The Art of Electroacoustic Music* (London: Associated University Press, 1989), 66.

57   Joel Chadabe, *Electric Sound: The Past and Promise of Electronic Music* (Upper Saddle River, NJ: Prentice Hall, 1997), 48.

58   As reported in Appleton and Perera (eds), *The Development and Practice of Electronic Music*.

59   Barry Shrader, *Introduction to Electro-Acoustic Music* (Englewood Cliffs, NJ: Prentice Hall, 1982), 179.

60   Luciano Berio, liner notes, *Electronic Music* (Turnabout, TV 34046S, 1966, New York).

61   Albert Mayr, "The Phonology Studio in Florence—S 2F M." *Musica/Tecnologia* 1 (2007), 333–8.

62   Rampazzi, liner notes, *Musica Endoscopica*.

63   Louis Niebur, *Special Sound: The Creation and Legacy of the BBC Radiophonic Workshop* (London: Oxford University Press, 2010), 35–6.

64   "Daphne Oram: An Electronic Music Pioneer," Goldsmiths and the Sonic Arts Network. Available online: http://daphneoram.org/oramarchive/bbc/ (accessed October 9, 2011).

65   Jo Hutton, *Radiophonic Ladies*. Available online: http://delia-derbyshire.dyndns.org/sites/ARTICLE 2000JoHutton.html (accessed August 2, 2011).

66   Niebur, *Special Sound*, 48–9.

67   Ray White, *BBC Radiophone Workshop: An Engineering Perspective*. Available online: http://whitefiles.org/rws/ (accessed June 12, 2011).

68   Nieber, *Special Sound*, 53.

69   Ibid., 127.

70   "Delia Derbyshire: Electronic Music Pioneer: Interview," *Surface*, May 2000. Available online: www.delia-derbyshire.org/interview_surface.php (accessed June 13, 2011).

71   Ibid.

3   Early Electronic Music in the United States and Latin America

1   Bebe Barron, interview with Thom Holmes, April 9, 2001.

2   Ibid.

3   Ibid.

4   Ibid.

5   Ibid.

6   David Tudor, interview with Teddy Hultberg, Dusseldorf, May 17–18, 1988. Available online: www.emf.org/tudor/Articles/hultberg.html (accessed May 12, 2007).

7   John Cage, interview with Thom Holmes, April 1981.

8   John Cage, *Imaginary Landscape No. 5* (score) (New York: Edition Peters 6719, Henmar Press, 1961).

9   Tudor, interview with Hultberg, May 17–18, 1988.

10   John Cage, *Werkverzeichnis* (New York: Edition Peters, 1962), 41.

11   Barron, interview with Holmes, April 9, 2001.

12   Ibid.

13   David Revill, *The Roaring Silence, John Cage: A Life* (New York: Arcade, 1992), 146.

14   Barron, interview with Holmes, April 9, 2001.

15   Richard Kostelanetz, *John Cage: An Anthology* (New York: Da Capo, 1991), 130.

16   The Wolff piece was identified by Matt Rogalsky and included in a personal communication with Thom Holmes, August 24, 2001.

17   Frederick S. Clarke and Steve Rubin, "Making *Forbidden Planet*," *Cinefantastique* 8(2–3) (1979), 42.

18   Barron, interview with Holmes, April 9, 2001.

19   Ibid.

20   Ibid.

21   Clarke and Rubin, "Making *Forbidden Planet*."

22   Cage, interview with Holmes, April 1981.

23   Ibid.

24   Ibid.

25   Ibid.

26   Otto Luening, *The Odyssey of an American Composer: The Autobiography of Otto Luening* (New York: Charles Scribner's Sons, 1980), 512–16.

27   Ibid., 513.

28   Ibid., 512.

29   Otto Luening, "An Unfinished History of Electronic Music," *Music Educator's Journal* 55(3) (November 1968), 48.

30   Luening, *Odyssey of an American Composer*, 528.

31   Ibid., 533.

32   David Sarnoff, liner notes, *The Sounds and Music of the RCA Electronic Music Synthesizer* (Radio Corporation of America, L16101 Experimental, 1955).

33   Harry F. Olson, *Music, Physics, and Engineering* (New York: Dover, 1952, reissued 1967), 424.

34   Ibid., 448.

35   Ibid., 434.

36   Gordon Mumma, personal communication with Thom Holmes, March 17, 2001.

37   Les Paul was among the first to use multiple tracking to build several guitar and vocal parts using just himself and his wife, Mary Ford.

38   Mumma, personal communication with Holmes, March 17, 2001.

39   Robert Ashley, interview with Thom Holmes, March 22, 2001.

40   Ibid.

41   Robert Ashley, "Autobiographie," *MusikTexte* MT88, February 2001, based on English draft version provided by the composer.

42   Ibid.

43   Lejaren A. Hiller and Leonard M. Isaacson, *Experimental Music: Composition with an Electronic Computer* (New York: McGraw-Hill, 1959), 4.

44   Ibid., 4–5.

45   Lejaren A. Hiller, liner notes, *Computer Music from the University of Illinois* (MGM Records, H/HS 25053, 1964).

46   Gordon Mumma, "Innovation in Latin-American Electroacoustical Music," *The Pacific Ring* (San Diego, CA: University of California Press, 1986).

47   Ricardo Dal Farra, *Latin American Electroacoustic Music Collection* (La fondation Daniel Langlois, 2004–2011). Available online: www.fondation-langlois.org/html/e/page.php?NumPage=556 (accessed October 9, 2011).

48   Aurelia de la Vega, Review: "Avant Garde Music at the American Art Biennial of Cordoba," *Anuario* 3 (1967), 85–100.

49   Farra, *Latin American Electroacoustic Music Collection*.

50   Vania Dantas Leite, *Musicians and Movements that Initiated Electroacoustics in Brazil* (Universidade do Rio de Janeiro, 2000). Available online: http://gsd.ime.usp.br/sbcm/2000/papers/leite.pdf (accessed October 9, 2011).

51 Farra, *Latin American Electroacoustical Music Collection*.

52 "Antunes" (UNESCO Culture, 2008). Available online: http://portal.unesco.org/culture/en/ev.php-URL_ID=16138&URL_DO=DO_PRINTPAGE&URL_SECTION=201.html (accessed October 9, 2011).

53 Neil Leonard III, "Juan Blanco: Cuba's Pioneer of Electroacoustic Music," *Computer Music Journal* 21(2) (Summer, 1997), 12–13.

54 Ibid., 14–15.

4   Early Electronic Music in Japan, Southeast Asia, and China

1 Koichi Fujii, "Chronology of Early Electroacoustic Music in Japan: What Types of Source Materials Are Available?," *Organized Sound* 9(1) (2004), 64.

2 Ibid.

3 Fujii, "Chronology of Early Electroacoustic Music in Japan."

4 Ibid., 66.

5 Takehito Shimazu, "The History of Electronic and Computer Music in Japan: Significant Composers and Their Works," *Leonardo Music Journal* 4 (1994), 102–6.

6 Koichi, "Chronology of Early Electroacoustic Music in Japan," 65.

7 Ibid.

8 Ibid., 71.

9 Emmanuelle Loubet, "The Beginnings of Electronic Music in Japan, with a Focus on the NHK Studio: The 1950s and 1960s," *Computer Music Journal* 21(4) (Winter, 1997), 16.

10 Julian Cope and Joji Yuasa, Japrocksampler.com. Available online: www.japrocksampler.com/artists/.../yuasa_joji/ (accessed October 9, 2011).

11 Emmanuelle Loubet, "The Beginnings of Electronic Music in Japan, with a Focus on the NHK Studio: The 1970s," *Computer Music Journal* 22(1) (1998), 53–4.

12 Ibid., 49.

13 Shimazu Takehito, "The History of Electronic and Computer Music in Japan: Significant Composers and Their Works, Music," *Leonardo Music Journal* 4 (1994), 103.

14 Ibid., 104.

15 Takahisa Kosugi, *MĀLIKĀ 5* (1964). Available online: www.artnotart.com/fluxus/tkosugi-malika5.html (accessed May 20, 2011).

16 Yoko Ono, *Painting for the Wind* (1961). Available online: www.artnotart.com/fluxus/yono-paintingforwind.html (accessed June 2, 2011).

17 Yamamoto Atsuo, *Space as a Catalyst* on Kosugi's *World of Sound* (1996). Available online: www.sukothai.com/X.SA.08/X8.Kosugi.html (accessed May 19, 2011).

18 Koichi, "Chronology of Early Electroacoustic Music in Japan," 71.

19 Bob Gluck, *Electronic Music in Indonesia* (EMF, 2006). Available online: http://emfinstitute.emf.org/articles/gluck.indonesia_06.html (accessed May 18, 2011).

20 Michael Tenzer, "José Maceda and the Paradoxes of Modern Composition in Southeast Asia," *Ethnomusicography* 47(1) (Winter, 2003), 103.

21 Bob Gluck, *Electronic Music in China* (EMF, 2006). Available online: http://emfinstitute.emf.org/articles/gluck.china_06.html (accessed May 18, 2011).

5   Tape Composition and Fundamental Concepts of Electronic Music

1 Alan Baker, *An interview with Pauline Oliveros* (American Public Media, January 2003). Available online: http://musicmavericks.publicradio.org/features/interview_oliveros.html (accessed August 23, 2007).

2 Hugh Davies, *Répertoire international des musiques électroacoustiques (International Electronic Music Catalog)* (Cambridge, MA: MIT Press, 1967), a joint publication of Le Groupe de Recherches Musicales de l'ORTF (Paris) and the Independent Electronic Music Center Inc. (Trumansburg, NY). Figures based on an analysis of the studio listings in this historic book.

3   H. H. Stuckenschmidt, "The Third Stage: Some Observations on the Aesthetics of Electronic Music," *die Reihe* 1(1) (English edition, 1955), 11–13.

4   Karl. H. Wörner, *Stockhausen: Life and Work* (Berkeley, CA: University of California Press, 1976), 123.

5   Wendy Carlos, interview with Thom Holmes, August 8, 2001.

6   Ibid.

7   John Cage, *Silence* (Middletown, CT: Wesleyan University Press, 1961), 68–9.

8   Igor Stravinsky, *Poetics of Music in the Form of Six Lessons* (New York: Vintage, 1947), 125.

9   Alvin Lucier, *I Am Sitting in a Room* (Middletown, CT: Wesleyan University Press, 1980).

10   Christopher Burns, *Realizations*. Available online: www-ccrma.stanford.edu/~cburns/realizations/lucier-2.html (accessed June 10, 2007).

11   Stravinsky, *Poetics of Music in the Form of Six Lessons*, 29.

12   Robert Ashley, interview with Thom Holmes, September 8, 1982.

13   Richard L. Gregory, "Perceptions of Knowledge," *Nature* 410 (March 1, 2001), 21.

14   Peter Shapiro (ed.), *Modulations* (New York: Caipirinha, 2000), 22.

15   John Cage, interview with Thom Holmes, April 1981.

16   David Paul, "Karlheinz Stockhausen," interview, *Seconds Magazine* 44 (1997). Available online: www.stockhausen.org/stockhausen%20_by_david_paul.html (accessed June 6, 2007).

17   Karlheinz Stockhausen, *On Music* (London: Marion Boyars, 1989), 95.

18   Brian Eno, liner notes, *Discreet Music* (EG Records Ltd, 1975).

19   Alvin Lucier, interview with Thom Holmes, February 24, 2001.

20   Pauline Oliveros, *Software for People: Collected Writings 1963–80* (Baltimore, MD: Smith Publications, 1984), 43.

21   Pauline Oliveros, personal communication with Thom Holmes, April 14, 2001.

22   Terry Riley, liner notes, *Music for the Gift* (Organ of Corti, 1, 1998).

23   Pauline Oliveros, liner notes, *Electronic Works* (Paradigm Discs, 4, 1997).

24   John Cage, *Fontana Mix* entry, New York Public Library repository of works by John Cage. Available online: www.johncage.info/workscage/fontana.html (accessed June 15, 2007).

25   John Cage, *Fontana Mix* (score) (New York: C. F. Peters Corporation, 1962).

26   Ibid.

27   Matt Rogalsky, personal communication with Thom Holmes, June 16, 2007.

28   Benjamin Robert Levy, *The Electronic Works of György Ligeti and Their Influence on His Later Style*. Doctoral dissertation submitted to the Faculty of the Graduate School of the University of Maryland, College Park (2006), 3. Available online: http://drum.umd.edu/dspace/handle/1903/3457?mode=simple (accessed June 14, 2007).

29   Gottfried Michael Koenig, "Ligeti und die elektronische Musik" in Otto Kolleritsch (ed.) *György Ligeti: Personalstil–Avantgardismus–Popularität* (Vienna: Universal Edition, 1987), 19.

30   Levy, *The Electronic Works of György Ligeti and Their Influence on His Later Style*.

31   Ibid.

32   Ibid., 42.

6   Early Synthesizers and Experimenters

1   Harry F. Olson and Herbert Belar, "Aid to Musical Composition Employing a Random Probability System," *Journal of the Acoustical Society of America* 33(9) (September 1961), 1163–70.

2   Harry F. Olson, *Music, Physics, and Engineering*, 2nd edn (New York: Dover Publications, 1967), 434.

3   Ibid., 431.

4   Ibid., 429.

5   Milton Babbitt, liner notes, *Columbia–Princeton Electronic Music Center* (Columbia, MS 6566, 1964).

6   Liner notes, *Columbia–Princeton Electronic Music Center Tenth Anniversary Celebration* (CRI SD 268, 1971), 3.

7   Herbert Russcol, *The Liberation of Sound* (Englewood Cliffs, NJ: Prentice Hall, 1972), 132.

8   Charles Wuorinen, liner notes, *Time's Encomium* (Nonesuch Records, H-71225, 1970).

9   Alice Shields, personal communication with Thom Holmes, June 27, 2007.

10   Otto Luening, *The Odyssey of an American Composer: The Autobiography of Otto Luening* (New York: Charles Scribner's Sons, 1980), 554.

11   Milton Babbitt, interview, *Oral History Project* by Eric Chasalow (1996). Available online: www.ericchasalow.com/oralhist.html (accessed June 27, 2007).

12   Wendy Carlos, interview with Thom Holmes, June 6, 2001.

13   Wendy Carlos, liner notes, *Electronic Music* (Turnabout, TV 24004S, 1965).

14   Babbitt, liner notes, *Columbia–Princeton Electronic Music Center.*

15   Halim El-Dabh, interview with Thom Holmes, July 9, 2007.

16   David Badagnani, personal communication with Thom Holmes, June 28, 2007.

17   Liner notes, *Columbia–Princeton Electronic Music Center Tenth Anniversary Celebration*, 2.

18   Alice Shields, personal communication with Thom Holmes, June 28, 2007.

19   Babbit, interview, *Oral History Project.*

20   Shields, personal communication with Holmes, June 28, 2007.

21   Josef Anton Riedl, liner notes, *Siemens Studio für Elektronische Musik* (Siemens Kultur Programm, 1994), German translation by the author.

22   Homer Dudley, "The Vocoder," *Journal of the Acoustical Society of America* 11(2) (1939), 169.

23   Harald Bode, "History of Electronic Sound Modification," *Journal of the Audio Engineering Society* 32(10) (October, 1984), 733.

24   Maurizio Erman Mansueti and Luca Luke Cirillo, "An Interview with Bob Moog" (Thereminovox. com, May 12, 2005). Available online: www.thereminvox.com/article/articleview/154/ (accessed June 30, 2007).

25   There were a few exceptions. Between 1975 and 1981, electronic music historian and former Moog employee Tom Rhea authored articles for *Keyboard* magazine about many hits and misses in the development of electronic musical instruments; ten paragraphs devoted to Scott appeared in reprint form in the book *The Art of Electronic Music* (1984), edited by Greg Armbruster. But it is only recently that Scott's work has gained more widespread attention by the reissuing of several recordings of his music and the handsome CD/book combination *Manhattan Research Inc.* (2000).

26   Gert-Jan Blom and Jeff Winner, liner notes, *Manhattan Research Inc.* (Holland Basta, 90782, 2000), 40–5. The liner notes refer to an article written by Joseph Kaselow for the July 19, 1960 edition of the *New York Herald Tribune.*

27   Robert Moog, interview with Thom Holmes, March 4, 2001.

28   Raymond Scott advertisement (*c.* 1957), liner notes, *Manhattan Research Inc.* (Holland Basta, 90782, 2000), 49.

29   George Martin (ed.), *Making Music* (New York: Quill, 1983), 229.

30   Greg Armbruster (ed.), *The Art of Electronic Music* (New York: Quill, 1984), 55.

31   Ibid.

32   Jeff E. Winner and Irwin D. Chusid, *Circle Machines and Sequencers: The Untold History of Raymond Scott's Pioneering Instruments.* Available online: http://raymondscott.com/em.html (accessed June 30, 2007).

33   Blom and Winner, liner notes, *Manhattan Research Inc.*, 20.

34   Winner and Chusid, *Circle Machines and Sequencers.*

35   Blom and Winner, liner notes, *Manhattan Research Inc.*, 54–5.

36   Ibid., 51.

37   Moog, interview with Holmes, March 4, 2001.

38   Gayle Young, liner notes, *Hugh Le Caine: Compositions, Demonstrations 1946–1974* (JWD Music, JWD 03, 1999), 1.

39   Blom and Winner, liner notes, *Manhattan Research Inc.*, 35.

40   Elliot Schwartz, *Electronic Music: A Listener's Guide* (New York: Praeger, 1975), 131.

41   Pauline Oliveros, personal communication with Thom Holmes, May 4, 2001.

42   Heidi von Gunden, *The Music of Pauline Oliveros* (Metuchen, NJ: Scarecrow Press, 1983), 57.

43   Oliveros, personal communication with Holmes, May 4, 2001.

44 Armbruster, *The Art of Electronic Music*, 54.
45 Canada Science and Technology Museum, "Early Synthesizers, Keyboard and Performance Instruments." Available online: www.science-tech.nmstc.ca/english/collection/music8.cfm (accessed June 17, 2007).
46 Gayle Young, "Hugh Le Caine Instruments" (Hugh Le Caine, 1999). Available online: www.hughlecaine.com/en/ (accessed June 17, 2007).

7 Principles of Analog Synthesis and Voltage Control

1 Ferruccio Busoni, "Sketch of a New Esthetic of Music (1911)" in *Three Classics in The Aesthetic of Music* (New York: Dover, 1962), 89–95.
2 Ibid., 77.
3 John Cage, *Silence* (Middletown, CT: Wesleyan University Press, 1961), 4.
4 Ibid., 9.
5 Ibid., 3–4.
6 Allen Strange, *Electronic Music: Systems, Techniques, and Controls* (New York: Wm. C. Brown, 1972), 32.
7 Table based on ideas from Strange, *Electronic Music*, 32.
8 Ibid., 7.
9 Robert Ashley, interview with Thom Holmes, September 8, 1982.
10 Ibid.
11 Steve Reich, interview with Jason Gross, *OHM: The Early Gurus of Electronic Music*. Available online: www.furious.com/perfect/ohm/reich.html (accessed July 2, 2007).
12 David Lee Myers, personal communication with Thom Holmes, April 4, 2001.
13 Strange, *Electronic Music*, 190.
14 Thom Rhea, *The Minimoog Synthesizer Operation Manual* (New York: Moog Music, 1972), 14.

8 The Voltage-Controlled Synthesizer

1 Robert Moog, interview with Thom Holmes, March 4, 2001.
2 Ibid.
3 Ibid.
4 Robert Moog, "Voltage-Controlled Electronic Music Modules," *Journal of the Audio Engineering Society* 13(3) (July, 1965), 200.
5 Ibid., 205.
6 Trevor Pinch, *Analog Days* (Cambridge, MA: Harvard University Press, 2002), 56.
7 Moog, interview with Holmes, March 4, 2001.
8 Joel Chadabe, remarks during "Electronic Music Pioneers @ Hofstra," a seminar sponsored by the Hofstra University Department of Music, New York, March 16, 2001, transcribed by Thom Holmes.
9 Ibid.
10 Robert Moog, remarks during "Electronic Music Pioneers @ Hofstra," a seminar sponsored by the Hofstra University Department of Music, New York, March 16, 2001, transcribed by Thom Holmes.
11 Moog, interview with Holmes, March 4, 2001.
12 Moog, remarks during "Electronic Music Pioneers @ Hofstra."
13 Wendy Carlos, *Bob Moog R.I.P.* Available online: www.wendycarlos.com/moog/index.html (accessed July 8, 2007).
14 Wendy Carlos, interview with Carol Wright, *New Age Voice* (November 1999). Available online: www.synthmuseum.com/magazine/0103cw.html (accessed July 6, 2007).
15 Wendy Carlos, interview with Thom Holmes, August 8, 2001, and correspondence with Thom Holmes, February 20, 2008.
16 Some of Carlos's photographs of solar eclipses are so exquisite that they have graced the cover and pages of *Sky and Telescope* magazine.
17 Moog, interview with Holmes, March 4, 2001.

18   Carlos, *Bob Moog R.I.P.*

19   Carlos, interview with Holmes, August 8, 2001.

20   Ibid.

21   Carlos, interview with Wright, *New Age Voice*.

22   Ibid.

23   Carlos, interview with Holmes, August 8, 2001. The homemade eight-track tape machine was created by cannibalizing off-the-shelf equipment. It was made from Ampex model 300 and 351 tape recorder parts, EMI tape heads, and a custom control panel for "Sel-Synching"—synchronizing—the tracks. Sel-Synching was an Ampex trademarked technique of routing the record head into the playback preamps so that you could monitor the same spot on the tape where you were recording instead of from the playback head itself, which was an inch or two to the right and was slightly delayed from the moment of recording. It was a critical feature for a multitrack tape machine, on which one could build a piece of music one track at a time. Sel-Synching enabled one to synchronize new tracks with previously recorded tracks.

24   Ibid.

25   Ibid.

26   Mark Vail, *Vintage Synthesizers* (San Francisco, CA: Miller Freeman, 2000), 41. Reprint of an interview with Bob Moog by Connor Freff Cochran called "The Rise and Fall of Moog Music," which originally appeared in *Keyboard* magazine. Moog was correct about the relative success of the three records, but was fooled by the so-called bowl of reefers. David Behrman, who was also in attendance at the press party, told me about the secret behind the bowl of joints: "My boss, John McClure, who was the head of Columbia Masterworks, made these fake marijuana cigarettes that had tobacco in them and put them in a big bowl. John McClure was being on the safe side."

27   Wendy Carlos, interview with Thom Holmes, June 6, 2001.

28   Glenn Gould, liner notes, *Switched-On Boxed Set* (East Side Digital, ESD 81422, 1999).

29   Gordon Mumma, "Foreword," in Allen Strange, *Electronic Music: Systems, Techniques, and Controls*, 2nd edn (Dubuque, IA: W. C. Brown, 1983), ix.

30   Moog, remarks during "Electronic Music Pioneers @ Hofstra."

31   Ibid.

32   William Maginnis, personal communication with Thom Holmes, 1984.

33   Vail, *Vintage Synthesizers*, 106–7.

34   Ibid.

35   Charles Cohen, personal communication with Thom Holmes, May 3, 2001.

36   Joel Chadabe, *Electric Sound: The Past and Promise of Electronic Music* (Upper Saddle River, NJ: Prentice Hall, 1997), 196.

37   Michel Waisvisz, *The Hands*. Available online: http://crackle.org/The%20Hands%201984.htm (accessed July 1, 2007).

38   Robert Ashley, liner notes, *Superior Seven* (New World Records, 80460–2, 1995, New York).

39   Ibid.

9   Early Computer Music (1953–85)

1   Max V. Mathews, "The Digital Computer as a Musical Instrument," *Science* 142 (November 1963), 553–7.

2   Computer History Museum, *Timeline of Computer History*. Available online: www.computerhistory.org/timeline/?year=1939 (accessed July 23, 2007).

3   C. E. Shannon, "A Mathematical Theory of Communication," *The Bell System Technical Journal* 27 (July, October, 1948), 379–423, 623–56.

4   Max V. Mathews, *The Technology of Computer Music* (Cambridge, MA: MIT Press, 1969), 37.

5   *Computer Music: Music1–V & GROOVE*. Available online: www.obsolete.com/120_years/machines/software/ (accessed July 23, 2007).

6   James Bohn, *Lejaren Hiller* (Experimental Music Studios, University of Illinois). Available online: http://ems.music.uiuc.edu/history/hiller.html (accessed July 25, 2007).

7   Joel Chadabe, *Electric Sound: The Past and Promise of Electronic Music* (Upper Saddle River, NJ: Prentice Hall, 1997), 278.

8   Ibid., 279.

9   Michael Koenig, *Project 1*. Available online: www.koenigproject.nl/indexe.htm (accessed July 25, 2007).

10 Chadabe, *Electric Sound*, 116.

11 Tom Darter, *John Chowning, an Interview*. Available online: www.maths.abdn.ac.uk/~bensondj/html/Chowning.html (accessed July 25, 2007).

12 Ibid.

13 Chadabe, *Electric Sound*, 117.

14 Darter, *John Chowning, an Interview*.

15 David F. Salisbury, *Yamaha, Stanford Join Forces on Sound Technology*, Stanford Online Report (July 16, 1997). Available online: http://news-service.stanford.edu/news/1997/july16/sondiusxg.html (accessed July 25, 2007).

16 Julius O. Smith, *Experiences with the Samson Box*. Available online: www-ccrma.stanford.edu/~jos/kna/Experiences_Samson_Box.html (accessed July 25, 2007).

17 Rozalie Hirs and Bob Gilmore (eds), *Contemporary Compositional Techniques and OpenMusic* (Paris: Editions Delatour and IRCAM Centre Pompidou, 2009), 1.

18 E. E. David, Jr., "Digital Simulation in Perceptual Research," *Bell Telephone System Monograph* 3405–1 (1958).

19 A press release from Bell Labs in November 1965 proclaimed the results of a listening test: "In listening to the computer-generated tones, 20 persons, several of whom were professional musicians, were unable to tell the difference between the computer trumpet sound and the real one."

20 Joel Chadabe, remarks during "Electronic Music Pioneers @ Hofstra," a seminar sponsored by the Hofstra University Department of Music, New York, March 16, 2001, transcribed by Thom Holmes.

10 The Microprocessor Revolution (1975–2011)

1   Nicolas Collins, interview with Thom Holmes, April 2, 2001.

2   Nicolas Collins is credited for coining this nickname for Behrman.

3   Collins, interview with Holmes, April 2, 2001.

4   David Behrman, interview with Thom Holmes, March 13, 2001.

5   Teddy Hultberg, interview with David Tudor, Dusseldorf, May 17–18, 1988. Available online: www.emf.org/tudor/Articles/hultberg.html (accessed July 26, 2007).

6   Gordon Mumma, personal communication with Thom Holmes, June 27, 2001.

7   Behrman, interview with Holmes, March 13, 2001.

8   Collins, interview with Holmes, April 2, 2001.

9   Tim Perkis, liner notes, *Wreckin' Ball: The Hub* (Artifact Recordings, ART 1008, 1994), 1.

10 Laurie Spiegel, personal communication with Thom Holmes, June 27, 2001.

11 Collins, interview with Holmes, April 2, 2001.

12 Ibid.

13 Mumma, personal communication with Holmes, June 27, 2001.

14 Julius O. Smith III, *Physical Modeling Synthesis Update* (Stanford, CA: Center for Computer Research in Music and Acoustics, Department of Music, Stanford University, 2005). Available online: https://ccrma.stanford.edu/~jos/pmupd/ (accessed October 9, 2011).

15 Hultberg, interview with Tudor, May 17–18, 1988.

16 Behrman, interview with Holmes, March 13, 2001.

17 Gordon Mumma, personal communication with Thom Holmes, August 6, 2001.

18 Ibid.

19 Behrman, interview with Holmes, March 13, 2001.

20 Hubert Howe, remarks during "Electronic Music Pioneers @ Hofstra," a seminar sponsored by the Hofstra University Department of Music, New York, March 16, 2001, transcribed by Thom Holmes.

21 Collins, interview with Holmes, April 2, 2001.

11 The Principles of Computer Music

1   Curtis Roads, *Foundations of Computer Music* (Cambridge, MA: MIT Press, 1991), 1.
2   Richard Boulanger, "Introduction," *Sound Design in Csound*. Available online: www.csounds.com/ chapter1/index.html (accessed July 18, 2007).
3   Jean-Claude Risset, *Computer Music: Why?* Available online: www.shawndecker.com/education/ programmingsound/risset_2.pdf (accessed July 20, 2007).
4   John M. Chowning, "Digital Sound Synthesis, Acoustics, and Perception: A Rich Intersection," *Proceedings of the COST G-6 Conference on Digital Audio Effects (DAFX-00)* (Verona, Italy, December 7–9, 2000). Available online: http://profs.sci.univr.it/~dafx/Final-Papers/pdf/Chowning.pdf (accessed July 19, 2007).
5   Julius O. Smith III, "Viewpoints on the History of Digital Synthesis," *Proceedings of the International Computer Music Conference* (Montreal, Canada, October 1991), 1–10. Revised with Curtis Roads for publication in *Cahiers de l'IRCAM*, 1992.
6   Chowning, "Digital Sound Synthesis, Acoustics, and Perception."
7   J. M. Chowning, "The Synthesis of Complex Audio Spectra by Means of Frequency Modulation," *Journal of the Audio Engineering Society* 21 (1973), 526–34.
8   Robert Rowe, *Digitally-Controlled Music Systems* (New York: New York University).
9   Charles Dodge and Thomas A. Jerse, *Computer Music: Synthesis, Composition, and Performance* (New York: Schirmer Books, 1985), 128–9.
10 Dennis Gabor, "Acoustical Quanta and the Theory of Hearing," *Nature* 159(4044) (1947), 591–4.
11 Roads, *Foundations of Computer Music*, 145.
12 Ibid., 149.
13 Thom Holmes (ed.) *The Routledge Guide to Music Technology* (New York: Routledge, 2006), 202–3.
14 Ted Painter and Andreas Spanias, *A Review of Algorithms for Perceptual Coding of Digital Audio Signals*. Available online: http://neutron.ing.ucv.ve/comunicaciones/Asignaturas/DifusionMultimedia/ dsp97.pdf (accessed July 20, 2007).
15 W. Speek, *Performance Comparison of Lossless Audio Compressors*. Available online: http://members. home.nl/w.speek/comparison.htm (accessed July 20, 2007).
16 Steve Jobs, *Thoughts on Music* (February 6, 2007). Available online: www.apple.com/hotnews/ thoughtsonmusic/ (accessed July 21, 2007).
17 Ibid.
18 John Walker, *The Digital Imprimatur* (September 13, 2003). Available online: www.fourmilab.ch/ documents/digital-imprimatur (accessed July 21, 2007).
19 Richard Stallman, *What is DRM?* Available online: http://defectivebydesign.org/about (accessed July 21, 2007).

12 Classical and Experimental Music

1   Pierre Boulez, "At the Ends of Fruitful Land . . .," *die Reihe* 1 (1955, English translation 1958), 19.
2   Herbert Eimert, "What is Electronic Music?," *die Reihe* 1 (1955, English translation 1958), 1.
3   Boulez, "At the Ends of Fruitful Land . . .," 19.
4   Igor Stravinsky, "Where is Thy Sting?," *New York Review of Books* (April 24, 1969), 3–8.
5   Jack Bornoff, "Technology, Techniques, Music," *Cultures* 1(1) (Unesco, 1973), 261–2.
6   Thom Holmes, *Electronic and Experimental Music* (New York: Routledge, 2002), 226.
7   Boulez, "At the Ends of Fruitful Land . . .," 28.
8   Forrest Warthman, "The Neural Network Synthesizer: For Neural Synthesis and Neural Network Plus" (1995). Available online: www.emf.org/tudor/Articles/warthman.html (accessed February 7, 2006).
9   Leigh Landy, *Electroacoustic Music Studies and Accepted Terminology: You Can't Have One Without the Other* (Electroacoustic Music Studies Network, Beijing presentation, 2006), p. 4. Available online: www.ems-netowrk.org (accessed June 10, 2011).
10 Brigette Robindoré, "Luc Ferrari: Interview with an Intimate Iconoclast," *Computer Music Journal* 22(3) (Fall, 1998), 8.

11   Marion Melius, "Music by Electricity," *The World's Work* (June, 1906), 7660–3.

12   Pierre Schaeffer, *Traité des objets musicaux* (Paris: Éditions du Seuil, 1966).

13   Landy, *Electroacoustic Music Studies and Accepted Terminology*, 4.

14   Ibid.

15   Alan Clayson, *Edgard Varèse* (London: Sanctuary, 2002), 160–1.

16   "Review of *Déserts*," *The Score* (International Music Association, March 1955), 68.

17   Clayson, *Edgard Varèse*, 165.

18   Louis Chapin, "Tape Music by Varèse at Conservatory Concert," *The Christian Science Monitor* (1955). Clipping from the collection of the Columbia Electronic Music Center.

19   Clayson, *Edgard Varèse*, 166.

20   Herbert Russcol, *The Liberation of Sound: An Introduction to Electronic Music* (Englewood Cliffs, NJ: Prentice Hall, 1972), 62.

21   Stephen Addiss, "Review of a concert of contemporary music at the Village Gate Café in New York City on November 9, 1958," *Musical America* (December 1, 1958), 29.

22   Russcol, *The Liberation of Sound*.

23   Vladimir Ussachevsky, letter to Edgard Varèse, February 18, 1960. From the archives of the Columbia Computer Music Center.

24   Vladimir Ussachevsky, letter to Dr. Jacques Barzun, January 22, 1963. From the archives of the Columbia Computer Music Center.

25   Ibid.

26   Otto Luening, "Tribute to Edgard Varèse," *Columbia University Forum* (Spring, 1966), 20.

27   Annea Lockwood, *The River Archive*. Available online: www.halcyon.com/robinja/mythos/AnneaLockwood.html (accessed July 30, 2007).

28   John Cage, interview with Thom Holmes, April 1981.

29   William Duckworth, *Talking Music* (New York: Da Capo, 1999), 197.

30   Pauline Oliveros, "The Roots of the Moment: Interactive Music," *NewMus MusicNet* 1 (April 1995; online journal).

31   Benjamin Robert Levy, *The Electronic Works of Gyögy Ligeti and Their Influence on his Later Style*. Doctoral dissertation, University of Maryland, College Park (2006), 94.

32   György Ligeti, "Metamorphosis of Musical Form," in *Form—Space*, *Die Reihe* 7 (English edn, trans. Cornelius Cardew, Bryn Mawr, PA: Theodore Presser, 1965), 15.

33   John Cage, personal communication with Thom Holmes, December 29, 1985.

34   Karlheinz Stockhausen, liner notes, *Telemusik, Mixtur* (Deutsche Grammophon, 137 012, 1967).

35   Karlheinz Stockhausen, liner notes, *Es und Aufwärts* (Deutsche Grammophon, 2530 255, 1972).

36   Ibid.

37   Thom Holmes, notes written on Sun Ra's personal copy of *Aus den sieben Tagen* (Deutsche Grammophon, 2720 073, 1973).

38   Stockhausen, liner notes, *Es und Aufwärts*.

39   John Cage, personal conversation with Thom Holmes, January 15, 1973.

40   Karl. H. Wörner, *Stockhausen: Life and Work* (Berkeley, CA: University of California Press, 1977), 61.

41   Ibid., 68.

42   Robin Maconie (ed.), *Stockhausen on Music: Lectures and Interviews* (London: Marion Boyars, 2000), 103–4.

43   Karlheinz Stockhausen, notes for *Sirius* (Stockhausen Edition No. 26). Available online: http://home.earthlink.net/~almoritz/sirius.htm (accessed April 29, 2007).

44   Wendy Carlos, interview with Thom Holmes, August 8, 2001.

45   Ibid.

46   Wendy Carlos, interview with Carol Wright, *New Age Voice* (November 1999). Available online: www.synthmuseum.com/magazine/0103cw.html (accessed July 6, 2007).

47   Ibid.

48   Wendy Carlos, interview with Thom Holmes, June 6, 2001.

49 Wendy Carlos, liner notes, *Digital Moonscapes* (East Side Digital, ESD 81542, 2000), 2–3.

50 Carlos, interview with Holmes, June 6, 2001.

51 Larry Fast, interview with Paul Clark, April 1997. Available online: http://electronicmusic. com/features/interview/larryfast.html (accessed July 6, 2007).

52 Carlos, interview with Holmes, June 6, 2001.

53 Wendy Carlos, personal correspondence with Thom Holmes, August 23, 2007.

54 Duckworth, *Talking Music*, 274.

55 Terry Riley, liner notes, *Music for the Gift* (Organ of Corti, 1, 1998).

56 Duckworth, *Talking Music*, 210.

57 Ibid., 233.

58 Michael Nyman, *Experimental Music: Cage and Beyond* (New York: Schirmer, 1974), 69.

59 Laura Kuhn, executive director of the John Cage Trust, quoted in *The Scotsman* (August 24, 2001). Available online: www.festival.scotsman.com URL (accessed July 30, 2007).

60 Nyman, *Experimental Music*, 70.

61 Duckworth, *Talking Music*, 253.

62 Ibid., 277.

63 Ibid., 282.

64 Steve Reich, *Music as a Gradual Process* (1968). Available online: http://ccnmtl.columbia.edu/ draft/ben/feld/mod1/readings/reich.html (accessed June 10, 2011).

65 Hugh Davies, *Répertoire international des musiques électroacoustiques* (*International Electronic Music Catalog*), (Cambridge, MA: MIT Press, 1967), a joint publication of Le Groupe de Recherches Musicales de l'ORTF (Paris) and the Independent Electronic Music Center Inc. (Trumansburg, NY), vii.

66 Brian Eno, liner notes, *Discreet Music* (Editions EG, EGS 303, 1975).

67 Duckworth, *Talking Music*, 296.

68 Steve Reich, liner notes, *Three Dances & Four Organs* (Angel Records, S-36059, 1973).

69 Alvin Lucier, liner notes, *Clocker* (Lovely Music Ltd., 1994), 1.

70 Ibid.

71 Laurie Spiegel, liner notes, *The Expanding Universe* (Philo Records, 9003, 1980).

72 Ibid.

73 Ibid.

74 Ibid.

75 Marina Rosenfeld, interview with Thom Holmes, February 2, 2001.

76 Xenakis, liner notes, *Electro-Acoustic Music*.

77 Makis Solomis, liner notes, *Xenakis: Electronic Music* (EMF Media, EMF CD003, 1997).

78 Pierre Schaeffer, *Regards sur Iannis Xenakis* (Paris: Stock, 1981), 85.

79 James Brody Mansback, liner notes, *Electro-Acoustic Music* (Nonesuch Records, H-71246, 1969).

80 Heidi Von Gunden, *The Music of Pauline Oliveros* (Metuchen, NJ: Scarecrow Press, 1983), 52.

81 Pauline Oliveros, *Software for People* (Baltimore, MD: Smith Publications, 1984),195.

82 Ibid., 196–7.

83 William Maginnis, personal communication with Thom Holmes, 1984.

84 Oliveros, *Software for People*, 197.

85 Maggi Payne, personal communication with Thom Holmes, May 18, 2001.

86 Oliveros, *Software for People*, 197. John Bischoff and Maggi Payne, personal communication with Thom Holmes, May 18, 2001.

87 Robert Ashley, interview with Thom Holmes, March 22, 2001.

88 Ibid.

89 Maggi Payne, personal communication with Thom Holmes, August 21, 2001.

90 Bischoff and Payne, personal communication with Holmes, May 18, 2001.

91 Ashley, interview with Holmes, March 22, 2001.

92 Payne, personal communication with Holmes, May 18, 2001.

93 Ashley, interview with Holmes, March 22, 2001.

94 Maggi Payne, personal communication with Thom Holmes, August 22, 2001.

13 Jazz, Live Electronic Music, and Ambient Music

1 Gil Mellé, liner notes, *Tome VI* (Verve, V6-8744, 1966).
2 Gunther Schuller, liner notes, *Jazz et Jazz: Jazz Experiments*, conducted by Andre Hodeir (Philips PHS 600-073, 1960.
3 Terry Riley, *Magnet Magazine* (May 2001). Available online: www.terryriley.net/magnet_article.htm (accessed May 8, 2011).
4 Bob Thiele, liner notes, *Head Start* (Flying Dutchman Records, FDS-104, 1969).
5 George Russell, liner notes, *Electronic Sonata for Souls Loved by Nature* (Flying Dutchman Records, FD-10124, 1969).
6 Mellé, liner notes, *Tome VI*.
7 Matt Rogalsky, *Live Electronic Music Practice and Musicians of the Merce Cunningham Dance Company*, master's thesis, Wesleyan University, Connecticut (May 15, (1995; revised November 1996), 2.
8 John Cage, interview with Thom Holmes, April 1981.
9 Ibid.
10 Merce Cunningham, *Changes: Notes On Choreography* (New York: Something Else Press, 1969), 28.
11 Rogalsky, *Live Electronic Music Practice and Musicians of the Merce Cunningham Dance Company*, 2–3.
12 Richard Kostelanetz (ed.), *Conversing with Cage* (New York: Limelight, 1988), 191.
13 Gordon Mumma, personal communication with Thom Holmes, March 17, 2001.
14 William Duckworth, *Talking Music* (New York: Da Capo, 1999), 196–7.
15 Richard Kostelanetz, *John Cage: An Anthology* (New York: Da Capo, 1991), 21.
16 Joel Chadabe, *Electric Sound: The Past and Promise of Electronic Music* (Upper Saddle River, NJ: Prentice Hall, 1997), 82.
17 Robert Moog, interview with Thom Holmes, March 4, 2001.
18 Ronald J. Kuivila, personal communication with Thom Holmes, March 12, 2001.
19 Gordon Mumma, personal communication with Thom Holmes, January 17, 2002.
20 Kostelanetz, *John Cage*, 54.
21 John Cage, *Silence* (Cambridge, MA: MIT Press, 1966), 18.
22 Cage, interview with Holmes, April 1981.
23 Zeena Parkins, interview with Thom Holmes, March 15, 2001.
24 Pauline Oliveros, "The Roots of the Moment: Interactive Music." Available online: www.deeplistening.org/pauline/writings/roots.html (accessed July 30, 2007).
25 Ibid.
26 Gordon Mumma, "The ONCE Festival and How It Happened," *Arts in Society* (Madison, WI) 4(2) (1967, minor revisions August 1970). Provided by Mumma.
27 Ibid.
28 Ibid.
29 Robert Ashley, "Autobiographie," *MusikTexte* 88 (February 2001).
30 Mumma, "The ONCE Festival and How It Happened."
31 Ibid.
32 This performance in 1968 was not one of the official ONCE festivals, but one of the follow-up concerts involving the ONCE group of performers.
33 Alvin Lucier, interview with Thom Holmes, February 24, 2001.
34 Gordon Mumma, personal communication with Thom Holmes, August 6, 2001.
35 Gordon Mumma, personal communication with Thom Holmes, March 15, 2001.
36 Lucier, interview with Holmes, February 24, 2001.
37 David Behrman, liner notes, *Wave Train—Music from 1959 to 1968* (Alga Marghen, Plana B 5NmN. 020, 1998, Italy), 10.
38 Robert Ashley, interview with Thom Holmes, March 22, 2001.
39 Rogalsky, *Live Electronic Music Practice and Musicians of the Merce Cunningham Dance Company*, 148.
40 Ashley, "Autobiographie."
41 Ibid.
42 Ashley, interview with Holmes, March 22, 2001.
43 Mumma, personal communication with Holmes, March 17, 2001.

44 Gordon Mumma, liner notes, *The Sonic Arts Union* (Mainstream, MS/5010, 1971).

45 Gordon Mumma, personal communication with Thom Holmes, June 27, 2001.

46 Ashley, interview with Holmes, March 22, 2001.

47 Robert Ashley, interview with Thom Holmes, September 8, 1982.

48 Ibid.

49 Ibid.

50 Ibid.

51 Lucier, interview with Holmes, February 24, 2001.

52 Ibid.

53 Ibid.

54 Ibid.

55 David Tudor, interview with Larry Austin, April 3, 1989 (included in the narrative material for the Larry Austin composition *Transmission Two: The Great Excursion* (1990).

56 David Behrman, interview with Thom Holmes, March 13, 2001.

57 David Behrman, liner notes, *Wave Train–Music from 1959 to 1968* (Alga Marghen, 10, 1998).

58 Behrman, interview with Holmes, March 13, 2001.

59 Cornelius Cardew, liner notes, *Live Electronic Music Improvised* (Mainstream, MS-5002, 1968).

60 Ikue Mori, interview with Thom Holmes, January 23, 2001.

61 Marina Rosenfeld, interview with Thom Holmes, February 2, 2001.

62 Lucier, interview with Holmes, February 24, 2001.

63 Cage, *Silence*, 8.

64 David Behrman, personal communication with Thom Holmes, August 19, 2001.

65 Wendy Carlos, liner notes, *Sonic Seasonings* (East Side Digital, ESD 81372, 1972/1998).

66 Annea Lockwood, interview with Thom Holmes, February 19, 2001.

67 Annea Lockwood, personal communication with Thom Holmes, July 25, 2001.

68 Annea Lockwood, *The River Archive*. Available online: www.halcyon.com/robinja/mythos/AnneaLockwood.html (accessed July 30, 2007).

69 Lockwood, interview with Holmes, February 19, 2001.

70 Brian Eno, liner notes to the vinyl release of *Music for Airports* (Editions EG, EGS 303, 1978).

71 Paul Schütze, "Strategies for Making Sense, an interview with Brian Eno," *The Wire* 139 (September 1995).

72 Harold Budd, interview with Thom Holmes, February 19, 2001.

73 Ibid.

74 Ibid.

75 Ibid.

76 Ibid.

77 "John Diliberto: Biography." Available online: www.echoes.org/ie.john.html (accessed August 1, 2007).

78 Klaus Schulze, correspondence with Thom Holmes, February 2007.

14 Rock, Space Age Pop, and Turntablism

1 Geoff Emerick, *Here, There, and Everywhere: My Life Recording the Music of The Beatles* (New York: Gotham Books, 2006), 111.

2 Mark Lewisohn, *The Beatles Recording Sessions* (New York: Harmony Books, 1988), 72.

3 Ibid., 74.

4 Georgie Rogers, "Beatles' Experiment: Macca Says He Wants 14 Minute Beatles' Avant-garde Track to See Light" (BBC Radio 4, November 17, 2008). Available online: www.bbc.co.uk/6music/news/20081117_macca.shtml (accessed November 28, 2008).

5 Mark Ellen, "Exclusive! Lost Beatle Track Unearthed!" (Rockingvicar.com, April 2002). Available online: www.abbeyrd.net/carnival.htm (accessed November 28, 2008).

6 Ibid.

7 Rogers, "Beatles' Experiment."

8 Lewisohn, *The Beatles Recording Sessions*, 74.

9 Rogers, "Beatles' Experiment."

10 Lewisohn, *The Beatles Recording Sessions*, 138.

11 Interview with George Martin, *Melody Maker* (1971). Available online: http://beatlesnumber9.com/martininterview1971.html (accessed November 28, 2008).

12 Bernie Krause, *Into a Wild Sanctuary* (Berkeley, CA: Heyday Books, 1997), 66.

13 Larry the O, "To Sir With Love: Conversations With and About Sir George Martin," *Electronic Musician* (February 1999). Available online: http://emusician.com/em_spotlight/sir_with_love/ (accessed November 28, 2008).

14 Lewisohn, *The Beatles Recording Sessions*, 138.

15 Ibid., 185.

16 Tony Macarthur, interview with John Lennon (Radio Luxembourg, September 27, 1969). Available online: http://homepage.ntlworld.com/carousel/pob03.html (accessed November 28, 2008).

17 Larry the O, "To Sir With Love."

18 Lisa Takeuchi Cullen, "Yoko Ono: Rebirth of a Renaissance Rebel," *Time Magazine* (April 28, 2003). Available online: www.time.com/time/asia/2003/heroes/yoko_ono.html (accessed July 30, 2007).

19 Yoko Ono, correspondence with Thom Holmes, February 2007.

20 Ibid.

21 Gary Numan, correspondence with Thom Holmes, February 2007.

22 Robert Moog, interview with Thom Holmes, March 4, 2001.

23 David Miller, personal communication with Thom Holmes, April 23, 2001. Miller is a personal acquaintance of both Paul Tanner and Robert Whitsell and has a web site dedicated to Theremins: www.geocities.com/Vienna/4611/.

24 David Miller, personal communication with Thom Holmes, May 5, 2001.

25 Ibid.

26 Cy Schneider, liner notes, *Music for Heavenly Bodies* (Omega, OSL-4, 1958).

27 Miller, personal communication with Holmes, May 5, 2001.

28 Ibid.

29 Robert Moog, personal communication with Thom Holmes, April 23, 2001.

30 Dick Hyman, personal communication with Thom Holmes, August 7, 2001.

31 Liner notes, *Song of the Second Moon* (Limelight, LS 86050, *c.* 1967).

32 Dana Countryman, "Interview with Jean-Jacques Perrey," *Cool and Strange Music! Magazine* 10 (1998). Available online: http://members.aol.com/coolstrge/perrey.html (accessed August 1, 2007).

33 Arnaud Boivin, "Interview with Jean-Jacques Perrey." Available online: www.fly.co.uk/jjp.html (accessed August 1, 2007).

34 Thurston Moore, liner notes, *Records, 1981–1989* (alp62cd, 1997), 4.

35 Herbert Russcol, *The Liberation of Sound* (Englewood Cliffs, NJ: Prentice Hall, 1972), 71.

36 John Cage, *Silence* (Cambridge, MA: MIT Press, 1966), 6.

37 Mike Doherty, "Interview with Christian Marclay," *Eye* (November 30, 2000). Available online: www.eye.net/eye/issue/issue_11.30.00/music/marclay.html (accessed July 30, 2007).

38 Nicolas Collins, interview with Thom Holmes, April 2, 2001.

39 Christian Marclay, liner notes, *Records, 1981–1989* (alp62cd, 1997).

40 Ibid.

41 Moore, liner notes, *Records, 1981–1989*, 4.

42 DJ Olive, interview with Thom Holmes, January 30, 2001.

43 Ibid.

44 Ikue Mori, interview with Thom Holmes, January 23, 2001.

45 DJ Spooky, liner notes, *Necropolis: The Dialogic Project* (Knitting, 67, 1996).

46 Jon Garelick, "Interview with DJ Spooky," *Boston Phoenix* (November 28–December 5, 1996). Available online: www.bostonphoenix.com/alt1/archive/music/reviews/11–28–96/DJ_SPOOKY.html (accessed July 30, 2007).

47 Marina Rosenfeld, interview with Thom Holmes, February 2, 2001.

Appendix I: The Evolution of Analog Synthesizers

1   Peter Forrest, *The A–Z of Analogue Synthesisers, Parts One and Two* (Crediton, UK: Surreal, 2003). Estimates for makes and models of analog synthesizers were derived from the information found in this excellent technical compendium by Forrest.

Notes on the Audio CD

Track 1   *Trickaufnahmen* (excerpt) by Paul Hindemith. ℗ 2004 by Martin Elste/SIMPK Berlin.

Track 2   *Symphonie pour un homme seul: Waltz* by Pierre Henry and Pierre Schaeffer. From the CD *Panorama of Musique concrète*, No. 2. Courtesy of Sinetone AMR.

Track 3   *Scambi* by Henri Pousseur. From the CD Electronic Music Sources. Courtesy of Sinetone AMR.

Track 4   *Studie II* by Karlheinz Stockhausen. From the CD *CE: #3: Elektronische Musik 1952–1960*. Used by permission of the Stockhausen Foundation for Music.

Track 5   *Thema—Omaggio a Joyce* by Luciano Berio. Used by permission of Sony Music Entertainment.

Track 6   *Duodeno normale* by Teresa Rampazzi. Courtesy of the University of Padova.

Track 7   *Four Aspects* by Daphne Oram. From *Electronic Music Sources, Volume 4.* Courtesy of Sinetone AMR.

Track 8   *Forbidden Planet: Overture* (reprise) by Bebe and Louis Barron. From the soundtrack to *Forbidden Planet.* © 1956 by Planet Music. Used by permission of GNP Crescendo.

Track 9   *Williams Mix* (excerpt) by John Cage. From the album *The 25-Year Retrospective Concert of the Music of John Cage.* Courtesy of WERGO/Schott Music & Media, Mainz, Germany, www.wego.de.

Track 10   *Linear Contrasts* by Vladimir Ussachevsky. From the CD *Vladimir Ussachevsky: Electronic and Acoustic Works 1957–1972*, NW 80654. Used by permission of New World Records ℗ & © 1998 Anthology of Recorded Music, Inc. Available at www.newworldrecords.org.

Track 11   *Postlude from Music for a Sacred Service* by Bülent Arel. From the CD *Columbia-Princeton Electronic Music Center 1961–1973*, NW 80521. Used by permission of New World Records Ⓟ & © 2007 Anthology of Recorded Music, Inc. Available at www.newworldrecords.org.

Track 12   *I of IV* (excerpt) by Pauline Oliveros. Published by Deep Listening Publications. Used by permission.

Track 13   *Numerology* by Max Mathews. Courtesy of Marjorie Mathews.

Track 14   *Stria* by John Chowning. WER 2012-50. Used by permission of Schott Music & Media.

Track 15   *Poème électronique* by Edgard Varèse. Produced by Andrew Cornall. Ⓟ 1998 Decca Music Group Limited. Courtesy of Decca Music Group Ltd under license from Universal Music Enterprises. GB-F07-98-10060.

Track 16   *Hymnen: Region III* (opening) by Karlheinz Stockhausen. From the CD *Hymnen*. Used by permission of the Stockhausen Foundation for Music.

Track 17   *Come Out* (Album Version excerpt) by Steve Reich. Ⓟ 1987 Elektra Entertainment. Produced under License from Nonesuch Records. ISRC: USEE10502361.

Track 18   *JazzEx* (excerpt) by Bernard Parmegiani. Courtesy of Bernard Parmegiani.

Track 19   *Song of the Second Moon* by Dick Raaijmakers and Tom Dissevelt. From the CD *Popular Electronics, Early Dutch Electronic Music*. Used by permission of Basta Music.

Index

Numbers in **bold** type indicate pages that contain figures and tables relevant to the topic.